# The Klingensmith Family Reunion

Including:
Klingenschmidt / Klingensmith
Steinle / Stanley
Carpenter
Müller / Miller and
Bischoff / Bishop Family Lines

Nancy M Ham

Copyright 2020

*The Klingensmith Family Reunion*
by Nancy M Ham

Published by Nancy M Ham

ISBN: 978-0-9970561-4-3 (paperback)
978-0-9970561-5-0 (e-Book)

All rights reserved. No part of this publication may be reproduced, stored in a retrieval system, or transmitted in any form or by any means without the prior written permission of the publisher. The only exception is brief quotation in printed reviews.

The author has relied on sources believed to be reliable, augmented with her own understanding and perceptions. The author may be contacted at nancymham@gmail.com with substantiated corrections.

# Preface

I have had a lifelong interest in history and the stories of older people. I was fascinated by the fact I had a German great-grandfather, even though I never met him. This interest in the past fostered many trips to search for information. In 1979, the family decided to take a family vacation out east to see if we could trace some of the information on the Sawyers, my mother's family, and find out something about the Bishops. We spent three weeks looking in libraries, court houses, museums and cemeteries. We found a wealth of information and have continued to collect information from time to time since then.

After my retirement, I decided to collect all our bits of information in a family history. This still required many trips like the first one and days at the Michigan State Library. It has become progressively easier to get information. Instead of so much time in libraries looking at books and microfiche, much information is available online. The information, however, is still hand written and frequently hard to read. The following is a combination of many types of research.

This book may not be easy to read. I encourage you to read it slowly and with imagination. Imaging how it felt to leave family and everything you have ever known to board a boat to a land you have only heard about. One branch of the family moved to Kansas and Oklahoma. Many were hit hard by the "dust bowl" which lasted from 1930 to 1939. McPherson, Kansas was on the edge of the worst hit area and many of the family were affected. The great depression was from 1929 until WW11. The 1930 census data often gives the value of homes, the value falls by 1940 for everyone with the exception of up-state New York dairy farmers. Some of the family moved to other areas, mostly California. Notice how increasing education made life easier. In the early years everyone farmed, later there are a variety of occupations. History isn't always pretty, sometimes it leaves scars. There are many scars!

There is a lot of census and other data but there are also many stories. From those who were incarcerated to an Olympic Gold winner. A boxer to an early automobile executive. And of course, a Revolutionary War Soldier.

My purpose in writing this book is to pass on what I know to the many descendants of the families I followed, to know where they came from, their family history.

I hope you read and enjoy my book and the Klingensmith family history it presents.

Nancy M Ham

# Contents

Preface ............................................................................................................................. iii
Introduction ....................................................................................................................... 1
Chapter 1    The Klingensmith Family Reunion ............................................................... 3
Chapter 2    Early Germany............................................................................................ 24
Chapter 3    The Steinles in Germany ........................................................................... 28
Chapter 4    The Klingenschmidt Family in America ..................................................... 33
Chapter 5    Mary Klingensmith and George Kester ..................................................... 41
Chapter 6    Elizabeth Klingensmith and John Steinle/Stanley ..................................... 60
Chapter 7    Catherine Klingensmith and John Arn ...................................................... 83
Chapter 8    Karl (Charles) Klingenschmidt and Sarah Ish .......................................... 158
Chapter 8    The Early Carpenters............................................................................... 186
Chapter 10  Phillip and Mary Rhodes Carpenter ........................................................ 200
Chapter 11  Orson Carpenter ...................................................................................... 337
Chapter 12  Fred Stanley and Ella Louise Carpenter .................................................. 369
Chapter 13  Christian Müller and Margaretha Essen................................................... 379
Chapter 14  Frank Bishof/Bischoff/Bishop and Mary Geiser/Kaiser ........................... 394
Chapter 15  Theodore Bishop and Katherine Müller.................................................... 417
Chapter 16  Charles Bishop and Mae Stanley............................................................. 435
References .................................................................................................................... 495

# Introduction

This book includes a number of features that may not be familiar to most people; therefore, an introduction is included with some explanations.

Each chapter begins with a lineage relating to that chapter. The numbers denote the generation. The lineage starts with the oldest direct line person in that chapter as number "1." followed by the name and years they were living. The following numbers denote successive generations, i.e. all the children of "1." are "2." a "+" indicates a marriage.

An example: 1. Jacob Klingenschmidt (1802-1889)
   + Charlotte Warner (1801-1872)
      2. Mary Klingenschmidt (1827-1899)

Jacob Klingenschmidt married Charlotte Warner and their first child was Mary Klingenschmidt. Couples are in bold when they tie into a later chapter.

There are many very large families which make it difficult to get the relationships correct. I have used the numbering system in the lineage chart to identify individuals and families in that chapter. I hope this helps the reader to keep everyone straight. Many details have been included that should be helpful for anyone who wants to continue the research.

As land was settled west of the original colonies, it was divided into townships, counties and ranges. A township was generally 6 miles in each direction enclosing 36 sections of about one square mile each. A chart of land divisions and measures follows.

Census records have township, county, state for rural areas and city, state for cities.

Research has changed drastically during the writing of this book. On line research at Ancestry.com and associated websites is not documented. I have referenced books and data that is not online by use of superscripts (book[6]). References are at the end of the book. Many comments and remembrances are my own.

The information is as complete as currently available. Some sources were not well documented when collected and others have sketchy documentation.

The family history will start with a little early German history that relates to the many German relatives. The various lines will be added as appropriate.

# LEGAL METHOD OF DESCRIBING FRACTIONAL PARTS OF A SECTION

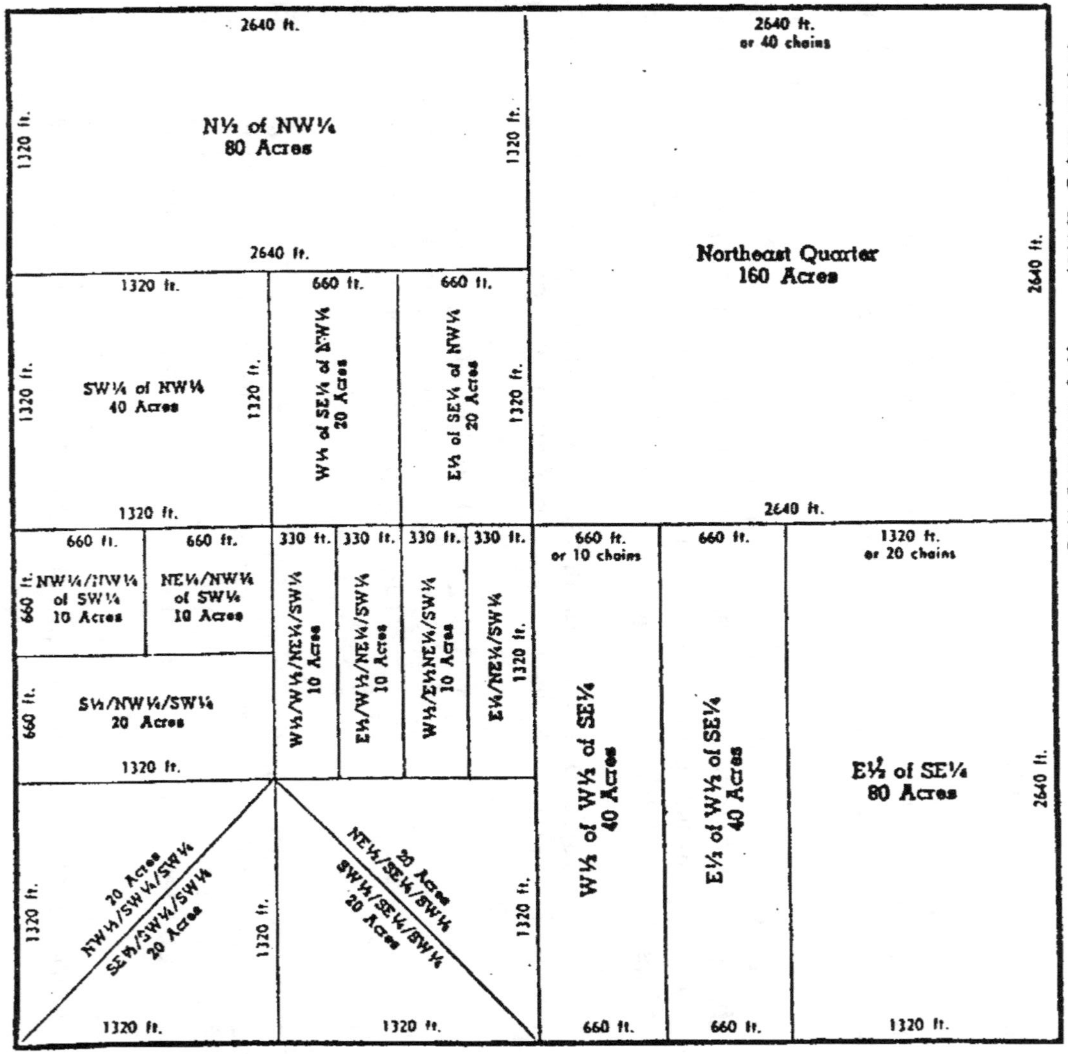

Diagram of a section showing:

- N½ of NW¼ — 80 Acres (2640 ft × 1320 ft)
- SW¼ of NW¼ — 40 Acres (1320 ft × 1320 ft)
- SW¼ of NW¼ subdivisions:
  - NE¼/NW¼ of SW¼ — 10 Acres (660 ft)
  - S½/NW¼/SW¼ — 20 Acres (1320 ft × 660 ft)
  - NE¼/NW¼ of SW¼ — 10 Acres
- Triangular subdivisions of SW¼:
  - NW¼/SW¼/SW¼ — 20 Acres
  - SE¼/SW¼/SW¼ — 20 Acres
  - NE¼/SE¼/SW¼ — 20 Acres
  - SW¼/SE¼/SW¼ — 20 Acres
- W½ of SE¼ of NW¼ — 20 Acres (660 ft)
- W½/W½/NE¼/SW¼ — 10 Acres (330 ft)
- E½/W½/NE¼/SW¼ — 10 Acres (330 ft)
- E½ of SE¼ of NW¼ — 20 Acres
- W½/E½/NE¼/SW¼ — 10 Acres (330 ft)
- E½/NE¼/SW¼ — (330 ft)
- Northeast Quarter — 160 Acres (2640 ft × 2640 ft, or 40 chains)
- W½ of W½ of SE¼ — 40 Acres (660 ft, or 10 chains)
- E½ of W½ of SE¼ — 40 Acres (660 ft)
- E½ of SE¼ — 80 Acres (1320 ft, or 20 chains)

## LINEAR MEASURE

| | |
|---|---|
| 7.92 inches | 1 link |
| 25 links | 1 rod, perch or pole |
| 16½ feet | |
| 100 links | 1 chain |
| 4 rods | |
| 66 feet | |
| 80 chains | 1 mile |
| 320 rods or poles | |
| 5,280 feet | |

## SQUARE MEASURE

| | |
|---|---|
| 208.708 x 208.708 feet | 1 acre |
| 43,560 square feet | 1 acre |
| 16 square rods or poles | 1 square chain |
| 10 square chains | 1 acre |
| 160 square rods or poles | 1 acre |
| 640 acres (one section) | 1 square mile |
| 36 square miles | 1 township |

Official Plat of Township Sectionized and Numbered With Adjoining Sections

| | 36 | 31 | 32 | 33 | 34 | 35 | 36 | 31 |
|---|---|---|---|---|---|---|---|---|
| | 1 | 6 | 5 | 4 | 3 | 2 | 1 | 6 |
| | 12 | 7 | 8 | 9 | 10 | 11 | 12 | 7 |
| | 13 | 18 | 17 | 16 | 15 | 14 | 13 | 18 |
| | 24 | 19 | 20 | 21 | 22 | 23 | 24 | 19 |
| | 25 | 30 | 29 | 28 | 27 | 26 | 25 | 30 |
| | 36 | 31 | 32 | 33 | 34 | 35 | 36 | 31 |
| | 1 | 6 | 5 | 4 | 3 | 2 | 1 | 6 |

# Chapter 1

## The Klingensmith Family Reunion

Some of my earliest memories are of the family reunions held every year just before the start of school. We would all gather at someone's house. There would be games, sometimes performances by the children, and always food. By the time, I became interested in this book, no one remembered why we had the Klingensmith Reunion or how they were related. This is the start of my story.

In 1926 the first Klingensmith Family Reunion was held. The following poem was written at that time and given to me by Helen Bishop. I have commented on relationships.

"Our First Reunion"

| | Comments |
|---|---|
| The first Klingensmith reunion<br>    Has finally got a date;<br>It is September 5th 1926<br>    I am happy to relate. | |
| On this date in the morning<br>    Didn't matter about the weather<br>The following to Fred Stanley's came,<br>    To have a visit together. | The Carpenter farm owned by<br>Ella Stanley, later Charles Bishop |
| George Klingensmith is the oldest;<br>    He married Clara Carl.<br>They haven't any children<br>    So with each other have to quarrel. | Son of Karl Klingensmith |
| Emma and Amaza of Hadley,<br>    On Saturday came thru;<br>Of all her eight grown children<br>    She only brought but two. | Emma Klingensmith, daughter of<br>Karl Klingensmith married Amaza Gee |
| One son, Elton of Detroit<br>    And Eva way out from Cal<br>Who use to stay with her grandpa<br>    When she was quite a gal. | Elton and Eva Gee, children of Emma<br>and Amaza Gee |
| When Libbie and Jay arrived,<br>    They were some surprised I'll say<br>To see so many of the relations<br>    That had come to spend the day. | Sarah Elizabeth Klingensmith, daughter<br>of Karl Klingensmith, married Jay<br>Southern |

| | |
|---|---|
| Phene's folks lives near Pittsford;<br>    Kester was her other name<br>'Till Charlie added the name of Clark;<br>    And Lela's still the same. | Josephine Kester, daughter of Mary Klingensmith and George Kester, married Charles Clark, one daughter Lela Clark |
| Emma Stanley came from Paw Paw<br>    She had her step grandson to come with.<br>Of course, she belongs to the family<br>    For her mother was a Klingensmith. | daughter of Elizabeth Klingensmith and George Steinle (Stanley) |
| Then there were the Snyders;<br>    In fact, to tell the truth<br>There is Mabel, Arthur and Harry,<br>    Walter, Helen and Ruth. | Mable Stanley daughter of Fred Stanley and Ella Louise Carpenter, married Arthur Snyder, children: Harry, Walter, Helen, Ruth |
| Blanche and Elvin and family<br>    Of course, were there on time<br>For she wanted this reunion<br>    And she succeeded, to, just fine. | Blanche Stanley daughter of Fred and Ella Stanley, married Elvin Gibbs |
| Mae who lives with Charles Bishop,<br>    She says it's no trouble at all<br>To get ready to come to the reunion<br>    With six little children small. | Mae Stanley daughter of Fred and Ella Stanley married Charles Bishop George was 12, Robert was 1 |
| Eddie, wife and children<br>    Big girl and sweetheart too<br>Started quite early in the morning<br>    And drove from Kalamazoo | Edwin son of John G Stanley, grandson Johann Georg Steinle, wife Blanch daughters Pauline, Maxine |
| Herman came down from Coldwater,<br>    Accompanied by his wife,<br>Who made him hustle along,<br>    You bet your life. | Homer Clyde "Herman" son of John G Stanley. Wife is Carrie, no mention of their 2 children |
| Louie and family from Battle Creek<br>    Came to the reunion, too,<br>To get a good big dinner, the most,<br>    I think, don't you? | Louis Kester son of J. George and Marie Kester, married Lois lived in Kalamazoo most of time |
| Fannie and Lee and two children<br>    From Camp Custer came thru,<br>No one thinks she looks like us<br>    Tho her grandmother was a Klingensmith too. | Fannie Kester, daughter of J. George and Marie Kester, married Lee Horton, children Edith & Eugene |

And such a time for handshaking
    Has never yet been told.
Some of us kissed all the babies,
    Many of them being pretty old.

Soon we got to visiting
    And getting acquainted too
With some of our kinfolks
    That we never knew.

Then dinner was ready
    And all did partake
Of meat, bread and potatoes,
    Beans, salad, pie and cake.

We didn't seem very hungry
    After we had all we could eat
Of such a wonderful dinner,
    Which would be hard to beat.

Then we had our pictures took
    All in one big family.
It seems strange being such pretty folks
    We didn't break the camera.

*This picture has not been found*

Russell and Arthur finally came,
    When the day was almost over.
They had trouble with their car,
    So couldn't come much sooner.

*Probably (Frank) Russell Gee and his younger brother Arthur Gee. In 1920 Russell, a millwright, was living in Detroit with two brothers, who were carpenters.*

The meeting was called to order,
    Thought we had better organize;
So Blanche was voted for President
    To run a company of our size.

Then plans were made for next year
    With Libbie at her home,
On Sunday before Labor Day,
    And everybody come.
The time of parting was at hand,
    My how the time did fly.
We have all had a good time,
    Hope to see you all next year, Good Bye.

    Composed by Mrs. Elizabeth Klingensmith Southern

A "p" after a name in the lineage charts, refers to this poem.

The tradition of a Klingensmith Family Reunion continued for many years, always just before Labor Day. As far as I know they happened every year although there may have been some missed years. The last Klingensmith reunion was held at George and Jean Bishop's home at 595 S. Meridian Rd. Hudson, Michigan in 1958. The "older folks" with Klingensmith connections were dying off and it became an occasional Bishop gathering.

I will start with reunion pictures I have found. Pictures were not available for most years. Many pictures with year and other notations were taken by Edward Bishop. The banner spells Klingensmith as Klinginsmith. There was some dispute as to the spelling but I believe the "e" is correct. Late finds may be from an early reunion.

This picture is labeled Marian Louise Bishop and George Klingensmith Sep 1939. The reunion was held at Gerald and Ruth Snyder Allen's home in North Adams, Michigan.

The picture was from Marian Bishop Allshouse's Family.

I visited Pam Bishop Smutek and saw the following picture stuck in a framed picture of Charles T Bishop when he was in the Army in the Philippines. It was behind glass. At first, I thought it was of Charles Bishop's brothers and sisters but that didn't fit. After finding this picture of George Klingensmith, I believe both pictures were taken at Klingensmith reunions. There were other pictures of the larger family in attendance but they were not clear.

This is probably a picture of the Klingensmith first cousins. They would be the children of the original Klingensmith family, Mary Klingensmith Kester, Elizabeth Klingensmith Stanley, Catherine Klingensmith Arn and Charles Klingensmith.

George Klingensmith is on the left, behind him is Charles Klingensmith Then Libbie Klingensmith Southern and Emma Klingensmith Gee on the far right. The entire back row has the children of Charles Klingensmith. The two in front are Fred Stanley son of Elizabeth Klingensmith Stanley and Josephene Kester Clark daughter of Mary Klingensmith Kester. I believe the picture was taken in 1932.

The reunion that year was held at the home of Merrill Southern, son of Libbie Klingensmith Southern. They had a potluck dinner followed by a business meeting called to order by George Klingensmith, president. They elected Elton Gee, president; Mrs. Merrill Southern, secretary-treasurer; Geraldine Snyder, Ruth Allen and Elsa Gibbs, program committee and Herman Kester, Walter Snyder and Lucille Gibbs, sports committee. They enjoyed a program with 6 acts including a short play. 66 persons were present. They collected $7.03 and expenses were $7.50.

Charles Klingensmith and Walter Snyder died before the next reunion.

There are no other "early" pictures of the Klingensmith Family Reunion to my knowledge. I did find a journal with records from the reunions

# The 1944 picture of the "Klingensmith" family

The 3 Sep 1944 reunion was at Charles and Mae Bishop's home. 46 were present. Pictured are; front row: Mickey Bishop, unknown, Marian Bishop, Nancy Bishop, unknown, unknown, unknown, unknown, Anna Mae Letherer; standing behind from left: unknown, Earl Bishop, Elvin Gibbs, unknown, George Klingensmith, unknown, Libbie Southern, Charles Bishop behind Mae Bishop, girl with baby, behind her Mabel Snyder looking to right, Edna Russel with baby, Blanche Gibbs behind baby, Jean Bishop, Agnes Letherer, George Bishop behind holding Carol, many partial faces and unknowns.

George Bishop called the meeting to order. Libbie Southern was elected president; Mae Bishop, vice president; Blanche Gibbs, secretary-treasurer; Agnes Letherer, program and Charlie Letherer, sports. 60 cents will be allowed for invitation cards. Next reunion at the home of Blanche Gibbs. $2.86 collected, $1.46 on hand for a total of $4.32.

This picture of the Stanley sisters; Mae Bishop, Blanche Gibbs and Mabel Snyder; was taken the same day as the 1944 reunion. Both Mae and Mabel died the following year.

The 1945 reunion was held at Blanche Gibbs house. There were lots of new babies and at least 2 deaths. Betty Bishop was elected to replace Mae Bishop. 67 cents was spent on paper plates (something new) and cards. 67 were present.

The 1946 reunion was held at Earl and Betty Bishop's home. Betty was in charge of the program. There were 6 recitations, music to welcome servicemen, piano solo and many songs. Libbie was in charge of getting a new banner.

The 1947 reunion was held at Merrill Southern's home. There was a long program with 46 present. Cards $0.10, ice cream $7.50, collection, $9.23 for a balance of $4.38.

By 1948, Ed and Helen Bishop had moved to Maple Grove Ave. in Hudson. The 1948 Klingensmith reunion was held there. This picture is of Wayne on a donkey (probably Charles Bishop's) Mickey is leading the donkey.

Here Mickey is on the donkey.

Pennies were hidden in a pile of sawdust for the kids to find. There seems to be quite a bit of interest from the adults as well. Grandpa, Charles Bishop, is standing to the right; Corabelle Bishop is the left of the two ladies. Note the seamed hose, the only option in the late forties and early fifties.

The adults had a three legged race. Jean Bishop is racing with her brother-in-law, Earl Bishop.

I believe everyone is getting ready for the tug-of-war. From the right: Elvin Gibbs is in front of the donkey, Ed Bishop is looking away from the camera, can't be sure about the two women, Earl Bishop with back to camera, Charles T. Bishop, not sure about rest or what they are looking at.

The children's tug-of war had Earl in the center, Betty facing him, and Jean Bishop on the porch, leaning on the post. Marian Bishop is the first girl on the near side. Nancy Bishop is just beyond Earl. The others are not identified. There was a program with recitations and music as well as the games.

The banner cost $13.60 so the hat had to be passed around several times to get enough money for the banner and ice cream.

Edna Russell riding the donkey is the last of the 1948 reunion pictures.

The 1949 reunion was held at Stanley Gibbs with the usual program and ice cream.

By 1950 asphalt siding had been added to Charles Bishop's house. Elvin and Blanche Gibbs had their picture taken during the reunion.

Fannie and Lee Horton were there from Paw Paw and had their picture taken as well. Notice the new banner.

Charles T Bishop had his mules, Jack and Jill, out for rides.

Libby Southern held Diane Bishop.

Robert Bishop gave Mickey (Earl Jr.) and Wayne (son of Ed) Bishop a ride on a mule.

Apparently, Aunt Ada Miller was there as well although she is not a Klingensmith. She was married to Henry Miller, the younger brother of Charles Bishop's Mother.

The very next day Mabel and Arthur Snyder's house burned.

Ed Bishop took the pictures. Fire equipment was not as effective in those days and most of the house appears to be a loss.

In 1951 the reunion was held at George and Jean Bishop's house on Oak Street in Hudson. Along with the usual picnic and games, several of the children played instruments and sang. No pictures have been found.

The 1952 reunion was at Charles Letherer's home. With the usual program of music and recitations. There was $1.42 left in the treasury after paying for ice cream.

1953 found us at Ed and Helen Bishop's house on Maple Grove Street in Hudson. There were lots of games that year.

Earl Bishop is with (Diane?)

Ed and Edith Horton Hinge

Digging for pennies in a sawdust pile! Marian Bishop is at top of picture, Robert Bishop below her.

Lee and Fanny Kester Horton
Fanny is the daughter of J. George Kester who was the son of George Kester and Mary Klingensmith

Clara Klingensmith was the wife of George Klingensmith who was the son of Karl Klingensmith. She is probably the oldest living Klingensmith at this point.

With her is Blanche Stanley Gibbs

From left back row: Corabelle and Robert Bishop, Ed & Edith Hinge, Lee and Fannie Horton, Betty Bishop in dark dress, Clara Klingensmith, Agnes Letherer to the front, Blanch and Elvin Gibbs slightly back, Jean Bishop, Earl Bishop with 2 unknowns in front, Charlie Letherer on the right. Mickey Bishop kneeling in front of Robert Bishop, 3 unknown boys (one a Hinge) Barry Bishop on his hands, Pam Bishop looking back, Carol Bishop sideways, Charles Bishop with Judy Bishop in front of him and Mary Letherer behind him, Nancy Bishop, Lucille Letherer with hands up, Anna Mae Letherer, and Margie Bishop holding Jackie

Diane Bishop, Edward Bishop's daughter

Pam Bishop, Robert bishop's daughter

A game is being organized

There was a program of popular and silly songs sung by a group of girls as well as the games.

Ice cream came in a 5-gallon cloth wrapped metal container that was a tall cylinder. It was purchased at the ice cream parlor. First come first served. Priority to children.

The 1954 reunion was held at George Bishop's. Lee and Libbie Horton stayed overnight at George's place. There is very little information and no pictures. I do know ice cream was served from the 5-gallon cylinder.

The 1955 Klingensmith Reunion was held at Blanche and Alvin Gibb's place near Manitou Beach North of Hudson.

From left – unknown, Agnes with Lucille Letherer, Corabelle Bishop, unknown, Blanche Stanley Gibbs, not sure of others

Near side Blanche Gibb's daughter, Edna Russell,
Helen Bishop is at far right, the children are being organized for a picture in the background.

Chairs were in short supply.

This is a picture of the children present. Back row: Marian Bishop, Nancy Bishop, Anna Mae Letherer, Judy Bishop, partially hidden and unknown. Middle in front and to the right of Judy is Barry Bishop with Mary and Shaila Letherer to his left (farther right). Lucille Letherer is in front of them. Pam Bishop is sitting on a small stool in the front with a white dress and dark sash, others unknown.

The children are less organized in this picture but "Mickey" Earl Bishop Jr. is behind Marian and Nancy Bishop. Carol Bishop is at the far right in back.

Another picture of the children, the older ones have left.

Clara Klingensmith, the oldest with the youngest

Overlapping pictures. From the left: unknown, Don Letherer, Mickey Bishop, Barry Bishop, Anna Mae Letherer, Nancy Bishop – also in picture to right, Jean Bishop, Marian Bishop, unknown Clara Klingensmith.

Edward Bishop read a poem brought by Clara Klingensmith and written by Libbie Southerland.

The 1956 Klingensmith Family Reunion was held at Roberta and Carl Mason's home. Fannie Horton was the oldest person present. Motion was made to buy an ice cream dipper. The program was:
"Jesus Loves Me" by the little folks and Mary, Shaila and Lucille Letherer.
"Skates Waltz" by Anna Mae Letherer on the accordion.
Dance by Leon and Kathy Gibbs
"Old McDonalds Farm" by Gibbs and Russell children
"Harvest Time" by Barry Bishop on the accordion
"Woody Woodpecker" by Cindy Liechty
"Little Feet be Careful" by Kathy, June, Peggy Gibbs and Barbra Russell
"The Bible Tells Me So" by Lucille Letherer
A fairly typical program for the reunion, although the entertainers changed through the years. There were 56 people present. Ice cream for all was $6.75.

The 1957 reunion was held at the home of Herbert Slusher. They voted to have the reunion 1 week earlier because people were taking vacation over the long weekend. There were 27 members present.

The 1958 Klingensmith Family Reunion was held at George Bishop's place on S. Meridian Road in Hudson. Fannie Horton had died in July. Fannie was the last connection to the early Klingensmith relatives. After that the occasional gatherings included only Bishops.

# Chapter 2

# Early Germany

Martin Luther wrote a set of 95 theses, criticizing abuses in the church, and nailed them to the door of the Wittenberg Cathedral 31 Oct 1517. This was an established practice to initiate debate but this time it became much more than that. People began following Luther's new way of looking at religion. The advent of the printing press helped spread the word throughout Germany. The Roman Catholic Church was no longer the only form of Christianity in Germany and they fought back. In spite of resistance, change to the way people worshiped was happening. This change in the church led to a desire for change in government.  At the time, Germany consisted of many small fiefdoms, monasteries and cities loosely held together by the "Holy Roman Empire of the German Nations".  They were still firmly rooted in the medieval feudal system. Small wars broke out as leaders sided with Luther or the Catholic Church. The people began demanding social and economic change. They didn't want to pay papal taxes when they were part of the new Lutheran Church. They wanted laws that were the same for everyone no matter what their religion. Luther's invitation for debate became more than a church. It began a reformation of the entire culture.[1]

The treaty of 1555 was intended to end the political unrest by keeping the Catholics and Lutherans in the areas they occupied.  Although other Protestant Leaders and beliefs were starting up, the treaty did not consider any of these other religions. You were either a Catholic or a Protestant Lutheran. The leaders of each area were allowed to determine the religion practiced on their land. They could not try to convert other principalities to their religion. The people under the rule of the Prince, Lord or Duke could not say which religion they preferred. If they did not want to abide by the local religion, they could move. This was not as easy as it sounds because they were indebted to the owner of the land under the feudal system. Most cities were independent and individuals could determine their religious preference.

In 1618, fighting began again in Germany between Protestants and Catholics. It soon spread across Europe. The 1648 "Peace of Westphalia" ended 30 years of war in Germany. The treaty attempted to settled two conflicts, the struggle between Catholics and Protestants and the struggle between the Emperor and the Principalities. The Principalities could still rule their lands and determine the religion practiced. Although "The Holy Roman Empire" still existed, the decision-making power lay with the individual rulers. The people could still not determine their own destiny. The Empire would remain until after the Napoleonic Wars. Individual Principalities eventually were united into a German state under Bismarck.[1]

All of this political maneuvering had little effect on the individual. They still had to work for a Master. Some were given small plots of land to work for themselves but they still had to work for the land owner. The few who had a small plot of land had to provide manual labor for the estate with little time to work the land that had been granted to them by their master. In the western and southern parts of Germany, the peasants were subject to taxation that was a complicated system of payment of money and produce and had remained intact from medieval times. In Prussia, in Northern Germany, the land owner controlled his goods and the peasants were bound to him in serfdom, in essence they were tied to his land as working possessions. Their children also worked for the land owner from a young age. The villages the serfs and peasants lived in were owned by the land owner. The peasants were even subject to the landowner's right to inflict corporal punishment.[2]

After the defeat of Napoleon, the Congress of Vienna met in 1814 to determine the new territorial and political structure of Europe. The result for Germany was a loose confederation of states or principalities without a sovereign. This ensured the independence of the states and suppressed the new political and social forces for change. The only national German institution was the Parliament in Frankfort which was not a people's representative assembly but a congress of delegates appointed by the German sovereigns and free cities. The people remained subservient.[2]

Serfdom was abolished by Napoleon in 1807 but remained at least partially in effect. Real changes to the status of serfs began in the smaller German states where they were able to devote more attention to domestic matters than rivalry with their neighbors. Constitutions were established by the monarchs in Baden, Württemberg and Bavaria as well as other smaller states. Status was no longer defined by birth and some middle-class individuals were able to buy land. The printing press and Luther's translation of the Bible into "high German" had led to the spread of education to those who were not aristocracy. Education had been only for the aristocracy and religious orders but by the mid-1800s many others were able to gain an education. Education was still only for males in most cases, just as it had always been except in rare cases. Literature, including the Bible, became more available to the newly educated middle class. This was true in most of the world at the time. With education, people could use their own reasoning to think independently and critically. This in turn led to advances in science, the arts and education.[1,2]

Prussia had a strong monarchy more concerned with military might than religion. Several forms of Protestantism and Catholicism were tolerated. A form of serfdom remained in Prussia until the revolution of 1848. Peasants were conscripted into the military where they were considered expendable. The aristocrats were also involved in the military service but as officers. This military power led to the establishment of Prussian Kings over Germany which lasted until WW1.[1]

Württemberg was able to resist the attempts of Dukes to establish a standing army leaving more resources for domestic issues. Württemberg maintained a functioning parliament from the 1500s right up to the formation of modern Germany. Peasants were relatively independent and both rural and urban interests were included in the parliament. It had a Lutheran Church tradition but in 1806 King Frederick granted religious freedom to all Christians.[1,3]

Bavaria (Bayern in German) was one of the 16 states created after the Napoleonic Wars. They were loosely combined with Baden and Württemberg. Most of the German ancestors came from these states. The Württemberg ancestors were Lutheran while most of the southern part of Germany was Catholic.[1] Maybe this independence led to their coming to America. The Bavarian criminal code of 1811 was the most progressive in Germany and contained the fundamental principal of modern jurisprudence - no punishment without a law. In 1809 Protestants were given the same rights as Catholics and in 1813 Jews were granted freedom to worship.[3]

Germany saw a considerable population growth in the early 1800s, most of it rural. The food supply of a still pre-industrial economy was insufficient to support a growing population. Food riots and rural unemployment brought migration to the towns. Industrialization brought factory and railroad building jobs but they did not provide sufficient wages to support a family. Generally, all of the family worked including children in order to provide a place to live and food. By 1847/48 the people began to demand freedom of the press, freedom in teaching, a leveling of economic differences and representation in the German Confederation. This German revolution failed mainly due to the lack of German unity.[2] However, the seeds of change had been planted.

For many people, emigration across the Atlantic to the land of opportunity seemed to be the only answer. The social and political unrest in 1848 may have led to the emigration of our ancestors. Many of our German ancestors came to the United States in the 1850s. They came from Württemberg, Bavaria, and Prussia. They also came with varying resources. The Klingensmiths could pay for passage as well as transportation inland. Frank Bishof, probably from Prussia, landed in New York and worked at menial labor all his life. It is not hard to see the difference in their circumstances. Coming from a progressive area that had access to education was very different from the area that had serfs until the mid-1800s.

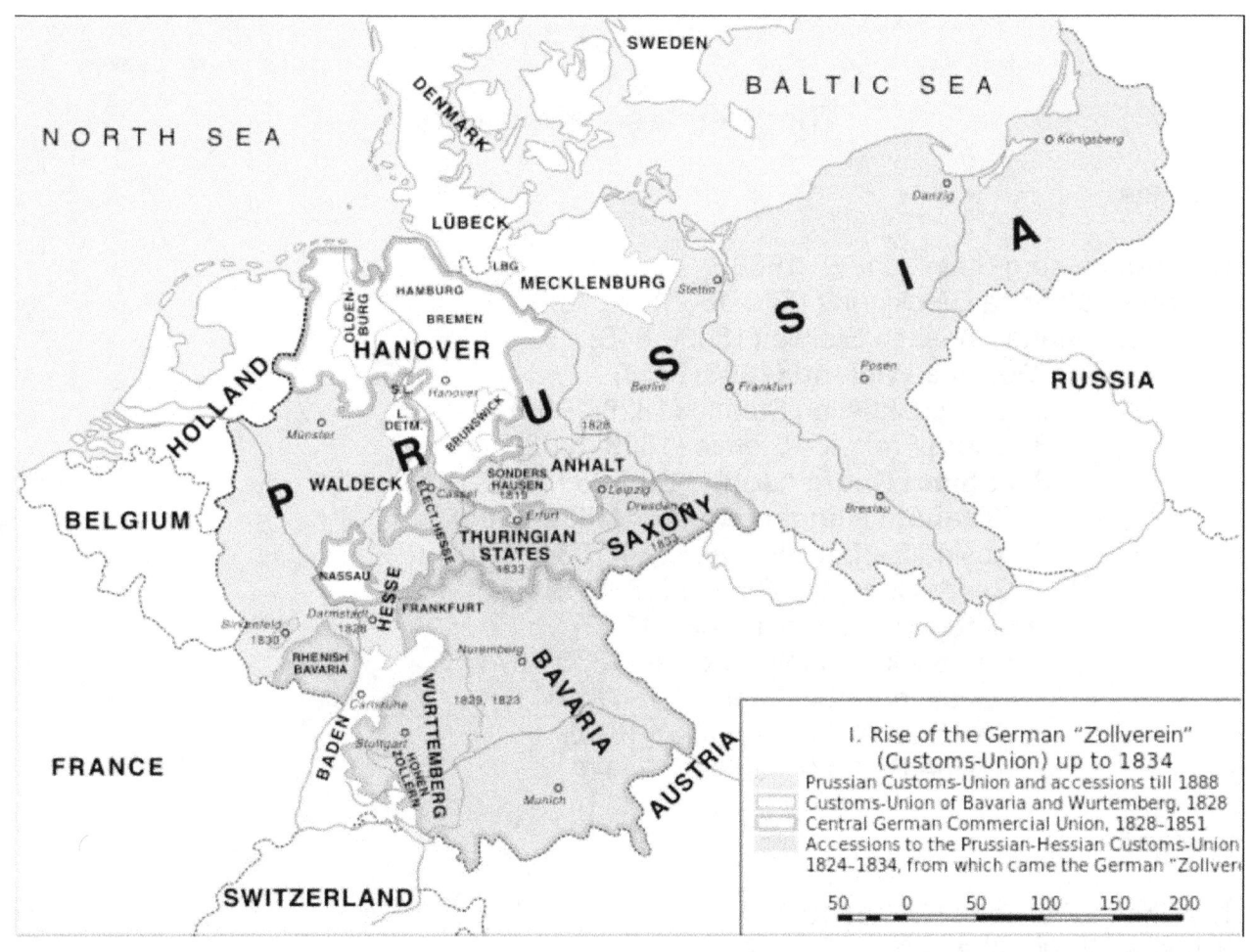

# Chapter 3

# The Steinles in Germany

**Steinles**

1. Johann Georg Steinle (1775-1838)
 + Maria Katharina Glocklerin (1775-1833)
     2. Johann Christian Steinle (1800-1846)
     **+ Ana Dorthea Wieland (1803-1856)**
         3. Georg Christian Steinle (1828-1909)
         3. Georg Freidrick Steinle (1829-1902)
         **3. Johann Georg "John" Steinle (1831-1911)**
         **+ Elizabeth Klingenschmidt (1830-1908)**
         3. Rosina Barbra Steinle (1834-1834)
         3. Georg Christoph Steinle (1835-1917)
          + Johanna C. Arnold (1839-1878)
         3. Frederick Wilhelm Steinle (1838-1871)
         3. Christina Barbra Steinle (1841-1841)
         3. Dorothea A. Steinle (1842-1842)
         3. Rosina Barbara Steinle (1844-)

**Wielands**

1. Wilhelm Wieland (1741-1810)
 + Maria Margaretha Lang (1742-1797)
     2. Johann Georg Wieland (1769-1852)
     + Anna Dorthea Mezger (1772-1817)
         **3. Ana Dorthea Wieland (1803-1856)**

**Mezgers**

1. Johann Heinrich Mezger (abt. 1750- )
 + Maria Magdalene Deizin (abt. 1750- )
     2. Anna Dorthea Mezger (1772- 1817)

The Steinles have lived in Scheppach, Jagst, Württemberg for many centuries. There are still descendants of Johann Christian Steinle (born 24 Dec 1800 in Scheppach) and Ana Dorthea Wieland Steinle (born 5 Dec 1803 in Scheppach) in Württemberg. Their history tells of Johann Georg Steinle (born 24 Aug 1831) who left for America but they know nothing about him after that. Either he was never heard from again or they were not interested in what happened to him so far away.

Ana Dorthea Wieland's history goes back farther than Johann Christian Steinle. Ana's grandfather was Wilhelm Wieland, born 9 Mar 1741 in Buchelberg, Jagst, Württemberg. He married Maria Margaretha Lang (born 9 Jun 1742 in Scheppach) on 17 Jan 1767 in

Scheppach, Jagst, Württemberg. Their son Johann Georg Weiland was born 21 Mar 1769 in Scheppach. Wilhelm Wieland died 9 Nov 1810 and Maria Lang Wieland died 19 Sep 1797.

On Ana Dorthea Wieland's mother's side, her grandfather was Johann Heinrich Mezger. He was born about 1750 in Scheppach. He was married to Maria Magdalene Deizin (born about 1750 in Scheppach) about 1770 in Scheppach. Their daughter Anna Dorthea Mezger was born 14 Mar 1772 in Scheppach. She married Johann Georg Wieland 9 May 1797 in Scheppach. Johann Georg Wieland died 25 Feb 1852 in Scheppach and Anna Dorthea Mezger died 22 Apr 1817.

Johann Christian Steinle married Ana Dorthea Wieland on 6 Nov 1827 in Waldbach, Jagst, Württemberg. They had nine children all while living in Scheppach, Johann Christian Steinle died 29 Jul 1846 and Ana Dorthea died 5 Feb 1856 in Scheppach.

The Lutheran Church in Scheppach, above, is probably where the Steinles worshipped. It was built in 1621 and is still in use. The date is visible over the doorway. The photos were taken in Scheppach by Jim Richardson, a descendant of Georg Christoph Steinle (1835-1917), during a visit in 1997. He visited with Elizabeth Steinle Claus and Paul Steinle who still live in Adolzfurt across the river from Scheppach. Below are the altar and choir loft on the left. The baptistery is on the right.

John Stanley would have been baptized Johann Georg Steinle here.

According to some German records, Johann Georg (1831) was married to Maria Glocklerin (1775). She was his grandmother. He probably was not married but lived with her after her husband died. It would not have been unusual to have one of the children take care of a grandmother. Considering the repetition of names, it is even possible the two people called Johann Georg (born 1775 and born 1831) were confused. It is helpful to attach a birth year when there are repeating names.

In the top picture, Jim Richardson is pictured on the right with, from the left his son Timothy, daughter Jenny, Herr Claus, and Elizabeth Steinle Claus.

The next picture is of Jim and his wife Anna.

The bottom picture is of the valley where the Steinles lived. Scheppach is mid photo and Adolzfurt is in the foreground. The valley has many vineyards and wine making seems to be the main livelihood. They have been making wine here for a very long time. It is possible, even probable, that the Steinles made wine. Jim Richardson's grandfather, who was born and grew up in Scheppach, liked a daily glass of Concord grape wine – probably similar to the wine made here.[5]

As the third son of a large family, Johann Georg (1831) would not have had the advantages of a first son. His father died in 1846 leaving 6 living children. The oldest child, a son, Georg Christian was 18 and would have inherited the land and been in charge of the household even though the mother was still alive. If Georg was doing something else, such as an apprenticeship, the second oldest would have taken over. With such bleak prospects, it is no wonder John felt he needed to leave. He would have had additional incentive if he was required to take care of his grandmother.

Johann Georg Steinle left Württemberg for La Havre, France in early 1854. He booked passage on the Pauline bound for New York. There were 438 passengers on the small wooden ship. It took several weeks under sail to reach their destination during which Johann would have had a small bunk low in the ship. He may have even had to share that bunk if he didn't have much money for the passage. He certainly would not have had a luxury cabin! Johann landed in New York on 25 May 1854.[4]

Georg Christoph Steinle a younger brother of John's born 2 Oct 1835 in Scheppach immigrated to the USA in 1881 with three children. His wife Johanna died in 1879. He lived in Cleveland, Ohio and died there 18 May 1917. I do not know if the brothers ever communicated or knew they lived so close together. Georg Christoph is the Great Grandfather of Jim Richardson.

# Chapter 4

## The Klingenschmidt Family in America

1. Konrad Klingenschmitt (1759-1827)
 + Marie Katrinen Sebastianin (1759-1837)
    2. Maria Katharina "Catherine" Klingenschmitt (1785-1871)
    + Johann Ludwig Sattler (1786-1862)
    2. Marie Elizabeth Klingenschmittin (1789-)
    + Jakob Ludwig Lich (1785-1839)
    2. Johann Philipp Klingenschmitt (1793-1796)
    2. Marie Sibylle Klingenschmitt (1795-1796)
    2. Anne Marie Klingenschmitt (1797-)
    2. Anna Catharina Klingenschmitt (1801-1881)
    **2. Johann Jakob "Jacob" Klingenschmitt (1802-1889)**
    **+ Charlotte Dortha Warner (1801-1872)**
        **3. Anna Marie "Mary" Klingenschmidt (1827-1899)**
        **+ Johann Geog "George" Kester (1820-1908)**
            4. Mary Kester (1854-1899)
            + Foster W. Rickard (1858-1941) (married in 1887)
            4. John George "J. George" Kester (1857-1923)
            + Maria Sieb (1864-1913)
            4. Charles P. Kester (3/1860- 10/1860)
            4. Sarah J. Kester (1861-1885)
            + Foster W. Rickard (1858-1941)
            4. Josephine "Phene" Kester (1864-1949) p
            + Charles Clark (1858-1949) p
        **3. Elizabeth Klingenschmidt (1830-1908)**
        **+ Johann C "John" Steinle (1831-1911)**
            4. Catherine Stanley (1854-) raised by grandparents
            + Johann Gothlich Schwany (1844-1927)
            4. Charlotte Steinle (1857-1864)
            4. John G. Steinle (abt. 1858-1924)
            + Jeanette Carrie Fry (1865-1927)
            4. Louisa Steinle (1860-1864)
            4. Anna Stanley (1862-1864)
            4. Fred Stanley (1864-1939) p
            + Ella Louise Carpenter (1858-1924)
            4. Emma Jane Stanley (1869-1935) p
            + John C. Kelley (1867-1893?)
            + William G Raymond (1873-before1940)
            + Phineas A Cole (1860-1940)
            4. Jacob Stanley (1872-)
            + Rhoda Phillips (1878-)
        **3. Catherine Klingenschmidt (1835-1904)**

  + Johann Ahrend (1830-1907)
    4. Charles J Arn (1857-1917)
    + Julina A Minter (1863-)
    4. Mary Ann Arn (1858-1928)
    + Thomas Jefferson Wise Jr. (1858-1922)
    4. Elizabeth Arn (1859-1938)
    + Charles Joseph Wilhelm (1845-1897)
    4. Franklin Arn (1862-1914)
    4. Ida Louise Arn (1865-1931)
    + A R Whiteman (1841-)
    + Jonas E. Likins (1849-1924)
    4. Julia C. Arn (1867-1946)
    4. John Jacob Arn (1870-1933)
    +Nellie M (1873- before 1920)
    + Hattie B Van Vliet (1870-)
    4. Frederick W. Arn (1872-1909)
 3. Karl "Charles" Phillip Klingenschmidt (1837-1917)
 + Sarah H. Ish (1835-1916)
    4. George Klingenschmidt (1862-1948) p
    + Clara Carl (1866-1960) p
    4. Emma Jane Klingenschmidt (1864-1941) p
    + Amaza L. Gee (1861-1941) p
    4. Ellen Klingenschmidt (1866-1870)
    4. Sara Elizabethm "Libbie" Klingenschmidt (1870-1953) p
    + Jacob "Jay" Southern (1861-1947) p
    4. Alice Eva Klingenschmidt (1871-1938)
    4. Charles Klingensmith (1874-1933)
    + Katherine M Baker (1870-1939)
    4. Frank L. Klingensmith (1879-1949)
    + Julia Myhrs (1880-1926)

A "p" after a name in the lineage chart refers to the Klingensmith Family Reunion Poem.

The name Klingenschmidt is German and means a person or smith who makes bells, especially hand bells, a Klingen Smith, (German dictionary). It can be spelled several different ways including added endings which may indicate male or female especially in baptismal records.

**1.Konrad Klingenschmit and Katerina Sebastian**

Johann Konrad "Konrad" Klingenschmittin was born 5 May 1759 in Morschheim, Bayern, Germany and died 24 Jan 1827 in Göllheim, Bayern, Germany. Marie Katrinen "Katharina" Sebastian was born 1759 and died 26 Jul 1837. Konrad Klingenschmidt married Katharina Sebastian 14 Sep 1784 at Evangelisch, Göllheim, Pfalz, Bavaria. They had at least 8 children including Johann Jakob Klingenschmitt, born 22 Sep 1802.

## 2. Maria Klingenschmittin and Johann Ludwig Sattler

Konrad and Katrina's oldest child, Maria Katharina Klingenschmittin was born 13 Okt (Oct) 1785, and baptized 14 Okt 1785 in Göllheim, Bayern, Preussen. She married Johann Ludwig Sattler 27 Jan 1811 in Göllheim, Bayern, Germany. They moved to Ashland County Ohio before 1862. Ludwick Sattler born 11 Jan 1786 in Bavaria, Germany, died 20 Aug 1862 in Ashland, Ohio and is buried in Ohl Cemetery. Catherine born 12 Oct 1785 in Germany, died 10 Aug 1871 in Ashland, Ohio and is buried with Ludwick. Their son Johann Ludwick Sattler was born 7 Feb 1813 and died 2 Oct 1889.

## 2. Maria Elizabethe Klingenschmittin and Jakob Ludwig Lich

Maria Elizabethe Klingenschmittin married Jakob Ludwig Lich on 11 Dec 1814 in Göllheim, Germany. They had a son Jakob Ludwig Lich; a daughter Anne Marie Lich; a daughter Barbra Lich born in 1824, died in 1895; and a son Conrad born in 1820 and died in 1903. All the children were born in Göllheim. A family tree has Jacob Ludwig Lich born 22 Apr 1785 and died 1839.
Another tree has Maria Elizabethe born about 1789.

Two of Konrad and Katrina's children died in 1796, probably from a disease. No information could be found on Ann Marie except her birth in 1797.

## 2. Anna Cathrina Klingenschmitt

Birth and death records were found for Anna Cathrina Klingenschmitt, born in 1801 and died in 1881 with the same name. Apparently, she didn't marry.

In Germany, frequently the boys were named Johann "John" something and the girls were named Maria or Anna something then they were called by their middle name most of the time. This made it difficult to find people and confirm that they were the same person. Names were also handed down in families so birth and death dates are crucial.

## 2. Johann Jacob "Jacob" Klingenschmidt and Charlotte Dorthe Warner

Jacob Klingenschmidt (it could also be spelled Klingelschmidt according to Trinity Lutheran Church records or even Klingelschmitt) was born 22 Sep 1802 and baptized 26 Sep 1802 at Evangelisch, Göllheim, Pfalz, Bavaria, now part of Germany. His father was Konrad Klingenschmitt and his mother Marie Katrinen Sebastianin. Evangelisch or Evangelisch Kirche is the protestant, Lutheran, church of the area.

Johann Jacob Klingenschmitt and Charlotte Dorthe Woerner were married 12 Nov 1826 according to a German marriage record. The place listed is Evangelisch, Göllheim, Donnersbergkreis (Donnersberg district), Rheinland-Pfalz (Pfalz is a principality), Germany. Charlotte's father was Johannes Woerner. The marriage would have been before the various areas of Germany were consolidated in to one country.

Anna Marie Klingenschmitt was born and baptized 22 Apr 1827 at Evangelisch, Göllheim, Pfalz, Bayern, Germany. Her father was Johann Jacob Klingenschmitt and her mother Charlotte Dorthe Woerner.

Elizabetha Klingenschmidt was born 17 Mrz (Mar) 1830 and baptized 21 Mrz 1830 in Evangelisch, Göllheim, Pflaz, Bavaria. Her parents are Charlotte Woerner and Jacob Klingenschmidt.

Katharina Klingenschmitt was born 7 Juni 1835 and baptized 8 Juni 1835 in Evangelisch Kirche, Göllheim (BA. Kircheimbolanden), Preussen. Göllheim is in present Bavaria or Rheinland – Pfalz but may have been considered Prussia as Prussia was used at times to include all of Germany. This is a slightly different date than the Hillsdale County History written in 1889. The German record is probably more accurate but was not what was remembered many years later.

Karl Phillip Klingenschmitt was born 27 Dec 1837 and baptized 31 Dec 1837 in Evangelisch, Göllheim, Pfalz, Bavaria. His parents were Jacob Klingenschmitt and Charlotte Wörner.

The church and city are the same but the ruling divisions have changed from time to time. There are also slightly different spellings of the last name.

The family lived in Bavaria until Karl was a youth of 16 years, then they all started for America, landing at New York City, 1 May 1856 and proceeding directly westward to Hillsdale County, Michigan. They were poor in pocket even having to borrow money to bring them to this country. While the father cultivated his little tract of land in Pittsford Township, Karl and his three sisters went out to earn money to pay the family debt, according to the History of Hillsdale County.[8] The facts have revealed a slightly different story.

Marie Klingenschmidt left Havre, France and arrived in New York on 11 Jun 1851 on the ship Bavaria. George Kester (Keister) arrived in New York, 25 Jul 1851. Mary Klingensmith married George Kester two years later in Erie County New York. They may have known each other before leaving Germany or just happened to both be in Erie and met there. The timing would allow either and there is no evidence. Mary may have come ahead to earn money for the others passage or she may have been an adventurous type. I would lean toward the theory that they knew each other before leaving Germany but just didn't take the same boat because they weren't married or their meeting in America was a secret. Göllheim is quite close to Kindenheim the probable birth place of Johann Georg "George" Kester. George would have been 30 when he left Germany and Mary would have been 24. Apparently, they didn't see a future in Germany.

Mary Klingenschmidt may have left Germany to go to the United States because her cousins were already there and could provide a place to live at least for a while.

Henry and Mary Klingenschmitt were living in Pendleton, Niagara County, New York in 1850. Their son Phillip Klingenschmitt was born in 1845 in New York. Henry was born in Bavaria about 1801. Henry's father was Johann Philipp Klingenschmitt. Who may have been an uncle to our Johann Jacob Klingenschmitt and a brother to Konrad Klingenschmitt. Konrad's son Johann Philipp Klingenschmitt may have been named after his father's brother which would be the connection, but there is no proof at this time. The towns in Germany where they were born are very close.

While looking for this connection, it became obvious the Klingenschmitts were active in the Lutheran Church and may have been deacons or pastors.

An 1850 census for Pendleton, Niagara, New York has Henry Klingenschmitt, 45, a farmer, born in Germany. Elizabeth is 45 and born in Germany. Their children are Jacob, 14, born in New York; Catherine, 17, born in New York; Henry,10; Phillip, 8 and Dolly, 1. This would put Henry in New York in 1833 long before Mary arrived.

The 1865 New York census for Erie County has Henry J. Klinghamsmith, 63, born in Germany, a farmer, a naturalized citizen and owner of land. Catharine Klinghamsmith is 37 born in Germany, has 9 children; Mary, 13, born in New York; John, 11; Elizabeth, 8; Dana, 6; Geny, 6; Dorothy, 3 3/12; Jacob, 2 4/12; Margaret, 11/12, and Peter, 73, born in Germany, widowed. Henry's first wife Elizabeth must have died and he married Catherine.

All of this leads me to the conclusion the Pendleton, New York Klingenschmitts were cousins to our Klingenschmitts and this is the reason Mary, and later the others, went to Erie County which is adjacent to Niagara County with the town of Pendleton right on the border. Mary may have lived with the Pendleton Klingenschmitts for a while then found a place of her own.

Mary Klingensmith and George Kester were married 6 Feb 1853 in Buffalo, Erie, New York then moved to Hillsdale County in 1854.

The date of Jacob and Anna's arrival given in the 1889 History of Hillsdale County is not the same as that found in ship records. The actual date may have been forgotten over the years or it may have been purposely changed.

Jacob Klingenschmidt 51, Charlotte 52, Elizabeth 25, Catherine 20, and Carl 10 arrived in the Port of New York on the ship Challenge on 11 May 1854 having left from Havre (France) 22 April 1854. This date would put them in the US earlier than the story told in 1889. It would also have them here in time for a baby, Catherine Stanley, to be born in June of 1854 in New York, either in New York City or more likely Erie County, before coming to Hillsdale. Mary Kester was born in July 1854 after the family moved to

Hillsdale County as she is always listed as being born in Michigan. John Steinle arrived in New York May 25, 1854 on the Pauline and went to Hillsdale County with a possible stop in Erie County, New York. The timing is way too coincidental to not have been at least in part to conceal the birth of an early baby. At this time, a pregnancy out of wedlock was scandalous indeed! The baby, Catherine Stanley must have been raised by her grandparents outside of the Lutheran Church. John Steinle and Elizabeth Klingenschmidt did eventually marry but not until 1856.

Göllheim the birthplace of the Klingenschmidts is 289 km or 179 miles from Scheppach, the birth place of Johann Steinle.

The 1860 census for Pittsford, Hillsdale, Michigan, taken 26 Jun has George Kester, 40, born in Germany, a farmer with $3000 in real estate. Mary is 33 and born in Germany. Their children are Mary E, 6; George, 3 and Charlie, 6/12. All the children were born in Michigan.

The same 1860 census has Jacob Klingensmith, 58, born in Germany, a farm laborer. Charlotte is 60 and born in Germany. Their children are Charley, 22, born in Germany and Catherine Stanley, 6, born in New York.

John and Elizabeth Steinle/Stanley were married in Trinity Lutheran Church in 1856 in Hillsdale. When Catherine Stanley was originally found in the 1870 census it was thought she could have been a helper in the home. A 6-year-old is not much of a helper. This may have been the reason everyone came to the US. The Klingensmiths may not have attended the Lutheran Church in Hillsdale at least not with Catherine Stanley and therefore the extra child would not have been obvious.

The 1870 census for Pittsford, Hillsdale, Michigan has Jacob Klingensmith, 67, born in Germany, a farmer with $750 in real estate. Charlotte is 70, keeping house and born in Germany. Catherine Stanley is 16 and born in New York.

It was a serious undertaking to pull up roots in Germany and make the long voyage in a wooden ship to a relatively unknown land. Our ancestors were courageous people and obviously, a family devoted to each other.

Charlotte Klingenschmidt died in Pittsford Township, 15 Sep 1872. Jacob was still living in 1889 and made his home with his son, Charles (formerly Karl). He retained, notwithstanding his great age (87), a goodly share of his old-time industry and activity according to the History of Hillsdale County.[8]

Jacob Klingensmith, born 22 Sep 1802, died in 1889 and is buried in Locust Corners Cemetery, Pittsford, Hillsdale, Michigan.

This picture was found on Ancestry under Charles Klingensmith. I believe the older man in the center is Jacob Klingensmith. The man on the left and woman on the right would be Charles and Sarah. Their three daughters are standing behind the others and the two small boys would be Charles Friedrich and Frank L. The oldest son George is missing and probably on his own. The picture may have been taken about 1884, estimating the children's ages.

HILLSDALE COUNTY MICHIGAN
Compiled & Published by
The American Atlas Co.
Geo. A. Ogle & Co.
Chicago 1894

This map may help in deciding where various people in the following chapters are living.

Townships of Hillsdale County

| Litchfield | Scipio | Moscow | Somerset |
|---|---|---|---|
| Allen | Fayette | Adams | Wheatland |
|  | Hillsdale |  |  |
| Reading | Cambria | Jefferson | Pittsford |
| Camden | Woodbridge | Ransom | Wright |
|  | Amboy |  |  |

# Chapter 5

## Mary Klingensmith and George Kester

1. Anna Marie "Mary" Klingenschmidt (1827-1899)
+ Johann Georg "George" Kester (1820-1908)
    2. Mary Kester (1854-1919)
    + Foster W. Rickard (1858-1941) (married in 1887)
        3. Cecil Leland Rickard (1892-1951) WW1
        + Eva M Gee (1893-1966) (granddaughter Charles Klingensmith)
    2. John George "J George" Kester (1857-1923)
    + Maria Sieb (1864-1913)
        3. Charles G. Kester (1883-1961)
        + Alice R. Hutcheson (1881-1937)
            4. Florence L. Kester (1909-2002)
            + Regner A Ekstrom (1908-1990)
                5. Ronald Ekstrom (1937-)
                5. Alice Ekstrom (1938-)
                5. Walter Ekstrom (1940-2001)
            4. Harold C. Kester (1910-2001)
            + Helen Oswald (1908-1991)
                5. Jean Louise Kester (1933-)
                5. Anita Kester (1938-)
            4. Bruce E. Kester (1913-1976)
            + Hazel Buck (1910-1991)
                5. Keith Kester (1940-)
        + Mable Mae Hutchison (1891-1971)
        3. Fannie Louise Kester (1885-1958) p
        + Lee Agustus Horton (1885-1968) p WW1
            4. Edith M. Horton (1923-) p
            + Edward Claire Hinga (1919-1987)
            4. Eugene Kester Horton (1925-1993) p
            + Margaret Bowers (1927-2005)
        3. Herman Kester (1887-1942)
        + Ida Elizabeth Ferguson (1893-)
        3. Louis Kester (1891-1936) p
        + Lois Rachel Fenner (1891-1966) p
            4. John George Kester (1916-) p WW11
            4. Frederick P. Kester (1924-) p
        3. Mary Kester (1892-1944) WW11
        3. Max Emil Kester (1895-1976) WW1
        + Wilma Florence Steadman (1893-1982)
    2. Charles P. Kester (1860-1860)
    2. Sarah J. Kester (1861-1885)
    + Foster W. Rickard (1858-1941)

                    3. Carlton George Rickard (1883-1920)
            2. Josephine (Phene) Kester (1864-1949) p
               + Charles Clark (1858-1949) p
                    3. Lela M. Clark (1896-1931) p

## 1. Mary Klingensmith and George Kester

George Kester, it may also be Keister in German, was born in Germany, 18 Jul 1820. His father, John Kester, was a mason by trade, and was a lifelong resident of Germany. George received an excellent education in the public schools of his native village, which he attended until fourteen years of age. He continued engaged in farming until the age of 16. He then served an apprenticeship of three years to learn the shoemaker's trade and followed it for one year after his apprenticeship expired, in his native country. He then ambitiously decided to try his fortunes in the United States of America, and set sail from Havre in June, 1851, for the Promised Land. He landed in New York after a voyage of seven weeks, and went directly to Erie County, where he arrived with but a few dollars in his pocket. But he was courageous and hopeful, and soon found work at his trade, which he pursued there the three succeeding years, when the state of his health would permit, for in his youth he was crippled with rheumatism, and often suffered from attacks of his old enemy. During his residence in that county, however, he obtained the cheerful and ready help of an active and able helpmate, to whom he gratefully acknowledges much of his success in life to be due, as after their union she sturdily put her shoulder to the wheel and went out to work that she might assist him in securing a home. His marriage to this devoted wife and faithful companion took place 6 Feb 1853. She was formerly Mary Klingensmith, daughter of Jacob and Charlotte Klingensmith and was born in Germany, 22 Apr 1827, coming to this country when 25 years of age according to the History of Hillsdale County.[8]

If my information that George was born in Kindenheim is correct, he would have been born on an estate or manor. His father's trade of mason would have given them some status. He did get some schooling, probably reading, writing and arithmetic. By the time, he was a teenager he would have been working on the estate's farm. Through good fortune or his earnings, he was able to serve an apprenticeship with a shoemaker. This gave him a trade and he could soon earn enough for passage to America.

I remember my father, George Bishop borrowing a metal shoe mold on a stand in order to repair some shoes. The bottom of the shoe mold faced upwards and was on a metal pole with a small plate at the bottom allowing it to stand on its own. By sitting in a chair with the pole between your legs, you could put nails in the bottom of the shoe which was supported by the mold. George Bishop fixed a shoe with a loose sole in this manner. This shoe mold may have belonged to George Kester originally and been passed down through the family. I do not know where it is now.

In June or early July of 1854 Mr. Kester and his wife came to Hillsdale County, where he first engaged on the farm with Mr. Long, in Pittsford Township. He afterward rented a log house on the northwest quarter of section 7, and in the fall of the year established himself at his trade of shoemaking. He lived there one and a half years, profitably employed at his trade, and then decided to turn his attention to farming, and bought seventeen acres of land that was included in the farm he held in 1889. There was a log house on the place, and after moving into it he commenced work on his farm, and at the same time made shoes. George and Mary by their untiring industry, wise economy, and sound management, became very prosperous, and besides building up a good home, reared their children in comfort, and sent them out into the world with the advantages of fine educations. In 1889, Mr. Kester owned one of the best and most productive farms in this locality; he added to his landed possessions, until he owned 147 acres of land and had two good sets of farm buildings. [8]

The 1860 census for Pittsford, Hillsdale, Michigan has George Kester, 40, born in Germany, a farmer with a farm worth $1000. Mary is 33 and born in Germany. The children are Mary E, 6; George, 3, and Charley 3/12. All the children were born in Michigan. Charley was born Mar 1860 and died Oct 1860 at the age of 7 months.

George Kester became a US citizen on 16 Sep 1861 in Hillsdale County Circuit Court, Hillsdale, Michigan.

The 1870 census for Pittsford, Hillsdale, Michigan has George Kester, 50, a farmer with $4200 in real estate and $1500 in personal property. Mary is 43 and keeping house. Their children are Mary, 16, at home; George, 10, at school; Sarah, 8, at school and Josephine, 5, at school.

The 1880 census for Pittsford, Hillsdale, Michigan has George Kester, 59, a farmer, born in Bavaria and had Rheumatism at the time the census was taken. Mary is 53 and was born in Bavaria. Their daughters are Mary, 25; Sarah, 18 and Josephine, 15. Foster Rickard, 22, a laborer is living with them.

This picture taken between 1880 and 1885 has seated left to right Sarah Kester, George Kester and Mary Klingensmith Kester. Standing are left to right Josephine, J George and Mary Kester.

Of George and Mary's five children, the following was recorded in the History of Hillsdale County written in 1889: Mary the wife of Foster Rickard, lives in Nebraska; George lives on the homestead; Josephine is a teacher in the public schools; Sarah died at the age of 23 years and Charles died at the age of seven months.[8]

A stone in Locust Corners Cemetery reads: Charly P died Oct 1860. The date is unclear and the rest is unreadable

The History of Hillsdale County continued with: George and Mary Kester were sincere members of the Lutheran Church and are widely respected for their kind hearts, blameless lives, and genuine worth and ability.[8]

Mary Klingensmith Kester, born 22 Apr 1827, died 26 Feb 1899 of La Grippe (flu) and heart failure. She is buried in Locust Corners Cemetery.

John George Kester, 88, born 18 Jul 1820, died 24 Jul 1908 of old age in Plainwell, Michigan. He is buried in Locust Corners Cemetery. He was widowed, was married 32 years and the father of 5 children, 3 of whom were living at the time of his death. George's father is listed as Mr. Kester and his mother as Abigail Messmer both born in

Germany. The certificate is signed by J G Kester. He was living in Plainwell with J George Kester at the time of his death.

George Kester left a hand written will dated 23 August 1898 which was probated 3 Aug 1908. He wanted all his bills paid then left everything firstly to his wife Mary. By the time he died Mary was already dead. The will continued with:

"3rd I leave devise and bequeath to my deceased daughter's son, Carlton George Rickard, from the reversion or remainder of my real estate's Buildings and it's appurtenances thereto the amount of four hundred (400) dollars in Real Estate or money. Provided the APPRAISED VALUATION OF PROPERTY IS TWO THOUSAND DOLLARS OR MORE. If it is less than two thousand dollars, he shall have equal to twelve and one-half percent (12 ½%) of the appraised valuation of the property and to have and hold the same to him the said Carlton George Rickard his heirs and assigns from and after the decease of my said wife to his and their use and behalf forever.

4th All the rest and residue of my Estate Real Personal and mixed of which I shall die seized and possessed unto which I shall be entitled at my decease or at the decease of my wife I give devise and bequeath to be equally divided between and among my three children as follows namely

Mrs. Mary E. Rickard
Mr. George Kester Jr.
Mrs. Josephine Clark

5th And lastly, I do Nominate and appoint Charles P. Klingensmith to be the Executor of this my last will and testament.

in witness whereof, I the said George Kester have to this my last will and testament consisting of three Sheets of Paper Subscribed my name and affixed my Seal this 23rd day of August in the year of our lord one thousand Eight Hundred and Ninety-Eight.

The will is witnessed by Almeron A. Case and Harry Case both of Pittsford Hillsdale Co. Mich. It appears to have been written by Almeron.

A probate paper for George Kester says:
I George Kester Jr reside in Plainwell; Allegan county am interested in the said estate and make this petition as son and devisee named in the last will and testament of 23 August 1898 which is deposited in said court etc. George had left Real Estate valued at $6000. The names of the devisees are as follows:
Mary Kester, wife died February 26th 1899
Carlton George Rickard Grandson, 24, Seattle, Washington

Mary E Rickard daughter Moscow, Idaho
Josephine Clark daughter Pittsford, Michigan
Your petitioner son Plainwell, Michigan
   All of legal age

Another paper grants Charles P Klingensmith the administration of said estate. He is ordered to appear 31 Aug 1908 at 10am. A copy of the order is to appear in the Pittsford Reporter for 3 weeks. Another paper has a copy of the information published in the paper, dates and signed by the publisher.

Another paper is signed by Harry Case saying that he was there and witnessed the will. The judge, Fred H Stone admitted the will 31 Aug 1908.

Next was an order admitting the will to probate with Charles Klingensmith as administrator. Dated 31 Aug 1908. A bond of $100 was paid

The will was finally approved by the Judge in another signed paper.

Next James Cousins and William A Williams were appointed to appraise the estate. Also, the executor is allowed one year in which to dispose of the estate and pay the debts of the deceased. Four months are allowed for creditors to present their claims to the court.

C P Klingensmith and the Judge signed a paper saying a full list of the deceased possessions would be given to the court in 30 days.

A legal description of George's land: 107 Acres on E ½ of section 6 Pittsford
W ½ of S E ¼ of Sec 6 Town 7 South of Range 1 West and 2 acres on West side of E ½ of SE ¼ of Section 6 Township Seven South Range one West, Also S ½ of S ½ of NE ¼ less 15 acres off East End of Sec. 6 Township Seven South Range One West.
Valued at and appraised at Five Thousand Dollars ($5,000.)
Appraised 9 Sep 1908 by Cousins and Williams
Inventory presented to Probate Court 2 Oct 1908

Charles Klingensmith had a notice to creditors that bills needed to be submitted by 31 Dec 1908 printed 4 times in paper and posted at 3 places where notices are conspicuously and securely posted, the post office, a jewelry store and Cole's Store.

Claims were submitted 31 Dec 1908:   D. M Keller         15.75
                                     George Kester Jr.   75.00
                                     C. R. Clark         75.00
With assets to pay the claimants, the claims were closed.

Next is a petition to the court that Charles P Klingensmith be allowed to settle the final account and have his bond discharged.

The petition is to be heard 1 Feb 1909 and a notice is to be published in the Pittsford Reporter for 3 successive weeks previous to said day.

Several creditors are paid small amounts totaling $150 including $ 34.04 to C. R. Clark, $15.75 to Dr. D McKellar, $43.12 in taxes, $2.98 for insurance, others hard to read.
This leaves    George Kester Jr. account paid    $75
               C R. Clark balance paid            $40.91
       Legacy to Carlton Geo. Rickard            $400

Final distribution of all that remains of the estate is to be made to Mary E Rickard, George Kester Jr. and Josephine Clark. It is noted that Mary Kester died before George Kester and that the value of the real estate exceeds the sum of two thousand dollars. All of the real estate be assigned to the above mentioned in equal shares as tenants in common or to their assigns. The executor is discharged and his bond cancelled. (this piece is typed; all the rest is hand written in printed forms)

Executor is discharged April 17th 1909.

The change from hand written to typed legal documents must have been made, in Hillsdale County, between 31 Dec 1908 and 1 Feb 1909 although hand written accounting and other forms were still allowed in other papers from 1 Feb 1909.

George and Mary Klingensmith Kester are buried in Locust Corners Cemetery.

## 2. Sarah / Mary Kester and Foster Rickard

Sarah J Kester married Foster W Rickard 6 Sep 1881 in Pittsford. Foster was 23, a farmer, from Bronson, Michigan and born in New York. Sarah was 19, from Pittsford and born in Michigan. R D Clark, minister, performed the ceremony. George Smith and Mary Smith witnessed the ceremony. They were married less than 4 years. A tombstone in Locust Corners Cemetery reads: Sarah J wife of F W Rickard died March 16, 1885 aged 23 yrs. 2 mo. 26 da. Foster and Sarah Rickard had a son Carlton born Oct 1883.

Mary Kester married Foster W. Rickard 10 April 1886 in Hudson, Michigan. They were married by J P Fanner, Pastor, Baptist Church. Their witnesses are William H Fanner and Kate Lang.

Mary and Foster went to Nebraska and were there when the 1889 History of Hillsdale County was written. They moved back from Nebraska before their son Cecil L Rickard was born Dec 1892 in Bronson, Michigan.

The 1900 census for Jefferson, Hillsdale, Michigan has Foster W Rickard, 42, born April 1858, married 13 years, a liveryman. Mary E is 45, born July 1854, and has had 1 child still living. Their sons are Cecil G, 7, born Dec 1892 and Carlton G, 16, born Oct 1883. Living with them is George Kester, 79, born July 1820, a widower, immigrated in 1852 and a naturalized citizen. They lived in a rented house not a farm. Carlton, Sarah and Foster's son, would have been 17 months old when Sarah died. Mary and Foster may have returned from Nebraska to take care of Mary's father, George Kester, who had retired from the farm to a rented house.

George Kester died in 1908 and by April of 1910 Mary and Foster Rickard had moved to Seattle with their two sons. The 1910 census for Seattle, Washington has Foster W Rickard, 52, married 24 years and a teamster in a lumberyard. Mary is 55. Carlton is 26 and a tailor in a shop. Cecil is 17 and an elevator operator in an office building.

A Seattle city directory for 1916 lists Rickards, Carlton G tailor, 334 Liberty Bldg. residence 4401 Phinney Ave. Cecil L machinist and Foster W (Mary) teamster all living at the same address.

Carlton George Rickards, 34, registered for WW1 on 12 Sep 1918. He is living at 4401 Phinney Seattle, Washington, was born 15 Oct 1883 and is a tailor with his own business at 312 Liberty Bldg. Seattle, Washington. He is short with a slight build, blue eyes and Brown hair.

Mary Kester Rickard died 26 Jan 1919 in Seattle, Washington. Her father is listed as George Kester and her mother Mary Clinkersmith (records are not always accurate).

The 1920 census for Seattle, Washington, taken 14 Jan 1920, has Foster W Rickard, 61, working in the ship yards. His sons are Carlton G, 35, a tailor who owns his own shop and Cecil L, 27, a miner in a copper mine.

Carlton Rickard died 7 Feb 1920 shortly after the census, possibly an accident. It could have been disease especially since his death was so close to his mother's. TB was prevalent and could not be cured.

### 3. Cecil Leland Rickard and Eva Mae Gee

Cecil Leland Rickard, 24, registered for WW1 on 5 Jun 1917. He is living at 1012 Superior in Toledo, Ohio and was born 7 Dec 1892 in Bronson, Michigan. He is working on the Hocking Valley Railroad as a fireman. He lists his mother as being dependent on him for support. He has been a private in the Washington Infantry (National Guard) for 3 years. Cecil is of medium height, medium build, blue eyes, brown hair and has lost the second finger of his right hand.

Cecil Rickard was in Company A at Ft Lawton, Washington from the time he was recruited until 13 Dec 1917; 130 Aero Squadron until 23 Jan 1918; 326 Aero Squadron until 23 Feb 1918; Kelly Field, Texas until 7 Aug 1918, then overseas 20 Oct 1918 to 18 Apr 1919. He left Pauillac, France 4 Apr 1919 and landed in Hoboken, New Jersey 18 Apr 1919. The United States Navy established a naval air station 1 Dec 1917 to operate sea planes during WW1.

Cecil was back in Seattle in 1920 or at least was counted in the census.

In the 1920 census for Flint, Michigan Eva Gee was living with her sister Ruth and Ruth's husband Elzie Remington. Both Eva and Elzie are working in the automobile industry.

Cecil Leland Rickard, 28, a dairyman from Spokane, Washington, married Eva Mae Gee, 28, a seamstress from Metamora, Michigan on 25 Aug 1921 in Hadley, Michigan. His parents are Foster Rickard and Mary Kester while hers are Amaza Gee and Emma Klingensmith. Samuel A Carey, Minister of the Gospel, performed the ceremony. Ruth and Elzie Remington were witnesses. Mary Kester and Emma Klingensmith were 1st cousins which would make Cecil and Eva 2nd cousins.

The 1930 census for South Gate, California has Cecil Rickard, 36, married at 28, a welder in an auto factory who owns his home worth $3000 and a radio. Eva is 36, married at 28 and a shirt maker in a shirt factory. Foster is 71, widowed and a watchman in a factory. After many years of moving around and working different jobs, they were finally settled in a place they would stay for many years. There was no retirement for Foster before Social Security.

The 1940 census for South Gate, California has Cecil L Rickard, 47, completed 8th grade, working at lunch delivery on a lunch wagon and owns a home at 3128 Elizabeth Ave. worth $2500. Eva is 46, graduated high school and working as a shirt maker for a wholesale shirt manufacturer. Foster is 81, completed 8th grade and no longer working. Foster Rickard died 29 May 1941 according to the California death index.

Cecil Leland Rickards, 49, registered for WW11 on 25 April 1942 in South Gate, California. He was living at 8130 Elizabeth Ave, born in Bronson, Michigan on 7 Dec 1892. The person who would know his address was Mrs. Rhoda Place of the same address, he was self-employed and working out of his home. He was 5'5 ¾ ", 206 lb. and had gray eyes and hair.

The 1947 Palm Springs, California City Directory has Rickards Cecil L (Eva M) farmer residence 1441 E Ramon Road. Apparently, they bought a farm.

Cecil L Rickards, born 7 Dec 1892, died 7 Apr 1951 in Maricopa, Arizona. He was working as a cook's helper in a restaurant. He died of a Heart Attack. They had been in Arizona 2 ½ years. Eva M Gee Rickards born 4 Feb 1893, died Oct 1966 in Grand Rapids, Michigan.

## 2. John George "J George" Kester and Marie Seib

J. George Kester, the son of George Kester and Mary Klingensmith, went to Colorado. The 1880 census for Bear Creek, Clear Creek, Colorado has J George Kester, 24, a farm laborer, born in Michigan, parents born in Bavaria. He is living with a hotel keeper. He must have returned (not having found his fortune?) and was living on the homestead in 1889 according to the Hillsdale County History.[8]

J George Kester married Marie Seib in 1882. All of their children were born in Hillsdale County. Charles G was born in 1883, Fannie in 1885, Herman in 1887, Louis in 1891, Mary E in 1892, and Max E in 1896.

A 1900 census has not been found.

The 1910 Census for Plainwell, Michigan has J George Kester, 53, married at 28, a laborer in the coal yards. Marie is 55, has had 6 children, all living and was born in New York of German parents. Their children are Fannie, 25, a Bell Telephone operator; Louis, 19, a rural school teacher; Mary, 18, and Max, 14 attended school.

Marie E Seib Kester, 58, born 13 Nov 1854, died 18 Jun 1913 in Plainwell, Michigan. Cause of death was inflammation and anemia due to gastritis. Her father was Charles Seib and her mother Katherine Eberhardt. Marie is buried in Hillside Cemetery, Plainwell, Michigan.

The 1920 census for Plainwell, Michigan has J George Kester, 63, widower, a laborer at a paper mill and living at 671 Bridge Street. Living with him are Mary E, 28, single, working as a nurse; Max E, 24, single, a school teacher; Lee Horton, 38, son-in-law, an engineer in a paper mill and Fanny L, 35, married.

John George Kester, 66, born 6 Mar 1857, died 5 Sep 1923 in Kalamazoo, Michigan.

### 3. Charles George Kester and Alice R. Hutcheson

I have never found a 1900 census for J George Kester and Charles had left the family by 1910.

Charles G Kester was discovered in Ancestry.com through a family tree and confirmed through his WW11 registration and marriage record. His registration has: Charles George Kester living at 1824 S 19th Ave. Maywood, Illinois, telephone Maywood 7431, age 58, born 12 Nov 1883 Pittsford, Michigan. The person who will know where you are is Bruce Kester 429 S Scoville Ave. Oak Park, Illinois. His employer is Jefferson Electric Co. 256 Madison, Bellwood, Illinois.

Charles G. Kester, 23, of Naperville, Illinois, born in Pittsford Michigan, an engineer married Alice R. Hutchison, 25, of Plainwell, Michigan, born in England, a clerk on 14 Aug 1907 in Plainwell. F M Coddington a Presbyterian Minister officiated. His parents were J G Kester and Maria E Seib. Her parents were Alfred G. Hutchinson and Rosa Lee. Witnesses were Herman Kester and Florence Hutchinson both of Plainwell, Michigan.

This is the very dapper Charles George Kester.

The 1910 census for Downers grove, Illinois has Charles G Kester, 26, Married 2 years, an engineer at an electrical company and renting a home at 87 Forest Ave. Alice R is 28, has had 2 children, both living and emigrated from England in 1888. Their children are Florence L 1 year 8 months and Harold C 1month old

Charles George Kester, 34, born 12 Nov 1883, registered for WW1 on 12 Sep 1918. He was living at 146 Prince Street, Donners Grove, Illinois. He was working as a Stationary Engineer at Chi Fuse Manufacturing Company of 1014 W Congress Street Chicago, Illinois. His nearest relative was Alice R Kester. He was of medium height and build with grey eyes and black hair.

The 1920 census for Downers Grove, Illinois has Charles G Kester, 35, an engineer at an electric company and renting a house at 146 Prince Street. Alice R is 37 and a naturalized citizen. Their children are Florence L, 11; Harold C, 9 and Bruce E, 7. All the children were born in Illinois.

There were a number of Electrical Companies in the area. Mr. Dicke, president of the Dicke Tool Co. that made electrical lineman tools is listed on the same page. It must have been a good neighborhood as several families had servants.

The picture to the right is of Bruce, Florence and Harold Kester. It was taken about 1920.

The 1930 census for Downers Grove, Illinois has Charles Kester, 46, married at 23, a stationary engineer for an electric company, renting a house at 4241 Main for $50 per month and owned a radio. Alice R is 48 and was married at 25. Their children are Florence L, 21, a stenographer in an attorney's office; Harold, 20, a pharmacist apprentice in a drug store and attended school and Bruce E, 17, attended school.

Alice Rosalee Hutchison Kester, 55, born 21 Jan 1882 in Hastings, England, died 14 Jul 1937 in Elmhurst, Illinois and was buried in Hillside Cemetery in Plainwell, Michigan. Her husband was Charles Kester, her father was Alfred George Hutchison born in England and her mother Rosa Lee born in London, England.

Charles George Kester, 55, of 7623 Evans Ave., Chicago, Illinois, an electrician married Mable Mae Hutchison, 48, of 321 Anderson Street, Plainwell, Michigan on 5 Sep 1939. Mable's parents are Alfred George Hutchison and Rosa Lee. She is a sister to Charles's first wife.

The 1940 census for Maywood, Illinois has Charles Kester, 56, graduated high school, an electrician at a manufacturer of electrical appliances for an income of $1,700 and renting an apartment at 526 17th Ave. Mae is 49 and completed 2 years of high school.

Charles George Kester, born 12 Nov 1883, died 15 Nov 1961 in Kalamazoo, Michigan. He is buried in Hillside Cemetery, Plainwell, Michigan.

## 4. Florence L Kester and Regner Ekstrom

Florence Kester married Regner Ekstrom.

The 1940 census for Chicago, Illinois has Regner Ekstrom, 31, completed 2 years college, born in Illinois, same place in 1935, working as a sales engineer for fire control instruments and renting part of a house at 7623 S Evans Ave. Florence is 31, graduated high school and lived in Downers Grove in 1935. Their children are Ronald, 3; Alice, 2 and Walter, 1 month.

## 4.Harold C Kester and Helen Oswald

The 1940 census for Naperville, Illinois has Harold Kester, 30, completed 3 years college, same house in 1935, a salesman for drug supplies and renting part of a house at 15 S Loomis. Helen is 31, graduated college and same house in 1935. Their children are Jean Louise, 7, attended school and Anita, 2.

Harold Kester born 13 March 1910, died 14 July 2001 in Naperville, Illinois.

## 4. Bruce E. Kester and Hazel

The 1940 census for Oak Park, Illinois has Bruce Kester, 27, completed 3 years of college, lived in Downers Grove in 1935, a chemist doing gypsum research and renting part of a house at 429 Scoville Ave. for $30 per month. Hazel is 29 completed 2 years college and lived in Villa Park, Illinois in 1935. Their son, Keith, is 6 months.

### 3. Florence "Fannie" L Kester and Lee A Horton

Florence "Fannie" Kester graduated from high school in 1901. This picture was taken about that time.

Her mother Maria E Sieb Kester died 18 Jun 1913 in Plainwell, Allegan, Michigan at the age of 58. Fannie took care of the family and her mother before she died.

Fannie L Kester, 33, born 25 Apr 1885, married Lee A Horton, 34, born 22 Sep 1885, an engineer on 3 Sep 1919 in Plainwell, Michigan. His parents were Charles Horton and Ella Gott. Her father is listed but not her mother.

Lee Horton enlisted for 3 years in the Army 9 Nov 1908 in Ohio. He was born in Middleville, Michigan. He was 23 years and 6 months at the time of enlistment with engineer as his occupation. He has brown eyes and hair with a sallow complexion and is 5' 9" tall. He was in Company D of the 7th Calvary. Lee was discharged 16 Nov 1911 at Fort McDowell, California with exemplary service. He was a private.

Lee Horton met Charles T Bishop in the Army. He is mentioned again in the Chapter on the Charles T Bishop Family. Chapter 1 has a picture of Lee and Fanny Horton taken in 1950. There is also a picture of Ed and Edith Horton Hinga.

Lee Horton reenlisted in troop B, 6th Calvary and was transferred to the 27th infantry where he is listed 31 Dec 1913. Lee left Hoboken, New Jersey 17 Feb 1918 with Company C, 126th Infantry of the Michigan National Guard on ship 35. He was a corporal and on his way to WW1. He must have been in some battles as he had shrapnel in his leg according to his WW2 registration. The war was over 11 Nov 1918. There is no record of his return but he was home by Sep 1919.

The 1920 census for Plainwell, Michigan has J George Kester, 63, a laborer in a paper mill who owns his home at 671 Bridge Street. Mary Kester is 28 and a nurse. Max E is 24 and a teacher in the school. Lee A Horton is 38 and an engineer in the paper mill. Fanny L Horton is 35 and her occupation is "none" although she must have been very busy taking care of the entire family.

The 1930 census for Galesburg, Michigan has Lee A Horton, 44, married at 34, a WW1 veteran, an engineer in a paper mill who owns his home at 152 New Street worth $900 and a radio. Fanny L is 44 and married at 34. Their children are Edith M, 7 and Eugene K, 4.

The 1940 census for Plainwell, Michigan has Lee A Horton, 55, completed 3 years high school, an electrician for a paper mill who owns his home at 671 W Bridge Street worth $1500. Fannie is 55 and graduated high school. Their children are Edith, 17, completed 2 years high school and Eugene, 14, completed 8th grade.

Lee Agustus Horton, 56, born 22 Sep 1885 in Middleville, Michigan, registered for WW11 on 27 Apr 1942. Lee was living at 671 W Bridge Street, Plainwell, Michigan. The person who would know his address was Edith Hinga of Cooper, Michigan. He was working for Kalamazoo Paper Co. on Lincoln Ave. in Kalamazoo, Michigan. He was 5'11" and weighed 160 lbs. with brown eyes and gray hair. The little finger of his left hand was missing and he had shrapnel wounds on his left leg.

Fannie Louise Kester Horton died 29 Jul 1958 in Plainwell, Michigan. Just before the last Klingensmith reunion.

Lee Augustus Horton died 11 Aug 1968 in Allegan, Michigan and is buried with Fannie in Hillside Cemetery, Plainwell, Michigan.

## 4. Edith M Horton and Edward C Hinga

Edith married Edward C Hinga on 27 Apr 1940 in Kalamazoo, Michigan. They had two children that I remember, Norman and Jean when they came to the Klingensmith Reunion.

The 1948 Kalamazoo City Directory says that Ed Hinga worked at International Paper in Kalamazoo and lived in Plainwell, Michigan. Lee Horton was an electrician at Kalamazoo Paper.

Ed Hinga died 7 Jun 1987 in Plainwell, Michigan and is buried in Hillside Cemetery. Edith was still alive in 1991 and living at 642 Bridge Street.

## 4. Eugene Kester Horton and Margaret Bowers

Eugene Kester Horton, 20, of Plainwell married Margret Bowers 29 May 1946 in South Haven, Michigan. Eugene Kester Horton died 6 Jan 1993.

## 3. Herman Kester and Ida Elizabeth Furguson

Herman was born 19 Feb 1887 in Pittsford but was not in the 1900 or 1910 census. He was in a 1911 Coldwater, Michigan City Directory working at the Tappan Shoe Company. By 1916 he was working at the Hoosier Shoe Company. I believe the shoe companies were making shoes in a factory.

Herman Kester married Ida Elizabeth Furguson in Hillsdale 28 Apr 1918.

The 1920 census for Coldwater, Michigan has Herman Kester, 36, renting a home on Walnut Street and working at a kraut factory for wages. Ida is 26.

The 1930 census for Coldwater, Michigan has Herman Kester, 48, a salesman at a garage who owns a home worth $3000 on Clay Street and a radio. Ida is 37.

The 1940 census for Coldwater, Michigan has Herman Kester, 53, completed 3 years of high school, a salesman at an auto supply store who owns a home on Clay Street worth $3000. Ida is 47 and completed 3 years of high school. They have a lodger, George Downton, 75.

Herman Kester died 25 Feb 1942 and is buried in Oak Grove Cemetery, Coldwater, Michigan. I found no further information on Ida. They did not have children.

### 3. Louis Kester and Lois R Fenner

The 1910 census for Kalamazoo, Michigan has Louis Kester, 20, a boarder and public-school teacher. Louis Kester was in the 1910 census for both Plainwell and Kalamazoo.

Louis Kester registered for WW1 in Allegan County 5 Jun 1917 with a wife and child.

The 1920 census for Kalamazoo, Michigan has Louis Kester, 29, a salaried cutter in a corset factory renting a home at 616 Oak Street. Lois is 28. Their son, John G is 3.

The 1930 census for Kalamazoo, Michigan has Louis Kester 39, married 24 years, not a veteran, an engineer in a factory who owns his home at 708 Maple Street. Lois R is 39. Their sons are George J, 14 and Fredrick P 5.

Louis Kester, 46, of 708 Mable Street. Kalamazoo, Michigan died at Bronson Methodist Hospital 9 Jun 1936. He was born 28 May 1890 in Pittsford, Michigan to John (George) Kester and Marie Sieb. His wife is Lois Kester and he was an engineer for Kalamazoo Paper. Louis had an operation for appendicitis on 12 Apr 1936. After the surgery he had generalized peritonitis, kidney problems, multiple abscesses of liver and the autopsy found a foreign body, wood, near his thyroid. In an age before penicillin infection claimed many lives. He was buried 12 Jun 1936 in Hillside Cemetery, Plainwell, Michigan. Lois died 9 Oct 1966 and is buried with Louis.

The 1940 census was not found but Lois was still living at 708 Maple in 1937 according to the Kalamazoo, Michigan City Directory. John G was living with her and working at Kalamazoo Paper Company. No other children were listed.

John George Kester, 26, son of Louis and Lois Kester, a U S Soldier, married Phyllis E Higdon, 25, a stenographer on 11 Nov 1942.

## 3. Mary Kester

Mary Kester was with her father in the 1920 census. She was working as a nurse.

The 1940 census for the US Marine Hospital, Riverside Drive, Detroit, Michigan has Mary Kester, 48, single, completed 2 years college, (nursing school) residence in 1935 was New Orleans, Louisiana. She worked 56 hours that week as a hospital nurse and made $1920 in 1939. Mary was living in the nurse's home.

Mary Kester born 15 Jan 1892, died 20 Feb 1944 in Detroit a WW11 veteran. She is buried in Hillside Cemetery, Plainwell, Michigan.

## 3. Max E. Kester and Wilma F Steadman

Max Emil Kester registered for WW1 on June 5, 1917. He was 21 years of age, born 8 Aug 1895 in Pittsford, Michigan and was a student at Western State Normal. His residence is 631 Davis Street. Kalamazoo, Michigan. He served from 15 Jun 1918 to 28 Jan 1919

Max is listed in the 1920 census for Gunplain, Allegan, MI with his father and sisters.

Max E Kester, 25, of Kalamazoo MI, a teacher, married Wilma Florence Steadman, 26 of Elsie, Michigan on 16 Oct 1920 in Elsie. Arthur W. Mumford, was the clergyman. Max's parents are John G Kester and Maria Sieb. Wilma's parents are Thomas P Steadman and unknown. Witnesses were T P Steadman of Elsie and J G Kester of Plainwell.

The 1930 census for Kalamazoo, Michigan has Max E Kester, 34, a veteran and a teacher who owns a house on Brook Drive worth $6000 and a radio. Wilma F is 36 and a teacher.

The 1940 census for Kalamazoo, Kalamazoo, Michigan Max Emil Kester, 44, completed 3 years college, a teacher in a public school who owns his home at 1928 Brook Drive. Wilma is 46, completed 2 years college and a substitute teacher in a public school. At that time a student could attend a year or two of "normal college" for a life time teaching certificate. The rules changed in the 1950's with school consolidation and stricter requirements.

Max Kester born 8 Aug 1895, died 28 Jan 1976 and is buried in Mount Ever-Rest Memorial Park South, Kalamazoo, Michigan. Wilma Steadman Kester died in 1982 and is buried with Max.

## 2. Josephine Kester and Charles R Clark

Josephine, known as Phene, was the youngest child of Mary Klingensmith and George Kester. She married Charles Clark 15 Nov 1893.

The 1900 census for Pittsford, Hillsdale, Michigan has Chas R Clark, 42, born Apr 1858, married 6 years, a farmer who owns his farm free and clear. Josephine is 35, born Aug 1864 and has had 1 child, still living. Their daughter, Lela M, is 4, born Jan 1896. George Kester is 79, born Jul 1820, widowed, immigrated in 1851 and a boarder.

The 1910 census for Jefferson, Hillsdale, Michigan has Charles R Clark, 52, married 16 years, well driller who is renting his home. Josephine is 45 and has had 1 child. Lela M is 14 and attended school.

The 1920 census for Jefferson, Hillsdale, Michigan has Charles Clark, 61, a farmer who owns his farm free and clear. Josephine is 53. A 1920 census could not be found for Lela.

The 1930 census for Jefferson, Hillsdale, Michigan has Charles Clark, 71, married at 35, not working but owns his farm worth $2000 and a radio. Josephine is 64 and married at 29. Lela M is 34 and single.

Lela taught school for many years in the Pittsford area according to Agnes Letherer. She may not have been working in 1930 because she was not well. Lela never married.

Lela Marie Clark, 35, born 29 Jan 1896, died 22 Mar 1931 in Jefferson, Hillsdale, Michigan of Tuberculosis of lungs. She had worked as a teacher and as a bank stenographer. Lela worked until 6 months before her death. She was buried in Leonardson Cemetery near Pittsford, Michigan on 25 Mar 1931.

The 1940 census for Pittsford, Michigan has Charles Clark, 82, completed 5th grade and living in a home he owns worth $2000, Josephine is 75 and graduated high school.

Josephine Kester Clark born 12 Aug 1864, died 27 May 1949 in Hillsdale, Michigan at the age of 84.

Charles R Clark, born 1858, died 25 Dec 1949 in Ypsilanti, Michigan. He is buried with Lela and Josephine in Leonardson Cemetery.

Charles Clark 1858-1949, 91 years

Josephine "Phene" Kester Clark 1864-1949, 85 years

Lela M. Clark 1896-1931, 35 years.

# Chapter 6

## Elizabeth Klingensmith and John Steinle/Stanley

1. **Elizabeth Klingenschmidt (1830-1908)**
 + **Johann Georg "John" Steinle (1831-1911)**
    2. Catherine Stanley (1854-1880) raised by grandparents
    + Johann Gothlich Schwany / Schwartz (1844-1927) Civil War
        3. Cottlied Schwartz (1880-1880)
    2. Charlotte Steinle (1857-1864)
    2. John George "John G" Steinle (1857-1924)
    + Jeanette Carrie Fry (1863-1927)
        3. Ellen Stanley (1883-1909)
        + William Leonard Snow (1872-1950)
            4. Charlotte "Lottie" Snow (1902-1977)
            + Roy Hancock (1899-1976)
                5. Marguerite Hancock (1920-)
                5. Robert Hancock (1922-)
                5. Elanor Hancock (1924-)
            4. Leone Snow (1904-1996)
            + Fred E. Cosley (1892-1935) WW1
                5. Betty Cosley (1920-1920)
                5. Letty Cosley (1920-1920)
            + John W. Ries (1905-1990)
            4. Frank Snow (1905-1981)
            + Gladys Belle Hamilton (1906-1998)
                5. Barbara D Snow (1926-2001)
                5. Beverly J Snow (1928-2012)
            4. Ruth Vivian Snow (1906-1992)
            + Marion Edward Wilkinson (1901-1972)
                5. Linda Wilkinson (1939-)
            4. Fern Snow (1908-1997)
            + Morton S Bailey (1903-1986)
        3. Edwin "Eddie" Frank Stanley (1886-1929) p
        + Blanch Lavina Snow (1885-1944) p (William Snow's sister)
            4. Pauline Stanley (1909-2002) p
            + James J Boulter (1902-1951)
                5. Sherman Boulter (1933-)
                5. Robert Boulter (1936-)
            4. Maxine Bertha Stanley (1912-) p
            + Bertrand Elmer Eifler (1909-)
                5. Edwin Eifler (1931-)
                5. Eilene Eifler (1931-)
                5. Charles Eifler (1932-)
                5. Elaine Eifler (1938-)

                5. Gerry Eifler (1939-)
            4. Betty Lynn Stanley (1922-)
            + Lyle Kizer (1919-)
                5. Ralph Kizer (1940-)
            4. L Kay Stanley (1923-)
            4. Jack Stanley (1925-)
        3. Leo Henry Stanley (1888-1918)
        + Hazel Snow (1891-1978) (William Snow's sister)
            4. Lois Verl Stanley (1910-)
            + Howard Glenn Stannard (1910-)
            4. Norman Laverne Stanley (1914-1990)
            + Mary Wilhelmena Olvitt (1917-)
            4. Juanita Stanley (1917-1986)
            + Robert E Stannard (1913-1980)
        3. Homer "Herman" Clyde Stanley (1890-1948) p
        + Carrie M. Cole (1889-1984) p
            4. Marvel Stanley (1912-1969) p
            + William R Krusell (1909-1969)
            4.Homer Arden Stanley (1914-1985) p
            + Violet E Thorpe (1918-)
        3. Rossamond Stanley (1892-1958)
        +Inez Davis (1878-1956)
        3. William Henry Stanley (1894-1941)
        + Ruth McKendrick (1894-1993)
            4. Wellington J Stanley (1916-2002)
            + Isabelle Beauchesne ()
        3. Bertha B Stanley (1896-1981)
        + William H Watson (1890-1978)
            4. Beatrice Ellen Watson (1915-1985)
            + Thomas Vandenberg (1915-2002) WW11
            + Lynn E Tuckey (1908-)
            4. Louise Watson (1916-)
            + Peter M VanLiere (1908-)
            4. Vivian Watson (1919-)
            + Peter Nordyke (1913-)
            4. Wilma Watson (1921-)
            4. Jean Watson (1923-)
2. Louisa Steinle (1860-1864)
2. Anna Stanley (1862-1864)
2. Fred Stanley (1864-1939) p
+ Ella Louise Carpenter (1858-1924)
        3. Mable Adell Stanley (1884-1945) p
        + Arthur Snyder (1879-1963) p
        3. Orson C. Stanley (1885-1919)
        + Clydia Altensee (1888-1943)

        3. Blanche Stanley (1887-1956) p
        + Elvin Sherman Gibbs (1878-1961) p
        3. Charlie Stanley (1889-1889)
        **3. Mae Louise Stanley (1892-1945) p**
        **+ Charles T. Bishop (1888-1954) p**
    2. Emma Jane Stanley (1869-1935) p
    + John C. Kelley (1873-1900)
    + William G Raymond (1871-1966)
    + Phineas A Cole (1860-1940)
    2. Jacob Stanley (1872-)
    + Rhoda Phillips (1878-)
        3. Frank William Stanley (1895-) WW1, Canada
        + Margaret Gorka (1903-)
        3. Ethyl Elizabeth Stanley (1902-)
        + J Lawrence Holstine (1897-)

A "p" after a name in the lineage chart refers to the Klingensmith Family Reunion Poem.

## 1. Elizabeth Klingensmith and Johann Georg "John" Steinle/Stanley

Elizabeth Klingensmith finally married John Steinle. Their marriage is recorded as: Steinle, John, son of Christian and Dorthea Steinle age 25 and Elizabeth Klingenschmidt daughter of Jacob and Charlotte Klingenschmidt (name later changed to Klingensmith) age 26, Hillsdale, June 8, 1856, Trinity Church Records (Lutheran Church, Hillsdale, Michigan).[9]

They lived on a farm in Wheatland Township. Their first acknowledged child was a daughter born in 1857. The Trinity Church Record is as follows: Steinle, Charlotte, daughter of John & Elizabeth was born 9 Apr 1857 Wheatland, Hillsdale, Michigan. Her death is recorded as follows: Stanley, Charlotte daughter of John & Elizabeth died September 20, 1864 aged 7 years 5 months 15 days, Pittsford, Hillsdale, Michigan. She is buried in Kane Cemetery, g.r.40 (grave record 40).[11]

The above is proof that Stanley was originally Steinle. This change was not known in the family before the discovery in Trinity Lutheran Church Records. The family name must have changed from Steinle to Stanley between 1857 and 1864. They probably used both names for a period of time. Steinle was used at the German speaking church. Stanley was used when dealing with the English-speaking community and official records.

The 1860 census for Wheatland, Hillsdale, Michigan has John Stanley 28 a farm laborer born in Germany. Elizabeth is 30 and born in Germany. Their children are Elizabeth, 5 and John, 3, both born in Michigan. Elizabeth 5 must have been Charlotte Elizabeth.

A daughter Louisa was born 26 Aug 1860. Her death is recorded as follows: Stanley,

Louisa daughter of John & Elizabeth, died 6 Sep 1864 aged 4 years, 11 days, Pittsford, Hillsdale, Michigan, burial Kane Cemetery, g.r.40.[11]

A daughter Anna was born Mar 1862. Her death is recorded as follows: Stanley, Anna, daughter John & Elizabeth, died 1 Sep 1864 aged 2 years 5 months 15 days, Pittsford, Hillsdale, Michigan, burial Kane Cemetery, g.r.40.[11]

The Kane Cemetery name must have been changed to Locust Corners Cemetery as their tombstones were found there. John Steinle/Stanley and Elizabeth Klingensmith Stanley were buried next to their daughters many years later. Marian Bishop Allshouse is holding up one of the three stones for the daughters.

Locust Corners Church has an inscription over the door that reads: New Baptist Church 1868. The Cemetery was there before the brick New Baptist Church which may have replaced an earlier wooden church. It remains a mystery as to why the girls were not buried in a Lutheran cemetery. Or was it Lutheran at the time?
All 3 daughters died within 20 days. It must have been to disease. There may have been an epidemic of measles, flu, TB or even the many diseases caused by the poor sanitation of the times. This was during the Civil War and more men died of disease than in the war.

Elizabeth was 6 months pregnant with a child when the girls died. Fred Stanley was born 14 Dec 1864. Losing 3 children in so short a time while pregnant must have been devastating for Elizabeth and John. It is no wonder they declined publicity and are not listed in the 1889 History of Hillsdale County.

Emma daughter of John and Elizabeth Stanley was born in Wheatland, Hillsdale, Michigan 15 Aug 1869 as recorded in Hillsdale County Records.[9]

The 1870 census for Wheatland, Hillsdale, Michigan has John Stanley, 40, a farmer, born in Germany, a citizen with $1000 in real estate. Elizabeth is, 41, keeping house, and born in Bavaria. Their children are John, 12, at school; Fred, 5, at school and Emma, 11/12, at home, all were born in Michigan. Much had changed since 1860.

The 1880 census for Wheatland, Hillsdale, Michigan has John Stanley, 49, a farmer from Wurttemberg. Elizabeth is 50, keeping house and from Bavaria. Their children are John, 22. farming at home; Fred, 15; Emma, 11 and Jacob 8. All the younger children were attending school and all were born in Michigan.

The 1900 census for Wheatland, Hillsdale, Michigan has John Stanley, 68, born Aug 1831, married 42 years, immigrated in 1854, a farmer who owned his mortgaged farm. Elizabeth is 70, born Mar 1830, has had 9 children, 4 are living, and immigrated in 1854. I only know of 8 children. There must have been one who was still born or died very young. The 4 living children would be John George, Fred, Emma and Jacob.

A picture was taken in front of the Carpenter/Stanley house in 1908. Elizabeth

Klingensmith Stanley was not well. It was decided a family picture should be taken. Elizabeth Klingensmith Stanley and John Stanley seated with great grandsons Harry Snider and Fred Gibbs Jr. Standing from left: Arthur Snider, Mabel Stanley Snider, Ella Louise Carpenter Stanley, Fred Stanley, Mae Louise Stanley, Blanch Stanley Gibbs with Leon and Fred Gibbs. The picture was taken between Leon's birth in Sept 1908 and Elizabeth's death on December 2, 1908. Possibly a nice October day.

Elizabeth Klingensmith Stanley, born 17 Mar 1830, died 2 Dec 1908 in Waverly, Van Buren, Michigan of apoplexy and arterial sclerosis. John and Elizabeth were living with their son Jacob. In the 1910 census John Stanley was still living with Jacob.

John George Steinle/Stanley born 24 Aug 1831, died 30 Oct 1911 in Waverly, Van Buren, Michigan of Apoplexy. He is buried in Locust Corners Cemetery with his wife Elizabeth Klingensmith Stanley and 3 daughters. Apoplexy is stroke.

## 2. Catherine M. Stanley and Johann Gothlich Schwany/ Schwartz

I believe John and Elizabeth's first child was Catherine Stanley born June 1854 in New York. Catherine was living with her grandparents in 1860 and 1870. Her grandmother, Charlotte Klingensmith died in 1872. Sometime after that her grandfather moved in with his son Karl or Charles Klingensmith, that left Catherine free to pursue her own life.

A marriage record was found for Catherine M Stanley, 24 of Wheatland, Michigan. She married Gothlich Schwany, 34, of Jefferson, Hillsdale, Michigan on 5 Dec 1878. He was born in Prussia and is a farmer while her birthplace is listed as Allen, Michigan. John Stanley of Wheatland and Charles Chinham of Wheatland were witnesses. John Stanley could have been her brother or father. Catherine's brother John G Stanley would have been 20 and it is most likely him. Catherine may have been living with John G in Allen, Michigan.

John Schwan, 19, of Lodi, Michigan, enlisted 2 Jan 1863 as a private in the Civil War. He enlisted in Company K, Michigan 1st light Artillery Battery. He was promoted to full Sargent. Transferred to Company A, U.S. Veteran Reserve Corps 6th Infantry Regiment on 15 Jan 1864. Mustered out on 2 Aug 1865 at Cincinnati, Ohio. Lodi is near Ann Arbor, Michigan.

The 1880 census for Wheatland, Hillsdale, Michigan has Gottlieb Schwarz, 35, farm laborer, born in Germany, both parents born in Germany; and Catherine M, 26, keeping house, born in New York, both parents born in Germany. The ages, occupation and nationality are right. The husband's name change seems reasonable. Names were easily changed long before social security and birth certificates. If the name was given verbally the spelling could change depending on the writer's interpretation.

Catherine had a son Gottlied Schwartz later in 1880. Gottlied died at 3 months. Catherine also died in 1880. The cause is not known. They are both buried in Lake View

Cemetery, Hillsdale, Michigan. The stones confirm Gotlieb's service in the Civil War.

Gottlieb Schwartz, born 8 Aug 1842, died 26 Aug 1927 at the age of 85 in the Michigan Soldiers' Home Hospital, Grand Rapids, Michigan. He died of old age, gangrene of toe and anemia. Born in Germany his father was Gottlieb Schwartz and his mother Christina Engel. Information from Soldiers' Home files.

## 2. John G. Stanley and Jeanette Carrie Fry

John G Stanley married Jeanette Carrie Fry 17 Sep 1882 in Rollin, Michigan. He was 24 and she was 17.

Their seven children were Ellen 1883-1909: Edwin Frank 1886-1929; Leo Henry 1888-1918; Homer Clyde 1890-1948; Rossamond 1892-1958; William Henry 1894-1941, and Bertha B 1896.

The 1900 census for Almena, Van Buren, Michigan has John G Stanley, 41, born July 1857, married 17 years, a farmer renting his land. Jeanette is 36, born April 1864 and has had 7 children all living. Their children are; Edwin F, 13, born June 1886; Leo H, 12, born May 1888; Homer C,10, born March 1890; Rossamond, 7, born July 1892; William H, 6, born Feb 1894 and Bertha B, 4, born May 1896.

See Jacob Stanley for the 1910 census as they are all living together with Jacob.

The 1920 census for Kalamazoo, Michigan has John G Stanley, 61, a policeman at the State Asylum who owns his home at 1809 Hudson Street. Jeanette is 56.

John G Stanley born 13 July 1858, died 22 May 1924 in Burlington, Calhoun, Michigan. He was a farmer according to his death certificate. His parents were John Stanley born in Württemberg, Germany and Elizabeth Klingensmith born in Bavaria, Germany. Cause of death was mitral regurgitate. They didn't know the duration. There was no operation, autopsy or testing. John was buried in West Oshtemo Cemetery 25 May 1924.

Jeanette Frye Stanley, 59, married William Leonard Snow, 52, her former son-in-law, 29 Dec 1924 in Kalamazoo. William had been married 3 times previously.

Jeanette E Stanley Snow, 63, born 10 April 1863, died 4 Feb 1927 of a cerebral hemorrhage confirmed by observation. Her parents were Ira Frye and Ellen Pittenger. She was buried in West Oshtemo Cemetery on 7 Feb 1927. Information by W H Stanley of 86 Maple Terrace, Battle Creek, Michigan where Jeanette was living.

## 3. Ellen E Stanley and William Snow

The 1900 census for Antwerp, Van Buren, Michigan has Ellen Stanley, 16, born Oct

1883 and working as a servant for William Eastman, a farmer, his wife and 2 children.

In the 1900 census William Snow, 27, born Aug 1872, divorced, was living as a boarder working at farm labor.

Ellen Stanley, 17, of Paw Paw, a domestic, married William Snow, 28, of Almena, a farmer, on 28 Mar 1901 in Almena, Michigan. His parents were Eber Snow and Verlinda Heller. Her parents were John G Stanley and E Klingensmith. Ellen's mother was Jeanette Frye not Elizabeth Klingensmith who was her grandmother. The form may have been confusing and "mother" was thought to be John G Stanley's mother. William Snow had been married previously. They were married by John W Shank a Minister of the Gospel. Witnesses were John Stanley and Janette Stanley of Almena. Almena is just west of Kalamazoo and north of Paw Paw.

Ellen and William had 5 children over the next 8 years before she died in 1909. The children were Lottie born 1902, Leone born 1904, Frankie born 1905, Ruthie born 1907 and Fern born 1908. Ellen had a short life filled with hard work, taking care of younger brothers and sisters, working taking care of children at a young age, marrying at 17, more children to care for, and dying at 25. It seems probable Ellen and William lived with Ellen's family most of this time. William Snow, the children and Ellen's parents were living with Jacob Stanley, Ellen's uncle, in 1910.

Ellen Stanley Snow, 25, born 11 Oct 1883, died 6 Sep 1909 in Waverly, Van Buren, Michigan of abscess on the kidney and Bright's disease. She was married at 17 had 5 children and 5 children were still living. Her parents were John Stanley and Jeanette Frye. Ellen was buried in Wildey Cemetery, Paw Paw, Michigan on 8 Sept 1909.

The 1920 census for Kalamazoo, Michigan has William Snow, 47, a truck driver for a coal yard who owns his mortgaged home at 527 Phillips Street. Hattie M is 37 and washing for a private family. The children are Leone H, 16, a sales lady in a dry goods store; Frank, 14; Ruth 13; Fern 12 all attending school and 2 step daughters 16 & 14, neither in school, the oldest doing general housework. Apparently, no one went to school beyond 16.

William L Snow married Hattie Mae Brown on 22 Oct 1910 and she divorced him 12 Mar 1921 for extreme cruelty. There needed to be a reason for a divorce and cruelty or adultery were the main reasons. William married Ellen's widowed mother, Jeanette Stanley in 1924.

William Snow married Mary E in Indiana 18 May 1929. His 5th marriage. A divorce was granted 10 Feb 1938 for non-support.

William Snow was living with his son Frank in 1940.

William Leonard Snow died 13 Feb 1950 and is buried in Wildey Cemetery, Paw Paw,

Michigan, the same place as Ellen. She may have been his real love after all.

### 4. Charlotte "Lottie" Snow and Roy Hancock

Lottie Snow, 17, married Roy Hancock, 20, a machinist on 3 Sep 1919 in Kalamazoo, Michigan. Her parents are listed as Will Snow and Hattie Brown. Hattie Snow is a witness and her address is 527 Phillips Street.

The 1930 census for Kalamazoo, Michigan has Roy Hancock, 30, married at 20, a laborer in ice and fuel renting a home at 505 Phillips for $24 per month and has a radio. Lottie is 28 and was married at 17. Their children are Marguerite, 10; Robert,8 and Elanor, 6.

Census records for 1920 and 1940 were not found.

Lottie M Snow Hancock born Mar 1902, died 1971 and is buried in Mount Ever-Rest Memorial Park South, Kalamazoo, Michigan. Roy Hancock born 1 May 1899, died 10 Sep 1976 and is buried with Lottie.

### 4. Leone Hattie Snow and Fred E. Cosley

Leone Hattie Snow, 16, of Kalamazoo, a paper sorter, married Fred E Cosley, 28, of Camp Custer, Michigan, a soldier, on 28 Mar 1920 in Kalamazoo, Michigan. Cecil E Pollock, M E Minister officiated. His parents were Andrew E. Cosley and Lettie. Her parents were William Snow and Ellen Stanley. Witnesses were Miss Helen Hosner and Mr. William Wily of Kalamazoo. Under the entry is: "In War Service Against Germany from St Louis, Mo."

Leone is in the 1920 census for Kalamazoo taken 16 Jan 1920 with her father.

Baby Cosley of 1835 S Bendix Street, Kalamazoo was born at Borgess Hospital and died 17 Oct 1920. She was premature. She is buried at Riverside Cemetery. The sign indicates twins, Betty and Letty Cosley.

Fred and Leone Cosley are listed in several Kalamazoo City directories from 1926 – 1934. Fred is working as a barber, in a lab and as a trucker.

Cosley, Fred E of RFD # 7 Kalamazoo, Michigan, born 24 Aug 1892 in Kansas City, Kansas, died 15 Dec 1935. His parents were Andrew Emile and Letty. Information is from Veterans Administration Facility, Camp Custer, Michigan. Cause of death is Chronic nephritis with anasarca, Chronic Myocarditis, Chronic valvular heart disease (mitral insufficiency). An autopsy was performed. His last work was as a barber.

His headstone reads: FRED COSLEY, KANSAS
Private 1C1 10 INF
14 DIV
DECEMBER 16, 1935

An Application for Headstone was made 19 Dec 1935 by Mrs. Leone Cosley of Kalamazoo, Michigan. Fred enlisted 5 Jun 1917 in the 14th Kansas, was discharged 9 May 1919, reenlisted 10 May 1919 and was Honorably discharged 9 May 1920. He was a Private 1st class in Company G of the 10th Infantry. He died 16 Dec 1935 and was buried in Riverside Cemetery, Riverside Drive, Kalamazoo, Michigan. The monument was approved 26 Dec 1935, ordered from Proctor, Vermont 15 Jan 1936, and shipped 4 Feb 1936.

Leone married John W Ries between 1940 and 1942. He is listed as single in a 1940 census for Detroit. John and Leone are listed in the Kalamazoo City Directory for 1942. John is an operator for Kalamazoo City Lines and they own a home at 40021 Laird Ave. They are listed again in 1959 at the same address and both working.

John W Ries, born 26 Jun 1905, died 22 Jan 1990 in Kalamazoo, Michigan.
Leone Hattie Ries, born 19 Aug 1903, died 13 Mar 1996 in Kalamazoo, Michigan.

### 4. Frank J Snow and Gladys Belle Hamilton

Frank J Snow, 19, of Kalamazoo, born in Paw Paw, Michigan working at casting, married Gladys Belle Hamilton, 18, of Kalamazoo, born in Lyons, Michigan on 15 Nov 1924 in Kalamazoo, John L Hollander, Judge of Probate presiding. His parents were William Snow and Ellen Stanley. Her parents were Frank Hamilton and Anna Stantz.

The 1930 census for Kalamazoo, Michigan has Frank J Snow, 24, married at 19, a helper in a paper mill who owns a house worth $3000 at 14 Blanche Ave but not a radio. Gladys B is 23 and married at 18 Their children are Barbara V, 4 and Beverly J, 3.

The 1940 census for Kalamazoo, Michigan has Frank J Snow, 34, completed 9th grade, a tinner in a Sheet Metal Company who owns a home at 505 Phillips Street worth $1500. Gladys B is 34 and completed 2 years high school. Their children are Barbara D, 14, completed 8th grade and Beverly J, 12, completed 7th grade. William L Snow, 67, father, completed 5th grade is living with them and not working.

Frank J Snow, born 28 May 1905, died 21 Jun 1981 in Citrus, Florida. Gladys B Snow, born 18 Apr 1906, died 13 Jun 1998 in Saint Joseph, Michigan.

## 4. Ruth Vivian Snow and Marion Edward Wilkinson

Ruth Vivian Snow, 18, of Kalamazoo married Marion Edward Wilkinson, 23, of Kalamazoo, a papermaker on 16 Oct 1924 in Kalamazoo, Michigan. His parents were Marion F Wilkinson and Lora Hosinger. Her parents were William L Snow and Ellen Stanley.

The 1930 Census for Kalamazoo, MI has Marion E Wilkinson, 28, a barber in his own shop who owns a house on Regent Street worth $3000. Ruth V is 23.

The 1940 census for Kalamazoo, Michigan has Marion Wilkinson, 38, completed 7th grade, the proprietor of a barber shop who owns a home at 624 Hutchinson Street worth $1500. Ruth is 33 and completed 8th grade. Their daughter, Linda, is 11/12.

Edward M Wilkinson died in 1971 and Ruth Vivian Snow Wilkinson, born 4 Oct 1906, died 9 Aug 1992 in Kalamazoo. They are buried in Mt. Ever-Rest Memorial Park South.

## 4. Fern Jeanette Snow and Morton S. Bailey

In 1930 Fern Snow, 22, was rooming at 509 Second St, single and a saleslady in a retail dry goods store.

Fern Jeanette Snow, 23, of Kalamazoo, a clerk married Morton S Bailey, 27, of Kalamazoo, born in Falmouth, Massachusetts, an assistant manager on 9 April 1931. His parents are George S Bailey and Florence Mary Osgood. Her parents were William L Snow and Ellen Stanley.

The 1939 Worchester, Mass. City Directory has Morton S. Bailey (Fern J) removed to Chicago, Illinois.

Morton S Bailey, born 15 Oct 1903, died 18 Sep 1986 in Hillsborough County, New Hampshire. Fern J Bailey, born 17 Sep 1907, died 27 Nov 1997. They are buried in Maplewood Cemetery, Antrim, Hillsborough, New Hampshire. They share a tombstone with his parents.

### 3. Edwin Frank Stanley and Blanch L Snow

Edwin F Stanley, 21, a farmer, married Blanche L Snow, 22, a housekeeper on 1 Jan 1908 in Paw Paw, Michigan. His parents are John G Stanley and Jeanette C Frye. Her parents are Eber Rice Snow and Verlinda Heller, Blanche was married before. Witnesses were Leo H Stanley and Hazel Snow. Blanche is William Snow's sister.

The 1910 census for Texas, Kalamazoo, Michigan lists Ed Stanley, 29, as head of the family living in a rented house, married 3 years, a laborer on a general farm. Blanche is 25, married twice and has 1 child. Their daughter, Pauline is 1. Leo, brother is 21, married 1 year and a laborer on a general farm. Hazel, sister-in-law, 18, has one child, Lois, niece, 3/12.

Edwin Frank Stanley, 30, born 9 Jun 1886, registered for WW1 on 5 Jun 1917. His occupation is steam engineer and he has a wife and children.

The 1920 census for Kalamazoo, Michigan has Edward Stanley, 33, an engineer in a paper mill who owns a home on Gale Ave. Blanch is 33 and a sorter in a paper mill. Their children are Pauline, 11 and Maxine, 8.

Edwin F Stanley, 43, born 9 Jun 1886 in Rollin, Michigan, died 28 Jul 1929 in Penfield, Calhoun, Michigan of myocarditis and acute cardiac failure. He was a stock man at United Motors. His wife was Blanche Stanley and his parents John Stanley and Jeanette Fry. He was seen by the doctor only on the day of death. He was buried in West Oshtemo Cemetery, Oshtemo, Michigan on 29 Jul 1929. Blanche Lavina Stanley, 59, born 3 Feb 1885, died 5 Oct 1944 in Kalamazoo, Michigan and was buried 7 Oct 1944 in West Oshtemo Cemetery.

The 1940 census for Kalamazoo, Michigan has Blanche Stanley, 55, widow, completed 8th grade, renting a home at 304 Darling Ave. for $15 per month. Her sons are L Kay Stanley, 17, completed 2 years high school and Jack, 15, completed 1-year high school. Lyle Kizar, 21, son-in-law, graduated high school, a planter at a nursery; Betty Lynn, 18, daughter, completed 3 years high school and Ralph, 7/12, are living with Blanche.

### 4. Pauline Stanley and James J Boulter

Pauline Stanley, 17, of Battle Creek, a clerk, married James J Boulter, 24, of Prairieville, a farmer, on 30 Dec 1925 in Battle Creek, Michigan. Quinton S Walker, clergyman, presided. His parents are Fredrick Boulter and Mary Winchester. Her parents are E F Stanley and Blanch Snow.

The 1930 census for Prairieville, Michigan has Mary L Boulter, 57, widow, working at housekeeping for a private family who owns a house worth $1000. James J, 28, son, married at 24, a laborer on a farm. Pauline is 21, daughter-in-law and married at 17.

The 1940 census for Prairieville, Michigan has James J Boulter, 39, completed 8th grade, a helper on a press in the Bliss factory who owns a house. Pauline is 32 and completed 10th grade. The children are Sherman, 7, completed 1st grade and Robert, 4.

## 4. Maxine Bertha Stanley and Bertrand Elmer Eifler

Maxine Bertha Stanley, 18, of 20 Ridgemont, Battle Creek Michigan, born in Kalamazoo, married Bertrand Elmer Eifler, 20, of 106 Inn Road, Battle Creek, Michigan, born in Coloma, Michigan, a spot welder, on 8 Jun 1929. H J Fennig, an Evangelical Lutheran Pastor, performed the ceremony. His parents are Frank Charles Eifler and Johanna Heier. Her parents are Edward Stanley and Blanche Snow.

The 1940 census for Battle Creek, Mi has Bertrand Eifler, 31, completed 8th grade, a machine operator at a steam pump company who owns a house at 78 Ave D worth $1300. Maxine is 29 and completed 3 years of high school. Their children are Eilene, 9 and Edwin, 9, completed 3rd grade; Charles, 8, completed 1st grade; Elaine, 2 and Gerry, son, 11/12.

## 3. Leo Harry Stanley and Hazel C Snow

Leo H Stanley, 21, of Paw Paw, a laborer, married Hazel C. Snow, 17 of Paw Paw, a housekeeper, on 17 Nov 1909 in Antwerp Township, Michigan. J. P. Bates Minister of the Gospel presided. His parents were John G Stanley and Jeanette Frye. Her parents were Eber A. Snow and Verlinda Snow. Witnesses were Roy Snow and Mable Thomas both of Paw Paw. Hazel was a sister to William Snow who married Ellen Stanley and Blanche Snow who married Edwin Stanley.

Leo and Hazel were found in the 1910 census living with his brother Ed Stanley.

Leo Harry Stanley, 29, born 23 May 1888, registered for WW1 on 5 Jun 1917. He was living at RFD # 10, Kalamazoo and working as a laborer for Clare Brown at same address. He had a wife and 3 children. He was tall, of medium build, gray eyes, and brown hair. He did not serve.

Leo Stanley, born 23 May 1888, died October 25, 1918 at 30 years of age. He was living at 405 Lincoln Ave. in Kalamazoo and working as a farmer. His parents were John G Stanley and Jeanette Frye. The informant was John G Stanley of the same address. The doctor certifies he saw Leo from Oct 22 to Oct 25 when he died at 10:30 am. The cause of death is Lobar Pneumonia from Influenza. Burial was in West Oshtemo Cemetery 28 Oct 1918. This would have been during the Spanish Flu epidemic. He was probably staying at his father's house to protect the children.

The 1920 census for Kalamazoo, Kalamazoo, Michigan has Eber Snow, 73, a laborer working out and living on Darling Ave. Liney is 66. Hazel Stanley is 29, daughter and working as a counter in a paper mill. Hazel's children are Lois, 9, attended school; Vern, 6, attended school and Juanita, 2 11/12. Juanita was a baby when her father died.

The 1930 census for Kalamazoo, Kalamazoo, Michigan has Elton J Crane, 31, married at 27, a papermaker at a paper mill who owns a house on Maple Ave worth $4500 and a radio. Hazel C is 39, first married at 16, a counter at a paper mill. The Stanley children are Lois V, 20, a laborer at a stationary company; Lavern N, 16, not attending school and not working and Juanita L, 14, attended school. Elton and Hazel must have been married in 1926.

The 1940 census for Kalamazoo, Michigan has Elton Crane, 44, completed 2 years high school, a cutter in a paper mill who owns a home at 3248 Michigan Ave. worth $1600. Hazel is 37 and a counter in a paper mill.

Hazel C Snow Stanley Crane, born 25 Jul 1892, died 16 Sep 1978 in Kalamazoo, Michigan. She is buried with Leo Stanley and Elton Crane in West Oshtemo Cemetery.

## 4. Lois Verl Stanley and Howard Glenn Stannard

Lois Verl Stanley, 22, of Kalamazoo, a stationary employee, married Howard Glenn Stannard, 22, of Kalamazoo, a salesman, on 14 Sep 1933 in Kalamazoo, Michigan. Elwin K Lewis, Minister of the Gospel, presided. Her parents were Leo Harry Stanley and Hazel Clair Snow. His parents were Glenn W Stannard and Odessa C Still. Witnesses were Juanita Stanley and Robert Stannard.

The 1940 census for Comstock, Kalamazoo, Michigan has Howard Stannard, 29, graduated high school, a machine operator at a medicine factory. Lois is 30 and completed 3 years high school.

## 4. Norman Laverne Stanley and Mary Wilhelmena Olvitt

Norman Laverne Stanley, 22, of Kalamazoo, a refrigeration serviceman, married Mary Wilhelmena Olvitt, 18, of Kalamazoo on 31 March 1936. Leroy M Whitney, a Methodist Pastor, presided. His parents are Leo Harry Stanley and Hazel Claire Snow. Her parents are Louis Olvitt and Mary Postlewaite.

The 1940 census for Portage, Kalamazoo, Michigan has Laverne Stanley, 26, completed 8$^{th}$ grade, working as a service man in the refrigerator industry and renting a home at 84 Ramona Park for $15 per month. Mary is 23 and completed 3 years high school.

## 4. Juanita L Stanley and Robert E Stannard

Juanita L Stanley, 18, of Kalamazoo, married Robert E. Stannard, 21, of Kalamazoo, a salesman and music teacher on 29 August 1935. LeRoy N Whitney, Methodist Pastor, presided. His parents were Glenn Stannard and Dessa Still. Her parents were Leo Stanley and Hazel Snow. Witnesses were Anna Mae Klinger and Laverne Stanley.

The 1940 census for Comstock, Kalamazoo, Michigan has Robert Stannard, 26, graduated high school, a musician renting a home at 270 Cooper for $25 per month. Juanita is 23 and graduated high school.

The 1945 Kalamazoo City Directory has Stannard, Robert E (Juanita L) music teacher home 1703 Grove. Also, Stannard Dessa L (widow Glenn W) residence 1703 Grove.

Juanita L Stannard born 23 Jan 1917, died 15 Jul 1986 in Kalamazoo, Michigan. Robert E Stannard died in 1980.

## 3. Homer Clyde Stanley and Carrie M. Cole

Homer C Stanley, 20, of Waverly, Van Buren, Michigan, a barber, married Carrie M Cole, 21, of Waverly, Kalamazoo, Michigan, a housekeeper, on 14 June 1910 in Schoolcraft, Michigan. G R Milland Pastor of M E Church presided. His parents were John G Stanley and Janette Frye. Her parents were Phineas Cole and Nellie Raymond. Carrie was the daughter of Emma Stanley's third husband by a previous marriage, not actually related. Homer may have met Carrie at his Aunt Emma's house.

Homer was living in a boarding house in Schoolcraft in 1910 just before the marriage.

Homer C Stanley, 27, born 23 Mar 1890 in Hudson, Michigan, a barber, registered for WW1 on 25 May 1917. His employer was Miller & Rinehart in Kalamazoo, Michigan. He has a wife and 2 children, is medium height, stout build, brown eyes, and slightly balding light brown hair.

The 1920 census for Salida, Colorado has Homer Stanley, 29, born in Michigan, a barber in a city shop and renting a home at 321 6th Street for $30 per month. Carrie is 30. Their children are Marvel, 7, attended school, born in Colorado and Arden, 5, born in Colorado. They must have been living in Colorado for at least 7 years and Homer went back to Kalamazoo to register for the WW1 draft.

The 1930 census for Battle Creek, Michigan has Homer Stanley, 40, married at 20, a salesman for autos who is renting a home at 181 N McKinley for $50 per month and has a radio. Carrie is 40 and was married at 20. Their children are Marvel, 17, attended school and Arden, 15, attended school.

The 1940 census for Battle Creek, Michigan has Homer C. Stanley, 50, completed 8th grade, owner of a gasoline station who owns a home at 163 Post Ave. worth $4000. Carrie is 50 and completed 8th grade. Arden Stanley, 25, graduated high school, a clerk in a bank and Violet E, 22, completed high school are living with his parents.

William H Stanley and Homer C Stanley, brothers, owned Stanley's Service Station on 315 E. Michigan Ave. in Battle Creek, Michigan according to the 1940 city directory. They had gasoline, oils, automobile repairing, greasing, tire repairing, washing and storage.

William H Stanley died in 1941 so the station went to Homer C Stanley. By 1946 the same service station was owned by Homer C and H Arden with the same advertisement except they dropped the washing. When Homer died in 1948, Arden continued to operate the station.

Homer C Stanley born 23 Mar 1890 in Hudson, Michigan, died 27 January 1948 in Battle Creek, and is buried in Memorial Park Cemetery, Battle Creek, Michigan.

Carrie M Cole Stanley born 1889 in Kansas, died 1984. Information was provided by H Arden Stanley born 1914.

## 4. Homer Arden Stanley and Violet E Thorpe

Arden Stanley, 22, of Battle Creek, born in Salida, Colorado, a bookkeeper married Violet Thorpe, 19, of Battle Creek, born in Valley, Wisconsin, a clerk on 18 Aug 1937 in Battle Creek. Henry N Jordan, clergyman presided. His parents were Homer C. Stanley and Carrie Cole. Her parents were Claude D Thorpe and Ella Newton.

Arden and Violet are living with his parents in the 1940 census.

Homer Arden Stanley, born 28 Oct 1914, died 21 Mar 1985 in Battle Creek, Michigan. He is buried in Memorial Park Cemetery. This stone was placed near his parents.

## 4. Marvel Stanley and William R Krusell

Marvel Stanley, 22, of Battle Creek, born in Colorado, a beauty operator, married William R Krusell, 26, of Middleville, born in Petoskey, Michigan, an assistant orderly, on 10 Apr 1935 in Battle Creek, Michigan. His parents were John Krusell and Bertha Norton. Her parents were Homer C. Stanley and Carrie Cole.

A 1940 census was not found. The 1949 Battle Creek City Directory has Krusell, Wm R (Marvel) tool maker, Clark's Equipment, home 348 N 34th. John and Bertha Krusell are living in an apartment in the same house.

William R. Krusell, born 1909, died 1969 in Battle Creek and is buried in Memorial Park

Cemetery. Marvel S Krusell also died in 1969.

### 3. Rossamond Stanley and Inez I Davis

Rossamond Stanley, 25, born 26 July 1892, in Hudson, Michigan registered for WW1 on 5 Jun 1917. He was living at Route 1 Oshtemo, Michigan, a farmer, employed by Joseph Haynes. He is medium height and build with brown eyes and light hair.

The 1920 census for Burlington, Calhoun, Michigan has Rossamond Stanley, 27, a farm laborer. He is living with his sister Bertha and her husband William Watson.

Rossamond Stanley, 31, of Burlington, Calhoun, Michigan, a farmer, married Inez Davis, 39, of Beaver, Oklahoma, on July 14, 1923 in Marshall, Michigan. Charles E Blanchard, clergyman presided. His parents were John G Stanley and Janette Fry. Her parents were James M Davis and Minerva T Payne.

The 1930 census for Paw Paw, Van Buren, Michigan has Rossamond Stanley, 38, married at 31, a laborer on a fruit farm renting a home. Inez is 49 and married at 36.

The 1940 census for Waverly, Van Buren, Michigan has Rossamond Stanley, 47, completed 1-year college, a farmer on a general farm, seeking work who owns a home worth $300. Inez is 62, completed 7th grade and, doing housework.

Inez I Davis Stanley born 28 Nov 1878 in Iowa, died 29 Jan 1956 in Paw Paw, Michigan and was buried in Wildey Cemetery. Rossamond Stanley born 26 Jul 1892, died 15 April 1958 in Hartford, Van Buren, Michigan and is buried with Inez.

### 3. William Henry A Stanley and Ruth McKendrick

William A Stanley, 21, of Paw Paw, Michigan, a barber married Ruth E McKendrick, 21, of Paw Paw, Michigan, a stenographer on 25 Oct 1915 in Kalamazoo, Michigan. James T L Gear, a Minister of the Bible officiated. His parents were John G Stanley and Janette Fry. Her parents were William McKendrick and Alice.

William Henry A Stanley, 23, born 13 Feb 1894 in Hillsdale, Michigan, registered for WW1 on 5 June 1917. He had a wife and child and was living at 115 Champion Street, Battle Creek, Michigan. William was a barber working for Charles Sutton in Battle Creek, Michigan. He was tall with a medium build, brown eyes and red hair.

The 1920 census for Battle Creek, Michigan has William Stanley, 26, a barber in a shop renting a house at 115 W Van Buren Street. Ruth is 26. Their son Wellington is 3 4/12.

The 1930 census for Battle Creek, Michigan has William Stanley, 36, married at 22, a sales manager for autos who owns a house at 86 Maple Terrace worth $5600 and a radio. Ruth is 36 and married at 22. Wellington is 13 and attended school. William McKendrick, 66, father-in-law, widowed is living with them.

The 1940 Census for Battle Creek, Michigan has William H Stanley, 46, completed 8th grade, an attendant at his own gas station who owns his home at 86 Maple Terrace worth $4000. Ruth E is 46 and graduated high school. Wellington J is 24, graduated high school and a laborer at an auto company. William E McKendrick is 76, widowed, completed 1-year high school and unable to work.

William H Stanley, 47, born Feb 1894 in Hillsdale, Michigan, died 1 Aug 1941 in Battle Creek, Michigan of coronary thrombosis. It was a sudden death in a car at 105 Central Ave. He was the owner and operator of a gas filling station. He was buried in Memorial Park, Battle Creek, Michigan on 4 Aug 1941.

The 1949 Battle Creek City Directory has Ruth E Stanley (widow Wm H) home 86 Maple Terrace. Just below that is Stanley's Service Station (H Arden Stanley) Gasolines, Oils, Used Cars, Automobile Repairing, Greasing, Tire Repairing, 315 E Michigan Ave, Tel 2-1894. This is the service station owned by Homer and William. Arden bought William's share after he died. It was owned by Arden and his father Homer until Homer died.

Ruth was still living at 86 Maple Terrace and Stanley's Service Station was still being run by Arden Stanley in 1960.

Ruth A McKendrick Stanley died in 1993 and is buried with William.

## 4. Wellington J Stanley and Isabelle Beauchesne

Wellington Stanley, 23, an engineer living in Lansing, Michigan married Isabelle Beauchesne, 23 on 30 Nov 1939 in Battle Creek.

The 1940 census for Lansing, Michigan has Wellington Stanley, 23, graduated college, a maintenance engineer in an auto factory renting part of a home at 422 Lapeer for $38 per month. Isabelle is 24 and graduated high school. It is not known why Wellington was listed with his parents in 1940.

### 3. Bertha B Stanley and William Watson

Bertha Stanley, 17, of Kalamazoo, Michigan, married William Watson, 21, of Kalamazoo, a papermaker, on 27 May 1913 in Kalamazoo. Her parents were John Stanley and Jeanette Fry. His parents were Charles Watson and Lydia Alexander. A witness was William Stanley of Kalamazoo.

The 1920 census for Burlington, Calhoun, Michigan has William H Watson, 30, born in Ohio, a farmer working by the year and renting a home. Bertha is 23. Their children are Beatrice, 5; Louise 4 and Vivian 1 4/12. Rossamond Stanley, 27, a farm laborer is living with them. Rossamond is Bertha's brother.

The 1930 census for Kalamazoo, Michigan has William H Watson, 40, married at 24, a trimmer in a paper mill, renting a home at 429 Bryant Street for $25 per month. Bertha is 33, married at 17 and a machine operator at a corset company. Their children are Beatrice, 15; Louise, 14; Vivian, 11; Wilma, 9; and Jean, 7, all attended school.

The 1940 census for Portage, Kalamazoo, Michigan has William Watson, 50, completed 8$^{th}$ grade, a trolley operator in the finishing department of a paper mill, renting a home on Ramona Park. Bertha is 43 and completed 8$^{th}$ grade. Their children are Wilma, 19, graduated high school, working as a paper sorter in the paper industry; Jean, 17, completed 11$^{th}$ grade; Vivian, 21, married, completed 9$^{th}$ grade, working as a paper sorter in the paper industry; and Peter Nordyke, 27, son-in-law, completed 11$^{th}$ grade, shop foreman in an insulating material factory.

### 4. Beatrice Ellen Watson and Thomas Vandenberg / Lynn Tuckey

Beatrice Ellen Watson, 21, of Kalamazoo, a clerk, married Thomas Vandenberg, 21, of Kalamazoo, a nailer, on 3 June 1936 in Kalamazoo, Michigan. Rev. J A Veldman, Pastor of Bethany Reformed Church, officiated. Her parents were William H Watson and Bertha Belle Stanley. His parents were Richard Vandenberg and Grace Kiel. Witnesses were Vivian Watson and Claus Vandenberg both from Kalamazoo.

Thomas served in the Navy in WW11 with a service start date of 7 Mar 1944. They were divorced 7 May 1946.

Beatrice E Vandenberg married Lynn E Tuckey 1 Jul 1946, in Kalamazoo. They are in the 1952 Kalamazoo City Directory as Tuckey, Lynn E (Beatrice E) working at Kalamazoo Stove Co.

Beatrice E Tuckey born 7 Jun 1914, died 27 Aug 1985 in Kalamazoo, Michigan

## 4. Louise Watson and Peter M VanLiere

Louise Watson, 20, of Kalamazoo, married Peter M VanLiere, 28, of Kalamazoo, working in Receiving Department, on 7 May 1936 in Kalamazoo, Michigan. Robert R. Tinkham, Baptist Minister, presided. Her parents were William Watson and Bertha Stanley. His parents were Marinus VanLiere and Johanna Zuidweg. Witnesses were Luke VanLiere and Beatrice Watson both of Kalamazoo.

A 1940 census has not been found.

## 2. Fred Stanley and Ella Carpenter

Fred Stanley married Ella Louise Carpenter in 1884. Their information will continue in Chapter 12 after the Carpenters.

## 2. Emma Stanley and John Kelley / William Raymond / Phineas Cole

Emma Stanley is an unusual woman for her time. She was married three times and divorced twice.

Emma Stanley, 19, of Wheatland, Michigan, married John C Kelley, 21, of Wheatland, a farmer, on 29 Nov 1888 in Hillsdale, Michigan. His parents were Charles Kelley and Sarah Cocklin. Her parents were John Stanley and Elizabeth Klingensmith. Witnesses were J Stanley and Libbie Klingensmith both of Wheatland. They were married less than 5 years before they were divorced.

Emma S Kelley, 23, of Wheatland, a dressmaker, married William G Raymond, 22, of Wheatland, a farmer, on 4 May 1893 in Hillsdale. Her parents are John Stanley and E Klingensmith. His parents are Geo Raymond and Lavina Barker. Witnesses were Geo C Barker and Ada S Bird both of Wheatland.

The 1900 census for Waverly, Van Buren, Michigan has George Raymond, 53, born May 1847, married 32 years, a farmer renting his farm. Lavina is 55, born Dec 1844 and has one child who is still living. Willie G is 27, son, born May 1873, married 7 years, a farmer. Emma is 30, daughter-in-law, born Aug. 1869 and has not had children.

Emma Raymond filed for divorce from Willie Raymond on 18 Jan 1904 for non-support. Divorce was granted 13 Jun 1904. It was not contested and there were no children.

Emma Raymond, 40, of Waverly, Van Buren, Michigan, a housekeeper, married Phineas A Cole, 49, of Waverly, Van Buren, Michigan, a farmer, on 23 Dec 1909 in Paw Paw, Michigan. His parents were Marvin Cole and Renia Tripp. Her parents were John Stanley and E Klingensmith. Phineas was married once before and Emma was married twice before.

Phineas' first wife was Nellie Raymond. Their children were Rania 19, Frank 14, Carrie M 11 and Carl 2. Nellie does not have the same parents as William G Raymond but being from the same area she may have been a cousin. Nellie died 11 Dec 1904.

The 1910 census for Waverly, Van Buren, Michigan has Phineas A Cole, 50, married for less than 1 year, a farmer on a general farm he owns. Emma is 40 and never had children. Phineas' son Carl is 12 and attending school. Carl served in WW1. He survived and died about 1970.

The 1920 census for Paw Paw, Van Buren, Michigan has Phineas A Cole, 59, a farmer who owns his own farm. Emma is 50.

The 1930 census for Waverly, Van Buren, Michigan has Phineas Cole, 70, a farmer on a farm he owns. Emma is 60. They do not have a radio.

Emma Stanley Kelley Raymond Cole, 64, born 15 Aug 1870, died March 24, 1935 in Paw Paw, Van Buren, Michigan of Angina Pectoris with contributory causes of Valvular heart disease, Nephritis and arthritis. Her parents were John Stanley and Elizabeth Klingensmith, both born in Germany. Informant is Phineas Cole. Burial was in Prospect Hill Cemetery, Paw Paw, Michigan on 27 Mar 1935. Phineas Cole died 27 Jul 1940 after an auto accident on 23 Jul and is buried with Emma and his first wife.

## 2. Jacob J Stanley and Rhoda Phillips

Jacob Stanley, 24, of Wheatfield, working at thrashing, married Rhoda Phillips, 17, of Wheatfield, doing housework, on 8 Aug 1894 in Hillsdale, Michigan. His parents were John Stanley and Elizabeth Klingensmith. Her parents were Taylor Phillips and Vine Rupley. Thrashing of wheat and oats occurred in August he may have been part of a group that went from farm to farm.

The 1900 census for Wheatland, Hillsdale, Michigan has Jacob Stanley, 28, born Sept 1871, married 5 years, a day laborer who is renting his home. Rhoda is 22, born Apr 1878 and has had 1 child still living. Their son is, Frankie, 4, born July 1895. John and Elizabeth Stanley are the previous listing. The parents were living on a farm they owned and Jacob's house appears to be on that farm.

The 1910 census for Waverly, Van Buren, Michigan has Jacob Stanley, 38, married 16 years, a general farmer who owns his mortgaged farm. Rhoda is 32 and has had 2 children who are living. Their children are Frank, 14 and Ethyl, 8. John Sr. is 78, widowed and not working. Also listed under Jacob Stanley is his brother J G Stanley's family but probably in a different house. John G Stanley, 51, married 29 years, a general farmer who owns his mortgaged farm. Jeanette is 48 and has had 7 children, 6 are living. Their children are Rossamond, 17, farm laborer; William, 16 and Bertha, 14.

All attended school. Willie Snow, son-in-law is 38 and a laborer at odd jobs. Willie's children are Lottie 8; Leone 6; Frankie 5; Ruthie 3 and Fern 2.

All are listed under Jacob Stanley so they may have been living in a double house or 2 houses and farming the same land. Jacob and his father John may have moved to Van Buren County to be near John G Stanley. Elizabeth Klingensmith Stanley died in 1908.

After his father died in 1911, Jacob and Rhoda moved to Kalamazoo where Jacob was listed in the city directory as a teamster. In 1913 Jacob and Rhoda moved to Canada.

After Jacob's father died, they may not have seen a need to stay in the US. Canada had the Dominion Lands Act that granted 65 hectares or 160 acres, a quarter section, for $10. Settlers had 3 years to build a house (sod or log) clear part of the land and live there at least 6 months each year. If they made progress on the quarter section, they might purchase a full section (640 acres). Robsart and Maple Creek are just North of central Montana. Undoubtedly good farm land.

Jake (Jacob) Stanley, 42, a farmer from Kalamazoo, Michigan crossed into Canada on a train headed for Winnipeg with $60 in his pocket on 2 Jul 1913. The rest of the family crossed 28 Sep 1913 after Jacob found land and built a "house". The family crossed into Canada by trail, with their possessions in a horse drawn wagon. Only train crossings left records.

Frank William Stanley went to Regina, Saskatchewan, Canada to enlist for WW1. He was born 6 Jul 1895 in Kalamazoo, Michigan, U.S. He was single, Lutheran, and a farmer. His father was Jacob Stanley and both lived in Robsart, Saskatchewan. He reported to Regina on 6 Jul 1918. He was 23, height 5' 7 ½ ", fair complexion, blue eyes and light hair. Frank was discharged 28 Mar 1919.

The 1921 census for Maple Creek, Saskatchewan, Canada has Jacob Stanley, 49, born in USA, immigrated in 1913, naturalized in 1917, living on section 15, township 3, range 25, meridian 3, in a wood house with 4 rooms that he owns. Rhoda is 43. Frank is 25 and farming. Maple Creek is an unorganized unit, number 21, part of district 9. The religion listed was Congregational. Jacob owned his farm and Frank was working for him. Jacob may have satisfied the requirements for his quarter section in Robsart and bought a section in Maple Creek. Ethyl, 19, is not listed and was married by then.

Jacob Stanley and Mrs. Jacob are on a 1940 voter list for Maple Creek. Agnes Bishop Letherer knew a Jacob Stanley had gone to Canada but nothing more. There may have been occasional contact with Agnes' grandfather Fred Stanley, Jacob's brother.

### 3. Frank William Stanley and Margaret Gorka

Frank William Stanley Age 27yr 4mo 16da; born 1895 in Michigan to Jacob Stanley and Rhoda Phillips was married Nov. 22, 1922 in Chinook, Blaine, Montana to Margaret

Gorka age 19 yr. 5 mo. 14 da.; born in Pennsylvania to Mike Gorka and Mary Riber. They were both from Robsart, Saskatchewan. The minister was from the Methodist Episcopal Church. It is interesting that they went to Montana to get married although crossing the border to get married has always been popular especially if the state allows quick marriages. They got the marriage license and married on the same day.

The 1958 voter lists for Brandon-Souris, Manitoba has Frank Stanley working for CNR Express and Mrs. Frank Stanley. They are living at 341 Ninth Street. A salesman William C Dagg is also living at this address. CNR Express would be the Canadian National Railroad freight service.

The 1962 Voter lists for Brandon-Souris, Manitoba has Frank William Stanley, retired and Mrs. Margaret Stanley living at 341 Ninth Street. Patricia Doreen Stanley, a student, and Peter Punak, a laborer, are living with them. It can be assumed Patricia is a daughter or granddaughter.

### 3. Ethel Elizabeth Stanley and J Lawrence Holstine

Ethel Elizabeth Stanley, 18, of Chinook Montana, born in Michigan married J L Holstine, 21 of Chinook, Montana, born in Kansas, on 9 Oct 1917. J L's parents were A E Holstine and Myrtle Bugg. Ethel's parents were Jacob Stanley and Rhoda Phillips. George W Glass, clergyman performed the ceremony in Havre Hill, Montana.

J L Holstine left Canada and reentered 13 Apr 1919. He was 22 and a farmer. The reason given for entering was take up homestead and locate well on farm. He was born in Beula, Kansas and his last permanent address was Pittsburg, Kansas. He was going to his father's in Robsart, Saskatchewan. He arrived on a train.

The 1921 census for Maple Creek, Saskatchewan, Canada has Archie Holstine, 46, living in a wood house he owns; Lawrence Holstine, 23; and Ethel Holstine, 20. All were born in the USA, immigrated in 1913, became naturalized citizens in 1916, are farming, and are Lutheran. Lawrence is working for his father.

# Chapter 7

## Catherine Klingensmith and John Arn

1. Catherine Klingenschmidt (1835-1904)
+ Johann Ahrend (1830-1907)
    2. Charles J Arn (1857-1917)
    + Julina Minter (1863-)
        3. Fred Louis Arn (1886-1949)
        + Effie May McNett (1886-1958)
            4. Ima Veda Arn (1907-1939)
            + Frank C Warta (1904-1979)
                5. Dorothy Warta (1925-)
                5. Frank Warta (1927-)
                5. Lawrence C Warta (1928-1987)
                5. Richard Warta (1932-)
        3. Odos "Otis" C. Arn (1893-1948) WW1
        + Gladys M. (1899-)
        + Eva (1901-)
    2. Mary Ann Arn (1858-1928)
    + Thomas Jefferson Wise Jr. (1836-1922)
        3. John Samuel Wise (1876-1937)
        +Hanna E. (1884-1956)
            4. Harold R Wise (1906-1979)
            + Marie G (1913-)
            + Juanita M Bybee (1910-1953)
                5. Charles Wise (1934-)
                5. Leon (1936-2005)
                5. Samuel Wise (1938-)
            4. Loren J. Wise (1908-1974)
            + Dorothy L. (1912-)
            + Esta L Fruits (1907-)
                5. Ray Wise (1929-)
                5.Carroll Wise (1930-)
                5. Bobbie Wise (1932-)
                5. Jamie Wise (1935-)
                5. William Wise (1937-)
                5. Wanita Wise (1937-)
                5. Jackie Wise (1939-)
            4. Beatrice "Juanita" Wise (1912-)
            4.John D Wise (1914-1988) WW11
            + Gladys (1914-1985)
                5. Wayne Wise (1935-)
                5. Joann Wise (1937-)
            4. Thomas Clifford Wise (1918-)

3. William W. Wise (1878-1970)
+Lela Ann McCandless (1888-1955)
    4. Joyce May Wise (1904-1989)
    + R F Puckett (1903-)
        5. Vernon Puckett (1928-)
        5. Richard Puckett (1933-)
        5. Shirley Ann Puckett (1939-)
    4. Lillard Leroy Wise (1907-1997)
    + Opal Cook (1913-)
    4. Earl W Wise (1909-1935)
    4. Lamoyne M Wise (1916-2011)
    + Hershel Smith (1913-)
        5. Charles K Smith (1913-)
    + Noel Lay (-)
3. Maude May Wise (1880-1946)
+ William Chester Kelsey (1875-1939)
    4. Edith Mildred Kelsey (1900-1986)
    + Oliver L Jackson (1896-1954) WW1
        5. Orral Jackson (1922-)
        5. Robert Jackson (1925-)
    + John J Zoller (1898-1967)
    4. Fern Alice Kelsey (1902-1977)
    + R D Fraidenburg (1898-1977)
        5. Alice May Fraidenburg (1920-)
        5. Ardath Fern I Fraidenburg (1923-)
    + Maurice Aubrey Nave (1901-1970)
    4. Chester L. Kelsey (1908-1975)
    + Evelyn Bernice Hagadorn (1911-1939)
        5. Clifford Kelsey (1933-)
        5. Lorene Kelsey (1936-)
        5. Carol Kelsey (1939-)
    4. Marion D. Kelsey (1911-1984)
    + Elsie Thelma Peepler Owen (1913-)
    4. Viola M. Kelsey (1914-2000)
    + Thomas E. Golden (1911-1973)
    4. Wanita M Kelsey (1916-2004)
    + Frank Plischke (1909-)
    4. Enos James Kelsey (1919-2009)
    + Vera Francis Frew (-)
3. Blanche E. Wise (1882-1963)
+ Jefferson Bromwell (1886-)
    4. Freddie LeRoy Bromwell Martin (1905-1975)
    + Mary Bonita Stewart (1908-1973)
        5. Lucille Martin (1929-)
        5. Helen Lois Martin (1931-1975)

                5. Patty Ann Martin (1936-2009)
                5. William Albert Martin (1942-1982)
        + Burton W Martin (1887-1958)
            4. Marie Norelle Martin (1909-1986)
            + William H Durbin (1905-1959)
                5. William Robert Durbin (1929-2016)
                5. Patricia Ruth Durbin (1931-)
            4. Evelyn C Martin (1917-2000)
            + Milton Lebbin (1914-1997)
        3. Thomas Jefferson Wise Jr (3rd) (1885-1928)
        + Bessie H Harrison (1879-1867)
            4. Thomas J Wise (4$^{th}$) (1907-1957)
            4. Kent H Wise (1910-1995)
            + Virginia L Gaskins (1907-)
        3. Mary Francis "Fannie" Wise (1888-1938)
        + Charles R Hamilton (1880-)
        + Charles G. Hilligoss (1880-1948)
        3. Rufus C. Wise (1896-1914)
        3. Earl Wise (1899-1902)
    2. Elizabeth Arn (1860-1938)
    + Charles Joseph Wilhelm (1845-1897)
        3. Laura Wilhelm (1878-1957)
        + Charles E Hammock (1875-1963)
            4. Edna Mae Hammock (1897-1991)
            + Charles R Garber (1891-1943) WW1
                5. George Wayne Garber (1918-2001) WW11
                5. Alene Garber (1921-)
                5. Laura Alice Garber (1931-)
            4. Alfred Leo Hammock (1902-1932)
            + Dixie Dowden (1902-2003)
                5. Alfred Leo Hammock (1929-2007)
            4. Gladys Marie Hammock (1906-1985)
            + Deward Henry Bates (1904-1944)
                5. Marie L Bates (1926-)
                5. Zella "Ella" Faye Bates (1929-)
            + George P Collins (1893-1968)
            4. Lester Hammock (1908-1994)
            + Hazel Hull (1908-1995)
            4. Gertrude Alice Hammock (1910-1988)
            + Floyd Harlan Roth (1907-1989)
                5. James H Roth (1929-)
                5. Charles H Roth (1932-)
            4. Everett W Hammock (1912-1977)
            + Gladys Richardson (1917-2011)
            4. Charles "Earl" Hammock (1914-1994)

  + Mary Ellen Lovell (1914-2011)
    5. Eleanor Lovell (1936-)
  4. Blanche E Hammock (1916-1999)
  + James Earl Lovell (1912-1992)
    5. Barbra J Lovell (1937-)
    5. Doris L Lovell (1939-)
  4. Ruth Catherine Hammock (1921-2000)
  + Rollie Morgan (1912-1993)
  4. Mary Francina Hammock (1923-2011)
  + Hugh Jones Gay (1919-2012) WW11
3. Katherine Wilhelm (1880-1936)
+ Fred Emery Raff (1874-1940)
  4. Percy George Raff (1902-1973) WW11
  4. Phylia E Raff (1908-1971)
  + Leo A Maxwell (1896-1994)
    5. Leo A Maxwell (1927-)
    5. Phylia Maxwell (1929-)
  4. Ethel Claudine Raff (1909-1937)
  + Ernest Miller (1907-1986)
    5. Robert Miller (1928-)
    5. Geraldine Miller (1931-)
  4. Gilbert Raff (1912-1974)
  4. Glenn A Raff (1914-1996)
  + Rita (1917-)
    5. Richard J Raff (1938-)
    5. Elizabeth J Raff (1939-)
  4. Datus Raff (1917-1918)
  4. Dayton Carl Raff (1917-2008)
  + Evelyn (1919-)
    5. William D Raff (1938-)
  4. John Lewis Raff (1919-1947)
3. Charlotte "Lottie" Wilhelm (1883-1891)
3. Minnie Mae Wilhelm (1885-1935)
+ Burton Folck (1880-1960)
  4. Leo Gilbert Folck (1903-1991)
  + Harriet Frances King (1908-2002)
    5. Richard L Folck (1931-)
    5. Carol Harriet Folck (1935-2004)
  4. Veda I Folck (1904-1988
  + Durward L Titus (1905-1967)
    5. Robert Alfred Titus (1922-2010)
    5. Lorraine M Titus (1924-)
    5. Maxine M Titus (1926-)
    5. Keith Wayne Titus (1927-1927)
    5. Lola L Titus (1928-2003)

            5. Cecil Owen Titus (1931-2005)
            5. Opal Jean Titus (1935-1992)
        4. Wilber A Folck (1906-1988)
         + Madaline Berry (1906-1994)
            5. Mae Belle Folck (1928-1928)
            5. Nadine Flock (1929-)
            5. Dora Lee Folck (1932-)
            5. Amy Elizabeth Folck (1933-)
            5. Wilbur William Folck (1934-1953) Korean War
            5. Roy Burton Folck (1938-2005)
        4. Ruby Marie Folck (1909-1944)
         + Donald Roe Arnold (1905-1973)
            5. Dwight Lassiter Arnold (1928-1983)
            5. Dwaine Lawrence Arnold (1929-1994)
            5. Daryl Dean Arnold (1931-2005)
            5. Gary Arnold (1934-)
            5. Dan Spencer Arnold (1934-1997)
            5. Barbara Lou Arnold (1935-2005)
            5. Lois Faye Arnold (1938-1938)
            5. Roger Arnold (1939-)
        4. Rosalee Folck (1916-1995)
         + John William Canfield (1914-1985)
        4. Genevieve Irene Folck (1918-1999)
         + Fred J Strouse (1898-1970)
        4. Lois Eileen Folck (1922-2001)
         + Robert C Gallmeister (1917-)
    3. Ernistine Wilhelm (1887-1941)
     + Warren Alva Landfair (1887-1977)
        4. Audrey Lois Landfair (1910-1982)
         + James F "Jesse" Wilson (1899-)
         + Marcus Miles Durfree (1905-1988)
        4. Ferne Landfair (1913-)
        4. Nellie Norene Landfair (1916-1956)
         + Waite
    3. Lewis Herman Wilhelm (1889-1958)
     + Clara Florence Ensminger (1891-1973)
        4. Lila Wilhelm (1911-2004)
         + Vincel O Kling (1909-1974)
        4. Wilber L Wilhelm (1914-2008) WW11
         + Lucille (1919-2011)
        4. Mildred L Wilhelm (1914-1997)
         + John Haskell Gibbons (1907-1984)
        4. Beulah Mae Wilhelm (1916-2011)
         + Leo Bernard Buffington (1918-1968) WW11
        4. Macel Dorthea Wilhelm (1919-2001)

                4. Faye Louise Wilhelm (1920-1970)
                 + Harry Milton Meyers (1917-1968) WW11
                4. Claude Joseph Wilhelm (1922-2011)
                4. Fern E Wilhelm (1923-1984)
                4. Galen E Wilhelm (1925-1931)
                4. Betty Lee Wilhelm (1928-)
                4. Mary Ann Wilhelm (1932-)
                4. Patsy Jean Wilhelm (1935-)
            3. Loretta Blanche Wilhelm (1892-1976)
             + Ewell Neff (1895-1972)
                4. James Wilhelm Neff (1918-1977)
            3. Claude J Wilhelm (1895-1918) WW1
    2. Franklin L Arn (1862-1917)
     + Isabell S. Dehoney (1864-1922)
            3. Nellie Arn (1884-1959)
             + Fred Eller Cannedy (1881-1959)
                4. Clarence Cannedy (1912-)
                4. Helen Cannedy (1914-)
            3. Oscar Arn (1890-before 1910)
            3. Earl Arn (1893-1957)
             + Alice H Refine (1899-1987)
                4. James Edward Arn (1921-1971)
            3. Alice Arn (1898-1970)
            3. Lawrence Arn (1901-1958) WW11
             + Wilmay Myrtle Arbrickle
                4. Lawrence Malcom Arn (1925-)
                4. Ralph Arn (1926-)
            3. Charles Arn (1906-1954)
             + Evelyn J Matern (1908-1994)
                4. Doris Jean Arn (1931-)
                4. Leona Mary Arn (1933-)
                4. Shirley Anne Arn (1936-)
                4. Joyce Elaine Arn (1939-)
            3. Margaret Marie Arn (1909-1924)
    2. Ida Louise Arn (1865-1931)
     + A R Whiteman (1841-)
            3. Nettie Whiteman (1879-1964)
             + Charles N. Auvigne (1871-1964)
                4. Leo Auvigne (1901-1919)
                4. Marie Auvigne (1903-)
                4. Laura Auvigne (1905-1920)
                4. Raymond Auvigne (1907-)
                4. Ida Auvigne (1909-)
                4. Floyd Auvigne (1914-)
                4. Fred Auvigne (1916-1985)

                4. Irene Auvigne (1918-)
                4. Clarence Auvigne (1919-)
                4. Carl Auvigne (1920-1921)
   + Jonas Ellsberry Likens (1849-1924)
        3. William Ellsberry Likens (1883-1938)
         + Serena Telva Simcox (1892-1928)
                4. Jessie Likins (1911-1994)
                 + Harry Ross Baldridge (1913-1989)
                4. Harold Leroy Likins (1913-1986) WW11
                 + Bertha Lucille Burch (1915-2003)
                4. Glenn Edwin Likins (1915-1988)
                 + Dorothy M Burch (1921-2004)
                      5. Glenmon Likins (1939-)
                      5. William J Likins (1942-)
                4. Clarence Likins (1917-1925)
                4. Floyd Raymond Likins (1921-1988) WW11
                4. Josie Irene Likins (1920-2006)
                 + Travis Ernest Turner (1919-2000) WW11
                4. Galen W Likins Childers (1922-1988) WW11
                4. Edna Mae Likins (1924-1998) WW11
        3. Carlinda Likens (1885-1908)
         + Elbridge C Moulds (1884-1936)
        3. Elmer Gene Likins (1887-before 1900)
        3. Frank Leslie Likins (1890-1947)
        3. Roy Likins (1893-1940)
         + Ada Partain (1895-)
        3. Robert Earl Likins (1896-1931)
         + Laura B Long (1900-1974)
                4. Alene L Likins (1919-)
                4. Earl Likins (1921-1982) WW11
                4. Billie N Likins (1924-)
                4. Mary Nell Likins (1928-1929)
        3. Walter Jonas Likens (1900-1976)
         + Eva Jane Holden (1910-1987)
                4. Walter Likins (1929-)
        3. Lewis Ray Likens (1902-1905)
        3. John Likins (1905-1914)
2. Julia C Arn (1867-1946)
 + Vallendingher "Val" Cox (1863-1940)
        3. Myrtle Cox (1885-)
         + Beryl Lewis Smith (1884-1964)
                4. Ida M Smith (1912-)
                4. Rena B Smith (1913-)
        3. Rilla Cox (1888-1941)
         + John Walter Alger (1876-1942)

   4. Russell A Alger (1906-1974)
   + Celia M Irvine (1908-1999)
     5. Dorothy M Alger (1930-)
     5. Russell A Alger Jr. (1931-)
     5. Ralph Alger (1933-)
     5. Deloris Alger (1935-)
     5. Carol J Alger (1937-)
   4.Claude Virgil Alger (1908-1949)
   + Ruth Helena Postier (1908-1980)
     5. Glenda Lee Alger (1940-)
   4. Wesley J Alger (1909-1928)
   4. Earl LeRoy Alger (1911-1946) WW11
   + Ethel Emmaline (1913-1991)
   4.Evelyn Alberta Alger (1913-1987)
   + James Harvey Poland (1907-1980)
   4. Hensley D Alger (1915-1958)
   + Lois L Durland (1918-2012)
     5. Myrna E Alger (1938-)
     5. Byron D Alger (1939-)
   4. LaVerda S Alger (1918-2017)
   + Donald W Brown (1919-2008)
   4. John Walter Alger Jr. (1920-1968)
   4. Nina Mae Alger (1926-1982)
 3. Clara Cox (1890-1972)
 + Fredrick J Mansfield (1878-1953)
   4. Edwin B Mansfield (1908-1973)
   + Florence Leta Willey (1909-1990)
     5. Victor Mansfield (1931-)
   4. Mary Elizabeth Mansfield (1910-1996)
   + Emery Hubbard (1909-1956)
   4. Ester F Mansfield (1918-1988)
   4. Ruth L Mansfield (1920-)
   4. Betty Mansfield (1932-)
 3. Clarence William Cox (1890-1963)
 + Emma Jean Ruth Starr (1892-1963)
   4. Julia M Cox (1913-)
   4. Ruth Irene Cox (1913-2001)
   + Gordon W Richey (1903-1970)
   4. Idena B Cox (1915-)
   4. Dorothy M Cox (1917-)
 3. Thomas Cox (1891-1902)
 3. John Roy Cox (1894-1911)
 3. Forest "Floyd" V Cox (1896-1964)
 + Stella J Lindquist (1895-1930)
   4. Darlene Retha Cox (1919-1991)

                4. William "Billy" Pierce Cox (1921-1991)
            + Julia A (1909-)
        3. Flossie Lenora Cox (1898-1979)
        + Clyde Raymond Embers (1900-1981)
        3. Nina M Cox (1901-1957)
        + Clyde Raymond Embers (1901-1981)
        3. Alta J Cox (1904-1983)
        + Robert Burkholder (1902-1958)
            4. Darlene Burkholder (1930-)
            4. Darwin Burkholder (1935-)
        3. Zelma Ann Cox (1907-)
        +Abram John Buller (1908-)
    2. John Jacob Arn (1870-1933)
    + Nellie McNamara (1866- before 1920)
        3. child born before 1910 died young
    + Hattie Van Vliet (1869-)
    2. Frederick W Arn (1873-1909)
    + Ada Brown (1878-1901)

## 1.Catherine Klingensmith and Johann "John" Arn

Catherine Klingensmith married John Arn (there are several spellings including Arn, Ahrend, and Arend) and lived in McPherson County, Kansas in 1889. Arn seems to be the most popular and will be used here unless it is spelled differently in a document.

Their marriage is recorded as: Klingelschmidt, Katherine, daughter of Jacob and Charlotte Klingelschmidt, (name later changed to Klingensmith), age 22, and John Arend (Ahrend), age 24, Hillsdale, 20 Jan 1856.[10] John was born 7 Mar 1830 in Switzerland as were both of his parents.

The 1860 census for Pittsford, Hillsdale, Michigan has John Aren, 30, born in Switzerland, a farmer. Catherine is 25 and born in Bavaria. Their children are Charles J born 4 Feb 1857; Mary Ann born 30 Jul 1858 and Elizabeth J born 12 Dec 1859. Two more children were born near Pittsford Michigan, Franklin in 1862 and Ida in 1865.

The Civil War was over and the west was opening to settlement. The prairie lured many to settle in Iowa with it's wonderful farm land. Catherine and John packed up their family and moved to Iowa in 1866. John found work near Iowa City so they stayed through the birth of their daughter, Julia in 1867. Then they moved to Grand Junction, Iowa where John was born in 1869 or 1870.

The 1870 Census for Grand Junction, Iowa has John Arn, 40, born in Switzerland, a laborer with $600 in real estate and $100 in possessions. Catherine is 35, born in Bavaria and keeping house. Their children are Charles, 13; Mary, 11; Elizabeth, 10; Frank, 8; Ida, 5; Julia, 3 and John, 10/12.

A son Frederick was born in 1872 in Iowa, probably Grand Junction. Catherine's mother, Charlotte Warner Klingensmith died 15 Sep 1872. Grand Junction was incorporated in 1873 just as the Arns were ready to leave.

Railroads now reached the west coast but they didn't go most places. John and Catherine heard about free land and started for Kansas about 1873. The distance is about 400 miles. Although they may have gone part way by train, it is likely they filled a wagon with all they had and headed south and west. They traveled through Iowa and Missouri before entering Kansas. It was a slow process with some walking and the rest riding in the wagon.

They would have stopped in Salina, Kansas. Salina was a frontier town by 1873 and had the only land office in central Kansas. A visit there would have told them where land was available. John and Catherine drove south of Salina to McPherson County and found their land on the West Branch of Sharps Creek. John traveled back to Salina to register the south west quarter of section 33 with the Land Office. Returning to the family, he started to work the land to fulfill the government contract.

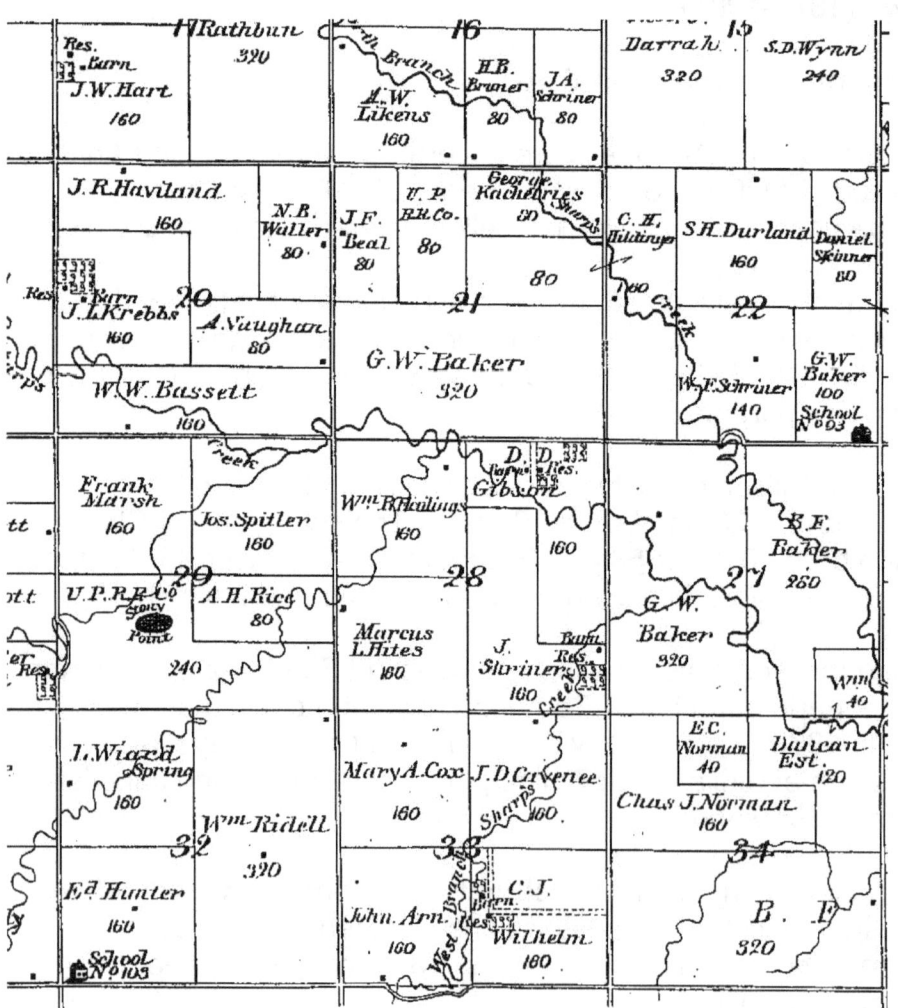

His farm was covered with tall prairie grass with a few trees near the creek. John and the boys used a sod breaking plow to plow the prairie grass and used the sod to build a house on the south side of their land using trees from the creek bank for the roof.

You can find the land along the south side of this map from 1884. There are other names on the map that will be found later in this chapter.

I found this land in 2019 west of McPherson on US 56 then north on 444 through Windom. East on Overland Road (bottom of map) 1 mile.

The dirt road becomes a 2 track.
Going up a hill we came to the corner of Arn's farm. All 3 roads from there were impassable but I took this picture. The land goes downhill to the creek where there are trees.

The school at the corner of 444 and Overland Road may be where some of the Arn's attended. I doubt there was a bridge near Arn's house but a low spot to drive through West Branch Sharp's Creek.

John and Catherine Arn lived in Sharps Creek, Kansas (later South Sharp's Creek) when a state census was taken on 1 Mar 1875. John Arn is 45, born in Switzerland, a farmer from Iowa with $1,400 in property. Catherine is 40 and born in Bavaria. Their children are Charles J, 18; Elizabeth 15; Franklin, 13; and Ida, 10, born in Michigan and Julia, 8; John J, 6 and Fred W, 3, born in Iowa. Mary has left home.

On 25 Oct 1879 John went to Salina to pay the last $4 due to record the land Patent. Patent Record for Salina, Kansas, Homestead Number 5020, Application 15342. "Johann Arn has been established and duly consummated to conformity to law for the South West Quarter of Section Thirty-Three in Township Eighteen South of Range five West in the district of lands subject to sale at Salina, Kansas containing one hundred and sixty acres. Now know ye that there is therefore granted by the United States unto Johann Arn the tract of land described; to have and hold, with the appurtenances thereof, unto the said Johann Arn and to his heirs and assigns forever. In Testimony Whereof I, Rutherford B Hayes President of the United States of America have caused these Letters to be made Patent, and the Seal of the General Land Office to be hereunto affixed. 30 Jun 1880. Recorded Vol 10 page 431."

The 1880 census for South Sharp's Creek, McPherson, Kansas has John Arn, 50, a farmer. Catharine is 45. Their children are Frank, 18, a laborer; Ida Whiteman, 15 with a daughter Nettie Whiteman, 1; Julia, 13; John, 10 and Fred, 8. Charles and Elizabeth have left home. Nettie Whiteman's father was born in Ohio but is not otherwise listed.

The 1885 Kansas State Census for Smoky Hill, McPherson, Kansas has John Arn, 55, a farmer. Catherine is 50. Their children are John Jr, 15 and Fred, 12. All are farmers.

On 6 Oct 1888 John Arn sold the land to his son John Jacob Arn for $3500 and paid off 2 mortgages for $850 and $85.

The 1895 Kansas State Census for Clear Creek, Marion, Kansas has John Arn, 65, a farmer. Catherine is 60.

The 1900 census for South Sharp's Creek, McPherson, Kansas has John Arn, 70, born March 1830 in Switzerland, married 44 years, immigrated 1853, a naturalized citizen, and a farmer renting his farm. Catherine is 64, born June 1835 in Germany, had 9 children with 8 still living and immigrated in 1854.

Catherine Klingensmith Arn born 25 Aug 1835 in Bavaria, died 7 March 1904 in Rice, Kansas. John Arn born Mar 1830 in Switzerland, died on 7 March 1907 in Picher, Oklahoma. John F Likins son of Ida Louise Arn Likins, John Arn's daughter said John J Arn died 7 March 1908 in Welch, Oklahoma. John is buried in the Welch Cemetery. This is probably accurate. Jonas and Ida Likins moved to Welch, Oklahoma between 1900 and 1910. They are buried in the same cemetery. Picher and Welch are only about 30 miles apart in North East Oklahoma.

This picture was taken around 1900. The caption is: John "Johann" 1830-1907 and Catherine (Klingensmith) Arn 1835-1904.

## 2. Charles J Arn and Julina Minter

The 1880 census for Sharps Creek, McPherson, Kansas has Charles Arn, 23, laborer He is listed with others working on a farm owned by Stephen Gilpin.

The 1885 Kansas State census for Smoky Hill, McPherson, Kansas has C J Arn, 25, single, born in Michigan, working for B F Baker.

Charles J Arn, 26, married Julina Minter 24 Dec 1885 in McPherson, Kansas.

The 1885 Kansas State census for Smoky Hill, McPherson Co. has William and Adline Minter with their daughter Julina and other children. Julina is not married.

The 1895 Kansas State census for South Sharps Creek, McPherson, Kansas has C J Arn, 37, born in Michigan, from Iowa, a farmer. J Arn is 31 and born in Iowa. Their children are Fred, 8, born in Kansas, attended school and O C, 1, born in Kansas.

The 1900 census for South Sharps Creek, McPherson, Kansas has Charles Arn, 43, born Feb 1857, married 17 years, a farmer renting a farm. Julina is 36 and born Aug 1863. Their sons are Freddie, 13, born Sept 1886 and Odos, 7, born May 1893. Both boys attended school 7 months during the last year.

The 1910 census for Castle, McPherson, Kansas has Charles J Arn, 53, married 24 years, a farmer on a general farm he is renting. Julina is 48. Their son, Odos, is 16 and a laborer on the home farm.

Charles J Arn born 4 Feb 1856 in Pittsford, Michigan, died 26 Dec 1917 and is buried in Excelsior Cemetery, Marquette, McPherson, Kansas. Charley was 61. Information was from his son Fred Louis Arn.

Julina is not buried with Charles and no record of her death has been found. She was 54 when Charley died and may have remarried.

## 3. Fred Louis Arn and Effie May McNett

Fred L Arn, 21, married Effie M McNett on 5 Sep 1906 in McPherson, Kansas.

The 1910 census for Castle, McPherson, Kansas has Fred L Arn, 23, married 3 years, a general farmer renting his farm. Effie M is 22. Their daughter, Ima V is 2.

Fred L Arn registered for WW1 in Marion Center, Kansas. He was born 5 Sep 1886. He is a self-employed farmer in Kanopolis with a wife and child of 9 years. He is tall, slender with brown eyes and hair.

Fred's daughter, Ima V Arn was born 1907. A 1920 census was not found and by 1925 she had left home.

The 1925 state census for Valley, Lincoln, Kansas has Fred Arn, 39, a general farmer renting his farm. Effie is 38.

The 1930 census for Marquette, McPherson, Kansas has Fred L Arn, 43, a laborer on a steam railroad and renting a house for $10 per month. Effie is 42 and they do not own a radio.

Fred and Effie moved to Brookville, Kansas by 1938. A 1940 census was not found.

Fred Louis Arn died 12 Jun 1949 at Brookville, Saline, Kansas and is buried in Brookville Cemetery.

Effie May McNett Arn born 1 Sep 1886, died 8 Apr 1958 in Brookville, Saline, Kansas and is buried with Fred.

### 4. Ima Veda Arn and Frank C Warta

Ima Veda Arn, 17, married Frank C Warta, 20, in 1924.

The 1930 census for Marquette Township, McPherson County, Kansas has Frank Warta, 25, married at 20, renting a farm, not a veteran. Ima is 22, was married at 17 and they have 3 children; Dorothy, 4 9/12, Frank, 3 1/12, Lawrence, 1 3/12. All were born in Kansas.

Ima Veda Effie Arn Warta, born 11 Sep 1907, died 14 Jul 1939. She is buried in Brookville Cemetery, Brookville, Saline County, Kansas. Frank C Warta died in 1979 and is buried with Ima.

The 1940 census for Brookville, Kansas has Frank Warta, 35, widowed, completed 8th grade and a laborer for public works. The children are Dorothy, 14, completed 7th grade; Frank, 13, completed 6th grade; Lawrence, 11, completed 5th grade and Richard, 8, completed 2nd grade.

### 3. Odos "Otis" C Arn

Odos Arn, 24, born 8 May 1893 registered for WW1 on 5 Jun 1917. He was single a farmer working for himself and lived in Windom, Kansas. Odos had poor eyesight, gray eyes, light brown hair and was tall with a medium build. A note says: defective eyesight not noticeable.

The 1920 census for Windom, Kansas has Odos Arn, 25, married, a laborer renting his home at 60 Murtte Street. Gladys M is 21.

The 1930 census for Lyons, Kansas has Otis Arn,34, divorced. a laborer in an ice plant and a lodger with another family. He is a veteran of WW1.

The 1940 census for Lyons, Kansas has Otis Arn, 43, married, graduated high school, a stationary engineer at a salt mine who owns his home at 215 East Trusdell worth $3500. Eva is 39, completed 1 year of high school and from Alabama.

Otis C. Arn born 8 May 1893 in Windom, McPherson, Kansas died 9 Sep 1948 and is buried in Lyons Municipal Cemetery, Lyons, Kansas. Otis was 55. He may have had problems resulting from WW1 as he is married twice for relatively short times and has no children. He is also buried by himself.

## 2. Mary Ann Arn and Thomas Jefferson Wise Jr

Mary Ann Arn married Thomas Jefferson Wise about 1875.

The 1880 census for Clear Creek, Marion, Kansas has Thomas J Wise, 44, farming. Mary is 22 and keeping house Their children are John, 4; William, 2; and Effie, 0. Joseph Hoover, 23, servant, laborer, and Annie Schnell, 19, servant are living with them. Effie was later called Maude. In the 1870 census Thomas J Wise had a wife Martha and a daughter Cora, 3. Martha and Cora probably died of disease.

The 1895 state census for Clear Creek, Kansas has T J Wise, 58, farmer; Mary A., 34; John S, 19; Wm W, 17; Maud, 15; Blanch, 13; T J Jr.,11; and Fannie, 6. The 4 younger children attended school for 8 months of the last year. John attended 4 months and William attended 5 months.

The following picture of Maude, Blanch and Fannie or Mary was taken about 1895.

Maude married William Chester Kelsey 12 Dec 1897 in Lincolnville, Kansas at the age of 17 and is not in the 1900 census with her parents.

The 1900 census for Clear Creek, Marion, Kansas has Thomas Wise, 63, born Dec 1836, married 25 years, a farmer who owns his farm. Mary is 41, born Jul 1858 and has had 9 children with 8 living. Their children are John, 24, born Mar 1876, a farmer renting his land; William W, 22, born Mar 1878, a farm laborer; Blanch, 19, born Jun 1882, attended school 4 months; Thomas, 17, born Dec 1882, a farm laborer, attended school 6 months; Mary, 12, born Mar 1888, attended school 7 months; Rufus C 4, born Feb 1896; and Earl 9/12, born Aug 1899. Fannie and Mary appear to be the same person.

The 1905 Kansas State census for Clear Creek, Marion, Kansas has T J Wise, 69 who owns his farm free and clear. Mary A Wise is 47. Their daughter Blanch Bromwell is 23; Jefferson Bromwell is 19 and Leroy Bromwell is 1. T J and Mary's other children are Fanny, 17 and Rufus, 8. Earl died 19 Aug 1902.

Blanch married Jefferson Bromwell, had a son Leroy, then something happened to Jefferson Bromwell. 30 Dec 1907 Blanche married Burton Wray Martin in Kansas City, Missouri.

The 1910 census for Wichita, Kansas has T J Wise living at 1116 S Wichita Street. He is 72, married 2 times, married 35 years, owns a mortgaged house and has his own income. Mary A is 52, married once, had 7 children, 7 are living. Their son Rufus is 14 and attending school. The number of children seems to keep changing but appears to actually be 8 or 9.

The 1920 census for Wichita, Kansas has Thomas J. Wise, 83, retired. owns a house at 1116 S Wichita Street free and clear. Mary is 61.

Thomas J. Wise died 5 Dec 1922 and Mary A. Wise died 5 Dec 1928 in Wichita, Kansas. They are buried in Maple Grove Cemetery.

The pictures are of Thomas Jefferson Wise to the right and Mary Ann Arn to the left.

### 3. John Samuel Wise and Hannah E Stolberg

John appears in the 1900 census living with his parents and farming rented land. Soon after the census John moved to Wichita to work on the railroads.

The 1910 census for Wichita, Kansas has John Wise, 33, married 7 years, a fireman on the railroad who is renting a house at 1024 Fannie Ave in Wichita. Hannah E is 26 and has had 3 children, 2 are living. The children are Harold R, 4 and Loren J, 2.

John Samuel Wise, 42, born 19 Mar 1876 registered for WW1 on 12 Sep 1918. He was living at 1425 S Dodge in Wichita, Kansas and working as a Hostler for Kansas City, Mexico And Orient Railroad at shops in the city. His next of kin is Hannah Wise. He has blue eyes, light hair and is short with a stout build.

Originally Hostler referred to one who takes care of horses at an inn or hotel. With railroads, it became one who drives train locomotives to designated stations in a railroad roundhouse to be cleaned, serviced or repaired. This seems to be a better job as fireman often meant one who shovels coal into the fire to make steam. The Kansas City, Mexico and Orient Railroad was started in 1900 with the line completed between Wichita, Kansas and Alpine, Texas. The shops were located in Wichita from 1910 to 1928 through several reorganizations and name changes. The railroad was acquired by the Atchison, Topeka and Santa Fe in 1928. The rail lines in Mexico and Texas were subsequently sold off.

The 1920 census for Wichita, Kansas has John S Wise, 42, a fireman in the RR Shops who owns a home free and clear at 1425 South Dodge in Wichita. Hannah E is 36 and was born in Kansas with parents from Sweden. Their children are Harold R, 14; Loren J, 11; Beatrice J, 8; J D, 5 and Tom Clifford, 2. The 3 older children attended school.

The 1929 Wichita City Directory Has John S Wise (Hannah) an engineer, residence 1425 S Dodge. Harold R Wise, painter, residence 1425 S Dodge. B Juanita Wise, student, residence 1425 S Dodge. Loren J Wise (Dorothy) working in a lab, residence 435 N Edward.

The 1930 census for Wichita, Kansas has John S Wise, 54, married at 27, not a veteran, an engineer on a steam railroad who owns his home worth $3500 at 1425 S Dodge and a radio. Hannah E is 45 and was married at 19. Their children are Juanita, 18; John D, 16; and Thomas C, 12. A daughter-in-law, Marie G is 17, married at 17, not attending school and was born in Missouri. John and Thomas are listed as single. Harold is 24 and may be the married son.

John S Wise died in 1937 and is buried in White Chapel Memorial Gardens, Wichita, Kansas. Hannah E Wise died in 1956 and is buried with John.

### 4. Harold R Wise and Marie G / Juanita M Bybee

The 1930 census for Hutchinson, Kansas has a Harold Wise, 24, married at 24, born in Kansas, an inmate at the Kansas State Industrial Reformatory.

In the mid-1880s Kansas recognized the need for a reformatory where sentences were not for a fixed time and early release could be had for good behavior. The reformatory was for young men 16-30 and was focused on reforming first-time offenders through education and vocational training. Prohibition was from 1920-1933. Kansas led the movement and had very stringent rules. Possibly Harold was caught in a raid. His brother is an auto mechanic so maybe they were transporting. Harold didn't serve more than 3 to 4 years so it could not have been a very serious offence.

The 1934 Wichita City Directory has Harold (Juanita M) home 607 S Sycamore Ave. Directories were often compiled before the year so Harold and Juanita were probably married in 1933. Marie G may have divorced Harold after he went to prison.

The 1940 census for Wichita, Kansas has Harold Wise, 34, graduated high school and a Real Estate Broker who owns his home at 1615 S Main Street. Juanita is 30 and completed 8th grade. Their children are Charles, 6, completed 1st grade; Leon, 4 and Samuel, 2. Harold's mother, Hannah, is 52, a widow, and completed 6th grade.

Juanita M Bybee Wise died in 1953 according to a family tree on Ancestry.

Harold R Wise born 4 Dec 1905, died 17 Feb 1979 in Los Angeles, California.

### 4. Loren J Wise / Dorothy L / Esta L Fruits

The 1930 census for Wichita, Kansas has Loren J Wise, 22, married at 18, an automobile mechanic who owns a house at 435 Richmond. Dorothy L is 18, married at 17 and a stenographer at the daily paper.

The 1936 Wichita City Directory has Loren J Wise (Esta L) an auto body man, home 2021 Jeanette, Ave.

The 1940 census for Wichita, Kansas has Loren Wise, 32, completed 8th grade, a metal man at an Automobile Body & Fender Shop, renting a home at 2110 S Wichita Street. Esta is 33, born in Oklahoma, and graduated high school. Their children are Ray, 11, completed 5th grade; Carroll, 10, completed 4th grade; Bobbie, 8, completed 1st grade; Jamie, 5; William, 3; Wanita, 3; and Jackie, 1. Working with automobiles would indicate this is the same Loren Wise. The name of the wife is different so Loren may have divorced, or Dorothy died, and he married again. Esta probably had some of the children before she married Loren.

Loren J. Wise born 5 Mar 1908, died 24 Oct 1974 and is buried in Mount Vernon Cemetery South in Cowley County, Kansas.

## 4. Beatrice Juanita Wise

Beatrice Wise attended Junction City High School. She is last found in her parent's 1930 Census record when she was 18. There are many marriage records for Beatrice or Juanita Wise, but none could be verified.

## 4. John D Wise and Gladys M

John D. Wise is listed in the 1936 Wichita City Directory with Gladys, working as a serviceman at Hockaday Auto Supply Co., home 1631 S Martinson Ave.

The 1940 census for Wichita, Kansas has John Wise, 26, married, completed 9th grade, a helper at a retail and wholesale tire shop who is renting a house at 1925 Montxell for $10 per month and made $1091 in the last year. Gladys is 25, completed 10th grade, born in Oklahoma, and doing housework in the home. Their children are Wayne, 5, attended school and Joann, 3.

John Delmar Wise, 26, born 5 Mar 1914 in Wichita, Kansas registered for WW11 on 16 Oct 1940. His next of kin is Gladys Marie Wise and his employer is Kenneth Administer. He is 5'9", weighed 165 lbs. with blue eyes and blonde hair. John served in the Navy from 20 Oct 1943 to 14 Dec 1945.

John D Wise, born 1914, died 1988 and is buried in Resthaven Gardens of Memory in Wichita, Kansas. Gladys M Wise born 1914, died 1985 and is buried with John.

## 4. Thomas Clifford Wise

The last record found of Thomas Clifford Wise was his parents 1930 Census record. There is a Thomas Rodney Wise born 1 May 1916 in Wichita, Kansas with parents John S Wise and Hannah Stolberg in Social Security records. Thomas Roger Wise, 23, born 1 May 1917 in Wichita, Kansas, registered for WW11 with next of kin John Delmer Wise. He is 5'10", 150 lbs. with gray eyes and blonde hair. There seems to be a family resemblance. Maybe Thomas was playing with different middle names,

## 3. William Wimer Wise and Lela Ann McCandless

The 1910 census for Cedar Valley, Blaine, Oklahoma has William Wise, 32, married 8 years, born in Kansas, a farmer on his rented farm. Lela is 28, has had 3 children, all living and was born in Kentucky. Their children are Joyce, 6, born in Kansas; Lillard, 3 born in Kansas and Earl, 1, born in Oklahoma.

William Wimer Wise, 40, registered for WW1 on 12 Sept 1918. He was born 19 Mar 1878 and is a farmer in Vincent, Grady, Oklahoma. His next of kin is Lela Ann Wise, wife, Blanchard, McClain, Oklahoma. He is medium height and build with blue eyes and brown/gray hair. It is signed W W Wise.

The 1920 census for Vincent, Grady, Oklahoma has W W Wise, 40, farming on his own account. Lela is 38 Their children are Joyce, 16, attended school; Lillard, 13, attended school; Earl, 10, attended school and Lamoyne, 3.

The 1930 census for Vincent, Grady, Oklahoma has William W Wise, 52, married at 24, a farmer who owns his farm and a radio. Lela A is 48 and was married at 21. Their children are Earl W, 21, a prize fighter in a prize ring and Lamoyne M, 13, attended school. Earl is also listed in Oklahoma City as a lodger working as a prize fighter in boxing. He must have lived at least part of the time in Oklahoma City

The 1940 Census for Vincent, Grady, Oklahoma has William W Wise, 62, completed 5th grade, owns his own farm. Lela Anne is 58 and completed 9th grade. The fact he owned his farm may be why he was able to keep it during the depression and dust bowl.

William Wimer Wise registered for WW11. His farm was 1 mile west of Blanchard, Oklahoma.

This is a picture of William W Wise and Lela A McCandless Wise on their farm in Oklahoma or more likely it was after they moved to California to be with their children.

Lela Ann McCandless Wise died 21 Sep 1955 in Tulare County, California.

William died in Lindsay, Tulare, California, 13 Apr 1970 at the age of 92.

Lindsay is a small town in a rural part of Tulare County near the mountains and Sequoia National Park. Although it is near mountains it is in the very productive Central Valley. It is a farming and olive growing region. No wonder the Wise family moved here from Kansas, Oklahoma and Texas.

### 4. Joyce May Wise and R F Puckett

Joyce Wise was born 1 Sep 1903 in Kansas. She worked as a second grade school teacher in Oklahoma before she married.

The 1930 census for Victor, McClain, Oklahoma has R F Puckett, 27, married at 21, born in Oklahoma, a farmer on a rented farm and owns a radio. Joyce is 26 and married at 19. Their son, Vernon, is 3 and born in Oklahoma.

The 1940 census for Bailey County, Texas has R F Puckett, 37, completed 9th grade, residence in 1935 a farm in Victor, McClain, Oklahoma and a farmer renting a farm for $25 per month. Joyce is 36 and completed 1 year college. Their children are Vernon, 12, completed 6th grade; Richard, 7, completed 2nd grade and Sirley Ann, 1. They have a hired hand living with them who also came from McClain, Oklahoma.

By 1950 Joyce Pluckett, born 1 Sep 1903 was living at 640 N. Elmwood Ave, Lindsay, California. Joyce May Wise Pluckett died 22 Feb 1989 in Lindsay, California.

### 4. Lillard Leroy Wise and Opal Cook

A 1930 census record for Lillard L Wise was not found.

The 1940 census for Lindsay, Tulane, California has Lillard Wise, 33, completed 8th grade, born in Kansas, living in the same house in 1935, and a farm laborer renting a house on Canne for $8 per month. Opal is 27, completed 10th grade, born in California, and a grader in an Olive plant.

Lillard Wise lived in rural Tulare County from 1935 until he died 1 Mar 1997. Opal Wise died 5 Dec 2005 in Lindsay, Tulare, California.

## 4. Earl W Wise

Earl was living part time with his parents in 1930 and starting his prise fighting career. Many newspaper articles chronicled his fights. Numbers in parathesis are rounds. My comments are also in paranthesis

Appleton Post Cresent, Appleton, Wisconsin 23 Sep 1930
Fights last night; Wichita, KS. Earl Wise, Oklahoma City and Chick Raines, Dodge City KS, draw (8).

The Chillicothe Constitution Tribune, 19 Feb 1931
Last Night Fights (by UP) Oklahoma City Feb 10 – Earl Wise, 174, Oklahoma City, knocked out "Battling" Woodward, 107, Kansas City (1).

Reno Evening Gazette, Reno, Nevada, 12 Feb 1932.
Sacramento, 12 Feb -(AP)- (two fights are described, Earl is the second) In the six round semi-windup. Earl Wise, Oklahoma lightweight, scored a technical knockout over Buddy Gorman of Vallejo in the last round. Wise was dropped in the first round for a four count. He outweighed Gorman ten pounds.

Reno Evening Gazette, 22 Oct 1932
(part of article) Earl Wise comes from Milwaukee and is a friend of King Tut. Tut recommended him highly. He has boxed such eastern boys as George Pavilick, Baxter Calmes, Jack Dillion and Buck Weaver. In his only coast appearance, he put a finish to Buddy Gorman's career by a knockout in four rounds. Wise is now training with Max Baer at Sacramento.

Reno Gazette, 11 Jan 1933
GEORGI-WISE BOUT WILL TOP CARD WEDNESDAY
Petro Georgi, young light-heavy-weight title contender, and Earl Wise will meet in the main event of a six-bout card at the Chestnut street boxing arena next Wednesday evening, January 18, according to an announcement made by Jake Garfinkle matchmaker. (the article goes on to say) Wise has an outside chance. – Wise, in addition to defeating Poloni, has won from Balee Hunt, Baxter Calmes, Bud Gorman and other first-rate fighters.

Reno 20 Jan 1933
Earl Wise young heavyweight, refused to appear in the main event against Pietro Georgi at the Chestnut street arena. Wise refused to fight on a percentage basis. (the arena was half full, apparently, he was smart enough to not risk a fight for little money)

**Tops Tonight's Fight Card**

Earl Wise, conqueror of Tony Poloni, will again step in fast company at the Chestnut Street Arena tonight, when he meets Pietro Georgi, Italian lightheavy, in a ten round contest.

Reno Evening Gazette, 9 June 1933
(parts of an article) Earl Wise meets Mickey McFarland in the ten round main event Friday. They are light heavyweights. Mickey McFarland was the best local drawing card of 1932. Earl Wise came here from Milwaukee where he beat some of the country's best-known fighters. In his only performance here, Wise gave Tony Poloni, local favorite, a trouncing, the only time Reno and Sparks have seen Poloni beaten.

This picture is Earl in his fighting prime.

Reno Evening Gazette, 29 June 1933
(parts of an article).
POLONI AND WISE READY TO MEET ON JULY 3
Fight interest rose to a new high in Reno today, bringing prospects of a record-breaking crowd for the Tony Poloni-Earl Wise bout in the new South Side Arena. Wise is doing his training in Sacramento his own stomping grounds but will probably come to Reno a few days before the battle to get used to the altitude. After his defeat of Mickey McFarland here two weeks ago Wise has taken a lay-off. He wants to prove his victory over Poloni here last summer was no fluke and will be at his best Monday night. He is insisting on a California referee.

(I didn't find articles on the outcome but apparently, he did win and another fight is planned for Sept 8 in the Southside Arena.)

Reno, 2 Sep 1933
Earl Wise, conqueror of Tony Poloni will meet the much-heralded Joe Zeman, French heavyweight, in a ten-round contest.

Reno Evening Gazette, 6 Sep 1933.
WISE-ZEMAN BOUT IS POSTPONED FOR ONE WEEK
(The problem seems to be that they do not have a strong supporting card. At this time there were 2 or more lesser known fights before the main event.)

Reno Evening Gazette, 21 Sep 1933
ACTION PROMISED IN BOUTS HERE TOMORROW
Promising fans the same action which has characterized his former appearances here, Earl Wise arrived in Reno today and expects to hand out a decisive defeat to Joe Zeman when the pair meet in the Southside Arena tomorrow night.
Wise a pleasing fighter who has drawn a large following because of his boxing form and ring mannerisms will be the favorite to take the French light-heavyweight into camp.

Reno Evening Gazette, 26 October 1933
WISE TO CONCEDE EDGE IN BOUT TONIGHT. (Parts of article) Earl Wise is confident that he will be in the winning corner when he meets Jimmy Darcy in the 10-round main event at Southside Arena tomorrow night. Darcy has had more fights and scored more wins. Wise in his last fight here, knocked out Joe Zeman after Zeman had him down twice.

Reno Evening Gazette, 28 Oct 1933.
KNOCKOUT CARD PRESENTED HERE
Concluding a knockout evening in which every bout on the card ended with one of the participants on the canvas, Earl Wise hooked his powerful right hand to the chin of Jimmy Darcy and sent the San Franciscan down for the count in the third round of their scheduled ten-round main event at Southside Arena last night.

Reno Evening Gazette, 29 Jan 1934
Earl Wise – Poloni top fight card Friday night.

Reno Evening Gazette, 3 Feb 1934
POLONI DEFEATS EARL WISE IN RENO RING
Proving to critics that he is still to be considered among the country's top-notch light-heavyweight boxers, Tony Poloni of Sparks scored a clear-cut decision over Earl Wise of Lindsey, Cal., in the ten-round main event at the Southside Arena last night. Poloni took seven rounds and Referee Frankie Neal said the other three were even. Ringsiders conceded that Wise may have had a shade the edge in the eighth.
Poloni with his shifty footwork, his straight jabs and heavy lefts and rights, proved himself too big a chunk for the rugged Californian to handle. Wise did not connect for a single solid blow although he jabbed Poloni's left eye repeatedly and had it open by the third round. On the other hand, Poloni counted with telling blows time after time. He knocked Wise off his feet only once, in the exciting third stanza, but damaged the Californian's ribs, midriff and face with heavy punches all through the fight.

Reno Evening Gazette, 1 Nov 1934, Oakland, Cal.
John Henry Lewis, negro of Prescott, Ariz., knocked out Earl Wise of Reno, Nev. (3).

The Zanesville Signal, Zanesville, OH, 15 Nov 1934
Fight Results, Noah Garrison, 195, Mexico City, knocked out Earl Wise, 180, Tulsa, OK. (1)

Reno Evening Gazette, 30 Nov 1934, Fights Last Night (by AP) Tacoma, Wash – "Sammy" Buxton, 175, Victoria, B.C. outpointed Earl Wise, 180, Reno (6).

Reno Evening Gazette, 8 Dec 1934; Fights Last Night, Boise, Id. – "Tiger" Ray Williams, 173, Negro, Spokane, outpointed Earl Wise, 175, Reno, Nev. (10) in the main event of a boxing card here.

Ada Weekly News, Ada Oklahoma, 22 Aug 1935
OKLAHOMAN KILLED, Porterville, Cal.,19 Aug. (AP) – Authorities were investigating today the death of Earl Wise, 26-year-old truck driver, who police said was the son of Mr. and Mrs. William Wise of Blanchard, Okla.

Nevada State Journal, Reno Nevada, 26 Aug 1939
Eddie Higgins, personable manager of Small Montana, is no stranger to Reno. He came here several years ago, with Earl Wise, the nifty light-heavy-weight who later was killed in an auto wreck. Wise fought Tony Poloni here.

The California Death Index has Earl Wise born 21 Mar 1909, died 18 Aug 1935, age 26 Porterville, Tulare, California.

Earl Wise boxed from 1930 to late 1934 with many matches. In Nov.1934 he fought on the 1st, 15th, 30th and again Dec. 8th. Far too many fights in too short a time. With little protection, he probably suffered head injuries which may have led to his accident.

Earl may have been living with his brother Lillard in Tulare County when he quit boxing and became a truck driver. Earl's parents moved there sometime in the late 40's or early 50's.

### 4. Mary LaMoyne Wise and Noel Lay

The 1940 census for Blanchard, Oklahoma has Hershel R Smith, 27, graduated high school, a manager in a retail gasoline station. Mary L is 23, graduated high school and a music teacher giving private lessons. Their son is Charles K, 3. This is believed to be LaMoyne Wise but there is no proof other than Ancestry family trees.

Mary LaMoyne Wise Lay, born 23 Dec 1916 in Oklahoma, died 18 Mar 2011 in Lindsay, California. An obituary has her parents as William and Leila Wise. She graduated from Blanchard, Oklahoma High School and worked as a piano teacher. Her husband was Noel Lay. Her son is Charles Smith.

## 3. Maude May Wise and William Chester Kelsey

Maud Wise and William Kelsey married 12 Dec 1897.

This picture of William and Maud was probably taken at the time of their marriage.

The 1905 Kansas State Census has W C Kelsey 30 a farmer renting his farm. Maud is 25. Their children are Edith, 4 and Fern, 3.

The 1910 Census for Englewood, Clark, Kansas has William C Kelsey, 35, married 12 years, born in Indiana, a farmer on a rented farm. Maud M is 29 and had 4 children, 3 are living, born in Kansas. Their children are Edith M, 9, attended school; Fern A, 7, attended school; and Chester L, 2. William's brother, John A, 25, is living with them and farming.

The 1920 census for Seattle, Washington has William C Kelsey, 45, a reamer in the shipyards and renting a home at 312a 2nd Street. Maud M is 39. Their children are Chester L, 12, born in Kansas; Marion D, 8, born in Kansas; Viola M, 6, born in Texas; Wanita M, 3, born in Washington; and Enos J, 5/12, born in Washington. The three older children attended school. They must have moved from Kansas to Texas between 1912 and 1916 as Viola was born there in 1914 then to Washington by 1917. Edith M, 19 and Fern A, 17 have left home.

The 1930 census for Seattle, Washington has William C Kelsey, 54, married at 23, a watchman renting a home at 3833 23rd Ave for $16 per month. Maud M is 51 and was married at 17. Their children are Wanita M, 13; Enos J, 10; and Marion D, 19. All the children attended school.

William Chester Kelsey, born 11 Jan 1875, died 6 Oct 1939 in Seattle, Washington and is buried in Forest Lawn Cemetery. His parents were Enos James Kelsey and Sarah Elizabeth Kelsey. He was married to Maude May Wise Kelsey.

The 1940 census for Mount View, Washington has Maud Kelsey, 59, widow, graduated high school and owns her home at 9800 30th Street S W worth $1000. Her granddaughter, Lorene, is 3 and born in Alaska.

This picture of Maud Kelsey seems to be with her granddaughter, Lorene. Taken about 1940.

Maude May Wise Kelsey, born 1 Jun 1880, died 16 Aug 1946 in Seattle, Washington and is buried with William.

## 4. Edith Mildred Kelsey and Oliver L Jackson

Oliver Jackson registered for WW1 on 5 Jun 1917. He was born in Montgomery County Kentucky 26 Mar 1896. He was currently working for his father in Guelph, Sumner, Kansas. He is single, tall, medium build, brown eyes and has dark hair.

The 1920 census for Seattle, Washington has Oliver L Jackson, 23, a bolter up in the shipyards and renting part of a home at 2815 First Ave. (there were 12 families or lodgers at this address). Edith M is 19.

The 1930 census for Seattle, Washington has Oliver Jackson, 34, married at 23, a veteran, a fireman for the city who owns a house at 9038 21$^{st}$ Ave. worth $2850 and a radio. Edith is 29 and married at 18. Their sons are Orral, 8, attended school and Robert, 5.

The 1940 census for Seattle, Washington has Oliver Jackson, 44, completed 10$^{th}$ grade, same house in 1935, a fireman for the municipal government who owns a house at 3528 W Holden worth $3500. Edith is 39, completed 9$^{th}$ grade and works as a filler in a peanut butter factory. Their sons are Orral, 18, completed 11$^{th}$ grade and Robert, 15, completed 8$^{th}$ grade. Clifford Kelsey, nephew, 6, born in Washington and lived in Ketchikan, Alaska in 1935 is living with them. Martina Woods is 29 and living with them as a housekeeper.

Oliver registered for WW11 on 27 April 1942 as Oliver L Jackson, 46, born 26 March 1896 in Kentucky and living at 3528 W Holden Street, Seattle, Washington. Person who will always know your address is Seattle Fire Dept. Seattle Washington. He is a truckman with the Seattle Fire Dept., Station 32, Seattle. His description is 5' 10", weight 165, complexion ruddy, eyes hazel, hair brown and scar on fourth finger right hand.

## 4. Fern Alice Kelsey and R D Fraidenburg / Maurice A Nave

Fern A Kelsey and R D Fraidenburg were married 23 Jan 1919 at the court house, King County, Washington. The witnesses were Mrs. W C Kelsey and J B Fraidenburg.

The 1921 Seattle City Directory has Fraidenburg R D (Fern) home 2607 1/2 Western Ave.

The 1930 census for Seattle, Washington has Clyde P Stocks, 24, divorced, a bookkeeper for Gilman Oil Company renting a home at 935 W 52$^{nd}$ Street. Fern A Fraidenburg is 27, married at 16, born in Kansas, and a housekeeper. Fern's daughters are Alice May Fraidenburg, 10 and Fern I, 7. Both girls were born in Washington and are attending school.

The 1940 census for Mount View, Washington has Maurice Nave, 39, widowed, completed 5$^{th}$ grade, born in Montana, a mill hand in a flouring mill. His son, Kenneth is 13 and completed 6$^{th}$ grade. Fern Fraidenburg is 37, divorced and born in Kansas. Alice Fraidenburg, 20, completed 7$^{th}$ grade, a new worker and Ardath Fraidenburg, 17, (Fern I from above), completed 6$^{th}$ grade, office assistant, NYA Public School, government work. Maurice Nave owns the house at 9710 30$^{th}$ Ave. S W and is living in the rear, Fern is renting the front of the house for $25 per month. Fern is living very close to her mother Maud Kelsey and her brother and his wife, Enos and Vera Kelsey.

M A Nave and Fern A Fraidenburg were married 4 Sep 1940.

Maurice Aubrey Nave born 10 Feb 1901 in Montana, died 8 Sep 1970 in Auburn, Washington and is buried in Forest Lawn Cemetery. He married Martha Elise Essex and they had 2 children then when she died in 1935, he married Fern Alice Kelsey.

Fern A Nave born 20 Sep 1902, died 13 Dec 1977 at the age of 75 in Seattle, Washington and is buried in Forest Lawn Cemetery with Maurice Nave.

## 4. Chester L Kelsey and Evelyn Hagadorn

Chester L Kelsey married Evelyn Hagadorn 8 Jun 1929 in Tacoma, Washington. Witnesses were Clyde Hagadorn and Lottie Hagadorn.

In the 1940 census for Ketchikan, Alaska, Chester Lee Kelsey, 32, rented a home, with 3 rooms, at 44A Second Ave. for $10 per month, born in Kansas, completed 10$^{th}$ grade, and was working as a foreman and truck driver for the city street department. Evelyn is 28, born in Washington and completed 11$^{th}$ grade. Their children are Clifford, 6, born in Washington, attended school; Lorene, 3, born in Alaska; and Carol, 5/12 born in Alaska. They lived in Alaska in 1934. They must have moved just about the time Clifford was born as his birth place is Alaska which is written over with Washington. The census was taken 17 Oct 1939.

Evelyn Bernice Hagadorn Kelsey born 19 July 1911 in Washington, died 6 Dec 1939 in Ketchikan, Alaska of a perforated gastric ulcer and peritonitis. She was 28 years, 4 months and 17 days old. The informant is Clyde J Hagadorn probably a brother. She is buried in Ketchikan.

All three children are listed somewhere else in the April 1940 census. Clifford Kelsey, 6, is living with his Aunt Edith and Oliver Jackson in Seattle. Lorene, 3, is living with her Grandmother, Maude Kelsey, in Mount View, Washington. Carol, 10/12, is living in Seattle with her Aunt Wanita and Paul Plischke at 10 months old.

Chester L Kelsey born 1908, died 5 Feb 1975 in Seattle, Washington.

## 4. Marion D Kelsey and Elsie T Peepler Owen

Marion D Kelsey, 26, married Elsie T Owen, 24, in Seattle Washington on 17 Nov 1937. Elsie had been married before. Her maiden name was Elsie T Peepler.

The 1940 census for Ketchikan, Alaska has Marion D. Kelsey, 28, married, completed 8th grade, born in Kansas, lived in Washington in 1934, a truck driver for the city street department and renting a 2-room apartment for $20 per month. There is no indication where Elsie is living.

Marion Denner Kelsey, born 4 Jan 1910 in Ingelwood, Kansas registered for WW11 in Ketchikan, Alaska. His next of kin is Thelma Elsie Kelsey and he works for Jack Cordell. He is 5' 7", blonde, weighs 145 lb. and has blue eyes. There is no indication he served.

Marion D Kelsey died 15 Feb 1984 in Pacific, Washington at the age of 73.

## 4. Viola M Kelsey and Thomas E Golden

Viola M Kelsey was born 31 Aug 1913 in Bloomington, Victoria, Texas.

Viola is listed in the 1920 census records with her parents.

The 1940 census for Mount View, Washington, lists Thomas E Golden, 29 graduated high school, seeking work as a stripper in a sawmill where he has worked before and renting a home at 2807 W Roxbury for $3 per month. Viola is 26 and completed 8th grade. Both Thomas and Viola lived in Seattle in 1935.

Viola M Kelsey of North Bend, Washington married Thomas E Golden of Snoqualmie, Washington on 31 Mar 1942 in Seattle. Officiated by K Simundman, minister of the Gospel. Witnesses were Waneta Plischke and Frank Plischke.

Viola M. Kelsey Golden born 31 Aug 1913, died 3 Jan 2000.

## 4. Wanita M Kelsey and Paul Frank Plischke

Wanita is listed with her parents in the 1920 and 1930 census reports.

Wanita is listed with Frank P Plischke in the 1938 Seattle, Washington Directory.

Waneta Kelsey Plischke applied for a Social Security Card in 1937. Her parents were William C Kelsey and Maud M Wise. She was born 5 Sep 1916 and died 17 Apr 2004.

The 1940 census for Seattle, Washington has Paul F Plischke, 31, completed 10$^{th}$ grade, born in Minnesota, a foreman in Seeds and Fertilizer who owns a home at 8602 17$^{th}$ Ave. S W worth $1800. Waneta is 23, completed 9$^{th}$ grade, born in Washington and working as a packer in Frozen Foods. Paul's family is living with them. Paul H, father is 72, completed 8$^{th}$ grade and born in Germany. Julia, mother is 60 and born in Minnesota. Otto, brother is 26, graduated high school, born in Minnesota and a musician in a band. Also living with them is Carol Kelsey, niece, 10/12.

Wanita may have divorced Frank and remarried. Her Social Security names include Wanita Balland. She was not buried with Frank Plischke

## 4. Enos James Kelsey and Vera Francis Frew

Enos James Kelsey of Seattle, Washington married Vera Francis Frew of Tacoma, Washington on 16 Mar 1940. K Simundman, Minister of the Gospel officiated. Witnesses were Wanita Plischke and Frank Plischke.

Enos James Kelsey born 3 Aug 1919, died 15 Nov 2009 in Everett, Washington.

## 3. Blanche Wise and Jefferson Bromwell / Burton Wray Martin

Blanche Wise was first married to Jefferson Bromwell. They had a son Leroy Bromwell. In 1905. They were living with her parents, Mary Ann and Thomas Wise in a 1905 Kansas State Census.

Blanche married Burton Wray Martin 30 Dec 1907.

The 1910 census for Kansas City, Missouri has Burton W Martin, 27, married 2 years, a jeweler in his own repair shop and living at 822 Spruce Ave. Blanche E is 27, married twice and has had 2 children that are still living. The children are Roy, 6, born in Kansas and. Marie N, 10/12, born in Missouri.

The 1920 census for Wichita, Kansas has Burton W Martin, 35, a chiropractor with his own practice renting a home at 1028 S Wichita Street. Blanch, 35, is keeping house. The children are Roy, 16, a driver for Jitney Co.; Marie N, 10, is attending school and

Evelyn C, 2. Their home is near Blanche's parents.

The 1930 census for Wichita, Kansas has Blanche E Martin, 47, owns her home at 1116 South Wichita Street worth $3000. She apparently inherited the home from her father when he died. Her daughter, Evelyn C is 12. William Durban, 24, son-in-law and a truck driver for a retail dairy; Marie N, daughter, 20 and William R, 11/12, grandson are living with Blanche.

The 1930 census for Florence, Kansas has Burton W Martin, married, born in Nebraska, a chiropractor in private practice renting his home at 416 Main Street for $25 per month. He is probably attending chiropractic school.

The 1940 census for Ellinwood, Kansas has Burton Martin, 54, completed 5 years college, born in Nebraska, a chiropractor in private practice who owns his home worth $3500. Blanche is 57, graduated college, and lived in the same place in 1935. A lodger, Dorothy Daniels, 37, completed 5 years college, a chiropractor, is living with them.

Burton and Blanche divorced and Burton married the lodger Dorothy Daniels in 1945. Burton Wray Martin died in 1958.

Blanche E Martin, born 11 Dec 1882 in Kansas, died 10 Feb 1963 in Josephine County, Oregon and is buried in Hawthorne Memorial Gardens. Her daughter, Marie Durban, was in Oregon at the time.

### 4. Freddie Leroy Bromwell Martin and Mary Bonita Stewart

No further information was found on Jefferson Bromwell; however, it appears Leroy was adopted by Burton Martin sometime before 1920.

The 1930 census for Concordia, Kansas has LeRoy Martin, 24, a lineman for the Telephone Company, renting a home at 517 East Ninth Street for $15 per month. Bonita is 21. Their daughter, Lucille is 1.

The 1940 census for Concordia, Kansas has F L Martin, 35, graduated high school, an electrician for the telephone company, renting a home for $20 per month. Mary is 32 and graduated high school. Their children are Lucille, 11, completed 4th grade; Lois, 9, completed 2nd grade, and Patty, 4. This is the same family even with some name changes.

Freddie LeRoy Martin, born 25 Sep 1905, died 2 Jan 1975 in Frankfort, Kansas and is buried in Frankfort Cemetery. His wife is Mary Bonita Stewart Martin. His children are Patty Ann Lewis, Helen Lois Hopkins and William Albert Martin.

### 4. Marie Norelle Martin and William H Durbin

Marie and William Durbin with their son William are living with her mother Blanche Wise in the 1930 census

The 1940 census for Great Bend, Kansas has William Durban, 34, completed 8th grade, the owner operator of a dairy, renting a home at 1018 Baker Street for $30 per month. Marie is 30 and graduated high school. Their children are William Robert, 10, completed 4th grade and Patricia Ruth, 9, completed 2nd grade.

William H Durbin born 29 May 1905, died 25 Jan 1959 in Grants Pass, Oregon and is buried in Hawthorne Memorial Gardens. Marie Norelle Martin Durbin born 9 Jun 1909, died 17 Nov 1986 and is buried with William.

### 4. Evelyn C Martin and Milton Lebbin

The 1940 census for Ellinwood, Kansas has Milton Lebbin, 25, graduated high school, a truck driver for a flour mill. Evelyn is 22 and graduated high school.

Evelyn C Martin Lebbin, born 11 Sep 1917, died 7 Jul 2000 in Ellinwood, Kansas and is buried in Lakin Comanche Cemetery. Milton W Lebbin born 10 May 1914, died 4 Feb 1997 and is buried with Evelyn.

### 3. Thomas Jefferson Wise (3rd) and Bessie Harrison

Jefferson Wise, 21, of Kansas City, Missouri married Bessie Harrison, 18, of Marion, Kansas on 24 Dec 1906.

The 1910 census for Kansas City, Missouri has Thomas J Wise, 24, married 3 years, born in Kansas, a stenographer in a law office who owns his mortgaged home at 2062 Hardesty Ave. Bessie is 28, had 1 child who is still living and was born in Kansas. Their son, Thomas J Jr. is 2 and was born in Missouri.

Thomas Jefferson Wise 33, born 17 Apr 1885 registered for WW1 on 12 Sep 18. He was living at 3809 Delaware, Gary, Indiana and working in building for Indiana & Illinois Land Co. at his home address. His nearest relative is Bessie Wise. He is medium height and build with blue eyes and brown hair.

The 1920 census for Gary, Indiana has Thomas J Wise, 34, a lawyer for a managing Company and living at 3825 Delaware Street. C Bessie is 34. Their sons are Thomas J, 12, and Kent H, 9. Both attended school and were born in Missouri.

Thomas J Wise Jr. (3), 43, born 17 Apr 1885, died 25 Jun 1928 in St Antonio Hospital, Gary, Indiana of Gastric Ulcer and a brain tumor. He worked in Real Estate and Insurance and was living at 715 West 8th Street in Gary. Thomas is buried in Maple Grove Cemetery, Wichita, Kansas. The same cemetery as his parents.

## 4. Thomas Jefferson Wise (4th)

The 1930 census for Scotts Bluff, Nebraska has Thomas J Wise, 22, a musician in an orchestra living with a family as a lodger.

The 1930 census for Wichita, Kansas has Bessie C Wise, 44, married at 22, a live-in maid.

The 1940 census for Los Angeles, California has Thomas Wise, 32, single, completed 1 year of college, a musician working in a Federal Music Program and living in an apartment house on Witmer Street. Bessie is 53, a widow, completed 2 years of college and living with Thomas.

Thomas Jefferson Wise, 33, born 10 Sep 1907 in Kansas City, Missouri, registered for WW11 in Los Angeles, California on 16 Oct 1940. His next of kin was Bessie Harrison Wise and his employer was WPA. He was 5'5", 155 lbs., with blue eyes and black hair.

Thomas Jefferson Wise born 10 Sep 1907, died 11 Dec 1957 in Los Angeles.
Bessie H Harrison Wise born 6 Sep 1879, died 10 May 1967 in Los Angeles.

## 4. Kent Harrison Wise and Virginia L Gaskins

The 1930 Wichita, Kansas census has Kent H Wise, 21, a salesman for the daily newspaper who is lodging at the YMCA.

Kent H Wise married Virginia L Gaskins on 10 May 1938 in California.

The 1940 census for Los Angeles, California has Kent Harrison Wise, 29, completed 3 years college, an auto parker in a parking garage renting an apartment on S Hartford Street. Virginia is 32, graduated college and a nurse in a hospital.

Kent Harrison Wise born 28 Jul 1910, died 17 Nov 1995 in Los Angeles.

## 3. Francis Mary Wise and Charles R Hamilton / Charles G Hilligoss

Mary Francis Wise, 20, married Charles R Hamilton, 25 on 15 Nov 1908 in Sedgwick,

Kansas. The marriage didn't last long as Francis is in the 1910 census with her parents.

Mary Francis Wise Hamilton married C G Hilligoss in Cooke, Texas on 8 May 1920. A 1920 census has not been found but they do appear in the 1923 Wichita, Kansas City Directory – Charles G Hilligoss (Frances M) occupation oil, 806 Faulkner Ave.

The 1925 Kansas State Census for Wichita has Charles G Hilligoss, 44, born in Kansas, working in oil for Vickers Refinery and renting a home at 125 ½ E 15th Street. Francis is 37 and born in Kansas.

The 1930 census for Wichita, Kansas has Charles G Hilligoss, 49, married at 21, a lease broker in the oil field industry renting a house at 1244 North Market Street for $50 per month. Frances is 45 and was married at 20. William Hilligoss is 48, brother, widowed and working as a driller in the oil fields William's children are L. Jack, 14, born in Oklahoma, attending school; and Wilma A, 6, born in Kansas, attending school.

Francis Mary Wise, born Mar 1888, died 30 Oct 1938 and is buried in White Chapel Memorial Gardens, Wichita, Kansas.

Charles G Hilligoss born 17 May 1880, died 15 Mar 1948 and is buried in Forest Lawn Memorial Park, Long Beach, California. He may have moved to L. A. to be near a son from his first marriage, Charles G born 1 Mar 1904, died 20 May 1947.

## 3. Rufus C Wise

The 1914 Wichita City Directory has Wise, Rufus living at 1116 S. Wichita, the same address as his parents.

Rufus C Wise born Feb 1896, died 23 Apr 1914 and is buried in Maple Grove Cemetery, Wichita, Kansas.

## 2. Elizabeth Arn and Charles Wilhelm

Elizabeth J Arn, 15, born 12 Dec 1859, married Chas Joseph Wilhelm, 32, born 5 Oct 1845, on 30 Apr 1877 in Salina, Kansas. They had a daughter Laura born 1879.

The 1880 census for South Sharp's Creek, Kansas has Charles J Wilhelm, 34, married, farming, from Mecklenburg as are both parents. (Mecklenburg is now part of Germany on the coast of the Baltic Sea close to Poland. At the time Charles Wilhelm was born it was its own country as Germany had not been unified yet. The main religion was Lutheran.) Elizabeth is 20 and keeping house. Their daughter, Laura, is 1. The listing is right below John Arn. C J Wilhelm's land is just East of John Arn. See map page 98.

The 1885 Kansas State Census for Smoky Hill has C J Wilhelm, 39, farmer born in

Germany, came from Indiana. Lizzie is 25, born in Michigan and came from Iowa. Their children are Laura, 6; Katie, 4 and Lottie, 2. William Wise, 24, a farmer is living with them. He may have been a brother of Thomas Jefferson Wise Jr.

Charlotte "Lottie" Wilhelm born 19 Feb 1883, died 31 Dec 1891.

The 1895 Kansas State Census for Castle, McPherson, Kansas has C J Wilhelm, 49, born in Germany, a farmer. Lizzie is 35 and born in Michigan. The children are Laura, 16; Katie, 14; Minnie, 9; Ernestine, 7; Lewis, 5; and Loretta, 2. All the children were born in Kansas.

Charles Joseph Wilhelm born in 1845, died 27 Jan 1897 in Windom, McPherson, Kansas. He is buried in Excelsior Cemetery.

The 1900 census for Windom, Kansas has Elizabeth J Wilhelm, 39, born Dec 1860, had 8 children, 7 are living, working as a washerwoman and owns her home on Main Street free and clear. Her children are Kate, 19, born Dec 1880, a servant girl; Minnie M, 15, born May 1885; Ernestine, 13, born Apr 1887; Louis J, 10, born Sept 1889; Loretta, 8, born Apr 1892; and Claude J, 4, born Oct 1895. All the children are at school except for Kate and Claude.

The 1910 census for Jackson, McPherson, Kansas has Louis H Wilhelm, 20, single, a farmer renting his farm. Elizabeth is 50 and a widow. Elizabeth's children are Loretta B 17; and Claude J, 15, attended school.

Claude J Wilhelm born 25 Oct 1895, died 15 Sept 1918 in France. He was a Corporal with the 17th Field Artillery Regiment, 2nd Infantry Division Battery D. He is buried in St Mihiel American Cemetery, Plot B Row 5 Grave 8, Thiaucourt, France. His mother, Elizabeth, applied to visit his grave in 1929. The trip was to be in 1930. A passenger list for the S.S. America has Elizabeth Wilhelm, 70, born 12 Dec 1860 in Hillsdale County, Michigan, currently from Windom, Kansas, leaving Cherbourg, France 10 Sep 1930 and arriving in New York Sep 1930. The trip of a lifetime to visit her son's grave.

The 1920 census for Windom, Kansas has Elizabeth Wilhelm, 59, a widow who owns her home at 37 Main Street free and clear. Also, under Elizabeth Wilhelm is the Windom Hotel at 38 Main Street with 6 boarders. Elizabeth has no occupation listed but she is still working taking care of others at her hotel.

The 1930 census for Windom, Kansas has Elizabeth Wilhelm, 70, a widow who owns her home on Main Street worth $2000. She is finally just taking care of herself.

Elizabeth J Arn Wilhelm born 12 Dec 1860, died 27 Mar 1938 in McPherson, Kansas.

### 3. Laura Belle Wilhelm and Charles Edgar Hammock

Laura Belle Wilhelm married Charles Edgar Hammock on 23 Dec 1896 in Lyons, Rice, Kansas.

The 1900 census for Castle, McPherson, Kansas has Charles Hammock, 24, born Oct 1875, married 4 years, a farmer renting his farm. Laura B is 21, born July 1878 and had 1 child who is still living. Their daughter is, Edna, 2, born Nov 1897.

The 1910 Census for Jefferson, Ellis, Oklahoma has Charles Hammock, 34, married 13 years, born in Kansas, a farmer who owns his farm free and clear. Laura is 31, has had 4 children, all are living. Their children are Edna, 12, born in Kansas, attended school; Alfred, 7, born in Kansas, attended school; Gladys, 3, born in Oklahoma; and Lester, 1 11/12, born in Oklahoma.

The 1920 census for Jefferson, Ellis, Oklahoma has C E Hammock, 43, a farmer with a mortgaged farm. Laura is 41. Their children are Alfred, 17, a laborer on the home farm; Gladys, 13; Lester, 11; Gertrude, 9; Everett, 7; Earl, 5; and Blanch, 3. All but the last 2 children attended school.

This picture is Laura Belle Wilhelm Hammock as a young mother.

The picture of Charles Hammock may have been taken about the same time.

The 1930 census for Jefferson, Ellis, Oklahoma has Charles E Hammock, 54, married at 21 and farming on a farm he owned. Laura B is 50 and was married at 17. The children are Everett W, 17; Earl C, 15; Blanche E, 13; Ruth C, 9; and Mary F, 6. All the children attended school. A total of 10 children. Edna, Alfred, Gladys, Lester and Gertrude have left home.

The 1940 census for Jefferson, Ellis, Oklahoma has Charles E Hammock, 64, completed 8th grade, a farmer on his own farm worth $1500. Laura B is 61 and completed 8th grade. Ruth is 19, graduated high school and a domestic servant in a private home. Everett W Hammock is 26, graduated high school, a farm laborer on his father's farm. Everett's wife, Gladys is 22 and graduated high school.

Laura Belle Hammock, born 7 Jul 1878 in Salina, Kansas, died 24 May 1957 in Woodward, Oklahoma and is buried in Gage Memorial Cemetery, Gage, Oklahoma.

Charles Edgar Hammock, born 14 Oct 1875 in Windom, Kansas, died 31 Jul 1963 in Gage, Oklahoma and is buried With Laura.

## 4. Edna Mae Hammock and Charles R Garber

Edna May Hammock, 19, married Charles R Garber, 22 in Jul 1917 in Ellis, Oklahoma.

The 1920 census for Liberal City, Kansas has Charles Garber, 28, a house carpenter, renting a home on New York Ave. Edna is 22. Their son, George is 1.

The 1930 census for Liberal City, Kansas has Charles R Garber, 38, married at 26, a veteran of WW1 and a carpenter renting a home on 3$^{rd}$ Ave. for $20 per month. Edna is 32 and was married at 19. The children are George W, 11 and Alene, 9, both attended school.

The 1940 census for Van Buren, Newton, Missouri has Charles Garber, 48, completed 2 years of high school, a carpenter. Edna is 42 and completed 8$^{th}$ grade. Their children are George Wayne, 21, single, completed 8$^{th}$ grade, a farmer; Alene, 19, graduated high school; Lura Alice, 9, completed 3$^{rd}$ grade. Alice Motley is 79, widow, aunt and never attended school. It is unclear if they are living on a farm and who owns the farm. A common provision in wills at that time was to give the farm or home to whoever took care of the individual during their lifetime.

Charles R Garber, born 21 Sep 1891 in Missouri, died 25 Dec 1943, in Ritchey, Missouri and is buried in Sarcoxie Cemetery, Sarcoxie, Missouri. He was a farmer and a carpenter. He died at his home from bronchial pneumonia as a complication of flu.

Edna May Hammock Garber, born 1 Nov 1897, died 30 Aug, 1991 in Missouri and is buried with Charles.

George W Garber, born 16 Dec 1918, died 18 Jan 2001. He was a corporal in the US Army in WW11 serving from 23 Sep 1942 to 9 Oct 1945. He is buried in the same cemetery as his parents.

## 4. Alfred Leo Hammock and Dixie Dowden

Alfred L Hammock, 20, born 1902, married Dixie Dowden, 20, on 4 Nov 1922 in Arnett, Oklahoma.

A 1930 census has not been found.

Alfred Leo Hammock, born 1902, died 1932, and is buried in Bickford Cemetery, Ellis County, Oklahoma. The parents are correct so this is the same Alfred Hammock.

Dixie Dowden applied for a Social Security number with Alfred L Hammock as her spouse and Alfred Leo Hammock as a child.

A Social Security record has Alfred Leo Hammock born 19 May 1929, died 14 Nov 2007, parents Alfred L Hammock and Dixie Dowden.

## 4. Gladys Marie Hammock and Deward Henry Bates / George P Collins

Gladys M Hammock was married to Deward Bates in Lipscomb, Oklahoma in 1922.

The 1930 census for Otter, Ellis, Oklahoma has Deward Bates, 25, married at 19, a farmer renting his farm. Gladys is 22 and married at 16. Their children are Marie, 4 and Zella Faye, 1. All were born in Oklahoma.

The 1940 census for Jefferson, Ellis, Oklahoma has Deward H Bates, 35, completed 8$^{th}$ grade, a farmer on his rented general farm. Gladys M is 33 and completed 8$^{th}$ grade. Their children are Marie L, 14, completed 7$^{th}$ grade and Ella F, 11, completed 3$^{rd}$ grade.

Deward Bates born 23 Jun 1904, died 4 Aug 1944 and is buried in Shattuck Cemetery.

Gladys M Bates married George P Collins 10 May 1950 in Ellis, Oklahoma. George P Collins born 1893, died 1968

Gladys Marie Hammock Bates Collins, born 26 Jun 1906, died 3 Apr 1985 in Amarillo, Texas and is buried in Shattuck Cemetery, Shattuck, Oklahoma. The stone reads mother of Marie Lanier and Zella Russell. She is buried next to George P Collins and in the same cemetery as Deward Henry Bates and her parents.

## 4. Lester Charles Hammock and Hazel L Hull

Lester Hammock, 19, married Hazel Hull, 18, 30 May 1927 in Woodward, Oklahoma.

The 1930 census for Jefferson, Ellis, Oklahoma has Lester C Hammock, 21, married at 19, a farmer. Hazel L is 21 and married at 19. They are living with her parents.

A 1940 census has not been found that can be verified. It is possible they were not counted or the census data has been lost. Lester and Hazel moved to Colorado before 1951 as his Social Security number was issued in Colorado before 1951.

Lester Charles Hammock, 32, born 1 May 1908, did register for WW11 in Cahone, Colorado. His next of kin is Hazel L Hammock.

A 1959 Grand Junction, Colorado City Directory has Lester Hammock (Hazel) equipment operator, Whitewater Sand & Gravel home 2893 Alta Vista Drive.

Lester Charles Hammock born 1 May 1908, died 29 Mar 1994 in Fremont, Colorado and is buried in Gage Cemetery, Gage, Oklahoma. Hazel L Hull Hammock born 6 Jun 1908, died 5 Jun 1995 in Fremont, Colorado and is buried with Lester.

## 4. Gertrude Alice Hammock and Floyd Harland Roth

Gertrude A Hammock married Floyd H Roth on 25 Aug 1928 in Ellis, Oklahoma.

The 1930 census for Otter, Ellis, Oklahoma has Floyd Roth, 23, married at 21, a farmer on a rented farm. Gertrude is 19 and married at 18. Their son, James, is 9/12.

The 1940 census for Woodrow, Ellis, Oklahoma has Floyd H Roth, 33, completed 7th grade, a farm laborer, worked 26 weeks in 1939, renting a home for $5 per month. Alice G is 29 and graduated high school. Their sons are James H, 12, completed 4th grade and Charles H, 8, completed 2nd grade.

Gertrude A Roth and Floyd H Roth obtained Social Security numbers in Missouri in 1951.

Gertrude Alice Hammock Roth born 19 Aug 1910, died 24 Mar 1988 and is buried in Lakeside Cemetery, Canon City, Colorado. Floyd H Roth born 20 Jan 1907, died 29 Dec 1989 and is buried with Gertrude.

## 4. Everett Wilbur Hammock and Gladys Richardson

Everett Hammock, 26, married Gladys Richardson, 23, in Aug 1939 in Woodward, Oklahoma.

Everett and Gladys were living with his parents in 1940.

Everett Wilbur Hammock born 23 Sep 1912, died Mar 1977 and is buried in Memory Gardens, McAlester, Oklahoma. Gladys Richardson Hammock born 1917, died 2011 and is buried with Everett.

## 4. Charles "Earl" Hammock and Mary Ellen Lovell

Charles Earl Hammock married Mary Ellen Lovell on 29 Jul 1933 in Beaver, Oklahoma.

The 1940 census for Blue Grass, Beaver, Oklahoma has Earl C Hammock, 25, graduated high school, a farm operator renting a home for $10 per month. Mary is 26 and graduated high school. Their daughter, Eleanor M, is 4.

Charles Earl Hammock born, 5 Oct 1914 in Gage Oklahoma, died 9 Sep 1994. His obituary reads: Charles Earl Hammock went by his middle name Earl. Earl was a farmer and also raised cattle just north of Shattuck, Oklahoma. Earl was a hard-working man, a loving father, grandfather and great grandfather and at times a practical joker. Earl and Mary had 3 daughters Laura, Eleanor and Joann.

Mary Ellen Lovell Hammock born 21 Feb 1914, died 22 Apr, 2011 and is buried with Earl in Gage Memorial Cemetery, Gage, Oklahoma.

### 4. Blanche Elizabeth Hammock and James Earl Lovell

Blanche Hammock, 18, married J Earl Lovell, 29, on 25 Jul 1933 in Beaver, Oklahoma. Blanche's brother Earl married J Earl's sister Mary Ellen. The Lovell farm was in Beaver County, Oklahoma.

The 1940 census for Lipscomb, Texas has Earl Lovell, 28, completed 1-year high school, a farmer renting a home for $6 per month. Blanche is 23 and completed 3 years high school. Their daughters are Barbra J, 3 and Doris L, 1. All are born in Oklahoma.

At some point the family moved to South Dakota.

James Earl Lovell, born 5 Apr 1912, died 6 Feb 1992 in Pierre, South Dakota and is buried in Riverside Cemetery. Blanche Elizabeth Lovell born 22 Nov 1916, died 18 Jun 1999 in Pierre, South Dakota and is buried in Riverside Cemetery with James Earl.

### 4. Ruth Catherine Hammock and Rollie Morgan

Ruth,19 is living with her parents in the 1940 census. She graduated from high school and is working as a domestic servant in a private home.

Ruth Hammock married Rollie Morgan.

Rollie Morgan born 14 Feb 1912, died 19 May 1993 in Fargo, Oklahoma and is buried in Fargo Cemetery, Fargo Oklahoma. Ruth Catherine Hammock Morgan born 29 Jan 1921 in Gage, Ellis, Oklahoma, died 16 Jun 2000 and is buried with Rollie.

### 4. Mary Francina Hammock and Hugh Jones Gay

The 1940 census for Rock, Ellis, Oklahoma has Hugh J Gay, 20, graduated high school, a farm operator on a farm. Mary F is 16 and completed 2 years high school.

Hugh J Gay born 1919 in Oklahoma enlisted (was drafted) in the Army 31 Jul 1944. His residence is Salt Lake City, Utah. This may be a continuance of an earlier enlistment. He had 4 years high school, a private, a machinist, and married.

Mary Francina Gay born 18 Aug 1923, died 24 Dec 2011 in Littleton, Colorado and is buried in Mountain Vale Memorial Park, Cannon City, Colorado. Hugh Jones Gay born 27 Nov 1919, died 17 Jun 2012 in Florence, Colorado. His obituary reads: Hugh Jones Gay served in WW11, Company M, 20th Infantry in Borneo, Philippines, and South Korea. He was a Staff Sargent in charge of fourteen men and two heavy fifty caliber machine guns. Hugh was awarded the Philippine Liberation Medal/Ribbon with two bronze stars. He retired after 22 years with the University of California where he worked as a machinist. He is survived by three sons; Rodney, Ben, and Wayne. He is buried with Mary in Mountain Vale Memorial Park.

### 3. Katherine L Wilhelm and Fred Emery Raff

Katie Wilhelm, 20, married Fred E Raff, 27, on 28 Nov 1901 in McPherson, Kansas.

The 1910 census for Rice County, Kansas has Fred E Raff, 36, married 8 years, a farmer. Kate is 29 and has had 3 children who are all living. Their children are Percy, 6, Phyla, 2, and Ethel 10/12.

Datus Raff born 15 May 1917 in Idaho, died 19 Apr 1918 in Nampa, Idaho. He was 11 month and 4 days old when he died of bronchial pneumonia.

The 1920 census for Nampa, Idaho has Fred Raff, 45, a farmer who owns a mortgaged farm on the South City Line. Kate is 39. Their children are Percy, 15, working on the farm; Phylia, 12; Ethyl, 10; Gilbert, 8; Glenn, 5, Dayton, 2; and John 1. Phylia, Ethel, and Gilbert are attending school. The last 3 were born in Idaho. They must have moved between 1912 and 1915.

The 1930 census for Young Nampa, Idaho has Fred E Raff, 56, married at 27, a farmer who owns his farm on Lake Shore Blvd. Katherine is 49 and was married at 20. Their children are Gilbert E, 18, farm laborer; Glen A, 15; Dayton C, 12; and John L,11. All the children except Gilbert are attending school.

Kathryn L Wilhelm Raff born 14 Dec 1880, died 22 Apr 1936 in Nampa, Idaho and is buried in Kohlerlawn Cemetery with Datus. Fred E Raff born 17 Mar 1874, died 20 Feb 1940 at Nampa, Idaho and is buried with Kathryn.

### 4. Percy George Raff

Percy G Raff enlisted in the marines 18 Nov 1920. He is a private serving in a Marine Detachment, Naval Ammunition Depot, Puget Sound, Washington. A June 1922 muster roll has Percy G Raff, private, Guard Company #1, Marine Barracks, Navy Yard, Puget Sound, Washington.

Percy Raff born 2 Feb 1902 served in the Army from 13 Sep 1930 to 27 May 1937.

Percy George Raff, 40, born 2 Feb 1902 in Windom, Kansas, registered for WW11 on 15 Feb 1942. He was living in Oakland, California and working for Pittsburg Equitable Meter Co. He is 6' with gray eyes and brown hair. His next of kin is Bud Long.

Percy G Raff born 2 Feb 1902 in Kansas, died 18 Jan 1973 in Almeda, California.

## 4. Phylia E Raff and Leo Alan Maxwell

Phylia E Raff married Leo A Maxwell on 5 Jul 1927 in Canyon, Idaho.

The 1930 census for Nampa, Idaho has Leo A Maxwell, 32, married at 30, born in Kansas, a cabinet maker in a Sash and Door Company who owns his home on Madison Ave. worth $4100. Phylia is 22 and was married at 20. They have 2 children, Leo A Jr., 2 and Phylia, 9/12. Leo's father, James, 58; mother, Helen, 58; and brother, James Jr., 15, are living with them.

Leo Alan Maxwell born 14 May 1896 in Salina Kansas, registered for WW11 on 27 Apr 1942 in Boise, Idaho. Leo was 45 and lived at R # 5 Boise, Idaho. Mark Maxwell would always know his address. Leo was working for Frank C Rathmen at 508 S. Fifth in Boise. Leo was 5' 7", weighed 170 lbs. and had black hair and hazel eyes.

A 1940 census for Leo Maxwell could not be found.

Phylia Maxwell is in the 1940 Boise, Idaho census. She is 32, married is crossed out, graduated high school, born in Kansas and is working as a maid in a private home.

Phylia Maxwell is found in the 1941 Boise, Idaho city directory living at 918 Krall. Leo is not listed. Leo remarried in 1942.

Phylia's death record was not found but an ancestry record has 1971.

Leo A. Maxwell born 14 May 1896, died 26 Oct 1994 in San Joaquin, California.

## 4. Ethel Claudine Raff and Ernest Miller

Ethel Raff married Ernest Miller on 25 Nov 1926 in Canyon, Idaho.

The 1930 census for Midway, Canyon, Idaho has Ernest Miller, 23, married at 19, born in Oklahoma and a laborer at a dairy. Ethel is 21 and was married at 17. Their son, Robert, is 2 and born in Idaho.

Ethel Claudine Raff Miller born 17 Jun 1909, died 1 Jul 1937 in Nampa, Idaho. She died of burns from an explosion of fireworks at a store. Her husband is Ernest Miller and parents are Katherine Wilhelm and Fred Raff.

The 1940 census for Young Nampa, Idaho has Ernest Miller, 32, widowed, graduated high school, a farmer. His children are Robert, 12 and Geraldine, 9. His sister Lenore, 21 is living with them.

## 4. Gilbert Earnest Raff

Gilbert Ernest Raff, 25, born 5 Nov 1912 in Windom, Kansas, entered the Idaho prison system 10 Jun 1937. He was convicted of second-degree burglary and sentenced to 1 ½ to 5 years. Gilbert went before the parole board and was released 5 Jan 1940.

Gilbert E Raff, 28, born 5 Nov 1912 registered for WW11 on 11 Mar 1941. He was living in Nampa, Idaho and his next of kin is Dayton Carl Raff.

## 4. Glen A Raff and Rita

The 1940 census for Dillon, Montana has Glen A Raff, 25, completed 3 years high school, a section laborer on the railroad. Rita is 23 and graduated high school. Their children are Richard J, 2 and Elizabeth J, 8/12.

## 4. Dayton Carl Raff and Evelyn

The 1940 census for Nampa, Idaho has Dayton C Raff, 22, completed 3 years high school, an apprentice in the railroad repair yards. Evelyn is 21 and completed 2 years high school. Their son, William D, is 2.

## 4. John Lewis Raff

John Lewis Raff, 18, born 8 Mar 1919 entered the Idaho prison system for second degree burglary on 10 Jun 1937. He was sentenced to 1 to 5 years. John was conditionally pardoned on 10 Jun 1938 after serving 1 year. Earnest and John were involved in the same burglary. Times were tough during the depression.

John Lewis Raff, 22, born 8 Mar 1919 in Nampa. Idaho registered for WW11 on 2 Aug 1941. He is unemployed and his next of kin is Dayton C Raff.

John Lewis Raff born 8 Mar 1919, died 10 Oct 1947 in Almeda, California.

## 3. Minnie Mae Wilhelm and Burton F Folck

Minnie Wilhelm, 18, married Burton Folck on 25 May 1902 in McPherson, Kansas.

The 1910 census for Castle, McPherson, Kansas has Burton Folck, 29, married 7 years, a farmer renting his farm. Minnie M is 24 and has had 4 children, all are living. Their children are Leo G, 7; Veda, 5; Wilber, 3 and Ruby 4/12.

The 1920 census for Winan, Rice, Kansas has Burton Folck, 39, a farmer who owns his mortgaged farm. Minnie is 34. The children are Leo G, 16; Veda, 15; Wilber A, 13; Ruby M, 10; Rosalee, 3 ½; and Jennie I, 1 ½. The 4 older children are attending school.

The 1930 census for Union, Rice, Kansas has Burton F Folck, 49, married at 21, a farmer who owns his farm. Minnie M is 44 and married at 17. The children are Rosalee, 13; Genevieve I, 11; and Lois E, 8. All the girls attended school.

Minnie Mae Wilhelm Folck, 49, born 3 May 1885, died 14 Mar 1935 at Little River, Rice, Kansas and is buried in Bean Cemetery.

An obituary said she was struck with rheumatism in 1910 and did not walk the last 10 years of her life. They lived on a farm near Little River until 1907 then moved to McPherson County 4 miles north of Windom. They stayed on that farm until 1919 when they returned to a farm north of Little River. The children are listed as Leo G of Winfield, Veda I Titus of Conway, Wilber of Genesso, Ruby Lee, Genevieve and Lois Ellen at home.

The 1940 census for Union, Rice, Kansas has Burton Folck, 59, completed 7th grade, a farmer renting his farm. His wife is Mary, 52.

Burton Folck born 22 Oct 1880, died Apr 1960 and is buried in Bean Cemetery.

## 4. Leo Gilbert Folck and Harriet Frances King

Leo G Folck of Little River attended Kansas State Teachers' College in 1925 with a major in Industrial Arts. He lettered in football and track and was in the YMCA.

The 1930 census for Clear Vale, Kansas has Leo G Folck, 26, married at 24, a teacher in a public school earning $9494 per year and renting a home on Walnut Street for $25 per month. Harriet F is 21 and married at 19.

The 1940 census for Winfield, Kansas has Leo G Folck, 37, 5 years of college, an industrial arts teacher at the high school renting a home at 904 Ann Street for $20 per month. Harriet F is 31 and graduated high school. Their children are Richard L, 9, completed 3rd grade and Carol H, 5.

Leo Gilbert Folck born 15 Apr 1903, died 6 Feb 1991 in Winfield, Kansas and is buried in Highland Cemetery. Harriet Frances King Folck born 23 Sep 1908, died 9 Oct 2002 and is buried with Leo.

## 4. Veda I Folck and Durward L Titus

The 1930 census for Odessa, Rice, Kansas has Durward L Titus, 24, married at 16, a farmer renting a farm and has a radio. Veda I is 25 and was married at 17. Their children are Alfred R, 8, attending school; Lorraine M, 6; Maxine M, 4; and Lola L, 1. Loraine was born in South Dakota. Everyone else is born in Kansas. They must have gone to South Dakota sometime between 1922 and 1926. Keith Wayne, born 1 Jan 1927, died 19 Jan 1927 and is buried in Bean Cemetery.

The 1940 census for Rockville, Rice, Kansas has Durward L Titus, 35, completed 8$^{th}$ grade, a farmer renting his farm. Veda I is 36 and completed 10$^{th}$ grade. The children are Robert A, 18, completed 8$^{th}$ grade, working as a laborer on the farm; Lorraine, 16, completed 9$^{th}$ grade, a hired girl on a farm; L Maxine, 14, completed 8$^{th}$ grade; Lola L, 11, completed 5$^{th}$ grade; Cecil O, 9, completed 2$^{nd}$ grade; and Opal Jean, 4.

Durward L Titus born 3 Jun 1905, died Mar 1967 in Little River, Kansas and is buried in Bean Cemetery. Veda I Folk Titus born 24 Sep 1904, died 4 Feb 1988 and is buried with Durward and their son Keith.

### 4. Wilber A Folck and Madeline Berry

Wilber Folck married Madeline Berry 15 Apr 1927 in Lyons, Kansas. They had a daughter, Mae Belle, born and died 26 May 1928. She is buried in Bean Cemetery.

The 1930 census for Trivoli, Ellsworth, Kansas has Wilber A Folck, 23, married at 20, a farmer on a rented a farm. Madeline is 23 and married at 20. Their daughter, Nadine N, is 8 months old.

The 1940 census for Odessa, Rice, Kansas has Wilber A Folck, 33, graduated high school, a farmer on his rented farm. Madeline is 33 and graduated high school. The children are Nadine, 10, completed 4$^{th}$ grade; Dora Lee, 8, completed 3$^{rd}$ grade; Amy Elizabeth, 7, completed 1$^{st}$ grade; Wilber William, 5; and Roy Burton 1.

Wilber W Folck born 12 Sep 1934, died 5 Jun 1953 in Korea of wounds. He was a Sargent First Class in the U.S. Army. He was a member of the 27$^{th}$ Infantry and was seriously wounded on 4 Jun 1953 and died of those wounds the following day. He was awarded the Purple Heart. Information from the Korean War Veterans Honor Roll. The body was returned and he is buried in Bean Cemetery.

Wilber Folck born 8 Dec 1906, died 27 May 1988 in Little River, Kansas and is buried in Bean Cemetery. Wilber was a member of the United Church of Christ, Lions Club and a lifelong farmer. Madeline Berry Folck born 15 Aug 1906 in Little River, died 25 Feb 1994 and is buried with Wilber.

### 4. Ruby Marie Folck and Donald Roe Arnold

Ruby Folck married Don Arnold on 31 Dec 1927.

The 1930 census for Odessa, Rice, Kansas has Don R Arnold, 24, married at 22, a farmer on his rented farm. Ruby M is 20 and married at 18. Their sons are Dwight L, 1 8/12 and Dwaine L, 7/12. Don's mother, Claudia L, 65, a widow, is living with them.

Ruby and Don's daughter, Lois Faye Arnold, was born and died 31 May 1938. She is buried in Bean Cemetery.

The 1940 census for Odessa, Rice, Kansas has Don Arnold, 34, graduated high school, a farmer, renting his home for $10 per month. Ruby is 30 and graduated high school. Their children are Dwight, 11, 5$^{th}$ grade; Dwaine, 10, 4$^{th}$ grade; Dean, 9, 3$^{rd}$ grade; Gary, 7; Spencer, 6; Barbra, 4 and Roger ½ year.

Ruby Marie Folck Arnold born 26 Dec 1909, died 25 May 1944 in Little River, Kansas. She was 34 and is buried in Bean Cemetery. Don Roe Arnold born 29 Jul 1905, died 17 Dec 1973 in Lyons, Kansas and is buried in Bean Cemetery.

### 4. Rosalee Flock and John William Canfield

The 1940 census for Stockton, California has John W Canfield, 25, born in Kansas, completed 9$^{th}$ grade, a fireman on a locomotive for a railroad and renting a home for $13 per month. Rosa L is 23, born in Kansas, completed 8$^{th}$ grade, and a piece worker in a cannery. The children are Shirley L, 3, born in Nevada and Helen R, 1, born in California. They have a lodger, Roy Street, 24 who is a service station operator. They must have left Kansas about 1936 or 1937 and Shirley was born on the way to California. Not unusual for the depression and dust bowl Kansas.

John William Canfield born 27 Jul 1914 in Little River, Kansas, died 18 Jul 1985 in Walla Walla, Washington and is buried in Shady Grove Cemetery, Portola, California. Rosa Lee Folck Canfield born 10 Jun 1916 in Little River, Kansas, died 17 Mar 1995 in Portola, California and is buried with John.

### 4. Genevieve Irene Folck and Fred J Strouse

Genevieve Irene Folck married Fred J Strouse on 21 Dec 1935.

Genevieve and Fred Strouse were living in Rice County, Kansas in 1940 according to county records but a census has not been found.

Fred Jacob Strouse born 10 Oct 1898 in Kansas, died 11 May 1970 in Rice county Kansas and is buried in Bean Cemetery. Genevieve Irene Folck Strouse born 26 Nov 1918, died 1 Mar 1999 in Little River Kansas and is buried with Fred.

### 4. Lois Eileen Folck and Robert C Gallmeister

Eileen Folck is listed in the 1940 Rice County Census by herself. Wilber is on the same page but she is not living with him. She is not listed in the federal 1940 census in the same area as Wilber.

Robert C Gallmeister was living in Oregon in 1940 and working as a lumber stacker.

Lois Ellen Folck married Robert Gallmeister on 6 Nov 1944 in Butte, Montana.

Robert Carl Gallmeister born 1 Jul 1917 in Little River, Kansas, died 15 Apr 1977 according to Social Security records. Lois Eileen Folck Gallmeister born 1922, died 2001 in Portola, California

### 3. Ernestine Wilhelm and Warren Alva Landfair

Ernestine Wilhelm, 22, a school teacher, married Warren A Landfair, 21, a farmer, on 3 Apr 1909 at the Methodist Episcopal parsonage in McPherson, Kansas.

The 1910 census for Groveland, McPherson, Kansas has Alva Landfair, 22, married 1 year, born in Michigan, a farmer renting a farm. Ernestine is 23, has not had children and was born in Kansas.

The 1920 census for St. John, Kansas has Warren Landfair, 32, not working and renting a home on Broadway Street. Ernestine is 32. Their daughters are Audrey, 9, born in Kansas; Ferne, 7, born in California and Nellie, 4, born in New Mexico. The 2 older girls are attending school. Warren's mother, Rosella Landfair is 60, a widow and living with them. There are 4 families living in the same house or apartment building.

The 1930 census for Hutchison, Kansas has Warren Landfair, 43, married at 22, a salesman for a light company and renting a home at 112 East A Street. Earnestine is 43, married at 22 and a clerk at an auction. The children are Audrey, 20, born in Kansas; Ferne, 17, born in California; and Nellie, 15, born in New Mexico. Ferne and Nellie are attending school.

The 1940 census for Hutchison, Kansas has Ernestine Landfair, 53, a widow, completed 2 years of college, a clerk at a Public Auction Sales who is renting a home at 300 First Street. Ferne is 27, single, graduated high school and is a long-distance operator at the telephone company. Ernestine is not a widow but may have been separated at the time.

Ernestine Wilhelm Landfair, born in 1887, died 1941 in Hutchison, Kansas and is buried in Fairlawn Burial Park, Hutchinson, Kansas.

Warren Alva Landfair, 55, born 16 Jun 1887 registered for WW11 on 11 Jul 1942. He is working for Pacific Bridge Builders, 341 Kearny Street, San Francisco, California. He is going to work in Pearl Harbor. His next of kin is Fern Landfair of Hutchison, Kansas. He is 6' and 200 pounds.

Warren A Landfair, 60, single, of 2173 Cal St. San Francisco, California is listed on a Pacific Overseas Airlines passenger manifest for 29 Apr 1947, originating in Shanghai, China destined for Ontario, California. He embarked at Guam, Marshal Islands. He is a clerk and was born in Leslie, Michigan 16 Jun 1887. His passenger weight is 200. The list is all men with occupations such as rigger. Warren Landfair born 16 Jun 1887, died Aug 1971 in Portland, Oregon.

## 4. Audrey Lois Landfair and James F Wilson / Marcus Miles Durfee

Audrey Lois Landfair married James F Wilson 18 Jun 1934 in Bonneville, Idaho.

A 1940 census has not been found.

Audrey Lois Landfair Wilson married Marcus Miles Durfee in 1952.

Audrey Lois Landfair Durfee, born 9 Sep 1910 in Kansas, died 27 Sep 1982 in Battle Mountain, Nevada and was buried in Burns Memorial Garden. Marcus Miles Durfee born 8 Sep 1905 in Utah, died 17 Sep 1988 in Elko, Nevada and is buried with Audrey.

## 4. Nellie Norene Landfair and Waite

Nellie married and divorced a man by the name of Waite.

Nell Norene Landfair Waite, 40, born 9 Apr 1915, died 16 Mar 1956 at Battle Mountain, Nevada. She had been there 3 months with Metastatic Cancer of Brain and Cancer of Bladder. The informant was Audrey Durfee of Battle Mountain, Nevada. Nellie's usual residence was San Francisco, California where she was a clerk in a hotel. She was divorced. Audrey made arrangements to bury Nell in Woodlawn, San Francisco, California. Burial costs were $165.06

## 3. Lewis Herman Wilhelm and Clara Florence Ensminger

The 1910 census for Jackson, Kansas has Lewis H Wilhelm, 20, single, a farmer on a rented farm. His mother, Elizabeth, is 50, a widow and living with him. A sister, Loretta B, 17 and a brother, Claude J, 15 are also living with him. Claude is attending school.

The 1920 census for Jackson, McPherson, Kansas has Lewis Wilhelm, 30, a farmer renting his general farm. Clara is 28 and their children are Lila, 8; Wilber, 6; Mildred, 5; Beulah, 3 and Macel, 1.

The 1930 census for Jackson, McPherson, Kansas has Lewis H Wilhelm, 40, married at 20, a farmer on his rented farm. Clara J is 38 and was married at 19. Their children are Wilber L, 16; Mildred L, 15; Beulah M, 13; Macel D, 11; Fay L, 9; Claude J, 8; Fern E, 6; Galen E, 4 1/12; and Bettie 2 1/12. All but the oldest 2 and youngest 2 attended school.

The 1940 census for Bonneville, McPherson, Kansas has Lewis Wilhelm, 50, completed 9th grade, a farmer who owns his farm worth $5000. Clara is 48 and completed 8th grade. Their children are Claude, 18, completed 11th grade; Fern, 16, completed 10th grade; Betty Lee, 12, completed 5th grade; Mary Ann, 8, completed 2nd grade; and Patsy Jean, 5.

Lewis H Wilhelm born 24 Sep 1889, died 9 Dec 1958 and is buried in McPherson Cemetery, McPherson, Kansas. Clara Florence Ensminger Wilhelm born 26 Jul 1891, died 6 Feb 1973 in Norwalk, California and is buried with Lewis.

### 4. Lila Wilhelm and Vincel O Kling

In the 1930 census for McPherson, Kansas has Lila Wilhelm, 18, single, a telephone operator and rooming at 315 S. Chestnut.

Lila Wilhelm married Vincel Kling in 1932. A 1940 census was not found.

Vincel O Kling born 8 Jun 1909, died 23 Apr 1974 and is buried in McPherson Cemetery, McPherson, Kansas. Lila A Wilhelm Kling born 3 Aug 1911, died 3 Oct 2004 and is buried with Vincel.

### 4. Wilber L Wilhelm and Lucille

Wilber is with his parents in 1930. He is listed as being born in Eastern Canada. This is strange. Could he be adopted or did they go to Canada for a short while? In the 1920 census Wilber is listed as born in Kansas. His mother, Clara, has a French father. Maybe Clara was visiting him when Wilber was born.

The 1940 census for Bonneville, McPherson, Kansas has Wilber Wilhelm, 26, completed 8th grade, born in French Canada, a naturalized citizen and a farmer who owns a home worth $500. Lucille is 21, born in Nebraska and completed 10th grade.

Wilbur Wilhelm born 15 Dec 1914, died 1 Jan 2008, and served in the army from 21 May 1942 to 1 Nov 1943.

### 4. Mildred Laurine Wilhelm and John Haskell Gibbons

The 1940 census for Bakersfield, California has John H Gibbons, 32, graduated college, lived in McPherson Kansas in 1935, a Chemist in a gasoline laboratory renting a house at 1521 Nile Street for $35 per month. Mildred is 25, completed 1-year college and lived in McPherson, Kansas in 1935.

John Haskell Gibbons, 33, born 7 Oct 1907 in Elk City, Oklahoma, registered for WW11 on 16 Oct 1940. He was unemployed at the time. He was living in Burbank, California with his wife Mildred Wilhelm Gibbons. He weighed 165 and was 6'1" with blue eyes and brown hair.

John Haskell "Tex" Gibbons born 7 Oct 1907 in Elk City, Oklahoma, died 30 May 1984 in La Habra, California and is buried in Rose Hills Memorial Park, Whittier, California.

His obituary follows: Gold Medal Olympic Champion. Gibbons was captain of the American basketball team which won the gold medal at the 1936 Olympics in Berlin, Germany. In the early 1930s, he played basketball at Southwestern College in Winfield, Kansas, and after graduating, he joined the Amateur Athletic Union league and played for several teams. It was as a member of the 1935 AAU National Champion McPherson Oilers, that he qualified for the 1936 Olympic team. The Berlin games saw basketball as an Olympic sport for the first time as the American team went 8-0 to capture the gold medal. Gibbons went on to teach at UCLA before joining Phillips Oil where he made his career in the petroleum industry.

Mildred Laurine Wilhelm Gibbons, born 4 Aug 1914 in McPherson, Kansas, died 27 Nov

1997 in La Habra, Orange, California and is buried with John.

## 4. Beulah Mae Wilhelm and Leo Bernard Buffington

The 1940 census for Newton, Kansas has Beulah Wilhelm, 25, graduated high school, a lodger, working as an operator in a Beauty Shop.

Beulah Wilhelm, 45, married Leo B Buffington, 42, on 22 Apr 1962 in Los Angeles, California.

A 1946 Salina, Kansas Directory has Leo B Buffington (Beulah M) living at 708 S Santa Fe Ave.

It appears Beulah may have been married to Leo before the 1962 marriage, was divorced and remarried.

Leo had a troubled life as shown in a Montana State Prison Record.
Leo had a 7-year suspended sentence to McPherson County Jail in 1938.
Leo Buffington arrested 11 Mar 1939 for forgery in McPherson, Kansas.
Leo B. Buffington arrested 24 Jan 1946 Newton, Kansas for investigation.
Leo Bernard Buffington arrested 26 Nov 1947 in Fort Riley, Kansas.
Leo Bernard Buffington arrested 16 Aug 1949 in Newton, Kansas for being drunk 15 days and $15 fine.
Leo Buffington arrested 11 Apr 1950 in Los Angeles for being drunk.
Leo Bernard Buffington arrested 25 Aug 1951 in Great Falls, Montana for being drunk, fined $10.
Leo Bernard Buffington arrested 21 Dec 1951 in Bozeman, Montana for forgery.
Leo Buffington, sentenced to 1 year in State Prison on 1 Jan 1952 for forgery. This last crime was committed 30 Nov 1951 in Bozeman. He wrote a forged check to Montgomery Ward in the amount of $100.

Leo was drafted in to the Army 6 Apr 1942 and honorably discharged 13 Aug 1945. He had been employed by Boeing Aircraft in Seattle, Washington for 1 month. Recently employed by Frank Wyatt in Bozeman, Montana for 1 ½ months as a farm hand. He is divorced and his father is Foster Buffington of Marquette, Kansas.

Leo Bernard Buffington, born 25 May 1918, died 6 Jan 1968 in Los Angeles and is buried in Rose Hills Memorial Park Cemetery, Whittier, California. Beulah Mae Wilhelm Buffington, born 13 Oct 1916, died 5 Mar 2011 in Norwalk, California and is buried in Rose Hills Memorial Park.

Beulah Mae "Buffy" Buffington has an obituary. She was married to her childhood sweetheart Leo until his death in 1968. They were parents to identical twins Ronald and Richard who preceded her in death. Buffy spent 30 years with the General Telephone Company retiring in 1980. She was chief operator in several Los Angeles area offices.

Buffy was a member of the First Baptist Church of Norwalk for 60 years.

### 4. Macel Dorthea Wilhelm

A Social Security record has Macel Doretha Wilhelm, born 21 Feb 1919 in McPherson, Kansas, died 13 Dec 2001. It lists her parents and that at one time she used the name Field. Nothing else has been found.

### 4. Faye Louise Wilhelm and Harry Milton Meyers Jr.

The 1940 census for Smoky View, Saline, Kansas has Faye Wilhelm, 19, single, graduated high school, a maid in a private home.

The 1940 census for San Francisco, California has Harry Meyers Jr., 22, graduated high school, an engineer for Army Transport. He has a brother and sister living with him.

Harry Milton Myers, 23, born in Washington, D C, single, registered 2 Dec 1940 with the Army. His current residence was Fort Mason, San Francisco, California. He is 5'8" and has blue eyes and red hair.

Harry Meyers, 27, born 26 May 1917 in Washington, D C, arrived in San Pedro, California on the USS General Mc Rae on 31 Dec 1944. He did not have a passport.

Harry M Meyers Jr., 36, a purser, sailed from Inchon, Korea and arrived in San Francisco, California on 14 August 1953. He had seen 13 years' service at sea.

Army Transport at the time was by ship. Harry may have liked being at sea and worked on ships for many years before changing to real estate salesman. A marriage record has not been found but a family tree has 1952 for their marriage.

Harry Meyers died 19 Feb 1968 and is buried in Cypress Lawn Memorial Park, Coloma, California. Carew and English Funeral Home records show he was a real estate broker for the last 4 years. His wife, Faye, was an RN. He was cremated and there was no service.

Fay Louise Wilhelm Meyers, born 2 Oct 1920 in Kansas, died 10 Jan 1970 at 11:15 pm in Park Emergency Hospital in San Francisco, California. She was a widow and the owner and operator of Laurel Heights Convalescent Hospital for 25 years. The cause of death is under investigation. She had multiple traumatic injuries from an automobile accident at 43rd and Fulton streets in San Francisco at 10:50 pm. The informant was her mother Clara Wilhelm of Norwalk, California. Faye was cremated and buried in Cypress Lawn Memorial Park, Coloma, California.

### 3. Loretta Blanche Wilhelm and Ewell Neff

The information for Loretta Blanche Wilhelm is confusing. There is another Loretta Blanche Wilhelm of nearly the same age whose father is George Wilhelm. The following information is consistent with other family trees but may not be correct.

L Blanche Wilhelm married Ewell E Neff on 27 Jul 1921 in Jackson, Missouri.

The 1930 census for Calexico, California has Ewell Neff, 34, married at 26, a brakeman on the railroad who owns his home at 103 E Seventh Street worth $7000. Loretta is 37 and, was married at 29. A son James is 11 and may be Ewell's son not Loretta's.

The 1940 census for Cass, Greene, Missouri has Ewell Neff, 44, completed 8th grade, a farmer who owns his farm worth $800. Loreta is 47 and graduated high school. It doesn't seem reasonable that a railroad worker would become a farmer right after the depression unless he was taking over his father's farm.

Ewell Neff born 1895, died 1972 and is buried in Bunkers Memory Gardens Cemetery in Las Vegas, Nevada. Loretta B Neff born 1892, died 1976 and is buried with Ewell.

## 2. Franklin L Arn and Isabelle Dehoney

Franklin Arn married Isabelle Dehoney about 1883.

The 1900 census for Springfield, Illinois has Frank Arn, 38, born May 1862, married 16 years, a teamster renting part of a home at 1217 Jackson Street. Bell S is 34, born Sept 1865 and has had 5 children, 4 are living. The children are Nellie, 15, born Oct 1884; Oscar, 9, born Aug 1890; Earl, 7, born Apr 1893 and Alice, 2, born Feb 1898. The three older children are attending school. All the children were born in Illinois.

The 1910 census for Springfield, Illinois has Frank L Arn, 48, married 20 years, a laborer at an ice company. Bell is 40 and has had 10 children, 6 are living. The children are Earl, 17, a clerk in a Cash Company; Lawrence, 9; Charley, 4; Alice, 12; and Marie, 1. Fred Cannedy is 29, son-in-law, married 4 years, a laborer in a Manufacturing Plant and renting a home at 824 East Mason. Nellie is 26 and has no children. Oscar Arn may have died before 1910. He is not mentioned in the 1917 obituary as a survivor and there are 6 children without Oscar in 1910.

Franklin L Arn, 55, born 1 May 1862 in Michigan, died 20 Sep 1917 in Springfield, Illinois and is buried in Oak Ridge Cemetery. He is survived by Isabelle; sons Earl, Charlie, and Lawrence; daughters Mrs. Fred Cannedy, Alice and Marie Arn. Death certificate states he was a teamster; son of John Arn who was born in Germany. Isabelle Dehoney Arn born 11 Sep 1864, died 3 Sep 1922 and is buried with Frank.

## 3. Nellie Arn and Fred Eller Cannedy

Fred Eller Cannedy, 37, born 16 Jun 1881 and living at 801 S. 11th Street, registered for

WW1 on 12 Sep 1918. Fred is driving a wagon for Swift and Company. His nearest relative is Nellie Cannedy. Fred is short with a slender build, grey eyes and light hair.

The 1920 census for Springfield, Illinois has Fred Cannedy, 38, a teamster renting a home at 801 South 11th Street. Nellie is 35. The children are Clarence, 8 and Helen, 6. A boarder is living with them.

The 1930 census for Springfield, Illinois has Fred Cannedy, 49, married at 24, a janitor in a store who owns his home at 628 Livingstone Ave. worth $1500 and a radio. Nellie is 46 and married at 21. Clarence is 19, single and a clerk in a bookstore. Alice Arn is 32, single, sister-in-law and working in a watch factory.

The 1933 Springfield, Illinois City Directory has Clarence Cannedy a salesman at Coe Brothers Inc. He is living with his parents at 628 Livingstone. Nothing further was found on Clarence or his sister Helen.

The 1940 census for Springfield, Illinois has Fred Cannedy, 58, completed 7th grade, renting a house at 608 North Stevens for $10 per month and working at street construction. Nellie is 55 and completed 8th grade.

Fred E Cannedy of 129 North Magnolia Drive, Springfield, Illinois, born Jun 1881, died 24 Sep 1959. He is buried in Roselawn Memorial Park. Nellie Cannedy born 1884, died 2 Oct 1959 and is buried with Fred.

### 3. Earl Arn and Alice H Refine

The 1930 census for Springfield, Illinois has Earl Arn, 37, married at 27, working in a furniture store and owns his home at 3119 Carpenter Street worth $1900. Alice, is 31 and married at 20. Their son is James Edward, 9, who attended school.

The 1940 census for Springfield, Illinois has Earl Arn, 47, completed 8th grade, a wood worker in furniture repair and owns their rural home worth $2000. Alice is 41 and completed 7th grade. James Edward is 19, graduated high school and a new worker.

Earl Arn born 1893, died 1957 and is buried in Roselawn Memorial Park, Springfield, Illinois. Alice H Refine Arn born 27 Apr 1899, died 12 Jan 1987 and is buried with Earl.

### 3. Alice Arn

Alice was living with her sister Nellie in 1930. A 1940 census has not been found.

The 1955 Springfield, Illinois City Directory has Alice G Arn, a waitress in Arn's Lunch Room and living at 3145 E Carpenter. In another listing, Evelyn Arn, widow of Charles, is the Lunch Room owner.

Alice Arn born 3 Feb 1898, died Dec 1970 in Springfield, Illinois.

### 3. Lawrence Arn and Wilmay Myrtle Arbrickle

The 1930 census for Springfield, Illinois has Lawrence Arn, 28, married at 22, a window cleaner at a window company, renting a house at 204 W Lawrence Ave. for $30 per month and they have a radio. Myrtle is 27 and was married at 21. Their children are Lawrence Jr.,5 and Ralph, 4 5/12.

The 1937 Springfield, Illinois City Directory has Lawrence S Arn (Myrtle) employee Illinois Window Cleaning Company, home 203 S Livingstone.

The 1940 census for Springfield, Illinois has Myrtle Arn, 38, a widow, completed 6th grade and renting a house at 628 Lancaster for $10 per month. The children are Lawrence M Jr, 15, completed 9th grade; Ralph E, 14, completed 7th grade and Franklin D, 6, completed 1st grade.

Lawrence Arn, the father, may have died between 1937 and 1940 or he may have left the family. It is possible that he served in WW11 and died in 1958. There are two Lawrence Arns or he had both S and M as middle initials. There could have been some mix-up with his son Lawrence who was old enough to serve in WW11. Lawrence Stanley Arn born 7 Aug 1901, died 3 Dec 1958 and is buried in Camp Butler National Cemetery, Springfield, Illinois. He served in TEC5 Co E, 474 QM TRK Regt, WW11. His widow is Edith Arn of Decatur, Illinois. I will leave this for others to sort out.

### 3. Charles E Arn and Evelyn J Matern

Charles Arn married Evelyn J Matern in 1926

The 1930 census for Springfield, Illinois has Charles Arn, 24, married at 21, working for a watch company and renting a home at 908 N 13th Street for $20 per month. Evelyn is 22, married at 19 and working in a laundry.

The 1940 census for Springfield, Illinois has Charles Arn, 34, completed 10th grade, a checker at a flour mill and owns a home at 1609 E Matheny worth $2000. Evelyn is 33 and completed 8th grade. Their children are Doris Jean, 9; Leona Mary, 7; Shirley Anne, 4 and Joyce Elaine, 1.

Charles E Arn born 1906, died 1954 and is buried in Oak Ridge Cemetery, Springfield, Illinois. Evelyn J Matern Arn born 5 Jul 1906, died 5 Jan 1994 and is buried with Charles.

### 3. Margaret Marie Arn

Margaret Marie Arn died 4 Aug 1924 at Lincoln State School, Lincoln, Illinois. She was survived by three brothers, Earl, Lawrence and Charles Arn and two sisters Alice Arn and Nellie Cannedy. Marie was born 17 Jun 1909 and was 15 when she died. She is buried in Oak Ridge Cemetery with her parents. Marie died just 2 years after her father. With both parents and Marie dying in so short a time they may have had TB or some other disease or maybe it was just coincidence. The Lincoln State School was for the mentally retarded.

**2. Ida Louise Arn and A R Whiteman / Jonas Likins**

Ida Louise was born March 11, 1865 in Pittsford Michigan. She went with her parents and family to Iowa and then Kansas.

Ida married A R Whiteman 4 Jul 1879 at 14. A daughter Nettie May was born 3 Oct 1878 in Parsons, Kansas. Ida is listed with her parents and daughter in the 1880 census. Apparently, Mr. Whiteman didn't stay around or didn't live long. According to some family trees, he went to Oregon and died there in 1914. There is an 1880 census listing of Abram Whiteman, 39, married, living with his mother Abigail, 78, in Sharps Creek, McPherson, Kansas. He has 2 daughters and a son but not a wife. The very next page has Ida living with her parents and Nettie the daughter. They may have been married but were not living together. The marriage may have been strictly to legitimize the baby. Abraham Whiteman may have left for Oregon after his mother died.

Jonas E Likins was in the 1880 Sharps Creek census one page over from the Arns. He was 30, a farmer and from Indiana. Jonas had a wife Maggie (Margaret Weeks), 30 and several children; Eva 10; Hattie 6; Eddie 3; Rosa 2 and Albert 7/12. All the children were born in Iowa except for the last. There is an A W Likens 3 miles North of John Arn on the 1884 map of Sharps Creek, Kansas. Possibly Jonas' parents.

Jonas Likins is in the 1870 census for Madison Co., Iowa. He is 20, Helen, his wife is 19 and they have a daughter Alice 7/12 born in Iowa. She may have been called Eva in the 1880 census. He had 3 marriages according to a later census. Helen would be first with a daughter Alice Eva; Maggie second with Hattie, Edward, Rosa and Albert.

Ida Louise married Jonas E Likins 20 Oct 1881 in Picher, Oklahoma. She was 16.

The 1885 Kansas State Census for Troy, Doniphan, Kansas has J E Likins, 35, a farmer. Ida is 21. The children are Eva 15; Edward, 8; Rosa, 6; Hattie Ball, 6; William, 2; and Carlinda less than a year. Apparently, Jonas' second wife, Maggie, died soon after the 1880 census as the children are living with Jonas. Hattie should be 11 and is missing as is the baby Albert. They may have all died due to disease. Of the 5 children from previous marriages, 3 are left. Hattie Ball is Nettie Whiteman. It is not known how she acquired the name Ball but all the names, Whiteman, Ball and Likins, are used later.

The 1900 census for Hackberry, Labette, Kansas has Jonas E Likins, 50, born Nov

1849 in Indiana, married 20 years, a farmer on a rented farm. Ida L is 39, born Mar 1865 in Michigan and had 9 children, 7 are living. The children are William E, 17, born Mar 1883 in Kansas, a farm laborer, attended school 3 months; Carlinda, 15, born Jan 1885 in Kansas, attended school 5 months; Leslie, son, 9, born Dec 1890 in Kansas, attended school 5 months; Roy, 6, born Aug 1893 in Kansas, attended school 3 months; Robert E 3, born Nov 1896 in Kansas and Walter, 3 months, born Feb 1900 in Indian Territory. The 6 children listed belonged to Ida along with Nettie Whiteman makes 7 living children. Elmer Gene Likins born 1887 died before 1900.

This picture is Ida and Jonas Likens probably taken in the early 1900s.

Starting in 1830 the present state of Oklahoma and some surrounding territory was set aside for relocation of Indians from the land east of the Mississippi. Several tribes were moved there in the 1830s. After the Civil War the land was also designated for resettlement of Negroes. The area was known as Indian Territory. By 1880 efforts were made to divide up the land and give it to individual Indians and Negroes. This left Unassigned lands. A bill was passed in 1879 to not relocate any more Indians or others to the land. With further rationalization, the unassigned lands were open for resettlement. On 23 Mar 1889, President Benjamin Harrison signed legislation which opened up 2 million acres of the Unassigned Lands for settlement on 22 Apr 1889. This was the first of many land runs. Because of widespread cheating, later land runs were held by lottery.

Ida and Jonas Likins were part of a later land run. They established a place in Indian Territory where Walter was born. Soon after Walter's birth they were forced to return to Kansas without the free land they envisioned. They were back to renting a farm in Kansas by June of 1900.

Oil was found in Oklahoma in 1850 but after the advent of the automobile, the oil business saw a big expansion. Ida and Jonas moved to Oklahoma to work in the oil fields.

The 1910 census for Welch, Oklahoma has Jonas E Likins, 60, 3rd marriage, married 28 years, born in Indiana, teaming on a pipeline and owns a mortgaged home. Ida, is 48, first marriage and has had 10 children, 7 are living. Their children are Roy, 16, born in Kansas, a farm laborer; Robert E, 13, born in Kansas, a farm laborer; Walter, 9, born in Oklahoma, attended school; John, 5, born in Kansas, attended school; Pearl, granddaughter, 8, born in Kansas, attended school.

Lewis Ray Likins born 1902, died 1905. John Likins born 1905, died 1914.

The 1920 census for Picher, Oklahoma has Jonas E Likins, 70, a house carpenter who owned his home. Ida is 59. Their children are Walter, 18, born in Oklahoma, laborer in a lead & zinc mine; Pearl, 18, born in Kansas, a saleslady; Ralph Nading, boarder, 17, born in Oklahoma, laborer in lead & zinc mine; Clifford, boarder, 13, born in Oklahoma.

Jonas Ellsberry Likins born 25 Nov 1849, died at the age of 74 on 6 Jul 1924, and is buried in Welch Cemetery, Welch, Oklahoma.

The 1930 census for Picher, Oklahoma has Ida Likins, 63, widow, landlady for a rooming home at 100 S Picker Street. Pearl Martin is 27, granddaughter, widow, born in Kansas and a saleslady for clothing. Pearl's son, J E is 7 and born in Oklahoma. There are three lodgers, all working in the mines.

Ida Louise Arn Likins born 11 Mar 1865 in Michigan, died 3 Feb 1931 in Oklahoma and is buried in Welch Cemetery with Jonas.

Ida Likins widow of Jonas is listed in the Oklahoma City Directory for 1934 (information out of date), living at 410 S Connell. Roy is at 100 S Picher and Walter is at 532 S Frisco with his wife Eva. They are both miners. This was the height of the Dust Bowl and mining was a much more profitable occupation than farming.

Lead and Zinc were discovered near Picher, Oklahoma in 1913. Picher's population reached a peak in 1926 then gradually declined. The Picher Lead Company produced 50% of the lead and Zinc used in WW1. It was a major supplier in WW11 as well. The tailings rose in huge piles for many years and the town was undermined so much buildings fell in. The nearby creeks run red with Cadmium and Arsenic. Operations ceased in 1967 and it has been an EPA Superfund site since. The mining jobs came at a price. Many died young.

### 3. Nettie Whiteman Ball and C N Auvigne

Nettie Whiteman Ball married C N Auvigne on 5 Nov 1900 in Labette, Kansas.

The 1910 census for Labette, Kansas taken 27 Apr 1910 has Charlie N Auvigne, 33, married 10 years, born in France, immigrated 1888 and farming a rented farm. Nettie is 31, has had 8 children, 5 are living. Their children are Leo, 9; Marie, 7; Laura, 5; Raymond, 2; and Ida 2 months. Nettie and all the children were born in Kansas.

Nettie Auvigne crossed the border into Saskatchewan, Canada in Aug 1910. She was going to join her husband in Red Deer. The children with her were Leo 9; Marie, 7; Laura, 5; Raymond, 3 and Ida 6 months.

Leo Datus Auvigne born 3 Jul 1899, died 6 Dec 1919. Laura May Auvigne born 28 Feb 1905, died 29 Feb 1920. They both died in Delburne, Alberta, Canada and are buried in Delburne Cemetery.

The 1921 census for Red Deer, Alberta, Canada has Charles Auvigne, 49, born in France and farming on a farm he owns. Nettie is 42 and born in USA. The children are Marie, 18; Raymond, 14; Ida, 11; and Floyd, 6 all born in USA. The parents and these children immigrated to Canada in 1915. The remaining children are Fredie, 4; Irene, 3; Clarence, 2; and Carl, 1 who were born in Canada.

Carl Auvigne died in 1921 and is buried in Delburne Cemetery.

Charles may have gone to Canada in 1910 or before to take up free land which he had to farm for part of the year. The family moved to Canada later in 1910.

There is very little census data in Canada at this time so nothing more is known about the children.

Nettie M Auvigne, maiden name Likins, born 3 Oct 1878, died 29 Mar 1964 in Delburne, Alberta, Canada and is buried in the Delburne Cemetery. Charles N Auvigne born 5 Aug 1872 in France, died 22 Apr 1964 in Delburne and is buried with Nettie.

### 3. William Ellsberry Likens and Serena Telva Simcox

Will Likens, 35, born 2 Mar 1883, registered for WW1 on 12 Sept 1918. He was living at 605 Columbus, Picher, Oklahoma and working as a miner for Premcie Mining Company. His nearest relative was Serena Likens. He was tall with a medium build, blue eyes and Light brown hair.

The 1920 census for Picher, Oklahoma has Will E Likens, 36, working as labor in a lead and zinc mine and renting a home on Main Street. Serena is 27. Their children are Jessie, 8; Harold, 6; Glenn, 4; Clarence, 3; and Floyd, 3/12.

The 1925 Kansas State Census for Canton, McPherson, Kansas has W E Likens, 42, renting a farm. His wife, Serena, is 32. Their children are Jessie, 13; Harold, 11; Glenn, 10; Floyd, 5; Josie, 4; Galen, 3; and Edna May, 1. Clarence died before 1925

Serena Telva Simcox Likens born 12 Aug 1892 in McPherson County, died 20 Jun 1928 in McPherson County and is buried in Canton Township Cemetery. She was a school teacher for 1 year before marrying Will. They had 10 children, 2 died young.

The 1930 census for Picher, Oklahoma has Will Likens, 47, a widower, married at 20, a miner working in a zinc mine and renting a home at 532 Frisco for $10 per month. Harold is 17 and, single.

William Ellsberry Likens born 2 Mar 1883 in Troy, Kansas, died 6 May 1938 and is buried in Canton Township Cemetery with Serena.

### 4. Jessie Louise Likins and Harry Ross Baldridge

The 1930 census for Acadia, Kansas has Jessie Likins, 18 a boarder, single, working as a clerk in a grocery store.

Jessie Likins, 26, married Harry Baldridge 25 Apr 1938 in Kay, Oklahoma.

The 1940 census for Wichita, Kansas has Harry Baldridge, 26, completed 8th grade, a carpenter's helper for a building contractor. Jessie is 28 and graduated high school. They are living with Harry's mother and step-father.

Harry Ross Baldridge born 26 Dec 1913 in Wichita, Kansas, died 30 Jul 1989 in McPherson, Kansas and is buried in the Canton Township Cemetery. Jessie Louise Likins Baldridge born 29 Oct 1911, died 18 Jul 1994 in Canton, McPherson, Kansas and is buried with Harry. They did not have children.

### 4. Harold Leroy Likins and Bertha Lucille Burch

The 1940 census for Canton, McPherson County, Kansas has Harold L Likins, 27, completed 8th grade, a mail carrier in the US Post office who owns his home on 1st Street worth $420. Bertha is 25 and completed 8th grade. Glenn E, brother, is 25, completed 8th grade and general labor crushing rock for roads. Glenn's wife is Dorothy M, 18, completed 8th grade. Glen and Dorothy have a son Glenmon,1. Bertha and Dorothy are sisters.

Harold Likins served in the US Army from 30 Dec 1942 to 13 Sep 1945 during WW11.

Harold Leroy Likins born 24 Mar 1913, died 24 Dec 1986 in McPherson, Kansas and is buried in Canton Township Cemetery. Bertha L Burch Likins born 16 Mar 1915, died 18 Mar 2003 and is buried in Canton Township Cemetery with Herold.

### 4. Glenn E Likins and Dorothy M Burch

Glenn and Dorothy are living with Harold in 1940. They had another son William J Likins in 1942. Glenn did not serve in WW11.

Glenn Edwin Likins born 1 Feb 1915, died 17 May 1988 in Canton, Kansas and is buried in Canton Township Cemetery. Dorothy M Burch Likins born 28 Sep 1921, died 25 Jul 2004 in Hutchison, Kansas and is buried with Glenn.

### 4. Floyd Raymond Likins

Floyd Raymond "Rosie" Likins was in the US Navy 5th Marine Regiment, 1st Marine Division during WW11. He served from 22 May 1943 to 28 Jan 1946.

Floyd Raymond Likins born 11 Oct 1919 in Picher, Oklahoma, died 2 Aug 1988 in Woodford, Virginia and is buried in Historyland Memorial Park.

## 4. Josie Irene Likins and Travis Earnest Turner

The 1930 census for Crawford, Crawford, Kansas has Martin and Hattie Schifferdecker, farmers, with Josie I Likins, 9, lodger, attending school.

The 1940 census for Crawford, Crawford, Kansas has Hattie Schifferdecker, 60, widow. Travis Turner, 21, son-in-law, is married, completed 1-year college and working on the farm. Josie is 19, daughter and graduated high school. Alfred Meyers is 28, nephew and working on the farm. His wife Hazel Meyers is 22. Apparently the Schifferdecker family took in several children. Josie may have been adopted when her father died.

Although a record was not found it can be assumed Travis was drafted or enlisted in the Merchant Marine early in WW11.

Travis Turner reenlisted 27 Apr 1945 and was discharged 15 Aug 1945.

The 1946 Wichita, Kansas City Directory has Travis E Turner (Josie I) USMM home 1517 S Pershing. Travis is still in the merchant marine.

Travis Earnest Turner born 20 Feb 1919 in Newton, Iowa, died 7 Oct 2000 in Frontenac, Kansas and is buried in Fort Scott Cemetery. He served in the US Merchant Marine during WW11. Josie Irene Likins Turner born 5 Dec 1920 in Picher, Oklahoma, died 9 Apr 2006 in Hutchison, Kansas and is buried with Travis.

## 4. Galen W Likins Childers

The 1930 Census for Sedgwick County, Kansas has Galen Likins, 8, a boarder, living with Gilbert and Edna Childers.

The 1940 census for Sedgwick County, Kansas has Gilbert Childers, 49, graduated college and working as a farmer on a farm he owns. Edna is 51 and graduated high school. Galen, 18, son, is attending school and has completed 10th grade. Galen has been adopted.

Galen W Childers, born 1921, enlisted 23 Dec 1940 in Wichita, Kansas, in the National Guard as a private. He graduated from high school and occupation is listed as actor. Galen was in the Army Medical Department during WW11. He served from 23 Dec 1940 to 12 Oct 1945. As a National Guard member, he may have finished high school and worked until the war started or he was needed.

Galen W Childers born 20 Dec 1921, died 23 Sep 1988 and is buried in Riverside National Cemetery in Riverside, California. He received a Purple Heart.

### 4. Edna Mae Likins and William Oscar Hatch

Edna Mae Likins, 6 was living with Howard and Margaret Simcox as a niece in 1930. Her mother, Serena Likins, and Margaret were sisters.

The 1940 census for Kansas City, Missouri has Howard Simcox, 37, graduated high school, the owner of a retail grocery. Margaret is 37 and graduated high school. There are several Simcox children. Edna Likins is 16 and completed 11th grade and was still with the same family.

Edna Mae Likins, born 4 Aug 1923 was admitted to the Cadet Nurse Corps 4 Sep 1944. The form is signed by Sister Rose Helene RN Director of School of Nursing. Edna withdrew on 1 Sep 1946. The St Joseph school of nursing was in Kansas City, Kansas.

Edna married William Oscar Hatch 20 Jan 1950 in Kansas City, Missouri.

William Oscar Hatch born 21 Dec 1926, died 19 Jul 1989 in Kansas City, Missouri. Edna Mae Likins Hatch born 4 Aug 1923 in Kansas, died 20 Jan 1998 in Kansas City, Missouri and is buried in Longview Memorial Gardens.

### 3. Carlinda "Chloe" Likins and Elbridge C Moulds

Carlinda Likins married Elbridge C Moulds on 11 Mar 1905 in Cherokee, Kansas.

Carlinda Likins Moulds born 9 Jan 1885, died 30 Dec 1908. She was 23. Her burial place is unknown.

The 1910 census for Cherryville, Kansas has Elbridge Moulds, 25, widowed, a boarder, working as a laborer at odd jobs. Elbridge Moulds married again to Mary Elizabeth Douglas. He died in 1936 and is buried with his second wife.

### 3. Frank Leslie Likins

The 1905 Kansas State Census for Cherokee County Has J E Likins, 55; Ida, 42; Frank, 14; Roy, 11; Robert Earl, 8; Walter, 5; Ray, 2; and Baby, 1.

He is not listed in the 1910 census with his parents.

Frank Likins, 23, born in the USA, a farmer, entered Canada on a train at Emerson, Manitoba, Aug 1915. He was from Walsh, Oklahoma and headed to Alberta with $25 in his pocket. He was probably going to join his sister Nettie Whiteman Auvigne.

Frank Leslie Likins, 27, born 16 Sep 1890 registered for WW1 on 28 Sep 1918. He was farming near Welch, Oklahoma.

Frank Leslie Likins born 16 Dec 1980 in Kansas, died 8 Mar 1947 in Delburne, Alberta, Canada and is buried in Delburne Cemetery. The same cemetery as his sister Nettie.

### 3. Roy Likins and Ada Partain

Roy Likins, 22, born 12 Aug 1894 in McPherson, Kansas, registered for WW1 on 5 Jun 1917 in Joplin, Missouri. He is working as a miner at the Hero Mining Company in Joplin, Missouri. He is married and has a crippled foot which he claims for an exemption. He is of medium height and weight with grey eyes and light brown hair.

The 1920 census for Picher, Oklahoma has Roy Likins, 25, married, a laborer in a Zinc & Lead mine. Ada is 25. His brother-in-law, Henry Partain and another boarder are working in the mines and live with them.

The 1929 Oklahoma City Directory has Roy B Likins (Ada) miner, home Broadway Interurban Heights Addition.

The 1930 census for Picher, Oklahoma has Roy Liken, 35, married, lodger, zinc miner.

The 1940 census for Tulsa Oklahoma has Roy B Likins, 45, completed 8$^{th}$ grade, divorced, a taxi driver living in a hotel.

Roy Likins born 12 Aug 1894, died 23 Oct 1940, no burial place is listed.

### 3. Robert Earl Likins and Laura Belle Long

Earl Likins, 19 married Laura Long, 18, on 23 Apr 1916 in Craig, Oklahoma.

Robert Earl Likins, 21, born 24 Nov 1896, from Welch, Oklahoma, registered for WW1 on 5 Jun 1918. He was working for Arthur Horn and his nearest relative is Laura Belle Likins. He is of medium height and weight with brown eyes and hair. He did not serve.

The 1930 census for Wagoner, Oklahoma has Earl Likins, 33, married at 19, a farmer on a rented farm. Laura B is 29 and married at 16. Their children are Alene L, 11, farm laborer; Earl, 9; and Billie N, 6. All the children attended school.

Robert Earl Likins born 24 Nov 1896 in Picher, Oklahoma, died 2 Feb 1931 in Deming, New Mexico and is buried in Welch Cemetery, Welch, Oklahoma.

A 1940 census was not found. After Earl's death, Laura married a McCaw.

Laura Belle Long McCaw born 17 Apr 1900, died 22 May 1974 in California. The children listed are Earl Likins (1921-1982) and Mary Nell Likins (1928-1929) Nothing could be found on Alene or Billie N.

## 4. Earl Likins

Earl Likins, single, born 1921 in Oklahoma, enlisted in the Army Medical Corps on 27 Nov 1940 in Fresno, California. He had completed 9th grade and was working as a cook.

## 3. Walter Jonas Likins and Eva Jane Holden

Walter Jonas Likins, 26, married Eva Holden, 22 on Jul 1926 in Ottawa, Oklahoma.

The 1930 census for Picher, Oklahoma has Walter Likins, 30, married at 26, a miner at a zinc mine who owns his home at 532 Frisco worth $100. Eva is 20 and married at 16. Their son Walter is 1 ½.

The 1940 census for Zincville, Oklahoma has Walter Likins, 40, completed 2nd grade, a cracker in a mine who owns a home worth $50. Eve is 30 and completed 6th grade. Walter is 11, completed 4th grade and attending school.

Walter Likins born 11 Feb 1900, died 21 Jul 1976 in Porum, Oklahoma. He is buried in Coleman Cemetery. Eva born 27 Jan 1910, died 10 Aug 1987 and is buried with Walter.

## 2. Julia C Arn and Vallendingher "Val" Cox

Julia Ann Arn, born in Des Moines, Iowa on 19 Mar 1867 married Vallendingher "Val" Cox, born Oct 1863 in Ohio on 19 Sep 1884 in McPherson, Kansas. The 1884 map of Sharps Creek has Mary A Cox, Val's mother, living in the next farm north of John Arn.

The 1885 Kansas State Census for Smoky Hill, McPherson, Kansas has Mary A Cox, 46, farming; Val Cox, 21, farming; Julia Cox 18; George Cox, 15; Dora Cox, 8; and Ira 4. Mary Cox must be a widow, Val is helping run the farm.

The 1900 census for South Sharps Creek, McPherson, Kansas has Val Cox, 36, born

Oct 1863 born in Ohio, married 16 years, a farmer renting his farm. Julia is 33, born March 1867 in Iowa and has 8 children, all living. The children are Myrtle, 14, born Oct 1885; Rilla, 12, born Feb 1888; Clarence, 10 born March 1890; Clara, 10, born March 1890; Thomas, 9, born May 1891; Roy, 5, born Jun 1894; Forest, 3, born Aug 1896; Flossie, 1, born Aug 1898. All the children were born in Kansas. All but the oldest and 2 youngest children attended school.

Thomas Cox, born May 1891, died 12 Jun 1902 and is buried in Excelsior Cemetery, Marquette, McPherson, Kansas.

The 1910 census for McPherson, McPherson, Kansas has Val Cox, 45, married 25 years, a farmer of small tracts, renting his home at 825 West Martin Street. Julia is 43 and had 11 children, 10 are living. The children are Clarence, 20, a laborer on the farm; Roy, 16, a laborer at odd jobs; Forest, 13; Flossie, 11; Nina, 9; Alta, 5; and Zelma, 3. All the children were born in Kansas. Forest, Flossie and Nina attended school.

Roy John Cox, born Jun 5, 1894, died Nov. 28, 1911 and is buried in Excelsior Cemetery, Marquette, McPherson, Kansas.

The 1920 census for Harper, McPherson, Kansas has Val Cox, 56, a framer renting his farm. Julia C is 53. The children are Flossie L, 21; Nina M, 18; Alta J, 15; and Zelma A, 12. None of the girls are working but only Zelma is in school.

The 1930 census for Castle, McPherson, Kansas has Val Cox, 66, married at 21, a farmer renting his farm and owns a radio. Julia C is 63 and married at 17. The others are Forest V, 33, widowed, a farm laborer, not a veteran; Flossie L, 31; Darlene R, 11, granddaughter; and Billy P, 5, grandson. Forest is the children's father. They were born in Kansas and went to school.

In the spring of 1937, they moved to Windom then to McPherson, Kansas.

The 1940 census for McPherson, Kansas has Val Cox, 76, completed 5th grade, not employed and renting a home at 571 S. Ash for $20 per month. Julia is 73 and completed 7th grade. Flossie is 41, single and completed 8th grade.

Val Cox died Sep 1940 and is buried in Excelsior Cemetery in Marquette, Kansas. Julia C Arn Cox died in 1946 and is buried with Val.

The following is a picture of Julia and Val Cox with their 9 living children taken in Sep 1939. Julia and Val are in front. From the left: Zelma, Alta, Flossie, twins Clarence and Clara, Forest, Rilla, Nina and Myrtle.

### 3. Myrtle M Cox and Beryl Lewis Smith

Myrtle Cox married Beryl Smith about 1910.

The 1910 census for Horton, Kansas has B L Smith, 26, married less than 1 year, born in Missouri, farming and renting a home. Myrtle is 23 and born in Kansas.

Beryl L Smith, 35, born 27 May 1883, a farmer living in Fairview Kansas, registered for WW1 on 12 Sep 1918. He was working in Powhattan, Kansas. Myrtle Smith was the nearest relative.

The 1920 census for Powhattan, Brown, Kansas has Beryl Smith, 35, a farmer renting his farm. Myrtle M is 33. Their daughters are Rena B, 9 and Ida M, 8, attended school.

The 1930 census for Craig, Nebraska has Beryl L Smith, 47, widowed, a medicine salesman renting a home for $12.50 per month. His daughters are Rena B, 19, attending school and training in a hospital; and Ida M, 18, attending school. Nothing more could be found on the two daughters.

One ancestry family tree has Myrtle Cox Smith dying in 1925. This could be true according to the above census but it seems she was still alive in 1939 as she is part of the family picture. There are the right number of women and men standing behind the parents. I believe she left the family around 1925 to pursue an education.

The 1940 census for Van Wert, Iowa has Myrtle Cox, 55, married (lightly crossed out) completed 5 years college, born in Kansas, a minister in a church who owns a house worth $1000. There is no proof this is or is not our Myrtle, only that the name, age and place of birth are the same. There is also a Myrtle Loricia Smith who died in Gray County Kansas and was buried 13 Dec 1925. The truth is a mystery.

The 1940 census for Hiawatha, Kansas has Beryl Lewis Smith, 56, completed 2 years college, a policy writer for an insurance company. He is married to Iva Moya, 50.

Beryl L Smith born 1883, died 1964 in Hiawatha, Kansas and is buried in Mount Hope Cemetery with his 2nd wife.

### 3. Rilla M Cox and John Walter Alger

Rilla Cox married John Alger about 1907. This is likely their wedding picture.

The 1910 census for Castle, McPherson, Kansas has Walter J Alger, 33, married 3 years, a farmer who owns his mortgaged farm. Rilla is 22 and has 3 children all living. The children are Russell, 4; Claude, 2 and Wesley, 5/12. Renzo Schiller, servant, 36, no trade, cannot read or write, is living with them. Clarence Cox, brother-in-law, 20, is working on the home farm. Clarence is listed with his parents as well as with Rilla and Walter. He may have been working on both farms. Renzo is a puzzle as he seems to be doing no work as a servant. He may be a relative and disabled.

The 1920 census for Castle, McPherson, Kansas has John W Alger, 43, a farmer who owns his mortgaged farm. Rilla M is 31. The children are Russel A, 13, a farmer on the home farm; Claude V ,11, a farmer on the home farm; Wesley J, 10; Earl L, 8; Evelyn A, 7; Hensley D, 4; and LaVerda S, 1 7/12. The five oldest attended school. Lorenzo Shiller is 44, a lodger, single, cannot read or write, a farm hand and still living with them.

The 1925 Kansas State Census for Castle, McPherson, Kansas has J W Alger, 48, a farmer who owns his mortgaged farm. Rilla M is 37. The children are Russell A, 18; Claude V, 17; Wesley J., 15; Earl L, 13; Evelyn A, 11; Hensley D, 9; LaVerda S, 6 and J W Jr., 4. All but Russell and J W attended school.

Wesley J Alger born 3 Nov 1909, died 7 Jul 1928 and is buried in Excelsior Cemetery, Marquette, Kansas.

The 1930 census for Castle, McPherson, Kansas has John W Alger, 54, married at 29, a farmer who owns his farm and a radio. Rilla M is 42 and was married at 18. Their children are Claude V, 22, farm laborer; Earl L, 19, farm laborer; Evelyn A, 16; Hensley D, 14; LaVerda S, 11; John W, 9 and Nina M, 4/12. Hensley, LaVerda and John attended school.

The 1940 census for McPherson, Kansas has John Alger, 63, completed 8th grade, a farmer on a farm he owns at 511 S Ash. Rilla is 52 and completed 6th grade. The children are Earl, 28, completed 7th grade, a laborer in building construction; John Walter, 19, completed 8th grade, an attendant at a gasoline filling station and Nina Mae, 14, attended school. The very next listing for 571 S. Ash is Val and Julia Cox.

Rilla Cox Alger born 12 Feb 1888, died 5 May 1941 and is buried in Excelsior Cemetery, Marquette, Kansas. John Walter Alger born 26 Sep 1876, died 17 Dec 1942 and is buried with Rilla.

### 4. Russell A Alger and Celia M Irvine

The 1930 census for Castle, McPherson, Kansas has Russel A Alger, 23, married at 22, a farmer renting his general farm. Celia M is 21 and married at 20. Their daughter, Dorothy M, is 7/12.

The 1940 census for Castle, McPherson, Kansas has Russel Alger, 33, completed 8th grade, a laborer on a farm renting a home for $4 per month. Celia is 31 and graduated high school. Their children are Dorothy, 10, completed 4th grade; Russel Jr., 9, completed 2nd grade; Ralph, 7, completed 1st grade; Deloris, 5 and Carol J, 3.

Russell A. Alger born 19 Sep 1906, died Jan 1974 and is buried in Excelsior Cemetery. Celia M Irvine Alger born 4 Jul 1908, died 26 Jan 1999 and is buried with Russell.

### 4. Claude V Alger and Ruth Helen Postier

The 1940 census for McPherson, Kansas has Claude Alger, 32, completed 7th grade, a common laborer at any kind of labor renting a home on N Chestnut for $12 per month. Ruth is 32, completed 8th grade and domestic labor and laundress, at a private home. Their daughter, Glenda Lee, is 5/12.

Claude Virgil Alger, 32, born 1 Feb 1908, registered for WW11 on 16 Oct 1940 in Kansas. He was working for J E Steele Truck Line. Next of kin is Ruth Helen Alger.

Claude Virgil Alger, born 1908, died 1949 and is buried in McPherson Cemetery, McPherson, Kansas. Ruth Helena Postier Alger, born 1907, died 1980 and is buried beside Claude.

### 4. Earl LeRoy Alger and Ethel Emmaline

Earl was living with his parents in 1940. Earl Leroy Alger, 29, born 28 Aug 1911, enlisted as a private in Company K of the 407th Infantry, 102 Division on 17 Nov 1942. He reported for active duty 26 Nov 1942. He was honorably discharged 28 Apr 1943.

He apparently married before or after his time in the service.

Mrs. Ethel Alger applied for a headstone on 4 Sep 1946 for Earl LeRoy Alger, born 28 Aug 1911 a private in Company K, 104th Infantry, 102nd Division. The stone was to be shipped to Mrs. Ethel Alger of RR#1 Marquette, Kansas for the Marquette Cemetery. The stone was approved 20 Sep 1946 and ordered 15 Oct 1946.

Earl Leroy Alger born 28 Feb 1911, died 2 Feb 1946 and is buried in Marquette Cemetery, McPherson Co., Kansas. His wife, Ethel Emmaline Alger Boggs born 13 Apr 1913, died 19 Feb 1991 is buried beside Earl. Ethel remarried after Earl died. Earl Boggs is buried on the other side of Ethel.

## 4. Evelyn A Alger and James Harvey Poland

Evelyn Alberta Alger married James Harvey Poland 10 Sep 1930 in McPherson, Kansas. They were both from Conway, Kansas. Claude Alger was a witness.

This picture may have been taken on or near their wedding.

James and Evelyn lived in Roseville, California in 1961 where he worked as a pipefitter for SP Company. They lived at 112 Donner Ave.

James H. Poland born 13 Feb 1907, died 5 Mar 1980 and is buried in Roseville Public Cemetery, Roseville, California. Evelyn Alberta Alger Poland, born 17 Jun 1913, died 20 Jun 1987 in El Dorado, California and is buried with James.

## 4. Hensley D Alger and Lois L Durland

Hensley D Alger married Lois L Durland 6 Feb 1937 in McPherson, Kansas.

The 1940 census for South Sharps Creek, McPherson, Kansas has Hensley D Alger, 28, completed 8th grade, a farmer, renting his home for $10 per month. Lois L is 22 and graduated high school. Their children are Myrna E, 2 and Byron D, 1.

Hensley Alger born 30 May 1915, died 24 May 1958 at the age of 42. His wife Lois went on to Work at Farmers Insurance for 22 years from 1959 to 1981, and married George Fry in 1988 who preceded her in death. She lived to be 94 and was buried with

Hensley Alger. Her only children were Myrna and Byron who survived her.

## 4. LaVerda S Alger and Donald W Brown

LaVerda S Alger and Donald W Brown were married 18 Nov 1939 in Lakin, Kansas.

The 1940 census for McPherson, Kansas has Donald W Brown, 21, completed 9th grade, an attendant at a gasoline filling station renting an apartment at 613 ½ N Main Street. LaVerda is 21 and completed 8th grade.

Donald W Brown born 23 Jan 1919, died 21 May 2008 in Saline, Kansas and is buried in McPherson Cemetery. LaVerda S Alger Brown born 3 Dec 1918, died 5 Jan 2017 at Inman, Kansas and is buried with Donald.

## 3. Clara A Cox and Fredrick J Mansfield

Clara Cox, 18, married Fred John Mansfield, 29, on 13 May 1908 in Oklahoma.

The 1910 census for Frisco, Texas, Oklahoma has Fred J Mansfield, 31, married 2 years, a farmer who owns his farm free and clear. Clara is 20 and has 2 children both living. The children are Edwin B, 1 1/12, born in Oklahoma; and Mary E, 1/12, born in Oklahoma.

The 1920 census for Blythe, California has Fred J Mansfield, 41, born in Illinois, a house painter renting his home. Clara A is 31 and born in Kansas. The children are Edwin B, 11, attending school, born in Oklahoma; Ester F, 2 1/2, born in California; and Ruth L, 1/12, born in California.

Mary E is not in the 1920 census it must have been an omission. Mary Elizabeth Mansfield, born 5 Mar 1910, married Emery Hubbard on 5 Mar 1928 in Pasadena, California. Her parents are Fredrick Mansfield and Clara Cox.

The 1930 census for Pasadena, California has Fredrick J Mansfield, 51, married at 28, a house painter who owns his home at 29 West Howard Street worth $4000 and has a radio. Clara is 41, married at 19 and a sales lady in ready to wear dry goods. Their daughters are Esther, 12 and Ruth, 10, both attended school.

The 1940 census for Pasadena, California has Fred Mansfield, 61, graduated high school, living in the same place in 1935, working as a chiropractor in private practice and renting a home at 1640 East Walnut Street for $33 per month. Clara is 50, completed 10th grade and is not working. Their daughters are Ruth, 20, graduated high school, a file clerk in a life insurance company and Betty, 8, attended school.

Fredrick John Mansfield, born 18 Aug 1878, died 22 Jan 1953 in Los Angeles, California. Clara Cox Mansfield, born 24 March 1890, died 6 Jun 1972 in Los Angeles,

California.

### 4. Edwin B Mansfield and Florence Leta Willey

The 1930 census for Alhambra, California has Edwin B Mansfield, 21, married at 20, a house painter, renting a home at 2416 Birch Street for $40 per month. Florence L is 20, married at 19 and not working.

The 1940 census for Pasadena, California has Edwin B Mansfield, 31, graduated high school, a salesman for a wholesale electric supply renting a home on North Wilson Ave. for $33 per month. Leta is 30, completed 11th grade and is working as a bookkeeper at the wholesale electric supply. Their son, Victor is 9 and completed 3rd grade. Leta's mother, Della Willey, 59 is living with them.

Edwin B Mansfield born 12 May 1908, died 7 May 1973 in Butte County, California and is buried in Paradise Cemetery. Florence L Mansfield born 20 Sep 1909, died 12 Mar 1990 in Butte County and is buried with Edwin.

### 4. Mary Elizabeth Mansfield and Emery Hubbard / Thomas Christian Jensen

Mary Elizabeth Mansfield married Emery Hubbard 5 Mar 1928 in Pasadena, California.

The 1930 census for Pasadena, California has Emery L Hubbard, 20, married at 18 and drives a truck doing roadwork. Mary is 20 and married at 18. They are living with his parents and sister. Emery A Hubbard, 65, married at 42 and not working. Minnie, is 55 and was married at 32. Their daughter Pearl is 22 and a clerk in a telephone office.

Social security records have Mary Elizabeth Mansfield born 5 Mar 1910 in Guymon, Oklahoma, died 29 Jun 1996, father Fredrick J Mansfield, mother Clara A. Cox.

Emery Leroy Hubbard born 11 Aug 1909, died 7 Jul 1956 in Idaho Falls, Idaho and is buried in Rigby Pioneer Cemetery. Mary Elizabeth Mansfield Hubbard born 5 Mar 1910, died 29 Jun 1996 in Idaho Falls, Idaho and is buried with Emery.

### 4. Esther Fern Mansfield

The 1940 census for Pasadena, California has Esther Mansfield, 22, single, graduated high school, a saleslady in a gift shop renting her home at 736 Sacramento Ave. for $26 per month.

The California death index has Esther Fern Mansfield born 27 May 1917, died 17 Feb 1988. She does not have a married name.

### 3. Clarence William Cox and Emma Jean Ruth Starr

Clarence William Cox married Emma Starr about 1911

Clarence William Cox, 27, registered for WW1 on 5 Jun 1917. His address is RR #1 Windom, Kansas and he has a wife and 4 children to support working as a farmer.

The 1920 census for Fairview, Butler, Kansas has C W Cox, 28, born in Kansas, a farmer renting his farm. E R is 28 and born in Nebraska. Their children are J M, 7; R I, 6; I B, 5; and D M, 3. All the children were born in Kansas.

The 1930 census for Dover, Vernon, Missouri has Clarence Cox, 40, married at 21, a farmer who owns his farm, not a veteran. Emma is 37, married at 18, and born in Nebraska. Their daughters are Julia 17, a housekeeper for a private family; Irene, 16; Idena, 15; and Dorothy, 13. All the children except Julia attended school.

In the 1940 census for Dover, Vernon, Missouri has Clarence Cox, 50, completed 8th grade, a farmer on a farm he owned worth $1000. Emma is 47 and completed 8th grade. Ruth Irene is 26 and completed 8th grade. All the other girls have left home and there is no further information on Idena B or Dorothy M Cox

Clarence W Cox born 24 Mar 1890, died Jul 1963 and is buried in Towanda Cemetery, Towanda, Butler, Kansas. Emma born 1892, died in 1963 and is buried with Clarence.

### 4. Julia M Cox

The 1940 Topeka, Kansas City Directory has Julia M Cox, cashier at Shawnee Tobacco Company, residence 1195 Garfield Ave.

### 4. Ruth Irene Cox and Gordon W Richey

Ruth Irene was living with her parents in 1940.

Gordon W Richey born Feb 1903, died 14 Aug 1970 and is buried in Welborn Cemetery, Moundville, Missouri. Ruth Irene Cox Richey born 29 Sep 1913, died 13 Aug 2001 and is buried with Gordon.

### 3. Forest "Floyd" Val Cox and Stella J Lindquist / Julia A

Forest Cox married Stella J Lindquist

Forest Val Cox, 21, born 19 Aug 1896, from R# 4 McPherson, Kansas registered for WW1 on 5 Jun 1918. His nearest relative was Mrs. Stella Cox of the same address.

The 1920 census for Harper, McPherson, Kansas has Forest V Cox, 23, a farmer renting his farm. Stella J is 23. Their daughter, Darlene R is 10/12.

A son, William "Billie" Pierce Cox, was born in 1921. Stella J Lindquist Cox born 1895, died in 1930.

The 1930 census for Castle, McPherson, Kansas has Forest V Cox, 33, widower, farm labor on his father's farm. His children are Darlene R,11 and Billy P, 5. They are living with his parents.

The 1940 census for Marquette, Kansas has Forest V Cox, 43, married, completed 8$^{th}$ grade, lived in the same place in 1935, proprietor of a dray renting a home on Lincoln Street. Julia A is 31 and completed 10$^{th}$ grade. Billie P is 18 and completed 11$^{th}$ grade. They have 2 lodgers.

The 1940 census for Hutcheson, Reno, Kansas has Darlene Cox, 21, niece, completed 8$^{th}$ grade and living with Fred and Myrtle Smith.

Apparently, Forest went to work in Kansas City during the war. Forrest Val Cox, 46, born 19 Aug 1896, of 108 S 17$^{th}$ St. Kansas City, Kansas registered for WW11 on 27 Apr 1942. The next of kin is Julia Cox of McPherson, Kansas. He is working for Vendo Company of 25 and Washington in Kansas City, Missouri.

Forest V Cox, born 19 Aug 1986, died Nov 1964 in Wyandotte, Kansas and is buried in Highland Park Cemetery, Kansas City, Kansas.

### 3. Flossie Lenora Cox and Clyde Raymond Embers

Flossie was living with her parents in 1940.

Flossie married Clyde after he sister Nina died in 1957. Flossie L Cox married Clyde R Embers in Clark County, Nevada 27 Jul 1964.

Flossie Lenora Cox Embers born 17 Aug 1898, died 27 Feb 1979 and is buried in McPherson Cemetery, McPherson, Kansas. Clyde Raymond Embers born 12 Aug 1900, died 15 Sep 1981 and is buried with both Cox sisters. They have matching headstones.

### 3. Nina Mable Cox and Clyde Raymond Embers

Nina Cox married Clyde Embers in 1922.

The 1925 Directory for Santa Monica California has Clyde R Embers (Nina) home 2451 ½ 117$^{th}$ Ave S.

The 1930 census for Santa Monica, California has Clyde R Embers, 29, married at 22, born in Kansas, a lather (putting up lath for plaster work) in buildings renting a home at 1430 Princeton Street for $35 per month and has a radio. Nina M is 29, married at 22, born in Kansas and occupation is nail (works in a nail salon?).

The 1940 census for Santa Monica, California has Clyde Embers, 39, graduated high school, a lather in construction who owns his home at 1437 Princeton worth $5000. Nina is 39 and completed 8$^{th}$ grade.

Clyde and Nina Embers went to England in the summer of 1955. They left Southampton 11 Jul 1955 and arrived in New York 20 Jul 1955. They traveled first class on the TSS New York. Their address is given as 1431 Princeton Street. Santa Monica, California. They were both born in Kansas.

Nina Mable Cox Embers, born 31 Mar 1901, died 3 Sep 1957 in Los Angeles, California. She is buried in McPherson Cemetery, McPherson, Kansas.

### 3. Alta J Cox and Robert W. Burkholder

Alta Cox and Robert Burkholder were married in 1922.

The 1930 census for Granada, Nemaha, Kansas has Robert Burkholder, 27, married at 19, a farmer renting his farm and has a radio. Alta J is 25 and married at 17. Their daughter, Darlene, is 3/12., William H Burkholder is 76, father, widowed and living with them.

The 1940 census for Harrison, Nemaha, Kansas has Robert Burkholder, 37, completed 8$^{th}$ grade, a farmer on a rented farm. Alta is 35 and completed 8$^{th}$ grade. The children are Darlene, 10, attended school; and Darwin, 5.

Robert W Burkholder born 11 Jun 1902, died 23 Aug 1958 and is buried in Fairview Cemetery, Goff, Kansas. Alta J Cox Burkholder born 30 Jul 1904, died Mar 1983 and is buried near Robert.

### 3. Zelma Ann Cox and Abraham John Buller

Zelma is listed with her parents, Val and Julia Cox in 1920 and 1925 but a 1930 census for Zelma could not be found. Zelma is in the 1939 photo.

The 1940 Census for Enid, Oklahoma has Abram J Buller, 31, completed 8$^{th}$ grade, a taxi driver for a taxi company renting a home at 615 West Park for $16 per month. Zelma A is 33 and completed 10$^{th}$ grade.

### 2. John Jacob Arn and Nellie McNamara / Hattie Van Vliet

John Arn married Nellie McNamara

The 1905 Kansas State Census for Blue Mound, Linn, Kansas has J J Arn, 35, born in

Iowa, a clerk for Implements renting a home. Nellie is 29 and born in Kansas. John Arn is 79 and retired.

The 1910 census for Blue Mound, Linn, Kansas has J J Arn, 42, married 18 years, born in Iowa, father born in Switzerland, Mother born in Germany, a Livery Man, renting his home. Nellie M is 37 and had 1 child, the number living is not filled in. The child is not listed and Nellie died before 1920.

The 1920 census for Kansas City, Missouri has John J Arn, 50, married, a truck driver for Hesse Carriage. He is living with a widow and her son as a boarder.

John J. Arn, 52, married Hattie Van Vliet, 53, on 14 Jan 1922 in Kansas City, Missouri.

The 1930 census for Blue, Jackson, Missouri has John J Arn, 60, first married at 23, born in Iowa, a janitor in a hospital. Hattie B is 61, first married at 20 and born in Kentucky. William A Van Vliet, step-son is 39, a widower, first marriage at 20, born in Missouri, a painter at odd jobs. They own their home worth $1500 at 20th Ashland. Two other families have the same address and all own their home

John Jacob Arn, 63 years, 9 months, 27 days, died 16 May 1933 in Jackson, Missouri. He was living at 2019 Ashland, his wife is Hattie Arn, his father, John Arn of Germany, his mother Catherine Klingensmith of Germany. He died of Acute Myocarditis and focal infection from teeth. He was buried in Forest Hill Cemetery 18 May 1933.

## 2. Fredrick W Arn and Ada Brown

Fred Arn, 24, married Ada Brown, 19 on 24 Nov 1897 in Northern District, Indian Territory.

The 1900 census for Township 28, Cherokee Nation, Indian Territory has Fred Arn, 27, born Feb 1873 in Kansas, married 2 years, both parents born in Germany, a farmer. Ada, 21, born Sep 1878, no children, born in Indian Territory, father born in Illinois, mother in Indian Territory. The next part of the page has Ada Arn a 7/8 Cherokee with a white father and Cherokee mother. They are living in a fixed dwelling with Ada's father and 4 of her siblings. This is the closest I could find. Fred was born in Iowa but who ever gave the information may have thought it was Kansas, otherwise it is very close.

A tombstone in Rogers Cemetery, Welch, Oklahoma has the inscription: Ada wife of F W Arn, died 1 Feb 1901, aged 23 y 4m 6d. Fred Arn born 1872, died 12 May 1909.

# Chapter 8

## Karl (Charles) Klingenschmidt and Sarah Ish

1. Karl (Charles) Philipp Klingenschmidt (1837-1917)
+ Sarah H Ish (1835-1916)
    2. George Urban Erwin Klingenschmidt (1862-1948) p
    + Clara Carl (1866-1960) p
    2. Emma Jane Klingenschmidt (1864-1941) p
    + Amaza L Gee (1861-1941) p
        3. Lorrin Jefferson Gee (1884-1958)
        + Nora Ellen Risden (1879-1915)
        + Anna M Cramer (1887-1966)
        3. Charles Howard Gee (1886-1968)
        + Ina Lucile Post (1892-1986)
            4. Robert Howard Gee (1915-1998)
            4. Carole Gee (1917-1997)
            + Edgar Sunderland (1911-1998)
                5. William P Sunderland (1938-)
            4. Elma Jane Gee (1919-)
            4. Richard Gee (1922-)
            4. Elizabeth Gee (1923-)
            4. Edward Gee (1926-)
            4. John Gee (1927-)
        3. Glenn D Gee (1888-1896)
        3. Elton G Gee (1891-1967) p WW1
        3. Eva M Gee (1893-1966) p
        + Cecil Rickard (1892-1951) grandson of Mary K Kester, WW1
        3. Frank Russell Gee (1894-1971) p WW1
        + Emma Schelles (1897-1973)
            4. Dorothy Gee (1922-)
            4. Patricia Gee (1923-)
            4. Charles Gee (1924-)
            4. Francis R Gee (1931-)
            4. Elsie L Gee (1932-)
        3. Lottie Ruth Gee (1898-1982)
        + Eljie Remington (1893-1971)
            4. Burdette Remington (1920-)
            4. Shirley M Remington (1924-)
            + Robert D Potter (-)
            4. Lois J Remington (1925-)
            4. Alan L Remington (1934-)
        3. Clara Elizabeth Gee (1897-1898)
        3. Un-named boy (1900-1900)
        3. Ralph E. Gee (1904-1975)

                3. Arthur L. Gee (1907-1929) p
         2. Ellen Maria Klingenschmidt (1866-1870)
         2. Sara Elizabethm "Libbie" Klingenschmidt (1870-1953) p – wrote poem
          + Jacob Elwood "Jay" Southern (1861-1947) p
             3. Charles Daniel Southern (1898-1971) WW1
              + Lois Isabel Green (1898-1957)
                 4. Charles D. Southern Jr. (1925-)
                 4. Barbara Southern (1929-)
                 4. Ernest Phillip Southern (1930-2011)
                 4. Agnes Ann Southern (1932-2001)
             3. Merrill Southern (1903-1974)
              + Lucile J Duryea (1904-1983)
                 4. Jack L Southern (1925-1989) WW11
         2. Alice Eva Klingenschmidt (1871-1938)
         2. Charles Klingensmith (1874-1933)
          + Fay Brown (1869-1904)
          + Katherine Baker (1869-1939)
             3. Julia Agnes Klingensmith (1908-1978)
              + Charles J. Frey (1906-1989)
                 4. Charles Lee Frey (1938-1995)
         2. Frank L Klingensmith (1879-1949)
          + Julia E. Myhrs (1879-1976)
             3. Thomas B. Klingensmith (1906-1976) WW11
              + Mary Margaret Emmons (1911-1968)
                 4. Marianne (1936-)
             3. Charles P Klingensmith (1910-1995)
             3. Elizabeth Ann Klingensmith (1914-1994)
              + Milo Kendell Winter (1913-)

A "p" indicates the person was mentioned in the Klingensmith Family Reunion Poem.

## 1. Karl Klingenschmidt / Charles P. Klingensmith and Sarah Ish

Karl received a very good education in his native tongue before coming to America, and after his arrival here he acquired the English language very readily and was not ashamed to go to the district school and add still farther to his fund of knowledge. By a steady course of reading he kept himself well informed upon general topics and was a man of more than ordinary intelligence in conversation.[8]

Karl stayed on the farm and assisted his parents until he was 24 years old. He managed to save something from his earnings and purchased forty-eight acres of land in Cambria Township, which he soon after sold. He continued buying and selling several times, making something with each sale, until he was enabled to secure possession of a 190-acre farm in Section 12 of Jefferson Township. The farm was valued at $75/acre in

1889.[8]

# THE PITTSFORD REPORTER

PITTSFORD, HILLSDALE CO., MICH., FRIDAY, JULY 7, 1911.

## Wedded Fifty Years

### AN AUSPICIOUS EVENT IN THE LIVES OF MR. AND MRS. CHARLES P. KLINGENSMITH

JULY 4, 1861

JULY 4, 1911

Karl Klingenschmidt married Sarah Ish on 4 Jul 1861 in Jonesville and had a very good home to offer his bride. Sarah was the daughter of Nicholas and Barbara (Vought) Ish, and was born in Wyandot County, Ohio 18 Aug 1836. Her parents were natives of Switzerland and came to the United States after their marriage. Sarah was the youngest of eight children. Mary, born Feb 1818; Nicolas, born 4 Aug 1820 and John, born 2 Dec 1821 were all deceased in 1889. Elizabeth, born 19 Nov 1823; Barbra, born 6 Dec 1825; Benjamin, born 18 Dec 1827 and Susan, born 15 Dec 1832. Nicholas Ish, Sarah's father, was born in Aug 1782 and died in 1880. Barbra Vought, Sarah's mother, was born Dec 1794 and died April 1871.[9]

The marriage of Charles and Sarah is recorded in county records. Charles P Klingensmith, 23, married Sarah Ish, 24, of Jonesville on 4 Jul 1861.[10] Apparently at this time he was using the name Charles P Klingensmith for county records but church records still used the German name Karl Klingenschmidt. He was using the new name when the Hillsdale County History was written in 1889.

Charles' farm was described as a beautiful and valuable farm which is finely located on section 12, in Jefferson Township, and which has been built up by his own industry and perseverance and is perhaps the most forcible illustration of the character of the man.

The fields are laid out with neat and well-kept fences; the buildings are of first-class description, the farm machinery of the most improved pattern, and the livestock of that description peculiar to the thrifty German farmer, being sleek, fat and well sheltered. The whole forms a most attractive homestead and is looked upon with admiring eyes by every traveler through this section of the country.[8]

Charles upon reaching his age of majority identified himself with the Democratic party and was one of the leading men in his community. Were it not that the Republicans were largely in the majority, he would have held important offices in his county. He was reared in the doctrines of the Lutheran Church by his excellent parents, and although not a member still adheres loyally to his early training.[8]

Mr. Klingensmith has been connected with the School Board of the district for the last nine years. Coming from an empire of compulsory education, the most admirable law ever established, he is naturally in favor of everything calculated to ensure the intelligence and usefulness of the rising generation, consequently the establishment and maintenance of schools have found him a zealous and liberal supporter. By the building up of one of the finest homesteads in the township, he has not only been of material value in its growth and progress, but on account of this alone has signalized himself as one of its best citizens.[8] The 1889 History of Hillsdale County paints a very rosy picture.

The 1880 census for Jefferson, Hillsdale, Michigan has Charles Klingensmith, 42, born in Prussia and a farmer. Sarah is 43, born in Ohio with both parents born in Prussia. The children are George U, 17, a farmer; Emma J, 16; Libbie S, 10; Alice E, 8; Charles F L, 6; and Frank L, 1. All the children are born in Michigan. Jacob Klingensmith is 77, father, born in Prussia and living with his son. Also, living with them is Ambrose Walter a laborer from England. Prussia was a name sometimes substituted for Germany.

Ellen Maria Helena Klingensmith, born 1866, died 1870.

This picture was taken some time between the two above pictures, possibly in the 1880's.

The 1900 census for Jefferson, Hillsdale, Michigan has Charles Klingensmith, 62, born Dec 1837, married 38 years, a farmer who owns his farm free and clear. Sarah is 63, born Aug 1836, and had 7 children, 6 are living. Alice Eva is 28 and born Dec 1871.

The 1910 census for Jefferson, Hillsdale, Michigan has Charles P Klingensmith, 72, married 48 years, a naturalized citizen who owns his home free and clear. Sarah is 73 and had 7 children, 6 are living. Eva A is 35, single and a clerk in a merchandise and hardware store.

Sarah H Ish Klingensmith, 79 years, 10 months and 28 days, died 16 Jul 1916 at her home. Cause of death was carcinoma of the liver. George Klingensmith signed the certificate. Burial was in Locust Corners Cemetery 19 Jul 1916.

Charles P. Klingensmith, 79 years 2 months and 6 days, born 27 Dec 1837 in Germany, died 3 Mar 1917 on his farm. The cause of death was carcinoma on the left side of his face. He was buried with Sarah on 6 Mar 1917. The information was given by Eva Klingensmith.

**2. George Erwin/Urban Klingensmith and Clara Belle Carl**

George was born in Hillsdale 14 Jul 1862. His birth is recorded by Trinity Church as George Erwin son of Karl and Sarah Klingenschmidt. His middle name is Erwin or Urban, depending on time and place but all are the same George Klingensmith.

George U Klingensmith, 26, a farmer married Clara Carl, 23, a teacher on 22 Jan 1889. Clara's father is William Carl and her mother is Fanny B Carl.

The 1900 census for Jefferson, Hillsdale, Michigan has George U Klingensmith, 37, born July 1862, married 11 years, a farmer. Clara is 35, born May 1865 and has not had children. George's parents, Charles and Sarah Klingensmith are living in the same house or next door with their daughter Alice E. The next house or farm has George's brother-in-law, Jay Southern, his wife Sarah Elizabeth, their son Charles, 2 and Jay's brother George B, 43. They are all farming.

The 1910 census for Jefferson, Hillsdale, Michigan has George U Klingensmith, 47, married 21years, a house and barn carpenter who owns his home free and clear. Clara B is 44 and has not had children.

The 1920 census for Jefferson, Hillsdale, Michigan has George Klingensmith, 57, a house carpenter who owns his home. Clara is 54.

George and Clara were at the 1926 Klingensmith reunion and are in many pictures.

The 1930 census for Jefferson, Hillsdale, Michigan has George Klingensmith, 67, married at 26, a house carpenter who owns his home and a radio. Clara B is 64 and married at 23.

The 1940 census for Pittsford, Michigan has George Klingensmith, 77, completed 8th grade, and a carpenter doing repairs in his carpenter shop. Clara Belle is 74 and completed 8th grade. Clara's sister Ola Chesley is 70, a widow, completed 8th grade and living with George and Clara.

George and Clara lived on Main Street in Pittsford in later life although they may have still owned the farm. George made his living as a carpenter most of his life. Clara was a teacher before they were married. Women could not teach after they were married. Teachers only had to complete 8th grade to teach in a country school.

This is a picture of George in 1948 not long before he died. The picture was taken by Ed Bishop

George Urban Klingensmith, 85, born 14 Jul 1862, died 31 May 1948. He is buried in Leonardson Cemetery near Pittsford, Michigan. Clara Belle Carl Klingensmith, 95, died in 1960 and is buried with George.

## 2. Emma Jane Klingensmith and Amaza Gee

Emma Klingensmith's birth is recorded in Trinity Church Records as Emma Jane, daughter of Karl and Sarah (Ish) Klingenschmidt, born in Hillsdale, 22 May 1864.[9]

Emma J. Klingensmith, 18, born in Hillsdale County, Michigan married Amaza S Gee, 22, born in Pennsylvania on 20 Mar 1883 in Pittsford, Michigan. G Price, a minister, officiated. Witnesses were George Klingensmith and Mary E Kester.

The 1880 Jefferson Twp. census records show Amaza Gee working as a 17-year-old farm laborer on a farm near Karl Klingensmith. Emma was 15 at the time and living at home. Most young people married someone close to home.

A picture was taken about 1887 of the Amaza Gee farm in Antrim County, Michigan. Charles H is seated on the stool, Lorrin Jefferson is on the stump, their mother, Emma is on the right, Amaza is with the oxen, Grandfather Charles Klingensmith on the left.

Antrium County is north of Traverse City, Michigan. Their farm may have been between Elmira and Alba. This is about the time the northern lower peninsula of Michigan was logged. The cabin burned shortly after this picture. Lorrin was playing in the fire but was able to save the baby and the canary hanging in the doorway, according to a family history by R Cook.

Lorrin Jefferson Gee was born 22 Jan 1884 in Hillsdale County, Michigan. The Gee's must have moved to Antrium County about 1885. Charles Howard Gee was born 18 Nov 1886 in Elmira, Michigan.

Glenn D Gee was born in 1888 and died in 1896. He is buried near his grandparents, Charles and Sarah Klingensmith, in Locust Corners Cemetery, near Pittsford, Michigan.

The 1900 census for Chestonia, Antrim, Michigan has Amaza Gee, 39, born Jan 1861, married 17 years, a day laborer renting his home. Emma is 36, born May 1864 and has had 8 children, 6 are living. The children are Howard G,13, born Nov 1886; Elton G, 9, born Feb 1891; Eva M, 7, born Feb 1893; Frank R, 5, born Nov 1894 and Lottie R, 1, born Sep 1898. Howard attended school 9 months. The other children are not listed as going to school. Lorrin had left home which made 6 living children out of 8 births.

Clara Elizabeth Gee, born 1897, died 9 Mar 1898 in Star, Antrim, Michigan.

The 1900 census for Star, Antrium, Michigan has Lorrin Gee, 16, born Jan 1884, single, farm laborer. He was working for Arthur Starks.

A death certificate from Alba, Atrium, Michigan has an unnamed boy, still born, 16 Aug 1900. The father is Amaza Gee and mother Emma Klingensmith. Burial or removal was 16 Aug 1900. Undertaker was self (A Gee). Cause of death was still birth. Contributory causes were cross presentation and manual delivery. Signed F L Kelley MD, Alba.

The 1910 census for Star, Antrim, Michigan has Amaziah L Gee, 49, married 27 years, a house carpenter, who owns his mortgaged home. Emma J is 46 and had 11 children, 8 still living. Their children are Elton, 19, a baggage man at a railway station; Eva M, 17; Frank R, 15, a newsboy; Lottie R, 11; Ralph E, 6 and Arthur L, 2.

The 1920 census for Hadley, Lapeer, Michigan has Amaza L Gee, 58, a farmer who owns his farm. Emma is 55. Their sons are Ralph,16, farm labor and Arthur, 12, attended school.

Emma and Amaza had 8 living children in 1926 as mentioned in the Klingensmith poem.

Amaza Gee's sons all left home early to work. Three sons, Charles Howard, a construction carpenter; Elton, a house carpenter and Frank Russell, a factory millwright were boarders living in Detroit in 1920.

The 1930 census for Hadley, Lapeer, Michigan has Amaza Gee, 69, married at 22, a farmer who owns his farm and a radio. Emma is 65 and married at 18. Their son, Elton is 39, single, and a carpenter for a house builder.

The 1940 census for Hadley, Michigan has Amaza Gee, 79, completed 8th grade and owns his home at 3315 First Street. Emma is 76 and completed 8th grade.

Emma J Klingensmith Gee, 77, born 23 May 1864, died 29 Mar 1941 in Flint, Michigan of arteriosclerosis and cardiac failure. Her parents were Charles Klingensmith and Sarah Ish. Amaza L Gee, 80, born 6 Jun 1861, died 19 Sep 1941 in Flint, Michigan of Uremic poisoning. His parents were Amaza Gee and Harriet Kane. The informant for both was Ruth Remington. They are buried in Greenwood Cemetery, Hadley, Michigan.

## 3. Lorrin Jefferson Gee and Nora Ellen Risden / Anna N Cramer

Lorrin Jefferson Gee, 23, a mason married Nora Risden, 27, doing housework on 19 Feb 1907 in Alba, Michigan. Fred Deighton, Elder Methodist Episcopal Church officiated. Lorrin's parents are Amaza Gee and Emma Klingensmith, Nora's parents are

John Risden and Mora Risden. Witnesses were Kenneth Park and Amy Deighton.

The 1910 census for Star, Antrim, Michigan has Loren J Gee, 26, Married 3 years, a house carpenter renting his home. Nora E is 30. The listing right before them is Amaza Gee. They may be renting a house on Amaza's property.

The Ludington Michigan City Directory for 1913 has Loren J Gee (Nora) car repair, residence 421 N William.

Nora Ellen Gee, 36, born 7 Aug 1879, died 9 Nov 1915 at home in Ludington, Michigan of lupus and paralytic dropsy. Her father's is John W Risden. Lorrin J Gee of 421 N William Street is the informant. The doctor is G W Hilton. She was buried in the city cemetery 11 Nov 1915.

Lorrin J Gee, 34, a carpenter married Anna M Cramer, 30, on 1 Jun 1918 by John Brock, minister of the Gospel, in Muskegon, Michigan. Lorrin's parents are Amaza L Gee and Emma Klingensmith while Anna's are John Cramer and Alice Huizenga. Witnesses were John Cramer and Mrs. Hattie Stark both from Muskegon.

Lorrin Jefferson Gee, 34, born 22 Jan 1884 registered for WW1 on Sep 12,1918. He lived at 175 Grand, Muskegon, Michigan with his wife Anna. He was a carpenter for Markle Cement & Coal Company. He was tall with a medium build, brown eyes and dark auburn hair.

The 1920 census for Muskegon, Michigan has Lorrin J Gee, 35, a house carpenter renting part of a house at 175 Grand Ave. Anna N Gee is 32.

The 1930 census for Laketon, Muskegon, Michigan has Lorrin J Gee, 46, married at 23, is not working and owns a home on Grand Road worth $2500. Anna M is 42 and married at 21. Lorrin was apparently between jobs at the beginning of the depression.

The 1940 census for Hadley, Lapeer, Michigan has Lorrin Gee, 56, completed 6th grade, a farm operator on his rented farm. Anna M is 52 and completed 5th grade. Lorrin's brother Elton is 48, graduated high school, a farm helper and living with Lorrin.

Lorrin Jefferson Gee, 58, born 27 Jan 1884 in Hillsdale County, registered for WW11 on 27 Apr 1942. His address was R#1 Metamora, Michigan. He was 5'10", weighed 170, and had brown eyes, gray hair and a ruddy complexion.

Lorrin Gee born 1884, died 1958 and is buried in Greenwood Cemetery, Hadley, Lapeer, Michigan. Anna born 2 Jul 1887, died Oct 1966 and is buried with Lorrin.

### 3. Charles Howard Gee and Ina Lucile Post

Charles Howard Gee, 27, a carpenter of Royal Oak, Michigan married Ina Lucile Post,

22, a teacher of Ovid, Michigan on 22 Sep 1914 in Ovid, Michigan. Frances W. Bates, minister officiating. Howard's parents are A L Gee and Emma J Klingensmith. Lucile's parents are Edward D Post and Alma G Barnes. Witnesses are Miss Vera Hathaway and Mr. Edward Post both of Ovid.

Charles Howard Gee registered for WW1 on 5 Jun 1917. He was born 18 Nov 1886 in Elmira, Michigan. He is married with a child under 2 years and is claiming an exemption for wife and child. Charles works as a Carpenter foreman at Davon Building Company in Detroit, Michigan. He is medium height and build with blue eyes and brown hair.

The 1920 census for Detroit, Michigan has Charles H Gee, 33, construction carpenter lodging on East Milwaukee Ave. with his brothers Elton, 28 and Frank Russell, 33.

The 1920 census for Ovid, Michigan has Edward Post, 83, not working, owns his home on West Street. Elma is 65 and a toilet goods agent (Avon Lady?). Their daughter, Lucile Gee, is 27. Their son-in law, Howard Gee, is 33 and a house carpenter. The three grandchildren are Robert, 4; Carole 2 1/12 and Elma Jane 9/12. Charles Howard was working in Detroit during the week to make money but visiting his wife and children, living with her parents, on weekends. The census records were taken at the same time.

The 1930 census for Knoxville, Tennessee has Charles H Gee, 43, married at 28, a line foreman in an auto shop renting his home at 116 Castle Street for $30 per month. Ina is 37 and married at 24. Their children, all born in Michigan, are Robert, 14; Carol, 12; Elma Jane, 11; Richard, 8; Elizabeth, 7; Edward, 4 and John, 2 8/12. All the older children are in school.

The 1936 Knoxville, Tennessee City Directory has Chas H Gee (Lucile) carpenter, residence 116 S Castle. Also, at the same address are Elma J, Carol M and Robert H Gee. Apparently, they only listed the older children, 17 and over.

The 1938 Knoxville, Tennessee City Directory has Charles H Gee (Lucile) carpenter TVA, residence 1145 Morris Ave. The listed children living with their parents are Elma Jane, a clerk at Comer Studio; G Richard, not working and Robert H, Armor & Co.

The 1940 census for Rhea, Tennessee has C H Gee, 53, completed 10th grade, a carpenter for the TVA renting a home for $15 per month. Ina is 48 and completed 10th grade. Their children are Richard, 19, graduated high school; Edward, 15, completed 6th grade and John, 13, completed 6th grade.

Apparently, Charles Gee and family moved to Knoxville just before 1930 to work for the Tennessee Valley Authority. They were building houses for workers as well as dams.

Charles Howard "Charley" Gee born 18 Nov 1886, died 8 Jun 1968 in Knoxville, Tennessee and is buried in Berry Highland Memorial Cemetery. Ina Lucile Gee born 25 Apr 1892, died 3 Sep 1986 and is buried with Charley.

## 4. Robert Howard Gee

The 1940 census for Nashville, Tennessee has Robert Howard Gee, 24, single, graduated high school, a sausage maker in the packing building and a lodger at 2115 Prince Street.

Robert Howard Gee, born 18 Aug 1915, died 5 Feb 1998.

## 4. Carole M Gee and Edgar F Sunderland

The 1940 census for Knoxville, Tennessee has E F Sunderland, 28, completed 10$^{th}$ grade, a laborer in a sheet mill renting a home at 122 Louise Street for $8 per month. Carol M is 22 and graduated high school. Their son, William P, is 2.

Edgar Fletcher Sunderland born 12 Apr 1911 in Tennessee, died 15 Feb 1988 in Huston, Texas and is buried in Davis Cemetery, Grapeland, Texas. Carole Marjorie Gee Sunderland, born 22 Nov 1917 in Ovid Michigan, died 17 Jun 1997 in Huston, Texas and is buried with Edgar.

## 4. Elma Jane Gee and Elizabeth Gee

Elma Jane Gee born 1919, is not found in the 1940 census. She may have married by then but no records are found. Elizabeth Gee born 1923 would have been 17 in 1940 and may have married by then. There is some evidence the girls may have returned to Michigan. Their 3 younger brothers are still living with their parents in 1940.

## 3. Elton Gee

Elton George Fredrick Gee, 26, born 18 Feb 1891, registered for WW1 on 31 May 1917. He was a carpenter at J M Campbell, Detroit, Michigan but his address is RFD # 3, Metamora, Michigan. Elton was medium height and build with brown eyes and black hair. Elton F Gee, private, company F, 337$^{th}$ infantry, sailed from New York on the Neleus on 22 Jul 1918. Amaza Gee, father, was next of kin.

By 1920, Elton was living in Detroit with his brothers Charles Howard and Frank Russell Gee and working as a carpenter.

Elton was a veteran according to the 1930 census. He is back with his parents and still working as a carpenter in the house building industry.

In 1940 Elton is living with Lorrin and his wife Anna in Lapeer, Michigan. He is now working as a farm helper.

Elton registered for WW11 on 27 Apr 1942. Born 18 Feb 1891, currently living at R#1, Metamora, Michigan. Lorrin Gee was the person who would always know his address. He was 5'7" weighed 148 lb. had Blue eyes and Black hair. It is interesting the color of his eyes changed between WW1 and WW11, maybe the registrar just saw things differently.

Elton George Frederick Gee born 18 Feb 1891, died Oct 1967 in Grand Rapids, Michigan.

### 3. Eva M Gee and Cecil Rickard

Eva Gee, 26, lived with her sister Ruth in 1920, working as a machine operator in the automobile industry.

Eva May Gee, 28, of Metamora, Michigan, a seamstress, married Cecil Leland Rickards, 28, of Spokane, Washington, a dairyman on 25 Aug 1921. Both were born in Michigan. Cecil's parents were Foster Rickard and Mary Kester. Eva's parents were Amaza Gee and Emma Klingensmith. They were married in Hadley, Michigan by Samuel A. Carey, Minister of the Gospel. Witnesses were Ruth and Eljie Remington of Flint, Michigan. Their mothers were first cousins. They lived in California. Eva did come back from California for the Klingensmith Reunion in 1926.

The rest of their story is under Cecil Rickard in Chapter 5 with the Kesters.

### 3. Frank Russell Gee and Emma Sarah Schelles

Russell Gee, chauffer, 1st sanitary squad, medical department, 83rd division left New York on 12 Jun 1918. His next of kin is Amaza Gee, father. Russell Gee was in Sanitary Squad #33 when he sailed from from Brest, France on 19 Jun 1919 in the USS America. His rank is wagoner or driver. (Ambulance or supply driver)

The 1920 census for Detroit, Michigan, Ward 7, 444 Milwaukee Ave. East was taken 10 Jan, 1920. This was a large rooming house called 149 Lyman Place. It has a family of 9 renting, followed by 27 people listed as lodgers. The lodgers include the 3 Gee brothers – Charles H, 33, married, working as a carpenter in construction; Elton, 28, single, working as a house carpenter and Russell, 25, working as a millwright in a factory.

Frank Russell Gee, 25, a millwright, of Detroit, Michigan married Emma Sara L Schelles, 22, a clerk, of Pittsford, Michigan on 23 Feb 1920 in Hillsdale, Michigan. Allen N McEvoy, Rector St Peters Church officiated. His parents were Amaza L Gee and Emma Klingensmith. Her parents were Henry Schelles and Kate Schwarz. Witnesses were Ellen Douglass and Mary D McEvoy both of Hillsdale.

The 1930 census for Detroit, Michigan has Frank Gee, 35, a fireman on a railway who owns his home on Helen Ave. worth $1000 and a veteran of WW1. Emma is 32. The children are Dorothy 8; Patricia, 7 and Charles, 6.

The 1940 census for Detroit, Michigan has Frank R Gee, 45, completed 10th grade, a utility person in the tire industry who owns his home at 13787 Stotter Street worth $2500. Emma S is 42 and graduated high school. Their children are Dorothy, 18, completed 10th grade and looking for work; Catherine P, 17, completed 10th grade; Charles R, 16, completed 9th grade; Francis R, daughter, 9, completed 4th grade; and Elsie L, 8, completed 4th grade.

Frank Russell Gee, 47, born 24 Nov 1894 in Alba, Michigan registered for WW11, 20 May 1942. He was living at 13787 Helen, Detroit, Michigan. He is 5' 7" weighs 156 lb., has brown eyes and black hair. He has a scar on his right forearm and a tattoo on his left forearm.

Frank R Gee born 24 Nov, 1894, died 6 Sep 1971 in Detroit, Wayne, Michigan. Emma S Gee born 6 Aug 1897, died 27 Oct 1973 in Madison Heights, Michigan.

### 3. Lottie Ruth Gee and Eljie Remington

Lottie Ruth Gee married Eljie Remington on 8 Jun 1918 in Flint, Michigan.

The 1920 census for Flint, Michigan has Eljie Remington, 26, a salvage clerk in the automotive industry who owns his mortgaged home at 903 Spencer Street. Ruth is 21. Their son, Burdette, is 6/12. Ruth's sister Eva, 26 is living with them and a machine operator in the automobile industry.

The 1930 census for Flint, Michigan has Eljie Remington, 37, married at 25, a production inspector in an auto factory who owns his home at 3014 Seneca worth $1600 and a radio. Ruth is 31 and was married at 19. The children are Burdette, 10; Shirley, 6 and Lois, 5. All the children attended school.

The 1940 census for Flint, Michigan has Eljie Remington, 47, graduated high school, a receiving clerk in an automobile factory who owns his home at 3301 Wisconsin worth $1500. Ruth is 41and completed 9th grade. Burdette is 20 and completed 11th grade. Shirley M Potter is 16 and completed 10th grade. Her husband, Robert D Potter is 18, graduated high school and a warehouse clerk in a retail grocery. Their other children are Lois J, 15, completed 8th grade and Alan L, 6. All of the children attended school except for Robert Potter.

Eljie Remington born 10 Mar 1893, died Mar 1971 in Lake County, Florida and is buried in Lakeside Memory Gardens, Eustis, Florida. Lottie Ruth Gee Remington born 5 Sep 1898, died 21 Sep 1982 in Flint, Michigan. She is listed on Eljie's stone.

### 3. Ralph E Gee

Ralph Gee was living with his parents in 1920.

The 1930 census for the US Naval Hospital, Navy Yard, Philadelphia, Pennsylvania has Ralph E Gee, F1c U S Navy, 28, single, born in Michigan, parents born in Michigan,

Ralph E Gee, 34, is found on a crew list for the Black Falcon. They left Antwerp 31 Jan 1937 arriving in New York 14 Feb 1937 and leaving for Antwerp 20 Feb 1937. He was working as a fireman.

The 1940 census for Amboy, Hillsdale, Michigan has a Ralph Gee, 47, completed 8th grade, a farmer renting a farm for $900 per month or the value is $900. Mable is 40 and completed 8th grade. I do not believe this is the right Ralph Gee. He should be 37 or 38.

Another 1940 census for Ralph Gee was not found. He may have still been at sea and wasn't counted. No other military records were found.

Ralph Gee born 16 Jun 1903, died Oct 1975 in Cape May, New Jersey. This may or may not have been our Ralph. There is no further information.

### 3. Arthur L Gee

Arthur was living with his parents in 1920. In 1929, he was single and may have still been living with his parents. Arthur L Gee, a farmer, born 13 May 1907 in Alba, Michigan, died 21 Sep 1929 in Goodland, Lapeer, Michigan of a fractured skull when struck by an automobile. He was buried 24 Sep 1929 in Greenwood Cemetery. His father was the informant.

### 2. Ellen Klingensmith

Ellen was born July 28, 1866. Her birth is recorded in the Trinity Church records as Ellen Maria Helena daughter of Carl and Sarah Klingenschmidt born Hillsdale, July 28, 1866.[9]

She died 28 Jul 1870 in Cambria, Hillsdale, Michigan. She is buried in Locust Corners Cemetery near her parents.

### 2. Sarah Elizabeth "Libbie" Klingensmith and Jacob "Jay" E Southern

Libbie was born 20 Mar 1870. Her birth is recorded in Trinity Church records as Sara Elisabethm daughter of Carl and Sara Klingenschmidt, born Cambria, 20 Mar 1870.[9]

Sarah Elizabeth Klingensmith married Jacob "Jay" E Southern about 1893.

The 1900 census for Jefferson, Hillsdale, Michigan has Jay Southern, 39, born May 1861, married 7 years, a farmer renting his farm. Sarah E is 39, born Jun 1869 and has had 1 child. Their son, Charles D is 2 and born Jan 1898. Jay's brother, George B Southern, 43, born Aug 1856, widower, was living with them.

The 1910 census for Wright, Hillsdale, Michigan has Jacob E Southern, 48, married 17 years, a merchant in a general store who owns his home free and clear. Sarah E is 40, had 2 children, both living and a dressmaker. Their children are Charles D, 12, and Merrill, 6.

Charles Daniel Southern, 20, born 1 Jan 1898, a student at Hillsdale College, registered for WW1 on 12 Sep 1918. He is living at 322 Hillsdale in Hillsdale, Michigan and his nearest relative is Elizabeth Southern. He is medium height and build with brown eyes and hair. According to his death certificate he did serve.

The 1920 census for Hillsdale, Michigan has Jay E Southern, 58, retired and renting a home. Elizabeth is 49. Their children are Charles, 22, attended school and Merrill, 16, attended school.

Elizabeth Klingensmith Southern wrote the Klingensmith poem in 1926 commemorating the first Klingensmith Reunion.

The 1930 census for Hillsdale, Hillsdale, Michigan has Jacob E Southern, 68, married at 31, a farmer Who owns his farm. Elizabeth is 60 and married at 23. The time in Hillsdale must have been so the boys could attend college and high school while living at home. They were still in Hillsdale in 1935.

The 1940 census for Pittsford, Michigan has Jacob E Southern, 78, completed 10th grade, unable to work and renting a home on First Street for $5 per month. Elizabeth is 70 and completed 9th grade.

Jacob E Southern born 1861, died 1947 and is buried in Locust Corners Cemetery, Pittsford, Hillsdale, Michigan.

Sarah Elizabeth "Libbie" Klingensmith Southern born 1870, died 1953 and is buried with Jay.

This picture is Libbie with Diane Bishop at the 1950 Klingensmith Reunion.

## 3. Charles Daniel Southern and Lois Greene

Charles D Southern, 24, a teacher, of Port Huron married Lois I Greene, 23, a teacher of Kansas City, Missouri on 24 Jun 1922 in Port Huron, Michigan. Charles' parents are J E Southern and Elizabeth Klingensmith. Lois' parents are C F Greene and Mabel Oberdorf. There is a second marriage application filed in Kansas City, Missouri on 27 Jun 1922. Charles D Southern, 24 and Lois Greene, 23, are both listed as being from Kansas City. The groom's signature is similar to the one on Charles' WW1 registration. Lois' parents may have wanted a wedding in Kansas City.

The 1926 Houston, Texas City Directory has Chas D Southern (Lois G) a teacher at George Washington Jr High School, residence 710 Wendel.

The 1930 census for Houston, Texas has Charles D Southern, 32, a mail carrier for U S Postal Department. Lois is 31. Their children are Charles D, 5 and Barbara, 1.

The 1935 Houston, Texas City Directory has Charles D Southern (Lois) carrier for Post Office home 510 W 21$^{st}$ Ave. They are also in the 1937 Directory but are living on Tidwell Rd.

The 1940 census for Harris County, Texas has Charles D Southern, 42, graduated college, born in Michigan, a letter carrier for the U S Post Office who owns a farm worth $2500 on Tidwell Road. Lois is 41, graduated college and born in New York. Their children are Charles D, 15, completed 8$^{th}$ grade; Barbara, 11, completed 6$^{th}$ grade; Ernest P, 9, completed 3$^{rd}$ grade; and Agnes A, 8, completed 2$^{nd}$ grade. All the children are born in Texas.

Lois Isabel Green Southern, 58, born 22 Dec 1898 in New York, died 22 Nov 1957 in St Joseph Hospital, Houston, Texas of coronary thrombosis, atherosclerosis and diabetes mellitus. She was buried 25 Nov 1957 in Brookside Cemetery, Houston, Texas.

Charles Daniel Southern born 1 Jan 1898 in Michigan, died 6 Sep 1971 in St Joseph Hospital, Houston, Texas. He was a veteran of WW1. Cause of death is acute myocardial infarction and coronary arteriosclerosis with a contributory cause of diabetes mellitus. He was buried in Brookside Cemetery with Lois.

It appears Charles D. Southern did serve in WW1, went back to Michigan to finish college, met Lois while teaching in Michigan or while in Kansas during the war, married in Michigan and Kansas, moved to Houston, worked as a teacher, mail carrier and finally ended up on a farm like his parents. If he was near the poisonous gas used in WW1, Texas may have been a better climate for any lung problems.

## 3. Merrill L Southern and Lucile J Duryea

Merrill Southern, 21, of Allen, Michigan, a clerk married Lucile Duryea, 20, of Allen,

Hillsdale, Michigan, a telephone operator, on 19 Apr 1924 in Hillsdale, Michigan. His parents were J E Southern and Elizabeth Klingensmith. Her parents were John Duryea and Rachel Moore

The 1930 census for Hillsdale, Michigan has Merrill Southern, 26, married at 20, a foreman in an engine works renting a home at 242 South Street for $16 per month and has a radio. Lucile is 25 and married at 19. Their son, Jack, is 4.

A 1940 census has not been found.

Jack Louis Southern, 18, born 29 Jun 1925 in Allen, Michigan registered for WW11 on 29 Jun 1943 in Hillsdale, Michigan. He was 5'10", 225 lbs. with hazel eyes and blonde hair. He served in WW11 from 3 Oct 1944 to 1 Jul 1946.

Merrill L Southern born 5 Jun 1903, died 4 Sep 1974 in Clare, Michigan and Lucile J Southern born 12 Apr 1904, died 17 Jul 1983 in Saginaw, Michigan with a residence of Clare, Michigan according to the Michigan Death Index. They are buried in Cherry Grove Cemetery, Clair, Michigan.

## 2. Alice Eva Klingensmith

Eva Klingensmith is living with her parents in 1910 and a clerk in a hardware store. She must have still been living with her father in 1917 as she signed his death certificate.

The 1920 census for Washington DC has A Eva Klingensmith, 47, single, born in Michigan, a clerk for the Federal Government.

The 1930 census for Washington DC has Eva Klingensmith, 58, a clerk for the government renting an apartment in Spring Place for $54.50 per month. Mary Kester is 36, cousin, single, a visiting nurse and living with Eva. Mary is J George Kester's daughter. Mary served as a nurse during WW11.

Alice Eva Klingensmith, 66, single, born 31 Dec 1871, died 5 Sep 1938 in University Hospital, Ann Arbor, Michigan. She was a clerical government employee for 18 years. She had brain surgery on 1 Sep 1938 and died from the surgery. The brain condition is not decipherable. George Klingensmith was the informant and burial was 7 Sep 1938 in Locust Corners Cemetery.

## 2. Charles Fredrick Levi Klingensmith

Charles Klingensmith's birth is recorded in Trinity Church records as Carl Fredrich Levi, son of Karl and Sarah (Ish) Klingenschmidt born in Hillsdale 12 Feb 1874.[9]

Charles F Klingensmith, 25, a druggist, of Prattville married Fay Brown, 29, of Pittsford on 22 Aug 1899 in Pittsford, Michigan. J C Jones, clergyman officiated. Frank

Klingensmith and Lucy Brown were witnesses.

The 1900 census for Wright, Hillsdale, Michigan has Charles L Klingensmith, 26, born Feb 1874, married less than 1 year, a druggist renting his home. Fay is 30, born Aug 1869 and has no children.

Fay Klingensmith, 34, born 25 Aug 1869, died 1 Feb 1904 in Hillsdale, Michigan of angio pretoris. She was buried in Oak Grove Cemetery, Hillsdale, Michigan. A stone has Charles L Klingensmith; Fay Brown his wife 1869-1904. Charles is not buried there.

Charles F Klingensmith, 31, a pharmacist in Lasing Michigan married Katherine M Baker, 30, of Lansing on 29 Jun 1905. It was his second marriage but her first. J A Schaad, rector, officiated. Edward W Baker and Eva Klingensmith were witnesses.

The 1910 census for Detroit, Michigan has Charles F Klingensmith, 37, married 5 years, a druggist in his own drug store and renting his home at 690 Mt. Elliot Street. Katherine is 40 and had 2 children, 1 is living. Their daughter, Julia Agnes, is 2. A brother-in-law Julius Lee Baker, 24, single and a manager for a real estate firm is living with them.

The 1920 census for Detroit, Michigan has C. Fred Klingensmith, 45, living in a rented house at 690 Mt. Elliot Ave., working as a pharmacist in his own drug store. Catherine M is 49 and Julia A is 10 and attended school.

The 1930 census for Detroit, Michigan has C Fred Klingensmith, 56, married at 30, a pharmacist at a drugstore who owns his home at 14310 Strathmore Ave. worth $15000. Katherine is 56 and married at 30.

This picture is of Charles, Katherine and Julia.

Charles Frederick Klingensmith, 59, of 14310 Strathmore, born 12 Feb 1874, died 18 Jun 1933 of septicemia and probable cancer at Providence Hospital. He was operated on 16 Jun 1933 for gall bladder. It was an exploratory operation which was very common at the time without any other way to find out what was wrong. He was buried in Mount Hope Cemetery, Lansing, Michigan.

Katherine Klingensmith, 68, born 15 Sep 1869, died 6 Dec 1939 of coronary thrombosis and is buried with Charles.

### 3. Julia Agnes Klingensmith and Charles J Frey

Julia A Klingensmith, 20, student, of Detroit, married Charles J Frey, 21, student, of Rome, New York on 5 May 1928 in Lucas County, Ohio.

The 1930 census for Boston, Massachusetts has Chas J Frey, 23, married at 21, an accountant for a public utility renting an apartment at 1160 Commonwealth Ave. for $50 per month. Julia is 22 and married at 20.

The 1940 census for Newton, Massachusetts has Charles J Frey, 33, graduated college, an accountant for the forestry industry. Julia is 31 and completed 1-year college. Their son Charles L is 2.

Julia Klingensmith Frey born 6 Mar 1908, died 29 Nov 1978 in Honolulu, Hawaii on a 50$^{th}$ anniversary trip. She is buried in Rose Hills Memorial Park, Whittier, California. Charles James Frey born 27 Aug 1906, died 15 Sep 1989 in Downey, California. He is buried with Julia.

### 2. Frank L Klingensmith and Julia E Myhrs

Frank L Klingensmith, 26, a bookkeeper, of Detroit, married Julia E Myhrs, 25, of Detroit on 17 Aug 1905 in Detroit, Michigan. G E Sharp, minister, officiated. Cora E Myhrs and John H Simpson were witnesses.

Frank was employed by Henry Ford in 1905 as a bookkeeper.

The 1910 census for Detroit, Michigan has Frank L Klingensmith, 30, married 4 years, a cashier for Ford Motor Company renting his home at 15 Gladstone Ave. Julia is 30 and had 1 child. Their son, Thomas, is 3.

Frank Klingensmith was in on the very beginning of the Ford Motor Company. The Model T was introduced in 1908. Production was moved to the Highland Park Plant in 1910 and the assembly line was introduced in 1913. Construction started on the River Rouge Complex in 1917 and the first truck was introduced just in time for WW1. The assembly line was developed to save time and costs. Frank Klingensmith was undoubtedly in the middle of calculating those costs and the changes needed to achieve cost reduction. His expertise may have been the reason he went from cashier to VP in 8 years. A time of opportunity if you had a good idea.

Detroit, Michigan, Dec. 21, 1916 – Beginning tomorrow the Ford Motor company will close its plant for seven days in order to relieve the railroad congestion here that carloads of food and fuel may be handled, it was announced today by Frank Klingensmith, vice-president. The suspension will mean a production loss of approximately 2,500 cars a day. Klingensmith said that the normal coal consumption of 13 cars daily will be curtailed to the amount needed to keep the plant above freezing temperature. Forty-two thousand men are made idle by the order, meaning a wage loss for the week of $1,400,000.

Frank Lewis Klingensmith, 39, born 18 May 1879, of RFD 3 Birmingham, Oakland, Michigan registered for WW1 on 12 Sep 1918. He is Vice President and Treasurer of Ford Motor Company, Highland Park, Wayne, Michigan. His nearest relative is Julia E Klingensmith. He is tall with a medium build, brown eyes and black hair.

Detroit, 14 Feb 1919, Fort Wayne News and Sentinel, Henry Ford is suing the Chicago Tribune for libel. The defense is saying Detroit is so dominated by Ford that they cannot get a fair trial. Frank Klingensmith gave most of the testimony. Ford had 51,000 employees and 12 firms supplied parts worth $26,500,000 in one year. The defense also made connection between various suppliers and Henry Ford's campaign for senator. They were supporting Ford, a Democrat, even though they had always voted Republican. Ford was a director of Big Dime Savings Bank and did much business there, the president of the bank said he supported Ford because of a 30 years' friendship not his large deposits. The article ended without a decision. They did change the venue as the trial continued in Mt. Clemens, Michigan.

The Reno Evening Gazette for 11 Jul 1919 has an article telling about Ford's reorganization. Edsel Ford is president of the company and sole partner along with his father Henry Ford and one other. The announcement was made by Frank L Klingensmith, vice-president and general manager of the company. Details of the stock sale and a loan are disclosed. The article also says the minimum wage for Ford Motor Company Employees will be raised to $7 a day.

The Daily Northwestern (Oshkosh, WI) 29 Jul 1919. A trial was being held in Mt Clemens, Michigan. Frank L Klingensmith was a rebuttal witness for Henry Ford. Henry Ford was suing the Chicago Daily Tribune for $1,000,000 on a charge of libel. Frank was being asked about Henry Ford. Ford was opposed to the war but was not opposed to the National Guard. The defense lawyer implied that was to protect Ford's Plant. Frank Klingensmith corrected previous testimony to read that Edsel Ford's salary remained at $10,000 until 1918 when he was made president of the company and it was raised to $73,000. Mr. Klingensmith was excused.

In another similar article, Frank said he tried to get Edsel's salary increased before he became president but Henry wouldn't do it.

Frank went on a trip by himself to Britain and Europe. He obtained his first passport for the trip. He traveled for the Ford Motor Company to promote export and trade. He left New York 6 Nov 1919 on the Carmania for England, Belgium, France, Sweden, Spain,

Portugal, Norway, Italy, Switzerland, and Denmark. Frank may not have gone to all these countries but his passport listed them so that he could visit. After his business was concluded, he sailed on the Mauretania from Southport, 18 Dec 1919 and arrived in Port of New York 25 Dec 1919. His passport application was signed by Edsel Ford and stated that the company had been in business 15 years and Frank Klingensmith had been employed by them 14 years which would mean he started with Ford in 1905.

By 1919, Henry Ford had bought out all his investors to make himself along with Edsel Ford and James Couzins, the millionaire Mayor of Detroit and former Ford Vice-President, the sole owners of Ford Motor. Frank's trip was an attempt to expand the overseas business. Ford opened assembly plants in England, France and Denmark in 1923. Ford opened plants in Germany and Austria in 1925.

A 19 May 1920 newspaper article by Associated Press is titled Detroit Factories Are Curtailing Operations. There is a shortage of raw materials. No factory is completely shut down but 30,000 to 40,000 men are out of work in Detroit. The Ford Motor Company has laid off 2,500 men, Vice President Frank Klingensmith said. He explained that this was not due to the results of the switchmen's strike but was done in the course of what he termed "a weeding out". Mr. Klingensmith denied that the company had cut the wages of its office forces 25 per cent, terming the report "ridiculous".

The 1920 census for Bloomfield, Oakland, Michigan has Frank L Klingensmith, 40, born in Michigan, father born in Germany, mother born in Ohio, Vice President for Ford Motor Company who owns his home on Lone Pine Road free and clear. Julia is 40, born in Michigan, father born in Norway and mother born in Michigan. Their children are Thomas,13, attended school; Charles, 9, attended school and Elizabeth, 5. Cora E Myhrs, sister-in-law, 44, is living with them. They also have Mary Smith, 47, a cook; Anna Sirka, 24, a maid and Gertrude Kaikkanen, 22, a waitress all living with them and working for a country home. There are two farms and two other families on this road. The next family has a Chauffer and laundress also working for a country home. Next is a family of 3 with the father working as a superintendent for a country home, a daughter is working as a book binder at a book factory. The next two families on Lone Pine are farmers on the home farm, one owns the farm and one is renting. It appears Frank bought a farm, built a large house, and has extra servants living in extra houses on a farm with limited farming activities remaining. The road just before Lone Pine Road is Cranbrook Road. Currently the NW corner of that intersection is Cranbrook Institute and Schools. Frank's house may have become part of that institute or is one of the large houses in the area. He was certainly coming up in the world!

Detroit Michigan 3 Jan 1921 – Frank L Klingensmith, vice-president and treasurer of the Ford Motor Company announced his resignation today because he is not in full accord with some of the business policies contemplated by the company. Klingensmith is the second Ford official to resign in the last week. Charles A Brownell advertising manager resigned last Friday. Iowa City Press Citizen and many other papers.

New York, 9 Mar 1921- The Dow Jones financial news service carried the following today: "Detroit – It is reported Ford Motor Company officials are conferring on what steps shall be taken toward refinancing and whether the plant shall be closed pending completion of these arrangements." Officials of the Ford Motor Company, Canada admitted they had heard a report that Henry Ford had sold his interest in the Canadian Company but that no actual transfer of stock had been made. The transaction is said to involve approximately $4,000,000 and with the sale go the rights to do business in all British possessions except England, Scotland and Wales.

"The formation of a new company is announced by Frank L Klingensmith, former vice president and general manager of the Ford Motor Company who will be president. The company is to be known as the Gray Motors Corporation. It is expected to get into production this summer or early fall."

E G Liebold, secretary to Henry Ford said today he had not heard anything about the report that Ford had sold or would sell his Canadian interests and that he had "absolutely nothing to say." Sandusky Star Journal

13 July 1921 Detroit, Mich.- A Holstein bull, a pedigree boar and a pedigreed rooster were prizes at stake in a "Knickers' tournament" played over the course of the Bloomfield Hills Golf Club yesterday. They were offered by Mayor James Couzins, Frank L Klingensmith and Clarence H Booth, respectively. Thirty members of the Detroit Club competed. Mr. Booth brought home the beef, Harry B. Mason, the bacon and the rooster went to Frederick Stockwell. (On the same page of the newspaper Babe Ruth is doing better than ever.)

Consolidated Press, New York 19 Oct 1922. Makers of medium and higher priced automobiles are not going to cut prices following the $50 reduction in the price of Ford cars. The Durant Star car is priced practically identical to Ford's car and will suffer the most from the reduction in price. The Gray Car sponsored by Frank L Klingensmith former Ford treasurer also is expected to be strongly affected. Other makers argue that with increased Ford production, "flivvers" will become so common that many present Ford owners will gladly pay the $50 to get a more distinctive car. A bigger concern is recent changes in process. Today it (Ford) is almost self-contained as the company makes parts from raw materials.

The River Rouge Plant was built from 1917 to 1928 and featured vertical integration (the entire process from raw materials to finished car were owned by Ford). Apparently, it was beginning to make a difference in 1922. On the same page is an article on building roads under the federal-aid highway system.

An advertisement for the Gray Motor Car appeared in the Davenport Democrat and Leader, 26 Nov. 1922, Davenport, Iowa. The advertisement says it was put on the market over a year ago and is now being distributed in Davenport.

3 Apr 1923 the following advertisement appeared in the Hammond, Indiana Times. Frank L Klingensmith is president of Gray Motor Corporation. He contributes ability in

large-scale organization, finance, and sales. It mentions his time with Ford helped him to put the Gray car before the public in the big way so good a car merited. Frank F Beall is Vice-President and General Manager. His experience is being in charge of production for the Packard Motor Company.

The Gray Car was put on the market a few months ago and is the lightest complete car

on the market. It gets 28 to 30 miles to a gallon of gas and takes hills easily. The factory is turning out 75 cars a day. It is also low cost. The company at the bottom of the ad is the local distributor.

Frank didn't take long to get his new company up and running.

29 Dec 1923 Detroit, Mich. An article on automobile prospects for 1924 was published. It is very optimistic and gives 10 reasons why. It predicts approaching the 5 million mark in cars manufactured. Ford will produce 55%, General Motors, Studebaker, Dodge Brothers, Willys Overland and Hudson Essex will make 30%, other companies will make the remainder. The new Gray group for 1924 is praised. Frank Klingensmith and Rex Glasson showed the new Gray which is stunning. It will be shown at the New York opening Saturday. "If you want an eyeful of grace, charm and balance in a low-priced automobile you will get 100% measure in the new closed job." The new touring car will sell for $630, the coupe at $735 and the sedan at $875. The company is unusually liberal in equipment. The gas tank has been increased to 10 gallons and moved to the rear of the frame and equipped with a gauge. The wheel base has been increased to 104 inches. The Gray motor corporation is now in production on the new group as well as the present line which will be continued. (It appears part of Frank's dispute with Henry Ford is expanding the offerings.)

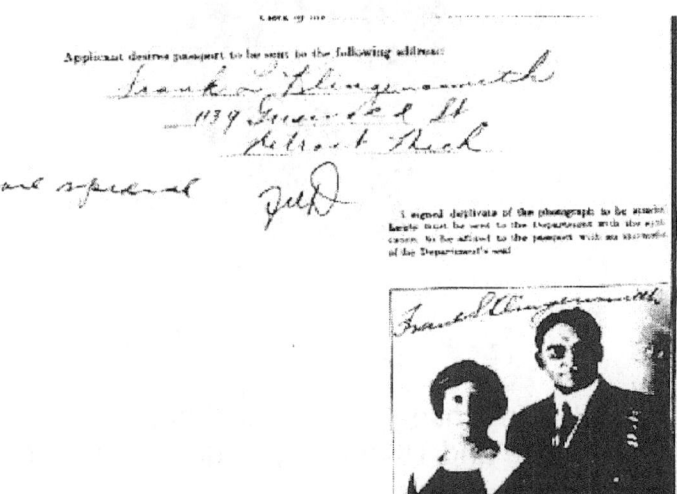

In 1924 Frank obtained another passport so that he could travel on business. He is President of Gray Motor Company. Frank applied for the passport on 20 Dec 1924 and wanted to leave on the first available steamer Jan 1925. At this time passports were for 1 trip only. Julia is on the same passport.

Frank and Julia sailed out of San Francisco on the Maui 7 Jan 1925 arriving in Honolulu on 13 Jan 1925, then traveling to Australia and New Zealand. After his business was completed, they sailed from Sidney, New South Wales, Australia on the Tahiti 26 Mar 1925 arriving at San Francisco 17 Apr 1925. They were living in Birmingham, Michigan at the time although the passport was sent to 1139 Griswold Street in Detroit. Frank must have had a plant or at least an office in Detroit.

A Ford Plant opened in Australia in 1925. Did Frank open a plant in competition and did Ford buy what Frank started? Gray Motor Car company did have the rights to manufacture in British possessions including Australia. All this maneuvering seems to be aimed at Henry Ford.

Detroit, 13 Jun 1925 – In an article about the future of the automobile trade, is the following paragraph: Most important in the news of the week in the capitol of motordom is the reorganization of the Gray Motor Company and the election of Earnest M Howe, widely known British transportation expert as president to succeed Frank L Klingensmith. The latter has resigned to go into another line of manufacturing.

Of special significance in the reorganization is the fact that the Gray Company becomes the sole manufacture in the United States for the Tilling-Stevens Gas Electric Motor bus. The move brings to Gray more than $1,000,000 in cash immediately available and means that Gray will go into motor bus production at once on a large scale. It goes on to say Gray cars will continue to be made as well as 3 sizes of buses including a double decker.

Frank then traveled to Europe returning on the Aquitania from Southampton 19 Sep, 1925 and arriving in New York 25 Sep 1925. His address is RFD No. 3 Birmingham, Mich.

This is a picture of Frank L Klingensmith probably taken for business purposes.

The Birmingham City Directory for 1926 has F L Klingensmith, businessman, Square Lake Road, Pontiac, R5. Also, in the listing are Julia and Thomas B, student, all with the same address.

On 18 Apr 1928 Julia Klingensmith, 49, and her son Charles, 17, left Southampton, England for New York on the Volendam arriving on 29 Apr 1928. Their address was Square Lake Road, Pontiac, Michigan. Square Lake Road is north of Lone Pine Road and Bloomfield. The boundary may have been changing at the time.

Frank L Klingensmith, 49, departed Southampton 5 Dec 1928 on the Berengaria and arrived in New York 11 Dec 1928. His address is 1139 Griswold Street, Detroit, Michigan. Eleanor Roosevelt was on the same ship.

The 1929 Pontiac, Michigan City Directory has Klingensmith, Frank L (Julia) home west Greenlawn Ave 1mile south of Square Lake Road.

The 1930 census for Bloomfield, Oakland, Michigan has Frank Klingensmith, 51, married at 25, President of American Pipe Company, owned his home on Square Lake Road worth $20,000 and a radio. Julia is 50, Their children are Thomas, 24, president of Klingensmith Laboratory Company; Charles, 18 and Elizabeth Ann, 15. The next listing is a butler in a private home but there is no indication it is the Klingensmith home.

The 1937 Birmingham, Michigan City Directory has Frank L Klingensmith (Julia) president-treasurer American Hume Concrete Pipe Company (Detroit) home east Orchard Ridge Road, 1mile south of W Long Lake Road (Bloomfield Hills).
Thomas B Klingensmith (Mary M Colegrove-Klingensmith Inc.) Tel 501, home 348 Greenwood, Tel 502.
Chas P Klingensmith, employed Ernst Kern Company (Detroit) home Frank L Klingensmith
Elizabeth A Klingensmith, student home Frank L Klingensmith

A Zanesville, Ohio newspaper article from 12 Mar 1938 refers to Frank Klingensmith president of the American Hume Concrete Pipe Co, Detroit. The article is about a court case involving possible bribes to Governor Davey of Ohio. One of the letters addressed to Lee Bradley as assistant governor of Ohio was from Frank Klingensmith of the American Hume Concrete Pipe company. Davey said he met Klingensmith in Detroit in June 1933 but denied there was any conversation about state business. Nothing more about Klingensmith but General Motors may have given a campaign contribution that led to business – "I don't remember". This is a politician's answer.

The 1940 Birmingham, Michigan City Directory has Frank L (Julia) president-treasurer American Hume Concrete Pipe Company (Detroit) home east Orchard Ridge Road 1mile south W Long Lake Road (Bloomfield Hills).
Charles P Klingensmith sales engineer Ernst Kern Company (Detroit) home Frank L Klingensmith
Elizabeth A Klingensmith assistant preparator Cranbrook Institute of Science (Bloomfield Hills) home Frank L Klingensmith.

Frank Lewis Klingensmith, 62, born 18 May 1879 in Pittsford, Michigan, registered for WW11 on 25 Apr 1942. He was living at 815 Southfield Road, Birmingham, Michigan and next of kin was Julia E Klingensmith. He worked for American Hume Concrete Pipe Company at 10228 Woodward Ave. Detroit, Michigan. He was 6' 0" weighed 190 with brown eyes, black or gray hair, and wore glasses.

The 1949 Birmingham, Michigan City Directory has Frank L Klingensmith (Julia) representative American Hume Pipe (Detroit) home 815 Southfield Road.

Frank Lewis Klingensmith died 28 Aug 1949 in Birmingham, Michigan at the age of 70. His obituary was in the New York Times:

### F L Klingensmith, Motor-Car Pioneer
### Successor to Senator Couzens as Ford Treasurer Dies at 70
### – joined Company in 1905
#### Special to the New York Times

Detroit. 28 Aug – Frank Lewis Klingensmith, automobile pioneer, died at the age of 70 today in his residence in suburban Birmingham after an illness of two weeks. He formerly was one of the top executives of the Ford Motor Company.

When he resigned from the firm in 1921, Mr. Klingensmith was vice president, general manager and co-director, with Henry and Edsel Ford. He had joined the company as a cashier in 1905.

In 1916, he succeeded the late United States Senator James Couzens as company treasurer. Since leaving the Ford company he had become president of the American Hume Concrete Pipe Company.

Born on a farm near Pittsford, Michigan, on 18 May. He came to Detroit in 1900 and obtained a job with the Detroit Safe Company at $8 a week.

Surviving are his widow, Julia; two sons, Thomas B of Royal Oak and Charles P, of Birmingham; a daughter, Mrs. Milo K. Winter Jr. of Providence, Rhode Island, and a sister Mrs. Elizabeth Southern of Pittsford.

A funeral service will be held at the Bell Funeral Home in Birmingham, at 3 P.M. on Wednesday. Burial will be in Greenwood Cemetery, Birmingham.

Julia Klingensmith born 6 Nov 1879, died 21 Feb 1976 in Avon, Michigan. Her last residence was 48009 Birmingham, Oakland, Michigan.

### 3. Thomas B. Klingensmith and Mary Margaret Emmons

Thomas B Klingensmith 27, a sales representative, of Bloomfield Hills married Mary Margaret Emmons, 23, of Grosse Pointe Farms on 14 June 1934 at the Presbyterian Church in Grosse Pointe Farms, Michigan. Edward H Pence officiated. Witnesses were Charles Marcotte and Frank Fitt. The bride's father was H H Emmons. The groom's parents were F L Klingensmith and Julia Myhrs.

The 1940 census for Birmingham, Michigan has Thomas Klingensmith, 34, graduated high school, a real estate salesman who owns his home at 339 Chesterfield worth $7000. Mary is 29 and graduated college. Their daughter, Marianne is 4.

The 1940 Birmingham, Michigan Directory has Thomas B Klingensmith (Mary M) real estate 339 N Chesterfield Rd home the same address.

Mary Margaret Klingensmith filed for divorce from Thomas B Klingensmith on 26 Feb 1942 cause was extreme and repeated cruelty. The divorce was granted on 1 Sep 1942 with Thomas paying support for a minor child. No information on custody but it was usually given to the mother.

Thomas Klingensmith served in WW11 from 12 Mar 1943 until 13 Nov 1945.

Thomas B Klingensmith born 7 Jun 1906, died 9 Aug 1976 in Royal Oak, Michigan.

Mary M Klingensmith born 13 Jan 1911 in Michigan, died 1 Apr 1968 in Riverside California. Probably the Mary Margaret Emmons who married Thomas.

### 3. Charles P. Klingensmith

Charles and his sister Elizabeth were living with their parents in 1940.

The 1954 Birmingham City Directory has Chas P Klingensmith, interior decorator J L Hudson (Detroit) residence 815 Southfield Road. Julia E (widow Frank L) home 815 Southfield Road. Thomas B residence 815 Southfield Road.

Chas P Klingensmith born 30 May 1910, died 28 Dec 1995 in Southfield, Michigan.

### 3. Elizabeth Klingensmith and Milo Kendall Winter

Elizabeth Ann Klingensmith, 26, married Milo Kendall Winter Jr. 27, a teacher at the Rhode Island School of Design, on 28 Dec 1940.

Elizabeth Klingensmith Winter, born 20 Oct 1914 in Detroit, Michigan, died Feb 1994. Her parents were Frank L Klingensmith and Julia Myhrs.

# Chapter 9

## The Early Carpenters

1. Jacob Carpenter (1739-1794)
   + unknown
     2. Jacob
     2. Peter (about 1761)
     2. Rhoda (about 1763)
     2. Philip Carpenter (1765-1836) Revolutionary War
      + Mary Rhodes (1772-1871)
         3. Daniel Carpenter (1791-before 1807)
         3. Asaph "Asa" Carpenter (1793-1874) War of 1812
         3. Jeremiah Carpenter (1796-1874)
         3. Rhoda Carpenter (1799-1883)
         3. Levi Carpenter (1799-1890) War of 1812
         3. Mary (Polly) Carpenter (1803-)
         3. Rebecca Carpenter (1805-before1844)
         3. Daniel Carpenter (1807-1893)
         **3. Orson (Orison, Orris) Carpenter (1809 or 1811-1899)**
         3. Cynthia C. Carpenter (1811-1887) 13 children
         3. Permelia Carpenter (1814-)

## 1. Jacob Carpenter

The earliest confirmed record of the Carpenters is that Philip Carpenter was born 29 Mar 1765 at Nine Partners, Dutchess County, New York, the son of Jacob Carpenter.[17]

We also know that Jacob, Peter, Philip, and Rhoda were Jacob's children.[17]

Jacob Carpenter was most likely born about 1739 in England, according to several family trees. If those family trees are correct, he died in Washington, New York in 1794. It is not certain if this is Washington County or Washington, the settlement in Dutchess County. Jacob Carpenter did not settle originally in Washington County which is farther north along the Hudson. Some Carpenters came from England to Long Island then moved to Dutchess County however most I found were later than Jacob Carpenter. There is no credible evidence as to the exact time or place of immigration of Jacob Carpenter, our ancestor.

The Finch Family Tree on Ancestry.com has Jacobs parents as John and Sarah Carpenter. Jacob was born about 1739 in Warminster, Wiltshire, England. He married Deborah Denton the daughter of Daniel Denton. Their children are listed as the same as our Jacob Carpenter with the additional information that Peter was born in 1761 and Rhoda in 1763. Other trees have Deborah Denton as his mother. I am not sure if this is our ancestor or the information is accurate. It might be worth researching further.

A search of the Dutchess County Library for Jacob Carpenter turned up only a reference to a Mrs. Jacob Carpenter working for the county in caring for the poor, a paid job hence the reference. This may very well have been our ancestor as it appears Jacob did not own land and therefore his wife may have worked outside the home for extra income.

From about 1680 to 1700 men who had influence enough with the provincial government, were able to get patent rights to all the vacant land along the Hudson River. Title to land came from the crown as either reward for service or as a sale. Dutchess County came from the old spelling of Dutchess Mary who became Queen Mary in 1685 upon her husband's accession to the English throne as King James II. The same King James authorized a "new translation" of the Bible. The King James Version of the Bible is still in use today. At that time land ownership was the key to personal and public success which made close ties to England imperative. One of the largest of these patents was for Nine Partners in Dutchess County granted 27 May 1697. All nine men involved in this transaction were in one way or another connected with the English or colonial government. The tract of land extended along the Hudson River from the Harmense and Sanders Patent (northern Poughkeepsie) to the Crum Elbow Creek, which flows into the river at what, is now Hyde Park. It was bounded in the East by Connecticut.[14]

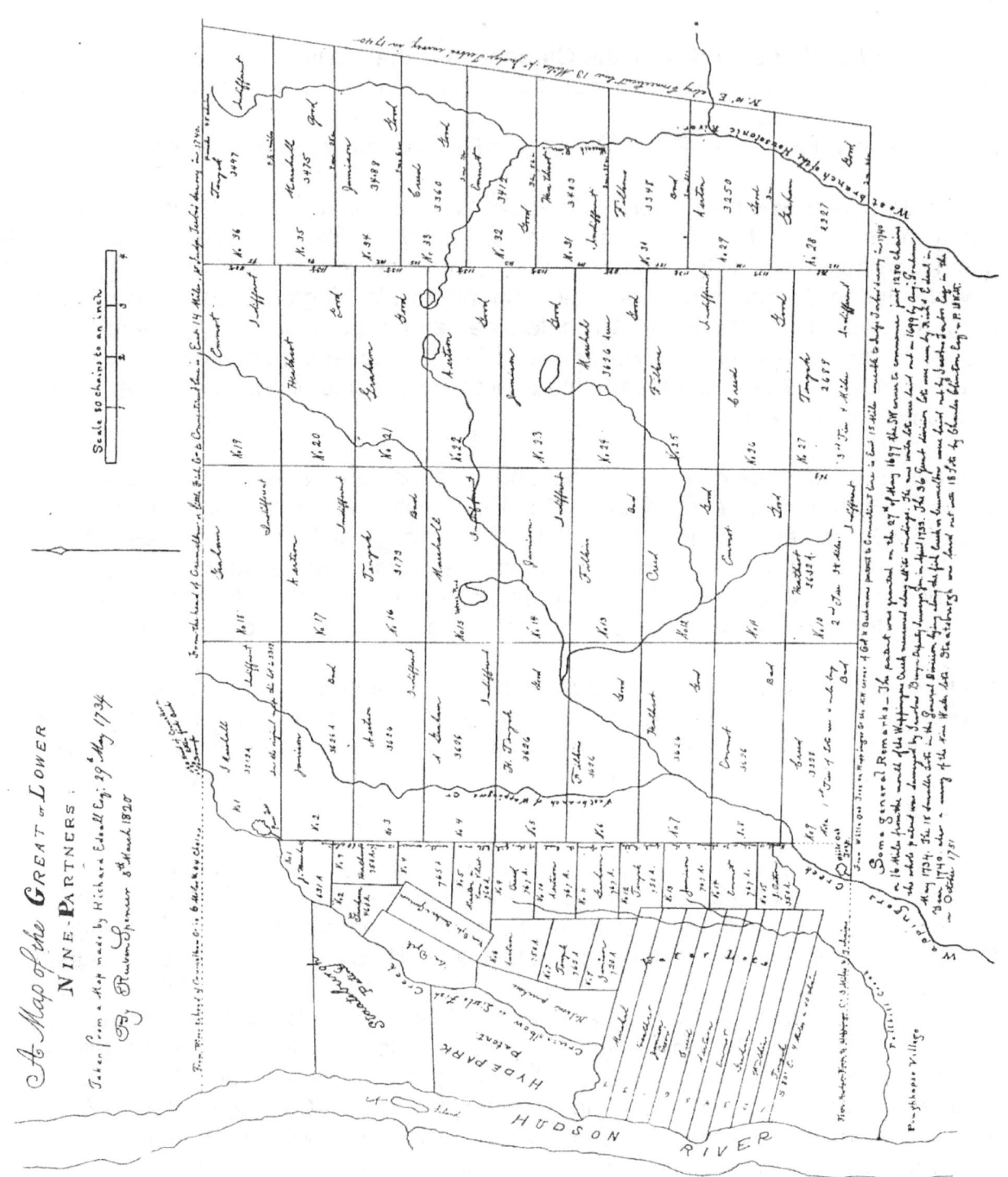

The Nine Partners were: Caleb Heathcote, Augustine Graham, James Emmott, John Arestin, Henry Filkin, Hendrick Ten Eyck, Jarvis Marshall, David Jamison and William Creed.[13]

The owners immediately divided the space along the Hudson into nine lots about ½ mile wide and extending inland about 4 miles. They were known as water lots and were the most valuable as the river was the easiest means of transportation. Nothing was done about the main body of the grant until after 1730 when David Jamison, the last survivor of the original patentees, called the owners of rights together and assessed them for money to pay for a survey to divide the main body of land into 36 equal shares, 4 shares went to each owner of a "water lot". The land was surveyed in 1734 by Richard Edsall. The Great Nine Partners Patent was issued 27 May 1697, but it was not until 4 Nov 1737 that a satisfactory deed was granted by the Indian owners of these lands. At that time, it was necessary to determine a correct boundary line between their lands and adjoining patents. By 1740 the differences were adjusted and agreements made on all the boundaries.[13,14]   Several of the original owners had land on Long Island, so it is entirely possible Carpenters may have been working land belonging to one of the owners and then were persuaded to move to Nine Partners to work other lands owned by the same person.

Henry Filkin held the 2nd water lot but lived on Long Island. After the patent was surveyed and boundaries established about 1740, three of Filkin's sons and a daughter came to live on their father's land in Dutchess County.[14] If you look closely at the above map, you will find four areas labeled Filkin.  This general area is where we first find Jacob Carpenter.

Nine Partners land was leased (rented) to homesteaders to build communities. It is very probable Jacob Carpenter leased land in Washington (as shown in the following map). The land was not owned by the farmers therefore there is no record of who lived on the land. When Washington County (farther north in New York State) opened up Jacob may have moved there to work his own land. There was an anti-rent resistance against wealthy land owners about 1766 which may have led to a desire to move. New York contained more Tories, people loyal to the crown, than any other colony. This may have been another reason to move as the Tories tended to be the wealthy land owners. The war didn't come to this area in part because they raised and sold food to the armies, or at least the land owners did, the farmers probably did not get a fair share of the profits.[14]

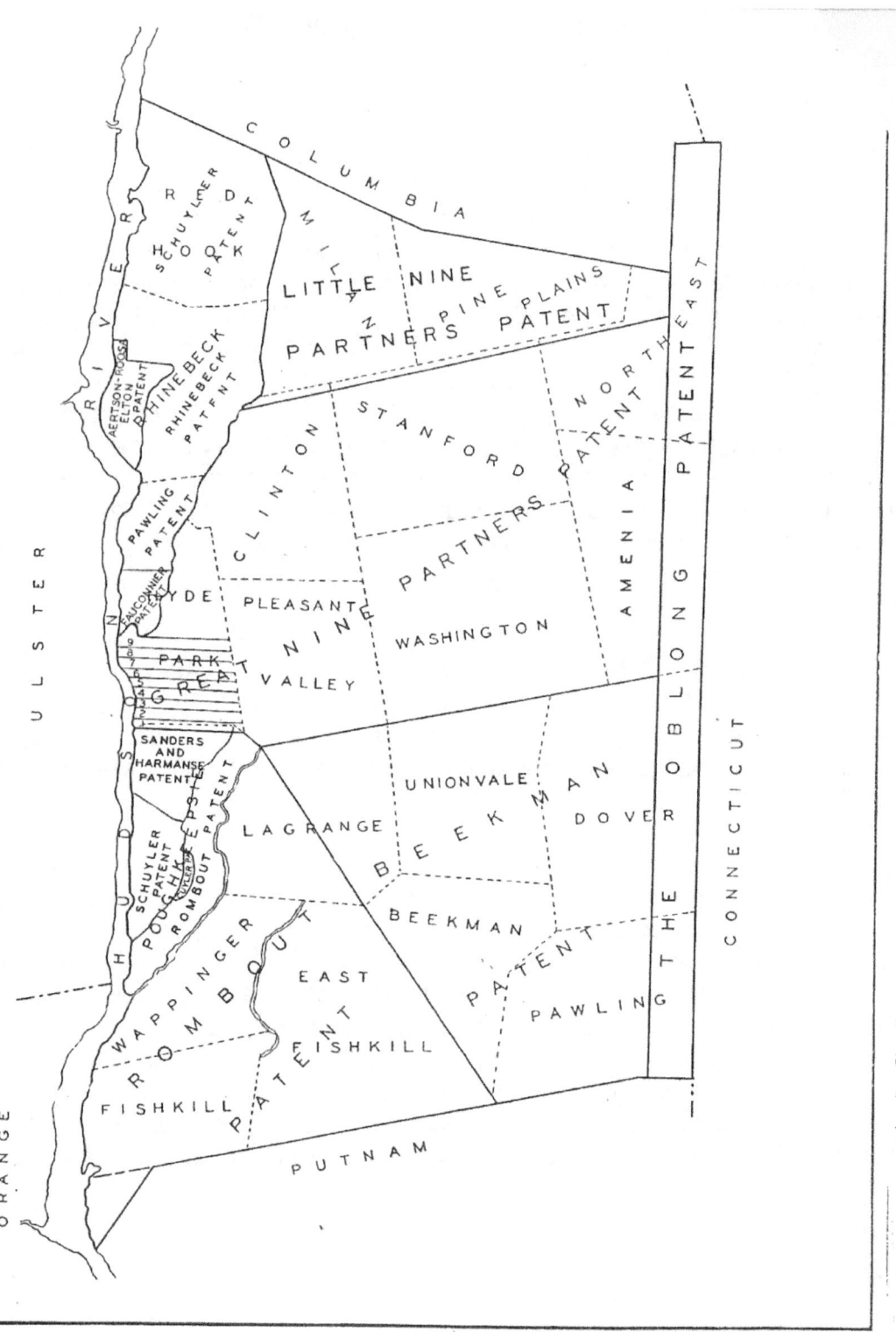

*Map of Dutchess County*

*Superimposed upon the townships of 1939 this map shows the patents for land that were issued in the seventeenth and eighteenth centuries.*

The map of the county with the towns was drawn by Emmett K. Hosier. The patents for land were superimposed by Mr. Hosier in accordance with information supplied by J. Wilson Poucher, M. D., George S. Van Vliet and Helen Wilkinson Reynolds.

The central portion of the above map is the Great Nine Partners Patent. The area of Nine Partners Patent labeled Washington is most likely where Jacob lived and probably died. This is often confused with Washington County which is much farther north along the Hudson. Jacob's son Philip was in Washington County by 1782. Philip was not a Tory but supported the revolution.

## 2. Phillip Carpenter and Mary Rhodes

Jacob's son, Phillip, may have moved to Washington County on his own. While residing in Salem, Washington County, New York. Philip enlisted 31 May 1782 to serve in the Revolutionary War. He served as a private in Captains Job Wright's and Cannon's companies, Colonel Marinus Willet's New York Regiment and was stationed at Fort Plain. Phillip was not in a battle while at Fort Plain. However, he broke his leg while at Fort Plain and was carried to the hospital in Albany. He was discharged from the hospital 1 Jan 1784. After the revolution, he lived in Hebron, Fort Ann, and Granville, New York. Philip married Mary Rhodes 1 Jan 1790 in Granville, New York. They were married in her father's house but his name is not given in the war records.[17]

In a deposition dated 3 Oct 1838, Nathan Rhodes of Dresden, testified that he was present when his sister Mary Rhodes married Phillip Carpenter on 1 Jan 1790, she then being 17 or 18 years of age.[17]

The above deposition was given to secure Phillip's Revolutionary War Pension for Mary. There are no records from 1790 or before in Washington County, New York.

Fort Plain was built in 1776 and became an important Revolutionary Fort in the center of the Mohawk Valley. Farmers in the area brought logs for the stockade, barracks, and blockhouses and helped build them. The fort was an irregular quadrangle about 250 by 375 feet with two small blockhouses on the southeastern and northwestern corners. The stockade also enclosed a large blockhouse, from an earlier fortification, and two barracks, one on the eastern and one on the western end. An octagonal blockhouse was built in 1780-81 and was located 400 feet northwest of the fort.[19] Actually, the blockhouse was of the common square variety as shown by excavations in 1960.[21]

The fort was on top of a hill so that it had a good view of the Mohawk Valley and all the area around. It was originally built as a refuge for settlers from the Indians. In the early part of the Revolutionary War, the military modified Fort Plain and additional buildings were erected in the manner described in the following illustration. Towers were erected at "b", a block house at "a", and housing at "c".

The following is a drawing of the fort

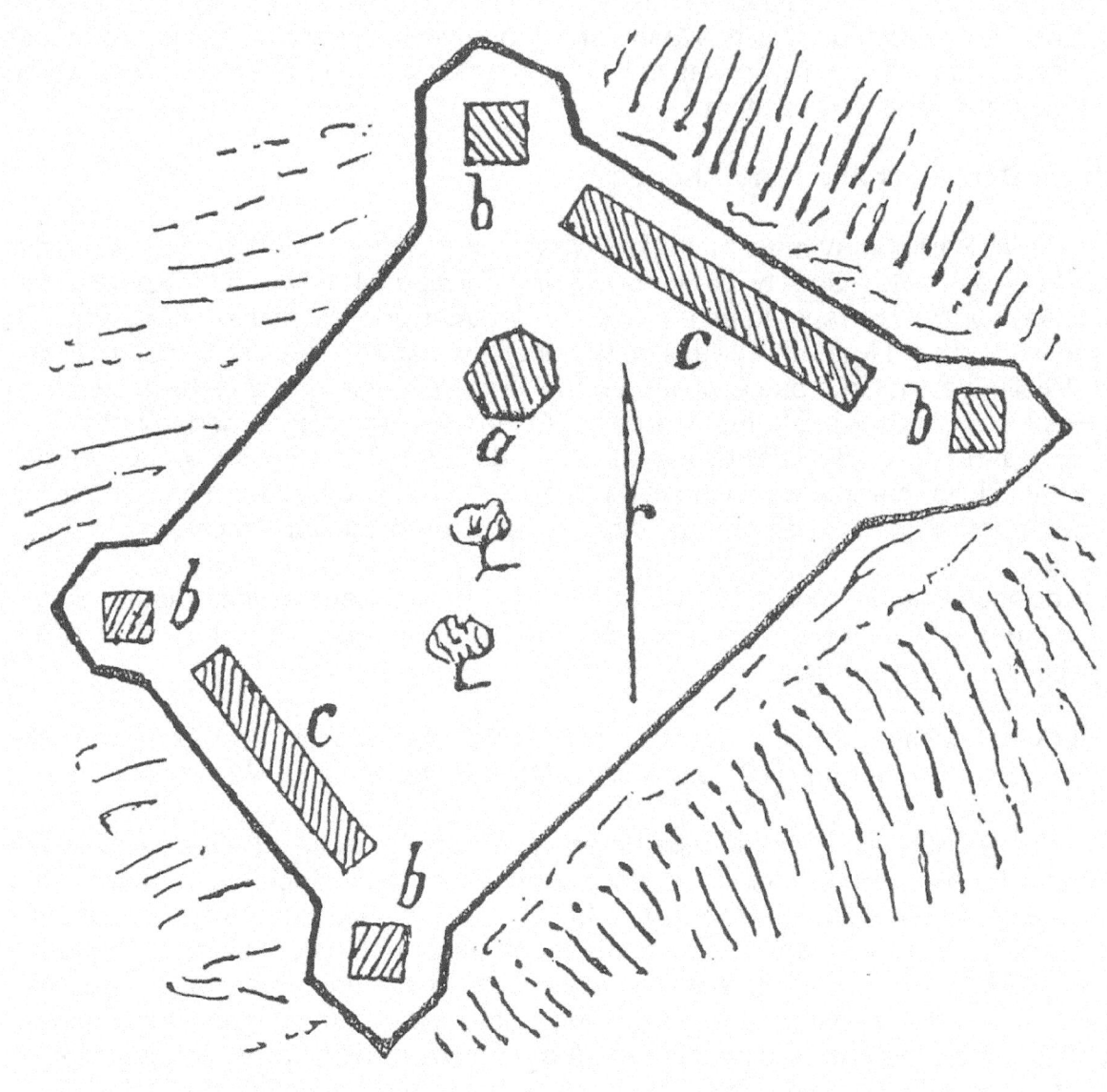

Lossing's Plan of Fort Plain, 1848. In 1848, Benson J. Lossing, famous American historian and historical artist visited the site of Fort Plain, with William Lipe, then an old man who knew the fort and its plan. Lossing went over the ground with Mr. Lipe and plotted the fort as above. – From Lossing's *Pictorial field Book of the Revolution.*

Lossing's Plan of Fort Plain, 1848
In 1848 Benson J Lossing, famous American historian and historical artist visited the site of Fort Plain, with William Lipe, then an old man, who knew the fort and it's plan. Lossing went over the ground with Mr. Lipe and plotted the fort as above.
From Lossing's "Pictorial Field Book of the Revolution."[19]

All able-bodied men in Tryon County, New York, were in the militia and commanded by General Nicholas Herkimer. In the summer of 1777, they battled a British-Tory-Indian-Hessian force under a Colonel Ledger. Herkimer's men were ambushed by the British. After the initial fighting, many were dead so the Americans stood behind trees, two behind each tree, alternating in loading and firing their muskets. This proved to be a very good means of defense as they could not be rushed while they were reloading. Eventually Colonel Willett came into the fight and destroyed the enemy's camp. In the end the Americans won the battle but General Herkimer was fatally wounded and Colonel Marinus Willet replaced him. Colonel Willet was made commander of all of the New York posts from Poughkeepsie north, including those of the Mohawk Valley and of all of the New York militia and levies in the same area. He had his headquarters at Fort Plain from 1781 until after the war. The battle of Johnstown, on 25 Oct 1781, was the last major battle in the area.[19]

Philip Carpenter enlisted 31 May 1782. Most of his service was spent at the fort so his broken leg was likely from an accident rather than military action. In February 1783, Colonel Willett did take a detachment of 500 men including the Fort Plain Garrison, on General Washington's orders, in an attempt to capture Fort Oswego which was held by the British. The Americans suffered terrible hardships on this winter journey and were unable to take the fort.[19] Philip Carpenter may have been on this expedition. He is listed as serving under Captain James Cannon at Fort Plain and would have been there at the time. Philip is also listed as serving under Capt. Job Wright. Captain Wright was known for ordering up to 150 lashes for various offences.[21]

In February 1783, Colonel Willett issued the following order: Every Saturday afternoon at 4 o'clock the men are to be paraded with their knapsacks & all their clothing then the officers commanding companies are not only to see that their men have all their clothing but that they are clean, whole, in good condition & neatly put up in their knapsacks. If a soldier loses a blanket, coat, boot, breeches, overalls, shirt or hat he is not only to be obliged to explain the articles lost but lose rations and pay and to receive thirty-nine lashes on his bare back. If stockings, shoes, or any lesser articles, they are to be replaced in like manner & he is to receive twenty lashes unless it shall be made to appear that the loss could not have been prevented. If it shall appear that he has disposed of either of the first mentioned articles, the corporal punishment shall be one hundred lashes & for either of the last-mentioned articles fifty lashes.[21] Serving in the military during the Revolution was not necessarily easy.

A list of enlisted men (according to the certificates of the muster-masters) who served either on the lines or the levies, having been hired by the several classes under the Land Bounty Rights at Fort Plain includes Prosper Carpenter and William Carpenter as well as Phillip Carpenter.[19] The list had to do with paying the men. It is not known if the other Carpenters are relatives.

A messenger arrived at Fort Plain on 17 Apr 1783 announcing the cessation of hostilities. The war was over. On the 4th of July 1783, a great Fourth of July celebration was held at Fort Plain. In celebration of the anniversary of our independence, each man was given a gill of rum.[20] Philip Carpenter was certainly there to get his ration of rum on the 4$^{th}$ of July as well as when George Washington arrived later in the month.

General Washington visited the fort 28 Jul (or 31) 1783 on a journey through the Mohawk Valley. General Washington was making a tour of forts and military installations to make sure the area was securely in American hands and defended against the British. He wanted to make arrangements for keeping the peace and chose Fort Herkimer as a supply post on the Mohawk River for westward expansion. Although Fort Plain was maintained for some time, it dwindled in importance after the war was over.[19,20]

Wounded men were usually cared for at the fort hospital if they were expected to recover. The fact that Philip was taken to Albany would indicate the war was over. He probably broke the leg in the late summer or early fall of 1783, was taken to Albany, and discharged in January 1784.[17,19]

The following picture is from George Washington's visit to Fort Plain.

After he was discharged, Phillip went back to Washington County. Where he married Mary Rhodes in 1790.

The page following the picture has a little background on the Rhodes family.

Washington at Fort Plain, July 31, 1783 – Drawing by Nelson Greene
(Topic 2: Fort Plain/ Fort Rensselaer)

The Rhodes family appears to goes back much farther than the Carpenters but the links are fuzzy. I have found little in actual records. Family Trees on Ancestry seem to differ considerably. The following is reasonably accurate and documented by Nathan Case's will.

1. Nathan Case
    2. Lucy Case (1728-1799)
    + Asa Rhodes (1724-1749)
        3. Dr. Nathan Rhodes (1) (1742-1859)
        + Phebe Foster (1750-1819)
            4. Dr. Nathan Rhodes (2) (1764-1861)
            + Mary
            + Anna Brown
            4. **Mary Rhodes (1772-1871)**
            **+ Philip Carpenter (1765-1836)**
            4. Rhoda Rhodes (1774-1855)
            + Thomas Wilson
            4. Rebecca Rhodes (1776-1858)
            + Nathan Parish (1774-1834)
                5. Nathan Parish Jr. (1797-1890)
                + Mary (Polly) Carpenter (1803-) Phillip & Mary's daughter
                5. Sanford Parish (1799-1864)
                + Rhoda Carpenter (1799-1883) Phillip & Mary's daughter
            4. Phebe Rhodes (1778-1844)
            + Jonathan Hayes (1756-1814) Revolutionary War, War of 1812
            4. Rachel Rhodes (1780-)
            + Mr. Wall
            4. Simeon Rhodes (1782-1844)
            4. Martha Rhodes (1784-)
            4. Eunice Rhodes (1786-)
            + Mr. Hayes

Nathan Rhodes (1) was the son of Asa Rhodes and Lucy Case. Nathan married Phebe and they had at least 6 children. They may have lived in Columbia County at one time.

Their oldest son Nathan Rhodes (2) was born 8 Dec 1764. He was a doctor in Dresden, Washington County, New York and lived most of his life there. He married Mary and second Anna Brown. Nathan's testimony was instrumental in Mary Rhodes Carpenter getting a Revolutionary War Pension. This is his picture.

Mary Rhodes was born on 4 Apr 1772, or possibly, 1769, in

Dr. Nathan Rhodes

Dutchess County, New York and married Philip Carpenter. Rhoda Rhodes married Thomas Wilson.

Rebecca Rhodes was born 14 Oct 1776 in Dutchess County, New York. She married Nathan Parish (1) and they had at least 2 sons. Nathan Parish Jr. (2) married Mary Polly Carpenter and Sanford Parish married Rhoda Carpenter. Both girls were daughters of Mary Rhodes Carpenter so the couples were first cousins.

Phebe Rhodes married Jonathan Hayes. Rachel Rhodes married a Mr. Wall. Simeon Rhodes was born in 1782, Martha Rhodes in 1784, and Eunice Rhodes in 1786, she married a Mr. Hayes.[16]

Philip and Mary Carpenter's first child was Daniel born in 1791 in Granville and died young (before 1807). Their other children were Asaph, also known as Asa born in 1793 in Granville; Jeremiah, born in 1796 in Granville; Rhoda, born in 1799 in Granville; Levi, born 10 Dec 1799 in Plattsburg, Clinton, New York; Mary (Polly), born in 1803; Rebecca, born in 1805; Daniel born 20 Sept 1807; Orson, born about 1809, Cynthia born in 1811 in Plattsburg, New York and Permelia, born in 1814.[16] Although Rhoda and Levi were both born in 1799 they are probably not twins but Rhoda was born early in the year and Levi late in the year. Mary was a very healthy woman to have so many children (11) over a period of 23 years.

Philip and Mary also lived in Martinsburg before moving to Brownville, Jefferson, New York about 1812. They were living in Brownville in 1813. Census records give the birth place of the older children as Washington County. Records for Cynthia and Permelia say Plattsburg, Clinton, New York.[16]

The Carpenters settled near Pillar Point in Brownville Township. Pillar Point is between Chaumont and Black Bays and owes its name to the peculiar manner in which the waters of Lake Ontario have worn grottos in the cliffs with intervening masses supporting the rock above.

The picture to the right shows the pillars.

The shores of this point have afforded important seine fisheries. A small village locally named Brooklyn, opposite Sacket's Harbor, is the post office of Pillar Point. It had a Methodist Church organized in 1836, and a small collection of shops and dwellings. The point has been somewhat important for its shipbuilding. Brownville was elected (removed) from Leyden 1 Apr 1802, embracing all north of Black River from a line running from the Northwest corner of Champion, North 45 E to the Southwesterly bounds of the County of St. Lawrence.[15]

Philip was allowed a Revolutionary War pension on his application executed December 6, 1832 while he was living in Brownsville, New York.

Philip Carpenter born 29 Mar 1765, died 13 Nov 1836.

This is his grave stone in Stone Cemetery, Pillar Point, New York.

There is a mistake on Phillip's marker or records as his marker shows he died 30 Nov 1836 and his Revolutionary War records give his death date as 13 Nov 1836.[17]

Mary Carpenter, the soldier's widow, married Jacob Brizee (or Bersie, Bersil, Berzil) about 1841. He died 26 Dec 1860 in Jefferson County, New York. In 1869 Mary was still living in Brownville, New York and stated that she was one hundred and seven years old. In 1871, her post office address was Watertown, New York. Mary Bersil, the name under which she was last pensioned, former widow of Philip Carpenter, certificate 6463, issued 27 May 1869, rate $166.66 per annum, commenced 20 Sept 1865, Act 2 Feb 1848, New York agency.[17]

Mary was allowed pension on her application executed September 15, 1838. She was living in Brownville and was aged 65 years. She was allowed bounty land in full satisfaction for the service of her husband, Philip Carpenter. Their children are referred to in the application. The following are the only names stated: Asaph, born in Dec 1793, Jeremiah, born 7 Feb 1796, and Levi, who was fifty-two years old in 1861.[17] They were her three oldest living sons.

The following is from the original hand-written records. The () indicates it could not be read.

Revolutionary Widows case
Office of E North,
Attorney at Law and U S Claim Agent
Watertown, New York 18 May 1871

Respectfully forwarded to the ()-Pensions with request that this case be made "Special" on grounds that this pensioner is about <u>112</u> years of age & wishes claim is soon settled. Will never need it.
Very Respectfully
E North
Atty-

The stone reads: Mary, relict of Phillip Carpenter, died June 22, 1871 age 112 y 2m 22days. Mary Rhodes Carpenter is buried in Stone Cemetery, Pillar Point, Jefferson, New York.

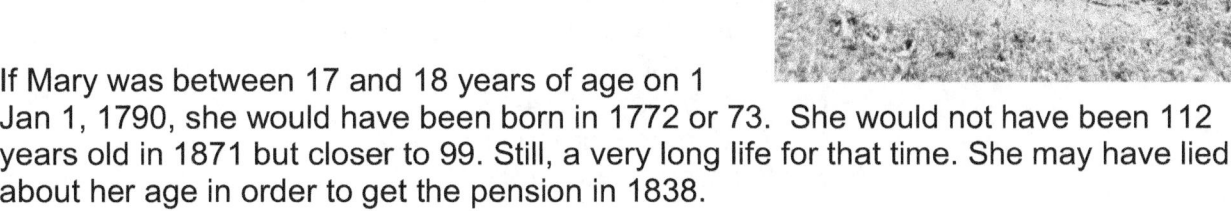

If Mary was between 17 and 18 years of age on 1 Jan 1, 1790, she would have been born in 1772 or 73. She would not have been 112 years old in 1871 but closer to 99. Still, a very long life for that time. She may have lied about her age in order to get the pension in 1838.

# Chapter 10

## Phillip and Mary Rhodes Carpenter

It is difficult to keep track of Phillip and Rhoda's 11 children. I have added a number indicating their order of birth after the 2 for Phillip's children. I hope this helps.

1. Philip Carpenter (1765-1836) Revolutionary War
 + Mary Rhodes (1772-1871)
     2.1 Daniel Carpenter (1791-1807)
     2.2 Asaph "Asa" Carpenter (1793-1874) War of 1812
     + Phoebe McGregory (1795-1842)
         3. James Asa Carpenter (1832-1915)
         + Dorcas Bennet (1834-1899)
             4. Franklin "Frank" Carpenter (1856-1929)
             + Harriett Cronk (1860-1953)
                 5. Lena May Carpenter (1878-1964) WW1
                 5. Roy Earnest Carpenter (1883-1952)
                 + Bertha L (1881-)
                 + Mertie Whitney (1894-1994)
                     6. Clinton Carpenter (1920-)
                 5. Scott T Carpenter (1891-1974)
                 + Clara Marie Stubberurd (1888-1965)
                     6. Gertrude Carpenter (1915-)
                     6. Ellen Jane Carpenter (1929-)
                 5. Leah Carpenter (1893-1961)
                 + William John Owen Phillips (1893-1964)
                     6. Clarence Phillips (1921-)
                     6. June Phillips (1923-)
                     + Donald Griffin (1917-)
             4. Sarah C Carpenter (1858-1878)
             4. Ida A Carpenter (1860-1930)
             + Bernard Schlough (1854-1934)
                 5. Flossie D Schlough (1886-)
                 5. Edna Mae Schlough (1897-1938)
                 + Ross D Flumo (1886-1938)
                     6. Natalie M Flumo (1922-)
                     6. Gladys K Flumo (1924-)
                     6. Arlene Flumo (1937-)
                 5. Nina D P Schlough (1899-1907)
                 5. Claudius B Schlough (1902-1903)
             4. James Martin Carpenter (1863-1931)
             + Sabrina Schimel (1858-1944)
             4. Delilah Carpenter (1867-1902)
             4. Clarence E Carpenter (1869-1870)

    4. Edwin Carpenter (1870-after 1880)
    4. Fredrick Carpenter (1871-1871)
    4. Betha M. Carpenter (1875-1875)
   3. Cordelia Carpenter (1839-1870)
 + Sophia Bennett (1820-1880)
   3. Elposa Carpenter (1853-)
2.3. Jeremiah Carpenter (1796-1874)
+ Mary Polly Belcher (1808-1829)
   3. Louisa Carpenter (1828-1867)
+ Mariah Weller (1808-1840)
   3. Priscilla Carpenter (1830-after 1870)
   3. Maria Carpenter (1832-)
   3. Jeremiah Carpenter (1833-1912)
    + Elizabeth M Underwood (1830-1911)
     4. Ella Louise Carpenter (1856-1899)
      + Willett H Vary (1854-1920)
       5. Earnest W Vary (1878-1962)
        + Mable Blanche McAdam (1887-1969)
         6. Earnest W Vary Jr (1915-1990) WW11
       5. Gertrude E Vary (1880-1957)
        + Charles Leigh Beecher (1881-1969)
         6. Hazel E Beecher (1904-1963)
          + Leonard Ambros Pfister (1901-)
           7. Beverly Pfister (1927-)
           7. Shirley Pfister (1929-)
           7. Natalie Pfister (1932-)
           7. Kenneth Pfister (1935-)
           7. Norma Jean Pfister (1937-)
         6. Robert W Beecher (1922-)
       5. Charles J Vary (1884-1976)
        + Florence Beecher (1888-1913)
         6. Doris L Vary (1907-1950)
          + William F John (1887-1958) WW1
           7. John L John (1933-)
           7. David W John (1935-)
           7. Harold A John (1939-)
         6. Ward C Vary (1911-1912)
        + Mary E Webb (1892-)
         6. Hugh Vary (1925-)
       5. Elizabeth S Vary (1892-)
        + John E Rienbeck (1878-1952)
         6. J Wesley Rienbeck (1911-1927) unknown mother
         6. Donald B Rienbeck (1918-)
         6. Ella L Rienbeck (1919-)
         6. Fredrick J Rienbeck (1922-)

      6. Kenneth H Rienbeck (1922-)
      6. Mary E Rienbeck (1926-)
     5. Willett H Vary (1899-1958) WW1
     + Muriel Margaret Huff (1898-)
      6. June E Vary (1927-)
      + Harry Hill (-)
   4. Watson F Carpenter (1862-1931)
   + Laura M McNitt (1867-1946)
     5. Bertha Laura Carpenter (1891-1946)
     + Earl Mason Gardner (1892-1963) WW1
      6. Barbara Gardner (1921-)
      6. Richard Gardner (1927-)
      6. Sally Gardner (1928-)
     5. Gladys Elizabeth Carpenter (1899-1959)
     + Philo Davis Clark (1901-1978)
      6. Patricia C Clark (1927-)
      6.Edward P Clark (1932-)
     5. Robert Watson Carpenter (1910-1985)
     + Muriel W Corbett (1912-2002)
      6. Judith Carpenter (1938-)
   4. Frank J Carpenter (1866-1938)
   + Mary A Brown (1866-1939)
     5. Harold J Carpenter (1900-)
     + Hattie Wilhelmina Vosburgh (1892-1976)
      6. Dorla Carpenter (1928-)
 3. Sylvester A Carpenter (1835-1919)
 + Carrie L Larkin (1837-1918)
   4. Nora Carpenter (1861-1913)
   + George Crittenton (1856-1932)
     5. Cora Stone (1888-)
     5. Emmitt C Crittenton (1893-1952) WW1
     5. Irma C Crittenton (1900-1990)
     + Harry V Liddy (1895-1967) WW1
      6. Donald G Liddy (1929-)
      6. Lorene J Liddy (1933-)
   4. Artie Carpenter (1871-1873)
 3. Adeline Carpenter (1838-1916)
 + James Ackerman (1836-1883)
   4. Adubelle "Addie" B Ackerman (1859-1928)
   + David S Baker (1847-1920)
     5. James E Baker (1875-1934)
     + Ruth C Leonard (1881-1960)
      6. Belle Ardis Baker (1901-1969)
      + Albert Walter Ayles (1903-1974)
       7. Leonard J Ayles (1925-)

                7. Hartwell W Ayles (1927-)
            6. Leonard D Baker (1907-1959)
            + Lulu M Stevens (1906-)
                7. Alice A Baker (1932-)
                7. David L Baker (1937-)
        5. Eva M Baker (1884-1961)
        + Adelbert C McLane (1875-1949) Spanish American War
            6. Addie Pearl McLane (1905-1986)
            + Clarence Everett Harris (1901-1986)
            6. James Aldebert McLane (1907-1970)
            + Elva Elizabeth Starr (1902-1983)
                7. Richard McLane (1933-)
                7. Sally McLane (1938-)
        5. Pearle Belle Baker (1888-)
        + Sherman Anderson (1894-1968) WW1
            6. Kathleen Pearle Anderson (1921-)
            + William Robert Corwin (1920-)
    + George R Kellogg (1854-1922)
+ Sarah Wilbur (1813-1886)
2.4. Rhoda Carpenter (1799-1883)
+ Sanford Parish (1799-1864)
    3. Melina Parish (1833-)
    3. Ephraim Adolphus Parish (1834-1919)
    + Margaret Van Patten (1840-1881)
        4. Lucinda Parish (1862-1884)
        4. Franklin L Parish (1864-before 1893)
        4. Alvin V Parish (1865-1886)
        4. Russell W Parish (1868-1928)
        + Elizabeth H Whitcomb (1869-1930)
        4. Luna M Parish (1869-1884)
        4. Ada E Parish (1873-1954)
        + Morris S Petrie (1870-1930)
        + Thomas Shannon (1875-)
        4. Worth W Parish (1883-1945)
        + Edith Minerva Waters (1887-1909)
            5. Clifford Worth Parish (1907-1947)
            + Lena Margaret Burdick (1911-1988)
                6. Barbara Parish (1933-)
                6. Minerva Parish (1935-)
                6. Francis Parish (1936-)
                6. Eli Parish (1938-)
                6. Margaret Parish (1939-)
                6. Clifford Parish (1940-)
        + Minerva R Pelow (1884-)
    + Anna Davis (1860-1943)

    4. Frank Parish (1893-1948)
    4. McKinley Alvin Parish (1896-1963) WW1
    + Iva Etta Michael (1904-1984)
     5. Jean Parish (1932-)
     5.Beverly Parish (1936-)
    4. Dewey Parish (1899-1952)
2.5. Levi Carpenter (1799-1890) War of 1812
+ Eunice Ayer (1802-1900)
   3. Lovina Carpenter (1829-between 1850 and 1860)
   3. Lucy Carpenter (1831-1917)
   + Joseph T Waterman (1821-1908)
     4. Henry Edwin Waterman (1848-1935) Civil War
     + Anna Fike (1854-about 1886)
       5. Ray Roland Waterman (1873-1945)
       + Ella E McGladrey (1879-1954)
        6. Effie Waterman (1897-)
        + Thomas Brennan (1894-)
         7. Barbra Brennan (1918-)
        + Harry E Jones (1897-)
       5. Levi W Waterman (1875-1957) Spanish American War
       + Olive "Ollie" Coy (1880-1947)
        6. Lyle Waterman (1895-)
        6. Millicent Waterman (1901-1981)
        + Wardlaw Douglas (1891-1957)
        + Livingstone (-)
       5. Lafayette Theron Waterman (1876-1971)
       + Laverna Hinds (1880-)
       + Elizabeth Samuels (1884-)
        6. Theron E Waterman (1906-1976)
        + Gladys D Bietner (1907-)
         7. Betty Lou Waterman (1926-)
         7. Theron Orin Waterman (1927-)
         7. Sandra Jean Waterman (1936-)
       + Lily M Ward (1891-1970)
        6. Lafayette Waterman (1918-) WW11
        6. Bertha Waterman (1920-)
        6. Moses Waterman (1922-1938)
        6. Joseph Waterman (1924-)
        6. Orlyn Waterman (1926-)
        6. Dolores Waterman (1929-)
       5. Moses Eugene Waterman (1877-1971)
        + Christie Oleva Rogers (1886-1966)
       5. Lulu Waterman (1881-1907)
     + Anna Sarah Rossiter (1850-1932)
       5. Nicolas Waterman (1888- between 1900 and 1910)

                5. Leslie Leonard Waterman (1889-1962)
                + Nellie Coon (1896-1970)
        4. Celia Eunice Waterman (1855-1938)
        + Israel Clark (1836 or 1838-1915) Civil War
                5. Allen Clark (1875-before 1900)
                5. Lilli Clark (1881-)
                + John McGhan (1880-)
                        6. Kathleen McGahn (1913-)
                        + Othell Hoffman
                + Harry J Marshall (1888-1971)
3. Mary Carpenter (1832-after 1910)
+ James Joseph Breeze (1826-1893)
        4. Edwin L Breeze (1855-1930)
        + Lamyra R Shattuck (1867-1919)
                5. Rosetta Breeze (1893-1935)
                + Edmund Wilson (1888-1966)
                        6. Gladys Leata Wilson (1908-1972)
                        + Leo Harold Card (1904-1984)
                                7. Leslie Card (1928-)
                                7. Wesley D Card (1929-)
                                7. Everett Card (1930-)
                                7. Leona Card (1934-)
                        6. Eva Jennettie Wilson (1911-)
                        + Francis Nevins Meyers (1907-)
                                7. Irene D Meyers (1929-)
                                7. Herbert Meyers (1933-)
                                7. Mary Meyers (1938-)
                        6. Herbert J Wilson (1912-1990)
                        + Ruth Lenard (1914-1968)
                                7. Eva Wilson (1936-1960)
                                7. Albert Wilson (1939-)
                        6. Ada M Wilson (1919-2001)
                        + Roland Green (1918-)
                5. Frank Breeze (1895-1980)
                + Florence Rita Hickox (1897-1969)
                        6. William Breeze (1918-1968) WW11
                        6. Edwin A Breeze (1923-)
                5. William R Breeze (1897-1970)
                + Eliza L Perigo (1897-)
                        6. Robert E Breeze (1926-)
                5. Nellie M Breeze (1904-1937)
                + Elon Brown Shattuck (1894-1937)
                        6. Charles Shattuck (1926-)
                        6. Fedrick Shattuck ((1929-)
                        6. Frances E Shattuck (1931-)

            6. Robert D Shattuck (1934-)
            6. Richard E Shattuck (1936-)
    4. Susan Breeze (1864-between 1885 and 1895)
     + Frederick Johnson (1859-)
        5. Julia Johnson (1880-1906)
         + Peter Ure (1880-1957)
            6. Howard Floyd Ure (1902-1980)
             + Loretta Inez Bowman (1906- 1988)
            6. Edith Ure (1903-1993)
             + Roy E Johnson (1891-1958)
                7. Mildred P Johnson (1923-)
                7. Charles H Johnson (1925-)
                7. Eleanor Johnson (1934-)
                7. Norma Johnson (1936-)
                7. Gerald Johnson (1938-)
                7. Geraldine Johnson (1938-)
            6. Harold V Ure (1905-1987)
             + Alice M Lumley (1910-1999)
                7. Janice M Ure (1928-1976)
                7. Vernon Ure (1933-)
                7. Lynn Ure (1939-)
        5. Chauncey Johnson (1882-1963)
         + Maude White (1887-1958)
            6. Roy V Johnson (1904-)
             + Gladys M Woodard (1909-)
                7. Doris Johnson (1926-)
                7. Roland Johnson (1927-)
                7. James Johnson (1929-)
                7. Richard Johnson (1931-)
                7. Joan Johnson (1933-)
                7. Donald Johnson (1934-)
                7. Ugene Johnson (1934-)
                7. Elizabeth Johnson (1938-)
            6. Clyde Johnson (1905-1982)
             + Rachel Pete (1914-)
                7. Nolan Johnson (1939-)
                7. Galen Johnson (1940-)
            6. Carl Johnson (1907-)
             + Marion Gamble (1913-)
                7. Carol Johnson (1935-)
                7. Linda Johnson (1940-)
            6. Grace Anna Johnson (1909-)
             + Milton Keech (1902-)
                7. Mary Keech (1936-)
            6. Clifford Johnson (1912-1974)

                + Jessie Brodie (1905-)
                    7. Nancy Jane Johnson (1936-)
            6. Florence M Johnson (1913-1956)
            + Joseph Peluso (1904-)
            6. Francis Johnson (1916-1982) WW11
            6. Kenneth Johnson (1919-)
            + Maude (1919-)
                7. Patricia Johnson (1940-)
        5. Maude Elizabeth Johnson (1885-1970)
        + Floyd Edward Ure (1882-1937)
            6. Ella Mae Ure (1903-1988)
            + Albert Irwin Blakeman (1901-1967)
                7. Jane Elizabeth Ure (1940-)
            6. Jettie Ure (1906-1920)
    4. Orin Breeze (1870-before 1900)
3. Wellington L Carpenter (1835-1872) Civil War
+ Emeline Kinney (1842-)
3. Rosetta Carpenter (1836-)
3. Absalom Carpenter (1838-before 1850)
3. Samuel Winfield Carpenter (1842-1916) Civil War
+ Anna Whaley (1844-before 1880)
    4. Levi Carpenter (1869-1947)
    + Johanna "Hannah" Madsen (1871-1942)
        5. Mabel Eunice Carpenter (1896-1944)
        + Ralph Lawhorn (1892-1918)
            6. Mildred Lawhorn (1916-2006)
            + Walter Ernest Rutishauser (1915-1983) WW11
                7. William Jack Rutishauser (1933-)
            6. Estella Lawhorn (1918-2007)
            + George Royce Freeman (1912-1966)
        + Theodore Sypus (1893-1961)
        + William S Saley (1890-1976) WW1
            6. Elizabeth Saley (1924-)
        5. Vera May Carpenter (1898-1973)
        + John "Jack" Eastman (1896-1968)
            6. Nellie Bernice Eastman (1919-)
            + Henry Brimhall (1917-)
                7. John H Brimhall (1939-)
            6. Leland J Eastman (1922-)
            6. LaVerne K Eastman (1923-)
            6. Frank Eastman (1924-)
            6. Gordon E Eastman (1926-)
            6. Harman L Eastman (1928-)
        5. Clifford Carpenter (1902-1933)
        5. Enid Carpenter (1905-1998)

+ Oscar Hendrickson (1898-1969)
    6. Jean Hendrickson (1932-)
    6. Enid Hendrickson (1937-)
5. Edna Carpenter (1908-2001)
+ Thomas Gunn (1905-)
+ Frank H Pickett (1901-1944) WW11
5. Lynn Winfield Carpenter (1910-1990)
+ Rachel Ann Brinchall (1910-)
+ Mildred Estella Peterson (1919-1980)
5. Howard Levi Carpenter (1913-1999)
+ Madge D Prince (1915-)
+ Melba Walker (1906-1998)
    6. Howard L Carpenter Jr. (1935-)
    6. Doyle La Marr Carpenter (1939-)
4. Eunice Carpenter (1870-1964)
+ Alexander Mc Arthur (1857-1901)
5. Edith Ann McArthur (1899-2001)
+ David E Greenwalt (1892-1974) WW1
    6. Jane Elizabeth Greenwalt (1919-2013)
     + Ethemer Eugene Mackey (1918-2004)
    6. Alice F Greenwalt (1921-)
    6. Marian Greenwalt (1922-)
    6. Neil Greenwalt (1938-)
5. Jean A McArthur (1901-1974)
+ Theodore C Wellsandt (1901-)
+ Albert J Larue (1890-1978)
+ Ester Griffis (1861-1943)
4. Jessie Syrenas Carpenter (1889-1972)
+ Grace Gladys Grimm (1894-1991)
5. William Carpenter (1918-) WW11
5. Mary E Carpenter (1933-)
4. Winfield A Carpenter (1893-1962) WW1
+ Dovie Williams Godwin (1898-1964)
4. Lucy Arcelia Carpenter (1895-1928)
+ Elmer G Johnson (1868-)
5. Hugh Johnson (1916-)
5. Neva M Johnson (1924-)
3. Orville Balora Carpenter (1842-1861) Civil War
3. Lafayette Carpenter (1847-1923) Civil War
+ Frances (1853-before 1873)
+ Carline Schloop (1853-1899)
4. Mildred Carpenter (1873-1953)
+ William W Smith (1875-1940)
5. Howard C Smith (1897-1959) WW1
+ Francis C Ballard (1903-1969)

                6. Irma Jean Smith (1931-)
            5. Gladys M Smith (1902-1978)
            5. Donald Gale Smith (1904-1971) WW11
             + Cora M Martin (1902-)
                6. Marvin Lee Smith (1928-)
            5. Paul Russel Smith (1905-1996)
             + Irene May Elizabetha Dannels (1912-2009)
                6. Melvin G Smith (1936-)
                6. Jimmy W Smith (1940-)
            5. Myrtle L Smith 1909-before 1920)
    4. Francis Carpenter (1877-)
    4. Jessie Carpenter (1880-)
     + Elizabeth (1884-)
            5. Pearl Carpenter (1904-)
    4. Mary Ann Carpenter (1881-1945)
     + Robert B Williams (1873-1955)
            5. Robert S Williams (1906-1971)
             + Louise Hill (1908-1996)
                6. Robert J Williams (1934-)
                6. Ronald H Williams (1938-)
                6. Grace K Williams (1939-)
            5. Mildred C Williams (1907-1987)
             + Gerald C Clemmons (1905-1987)
                6. Helen L Clemons (1929-)
                6. Geraldine R Clemmons (1932-)
                6. Patricia A Clemons (1937-)
                6. Larry C Clemons (1939-)
                6. James O Clemons (1940-)
            5. Helen G Williams (1909-1997)
             + Herbert L Rector (1910-1975)
                6. Susan J Rector (1939-)
    4. William Carpenter (1883-)
    4. Harriett "Hattie" Carpenter (1885-1958)
     + Herbert S Morse (1885-1960)
            5. Gilbert L Morse (1907-1960)
             + Marguerite Buckley (1907-2001)
            5. Ethel Sarah Morse (1908-1984)
             + Francis Charles Johnson (1906-1970)
                6. Shirley A Johnson (1928-1950)
    4. Grace Louise Carpenter (1886-)
     + Earl C Ferguson (1890-)
            5. Gerald Ferguson (1912-)
            5. Harold C Ferguson (1914-)
             + Emeline Washer (1914-1999)
    4. Clinton Carpenter (1889-1954)

    + Sophia R Chafee (1889-1972)
        5. Elizabeth C Carpenter (1913-)
        5. Howard R Carpenter (1920-)
        5. Robert J Carpenter (1926-)
    4. Hazen Carpenter (1890-1956)
    + Ina O Vincent (1892-1967)
        5. Marguerite Elanor Carpenter (1915-1998)
        + Daniel Matthew Canell (1916-2007)
            6. Barbara Canell (1939-)
            6. Grovine Canell (1940-)
        5. Charles Carpenter (1918-)
        + Thelma (1922-)
        5. Carlton Carpenter (1921-)
        5. Marceline Carpenter (1929-)
  + Jennie Shattuck (1864-1920)
  3. Bruce Carpenter (1853-)
  + Sharlotte (1852-1896)
2.6. Mary (Polly) Carpenter (1803-after 1865)
+ Nathan Parish Jr. (1793-1890)
  3. Elisha Parish (1823-1911)
  + Eliza Jane Hooper (1826-1919)
    4. Marcia Parish (1845-1935)
    + George A Gallinger (1837-1871)
        5. Louise "Lulu" Gallinger (1871-1952)
        + Willie C Smith (1862-)
        + Charles F Crawford (1880-)
    + Edwin Pearson (1843-1882) Civil War
    4. Elisha K Parish (1846-1932)
    + Francis S Swan (1849-1929)
        5. Annie Parish (1872-after 1910)
        5. Martin Kite Parish (1879-1959)
        + Alma R Fields (1885-1934)
            6. Elisha B Parish (1905-1968)
            + Rose Ella Stanford (1911-1994)
                7. Beverly M Parish (1928-2002) WW11
                7. Leroy Parish (1933-)
                7. Verna Mae Parish (1938-)
            6. Bernice L Parish (1908-1953)
            + Leroy L Hooker (1887-1960)
                7. Roger A Hooker (1937-)
            6. Albert Martin Parish (1909-1965)
            + Myrtle Irene Adams (1915-2000)
                7. Bettie Irene Parish (1939-)
        5. Harry S Parish (1888-1919)
    4. Nathan Parish (1849-1920)

         + Nellie M Austin (1860-1927)
             5. Alvin Edwin Parish (1878-1943)
              + Fannie B Cool (1886-)
                 6. Velma R Parish (1913-)
                  + Lloyd Woodham (1911-)
                     7. Beverly Blanche Woodham (1933-)
             5. William N Parish (1890-1952)
              + Esther M Comstock (1906-1975)
                 6. Imogene Parish (1928-)
                 6. Arlene Parish (1931-)
                 6. Franklin Parish (1932-1995) Korean War
                 6. Robert Parish (1936-)
                 6. Gary L Parish (1940-1942)
         4. Louisa Parish (1853-after 1870)
         4. Electa Parish (1859-1924)
          + James C Richardson (1847-1920)
             5. Elisha C Richardson (1882-1937)
              + Mary Tena Mitchell (1885-1915)
                 6. Leroy C Richardson (1905-)
                  + Florence K Deible (1905-)
                     7. Eugene Richardson (1931-)
              + Florence Richmond (1893-)
         4. Albert A Parish (1863-1929)
          + Mary L Keyes
          + Viola Englehart Richardson (1861-1920)
   3. Lemuel Parish (1833-about 1890)
    + Mary Jane Phillips (1837-before 1920)
       4. Mary E Parish (1853-after 1878)
        + William T Carsen (1838-)
       4. Olive Parish (1855-1916)
        + Ezra Parrish (1850-1934)
           5. William S Parrish (1875-1950)
           5. Adalbert Parrish (1878-1881)
           5. Ezra Parrish (1879-before 1900)
           5. Cora Parrish (1884-1955)
            + George Henry Couch (1891-after 1930)
               6. Olive Eloise Couch (1901-1970)
                + William E Pierce (1897-)
                   7. Donald L Pierce (1920-)
                   7. Elaine J Pierce (1925-)
            + Botzman
           5. Eva Mae Parrish (1886-1935)
            + Ira Conant Brainard (1895-1957)
               6. Clyde Brainard (1907-1966)
                + Kathryn Marjorie Conklin (1909-1980)

             7. Clyde Brainard Jr. (1929-)
             7. Marjorie Brainard (1931-)
             7. Katherine Brainard (1933-)
             7. Carol Brainard (1936-)
             7. Larry Brainard (1939-)
          6. Glenn Brainard (1909-1984)
           + Marie Edna Starliper (1912-1964)
             7. Glen Brainard (1928-)
             7. Eva Marie Brainard (1932-)
             7. Shirley Brainard (1937-)
          6. Lottie Pauline Brainard (1912-1992)
           + Charles E Brown (1908-1975)
             7. Charles E Brown Jr. (1929-)
             7. Marilyn Brown (1932-)
             7. Marvin Brown (1936-)
             7. Stanley Brown (1937-)
          6. Alfred Brainard (1914-1964)
           + Anna Gergely (1913-1989)
             7. Joseph Brainard (1936-)
             7. Lois Jane Brainard (1938-)
          6. Olive Brainard (1923-)
       5. Lottie Parrish (1890-1947)
          6. Violet Parrish (1906-)
           + Ludwig A Santti (1901-1924)
           + John R Hemming (1900-1951)
             7. Gloria Hemming (1929-)
             7. Joanne Hemming (1932-)
        + Arthur G Allen (1888-1930)
        + Fred W Korth (1891-)
        + Bert Peterson (1878-)
        + George E Forgason (1882-1935)
        + David Loveland (1878-)
       5. Alfred E Parrish (1893-1979)
        + Mildred M Alfard (1901-1981)
          6. Albert Parrish (1920-)
          6. George Parrish (1934-)
  4. Charles Parish (1856/7-1931)
   + Emma Jane Lamar Stafford (1859-1896)
       5. Walter Parish (1881-1948)
        + Gladys H Friend (1907-1944)
  4. Chester Parish (1859-1923)
   + Almina Allen (1869-)
   + Hallie Brannon (1876-)
  4. Harriet Parish (1866-1915)
   + Edward Whitley (1862-1911)

5. Jennie Whitley (1886-after 1940)
 + George L Moyer (1886-1916)
  6. Paul Moyer (1914-)
  6. George Moyer (1917-)
   + Louise (1918-)
    7. Robert Moyer (1939-)
 + James A Smith (1886-)
 + Wilbert L Clipp (1878-1937)
5. Mary Mamie Whitley (1887-1937)
 + Grover C Leigh (1884-1958)
  6. Evelin M Leigh (1911-)
  6. Francis Leigh (1921-)
5. Jackie Whitley (1889-before 1910)
5. Laura Whitley (1892-before 1910)
5. Edward B Whitley (1894-1965)
 + Margaret Carroll (1896-)
  6. John Whitley (1918-)
  6. Mary Ellen Whitley (1921-)
  6. Margie Ann Whitley (1923-)
  6. Richard Whitley (1925-)
  6. Ronald Whitley (1932-)
5. George A Whitley (1897-1954)
 + Leona M Turner (1896-)
  6. Evelyn Whitely (1920-)
  6. Jean Whitley (1936-)
5. Mable Whitley (1899-1968)
 + Thomas Morrison Lynch (1896-1967)
  6. James Lynch (1919-)
  6. Thomas Lynch (1923-)
  6. Jack Lynch (1926-)
  6. Jane Lynch (1927-)
  6. Donald Lynch (1932-)
  6. Sally Lynch (1935-)
  6. Richard Lynch (1938-)
5. Chester J Whitley (1903-1968)
 + Laura Conley (1901-1958)
 + Helen Cricket (1902-1979)
  6. William E Whitley (1929-)
  6. Ann M Whitley (1932-)
  6. Carol J Whitley (1933-)
  6. Raymond E Whitley (1939-)
4. Thomas Parish (1870-)
 + Ruth E Green (1901-)
  5. Marian A Parish (1918-)
  5. Stanley Paul Parish (1923-)

                5. Richard R Parish (1925-)
                5. Grace F Parish (1928-)
                5. Eileen Parish (1929-)
                5. Lloyd Parish (1933-)
                5. Marlene Parish (1935-)
                5. William Parish (1937-)
            4. Wayne Parish (1871-1951)
            + Myrtle Green (1903-)
                5. Lucille Parish (1923-)
                5. Juanita Parish (1924-)
            4. Nathan Parish (1875-after 1880)
            4. Lemuel Parish (1878-1910)
            + Mary E "Mammie Mack (1880-)
                5. Frank Ray Parish (1899-1963)
                + Lydia Cone (1900-)
                    6. Raymond Parish (1918-)
                + Dorothy L Deerring (1900-)
        + Bessie Brainard (1889-)
    + Racy Hartel (-)
3. Deforest Parish (1836-)
+ Adelia (1840-)
        4. Fred Parish (1859-before 1865)
        4. Everett Parish (1863- before 1870)
+ Esther (1833-)
+ Mary Jane Phillips (1836-before 1920) former wife of Lemuel Parish
3. Nathan Parish 3rd (1842-1917) Civil War
+ Amelia (1844-1865)
        4. Edwin Parish (1859-1870)
+ Diantha Jewett (1844-1908)
        4. Frank Parish (1865-1881)
        4. Isabel "Belle" Parish (1866-1914)
        + Freeman Fiefield (1866-1934)
            5. Estella Fiefield (1885-)
            + Edward R Sterne (1884-)
            5. Bessie Eugene Fiefield (1890-1991)
            + Andrew William Manning (1888-)
            + John "Jack" E Mog (1889-)
                6. Faith Natalie Mog (1912-1922)
                6. June P Mog (1925-)
        4. George Riley Parish (1867-1937)
        + Claudous C Joiner (1875-1946)
            5. George W Parish (1893-1971)
            + Elma H Hallen (1894-1963)
                6. George Parish 3rd (1934-)
            5. Loretta J Parish (1895-)

          + A J Dewey
                6. Lucille Dewey (1918-1994)
                  + Bauer (-)
                  + Ray A Hendershot (1918-)
            + Frank B Reid (1896-)
        5. Gilbert Parish (1897-)
          + Cora E Barnes (1896-1941)
                6. Raymond Parish (1919-)
                6. Eileen Parish (1920-)
  4. Orrin Parish (1873-1927)
  4. Louise Parish (1871-1958)
   + Henry Leitze (1862-)
        5. George Leitze (1892-1967)
          + Mary (1901-)
          + Katherine (1895-)
        5. Launa Leitze (1896-before1910)
   + Alfred Lewis Jr. (1873-)
        5. David Lewis (1907-1979)
          + Thelma Helen Herpy (1910-)
                6. Jeanette Lewis (1929-)
                6. David Lewis (1933-)
          + Emma (-)
        5. Albert Lewis (1911-)
          + Gladys Evans (1911-)
                6. Donald N Lewis (1929-)
          + Alma C Kerr (-)
          + Dorothy (1915-)
                6. Penelope Lewis (1938-)
  4. Sarah Parish (1875-)
  4. Martin Van Buren Parish (1876-1942)
   + Sadie Wier (1876-1952)
        5. Clarence Ray Parish (1896-1988)
          + Lillian Marie Johnson Randasaw (1899-1967)
                6. Donna Johnson Parish (1916-1963)
        5. Lloyd Parish (1897-1986) WW1
          + Bessie P Petrie (1909-)
                6. Saundra Parish (1938-)
        5. James Nathan Parish (1900-1934) WW1
          + Sadie Gibson (1898-)
        5. Sadie Parish (1903-)
          + Seth Donald Barkinen (1903-)
                6. Evalyn Joy Barkinen (1924-)
          + Thomas G Dunn Jr. (1904-)
        5. Martin "Buster" Parish (1905-1972)
          + Norma Smith (1908-1997)

    5. Lillian Parish (1908-)
     + Clarence B Maltbie (1906-)
      6. Martin Maltbie (1932-)
      6. William B Maltbie (1933-)
    5. Jenetta Parish (1910-1913)
    5. Diantha Parish (1913-)
     + Sam Sterling (1905-)
      6. Darlyne Sterling (1934-)
   4. Fred Parish (1877-1907)
   4. James Arthur Parish (1882-1967)
    + Esther Elsie Miller (1892-)
   4. Nathan Parish 4th (1884-1968)
    + Frances L Ganter (1888-1969)
    5. Iris Parish (1912-)
     + Robert Myers (1914-)
      6. Frances Jane Myers (1936-)
      6. Robert N Meyers (1939-)
   4. Chester Parish (1888-1961)
    + Mary N Willberg (1896-1938)
    5. Ronald V Parish (1916-1938)
  3. Margarette Parish (1840-)
  3. George R Parish (1846-1904)
   + Eliza J Dorsey (1848-1927)
   4. Eliza G Parish (1869-)
    + John F Heiber Jr (1868-1926)
    5. Donald G Heiber (1901-)
     + Virginia A Westgate (1909-)
   4. George R Parish Jr (1875-1931)
    + Minnie Stelzer (1874-)
    5. Dorothy M Parish (1898-)
  3. Mary Etta Parish (1844-1915)
   + Brown (-)
   4. Mary Etta Brown (1875-)
2.7. Rebecca Carpenter (1805-before1844)
2.8. Daniel Carpenter (1807-1893)
 + Elmina P Shepard (1817-1867)
  3. William Wallace Carpenter (1837-1885)
   + Florence M Bowman (1846-1928)
   4. Minnie Seacf Carpenter (1868-1950)
    + William H Hall (1867-1949)
    5. Carl Hall (1895-1984)
     + Pauline E Bass (1897-)
      6. Shirley E Hall (1925-)
  3. Olive Carpenter (1840-)
  3. Delina Carpenter (1843-)

+ Mary (1843-)
**2.9. Orson (Orison, Orris) Carpenter (1809-1899)**
**+ Nancy Jane Duffin (1815-1848) (m.1830)**
**+ Maria (Meriah) Phillips (1827-1857) (m. 1848)**
**+ Mary M Smith (1822-1889)**
2.10. Cynthia C. Carpenter (1811-1887)
 + Jonathan Elmer (about 1803-1885) Civil War
  3. Minerva Elmer (about 1828-)
  3. Silas Elmer (1828-1905)
   + Hannah (1830-1919)
    4. Harriet "Hattie" Elmer (1860-1934)
     + George Petrie (1859-1956)
      5. Lulu May Petrie (1880-1976)
       + Kirke Henry White (1881-1969)
        6. Kirke M White (1905-1985)
        6. Virginia L White (1911-2014)
         + Stedman D Tuthill (1909-1993)
        6. Niel S White (1918-)
      5. Maude Petrie (1885-1970)
    4. William Elmer (1865-1951)
    4. Fredrick Elmer (1871-1899)
  3. William M Elmer (1832-1911)
   + Mariette A Scott (1843-1919)
    4. William Henry Harrison Elmer (1864-1927)
     + Hattie M Lonsdale (1869-1888)
      5. Frank Monroe Elmer (1888-1960) WW1
       + Lillian Edith Hobbs (1887-1973)
       + Ruth E Dorothy (-)
     + Martha "Mattie" Poole Hurd (1869-1943)
      5. Mildred I Elmer (1890-1960)
       + Fredrick A Isley (1885-1955)
        6. Fredrick E Isley (1918-) New York National Guard
        6. Dorothy A Isley (1922-)
      5. Lincoln Grant Elmer (1891-1979)
       + Anna Martha Witt (1894-)
        6. Ralph Elmer (1920-)
        6. Richard Elmer (1922-)
        6. Robert Elmer (1930-)
      5. Maryette Elmer (1898-before1910)
    4. Fred M Elmer (1866-1919)
     + Minnie Shaffert (1870-1921)
    4. Frank N Elmer (1871-1876)
  3. Melissa Elmer (1834-before 1900)
   + Charles N Osborn (1811-before 1900)
    4. Elnora Osborn (1853-before 1860)

    4. Charles A Osborn (1860-1914)
      + Ada Hill (1861-1946)
  3. Wellington H Elmer (1837-1859)
  3. Washington Rufus Elmer (1837-1925) Civil War
   + Helen V Burlingame (1846-1930)
    4. Lewis H Elmer (1869-1918)
  3. Roxanna Elmer (1841-1903)
   + Benjamin T Glassford (1837-1917) Civil War
    4. Frank Jule Glassford (1873-1959)
      + Emma A Foley (1875-)
      5. Lola Glassford (1896-)
       + Raymond Miehl (1896-1973)
        6. Lillian Ruth Miehl (1915-2002)
         + Oscar Held (1914-1996)
          7. Raymond Held (1939-)
      5. Harold F Glassford (1897-1966)
       + Albina Fronek (1897-1931)
        6. Leona May Glassford (1920-1992)
         + Vernon C Wheeler (1912-)
        6. Marie Glassford (1925-)
        6. Harold Glassford (1931-1931)
       + Rose Keenan (1901-)
      5. Venita Glassford (1915-1987)
    4. Fred Foster Glassford (1879-1941)
     + Mary Ann Moore (1880-1963)
      5. Marion Roxanne "Roxie" Glassford (1905-1983)
       + George Corke (1902-)
        6. Anita Corke (1937-)
      5. Lawrence Glassford (1906-1975)
       + Leona Frances Wall (1906-)
      5. Joseph Richard Glassford (1908-2005)
       + Ann Humphreys (-)
      5. Edwin F Glassford (1910-1975)
       + Elizabeth M Robarge (1914-)
        6. Marilyn Glassford (1939-)
      5. Harriet Glassford (1913-)
      5. Mary Agatha Glassford (1914-)
       + Herbert Finch (1914-)
        6. Robert Finch (1937-)
      5. Hazel Glassford (1918-)
  3. Adeline Adalaide Elmer (1845-1925)
   + Henry A Read (1838-1906)
    4. Minnie C Read (1873-1918)
     + James W Ackerman (1868-1941)
      5. Hazael Read Ackerman (1899-1924)

                + Maude A Burdick (-)
            3. Arvilla Elmer (1846-)
            + Azariah Ackerman (1826-1875)
                4. James W Ackerman (1868-1941) see above
                + Minnie C Read (1873-1918)
                + Luella P Stone (1866-)
                4. Minnie Ackerman (1872-1951)
                + John Philips (1845-1921)
                    5. Flora A Philips (1890-1916)
                    + William H Dopking (1861-)
            + William Phillips (1931-)
                4. Willis Philips (1876-)
                4. Fanny Philips (1879-)
            3. Elvira Elmer (1848-1924)
            + Alexander Johnston (1835-1913)
                4. Minnie Johnston (1873-before 1900)
                4. Mannoah Johnston (1878-before 1900)
                4. Goldie Johnston (1880-)
                4. Everett E Johnston (1882-)
                + Ella (1899-)
            3. Edward D Elmer (1850-1875)
            3. Ruth Elmer (1853-1856)
            3. Alice Elmer (1855-)
            + George Loyd (1853-)
                4. Charles Wellington Loyd (1874-1942)
                + Lillie M Starker (1880-1910)
                    5. Rollin Morrison Loyd (1904-1970)
                + Louise (1901-)
                    5. Ann Loyd (1920-)
                    5. Nancy Loyd (1928-)
2.11. Permelia Carpenter (1814-)


## 2.1. Daniel Carpenter

Daniel Carpenter born 1791, died 1807. He is probably buried in Washington County, New York.

## 2.2. Asaph "Asa" Carpenter and Phoebe McGregory / Sophia Bennett

Asa Carpenter married Phoebe McGregory about 1815 according to several family trees. There may have been more children to this marriage but they are not known. The children I can document are listed in the lineage. The family trees also list Phoebe's death as 1842. Census records before 1850 do not list anyone except the head of household. The rest of the family is noted by marks in male or female age groups.

The 1850 census for Brownville, New York has Asa Carpenter, 55, born in Vermont, a farmer with $300 in real estate. His daughter, Cordelia is 12 and born in New York. Phoebe has died. Asa was born in Granville, New York which is very near the Vermont border. The boundary between the states was in dispute when Asa was born.

The 1855 State of New York Census for Brownville, Jefferson, New York has Asa Carpenter, 61, a farmer, able to vote and living in a log house worth $50. Sophia, is 35 and born in Saratoga County. The children are Orison Kincon, 10, step child, born in Jefferson County and Elposa, 2, born in Jefferson County.

Another line has (James) Asa Carpenter, 22, born in Oswego County, a laborer, living in a log house worth $50. Dorcas is 20 and born in Oswego County. Asa's sister, Cordelia, is 16 and born in Jefferson County. James Asa is Asaph and Phoebe's son.

The 1860 census for Brownville, Jefferson, New York has Asa Carpenter, 66, a farmer with $350 in real estate. James Carpenter is 27 and a farmer. Dorcas is 26. The children are Franklin, 4 and Sarah, 2. Relationships and place of birth are not listed. The whereabouts of Sophia and Elposa are not known.

The 1860 census for Lebanon, Madison, New York has a John Carpenter with a wife and 3 children. Cordelia Carpenter is working as a domestic. Cordelia Carpenter born 18 Jun 1839, died 5 Oct 1870 according to some family trees.

The 1870 census for Brownville, New York has Asa Carpenter, 80, a farmer with $200 in real estate. Sophia is 50. Elposa is 16. Nothing more was found on Elposa Carpenter.

War of 1812 Pension Application Files have Asa Carpenter, a Private in Capitan Shumway's Company of the New York Militia. He enlisted 11 Sep 1814 and was discharged 22 Sep 1814. First wife was Phebe McGregory. Asa's widow is Sophia Bennett who Asa married 16 Mar 1853 in Brownville, New York. Asa died 2 Sep 1874 in Lorraine, Jefferson, New York. Sophia died 14 Jan 1880 in Redfield, New York. There is a reference to bounty land.

### 3. James Asa Carpenter and Dorcas Bennet

James Asa and Dorcus are listed in the 1855 and 1860 censuses with his father.

The 1870 census for Brownville, New York has James A Carpenter, 38, a farmer with $200 in real estate. Dorcas is 36. The children are Frank, 14; Sarah C, 12; Ida A, 10; Martin, 7; Delilah, 3 and Edwin, 1. All the children except the two youngest attended school.

An 1875 New York State census has James A Carpenter, 43, born in Oswego County, a farm laborer. Dorcas is 40 and born in Oswego County. The children are Ida, 15; James

M, 12; Delilah, 8 and Edward, 4. All the children were born in Jefferson County.

Clarence E Carpenter, born 1869, died 1870. Sarah C Carpenter, born about 1858, died in 1878 and may have left home in 1875.

The 1880 census for Brownville, New York has James Carpenter, 48, a laborer. Dorcas is 45. The children are Martin, 17, laborer; Delilah, 13, at school and Edwin, 9, at school. Ida has left home. Nothing more was found on Edwin Carpenter.

Dorcas Bennet Carpenter born 1834, died 1899 and is buried in Dexter Cemetery, Dexter, New York.

The 1900 census for Brownville, New York has James A Carpenter, 68, born May 1832, widowed, a stone mason who owns his house free and clear. His daughter, Delia H, is 33, born May 1867 and single.

Delia Carpenter born 1867, died 17 Feb 1902 and is buried in Dexter Cemetery.

James Asa Carpenter born 1832, died 1915 and is buried in Dexter Cemetery along with several children who did not live long; Sarah (1858-1878), Clarence E (1869-1870), Fredrick (1871-1871) and Bertha M (1875-1875).

Edwin Carpenter was with his parents in 1880 but nothing more could be found on him. There are several other Edwin Carpenters in the area but those with the middle initial W, P, H and B have been ruled out. Edwin son of James Asa probably died young.

## 4. Franklin Carpenter and Harriett Cronk and daughter Lena Carpenter

The 1880 census for Ellisburg, Jefferson, New York has Frank Carpenter, 23, married, a servant working as farm labor for the Bigelow family. His family is not listed.
Harriett's father died in 1878 and her mother had remarried by 1880. Harriett is not with her. The 1880 census for Belleview, Jefferson, New York has Harriett Carpenter, 20, married and keeping house. Her daughter, Lena, is 1. For some reason Frank is listed with his work although he was only about 3 miles from Harriett. He may have stayed on the farm part time.

The 1900 census for Henderson, Jefferson, New York has Frank Carpenter, 43, born Jul 1856, married 22 years, a farmer who owns his mortgaged farm. Harriett is 40 born Apr 1860 and has had 4 children who are still living. The children are Lena M, 21, born Nov 1878; Roy, 16, born Aug 1883, a farm laborer; Scott, 9, born Feb 1891, attended school and Leah, 6 born Aug 1893, attended school.

The 1910 census for Henderson, Jefferson, New York has Frank Carpenter, 54, married 33 years, a dairy farmer who owns his mortgaged farm. Harriett C is 50, had 4 children and all are living. The children are Scott, 19, working on the home farm and Leah, 16.

Both attended school.

The 1915 New York State Census for Utica has Lena M Carpenter, 36, a school teacher rooming at 10 Court Street.

Lena M Carpenter, Rochester Homeopathic Hospital Rochester, New York was called into active service 3 May 1918. She served overseas form 3 Jun 1918 to 19 Jun 1919. She was honorably discharged 31 Jul 1919 but a note says relieved from active duty, not discharged.

Lena M Carpenter was a resident nurse at base hospital # 19. The nurses left New York, New York on the Army Transport Ship Baltic on 4 Jun 1918. Lena M Carpenter, Army Nurse Core, Casual Nurse Detachment # 29, left Brest, France on 10 Jun 1919 on the Army Transport ship Kasserin Aguste Victoria and arrived in New York, New York.

The 1920 census for Henderson, Jefferson, New York has Frank Carpenter, 63, a dairy farmer. Harriett is 59. Frank died 8 Aug 1929.

The 1920 census for Utica, New York has Lena M Carpenter, 40, single, a school teacher rooming at 310 Court Street with other teachers.

The 1930 census for Henderson, New York has Harriett Carpenter, 70, a widow, renting a home on Park Street. Her daughter Lena, 51, single is living with her.

The 1940 census for Henderson, New York has Harriett Carpenter, 79, widow, completed 8th grade. Lena is 61, single and completed 11th grade. Harriett died 18 Jan 1953 and Lena died 11 Dec 1964.

## 5. Roy Earnest Carpenter and Bertha / Mertie Whitney

The 1910 census for Henderson, Jefferson, New York has Roy E Carpenter, 26, married 3 years, a dairy farmer. Bertha L is 29. She has not had children.

Roy Earnest Carpenter, 35, born 22 Aug 1883, of 511 Robert Street, Camden, New Jersey registered for WW1 on 6 Sep 1918. He was working as a carpenter at Tidewater Building Company in Camden. His nearest relative is Mertie Carpenter. He is of medium height and build with blue eyes and brown hair.

The 1920 census for Henderson, Jefferson, New York has Roy E Carpenter, 36, a farmer who owns his mortgaged farm. Mertie is 25.

The 1930 census for Henderson, Jefferson, New York has Roy Carpenter, 46, married at 26, a carpenter in building construction who owns his home worth $1500 and a radio. Mertie is 36 and was married at 16. They have an adopted son, Clinton, 10.

The 1940 census for Henderson, Jefferson, New York has Roy Carpenter, 57, completed 11th grade, a carpenter working for a contract building company who owns his farm worth $2000. Mertie is 46 and completed 8th grade. Their son Clinton is 20, graduated high school and is an apprentice carpenter with his father.

Nothing is known about Roy's first wife Bertha. Roy Carpenter born 22 Aug 1883, died 1952. Mertie Whitney Carpenter born 13 Jun 1894, died Mar 1994 at almost 100.

## 5. Scott Carpenter and Clara Marie Stubberud

Scott Carpenter, 23, married Clara Marie Stubberud, 27, on 20 Mar 1914 in Winnebago, Illinois.

The 1920 census for Henderson, Jefferson, New York has Scott Carpenter, 28, working on a mortgaged farm he owns on Butterville Road. Clara is 32, born in Norway and immigrated in 1904. They have a daughter, Gertrude, 5.

The 1930 census for Henderson, Jefferson, New York has Scott Carpenter, 39, married at 23, a farmer who owns his dairy farm worth $1000 and a radio. Clara is 43 and married at 27. Their two daughters are Gertrude, 15, attended school and Ellen 4/12. Ellen Jane Carpenter was born 2 Dec 1929 and baptized 25 Nov 1930 in Bethel Lutheran Church, Madison, Wisconsin. They traveled to Clara's parents church to baptize Ellen.

The 1940 census for Henderson, Jefferson, New York has Scott Carpenter, 48, graduated high school, a farmer who has a farm that is now worth $5000. Clara is 52 and completed 8th grade. Ellen is 10 and has completed 4th grade.

The 1940 census for Ellisburg, Jefferson, New York has Gertrude Carpenter, 25, single, graduated high school, a hired hand in a private home for a doctor and school teacher.

Scott Carpenter born 10 Feb 1891, died Jun 1974. Clara Stubberud Carpenter born 1888, died Feb 1965 in Hillsborough, Florida.

## 5. Leah Carpenter and William John Owen Phillips

Leah Carpenter, 23, of Henderson, New York, married William John Owen Phillips, 23, of Mannsville, New York, on 20 Sep 1916 in Detroit, Michigan.

The 1920 census for Henderson, New York has Owen Phillips, 26, born in Canada, renting a dairy farm. Leah is 26. Just above in the listing are Frank and Harriett, Leah's parents. Owen may have been renting part of their farm.

The 1930 census for Henderson, Jefferson, New York has Owen Phillips, 37, married at 23, born in Canada, a dairy farmer who owns his farm worth $1200 and a radio. Leah is

36. The children are Clarence, 9, and June, 7. Leah's father Frank Carpenter died in 1929 so they may be running his dairy farm.

The 1940 census for Henderson, Jefferson, New York has Owen Phillips, 46, graduated high school, a dairy farmer who owns his farm worth $2000. Leah is 46 and graduated high school. Clarence is 19, completed 2 years high school and laborer on a dairy farm. Donald Griffin, 23, son-in-law, completed 8th grade and laborer on a dairy farm. June Phillips Griffin is 17 and graduated high school. Warren Griffin, 18, completed 8th grade, and is a hired hand.

Leah C Phillips born Aug 1893, died Feb 1961 in Hillsborough, Florida and is buried in Oakwood Cemetery, Teresa, Jefferson, New York. Owen Phillips born 21 Apr 1893, died Nov 1964 in Florida.

## 4. Ida A Carpenter and Bernard Schlough

The 1900 census for Brownville, Jefferson, New York has Bernard Schlough, 45, born Dec 1854 in Germany, married 15 years, immigrated 1871, a naturalized citizen, a mill watchman who owns his mortgaged home. Ida A is 39 born Jul 1860 in New York, has had 2 children, both are living. The children are Flossie D, 13, born Jun 1886, adopted daughter; Edna M, 3, born Jul 1897; and Nina P, 11/12, born Jun 1899. All the children were born in New York and Flossie was attending school.

Nina P Schlough born 1899, died 1907 and is buried in Dexter Cemetery Dexter, New York. Claudius B Schlough born 1902, died 1903 and is buried in Dexter Cemetery.

The 1915 New York State Census for Dexter, New York has Bernard Schlough, 58; Ida, 54; and Edna 18.

The 1920 census for Dexter, New York has Bernard Schlough, 63, immigrated 1874, naturalized 1885, watchman at a sulfite mill who owns his home. Ida A is 59.

Ida A Carpenter born 1860, died 1930 and is buried in Dexter Cemetery. Bernard Schlough born 1854, died 1934 and is buried with Ida.

Nothing more is known about Flossie D Schlough.

## 5. Edna Mae Schlough and Ross D Fluno

Edna Mae Schlough, 21 married Ross D Fluno, 32 on 8 Oct 1918 in Brownville, Jefferson, New York.

The 1920 census for Brownville, Jefferson, New York has Ross Flumo, 33, a farmer. Edna is 22. Mary, Ross' mother, is 61. Edward Fisher is 44 and a half-brother.

The 1930 census for Brownville, Jefferson, New York has Ross Flumo, 43, married at 32, a farmer renting a dairy farm on Perch Lake Road. Edna M is 33 and married at 21. Their children are Natalie M, 8; Gladys K, 6, and Arlene, 3.

Edna Mae Schlough Fluno and Ross D Fluno both died on 24 Jun 1938 at Sacketts Harbor, New York. The New York Death Index has Hounsfield, New York. They are both buried in Dexter Cemetery. I could not find a story but they may have been on an outing to Sacketts Harbor on Lake Ontario and had an accident officially dying in Hounsfield. Sacketts Harbor is 7 miles from Dexter. Hounsfield is on an island in Lake Ontario.

The 1940 census for Watertown, New York has Natalie Flumo, 18, completed 10th grade and a maid for the Dr. Calkins family.

The 1940 census for Hounsfield, Jefferson, New York has Gladys Flumo, 16, completed 8th grade, attending school Arlene Flumo is 13, completed 8th grade, attending school. They are both lodgers with Horace and Mary Cole. They were living in the same place in 1935 so it is possible the family moved to Hounsfield before the accident.

## 4. James Martin Carpenter and Sabrina M Schimel

The 1900 census for Orleans, Jefferson, New York has James Carpenter, 37, born Apr 1863, married 16 years, a farmer who owns his mortgaged farm. Sabrina is 42, born May 1858 and has not had children. Sabrina's mother is living with them.

The 1910 census for Watertown, New York has James M Carpenter, 47, married 26 years, working as a house carpenter and renting a home. Sabrina M is 51.

The 1920 census for Carthage, New York has James M Carpenter, 56, renting his home and working with wood in a blacksmith's shop. Sabrina M is 61.

The 1925 census for Champion, Jefferson, New York has James Carpenter, 62, and Sabrina, 66. A 1930 census was not found.

James M Carpenter, born 1863, died 1931 and is buried in Old Evans Mills Cemetery, Evans Mills, Jefferson, New York.

The 1940 census for Evans Mills, New York has Sabrina M Carpenter, 82, widowed, completed 8th grade and renting a home on Willow Avenue. Anna Bowman, 70 is living with her.

Sabrina Schimel Carpenter born May 1858, died 11 Dec 1944 at the age of 86 and is buried with James.

## 2.3. Jeremiah Carpenter and Mary Belcher / Mariah Weller / Sarah Wilber

Jeremiah Carpenter married Mary Belcher about 1827. They had a daughter Louisa in 1828. Jeremiah married Mariah Weller about 1829. They had 5 children before she died in 1840. Jeremiah married Sarah Wilber between 1840 and 1850.

The 1850 census for Brownville, New York has Jeremiah Carpenter, 58, born in Vermont, a farmer who owns a farm worth $6000. Sarah, is 38. The children are Louisa, 22; Priscilla, 20; Maria, 18; Jeremiah, 16; Sylvester, 14; and Adeline, 12.

The 1855 New York State census for Brownville, New York has Jeremiah Carpenter, 60, a farmer who owns a frame house on a farm worth $1500. Sarah is 42. The children are Louisa, 27; Pricilla, 25, a teacher; Jeremiah, 22; Sylvester, 19; and Adeline ,16. There is also a grandson, Ervin Dempsey, 9. Louisa and Priscilla are old enough to have a child but they aren't married so any child would be a Carpenter. He may be Sarah's grandson.

The 1860 census for Brownville, Jefferson, New York has Jeremiah Carpenter, 68, a farmer with $1500 in real estate. Sarah is 47. Louisa is 27 and a teacher. Priscilla is 24. Geo H Hucksom is 20 and working on the farm. Sylvester Carpenter is the next listing.

The 1870 census for Brownville, New York has Jeremiah Carpenter, 72, a farmer with $10,700 in real estate. Sarah is 56 and keeping house.

Find a Grave has Jeremiah Carpenter born 7 Feb 1796, died 11 Sep 1874; Mariah, his wife, died 10 May 1840; Sarah his wife died 5 May 1886. A daughter Louisa Carpenter died 14 Aug 1867 aged 38 years. All are in Dexter Cemetery, Dexter, New York. Louisa's mother was Mary Belcher (1808-1829) according to Ancestry trees. This is a picture of their stone.

Priscilla Carpenter is living with her brother Sylvester in 1870. Sarah Carpenter is living with her step-son, Sylvester, in 1880. Nothing more could be found on Priscilla or Maria Carpenter. Without marriage licenses it is almost impossible.

### 3. Jeremiah P Carpenter and Elizabeth M Underwood

Jeremiah Carpenter is with his parents in the 1850 census and 1855 state census. In 1855 Jeremiah is 22, a farmer, a voter and owns land. Jeremiah and Elizabeth must have been married later in 1855 or early 1856.

The 1865 New York State Census for Pinckney, Lewis, New York has Jeremiah P Carpenter, 33, a farmer who owns land and a frame house worth $150. Elizabeth is 32 and has 2 children. The children are Ella, 9 and Watson 3. They also have a hired hand.

The 1870 census for Pinckney, Lewis, New York has Jeremiah Carpenter, 36, a farmer with $9360 in real estate. Elizabeth is 37 and keeping house. The children are Ella, 14, at school; Watson, 8, at school; and Frank, 4.

The 1900 census for Antwerp, Jefferson, New York has Jeremiah P Carpenter, 67 born May 1833, married 45 years, owns his farm free and clear. Elizabeth M is 69, born Aug 1830 and has had 3 children, 2 are living.

The 1910 Census for Oxbow, New York has Jeremiah P Carpenter, 76, married 54 years, a farmer who owns his farm free and clear. Elizabeth is 80 with 2 living children.

Elizabeth Carpenter, born 1830, died in 1911 and is buried in New Oxbow Cemetery, Oxbow, New York. Jeremiah P Carpenter born 1833, died 25 Feb 1912 in Gouverneur, New York and is buried with Elizabeth.

## 4. Ella Louise Carpenter and Willett H Vary

Ella Louise Carpenter married Willett H Vary about 1877.

The 1880 census for Harrisburg, New York has Willett Vary, 26, a cheese maker. Ellen is 23. Their son, Earnest, is 2.

Ella Louise Carpenter Vary born 1856, died 10 Mar 1899 (probably from complications due to childbirth, she had a 2-week-old son) and is buried in Huntingtonville Rural Cemetery (North Watertown), Watertown, Jefferson, New York.

The 1900 census for Watertown, New York has Willett H Vary, 46, born Apr 1854, widowed, secretary of Jefferson County PFA (Patrons Fire Relief Association) Insurance who owns his home at 127 Franklin Street free and clear. His children are Earnest W, 22 born May 1878, a dry goods salesman; Gertrude E, 19 born Aug 1880; Charles J, 15 born Sep 1884, clerk in a dry goods store; Lizzie S, 7 born Nov 1892 and Willett H Jr, 1 born Mar 1899.

The 1910 census for Watertown, New York has Willett H Vary, 55, widowed, secretary of insurance company who owns his home at 1119 Franklin Street. Elizabeth S is 17 and Willett H Jr is 11.

The 1920 census for Watertown, New York has Willett Vary, 65, insurance agent who owns his mortgaged home at 332 South Indiana Ave. Agnes C (2nd wife) is 55 and Willett Jr is 21 and single.

Willett H Vary born 26 Apr 1854, died 16 Mar 1920 in Southern Pines, South Carolina of a pulmonary hemorrhage and is buried with Ella Louise.

## 5. Earnest W Vary and Mable Blanche McAdam

The 1910 census for Watertown, New York has Earnest Vary, 32, a salesman in a department store, boarding at 416 Broadway Ave.

Earnest W Vary, 36, married M Blanche McAdam, 26, on 30 Jun 1914 in Brownville, Jefferson, New York.

Earnest Willet Vary, 40, born 23 May 1878 registered for WW1 on 12 Sep 1918. He was employed as a clerk by his father. His wife is Mabel Blanch Vary.

The 1920 census for Watertown, New York has Earnest W Vary, 41, an insurance salesman renting his home at 437 Broadway Ave. M Blanche is 32 and a music teacher. Their son, Earnest Jr., is 4.

The 1930 census for Watertown, New York has Earnest W Vary, 51, married at 36, a secretary for an insurance company who owns his home at 414 Grand Ave. and a radio. M Blanche is 42 and married at 27. Earnest W Jr. is 14.

The 1940 census for Watertown, New York has Earnest W Vary, 62, completed 9th grade and an insurance agent who owns his home at 414 Grand Ave worth $5000. M Blanche is 52 and graduated high school.

Earnest W Vary Jr born 27 Apr 1915, joined the US Navy 22 Sep 1939 and was released 9 Feb 1946. He reenlisted and continued to serve in the Navy eventually becoming a Commander.

The 1940 census for the US Naval Air Station Cadet Quarters, Escambia, Florida has Earnest W Vary Jr, 24, graduated college, Potsdam, St Lawrence, New York in 1935, an aviation cadet with the US Navy.

Earnest W Vary born 23 May 1878, died 1962 and is buried in North Watertown Cemetery, Watertown, New York. M Blanche McAdam Vary born 5 Aug 1887, died 16 Jan 1969 and is buried with Earnest.

## 5. Gertrude E Vary and Charles Leigh Beecher

Gertrude Vary and Leigh Beecher were married 4 Sep 1902 in Watertown, New York.

The 1910 census for Watertown, Jefferson, New York has Charles L Beecher, 28, married 8 years, a dairy farmer who owns his mortgaged farm. Gertrude E is 29 and has 1 child. Their daughter, Hazel E, is 6.

This is Gertrude about 1910.

The 1920 census for Watertown, Jefferson, New York has Charles L Beecher, 38, a farmer with his own mortgaged farm on East Water Road. Gertrude is 39. Hazel E is 16.

The 1930 census for Watertown, Jefferson, New York has C Leigh Beecher, 48, married at 20, a farmer on the farm he owns on Hadcock Road worth $8000. Gertrude E is 49 and was married at 21. Robert W, an adopted son, is 8. No more is known about him.

The 1940 census for Ogdensburg, New York, St Lawrence State Hospital has C Leigh Beecher, 58, completed 8th grade, patient. No illness is listed.

The 1940 census for Watertown, New York has Gertrude E Beecher, 59, completed 9th grade, a housekeeper in a private home at 217 Franklin Street.

Gertrude E Vary Beecher born Aug 1880, died 12 Feb 1957 and is buried in Huntington Rural Cemetery, Watertown, New York. C Leigh Beecher born 24 Sep 1881, died 1 Oct 1969 and is buried with Gertrude.

### 6. Hazel E Beecher and Leonard Ambrose Pfister

Hazel E Beecher, 16, married Leonard Ambrose Pfister, 19, on 20 Aug 1920 in Watertown, New York.

The 1930 census for Watertown, New York has Leonard Pfister, 28, married at 19, a foreman for street repairs renting a home at 427 Grove Street for $29 per month. Hazel E is 26 and married at 17. Their daughters are Beverley L 3 and Shirley 1.

The 1940 census for Watertown, New York has Leonard Pfister, 38, completed 8th grade, a truck driver for the Department of Public Works who is renting a home at 503 Cooper Street for $12 per month. Hazel is 36 and graduated high school. Their children are Beverly, 13, completed 7th grade; Shirley, 11, completed 6th grade; Natalie, 8, completed 3rd grade; Kenneth, 5 and Norma Jean, 3.

### 5. Charles J Vary and Florence Beecher / Mary Elizabeth Webb

Charles J Vary and Florence Beecher were married 4 Sep 1906. Florence's brother is C L Beecher who married Gertrude Vary. Florence had 2 children, Doris L in 1907 and

Ward C in 1911.

Ward C Vary born 1911, died 1912 at 10 months of age. Florence was in failing health after his death.

Florence Beecher Vary born 29 Feb 1888, died Feb 1913 and is buried in Huntington Rural Cemetery, Watertown, New York.

The 1915 New York State Census for Watertown, Jefferson has C Leigh Beecher, 33, a farmer. Gertrude E is 34. The children are Hazel E, 11 and Doris L Vary, 8.

Charles J Vary, 30, married Mary E Webb, 23, on 18 Aug 1915 in Watertown, New York.

Charles Vary, 35, an accountant, crossed into Canada on 2 Dec 1919 to work in Ontario for a paper company. Doris, 12 was with him.

A 1920 census has not been found. They may have moved to Menominee, Michigan while the census was taken. A 1924 City Directory for Menominee, Michigan has Charles J Vary, secretary-treasurer for Hoskins-Morainville Paper Company and living at 1064 Sheridan Road. His wife is Mary E and Doris L is a student.

The 1930 census for Menominee, Michigan has Charles J Vary, 46, married at 30, secretary-treasurer of a paper mill, renting his home at 220 Sheridan Road for $40 per month and owns a radio. Mary E is 38 and was married at 23. Their children are Doris L, 22, an assistant librarian at the public library and Hugh, 5.

The 1940 census for Menominee, Michigan has Charles Vary, 52, completed 8th grade an accountant for a paper mill who owns his home at 234 Sheridan Road worth $20,000. Mary is 48 and graduated high school. Hugh is 15 and completed 9th grade.

Charles J Vary born 29 Sep 1884, died 17 Aug 1976 in Menominee, Michigan and is buried with his first wife, Florence, in Watertown, New York.

### 6. Doris Louise Vary and William Francis John

The 1940 census for Marinette, Wisconsin has William F John, 51, graduated high school, a senior clerk for a tract index who owns his home at 1328 Prescott Street worth $3500. Doris L is 31 and completed 1-year college. Their sons are John L, 7, completed 1st grade; David W, 5 and Harold A, 1.

Doris Louise Vary John born 3 Jun 1907, died 6 Jun 1950 in Marinette, Wisconsin and is buried in Forest Home Cemetery. William Francis John born 18 Nov 1887, died 27 Apr 1958 and is buried with Doris. William was a private in the Wisconsin 161st Depot Brigade during WW1.

## 5. Elizabeth S Vary and John E Rienbeck

Elizabeth S Vary, 24, married John E Rienbeck, 38, on 8 Nov 1916 in Jefferson County, New York. This picture was taken at their wedding.

The 1920 census for Cape Vincent, New York has John E Rienbeck, 42, a farmer with a truck farm on James Street. Elizabeth is 37. The children are J Wesley, 9; Donald B, 2 and Ella L less than a year. John Wesley Rienbeck born 20 Nov 1910, died 16 Jan 1927 in Cape Vincent, New York.

The 1930 census for Cape Vincent, New York has John Rienbeck, 52, married at 28, farming on James Street. Elizabeth is 37 and married at 24. The children are Donald B, 12; Ella L, 11; Fredrick J, 9; Kenneth H, 8 and Mary E, 4.

The 1940 census for Cape Vincent, New York has John E Rienbeck, 62, completed 9th grade and owns his farm on James Street worth $5000. Elizabeth is 47 and completed 8th grade. Their children are Donald B, 22, completed 2 years college, a farm hand; Ella, 21, completed 3 years college; Fredrick, 19, completed 2 years college, a farm hand; Kenneth, 18, graduated high school, a farm hand and Mary, 14, completed 8th grade.

## 5. Willett Hart Vary and Muriel Margaret Huff

Willet Hart Vary Jr, 18 years 9 months, enlisted at the recruiting station in Syracuse, New York as an apprentice seaman on 27 Dec 1917. He went to the Newport Rhode Island Naval Training Station from 19 Jan 1918 to 14 Mar 1918. He trained on a ship at Boston, Massachusetts, 14 Mar 1918 and left 7 Apr 1918. He trained on another ship at Philadelphia, Pennsylvania form 7 Apr 1918 to 22 Apr 1918. Willet then served on the USS Carola from 22 Apr 1918 to 9 May 1918 and the USS Remlik from 9 May 1918 to 11 Nov 1918. He was discharged from the USS Remlik on 29 Aug 1919 at Newport News, Virginia with a rank of Fireman 1st class.

Willett Hart Vary, 23, a chauffeur, married Muriel Margaret Huff, 23, a school teacher, on 20 Jul 1921 in Dexter, New York.

The 1930 census for Harrisburg, Lewis, New York has Willett H Vary, 31, married at 22, a farmer who owns his home on West Road and a radio. Muriel M is 32 and married at 23. Their daughter is June E, 7.

The 1940 census for Caroline, Tompkins, New York has Willett Vary, 41, completed 10th grade, a farm manager renting his home on Slaterville Road for $18 per month. Muriel is 42 and graduated high school.

June E Vary married Harry Hill on 2 Jun 1940 in West Carthage, New York.

## 4. Watson F Carpenter and Laura M McNitt

The 1900 census for Antwerp, New York has Watson Carpenter, 38, born May 1862, married 11 years, a cheese maker who owns his home. Laura is 32, born Sept 1867 and has two children both living. The children are Bertha, 8, born Nov 1891 and Gladys, 11/12, born Jun 1899. They have a servant Edith, 15.

The 1910 census for Gouverneur, New York has Watson F Carpenter, 47, married 21 years, a commercial traveler selling dairy equipment. Laura is 42 and has 3 children all living. The children are Bertha, 18; Gladys, 10; and Robert W a new born.

The 1920 census for Gouverneur, New York has Watson F Carpenter, 57, a salesman who owns his home on Clinton Street. Laura M is 52. Gladys E is 20 and Robert W is 9.

The 1930 census for Gouverneur, New York has Watson F Carpenter, 67, married at 27, a traveling salesman for dairy supplies who owns his home worth $7000 on Clinton Street and a radio. Laura M is 62 and married at 21. Robert W is 20.

According to his obituary, Watson was a traveler (traveling salesman). He was educated at Ives Seminary in Antwerp, New York and Perkins Academy in Copenhagen, New York. He started manufacturing butter and cheese in Jefferson County in 1884, continuing in Frankfort, New York until 1889. He married Laura McNitt and moved to Oxbow in 1889 where they lived until 1901. After that he sold dairy and agriculture equipment for a company in Little Falls, New York.

Watson F Carpenter born 1862 in Brownville, New York, died 1931 in St Lawrence County, New York and is buried in Riverside Cemetery, Gouverneur, New York. Laura M McNitt Carpenter born 1867, died 1946 and is buried with Watson.

## 5. Bertha Laura Carpenter and Earl Mason Gardner

Bertha L Carpenter, 26, married Earl Mason Gardener, 25, on 21 May 1918 in Ross County, Ohio. They were married by the base Chaplain at Camp Sherman.

Earl M Gardner, born 26 May 1892, of 9 University Ave. Canton, New York was called into active service 15 Aug 1917 as a 2$^{nd}$ Lieutenant and was assigned to the 3$^{rd}$ Infantry New York National Guard. He served overseas from 12 Jun 1918 to 21 Jan 1919 and discharged 4 Feb 1919.

The 1930 census for Gouverneur, New York has Earl M Gardner, 37, a veteran, a salesman for Tale Corporation renting a home on Oak Square Street for $30 per month. Bertha is 38 and married at 26. The children are Barbara, 9; Richard, 3; and Sally, 2.

The 1940 census for Gouverneur, New York has Earl M Gardner, 47, graduated college, a salesman for mining products renting a home at 145 Main Street. Bertha is 48, graduated high school and a saleslady for a retail grocery. The children are Barbra, 19, graduated high school, a waitress in a restaurant; Richard E, 13, completed 8$^{th}$ grade; and Sally, 12, completed 7$^{th}$ grade.

Bertha Carpenter Gardner born 1891, died 22 Mar 1946 in Watertown, New York and is buried in Riverside Cemetery, Gouverneur, New York. Earl Gardner born 26 May 1892, died 28 Aug 1963 in Cambridge, Ohio and is buried with Bertha.

## 5. Gladys Elizabeth Carpenter and Philo Davis Clark

Gladys Elizabeth Carpenter, 26, married Philo Davis Clark, 24, on 29 Aug 1925 in St Lawrence County, New York.

The 1930 census for Rumford, Maine has Philo Clark, 28, born in Maine, a teacher in a paper mill who owns a home at 219 Wheeler Street worth $7000. Gladys is 29. Their daughter, Patricia is 3.

The 1940 census for Watertown, New York has Philo D Clark, 38, graduated college, a proprietor of a retail gent's shop renting a home at 325 South Massey Street for $45 per month. Gladys is 39 and graduated college. The children are Patricia C, 13, completed 7$^{th}$ grade and Edward P, 8, completed 2$^{nd}$ grade.

Gladys Carpenter Clark died 6 Oct 1959 in Seattle, Washington and is buried in Riverside Cemetery, Gouverneur, New York. Philo Davis Clark died in 1978 and is buried with Gladys.

## 5. Robert W Carpenter and Muriel W Corbett

Robert W Carpenter and Muriel W Corbett were married 19 Dec 1936 in Ogdensburg, New York. They may have been attending college in Ogdensburg.

The 1940 census for Watertown, New York has Robert W Carpenter, 29, graduated college and a credit adjuster at a small loan company and renting a home at 150 Bishop Street for $45 per month. Muriel is 27, graduated high school and a secretary at an investment banking firm. Their daughter, Judith is 2. They have a live-in servant.

Robert Watson Carpenter born in 1910, died in 1985 and is buried in Riverside Cemetery, Gouverneur, New York. Muriel died in 2002.

## 4. Frank J Carpenter and Mary A Brown

The 1900 census for Palmyra, New York has Frank Carpenter, 34, born May 1866, married 3 years, a blacksmith renting his home at 7 Main Street. Mary is 34, born Mar 1866 and had 1 child. Their son, Harold, born Feb 1900 is 3/12.

The 1910 census for Oxbow, Antwerp, New York has Frank J Carpenter, 43, married 13 years, a blacksmith in the horseshoe industry. Mary is 44. Their son, Harold J is 10.

The 1920 census for Antwerp, New York has Frank J Carpenter, 53, a dairy farmer with a farm on Beartown Road. Mary A is 53. Harold J is 19 and a laborer on his father's dairy farm.

About the time of his marriage, Frank and Mary's only son moved to Trumansburg in the finger lakes region of New York. Frank and Mary moved to the area soon after.

The 1930 census for Seneca County, New York has Frank J Carpenter, 63, married 30 years, a farmer on a rented farm. Mary A is 64 and married at 30.

Frank J Carpenter born 1866, died 31 May 1938 and is buried in New Oxbow Cemetery, Oxbow, New York. Mary A Carpenter born Mar 1866, died 11 Nov 1939 and is buried with Frank.

## 5. Harold J Carpenter and Hattie Wilhelmina Vosburgh

Harold Jerry Carpenter, 23, married Hattie Wilhelmina Vosburgh on 27 Aug 1923 in Trumansburg, New York. Trumansburg is on the Seneca and Ulysses County line

The 1925 New York State Census for Ulysses, Tompkins, New York has Harold Carpenter, 25, a carpenter living on Lake Street. Hattie W is 33. Hattie's mother, Anna Vosburgh, 69, is living with them.

The 1930 census for Trumansburg, New York has Harold Carpenter, 30, married at 23, a mechanic at a chain works. Hattie is 38 and married at 31. Their daughter, Dorla M is 2. Anna Vosburgh is 74 and living with them.

The 1940 census for Trumansburg, New York has Harold Carpenter, 40, completed 11th grade, a machinist for a chain works who owns his home worth $1000. Hattie is 48 and completed 8th grade. Their daughter, Dorla is 12 and completed 6th grade.

## 3. Sylvester A Carpenter and Carrie L Larkin

The 1860 census for Brownville, Jefferson, New York has Sylvester Carpenter, 23, a farmer. Carrie is 22. Sylvester's father, Jeremiah, is the next listing.

Sylvester Carpenter, 28, of Brownville, New York, married, a laborer, registered for the Civil War 3 Jul 1863. It is not known if he served. This is a picture of Sylvester Carpenter.

The 1870 census for Brownville, New York has Priscilla Carpenter, 38, keeping house; Sylvester, 33, a sailor; Carrie, 30 a school teacher and Elnora, 9, attended school. Priscilla is listed first and may have owned the house. She is Sylvester's sister.

Artie Carpenter was born in 1871 and died in 1873.

The 1880 census for Brownville, New York has Sylvester Carpenter, 44, a farmer. Carrie is 42; Nora is 18 and teaching school and Sarah, Sylvester's step-mother is 67.

The 1900 census for Brownville, New York has Sylvester Carpenter, 64, born Nov 1835, married 41 years, owns his home free and clear. Carrie L is 63, born Feb 1837, had 2 children, one is still living.

The 1910 census for Brownville, New York has Sylvester Carpenter, 74, married 51 years, a retired farmer who owns his home. Carrie L is 73 and has had one child who is still living.

Carrie L Carpenter died 15 May 1918 and is buried in Dexter Cemetery, Dexter, New York. The large stone has S A Carpenter, died 16 Jul 1919, Artie A their son, died 30 May 1873 aged 2 years 4 months. George Crittenton died 25 Jan 1932 and Nora E Carpenter, his wife, died 23 Apr 1913; their son C Emmitt Crittenton born 1893, died 1952.

## 4. Nora E Carpenter and George M Crittenton

The 1900 census for Brownville, New York has George Crittenton, 43, born Aug 1856, married 15 years, a farmer who owns his farm. Nora E is 38, born Sep 1861 and has two children, both alive. The children are Emmett C, 6, born Sep 1893; an unnamed daughter, 1/12, born Apr 1900; and Cora M Stone, 11, born Sep 1888, adopted daughter. Nothing more is known about Cora Stone.

The 1910 census for Dexter, New York has George M Crittenton, 53, married 24 years, a laborer in a coal yard who owns his home. Nora E is 48 and has had 2 children both living. The children are Emmitt C, 16 and Irma F C, 9. Both attend school.

Emmitt Carpenter Crittenton born 1 Sep 1893 in Pillar Point, New York registered 5 Jun 1917 for WW1, enlisted 22 Nov 1917 at Madison Barracks, New York. He was assigned to 306 Supply company Quarter Masters Corp as a private then promoted to private first-class 9 Dec 1917. He went overseas from 12 Jan 1918 to 4 Jul 1919. Emmitt was honorably discharged 16 Jul 1919 from Camp Upton, Long Island.

The 1920 census for Dexter, New York has George Crittenton, 55, widower, teamster in a coal yard and boarding with another family.

The 1930 census for Dexter, New York has Harry V Liddy, 34, married at 26, a laborer for a coal company who owns his home worth $3500. Irma C is 29 and married at 22. Their son, Donald G is 1 10/12. Irma's father, George Crittenton, 73, widower and brother, Emmitt C, 36, single, a farm laborer are living with them.

Emmitt is still living with his sister Irma in 1940. It appears he never married.

## 5. Irma F Crittenton and Harry V Liddy

Irma F Crittenton, 22, married Harry V Liddy on 17 Nov 1922 in Jefferson, New York.

The 1940 census for Dexter, New York has Harry Liddy, 34, completed 6th grade, a truck driver for a coal and wood company. Irma is 39 and completed 11th grade. The children are Donald, 11, completed 6th grade and Lorene J, 7, completed 2nd grade. Emmitt Crittenton is 46, graduated high school and working in a sulphite mill.

Harry V Liddy born 1895, died 1967 and is buried in Dexter Cemetery, Dexter, New York. Irma Crittenton Liddy born 25 Apr 1900, died 13 Nov 1990 and is buried with Harry.

## 3. Adeline Carpenter and James B Ackerman / George R Kellogg

The 1860 census for Brownville, Jefferson, New York has James Ackerman, 24, a farmer, born in New York. Ada is 21. Their daughter Ada is 1. James' father and 2 brothers are living with them.

James B Ackerman, 27, a married farmer was registered for the Civil War on 4 Jul 1863. There is no indication he served.

The 1865 New York State Census for Brownville has James B Ackerman, 29, a farmer. Adaline is 26. Their daughter, Adubelle is 6. James' mother, Rhoda is 65.

The 1880 census for Brownville, Jefferson, New York has James Ackerman, 40, a farmer. Addie is 41 and keeping house.

The will of James B Ackerman was proved on 7 Aug 1883 in Watertown, New York. The widow Adaline and only child Addie B Baker would inherit everything.

Adeline Carpenter Ackerman married George R Kellogg about 1885.

The 1900 census for Dexter, New York has George Kellogg, 45, born Oct 1854, married 15 years, a sawyer in a pulp mill. Addie is 59, born Jan 1841 (earlier census records have about 1838 to 1840), had 2 children, 1 is still living. Two boarders who work in the pulp mill and a female servant are living with them.

The 1910 census for Dexter, New York has George Kellogg, 56, 1st marriage, married 25 years, a county debt sheriff who owns his home on Grove Street free and clear. Addie B is 70, 2nd marriage, had 2 children, one is living. It is not known when the 2nd child was born or it's name.

Adeline Carpenter Ackerman Kellogg born 1838-40, died 1916.

George R Kellogg died 9 Aug 1922 in Watertown, New York and is buried in Dexter Cemetery, Dexter, New York. There is no stone for either.

## 4. Adubelle "Addie" B Ackerman and David S Baker

The 1880 census for Brownville, Jefferson, New York has David Baker, 35, born in Canada, a laborer. Belle is 22. Their son, James is 3.

The 1900 census for Dexter, New York has David S Baker, 53, born June 1847 in Canada, married 25 years, immigrated 1865, the proprietor of a grocery who owns his mortgaged home. Addie Belle is 40, born Feb 1860, had 3 children, 3 are living. The children are Eva M, 15, born Aug 1884 and Pearle B, 12, born May 1888. There are 5 boarders living with them.

The 1910 census for Dexter, New York has David S Baker, 62, married 35 years, a day laborer who owns his home on Bradley Street free and clear. Addie B is 50 and a boarding house keeper with 5 boarders. Pearl B is 21 and a bookkeeper at a clothing store.

The 1920 census for Dexter, New York taken 6 Jan 1920 has David Baker, 74, a truck gardener who owns his home on Bradley Street. Belle is 58 and a boarding house keeper with 5 boarders. Sherman Anderson, son-in-law, 25, is a foreman at the paper mill. Pearl, 30 is a bookkeeper for a furniture store.

David S Baker died 12 Feb 1920 in Watertown, New York. Addie died about 1928.

## 5. James E Baker and Ruth E Leonard

The 1900 census for Watertown, New York has James Baker, 24, born Sep 1875, married 2 years, a salesman renting a home. Ruth is 18 and born Sep 1881.

The 1910 census for Brownville, New York has James Baker, 32, married 12 years, a manufacturer of soap who owns his home free and clear. Ruth is 28 and has 2 children, both living. The children are Bell A, 9, and Leonard D, 3.

The 1920 census for Watertown, New York has James E Baker, 43, a taxi driver who owns his home at 202 Chestnut Street. Ruth E is 38. The children are Bell A, 18, a worker in a corset factory and Leonard D, 13, attended school.

The 1930 census for Watertown, New York has James Baker, 53, married at 21, a salesman for a soap company who owns his home at 202 Chestnut Street worth $5000. Ruth is 48, married at 16 and a saleslady for a knitting company. Leonard is 23, single and a life insurance agent.

James E Baker born 7 Sep 1876, died 6 Oct 1934 and is buried in Dexter Cemetery, Dexter, New York. A Watertown City Directory for 1935, information from 1934, has James E Baker as a soap manufacturer. It is not clear whether he owned the company and worked at various jobs or worked for the owner of the soap company.

The 1940 census for Watertown, New York has Ruth E Baker, 58, widow, completed 10th grade and keeping 2 lodgers in the house at 202 Chestnut.

Ruth E Baker born 2 Sep 1881 in Dexter, New York, died 4 Nov 1960 in Kalamazoo, Michigan. She is buried in Dexter Cemetery with James.

## 6. Belle Ardus Baker and Albert Waldo Ayles

Belle Ardus Baker, 23, married Albert Waldo Ayles, 21, a student, on 21 Jun 1924 in Watertown, New York.

The 1930 census for Dexter, New York has Albert W Ayles, 26, married at 20, an insurance agent who owns his home on Brown Street worth $5000 and a radio. Ardis B is 29 and was married at 23. The children are Leonard J 5, and Hartwell W 3. Lucy A Leonard, grandmother, 78, widow, is living with them.

The 1940 census for Dexter, New York has Walter Ayles, 36, completed 2 years college, a chemist in a sulphite mill who owns a home worth $4000. Ardis is 39, graduated college and a cutter girl in a paper mill. Their sons are Leonard, 15, completed 8th grade and Hartwell, 13, completed 8th grade.

## 6. Leonard D Baker and Lulu N Stevens

Leonard D Baker married Lulu N Stevens on 6 Apr 1931 in Watertown, New York.

The 1940 census for Geddes, Onondaga, New York has Leonard D Baker, 33, completed 11th grade, a salesman for a utility renting a home at 120 Meadow Road for $35 per month. Lulu N is 34, born in Canada and graduated high school. Their children are Alice A, 8, completed 1st grade and David L, 3.

## 5. Eva M Baker and Adelbert C McLane

The 1910 census for Watertown, New York has Delbert C McLane, 34, married 6 years, a house mason renting a home at 212 Phelps Street. Eva M is 24 and has 2 children who are living. The children are Addie P, 4, and James A, 3.

The 1920 census for Dexter, New York has Albert McLane, 44, working in the shipping department of a sulphite mill and renting a home on Water Street. Eva M is 35. Their children are Addie, 14 and James, 13.

The 1930 census for Watertown, New York has Adelbert McLane, 54, married at 28, a brick layer in the building trades renting a home at 101 South Hamilton for $40 per month and owns a radio. Eva is 45, was married at 19 and a sales lady in a department store. James is 23, single and teaching at a university.

The 1940 census was not found but a 1944 Watertown, New York City Directory has Adelbert C McLane living at 513 Hamlin. Eva M is a buyer at Smith & Percy Inc.

Adelbert "Delbert" C McLane born 16 Jun 1875, died 7 Nov 1949 and is buried in Dexter Cemetery. An application for headstone signed by Eva says he served in the 9th Infantry Regiment from 15 Jun 1898 to 21 Jan 1900 as a private. He joined the Army at Madison Barracks near Sacketts Harbor, New York for a three-year enlistment. He was assigned to Company I, 11th Regiment; Company I, 19th Regiment; and Company M, 9th Regiment. This was during the Spanish American War. Part of this time was served in the Philippines.

Eva M Baker McLane born 1884, died 1961 and is buried with Adelbert.

## 6. Addie Pearl McLane and Clarence Everett Harris

Addie Pearl McLane, 22, a teacher, married Clarence Everett Harris, 25, a teacher, in Watertown on 25 Jun 1927.

The 1930 census for Highland Park, Michigan has Clarence E Harris, 28, married at 25, a teacher at a private school renting part of a home at 119 Grove for $50 per month. Addie P is 24 and married at 22. A 1940 census was not found.

Clarence Harris born 3 Jul 1901, died 17 Jan 1986. Addie Harris born 6 Jun 1905, died 25 May 1986. They were living in Pinellas, Florida and are buried in Dexter Cemetery, Dexter, New York.

## 6. James Adelbert McLane and Elva Elizabeth Starr

James Adelbert McLane married Elva Elizabeth Starr in 1931 in Champaign, Illinois.

The 1940 census for Alfred, New York has James A McLane, 33, graduated college, director of a college athletic department who owns his home at 99 North Main Street worth $5000. Elva is 38 and completed 5 years college. Their children are Richard, 7, completed 1st grade and Sally, 2.

James A McLane born 1906, died 1970 and is buried in Alfred Rural Cemetery, Alfred, New York. Elva died 6 Sep 1983 and is buried with James.

## 5. Pearle Belle Baker and Sherman Anderson

Pearle Belle Baker, 26, married Sherman Anderson on 23 Sep 1915 in Jefferson County, New York.

Sherman Anderson, 22, born 23 Sep 1894 in Red Wing, Minnesota, with both parents born in Denmark registered for WW1 on 5 Jun 1917 in Dexter, New York. His occupation was paper maker at Dexter Sulphite Pulp and Paper Company. Sherman was inducted 11 May 1918 at Adams, New York and sent to Ft. Slocum, New York where he was assigned 9th Company D Battalion as a private. He was transferred 18 Jul 1918 to Camp Upton, Long Island, 101st M G B then to Camp Hancock. Sherman was sent overseas 27 Jul 1918 to 15 Feb 1919. He fought at St Mihiel, Meuse-Argonne where he was gassed 28 Oct 1918. He was hospitalized in a field hospital and 3 base hospitals. Sherman Anderson was honorably discharged 25 Feb 1919 at Camp Upton, Long Island. Claude Wilhelm died 15 Sep 1918 in the same area and is buried in St Mihiel Cemetery. He is a Klingensmith - Arn descendant.

The 1925 census for Dexter, New York has Sherman Anderson, 30, a mill foreman. Pearl B is 36. Their daughter, Kathleen P is 4. Addie B Baker, 65 is living with them.

The 1930 census for Dexter, New York has Sherman Anderson, 34, married at 21, a foreman at a paper mill. Pearle B is 39, married at 25 and a bookkeeper in a paper mill office. Kathleen is 9 and attending school. They are living on Bradley Street probably in the home owned by Addie and David Baker.

The 1940 census for Watertown, New York has Sherman Anderson, 45, completed 6th grade, a foreman in a paper mill renting part of 213 Stone Street. Pearle is 51, completed 8th grade and a bookkeeper in a paper mill.

Kathleen Pearle Anderson, 21 married William Robert Corwin on 10 Jul 1942 in Fort Wayne, Indiana. Kathleen is in the 1942 Fort Wayne City Directory. She was a stenographer for Norwalk Truck Line. Her residence was 733 W. Wayne Apt 205.

## 2.4. Rhoda Carpenter and Sanford Parish

The 1850 census for Brownville, New York has Sanford Parish, 53, a farmer. Rhoda is 52. Their children are Melina, 17 and Ephraim, 16.

Nothing more was found on Melina Parish. It is not known if there were other children.

The 1860 census for Pitcairn, St Lawrence, New York has Sanford Parish, 61, a farmer with $200 in real estate. Rhoda is 60. Ephraim is 26 and a farmer. His wife, Margaret is 19 and a school teacher.

An 1870 census has not been found. Rhoda is with Ephraim in 1880 so Sanford must have died between 1860 and 1880. Ancestry trees have 1864.

Rhoda C Parish died 28 Jun 1883 in Pitcairn. No cemetery records were found.

## 3. Ephraim Adolphus Parish and Margaret Van Patten / Anna Davis

Ephraim is listed with his parents in 1860. He was successful enough as a farmer and joiner (carpenter) that he paid for a substitute during the civil war. Maybe his parents paid for the substitute.

The 1870 census for Pitcairn, New York has Ephraim Parish, 36, a farmer with $400 in real estate. Margaret is 29 and keeping house. The children are Lucinda, 8; Franklin, 7; Alvin, 5; Russell, 3; and Luna, 1.

The 1880 census for Pitcairn, New York has Ephraim A Parish, 43, a farmer. Margaret is 39. The children are Lucinda, 19, works out; Frank L, 16, works out, Alvin V, 14; Russell W, 13; Luna M, 11; Ada E, 5; and Worth, 3/12. Rhoda, 86, is living with them. All the children except the 2 oldest and 2 youngest attended school. Ephraim's wife, Margaret, died in 1881.

Lucinda Parish died in 1884. Nothing definite could be found for Frank L Parish after 1880. I suspect he died before the second Frank Parish was born in 1893. Alvin Parish died 1886.

The 1900 census for Diana, Lewis, New York is so faint it is unreadable. Ancestry has

Ephraim Parish, born Oct 1834, married 1887. His wife is Anna and children Frank, McKinley, and unknown.

The 1910 census for Champion, Jefferson, New York has Ephraim A Parish, 65, married 22 years, a farmer renting his farm. Anna is 50, born in England and had 3 children, all living. The children are Frank, 17, a farm laborer; McKinley, 13; Dewey, 10 and grandson, Alvin Parish, 1. McKinley and Dewey attended school.

Ephraim Parish born 25 Oct 1833 at Pillar Point, New York, died 10 Sep 1919 at Adams, Jefferson, New York and is buried in Pitcairn Cemetery, Pitcairn, New York with his 2 wives; Margaret Van Patten Parish born 1840, died 1881; and Anna Davis Parish born 1860, died 1943. Lucinda Parish born 1862, died 1884 and Alvin Parish born 1865, died 1886 are in the same cemetery. Luna M Parish, born 1869 may have died 1884.

## 4. Russell W Parish and Elizabeth Whitcomb

Russell W Parish, 25, of Rutland, Vermont, a jeweler, born in Gouverneur, New York, married Elizabeth H Whitcomb on 7 Oct 1895 in Rutland, Vermont. Gibbs Brasilin, Pastor, Baptist Church, officiated.

The 1900 census for Rutland, Vermont has Russell W Parish, 32, born May 1868, married 4 years, a jeweler, renting his home. Lizzie H is 30, born Jul 1869 and a bookkeeper.

The 1910 census for Burlington, Vermont has Russel W Parish, 42, married 14 years, born in New York, a jeweler in his jewelry store. Elizabeth, 39, born in Vermont, has not had children. They have a boarder and are living in a mortgaged home they own.

The 1920 census for Burlington, Vermont has Russell W Parish, 53, owner jewelry store who owns a home at 1 Brooks Ave. free and clear. Elizabeth is 50 and her father, Vernon Whitcomb, 76 is living with them. They also have a male nurse living with them presumably taking care of the father. Elizabeth's father died 27 Jan 1924.

Russell White Parish born 31 May 1868, died 24 Jul 1928. He was in the hospital for 1 week and died of Chronic Myocarditis and cerebral hemorrhage. Elizabeth Whitcomb Parish born Jul 1869, died 1930 in Pinellas, Florida. They are both buried in Lakeview Cemetery, Burlington, Vermont.

## 4. Ada E Parish and Morris S Petrie /Thomas Shannon

Ada E Parish married Morris S Petrie on 14 Feb 1894 in Oxbow, New York.

The 1900 census for Diana, Lewis, New York is so faint it is unreadable but Ancestry has recovered the following. Ada Petrie, born Jan 1873, married in 1894 and Nora Petrie. Nora may be Morris' daughter by a previous marriage as Ada did not have children.

The 1910 census for Le Ray, Jefferson, New York has Morris S Petrie, 40, married 16 years, a farmer renting his farm. Ada M is 35 and has not had children. Clifford Parish, 3, a nephew is living with them.

The 1930 census for Lorraine, Jefferson, New York taken 27 May 1930 has Morris S Petrie, 60, married at 22, a farmer on a farm he owns and a radio. Ada is 55, married at 19. They also have a school teacher boarding with them.

The Syracuse, New York City Directory has Morris S Petrie (Ada P) died 13 Sep 1930.

Ada Parish Petrie, 57, married Thomas Shannon on 17 May 1932 in Onondaga, New York

The 1940 census for Rutland, Jefferson, New York has Thomas Shannon, 64, completed 7$^{th}$ grade, a farmer on his own farm. Ada is 65 and completed 6$^{th}$ grade.

Ada Parish Petrie Shannon died 11 Oct 1954 in Watertown, New York.

## 4. Worth W Parish and Edith M Waters / Minerva R Pelow

Worth Parish, 24, was living with his father in 1905. Worth Parish married Edith M Waters about 1906 and Clifford was born in 1907.

Edith Waters, born 1887, died 17 Apr 1909.

The 1910 census for Watertown, New York has Worth Parish, 28, widowed, a teamster, and a boarder, in a boarding house on West Main Street. Clifford is living with his Aunt Ada Parish Petrie in 1910.

Worth W Parish, 35, born 24 Feb 1883 of Watertown, New York, a taxi driver, registered for WW1 on 12 Sep 1918. His nearest relative is Clifford W Parish of Adams, New York.

Worth W Parish, 35, married Minerva R Pelow on 8 Feb 1919 in Jefferson, New York.

The 1920 census for Watertown, New York has Worth Parish, 36, an automobile chauffer renting a home at 117 Gale Street. Minerva is 36.

The 1930 census for Watertown, New York has Worth Parish, 47, a chauffeur for an omnibus renting a home at 638 Mundy Street for $31 per month and owns a radio. Minerva is 46.

The 1940 census for Pamelia, Jefferson, New York has Worth W Parish, 57, completed 5$^{th}$ grade, a salesman in his gas station renting a home at 51 Ogdensburg Road.

Minerva R is 56 and completed 6th grade.

Worth W Parish born 1883, died 28 Sep 1945 in Watertown, New York. He is buried in North Watertown Cemetery, Watertown, New York.

## 5. Clifford Worth Parish and Lena Margaret Burdick

Clifford is living with his aunt Ada in 1910.

The 1925 census for Ellisburg, New York has Clifford Parish, 19, a farm laborer.

Clifford Worth Parish, 22, born in Watertown, New York, married Margaret Burdick, 18, born in Sacketts Harbor, New York, on 1 May 1929 in Savannah, New York. Clifford's father was Worth Parish and his mother Edith Waters, born in France.

The 1940 census for Sandy Creek, Oswego, New York has Clifford Parish, 32, completed 8th grade, a laborer in a gravel pit renting a home for $8 per month. Lena is 29 and completed 7th grade. The children are Barbara, 7, attended school; Minerva, 5; Francis, 4; Eli, 2; Margaret, 1; and Clifford, 2/12.

Clifford Parish born 1907, died 1 Nov 1947 in Syracuse, New York and is buried in North Watertown Cemetery, Watertown, New York. Margaret Lena Burdick Parish born 1911, died 1988.

## 5. Frank S Parish, Dewey E Parish and their mother Anna Davis Parish

Frank is listed with his parents in 1910.

The 1920 census for Adams, Jefferson, New York has Frank S Parish, 26, head of the family, single, a farmer renting a farm on Henderson Road. His mother, Anna, is 60, a widow and immigrated from England. His brothers McKinley, 23, and Dewey, 20 are working on the farm.

The 1930 census for Adams, New York has Anna Parish, 70, a widow, married at 28, immigrated in 1870 and renting their home at 34 Church Street for $19 per month. Frank S is 36, single and a foreman in a truss factory. Dewey C is 30, single and driving truck for the New York State Highway Department.

The 1940 census for Adams, New York has Anna Parish, 80, a widow, completed 4th grade and renting their home on Church Street for $15 per month. A decrease in value due to the depression. Frank is 46, single, completed 8th grade and working as a shipping clerk in the truss factory. Dewey is 40, single, completed 7th grade and driving truck for the New York State Highway Department.

Anna Davis Parish born 31 Jan 1860 in England died 6 Sep 1943 in Watertown, New

York and is buried in North Watertown Cemetery with Ephraim Parish.

Frank Sanford Parish born 16 Apr 1893, died 28 Oct 1948 in Watertown, New York and is buried in North Watertown Cemetery.

Dewey Ephraim Parish born 24 May 1899, died Jun 1952 in Watertown, New York and is buried in North Watertown Cemetery.

## 5. McKinley Alvin "Mac" Parish and Iva Etta Michael

McKinley Alvin Parish, 21, from Adams, New York, enrolled at the recruiting station in Syracuse, New York on 23 May 1918. His rate was Seaman $2^{nd}$ Class. He served at Pelham Bay Park, New York from 22 Aug 1918 to 11 Nov 1918. He was discharged 15 Apr 1919 at Fleet Supply Base, Brooklyn, New York.

McKinley Alvin Parish, 29, married Iva Etta Michael, 22, on 15 Aug 1925 in Oswego, New York.

The 1930 census for Fulton, New York has McKinley A Parrish, 33, married at 29, a truck driver for a trucking company renting a home on Third Street for $30 per month and they have a radio. Iva E is 26, married at 22 and a teacher in a public school.

The 1940 census for Fulton, New York has McKinley Parish, 43, completed $8^{th}$ grade, a substation agent for an oil company renting a home at 8 West Third Street for $30 per month. Iva is 36 and graduated college. Their daughters are Jean, 8, completed $3^{rd}$ grade and Beverly, 4.

McKinley Alvin "Mac" Parish born 24 Jul 1896, died 24 Nov 1963 in Watertown, New York and is buried in North Watertown Cemetery. He served in WW1. Iva died in 1984 and is buried with McKinley.

## 2.5. Levi Carpenter and Eunice Ayer

Levi Carpenter born 10 Dec 1799 in Plattsburg, New York, served in the War of 1812. Levi Carpenter, private, is listed with Capt. Peter Miller's Company of Col. Samuel Hawken's $2^{nd}$ U S Volunteer Regiment. A payroll abstract for New York State Militia has Carpenter, Levi, private, paid from 8 Nov to 31 Dec 1812, $8.83; 1 Jan to 28 Feb 1813, $16; and 1 May to 1 Jul 1813, $16. Levi would have been 13 and 14 years old. He seems a little young but could have been a drummer boy or lied about his age. His older brother Asaph was also in the War of 1812.

Levi Carpenter came to Brownville Township, New York with his parents after serving in the War of 1812. Levi Carpenter married Eunice Ayer and they had 10 known children.

The 1850 census for Brownville, New York has Levi Carpenter, 39, born in New York, a farmer with $312 in real estate. Eunice is 39 and born in Vermont. Their children are Lovina, 21; Lucy, 18; Mary, 17; Wellington, 16; Rosetta, 13; Winfield, 11 and Lafayette, 3, all born in New York. Lovina either married or died between 1850 and 1860. Nothing more is known.

The 1860 census for Brownville, Jefferson, New York has Levi Carpenter, 53, a farmer with $400 in land Eunice is 52. The children are Wellington, 28, sailor; Rosetta, 23, housekeeping; Winfield, 19, farmer; Orville, 16, farmer; Lafayette, 12 and Bruce, 7.

In1860 Levi Carpenter and Eunice had 5 living sons. Within a few short years, 4 would serve in the Civil War: Wellington L, Winfield, Orville, and Lafayette.

The 1865 census for Brownville, Jefferson, New York has Levi carpenter, 59, a farmer living in a frame house worth $200. Eunice is 56 and had 10 children. The children with them are Rosetta, 27, single; Winfield, 24, single, farmer, owned land; Lafayette, 18 a farmer; and Bruce, 12. Winfield and Lafayette were voters and in the army.

The 1870 census for Brownville, Jefferson, New York has Levi Carpenter, 64, a farmer. Eunice is 62. Their son, Bruce is 17 and a farmer.

The 1880 census for Brownville, Jefferson, New York has Levi Carpenter, 80, a farmer. Eunice is 80.

Levi Carpenter, born 10 Dec 1799, died 28 Aug 1890 age 91 years and is buried in Stone Cemetery.

This is his stone.

Eunice Ayer Carpenter, born June 1802 in Vermont, moved to Denver, Newago, Michigan to be with her daughter Lucy Carpenter Waterman after Levi died.

Eunice Ayers Carpenter died, 13 Aug 1900 in Denver, Newago, Michigan. She is buried in the East Hesperia Cemetery.

### 3. Lucy Carpenter and Joseph T Waterman

Lucy Carpenter married Joseph T Waterman in 1847.

The 1850 census for Brownville, Jefferson, New York, has Joseph Waterman, 26; Lucy, 17; and Edwin, 1. Lucy is also listed with her parents in 1850.

The 1860 census for Brownville, Jefferson, New York has Joseph Waterman, 38, a day laborer with $200 in real estate. Lucy is 27. Their children are Henry, 11 and Eunice, 5. Cynthia Waterman, 76, Joseph's mother, and Viola Rogus, 17, are living with them.

The family moved to Hesperia, Michigan in the fall of 1868 or 1870 after Joseph's parents died.

The 1880 census for Denver, Newago, Michigan is mostly unreadable. Joseph Waterman and Lucy are farming. The next entry is Israel Clark, 36, carpenter; Celia, 25; and Allen, 5.

The 1900 census for Denver, Newago, Michigan has Joseph B Waterman, 79, born Mar 1821, married 54 years, a farmer who owns his farm free and clear. Lucy is 69, born May 1831 and had two children, both are living. Eunice Carpenter, 97, a widow, mother-in-law, born Jun 1802, had 10 children, four are living. Lucy took care of her mother until her death in 1900 and then her husband until his death in 1908.

Joseph Waterman born 10 Mar 1821, died 22 Aug 1908 in Hesperia, Michigan and is buried in East Hesperia Cemetery. Lucy Carpenter Waterman born 25 May 1831 Pillar Point, New York, died 14 Apr 1917 in Hesperia, Michigan. She was living with her daughter Celia Clark at the time of her death.

## 4. Henry Edwin Waterman and Anna Fike / Anna Sarah Rossiter Dailey

Henry Edwin Waterman born Mar 1848 left for the Civil War Sep 1864. He was 16.

The 1865 census has Henry living with his parents and sister. He is listed as formerly in military.

Henry Edwin Waterman and Anna Fike were married about 1871.

The 1880 census for Dayton, Newago, Michigan has H E Waterman, 31, farmer. Anna is 26. Their children are Ray, 6; Levi, 5; Lafayette, 3; and Moses, 2. Anna Fike Carpenter died sometime after Jun 1881 and before 1887, possibly from childbirth.

Lulu Waterman was born 1 Jun 1881. She died 4 Jun 1907 of appendicitis in Grand Rapids, Michigan. Lulu had been working as a domestic. She was living with her brother Ray R Waterman in 1900.

Henry Edwin Waterman married Anna Sarah Rossiter about 1887.

The 1900 census for Denver, Newago, Michigan has Edward Waterman, 52, born Mar 1848, married 13 years, a farmer who owns a mortgaged farm. Anna is 49, born Mar 1851, had 9 children, 8 are living. The children are John Dailey, 21, farm laborer; Jessie Dailey, 18; Mary Dailey, 15 and Nicholas Waterman, 11, born Nov 1888. The Dailey children are from Anna Sarah Rossiter's previous marriage. Where is Leslie?

The 1910 census for Denver, Newago, Michigan has Henry E Waterman, 62, married 22 years, a farmer who owns his mortgaged farm. Annie S is 58 and had 9 children 7 are living. Their son Lessie is 21. Lessie is Leslie Leonard, born 7 Nov 1889.

The 1920 census for Hesperia, Michigan has E H Waterman, 71, renting his home. Anna is 67 and immigrated in 1852 from Ireland. The next listing has their son, Leslie Waterman, 30, renting his home and working as a laborer. Leslie's wife, Nellie is 23.

The 1930 Census for Hesperia, Michigan has Ed H Waterman, 82, first married at 21, owns his home worth $1000 and is a veteran of the Civil War. Anna is 78, first married at 16 and was born in the Irish Free State. Leslie L Waterman, 40, was married at 26, a meat cutter in a meat market who owns his home worth $1000. Nellie O is 33, was married at 19 and a bookkeeper in a creamery. They are living next door. The homes and streets are not numbered. Most numbers were assigned by electric companies.

Anna S Rossiter Waterman born 4 Mar 1850 in Wexford County Ireland, died 10 Sep 1932 in Hesperia, Michigan of aortic insufficiency and arterial sclerosis. The informant was Leslie Waterman. She was buried in East Hesperia Cemetery.

Henry E Waterman born 20 Mar 1848, died 6 Sep 1935 in Hesperia, Michigan. He died of aortic insufficiency and arterial sclerosis. Henry is buried in East Hesperia Cemetery. Informant is Leslie Waterman, child.

An application for a headstone was made 8 Jun 1940 by Leslie Waterman. Henry E Waterman was a private in Company I of the 186th New York Infantry from 21 Sep 1864 to 2 Jun 1865. Pension number was A G 201. Henry would have been 16 when he left for the Civil War. His company served in the trenches before Petersburg, Virginia and two other places in Virginia. Their toughest battle, with the most men lost, was the Appomattox Campaign that ended the war.

### 5. Ray Roland Waterman and Esther Ellen McGladrey

Ray Waterman, 22, a farmer married Ella E McGladrey, 18, a domestic on 14 Nov 1896 near Hesperia, Michigan.

The 1900 census for Leavitt, Oceana, Michigan has Ray R Waterman, 26, born Nov 1873, married 3 years, a day laborer and renting his home. Ella E is 20, born Aug 1879. Their daughter, Effie is 2 and born Aug 1897. Ray's sister Lula is 19, born Apr 1881 and working as a housekeeper. They have a boarder living with them.

Lulu Waterman born 1 Jun 1881, died 4 Jun 1907 of appendicitis. She was single and working as a domestic. She was buried 6 Jun 1907 in Hesperia, Michigan. Her father, Henry E Waterman was the informant.

The 1910 census for Edgecomb, Washington has Ray R Waterman, 36, married 13 years, a sawyer in a shingle mill and renting a home. Esther is 30 and had 1 child, still living. Effie is 12. Edgecomb is North of Seattle.

The 1920 census for Mukilteo, Washington has Ray Waterman, 46, a laborer in a lumber mill and renting a home. Esther E is 40 and they have a girl, 15, boarding.

The 1930 census for Edgecomb, Washington has Rolan R Waterman, 56, married at 23, a farmer who owns his farm. Esther E is 50 and married at 17.

The 1940 Census for Edgecomb, Washington has R R Waterman, 66, completed 5$^{th}$ grade, a farmer who owns his home worth $100. Ester E is 60 and completed 4$^{th}$ grade.

Ray Roland Waterman born Nov 1873, died 30 Oct 1945 in Arlington, Snohomish, Washington. Ester Ellen McGladrey Waterman born Aug 1879, died 11 Apr 1954.

## 6. Effie Waterman and Thomas Brennan / Harry E Jones

The 1920 census for Mukilteo, Washington has Thomas Brennan, 26, a weaver in a shingle mill renting his home. Effie is 22. Their daughter, Barbra is 2.

Effie and Thomas were divorced before 1930.

The 1930 census for Edgecomb, Washington has Harry E Jones, 33, first married at 18, a laborer in a lumber mill. Effie is 32 and first married at 18. Barbra Brennan is 13 and step-daughter. Apparently, this marriage didn't work either.

The 1940 census for Seattle, Washington has Effie Brennan, 39, divorced, completed 10$^{th}$ grade and a housekeeper in a layaway department renting a home on Ninth Avenue. Her daughter, Barbara Rodal is 23, married and completed 11$^{th}$ grade.

## 5. Levi W Waterman and Olive "Ollie" A Coy

Levi W Waterman, 24, of Denver, Michigan married Ollie Cay, 20, of Newfield, Oceana, Michigan on 3 Jul 1899 in Newfield, Michigan

The 1900 census for Newfield, Oceana, Michigan has Levi Waterman, 25, born May 1875, married less than a year, a farm laborer. Olive is 20, born Oct 1880. They are living with Olive's parents and their children and grandchildren. One of the grandchildren is Lyle, 5, born May 1895.

The 1910 census for Grand Rapids, Michigan has Levi Waterman, 33, married 15 years, a sawyer in a factory and renting his home at 871 Canal Street. Ollie is 31 and had 2 children, both living. Their children are Lyle, 14 and Millicent, 9. Olive's parents are living with them. They were married in 1899. If they were married 15 years, it would be 1895. Their marriage date may have been changed to coincide with Lyle's birth.

Levi Waterman was a private in Company A of the 35th Michigan Infantry during the Spanish American War. The record is from 1898. The real story may be that Lyle was conceived before Levi went to the War and they were married when he was discharged.

The 1920 census for Tampa Florida has Levi W Waterman, 45, a butcher in his own meat market and renting his home on North Weiland Ave. Olive is 41. Lyle is 24, single, and a clerk at a hotel. Douglas Wardlaw is 29, son-in-law, immigrated from Scotland and a traveling salesman for a packing house. Millicent is 19 and married to Douglas.

The 1930 census for Tampa Florida has Levi W Waterman, 55, married at 19, a veteran of the Spanish American War, a barber in a barber shop renting a home at 313 Labright Hanna for $15 per month. Ollie is 50 and married at 14. Millicent Livingstone, 29, married at 21, is living with them.

The 1940 census for Tampa, Florida has L W Waterman, 65, completed 4th grade and renting a home at 4103 E Ida Street. Ollie A is 60 and completed 9th grade.

Ollie Coy Waterman died in Tampa Florida in 1947. Levi Waterman born 30 May 1875, died 19 Nov 1957 in Philadelphia, Pennsylvania of congestive heart failure and arteriosclerotic heart disease. The informant is G W Barker, son-in-law.

## 6. Lyle Henry Waterman

Lyle Henry Waterman, 22, born 4 May 1895 in Hesperia, Michigan, living in Grand Rapids, an unemployed clerk, registered for WW1 on 5 Jun 1917 in Grand Rapids, Michigan.

In 1920 Lyle was living with his parents in Tampa Florida. He is in a 1919 city directory for Grand Rapids, Michigan so the family must have moved in 1919 or early 1920.

No more was found.

## 6. Millicent Waterman and Douglas Wardlaw / Livingstone / G W Barker

Millicent and Douglas Wardlaw are living with Millicent's parents in 1920. Millicent Livingstone is living with her parents in 1930. She was in Philadelphia when her father died married to G W Barker.

A California death certificate has Millicent T Carrisoza (Millicent T Waterman) born 16 Sep 1901 in Michigan, died 11 Feb 1981 in San Bernardino, California. Mother's maiden name Coy.

## 5. Lafayette T Waterman and Laverna Hinds / Elizabeth Samuels / Lily M Ward

Lafayette Waterman married Laverna Hinds 25 Sep 1897 in Hart, Michigan. Laverna filed for divorce on 8 Nov 1902 because of desertion, cruelty and non-support. The action was pending in Oceana County Circuit Court on 31 Dec 1902. It must have been granted by 1905.

Lafayette Waterman married Elizabeth Samuels 30 Nov 1905 in Grand Rapids, Michigan.

The 1910 census for Wyoming, Michigan has Lafayette Waterman, 33, married 5 years, a teamster. Lizzy is 26 and has 1 child still living. Theron is 4. Charles Albright, 18, brother-in-law is living with them.

Elizabeth Waterman filed for divorce on 4 Sep 1914, they had 1 child. Extreme and repeated cruelty was alleged. It was contested but the divorce was granted 9 Jul 1915 in Kent Michigan.

Lafayette T Waterman, 40, married Lily M Ward, 25, 10 Mar 1917 in Grand Rapids, Michigan.

The 1920 census for Wyoming, Michigan has Lafayette Waterman, 43, a watchman at a refrigerator plant renting a home on Clyde park Ave. Lillie is 28. Their children are Theron, 13, attended school and Lafayette, 1 5/12.

The 1930 census for Hudsonville, Michigan has Lafayette Waterman, 53, married at 21, a checker in a refrigerator factory who owns his home. Lily is 38 and married at 25. Their children are Lafayette, 11; Bertha, 10; Moses, 8; Joseph, 6; Orlyn, 4; and Dolores, 1. Also living with them are Ruth Murphy, 3 and James Murphy, 1 a niece and nephew.

Moses Eugene "Mosie" Waterman born 7 Feb 1922, died 24 Oct 1938. He lived 2 days before dying from Shock and cerebral damage due to fracture of base of skull. He was kicked by a horse against a cement wall. The accident occurred at home in Hudsonville, Michigan. He is buried in Georgetown Township Cemetery, Hudsonville, Michigan.

The 1940 census for Hudsonville, Michigan has Lafayette T Waterman, 63, completed 2nd grade, a farmer who owns his home on Townline Road. Lillie M is 48 and completed 9th grade. The children are Lafayette T, 21, completed 9th grade, a buffer in a bran factory; Bertha H, 20, completed 8th grade and an inspector in a meter factory; Joseph D, 16, completed 8th grade; Orlyn M, 14, completed 5th grade; and Dolores, 10 completed 4th grade.

Lillie May Ward Waterman born 5 Sep 1891, died 7 Aug 1970 and is buried in Georgetown Cemetery, Hudsonville, Michigan. Lafayette Theron Waterman born 8 Aug 1876, died 12 Jun 1971 and is buried with Lillie.

## 6. Theron E Waterman and Gladys D Beitner

Theron Waterman, 18, a factory worker, married Gladys Beitner, 18 on 15 Dec 1924 in Grand Rapids, Michigan.

The 1930 census for Grand Rapids, Michigan has Theron Waterman, 24, married at 19, a laborer in a factory renting his home on Sixth Street for $35 per month and they own a radio. Gladys is 23 and married at 18. The children are Bettie, 4 and Theron 3.

The 1940 census for Grand Rapids, Michigan has Theron Waterman, 34, completed 9th grade, an upholster at an auto body manufacturer renting a home at 604 Turner Ave. for $15 per month. Gladys is 33 and completed 8th grade. The children are Betty Lou, 14, completed 7th grade; Theron Orin, 13, completed 6th grade and Sandra Jean, 4.

Theron E Waterman born 2 Mar 1906, died 6 Nov 1976 in Lansing, Michigan.

## 5. Moses Eugene Waterman and Christie Oleva Rogers

The 1900 census for Colfax, Oceana, Michigan has Moses Waterman, 22 born Nov 1877, a lodger and a laborer in a lumber camp.

Moses E Waterman, 26, a farmer, married Oleva Rogers, 18, on 21 Apr 1904 in Hesperia, Michigan.

The 1930 census for Arlington, Washington has Moses E Waterman, 52, married at 26, a stationary engineer at a logging camp who owns his home on Third Street worth $1200 and a radio. Christie O is 43 and was married at 21.

The 1940 census for Arlington, Washington has Moses E Waterman, 62, completed 3rd grade. Christie O is 53 and completed 10th grade.

Christie Rogers Waterman born 18 Jul 1886, died Oct 1966 and is buried in Arlington Municipal Cemetery, Arlington, Washington. Moses Waterman born 30 Nov 1877, died 29 Mar 1971 in Grand Rapids, Michigan. He is buried in Arlington with Christie.

## 5. Nicolas Waterman

Nicolas born Nov 1888, died between 1900 and 1910 or at least nothing more was found.

## 5. Leslie Leonard Waterman and Nellie O Coon

Leslie Waterman, 26, a farmer married Nellie Coon, 19, on 19 Oct 1915 in Muskegon, Michigan.

The 1920 census for Hesperia, Michigan has Leslie Waterman, 30, a laborer renting a home. Nellie is 23.

The 1930 census for Hesperia, Michigan has Leslie L Waterman, 40, married at 26, a meat cutter in a meat market who owns his home worth $1500. Nellie O is 33, married at 19 and a bookkeeper at a creamery.

The 1940 census for Hesperia, Michigan has Leslie L Waterman, 50, completed 9$^{th}$ grade, a meat cutter in a meat market who owns his home worth $3500. Nellie O is 43 and graduated high school.

Leslie L Waterman born 7 Nov 1889, died 1962 and is buried in East Hesperia Cemetery, Hesperia, Michigan. Nellie O Coon Waterman born 1896, died 1970 and is buried with Leslie.

## 4. Celia Eunice Waterman and Israel Clark

The 1880 census for Hesperia, Michigan has Israel Clark, 41, a carpenter. Celia is 25. Their son Allen is 5. They are living next to her parents.

The 1900 census for Denver, Newago, Michigan has Israel Clark, 61, born Jun 1838, married 21 years, a farmer on his own farm. Celia is 45, born Jan 1855 and had I child no longer living. Allen Clark died before 1900.

The 1910 census for Hesperia, Michigan has Israel Clark, 71, married 31 years, a retired carpenter who owns his home free and clear. Celia is 55, had 1 child not living, and a dressmaker. Celia's mother, Lucy Waterman, 78, widowed, is living with them.

Israel Clark, born 16 Jun 1836, died 18 Nov 1915 of arterial sclerosis in Hesperia, Michigan. He is buried in East Hesperia Cemetery. He was a carpenter and served in the Civil War. He was in company H, 68$^{th}$ Illinois Infantry.

Lucy Carpenter Waterman died in Hesperia, 14 Apr 1917.

The 1920 census for Hesperia, Michigan has 3 women living together. Mary Mena is 90 and a widow. Isabel Becker is 79 and a widow. Celia Clark is 65, a friend, a widow and a nurse in a private home.

The 1930 census for Garfield, Newago, Michigan has Celia Clark, 75, widow, servant for a very large family with parents, 8 children and a widowed mother.

Celia Clark, 83, born 8 Jan 1855, died 17 Dec 1938 of arterial sclerosis and myocarditis. She was a domestic. Parents are Joseph Waterman and Lucy Carpenter.

A Lilli Clark, 16, married John McGhan, 19 in Hesperia, Michigan on 9 Nov 1899. Lilli's parents are Celia Waterman and Israel Clark. Celia and Israel may have adopted Lilli after Allen died. A family tree has her father as J C Clark. Relatives were often adopted when their parents died. Celia may also have misinterpreted the census and had 1 living, 1 deceased child rather than 1 child who is deceased.

Lilli Clark and John McGhan had a daughter Kathleen in 1913. Lillie married Harry J Marshall in 1930 and divorced him in 1939. Lillie Marshall is living with her daughter Kathleen and husband Fred Seggett in 1940.

### 3. Mary M Carpenter and James Joseph Breezee

Mary Carpenter married James Breezee about 1853

The 1870 census for Croghan, Lewis, New York has Joseph Breeze, 40, a farmer. Mary is 37. The children are Edwin, 16; Susan, 6 and O, 7/12, born in Oct 1869. E Carpenter, 18, a school teacher is living with them.

The 1880 census for Croghan, Lewis, New York has James Breezee, 54, a farmer. Mary is 48 and keeping house. Orin is 10 and works at home. Fredrick Johnson is 21, son-in-law, married less than a year and a laborer. Susan Breezee Johnson is 16.

The 1892 New York State Census has James Breezee, 65; Mary Brazee, 59; Julia Johnson 11 and Orin Breezee, 23, labor.

James J Breezee died 4 Jan 1893 and is buried in Sand Hill Cemetery at Natural Bridge, Jefferson, New York.

Orin died sometime between 1892 and 1900 as Mary says she only has 1 living child. The child would be Edwin.

The 1900 census for Croghan, Lewis, New York has Mary Breezee, 68, born Apr 1832, a widow, had 3 children, 1 is still living and owns her own home free and clear. Living with her are Julia, 19, born Oct 1880; Channcy, 17, born Jun 1882 and Maude, 14, born Sep 1885. The children are all Johnsons. Susan Breeze Johnson died in 1886.

Mary M Breezee is living by herself in a 1905 State of New York census. She is also found in 1910 living with Peter Ure.

Mary M Carpenter Breeze died sometime after 1910 and is buried with James in Sand Hill Cemetery.

### 4. Edwin Breeze and Lamyra R Shattuck

Edwin Breeze married Lamyra R Shattuck in 1891

The 1900 census for Croghan, Lewis, New York has Edwin L Breeze, 45, born Mar 1855, married 9 years, a day laborer who owns a mortgaged home. Elmira, 32, born Oct 1867, has had 4 children and three are living. The children are Rosettie, 6, born Jun 1893; Frankie, 5, born Mar 1895 and William, 2, born Sep 1897.

The 1910 census for Croghan, Lewis, New York has Edwin L Breezee, 54, married 19 Years, a farmer who owns his mortgaged farm. Lamyra R is 41 and has had 7 children, 4 are living. The children are Frankie, 14; Willie R, 13 and Nellie M, 7.

Lamyra R Shattuck born 1867, died 1919 and is buried in Sand Hill Cemetery, Natural Bridge, New York.

The 1920 census for Harrisburg, Lewis, New York has Edwin L Breeze, 63, widowed, a dairy farmer. William R, 22, a laborer on the dairy farm and Nellie M, 14, are living with their father.

Edwin L Breezee born 1855, died 1930 and is buried with Lamyra.

## 5. Rosetta M Breeze and Edmund Wilson

Rosetta Breeze and Edmund Wilson were married 23 Jul 1908 in Croghan, New York.

The 1920 census for Croghan, Lewis, New York has Edmund Wilson, 32, immigrated from Canada in 1900, naturalized citizen in 1901 and a farmer. Rosetta is 26. The children are Gladys, 10; Eva, 9; Herbert, 7 and Ada, 11/12. Edmund's uncle Samuel is living with them.

The 1930 census for Croghan, Lewis, New York has Edmund Wilson, 42, married at 21, a dairy farmer living on Boardman Road. Rosetta M is 36 and was married at 15. The children are Herbert J, 17, labor on the dairy farm and Ada M, 11. Edmund's mother is living with them.

Rosetta M Breezee Wilson born 1893, died 12 May 1935 and is buried in Pulaski Village Cemetery, Pulaski, New York. Edmund Wilson died 13 Nov 1966 and is buried with Rosetta.

## 6. Gladys Leata Wilson and Leo Harold Card

Gladys Leata Wilson, 16, married Leo Harold Card, 20, on 3 Jun 1925.

The 1930 census for Croghan, Lewis, New York has Leo H Card, 25, married at 21 a laborer at the Sugar Orchard. Gladys L is 21 and was married at 17. The children are Leslie, 2 and Wesley D, 1 7/12.

The 1940 census for Croghan, Lewis, New York has Leo Card, 35, completed 8$^{th}$ grade, a farm laborer. Gladys is 32 and completed 7th grade. The children are Leslie, 12, completed 5th grade; Wesley 11, completed 3rd grade; Everett, 10, completed 3rd grade and Leona 6, completed 1st grade.

Gladys Wilson Card born 1908, died 1972 and is buried in Sunnyside Cemetery, Lewis County, New York. Leo H Card born 1904 died 1984 and is buried with Gladys.

### 6. Eva Jennettie Wilson and Francis Nevins Meyers

Eva J Wilson, 18, married Francis N Meyers on 7 Jul 1928.

The 1930 census for Croghan, Lewis, New York has Francis Meyer, 23, married at 21, born in New Jersey, farming a rented farm. Eva J is 19, married at 18. Their daughter, Irene, is 1.

The 1940 census for Jersey City, New Jersey has Francis Meyer, 33, completed 8th grade, a driver for a public utility. Eva is 29 and completed 8th grade. The children are Irene, 10, completed 4th grade; Herbert, 7, completed 2nd grade and Mary, 2. The 2 younger children and their father were born in New Jersey.

### 6. Herbert Wilson and Ruth Lenard

Herbert Wilson, 21, married Ruth Lenard, 20, on 25 Aug 1934 in Lewis Co., New York.

The 1940 census for Tewksbury, Hunterdon, New Jersey has Herbert Wilson, 27, completed 8th grade, working as a farmhand. Ruth is 26 and graduated high school. The children are Eva, 4 and Albert, 1.

Ruth Leonard Wilson died 10 Nov 1968. Herbert Wilson born 31 Aug 1912, died 10 Oct 1990. They are buried in Pulaski Village Cemetery, Pulaski, New York. Both died in car accidents. Eva Ruth Wilson died in 1960.

### 6. Ada M Wilson and Roland Green

Ada M Wilson married Roland Green 25 Jun 1945. A 1940 census was not found.

### 5. Frank Breezee and Florence Rita Hickox

The 1920 census for Harrisburg, Lewis, New York has Frank Breezee, 25, a dairy farmer who owns his mortgaged farm. R Florence is 22. Their son H William is 2.

The 1930 census for Croghan, Lewis, New York has Frank Breezee, 36, married at 21, a dairy farmer living on Beantown Road. Florence is 33 and was married at 18. The children are William H, 12 and Edwin A, 7. William H Hickox, 75, is living with them.

The 1940 census for Croghan, Lewis, New York has Frank Breezee, 45, completed 11th grade, a farmer who owns his farm on Beantown Road. Florence is 43 and completed 6th grade. Their sons are William, 22, and Edwin, 18, both completed 8th grade and are working on the farm.

Frank J Breezee born 1895, died 1980 and Florence Hickox Breezee born 1897, died 1969. They are buried in Sand Hill Cemetery, Natural bridge, New York. Their son William H Breezee born 1917, died 1968 and is buried near them. William served in WW11

### 5. William R "Willie" Breeze and Eliza L Perigo

Willis Breezee, 24, married Eliza L Perigo, 26, on 21 Jul 1922 in Lewis, New York.

The 1930 census for Croghan, Lewis, New York has Willie R Breezee, 32, married at 24, a dairy farmer. His wife Eliza is 33 and married at 26. Their son is, Robert E, 4.

The 1940 census for Croghan, Lewis, New York has Willie Breeze, 42, completed 6th grade, a farmer who owns his farm on Beantown Road. Eliza is 43 and completed 6th grade. Robert is 14 and completed 8th grade.

### 5. Nellie Mae Breezee and Elon Brown Shattuck

Nellie Mae Breeze, 19 married Elon B Shattuck, 30, on 9 Aug 1924 in Lewis, New York.

The 1930 census for Wilna, Jefferson, New York has Elon Shattuck, 35, married at 30 and a laborer in a mill renting a home for $12 per month. Nellie is 25 and was married at 19. Their children are Charles, 4 and Fredrick, 1 ½.

Nellie M Shattuck born 1904, died 30 Apr 1937. Elon Brown Shattuck born 25 Jul 1894, died 6 May 1937.

The 1940 census for Alexandra, Jefferson, New York has Lyman J Foster, 65, and his wife Juliaette, 58 living on a farm on State Road. They have a lodger, 16 and 4 other children. They are Fredrick Shattuck, 11, completed 3rd grade; Frances E, 9, completed 2nd grade; Robert D, 6 and Richard E, 4. These are believed to be Nellie and Elon's children. The children are boarders. Charles Shattuck, 14, completed 5th grade, is a hired hand living with Raymond and Bertha Weaver in Richland, Oswego, New York.

### 4. Susan Breezee and Fredrick Johnson

Susan and Fredrick Johnson are living with her parents, James Breezee and Mary

Carpenter, in 1880 less than a year after they were married.

Susan died between 1885 and when Frederick remarried in 1895.

In 1900 the Johnson children were living with their grandmother Mary Carpenter Breezee. The children are Julia, 19, born Oct 1880; Channcy, 17, born Jun 1882; and Maude, 14, born Sep 1885.

## 5. Julia Johnson and Peter Ure

The 1905 State of New York census has Peter Ure, 25, a farmer; Julia M, 24; Howard F, 3 and Edith M, 1.

Harold V Ure was born 14 Aug 1905.

Julia Johnson Ure born Oct 1880, died Oct 1906 of consumption (tuberculosis). She is buried in Sand Hill Cemetery although there is no stone.

The 1910 census for Croghan, Lewis, New York has Mary Breezee, 83, a widow, had 8 children, three are living and she owns the farm. Pete Ure, 33, son-in-law, a widower, is working out as farm labor. The grandchildren are Howard, 9 and Edith, 8. In 1915 Harold Ure, 4, son of Peter Ure, is living with Nettie Whitehead.

The 1920 census for Croghan, Lewis, New York has Peter Ure, 41, widowed, a farmer who owns his mortgaged farm on Beartown Road. The children are Howard, 17, working out as farm labor; Edith, 16, housekeeper for a private family; and Harold, 14. Lydia Mood, 39, housekeeper and Marie Matson, 3, ward.

Peter Ure died Feb 1957 in Carthage, New York and is buried in Sand Hill Cemetery.

## 6. Howard Floyd Ure and Loretta Inez Bowman

Howard Floyd Ure, 23, married Loretta Inez Bowman, 19, on 30 Jun 1926 in Lowville, New York. His parents were Julia Johnson and Peter Ure.

The 1930 census for New Bremen, Lewis, New York has Howard Ure, 26, married at 22, a chauffeur driving a road truck who owns his home on Wagner Road and a radio. Loretta is 23, married at 20 and works transplanting at a nursery.

The 1940 census for Lowville, New York has Howard F Ure, 37, completed 8th grade, a truck driver for the town highway department who owns his home on Croghan Road. Loretta I is 32, completed 7th grade and not working.

Howard F Ure bon 14 May 1902, died 1980 and is buried in Beaches Bridge Cemetery, Watson, New York. Loretta I Bowman Ure born 1906, died 1988 and is buried with

Howard.

## 6. Edith M Ure and Roy E Johnson

Edith Ure, 19, married Roy E Johnson, 32, on 14 Apr 1923 in Jefferson, New York.

The 1930 census for Sodus, Wayne, New York has Roy E Johnson, 38, married at 30, a farmer who owns his farm and a radio. Edith M is 26 and was married at 18. The children are Mildred P, 7 and Charles H, 5.

The 1940 census for Sodus, Wayne, New York has Roy Johnson, 48, completed 7$^{th}$ grade, a farmer renting his farm on Rotterdam Road. Edith is 36 and completed 8$^{th}$ grade. The children are Mildred, 17, completed 10$^{th}$ grade; Charles, 15, completed 9$^{th}$ grade; Eleanor, 6; Norma, 4; Gerald, 2 and Geraldine, 2.

Roy E Johnson born 1891, died 1958 and is buried in Sodus Rural Cemetery, Sodus, Wayne, New York. Edith M Johnson born 1903, died 1993 and is buried with Roy.

## 6. Harold V Ure and Alice M Lumley

Harold Ure, 21, a paper maker, married Alice M Lumley, 17 on 4 Dec 1926.

The 1930 census for Wilna, Jefferson, New York has Harold Ure, 24, married at 21, a laborer in a paper mill who owns his home worth $1400 and a radio. Alice is 20 and was married at 17. Janice M is 2.

The 1940 census for Croghan, Lewis, New York has Harold, 34, completed 8$^{th}$ grade, a paper maker in a paper mill who owns a home worth $500. Alice is 29 and graduated high school. The children are Janice, 12, completed 6$^{th}$ grade; Vernon, 7, completed 3$^{rd}$ grade and Lynn, 1.

## 5. Chauncey Johnson and Maude White

The 1910 census for Rutland, New York has Chan Johnson, 26, married 7 years, a laborer in a paper mill renting his home. Maude is 24 and has had 4 children all are living. The children are Roy, 6; Clyde, 5; Carl, 3 and Grace, 1.

The 1920 census for West Carthage, New York has Chauncey Johnson, 37, a foreman in a paper mill who owns his home on Main Street. Maude is 34. The children are Roy, 16, a teamster; Claude, 14; Carl, 12; Grace, 10; Clifford, 8; Florence, 6; Frances, 4; and Kenneth 9/12.

The 1930 census for Carthage, New York has Chauncey Johnson, 47, married at 22, a fireman in a paper mill renting his home at 635 West End Ave. for $22 per month. Maude is 42 and married at 17. The children are Carl, 22, working at odd jobs; Clifford,

18, laborer in paper mill; Grace, 20, paper mill worker; and Florence, 17, paper mill worker; Francis, 15 and Kenneth, 11.

The 1940 census for Carthage, New York has Chauncey Johnson, 58, lodger, widowed, completed 6th grade and a fireman in the paper mill. Most of the children have married. Francis is living with Carl. Maude did not die but left Chauncey between 1930 and 1940, maybe 1933 as many of the children are married in 1934. A photo shows Maude Remington Johnson and James Blackwell, longtime companion of Maude Marion White Johnson. Maude died in 1958.

Chauncey Johnson born 6 Jun 1882, died 31 Mar 1963 in Carthage, New York.

### 6. Roy V Johnson and Gladys M Woodard

Roy V Johnson, 22, married Gladys M Woodard, 16, on 21 Nov 1925 in Jefferson, New York.

The 1930 census for Syracuse, New York has Roy Johnson, 27, married at 21, a driver for a milk factory renting a home for $20 per month. Gladys is 21 and married at 16. The children are Doris, 4; Roland, 3 and James, 1 4/12.

The 1940 census for Wilna, Jefferson, New York has Roy Johnson, 38, completed 8th grade, working for the WPA and renting a home for $10 per month. Gladys is 32 and completed 8th grade. The children are Doris, 14, completed 9th grade; Roland, 13, completed 7th grade; James, 11, completed 3rd grade; Richard, 9 completed 4th grade; Joan, 7, completed 2nd grade; Donald, 6 completed 1st grade; Ugene, 5, completed 1st grade and Elizabeth, 2.

### 6. Clyde Johnson and Rachel Pete

The 1930 census for Fort Wadsworth, New York has Clyde Johnson, 24, employed by the US Army.

The 1940 census for Carthage, New York has Clyde Johnson, 33, completed 3rd grade, working for the WPA and renting a home for $12 per month. Rachel is 26 and completed 9th grade. The children are Nolan, 1 and Galen, 8/12.

The picture was taken sometime later possibly 1940's or 1950's.

Clyde and Rachel Pete Johnson, Son of Chauncey and Marion Maude White.

### 6. Carl Johnson and Marion Gamble

Carl Johnson, 27, married Marion Gamble, 21, on 12 Feb 1934 in Jefferson, New York.

The 1940 census for Carthage, New York has Carl Johnson, 32, completed 4th grade, a paper mill laborer renting a home at 449 South Washington for $19 per month. Marion is 27 and completed 10th grade. Their children are Carol, 5 and Linda new born. Francis, 24, Carl's brother, completed 8th grade, a new worker is living with them.

### 6. Grace Anna Johnson and Milton G Keech

Grace Johnson, 25, married Milton Keech, 32, on 30 Nov 1934 in Carthage, New York.

The 1940 census for Carthage, New York has Milton Keech, 37, completed 9th grade, a line inspector for a power and light company renting a home on State Street for $14 per month. Grace is 30 and completed 8th grade. Their daughter, Mary is 4.

### 6. Clifford Johnson and Jessie Brodie

The 1940 census for Riga, Monroe, New York has Clifford Johnson, 28, graduated high school, a shovel operator on the roads and living with his father-in-law. Jessie is 35 and completed 11th grade. They have a daughter, Nancy Jean, 4.

### 6. Florence M Johnson and Joseph Peluso

Florence M Johnson, 21, married Joseph Peluso, 30, on 30 Nov 1934 in Carthage, New York. It must have been a double wedding with her sister Grace. Joseph Peluso was born 23 Oct 1904 in Naples, Italy and working in a restaurant.

The 1940 census for Carthage, New York has Frank Peluso, 59, completed 3rd grade, born in Italy, restaurant owner. Bridget is 60, completed 3rd grade, restaurant cook. Their son, Fio is 28 and a beater man in a paper mill. Joseph is 38, completed 10th grade and a waiter in his father's restaurant. Florence is 27 and completed 8th grade. Joseph has two sons, Anthony, 15, completed 10th grade and James, 13, completed 8th grade. They were all living over the restaurant at 227 State Street.

Joseph and Florence Peluso Johnson

### 6. Francis Lewis "Manny" Johnson

Francis was living with his brother Carl during the 1940 census for Carthage, New York. He was 24, single, completed 8th grade and a new worker.

Francis I Johnson, born 1915, enlisted in the army on 20 Feb 1941 in Syracuse, New York as a private. Manny was an artillery repairman. He served in North Africa and Europe. He was a technician 4th grade when he was honorably discharged from Fort Dix, New Jersey on 16 Sep 1945. The picture was taken while he was in the Army.

## 6. Kenneth Johnson and Maud

The 1940 census for Carthage, New York has Kenneth Johnson, 20, completed 8th grade, a cutter in the paper mill renting a home at 541 West End Ave. for $12 per month. Maude is 21 and graduated high school. Their daughter, Patricia, is 3/12.

## 5. Maude Elizabeth Johnson and Floyd Edward Ure

The 1905 New York State Census for Croghan, New York has Floyd Ure, 23, a teamster; Maude E, 20 and Ella L, 1.

The 1910 census for Seneca, New York has Floyd Ure, 28, married 8 years and a farm laborer. Maude E is 25. The children are Ella M, 6, and Jettie, 4.

A 1920 census has not been found. Jettie died 16 May 1920 in Geneva, New York.

The 1930 census for Galen, Wayne, New York has Floyd E Ure, 48, married at 22, a farmer who owns his farm on Dutton Road and a radio. Maude E is 44 and was married at 18. Ella M is 26, single and a teacher at a district school.

Floyd Edward Ure born 20 Jun 1880 in Carthage, New York, died 6 Oct 1937 in Ithaca, New York and is buried in Whitney Cemetery, Seneca, New York. Maude Elizabeth Johnson Ure born 21 Sep 1883 in Natural Bridge, New York, died 26 Sep 1970 in Lyons, New York and is buried with Floyd. Other sources have Maude's birth 26 Sep 1985 which seems to agree with the census records.

## 6. Ella Mae Ure and Albert Irwin Blakeman

The 1940 census for Galen, Wayne, New York has Albert Blakeman, 39, graduated high school, a farmer who owns his farm worth $4000. Ella Mae is 36 and completed 2 years college. Their daughter is Jane Elizabeth a new born. Maude Ure, 56, Ella's mother, a widow, is living with them.

Albert Irwin Blakeman born 6 Jan 1901 in Galen, New York, died 12 Apr 1967 in Galen and is buried in Maple Grove Cemetery, Clyde, New York. Ella Mae Ure Blakeman born 25 Nov 1903, died 18 Mar 1988 in Galen, New York and is buried with Albert.

## 3. Wellington L Carpenter and Emeline Kinney or Pinney

Wellington is living with his parents in 1855 and 1860. He was a sailor in 1860.

Wellington Carpenter, 27, a sailor, married, from Brownville, New York is listed with those eligible to serve. A note has him in the Michigan 7th Infantry in Jun 1863. It is not known when he started serving or when he was discharged.

The Michigan 7th was organized in Monroe Michigan during Aug 1861. Wellington may have enlisted at that time if he was in Monroe on one of his sailing trips. This regiment was in many famous battles. The Peach Orchard Jun 62; Antietam Sep 62; Fredericksburg Dec 62; Gettysburg Jul 63; Wilderness May 64; Spotsylvania May 64; Cold harbor Jun 64; Petersburg Jun 64; Fall of Petersburg Apr 65; and Appomattox Court House Apr 65. There were many other less well-known battles. The unit mustered out 5 Jul 1865.

The 1865 New York State census for Brownville has Wellington Carpenter, 29, living in a frame house worth $75 and working as a sailor. His wife, Emeline is 23.

The 1870 census for Brownville, New York has Wellington Carpenter, 34, a sailor with real estate worth $2925. Emeline is 28.

Wellington Carpenter a sailor on the Great Lakes, left Chicago 27 Sep 1872 on the Whitney and was never heard from again. (paper dated 30 Nov 1872.)[16]

The schooner George J Whitney sunk at Sugar Island reef according to a list of ship wrecks. The Whitney was a wooden sailing ship.

## 3. Roxana / Roseanna / Rosetta Carpenter

Roxanna or Roseanna may be the same person as Rosetta. Roxanna is listed with her parents in the 1850 census. Roseanna is in the 1855 census records. Rosetta is living with her parents in 1860 and 1865. Although information in the Watertown Library has two girls born in 1836 and 1837, census records have one girl with a name starting with "R" after Wellington and a total number of children that is right with only one "R" girl. Nothing more could be found.

## 3. Absalom Carpenter

Absalom Carpenter was born in 1838 but is not in the 1850 census. He must have died young.

## 3. Samuel Winfield Carpenter and Anna Whaley / Esther M Griffis

A record of men who served in the Civil War has Samuel Winfield Carpenter of Pillar Point, born 24 Feb 1842 in Brownville a private in Company I, 20th New York Calvary. He enlisted 11 Aug 1863 at Sacketts Harbor and was discharged at Manchester, Virginia 31 Jul 1865. His unit flag is pictured.

Winfield Carpenter, 24, was with his parents in the 1865 census and working as a farmer.

The 1870 census for Rodman, New York has Samuel Carpenter, 26, a farm laborer, eligible to vote. Ann, is 26. Their children are Levi, 3, and Eunice, 1.

The 1880 census for Edison, Furnas, Nebraska, taken 19 Jun 1880 has Samuel Carpenter, 37, widower, a farmer. The children are Levi, 13, at school and Eunice, 11, at school. All were born in New York.

Samuel Winfield married Esther Griffis about 1888 and raised her children, Victor, Della, and James Butterfield, as his own. They moved to Michigan about 1895.

The 1900 census for Denver, Newago, Michigan has Samuel W Carpenter, 58, born Feb 1842, married 11 years, a farmer who owns his farm free and clear. Esther M is 39, born Feb 1861, had 6 children and 6 are living. The children are Victor Butterfield, 20, born Feb 1880, a farm laborer; Della Butterfield, 16, born Sep 1883; James Butterfield, 12, born Nov 1887, at school; Jessie Carpenter, 10, born Dec 1889, at school; Winfield, 7, born Apr 1893; and Celia, 5, born May 1895. The older children were born in Nebraska and Celia was born in Michigan.

The 1910 census for Denver, Newago, Michigan has S Winfield Carpenter, 68, 2nd marriage, married 21 years, a farmer who owns his mortgaged farm. Ester is 49 and 2nd marriage. The children are Jessie, 20, born in Nebraska, farm labor; Winfield, 17, born in Nebraska, farm labor; and Lucy R (Celia), 14, born in Michigan.

Pvt Samuel Winfield Carpenter, 74, born 24 Feb 1842 in Brownville, New York, died 8 Jun 1916 in Muskegon, Michigan and is buried in East Hesperia Cemetery, Hesperia, Michigan. Winfield broke his leg in May followed by amputation. Gangrene set in and he died 8 Jun 1916 in Hachley Hospital.

The 1920 census for Hesperia, Michigan has Esther Carpenter, 59, a widow who owns her home free and clear. Winfield Carpenter is 26, single and a farm laborer. Helena Robbins, 60, a friend, is living with them.

The 1930 census for Hesperia, Michigan has Esther Carpenter, 69, widow, married at 18, owns her home worth $2000 but not a radio. Winfield is 36, single and a laborer.

Ester is living with Winfield in 1940.

Ester M Griffis Butterfield Carpenter born 7 Feb 1861, in Boon County, Illinois, died 26 Jun 1943, in Newago, Michigan and is buried with Samuel. Ester's first husband was Nathan Butterfield.

## 4. Levi W Carpenter and Johanna Madsen

The 1900 census for Provo, Utah has Levi Carpenter, 31, born Jan 1869, married 6 years, a plumber renting his home. Hannah is 29, born Jan 1871, had 3 children, 2 are living. The children are Mabel, 4, born Dec 1895 and Vera, 2, born May 1898.

The 1910 census for Provo, Utah has Levi W Carpenter, 41, married 16 years, a steam fitter who owns his home at 994 West Center Street. Hannah is 39 and had 7 children, 5 are living. The children are Mabel, 14; Vera, 11; Clifford, 8; Enid, 5 and Edna, 2.

The 1920 census for Provo Utah has Levi Carpenter, 51, a hunter of wild animals who owns his home at 994 West Center free and clear. Hannah is 49. The children are Clifford, 17, working in a sugar factory; Enid, 15; Lynn, 10 and Howard 7.

The 1930 census for Provo, Utah has Levi W Carpenter, 60, married at 25, not working but owns his home at 994 West Center worth $1500. Hannah is 58 and married at 23. The sons are Lynn, 19 and Howard, 17.

The 1940 census for Provo, Utah has Levi W Carpenter, 71, did not attend school but owns his home at 994 West Center worth $2000. Hannah is 69 and completed 5th grade.

Johanna Madsen Carpenter born 1871, died 1942 in Provo Utah and is buried in Provo City Cemetery. Levi W Carpenter, born 8 Jan 1869 at Pillar Point, New York, died 21 Jul 1947 in Provo, Utah and is buried with Hannah.

## 5. Mabel Eunice Carpenter and Ralph Lawhorn / Theodore Syphus / William Saley

Mabel Carpenter, 19, married Ralph Lawhorn, 22, on 11 Sep 1914 in Provo, Utah.

Ralph registered for WW1 on 31 May 1917. He is married with one child and claimed an exemption for poor eyesight. His occupation was teamster so his eyesight must have been good enough to drive.

Ralph Lawhorn born 20 Apr 1892, died 19 Oct 1918 in Salt Lake City, Utah and is buried in Provo City Cemetery. Considering there is no evidence he went to WW1, he may have died of Spanish Flue or in an accident. There was no death certificate.

Mabel Carpenter Lawhorn, 24, widowed, married Theodore Syphus, 27, widowed, on 26 Aug 1919 in Salt Lake City, Utah.

The 1920 census for Rains, Utah has Theodore C Syphus, 27, a mechanic in a coal mine renting a house. Mable E is 24. The children are Mildred, 4 and Estella E, 2. They have a boarder who is working in a coal mine.

Theodore left or they were divorced as he married again in 1921 in California. They may have been divorced due to violence. Theodore was accused of threatening to kill his first wife according to the Salt Lake Tribune.

Mabel Lawhorn, 26, married William Saley, 31, in 1921 in Bannock, Idaho.

The 1930 census for Salt Lake, Utah has William Saley, 40, married at 31, a laborer at odd jobs owns his home at 3490 South 4th West Street worth $5250. Mabel is 34 and married at 26. The children are Mildred, 15; Stella, 13 and Elizabeth, 6.

The 1940 census for South Jordan, Utah has William S Saley, 50, completed 5th grade, a laborer for Utah Portland Cement who owns his home. Mabel is 44 and completed 8th grade. Elizabeth is 16 and completed 9th grade. Mabel's grandson, William J Rutishauser, 7, is living with them.

Mabel Eunice Carpenter Saley born 13 Dec 1895, died 11 Oct 1944 in Salt Lake, Utah. She died of carcinoma of the uterus which was removed with surgery; however, it had spread to the bowel and brain causing partial blindness. Mabel was buried in West Jordan Cemetery, South Jordan, Utah. Stella Freeman was the informant. William S Saley born 8 Dec 1889 in Salt Lake, Utah, died 18 Jan 1976 in Riverton, Utah and is buried with Mabel. William S Saley served as a cook in the army during WW1. He was stationed at Fort Bradley, Sault Ste Marie, Michigan in 1920 and is a cook.

## 6. Mildred Lawhorn and Walter E Rutishauser

Mildred Lawhorn married Earnest Walter Rutishauser on 28 Mar 1933.

William Jack Rutishauser was born 19 Aug 1933 in Salt Lake, Utah.

The 1939 Salt Lake City Directory has Walter E (Mildred) oiler Utah Copper Company. By 1940 Mildred and Walter's son, William Jack Rutishauser is living with his grandparents. No other 1940 census has been found.

Walter Rutishauser born 20 Mar 1915 registered for WW11 in 1940. He served from 5 Feb 1941 to 24 Nov 1945. According to Utah Military Records, Walter was married to Mildred at the time.

## 6. Estella Enid Lawhorn and George Royce Freeman

Estella Enid Lawhorn married George Royce Freeman on 15 Oct 1938 in Salt Lake, Utah.

George Royce Freeman born 21 Aug 1912, registered for WW11 in 1940. His next of kin was Stella Enid Freeman. They were living in Herriman, Utah. A 1940 census was not found. There is no evidence he served.

## 5. Vera May Carpenter and John "Jack" Eastman

Vera Carpenter, 19, married Jack Eastman, 20, on 25 Jul 1917 in Provo Utah.

The 1920 census for Bremerton, Washington has J Eastman, 23, a machinist renting a home at 856 ½ Park Ave. Vera M is 21 and Nellie B is a new born.

The 1930 census for Provo, Utah has Jack Eastman, 34, married at 20, a peddler on a truck farm who owns his home at 727 7 W 3 N, worth $1250 and a radio. Vera M is 32 and married at 18. The children are Bernice, 11; Leland J, 8; LaVerne K, 7; Frank, 6; Gordon E, 4 and Harman L, 2.

The 1940 census for Springville, Utah has Jack Eastman, 43, completed 8th grade, a peddler for hides and pelts trading who owns his home worth $1000. Vera is 41 and completed 8th grade. The children are Leland, 18, completed 11th grade; LaVern, 17, completed 11th grade; Frank, 16, completed 8th grade; Gordon, 14, completed 7th grade and Harman, 12, completed 5th grade.

John Eastman born 18 May 1896 in Ogden, Utah, died 19 Jan 1968 in Mapleton, Utah and is buried in Provo City Cemetery, Provo, Utah. Vera May Carpenter Eastman born 5 May 1898 in Provo, Utah, died 29 Dec 1973 in Payson, Utah and is buried with John.

## 6. Nellie Berniece Eastman and Henry Brimhall

Nellie Bernice Eastman married Henry Brimhall on 12 Oct 1938 in Utah.

The 1940 census for Provo, Utah has Henry Brimhall, 23, graduated high school, a barber in a barber shop renting his home for $8 per month. Bernice is 20 and graduated high school. Their son, John H is 9/12.

## 5. Clifford Carpenter

The 1930 census for Grafton, Yolo, California has Clifford Carpenter. 28. Single living at 730 Reclamation District, born in Utah, working as a laborer for State Reclamation. Reclamation Districts were wetlands that were being reclaimed as agricultural land generally in the Central Valley. They built levees and dams.

A California death index has Clifford Carpenter, 31, born about 1902, died 10 Apr 1933, in Sacramento, California.

## 6. Enid Carpenter and Oscar Hendrickson

The 1930 census for Salt Lake City, Utah has Oscar Hendrickson, 30, married at 25, a foundry man at American Foundry owns his home at 503 Montague worth $2000 and a radio. Enid is 25 and married at 20. Oscar's brother, Edward, is 40, single, works at basket weaving at the blind school and is living with them.

The 1940 census for Salt Lake, Utah has Oscar Hendrickson, 42, completed 8$^{th}$ grade, a steel chipper in a foundry who owns his home at 945 South Second West worth $1500. Enid is 35 and completed 10$^{th}$ grade. The children are Jean, son, 8, completed 1$^{st}$ grade and Enid, 3.

Oscar Hendrickson born 6 Jul 1898 in Salt Lake City, Utah, died 19 May 1969 in Salt Lake, Utah and is buried in Salt Lake City Cemetery. Enid Carpenter Hendrickson, born 10 Jan 1905 in Provo Utah, died 28 Jan 1998 in Murry, Utah and is buried with Oscar.

## 5. Edna Carpenter and Thomas Gunn / Frank H Pickett

Edna Carpenter, 18, married Thomas Gunn, 20, on 31 Mar 1926 in Salt Lake, Utah.

It appears this marriage didn't last long as Thomas Gunn married Thurza Jenkins in 1927. Their baby was born and died 19 Apr 1928. The child was buried in Salt Lake City Cemetery.

The 1930 census for San Diego, California has Frank H Pickett, 30, married at 27, an engineer for the US Navy renting a home on F Street for $20 per month. Edna is 22 and married at 19.

The 1940 census for San Diego, California has Frank H Pickett, 40, completed 8$^{th}$ grade, a machinist for the US Navy renting a home at 3228 National Ave. for $25 per month. Edna is 32 and completed 7$^{th}$ grade.

Frank H Pickett presumably died 18 Dec 1944. There is a monument that lists his name at Fort William McKinley, Manilla, Philippines. He is listed as missing and received a Purple Heart. He spent his career in the US Navy. Utah Military Service Records have Frank Hulse Picket, born 14 Mar 1901 in Hopkinsville, Kentucky. He enlisted in Dallas, Texas 26 Jun 1919. He was discharged in Seattle, Washington 26 Dec 1944. His wife is Edna Pickett

Edna C Pickett born 10 Jan 1908, died 8 Feb 2001 and is buried in Provo City Cemetery, Provo, Utah.

## 5. Lynn Winfield Carpenter and Rachel Ann Brinchall / Mildred Estell Peterson

Lynn Winfield Carpenter, 22, married Rachel Ann Brinchall, 22, on 5 Aug 1932 in Utah County, Utah. It didn't last long.

Lynn Winfield Carpenter married Mildred Estell Peterson 20 Feb 1937 in Salt Lake, Utah.

The 1940 census for Salt Lake, Utah has Lynn Carpenter, 29, completed 10th grade, a helper in a molding foundry who owns his home at 1320 Emery Street worth $1000. Mildred is 21 and completed 9th grade.

Mildred Estella Peterson Carpenter born 21 Feb 1919 in Neola, Utah, died 10 Sep 1980 in Salt Lake, Utah and is buried in Redwood Cemetery, West Jordon, Utah. Lynn Winfield Carpenter born 4 Jun 1910 in Provo, Utah, died 3 Jun 1990 in Salt Lake, Utah and is buried with Mildred.

## 5. Howard Levi Carpenter and Madge D Prince / Melba Walker

Howard Levi Walker, 20, married Madge D Prince, 18 on 20 Feb 1933 in Utah.

Howard Levi Carpenter, 23 married Melba Walker, 27, on 10 Oct 1934 in Summit, Utah.

The 1940 census for Salt Lake, Utah has Howard L Carpenter, 27, completed 9th grade, a laborer in copper who owns a home at 1148 9th East worth $600. Melba is 32 and graduated high school. The children are Howard L Jr, 5 and Doyle La Marr, 1.

Howard Levi Carpenter, 27, registered for WW11 in 1940. He was born 16 Feb 1913, lives in Salt Lake, Utah and works for the Utah Copper Company. His next of kin is Melba Walker Carpenter.

Howard Carpenter born 6 Feb 1913 in Provo, Utah, died 28 Oct 1999 in Salt Lake, Utah and is buried in Lake Hills Cemetery, Sandy, Utah.

## 4. Eunice A Carpenter and Alexander McArthur / Albert J Larue

Eunice Carpenter, 27, married Alexander McArthur, 38, on 27 Jan 1897 in Spokane, Washington. It was the first marriage for both.

The 1900 census for Spokane, Washington has Alexander McArthur, 42, born Oct 1857 in Canada, married 3 years, working at bridge construction and owns a home at 427 Mission. Eunice is 30, born Feb 1870 in New York and has 1 child still living. Their daughter, Edith is 1 and was born Feb 1899 in Washington.

Alexander McArthur born 30 Nov 1857, died 18 Jul 1901 according to Washington

Death Records. There is a large blank area where cause of death, occupation, etc. should be for 11 people. Find a Grave indicated his body was never found. He may have died while working on a bridge.

The 1910 census for Spokane, Washington has Eunice A McArthur, 40, widow, had 2 children, both are living and owns her home at 427 Mission free and clear. The children are Edith H, 11, and Jean A, 9. There are also 4 boarders living with them.

Eunice A McArthur married Albert J Larue in 1914 in Pend Oreille, Washington.

The 1920 census for Ritzville, Washington has Albert J Larue, 37, a machinist in his own shop who owns his mortgaged home at 66 5th Street. Eunice A is 49 and Jean A McArthur is 19.

The 1930 census for Tumwater, Washington has Albert Larue, 46, married at 32, a mechanic in an auto supply company who owns his home worth $4300. Eunice is 60 and was married at 27. Jean Wellsandt is 29, was married at 24 and a stenographer for the State Department.

The 1940 census for Tumwater, Washington has Albert J Larue, 56, completed 6th grade, a carpenter in building construction who owns his home worth $3500. Eunice is 70 and completed 4th grade.

Eunice McArthur Larue born Feb 1870, died 14 Feb 1964 in Tacoma, Washington. Albert Jay Larue born 1890, died 1978.

## 5. Edith Ann McArthur and David E Greenwalt

A German Lutheran record has Jane Elizabeth Greenwalt born 22 Jan 1919 and baptized 13 Mar 1921. Parents are Dave Greenwalt and Edith Ann McArthur.

The 1920 census for McQueen, Adams, Washington has David Greenwalt, 27, a farmer. Edith is 21. Their daughter, Jane E is 11/12.

The 1930 census for Shelton, Washington has David Greenwalt, 37, married at 26, a veteran of WW1, a mechanic at a timber company who owns his home worth $6000 and a radio. Edith is 31 and married at 19. The children are Jane, 11; Alice, 9; and Marian, 8.

The 1940 census for Lincoln, Chelan Washington has Dave E Greenwalt, 48, completed 9th grade, operator of a fruit park who owns his farm worth $6000. Edith is 41 and completed 11th grade. The children are Marian, 18, completed 10th grade and Neil, 2.

David Greenwalt born 13 Apr 1892 in Culbertson, Nebraska, died 20 Feb 1974 in Wenatchee, Washington and is buried in Wenatchee City Cemetery. Edith Ann

McArthur Greenwalt born 11 Feb 1899 in Spokane, Washington, died 18 Jul 2001 in Shelton, Washington at the age of 102 and is buried with Dave.

### 6. Jane Elizabeth Greenwalt and Ethemer Eugene Mackey

The 1940 census for Shelton, Washington has Ethemer Mackey, 22, graduated high school, working as a clerk in a grocery. Jane Greenwalt's 1940 census was not found.

Jane Greenwalt, 21, a bookkeeper, married Ethemer Eugene Mackey, 22, a grocer, on 1 Jul 1940 in Mason County Washington.

### 6. Alice F Greenwalt

The 1940 census for Wenatchee, Washington, St. Anthony's Hospital and Nurses' Home has Alice Greenwalt, 19, graduated high school and a nursing student.

### 5. Jean A McArthur and Theodore C Wellsandt

Jean A McArthur, 24, a stenographer, married Theodore C Wellsandt, 24, a mechanic, on 19 Jun 1925 in Olympia, Washington.

The 1930 census has Jean Wellsandt, 29, married, living with her mother and working as a stenographer. Jean must have been married about 5 years before the divorce.

The 1940 census for Newport, Washington has Jean McArthur, 39, lodger, divorced, completed 2 years college and working as a bookkeeper for a commercial bank. Additional information has that she was married at 24 but never had children.

Jean A McArthur born 22 Mar 1901 in Spokane, Washington, died 27 Jul 1974 in Shelton, Washington and is buried at Fairmount Memorial Park, Spokane, Washington.

### 4. Jessie Syrenas Carpenter and Grace Gladys Grimm

Jessie S Carpenter, 27, married Grace Gladys Grim, 22, in 1916 in Boone Illinois.

Jessie Syrenas Carpenter, 27, born 20 Dec 1889 in Arapahoe, Nebraska, married, a farmer, was living in Hesperia, Michigan when he registered for WW1.

The 1920 census for Newfield, Oceana, Michigan has Jessie Carpenter, 30, a farmer who owns his farm. Grace is 24. Their son, William is 2.

The 1930 census for Newfield, Oceana, Michigan has Jessie Carpenter, 40, married at 27, a farmer who owns his farm but not a veteran. Grace is 33 and married at 20. William is 12.

The 1940 census for Newfield, Oceana, Michigan has Jessie Carpenter, 50, completed 8th grade, a blacksmith in his own shop who owns his home worth $650. Grace is 44 and completed 9th grade. The children are William, 22, completed 8th grade, a blacksmith's helper and Mary E, 7, completed 1st grade.

Jessie Syrenas Carpenter born 20 Dec 1889 in Arapahoe, Nebraska, died 15 Jan 1972 in Hart, Michigan and is buried in East Hesperia Cemetery, Hesperia, Michigan. Grace Gladys Grimm born 5 Jul 1894 in Elgin, Iowa, died 19 Jul 1991 in Hesperia, Michigan and is buried with Jessie.

William Harold "Bill" Carpenter served from 8 Aug 1941 to 29 Oct 1945 in the Army during WW11.

## 4. Winfield A Carpenter and Dovie Williams Godwin

Winfield Algeman Carpenter, 24, born 7 Apr 1893 in Nebraska, living in Hesperia, Michigan, single, registered for WW1 on 5 Jun 1917. He was of medium height and build with grey eyes and brown balding hair. Winfield served as a private in Company B of the 339th Infantry 85th Division from 28 Apr 1918 to 18 Jul 1919.

The 1920 census for Hesperia, Michigan has Esther Carpenter, 59, a widow who owns her home free and clear. Winfield is 26, single and working as a laborer. A widowed friend is living with them.

The 1930 census for Hesperia, Michigan has Esther Carpenter, 69, married at 18, a widow who owns her home worth $2000. Winfield is 36, single and working as a laborer.

Winfield A Carpenter, 45, of Hesperia, Michigan, married Dovie Williams Godwin, 40, of Hesperia on 17 Dec 1938 in Hart Michigan. Winfield was never married before and his parents are Samuel W Carpenter and Esther Griffis. Dovie is a nurse.

The 1940 census for Hesperia, Michigan has Winfield Carpenter, 46, completed 8th grade, a carpenter for a building contractor who owns his home worth $1000. Dovie is 41 and completed 8th grade. Ester, mother is 79, a widow, and completed 5th grade. Esther died in 1943.

Winfield A Carpenter born 7 Apr 1893 in Arapahoe, Furnas County, Nebraska, died 8 Feb 1962 in Hesperia, Michigan and is buried in East Hesperia Cemetery. Dovie Godwin Carpenter born 17 Nov 1898, died 15 Feb 1964 and is buried with Winfield.

## 4. Lucy Arcelia Carpenter and Elmer G Johnson

The 1900 census has Celia Carpenter, 5, born May 1895. The 1910 census has the youngest child of Samuel Winfield and Ester Carpenter as Lucy R Carpenter, 14. An Ancestry Tree has Lucy Arcelia Carpenter.

Lucy Arcelia Carpenter, 16, a domestic, married Elmer G Johnson, 43, a farmer, both of Denver Township on 20 May 1911 in White Cloud, Michigan.

The 1920 census for Denver, Newago, Michigan has Elmer G Johnson, 52, a farmer who owns his mortgaged farm. Lucy is 25. Elmer has 2 sons Walter, 21 and Orville, 19 who are helping on the farm. The youngest son is Hugh, 4.

Celia was sent to the Traverse City State hospital in 1926. The hospital was known for kindness, comfort, and "work is therapy". It is not known why she was sent there but the hospital was used for many illnesses. Picture is from 1930.

A Michigan Death Record has Arcelia Johnson, 33, of Hesperia, Michigan, born 25 May 1895, died 15 Nov 1928 in Traverse City State Hospital. The cause of death was Epilepsy a clinical diagnosis. She had been in the State Hospital since 6 Jun 1926. Arcelia's parents are Samuel Carpenter and Esther Griffis. Her husband is E G Johnson. Informant is hospital records.

The 1930 census for Denver, Newago, Michigan has Elmer G Johnson, 62, widowed and farming a general farm. The children are Hugh W, 15 and Neva M, 6.

The 1940 census for Denver, Newago, Michigan has Elmer G Johnson, 72, widowed, completed 4th grade, a farm operator who owns his farm worth $750. Hugh is 24, single and completed 8th grade. Neva is 16 and completed 9th grade.

### 3. Orville Balora Carpenter

Orville was 16 and living with his parents in 1860.

The Town Clerk's Register of men who served in the Civil War has Orville Balora Carpenter, born 15 Apr 1842, of Pillar Point, enlisted Apr 1861. He was in the 35th Infantry, Company I and mustered in 11 Jun 1861. He was single and the son of Levi and Eunice Ayer Carpenter. Orville was not in any battles but died of disease at Alexandria, Virginia and is buried there.

Pvt. Orville Carpenter, Company K 35th New York Infantry, died 17 Jul 1861 and is buried at Arlington National Cemetery, Virginia. Grave number 13209, Civil War.

Pvt. Orville Balora Carpenter born 15 Apr 1842 in Brownville, New York, died 17 Jul 1861 of disease in Washington, District of Columbia. He is buried (or at least has a stone) in Brownville Cemetery, Brownville, New York.

I believe he is buried in Arlington not Brownville as there are several confirming military records.

### 3. Lafayette Carpenter and Francis / Caroline Schloop / Jennie Shattuck

The Town Clerk's register of men who served in the Civil War has Layfayette Carpenter born 25 May 1847 in Brownville, from Pillar Point, enlisted as a private in Company H of 186th Infantry on 22 Aug 1864, mustered in Sep 1864 at Sackett's Harbor. His parents are Levi and Eunice Ayer Carpenter. He was at the siege of Petersburg. Lafayette was discharged 2 Jun 1865 and paid one quarter of land in Lewis County and received $800. P.O. address Pillar, Point, New York.

The 1870 census for Diana, Lewis, New York has L Carpenter, 24, a farmer with $700 in real estate and a personal estate of $290. His wife is Frances, 17. Post office is Indian River. I have no other information on Francis.

Lafayette married Caroline Schloop about 1873.

The 1880 census for New Bremen, Lewis, New York has L F Carpenter, 29, a farmer. Caroline is 27. The children are Milly, 7; Frankie, 3; and Jessie, 3/12.

The 1892 New York State census has Lafayette Carpenter, 46, a laborer. Caroline is 38. The children are Mildred, 19; Francis, 15; Jessie, 12; Mary, 11; Hattie, 9; Grace, 7; Willie, 10; Clinton, 3; and Hazen, 1.

The 1900 census for Croghan, Lewis, New York has Lafayette Carpenter, 53, born Jan 1847, widowed, working as a commercial traveler (salesman). The children are Jessie, 20, born Feb 1880, nailing boxes; Mammie (Mary), 18, born Oct 1881, housekeeping; William, 16, born Jun 1883, handling lumber; Hattie, 15, born Feb 1885; Grace, 13, born Jul 1886; Clinton, 11, born Mar 1889; and Hazen, 8, born Oct 1891.

Carline Schloop Carpenter born 1853, died 1899, and is buried in Croghan Apostolic Christian Cemetery, Croghan, New York. Most places have the name Caroline.

The 1910 census for Denmark, Lewis, New York Has Lafayette F Carpenter, 62, married 3 times, completed 8th grade, a farmer renting a farm at Denmark and Deer River Roads. Jennie A is 45, married twice and completed 8th grade. Jennie has two children from her previous marriage that are living with them, Carrie A, 14 and Loren J Laupher. All the Carpenter children have left.

Jennie Shattuck Carpenter born 1864, died 1920 and is buried in Swinburne Cemetery, Denmark, New York. Lafayette F Carpenter born 1849, died 1923 and is buried with Jennie.

### 4. Mildred A Carpenter and William Wadsworth Smith

The 1900 census for Lowville, New York has William W Smith, 24, born Aug 1875, married 5 years, a tailor renting a home on Stewart Street. Mildred is 25, born Mar 1873 and has 1 child still living. Howard is 3 and born Feb 1897.

The 1910 census for Independence, Kansas has William W Smith, 35, married 14 years, a tailor renting a home at 207 South 15th Street. Mildred is 36 and has had 5 children all living. The children are Howard, 13; Gladys M, 8; Donald G, 6; Russell P, 4 and Myrtle L, 1.

The 1920 census for Independence, Kansas has William Smith 45, a tailor for a cleaning and pressing company who owns his mortgaged home at 510 North 9th Street. Mildred A is 46. The children are Howard C, 22, single, figuring (bookkeeping) in an oil office; Gladys M, 18; Donald G, 15 working at a soda fountain in a pharmacy and Paul Russell, 14. Myrtle is not listed and may have died.

The 1930 census for Independence, Kansas has W W Smith 55, married at 21, cleaning and pressing in his own shop and owns his home at 510 N 9th worth $3000. Mildred is 57 and married at 23. Gladys is 27 and a teacher in a public school. Paul is 24, single and a clerk in a department store.

The 1940 census for Independence, Kansas has W W Smith, 64, completed 9th grade, a tailor in a clothing store who owns his home at 510 9th Street now worth $800. Mildred is 67 and completed 8th grade. Gladys is 37, graduated college and teaching in a public school.

Wadsworth W Smith born 1875, died 1940 and is buried in Mount Hope Cemetery, Independence, Kansas. Mildred A born 1873, died 1953 and is buried with WW.

## 5. Howard Launcelot Carpenter Smith and Francis C Ballard

Howard L C Smith, 21, born 27 Feb 1897 in Watertown, New York, a student at Olson College, registered for WW1 on 5 Jun 1918. He was enlisted 5 Sep 1918 in Company C 87th Engineers as a private and was discharged 6 Dec 1918.

Howard C Smith, 32, married Francis C Ballard, 26, on 30 Dec 1929.

The 1930 census for Independence, Kansas has Howard L Smith, 33, married at 33, a cleaner in cleaning and pressing who owns his home worth $3000 and a radio. Francis is 27 and was married at 27.

The 1940 census for Independence, Kansas has Howard C Smith, 43, graduated high school, an assistant in a dry-cleaning company renting a home at 819 South 2nd Street for $10 per month. Francis is 37 and completed 7th grade. Their daughter, Irma Jean is 9 and completed 2nd grade.

Howard L C Smith born 27 Feb 1897, died 30 Apr 1959 and is buried in Mount Hope Cemetery, Independence, Kansas. Francis may have died in 1951 or 1969. She is not buried with Howard.

### 5. Gladys M Smith

Gladys was with her parents in 1940 and working as a public-school teacher. Francis C Smith (Howard Smith's wife) may have lived with Howard's sister Gladys after Howard died. There is a Francis C Smith, born 1907, died 1977 in Wichita, Kansas and buried in Resthaven Gardens of Memory. Gladys M Smith born 1902, died 1978 and is buried with Frances C Smith. It is difficult to track Smiths.

### 5. Donald Gale Smith and Cora M Martin

The 1930 census for Independence, Kansas has Donald G Smith, 26, married at 21, a delivery man for a tailor shop renting a home at 819 South 2$^{nd}$ Street for $15 per month. Cora M is 28 and was married at 23. Their son, Marvin, is 1. Isabell Martin, 64, a widow and mother-in-law is living with them.

The 1940 census for Tulsa, Oklahoma has Donald Smith, 36, graduated high school, a fountain manager at a chain drug company who owns a home at 125 East Haskell Place worth $2100. Cora is 37 and completed 9$^{th}$ grade. Marvin Lee is 11 and completed 5$^{th}$ grade.

Donald Gale Smith, 38, born 9 Jan 1904 in Utica New York, registered for WW11 on 16 Feb 1942. He is 6 ft with blonde hair and blue eyes and employed by Crown Drug Company. He served in the Navy.

### 5. Paul Russell Smith and Irene Dannels

Paul Russel Smith married Irene Dannels on 21 Oct 1934 in Fredonia, Kansas.

The 1940 census for Center, Wilson, Kansas has Paul R Smith, 34, completed 10$^{th}$ grade, a salesman in a drug store renting a home for $10 per month. Irene is 27 and graduated high school. Their sons are Melvin G, 4 and Jimmy W, 2/12.

Paul Russell Smith born 23 Jun 1905, died 7 May 1996 and is buried in Fredonia City Cemetery, Fredonia, Kansas. Irene May Elizabetha Dannels born 25 May 1912, died 13 Mar 2009 and is buried with Paul.

### 4. Francis Frankie Carpenter

Francis / Frankie Carpenter appeared with his parents in 1892 but nothing definite could be found after that. He may have died young or just was not found in the records.

## 4. Jessie/Jess/Jesse Carpenter and Elizabeth

The 1910 census for Champion, New York has Jess Carpenter, 30, married 8 years, a mill laborer renting his home at 21 Champion Street. Elizabeth is 27 and has 1 child still living. Their daughter is Pearl, 7.

A birth index has Pearl Carpenter born 1 Nov 1904, Stockholm, New York. Nothing more was found on Pearl.

Jesse Carpenter, 38, born 27 Feb 1880 of 21 Champion Street, Carthage, New York registered for WW1 on 12 Sep 1918. He was a millwright at Brahman Manufacturing Company, 531 Boyd Street Carthage, New York. His nearest relative is Elizabeth Carpenter.

The 1920 census for Champion, New York has Jessie Carpenter, 40, a laborer in a wood mill renting his home at 21 Champion Street. Elizabeth is 36.

The 1930 census for Watertown, New York has Jessie Carpenter, 50, married at 25, a barber in a barber shop renting part of a home on Boyd Street for $20 per month. Elizabeth M is 45 and was married at 20. Nothing more was found for Jessie Carpenter.

## 4. Mary Ann "Mammie" Carpenter and Robert B Williams

Mary Ann Carpenter married Robert B Williams in 1903.

The 1910 census for Denmark, Lewis, New York has Robert B Williams, 37, married 6 years, a farmer who owns his mortgaged farm. Mary E is 29 and has 3 children all living. The children are Robert S, 5; C Mildred, 3 and Helen Grace, 4/12.

The 1920 census for Denmark, Lewis, New York has Robert B Williams, 46, a dairy framer who owns his farm free and clear. Mary A is 38. The children are Robert S, 14; Mildred C, 13 and Helen G, 10. All the children attended school.

The 1930 census for Denmark, Lewis, New York has Robert B Williams, 57, married at 30, a farmer who owns his farm worth $7000 and a radio. Mary is 47 and married at 22. Helen G is 20, single and working for a private family.

The 1940 census for Denmark, Lewis, New York has Robert Williams, 67, completed 8th grade, a farmer who owns his farm worth $1500. Mary A is 58 and completed 8th grade.

Mary Ann Carpenter Williams born 1881, died 1945 and is buried in Swinburne Cemetery, Denmark, New York. Robert B Williams born 14 Jan 1873 in Wisconsin, died 1955 and is buried with Mary.

## 5. Robert S Williams and Louise Hill

Robert S Williams, 23, and Louise Hill, 20 were married 1 Nov 1928 in Lewis, New York.

The 1930 census for Castorland, New York has Robert S Williams, 25, married at 23, a feed mill laborer renting his home on Church Street for $10 per month. Louise B is 21 and married at 20. Their son, Robert J is 4/12.

The 1940 census for Denmark, Lewis, New York has Robert S Williams, 35, completed 8th grade, a laborer for State Petrol who owns his home on State Road worth $1000. Louise B is 32 and completed 10th grade. The children are Robert J, 10, completed 3rd grade; Ronald H, 2 and Grace K, 1.

Robert S Williams born 1905, died 1971 and is buried in Swinburne Cemetery, Denmark, Lewis, New York. B Louise Hill Williams born 1908, died 1996 and is buried with Robert.

## 5. Mildred C Williams and Gerald C Clemons

Mildred C Williams, 19, a teacher married Gerald C Clemons, 20, creamery, in Denmark, New York on 15 Aug 1925.

The 1930 census for Denmark, Lewis, New York has Gerald C Clemons, 25, married at 20, a farmer who owns his farm. Mildred C is 23 and was married at 19. Their daughter, Helen L is 11/12. They have a live-in farm hand.

The 1940 census for Denmark, Lewis, New York has Gerald C Clemons, 35, completed 8th grade, a farmer who owns his farm. Mildred is 33 and graduated high school. The children are Helen L, 11, completed 6th grade; Geraldine R, 8, completed 3rd grade; Patricia A, 3; Larry C, 1 and James O, 9/12.

Mildred C Williams Clemons born 1906, died 1987 and is buried in Swinburne Cemetery, Denmark, Lewis, New York. Gerald C Clemons born 1905, died 1987 and is buried with Mildred.

## 5. Helen G Williams and Herbert L Rector

The 1940 census for West Carthage, New York has Herbert L Rector, 29, completed 8th grade, as a grinder man in a paper mill renting a home for $16 per month. Helen is 30 and graduated high school. Their daughter, Susan J, is 1.

Herbert L Rector born 1910, died 1975 and is buried in Talcottville Village Cemetery, Talcottville, New York. Helen Williams Rector born 1909, died 1997 and is buried with Herbert. An infant son born and died in 1944 is buried with them.

## 4. William Carpenter

William Carpenter was in the 1900 census with his parents. A William Carpenter, 27 was found in a 1910 census for the St Lawrence State hospital in Ogdensburg, New York. This William Carpenter, 56, was still at Ogdensburg in the State Hospital in 1940. People were put in the hospital for various mental illnesses and epilepsy. They were often provided with work and allowed to wander the grounds. Although this may not be the right William Carpenter, nothing else was found that could be verified.

## 4. Harriet "Hattie" C Carpenter and Herbert S Morse

The 1910 census for Lowville, New York has Herbert Morse, 24, married 4 years, a telephone lineman living with his parents. Hattie is 25 and has 2 children both living. The children are Gilbert L, 3 and Ethel, 1.

The 1920 census for Lowville, New York has Herbert D Morse, 34, a wire chief at the telephone company renting a home on State Street. Hattie is 33. The children are Gilbert, 13 and Ethel, 11.

The 1930 census for Lowville, New York has Sarah Morse, 70, a widow who owns her home on Trinity Ave. worth $3000 and a radio. Herbert S is 44, married at 20 and a foreman for the highway department. Harriett is 44 and married at 19. Gilbert L is 23, married at 23, a lineman for utilities. Marguerite H is 22, married at 22, a rural school teacher. A 1940 census was not found.

Herbert S Morse, 56, born 17 Sep 1885 in Lowville, New York registered for WW11 on 26 Apr 1942. He is working for the New York State Highway Department.

Harriet C Morse born 1885, died 1958 and is buried in Lowville Rural Cemetery, Lowville, New York. Herbert S Morse born 1885, died 1960 and is buried with Hattie.

## 6. Gilbert L Morse and Marguerite Buckley

Gilbert Morse, 23, lineman married Marguerite Buckley, teacher on 25 Nov 1929 in Leyden, New York.

They are living with his parents and grandmother in 1930. A 1940 census was not found.

Gilbert Morse born 1907 in Lowville, New York died 24 Jan 1960 and is buried in Lowville Rural Cemetery, Lowville, New York. H Marguerite born 1907, died 2001 and is buried with Gilbert.

## 5. Ethel Sarah Morse and Francis Charles Johnson.

Ethel Sarah Morse, 19, married Francis Charles Johnson, 20, in Lowville, New York on 18 May 1928.

The 1930 census for Lowville, New York has Frances C Johnson, 23, married at 22, a utilities company worker renting a home for $13 per month. Ethel S is 21 and married at 19. Their daughter, Shirley A is 1 3/12.

The 1940 census for Border City, New York has Charles Johnson, 37, completed 8th grade, a foundry worker who owns a home worth $800. Sarah is 37 and completed 8th grade. Their daughter, Shirley is 10 and completed 4th grade.

Francis C Johnson born 1906, died 1970 and is buried in Lowville Rural Cemetery, Lowville, New York. Ethel born 1908, died 1984 and is buried with Francis. Their daughter, Shirley A, born 22 Dec 1928, died 7 Sep 1950 at Jefferson County Hospital for Polio.

### 4. Grace Louise Carpenter and Earl C Ferguson

Grace L Carpenter married Earl C Ferguson on 15 Aug 1907 in Copenhagen, New York.

The 1915 New York State Census for Watertown, New York has Earl C Ferguson, 24, an electrician living at 118 West Main Street. Grace L is 27. Their sons are Gerald, 3 and Harold C, 6/12.

A New York Guard Service Card has Earl Charles Ferguson, 23, living at 118 West Main Street, Watertown, New York, enlisted 13 Oct 1913 as a private in Company C 1st Infantry. Grace and Earl apparently parted ways after his time in the Guard.

The 1920 census for Watertown, New York finds Earl C Ferguson, 29, married, an electrician in a paper mill living with his parents. Gerald C, 8 is living with him.

The 1930 census for Watertown, New York has Grace Ferguson, 43, married at 20, renting part of a home at 520 Mundy Street. Her sons are Gerald C, 18, a helper in a machine manufactory and Harold C, 15. She also has a boarder.

The 1940 census for Watertown, New York has Grace Ferguson, 52, widow, completed 8th grade and living at 664 Cooper Street. Gerald is 29, single, completed 9th grade, an attendant at a gas station. Earl C Ferguson registered for WW11. They may have been separated but not divorced.

### 5. Harold C Ferguson and Emeline Washer

The 1940 census for Watertown, New York has Harold C Ferguson, 26, graduated high school, a service station attendant renting part of a home at 211 East Hoard Street.

Emeline, his wife, is 26 and completed 11th grade.

### 4. Clinton Charles Carpenter and Sophie R Chaffee

Clinton C Carpenter, 21, married Sophie R Chaffee, 21, on 30 Jul 1910.

Clinton Charles Carpenter, 28 born 31 Mar 1889 registered for WW1 on 5 Jun1917. He was working as farm labor in Martinsburg, New York and had a wife and child.

The 1920 census for Diana, Lewis, New York has Clinton Carpenter, 30, a farmer renting his farm. Sophie is 30. Their children are Elizabeth, 7 and Howard, 3/12.

The 1930 census for West Carthage, New York has Clinton C Carpenter, 41, married at 21, a truck driver for a lumber yard who owns his home at 13 Jefferson worth $2600 and a radio. Sophie is 40 and was married at 20. The children are Elizabeth C, 17, working as a saleslady at a Woolworth Store; Howard R, 10 and Robert J, 4.

The 1940 census for West Carthage, New York has Clinton C Carpenter, 51, completed 5th grade, a Street Commissioner for the Village who owns his home at 15 North Jefferson Street worth $3000. Sophie is 50 and completed 8th grade. Their children are Howard R, 20, completed 1-year college, a laborer in a school building and Robert J, 14, completed 8th grade.

A 1940 census or marriage record was not found for Elizabeth C Carpenter.

Clinton Charles carpenter born 31 Mar 1889, died 1954 and is buried in Hillside Cemetery, Natural Bridge, New York. Sophie Chaffee Carpenter born 1889, died 1972 and is buried with Clinton.

### 4. Hazen Carpenter and Ina O Vincent

The 1915 New York State Census for West Carthage, New York has Hazen A Carpenter, 25, a mill laborer. His wife, Ina, is 23. They are living with her parents William and Jennie Vincent and their children.

Hazen A Carpenter, 26, born 21 Oct 1890 in Croghan, New York, married, farmer registered for WW1 on 5 Jun 1917. His address was RFD#3, Carthage, New York. He is working in Champion, New York. Hazen is tall with a slender build, brown eyes and hair.

The 1920 census for Croghan, Lewis, New York has Hazen Carpenter, 30, a farmer working out renting his home. Ina is 27. The children are Margaret, 4 and Charles, 2.

The 1930 census for Carthage, New York has Hazen Carpenter, 39, married at 20, a wood worker in a brush factory who owns his home worth $2200 and a radio. Ina O is 38 and married at 18. The children are Marguerite, 14; Charlie, 12; Carlton, 9; and

Marceline 1 9/12.

The 1940 census for Carthage, New York has Hazen Carpenter, 49, completed 8th grade, a millwright for a wood working company who owns his home worth $3000. Ina is 48 and completed 11th grade. The children are Charles, 22, completed 11th grade, an operator in a wood working company; Carlton, 20, completed 9th grade, working with Charles; and Marceline, 11, completed 6th grade. Thelma, 18, completed 8th grade, daughter-in-law is living with them. Thelma and Charles were married in 1938.

Hazen Carpenter born 1890, died 1956 and is buried in Swinburne Cemetery, Denmark, New York. Ina O Vincent Carpenter born Feb 1892, died 1967 and is buried with Hazen.

### 5. Marguerite Elanor Carpenter and Daniel Matthew Canell

Marguerite E Carpenter married Daniel M Canell on 31 Dec 1936.

The 1940 census for Carthage, New York has Daniel Carnell, 23, completed 11th grade, a laborer in a lumber mill renting a home at 998 Alexander Street. Marguerite is 24 and completed 11th grade. The children are Barbara, 1 and Grovine a new born.

Marguerite Eleanor "Peg" Carpenter born 23 Dec 1915, died 17 Apr 1998 and is buried in Swinburne Cemetery, Denmark, New York. Daniel Mathew "Happ" Canell born 26 Mar 1916 in Carthage, New York, died 23 Jul 2007 in Carthage and is buried with Peg.

### 3. Bruce Carpenter and Sharlott or Charlotte

Bruce is living with his parents in 1870 and 1875.

The 1880 census for Brownville, New York has Bruce Carpenter, 28, a farmer; and Charlotte, 29, keeping house. They are living with Bruce's parents Levi and Eunice Carpenter.

Sharlotte I Carpenter died 24 Jul 1896 in Hornellsville, New York. Nothing more could be found on either Bruce or Sharlotte Carpenter.

### 2.6. Mary "Polly" Carpenter and Nathan Parish Jr.

Polly Carpenter married Nathan Parish about 1820.

The 1850 census for Brownville, New York has Nathan Parish, 52. Mary is 47 Their children are Lemuel, 17; Deforest, 16; Nathan, 13; Margarette, 10 and George R, 8.

The 1860 census for Brownville, New York has Nathan Parish, 62, born in Vermont, farmer. Polly is 60 and born in Vermont. The children are Sarepta (Margarette), 19, born in New York, seamstress and George, 17, born in New York.

The 1865 New York State Census for Watertown has Nathan Parish, 65, born in Vermont with a frame house worth $300. Mary is 65 and born in Vermont. The children are Mariette, 23, a widow; George R, 22 and Sabra, 18. George and Sabra are married.

Most of the family moved to Michigan around 1870. A census has not been found. Polly may have died before or after the move sometime between 1865 and 1880.

The 1880 census for Adrian, Michigan has Nathan Parish, 84, living with his son George and family.

Nathan Parish died 1 Jan 1890 in Adrian, Michigan of old age.

### 3. Elisha Parish and Eliza Jane Hooper

Elisha Parish is an older son of Nathan and Polly Parish not listed in 1850. He married Eliza Jane Hooper about 1845.

The 1860 census for Brownville, Jefferson, New York has Elisha Parish, 37, a farmer with $500 in real estate. Eliza is 34. The children are Marcia, 14; Elisha, 13; Nathan, 11; Louisa, 7 and Electa, 4/12.

The 1870 census for Geneva, Ashtabula, Ohio has Elisha Parish, 48, born in New York, a laborer. Jane is 44. The children are Lousia, 17; Electa, 10 and Albert, 7. Nothing more could be found on Louisa.

The 1880 Census for Dover, Lenawee, Michigan has Elisha Parish, 55, a farmer. Eliza is 53. Their children are Electa, 18; Albert A, 16; Francis, 31, daughter-in-law and her children Anne, 9 and Martin, 10/12.

The 1900 census for Dover, Lenawee, Michigan has Elisha Parish, 75, born Feb 1825, married 54 years, a farmer who owns his farm free and clear. Eliza is 72, born Jun 1827 and has had 8 children with 6 still living. Albert A is 36, born Jun 1863, married 9 years and a farm laborer. Viola is 39, born Apr 1861 and has not had children. There are 2 boarders living with them.

The 1910 census for Dover, Lenawee, Michigan has Elisha Parish, 86, married 65 years and owns his farm free and clear. Eliza is 83 and has had 8 children with 6 still living. Albert E is 47, second marriage, married 18 years and a house mason. Viola is 52 and has not had children.

Elisha Parish, 88, born 29 Feb 1823, died 6 Apr 1911 in Dover, Lenawee, Michigan. He was married, a farmer and died of La Grippe (pneumonia). He is buried in Dover Center Cemetery, Lenawee County, Michigan. Eliza died 2 Jun 1919 in Palmyra, Michigan.

## 4. Marcia Parish and George A Gallinger / Edwin Pearson

Marcia Parrish, 25, born in Jefferson County, New York, married George A Gallinger, 33, born in Ontario, a farmer, on 24 Apr 1870. They are both from Marathon, Lapeer, Michigan and were married by a Justice of the Peace.

The 1870 census for Marathon, Lapeer, Michigan has George Gallinger, 33, a farm laborer and Marcia, 25. They are living with his brother and family.

George Gallinger born 1839, died 6 Dec 1871, of consumption, in Lapeer, Michigan.

The 1880 census for Marathon, Lapeer, Michigan has Marcia Gallinger, 34, widowed, a farmer and Louise, 9, attended school.

Marcia Parish Gallinger, 36, married Edwin Pearson, 39, a farmer, in Marathon, Lapeer, Michigan on 21 Mar 1882.

Pvt Edwin Pierson born 12 Dec 1843, died 12 Apr 1882 and is buried in Woodlawn Cemetery, Columbiaville, Michigan. He was in Company E, 7th Michigan Infantry. He was wounded 5 May 1864 at Wilderness in Virginia, Enlisted 12 Aug 1861, discharged 21 Jan 1865.

The 1900 census for Marathon, Lapeer, Michigan has Marcia Pierson, 55, born Mar 1845, a widow, has had 1 child, still living and owns her home. Lulu Gallinger, 29, born Feb 1871 is single and a seamstress.

The 1910 census for Marathon, Lapeer, Michigan has Marcia Pearson, 64, widow, had 1 child still living and owns her home. Louise Gallinger, 38, divorced, no children and working as a dress maker.

The 1920 census for Marathon, Lapeer, Michigan has Marcia Pearson, 74, widowed and a farmer. Lula G Crawford is 48 and married.

Marcia Parish Gallinger Pierson, born 1845, died 1935 and is buried with Edwin.

## 5. Louise "Lulu" Gallinger and Willie C Smith / Chas F Crawford

Louise Gallinger, 18, married Willie C Smith, 27, on 6 Mar 1889 in Columbiaville, Michigan. Louise left Willie by 1900. Lula is in the 1900, 1910 and 1920 census records with her mother.

Lulu G Gallinger, 47, married Chas F Crawford, 37, on 8 Nov 1917 in Flint, Michigan.

Lulu Crawford filed for a divorce 10 Feb 1922. The absolute divorce was granted 8 Aug 1922 for extreme cruelty. There were no children.

The 1930 census for Marathon, Lapeer, Michigan has Louise Crawford, 59, divorced and a farmer who owns the farm. Marcia Pierson is 85 and a widow.

Lulu Gallinger born 1871, died 1952 and is buried in Woodlawn Cemetery near her mother.

## 4. Elisha K Parish and Francis S Swan

Elisha Parish Jr., 23, a farmer, married Francis S Swan, 21, on 17 Feb 1870 in Lapeer, Michigan.

The 1910 census for East St Louis, Illinois has Elisha parish, 63, married 40 years, born in New York, a commissioner of horses who owns his home at 1416 Baugh Ave. free and clear. Francis is 61, born in New York and has 3 children all living. Annie is 38, born in Michigan, married once; Martin is 30, married once for 6 years, born in Michigan and a commissioner of stock; and Harry is 22, single, born in Kentucky and a stock clerk. Alma is 24, daughter-in-law, married to Martin and has 3 living children. The children are Elisha, 4; Bernice, 2 and Albert, 9/12. All the grandchildren were born in Illinois.

The 1920 census for East St Louis, Illinois has Elisha parish, 73, owns his home at 1416 Baugh Ave. a stock dealer at the stock yards. Francis is 70. Martin K Parish is 39, renting part of the house and a stock dealer at the stock yards. Alma is 36. The children are Elisha, 14; Bernice, 12 and Albert, 10. The children are all attending school and there are 2 maids in the house.

The 1930 census for Monroe County, Mississippi has Elisha B Parish, 24, born in Illinois, married at 21 and a farmer. Rose is 18, married at 15 and born in Alabama. Beverly, their son, is 1 8/12 and born in Mississippi. Elisha is 83, grandfather, widowed and married at 23.

The stock in the above census' are Horses and Mules. The need for horses diminished with the advent of the automobile, trucks and tractors. Elisha and Frances moved to Mississippi to be with the grandson Elisha. Mississippi would be a better place to sell horses and mules. Martin stayed in Illinois to sell the house and wrap up the business.

Francis S Parish, grandmother, born 10 Mar 1849, died 20 Aug 1929 and is buried in Masonic Cemetery, Amory, Mississippi. Elisha K Parish, grandfather, born 24 Oct 1846, died 17 Apr 1932 and is. buried with Francis.

Alma F Parish, wife of Martin, born 27 Sep 1885, died 29 Oct 1934 and is buried in Masonic Cemetery. Martin K Parish born 22 Jul 1879, died 26 Feb 1959 and is buried with Alma.

Elisha Beverly Parish, husband, (grandson of Elisha K) born 7 Sep 1905, died 23 May

1968 and is buried in Masonic Cemetery. His son Beverly M Parish served in the Air Force in WW11, born 8 Aug 1928, died 21 Mar 2002 and is buried with him.

### 5. Annie Parish

Annie, 38, is living with her parents in 1910. Nothing more could be found.

### 5. Martin Kite Parish and Alma R Fields

Martin Parish married Alma Fields 12 Mar 1904 in St Clair, Illinois.

Martin Kite Parish born 22 Jul 1879, living at 1416 Bough, East St Louis, Illinois, registered for WW1 on 12 Sep 1918. He was working in the horse and mule business for E Parish & Son. He did not serve.

Martin and Alma are living with his parents in 1910 and 1920.

The 1930 census for East St Louis, Illinois has Martin K Parish, 51, married at 24, owns the Baugh Ave house worth $3500 and is a salesman in the horse and mule stock yards. Alma R is 44 and married at 18. Bernice L is 22, single and a clerk in a real estate office. Albert W is 20, single and a laborer in a service manufacturing plant.

Alma Fields Parish died in 1934 and is buried in Mississippi.

### 6. Elisha B Parish and Rose Ella Stanford

Elisha B and Rose were living in Mississippi with Elisha K his grandfather in 1930.

The 1940 census for Monroe, Mississippi has Elisha B Parish, 34, completed 10th grade, a truck driver doing general hauling who owns his farm on Gravel Road worth $300. Rose is 27 and completed 8th grade. The children are Beverly M, 10, completed 5th grade; Leroy, 7, completed 2nd grade and Verna Mae, 2. All but Elisha were born in Mississippi.

Rose Parish, born 19 Nov 1911, died 12 Jun 1994 and is buried in Masonic Cemetery in Amory, Mississippi with Elisha B and his parents and grandparents.

### 6. Bernice Parish and Leroy Hooker

Bernice is with her parents Martin and Alma in 1920 and 1930.

The 1940 census for Gates Mills, Ohio has Leroy L Hooker, 53, completed 8th grade, a salesman for a printing house who owns their home on Riverview Road worth $8,500. Bernice L is 33, born in Missouri and complete10th grade. Leslie A is 27, graduated college and a sales man for a printing house. Melvin L is 26, graduated college and a production man for an advertising agency. Roger A is 3 and Bernice's son. The 2 older boys are Leroy's sons. Bernice is listed as born in Illinois in previous records but Missouri is across the river from East St Louis and a possibility.

## 6. Albert M Parish and Myrtle Irene Adams

The 1940 census for Monroe County, Mississippi has Albert M Parish, 30, completed 8th grade, working for the WPA and renting a home on Gravel Road. Myrtle, is 25 and completed 7th grade. Their daughter, Bettie Irene, is 1. Martin Parish, Albert's father, is 58, widowed and completed 4th grade.

Albert Martin Parish born 12 Jul 1909, died 20 Jun 1965 in Jackson, Mississippi and is buried in Haughton Memorial Park, Armory, Mississippi. His wife Myrtle Irene Adams died in 2000 and is buried with him.

## 5. Harry S Parish

Harry Parish, 29, single, born 4 Mar 1888 in Louisville, Kentucky registered for WW1 on 5 Jun 1917, He is a horse dealer for E Parish & Sons in East St Louis, Illinois.

Harry S Parish born 1888, died 2 Feb 1919 in East St Louis, Illinois. His parents were Eliza Parrish and Francis Swan. There is no burial place. He may have had an accident or died of the Spanish Flu. Nothing more was found.

## 4. Nathan A Parish and Nellie M Austin

Nathan A Parish, 28, and Nellie Austin, 17, were married 5 Oct 1877 in Hillsdale, Michigan.

The 1880 census for Palmyra, Michigan has Nathan Parish, 31, a farmer. Nellie is 20. Their son, Alvin E is 2.

The 1900 census for Adams, Hillsdale, Michigan has Nathan Parish, 51, born Jan 1849 in New York, married 23 years, a farmer who owns his farm free and clear. Nellie M is 40, born Mar 1860 in Michigan and has 2 children, both living. Their son, William is 10, born May 1890.

The 1910 census for Jefferson, Hillsdale, Michigan has Nathan A Parish, 61, married 32 years, a farmer who owns his mortgaged farm. Nellie M is 50 and has 2 children both are living. William N is 19, single and working as farm labor.

The 1920 census for North Adams, Michigan has Nathan A Parish, 70, renting a home on Main Street. Nellie M is 59. William N is 29 and a repair man in a garage.

Nathan A Parish born 10 Jan 1849, died 6 Nov 1920 in North Adams, Michigan. He had chronic Bronchorrhea and Cirrhosis of Liver. He is buried in Northlawn Cemetery, North Adams, Michigan. Nellie M born 1860 died 1927 and is buried with Nathan

## 5. Alvin E Parish and Fannie B Cool

The 1900 census for Kingston, DeKalb, Illinois has Alvin Parish, 22, born May 1878, a farm laborer for a large family.

Alvin E Parish, 25, a farmer, married Fannie B Cool, 18, on 11 Feb 1904 in Hudson, Michigan.

The 1910 census for Adams, Hillsdale, Michigan has Alvin E Parish, 31, married 6 years, a blacksmith. Fannie is 24.

Alvin Edwin Parish, 40, born 2 May 1878, an auto worker for Ford Motor Company, registered for WW1 on 12 Sep 1918. The nearest relative is Fannie Bell Parish. They are living at 1261 Iroquois, Detroit, Michigan.

The 1920 census for Royal Oak, Oakland, Michigan has Alvin E Parish, 43, owns his mortgaged home at 33 13 Mile Road and is a foreman in a factory. Fannie B is 34 and their daughter, Velma is 7.

The 1930 census for Royal Oak, Michigan has Alvin E Parish, 52, married at 24, a shipper in an auto factory who owns his home at 33 13 Mile Road worth $8000 and a radio. Fanny B is 42 and was married at 17. Their daughter, Velma R is 17.

Velma Parish, 19, married Lloyd Woodham, 21 on 6 Sep 1932 in Mt Clemens, Michigan. Velma filed for divorce on 10 Jan 1941 which was granted 3 Mar 1941.

The 1940 census for Clawson, Michigan has Alvin Parish, 61, completed 8th grade, a watchman at an aluminum factory who owns his home at 221 Cresson Road. Fannie is 53 and completed 8th grade. Velma Woodham is 27, married, graduated high school and a stenographer in an aluminum factory. Velma's daughter, Beverly is 6.

Alvin Edwin Parish born 2 May 1878, in Adrian Michigan, died 4 Nov 1943 in Detroit, Michigan.

## 5. William N Parish and Esther Marie Comstock

William N Parish, 27, born 27 May 1890 in Adrian, Michigan registered for WW1 on 5 Jun 1917. He was working on his father's farm and claimed partial support of his parents. There is no evidence he served.

William N Parish, 32, married Esther M Comstock, 22 on 26 Nov 1928 in Williams, Ohio.

The 1930 census for North Adams, Michigan has William N Parish, 39, married at 32, a house carpenter. Esther M is 23 and was married at 18. Imogene F is 2.

The 1940 census for Somerset, Hillsdale, Michigan has William Parish, 49, completed 8th grade and a building carpenter. Esther is 33 and completed 8th grade. The children are Gene (Imogene) 13, completed 6th grade; Arlene, 9, completed 3rd grade; Franklin, 7, completed 2nd grade and Robert, 4.

William N Parish born 27 May 1890, died 16 Aug 1952 in Hanover, Michigan and is buried in Northlawn Cemetery, North Adams, Michigan. Esther M born 1906, died 1975 and is buried with William. A son Gary L was born 1940 and died 1942.

William Franklin Parish born 1932, died 1995 and is buried in Northlawn Cemetery, North Adams, Michigan. William served in the US Air Force during the Korean War.

## 4. Electa Parish and James Clark Richardson

Electa Parish, 21, married James C Richardson, 33, on 18 Sep 1881 in Blissfield, Michigan. They were both living in Palmyra, Michigan.

The 1900 census for Palmyra, Lenawee, Michigan has Clark Richardson, 53, born Apr 1847, married 19 years, a farmer who owns his farm free and clear. Electa is 40, born Jan 1860 and had 1 child, still living. Their son Elisha C, 18, born Jun 1881 is at school. Charles Richardson, Clark's father, 86, born Apr 1814, a widow is living with them.

The 1910 census for Palmyra, Lenawee, Michigan has J C Richardson, 63, married 26 years, a mason contractor. Electa V is 50 and has 1 child still living.

The 1920 census for Palmyra, Lenawee, Michigan has Elisha Richardson, 37, widowed, a building contractor. Clark, 73 is a stone mason. Electa is 59. They are all living on a farm and have a farm laborer living with them.

James Clark Richardson, born 2 Apr 1847, died 13 Jan 1920 in Palmyra of mitral insufficiency and is buried in Oakwood Cemetery, Adrian, Michigan. Electa V Richardson, born 28 Jan 1859, died 1 Feb 1924 of capillary bronchitis following severe hemorrhage due to carcinoma of stomach. Electa is buried with James.

## 5. Elisha C Richardson and Mary Tena Mitchell / Florence Richmond

Elisha C Richardson, 20, married Mary Tena Mitchell, 20, on 13 Mar 1905 in Lucas County, Ohio.

The 1910 census for Palmyra, Lenawee, Michigan has Elisha Richardson, 27, married 7 years and a farmer renting his farm. Mary T is 25 and has 1 child, still living. Leroy C is 5.

Elisha is living with his parents in 1920 as a widower.

Elisha Clark Richardson, 38, a contractor, married Florence Richmond on 6 Apr 1921 in Palmyra, Michigan.

The 1930 census for Adrian, Michigan has Elisha Richardson, 47, married at 21, a contractor for building construction who owns his home at 110 West Abbott Street worth $2600 and a radio. F Rose is 39, married at 29 and a laundress at a laundry.

Elisha C Richardson, born 16 Jun 1882, died 17 Aug 1937 of cerebral hemorrhage. The informant was Florence Richardson. He is buried in Palmyra Cemetery.

### 6. Leroy C Richardson and Florence K Deible

The 1920 census for Cleveland, Ohio has Leroy Richardson, 13, living with his mother Mary and step father William Dial. Mary didn't die but left Elisha.

Leroy C Richardson, 23, a dry cleaner, married Florence K Dibble, 22, on 15 Jun 1927 in Adrian, Michigan.

The 1930 census for Adrian, Michigan has Leroy C Richardson, 25, married at 22, owns his house at 512 Division Street worth $3000 and a radio. Florence is 24 and was married at 21.

The 1940 census for Adrian, Michigan has Leroy C Richardson, 35, graduated high school, a presser at a dry cleaner who owns his home at 512 Division Street. Florence K is 34, completed 11th grade and labor in a cable factory. Eugene is 9 and completed 4th grade.

### 4. Albert Parish and Mary L Keyes / Viola Richardson

Albert A Parish married Mary L Keyes about 1887.

Albert A Parish, 29, a farmer, of Dover, married Viola Englehart Richardson, 32, of Madison, on 14 Dec 1891. Both were married previously. Viola is the daughter of Isaac Englehart.

The 1900 census for Dover, Lenawee, Michigan has Albert A Parish, 36, born Jun 1863 in New York and Viola E, 39, born Apr 1861 living with Albert's parents. They have been married 9 years and have no children.

The 1910 census for Dover has Albert and Viola living with his parents, Elisha and Eliza. Albert's father died in 1911 and his mother in 1919.

A 1920 census could not be found. A 1921 Adrian, Michigan City Directory has Albert A Parish, a mason, living at 815 Vine Street. Viola must have died and Albert was in the process of moving during the 1920 census. Albert lived on Vine Street until his death.

Albert A Parish, 66, born Jun 1863 in New York, died 11 Mar 1929 in Adrian, Michigan, of Bronchial Pneumonia, La Grippe. He is widowed and buried in Dover Cemetery.

### 3. Lemuel Parish and Mary Jane Phillips / Racy Hartel

Lemuel parish married Mary Jane Phillips about 1853.

The 1860 census for Limerick, New York has Lemuel Parish, 29, a peddler. Mary is 23. The children are Maryette, 8; Olive, 6; Charles,3 and Chester 5/12.

The 1865 census for Watertown, New York has Lemuel Parish, 32, born in New York, a teamster. Mary J is 29, born in Canada and has 4 children. The children are Mary E, 12; Olive,10; Charles, 8 and Chester, 5. Nothing more was found on Maryette or Mary E.

The 1880 census for Fairport, Ohio has Lemuel Parish, 49, born in New York, a fish peddler. Mary J is 43. The children are Harriet, 14; Thomas, 10; Wayne, 6; Nathan, 4 and Lemuel, 1.

Lemuel Parish married Racy Hartel on 13 Sep 1886 in Lake County, Ohio. Lemuel and Mary have divorced. Mary Jane Phillips Parish married Deforest Parish 17 Aug 1891.

Lemuel Parish born 1831 in New York, died and is buried in Evergreen Cemetery, Painesville, Ohio. There is no death date but he is not found in 1900.

### 4. Olive Parish and Ezra Parrish

Olive and Ezra were married 1875 or 1879 (1900 census). They are probably cousins.

An 1880 census for Painesville, Ohio has Ezra Parrish, 29, a fisherman. Olive is 25. Their children are Ida, 9; William, 6; Adalbert 2 and Ezra, 9/12. The parents are born in New York and children are born in Ohio. Adalbert died 12 Jan 1881. Ezra also died young and is buried in the Potters Field section of Evergreen Cemetery.

The 1900 census for Painesville, Ohio has Ezra, Parrish, 49, born Jun 1850, married 21 years. Olive is 45, born Jan 1855 and has had 8 children, 6 are still living. The children are William, 25, born Jan 1875, a basket maker; Cora, 16, born Mar 1883; Eva, 13, born Jun 1886; Lottie, 9, born Nov 1890 and Alfred, 6, born Nov 1893. Ida, William and Adalbert may be Ezra's children by an earlier marriage. Nothing more was found on Ida.

The 1910 census for Fairport, Ohio has Ezra Parrish, 55, married 31 years, a fish peddler who owns his home on Vine Street. Olive is 52, and has had 10 children, 5 are living. William, 34 and Alfred, 16 are living with them.

The 1920 and 1930 census have Ezra Parrish, widowed, living with his son, Alfred.

Olive A Parish, born 1 Jan 1855 in New York, died 23 Mar 1916 and is buried in Evergreen Cemetery, Fairport Harbor, Ohio. Ezra Parrish, born 22 Jan 1850 in Watertown, New York, died 29 Sep 1934 and is buried with Olive.

## 5. William Parrish

William Parrish was never married and lived with family most of his life. He died after walking into the side of a passenger train. The accident fractured his skull, broke his neck, and other wounds. Mrs. Alfred Parish signed his death certificate.

William S Parrish born 30 Jan 1875, died 15 Dec 1950 in Painesville, Ohio and is buried in Evergreen Cemetery.

## 5. Cora Parrish and George Henry Couch / Botzman

The 1910 census for Madison, Ohio has G H Couch, 29, married 10 years and a blacksmith who owns his own shop. Cora is 26 and had 1 child still living. Olive is 8. A cousin is living with them.

The 1920 census for Middlefield, Ohio has George H Couch, 38, a blacksmith. Cora is 35. They have a blacksmith helper living with them.

The 1930 census for Painesville, Ohio has George H Couch, 49, married at 19, a building contractor who owns his home at 95 Kerr Ave., worth $4000 and a radio. Cora is 46 and married at 16. George died 1936 according to several Ancestry trees.

Cora moved to California by 1948 and married a Botzman. Cora Parrish Couch Botzman born 22 Nov 1884, died 29 Jul 1955 in Los Angeles, California

The picture is Cora on the right and her daughter Olive.

## 6. Olive Eloise Couch and William E Pierce

The 1920 census for Middlefield, Ohio has William Pierce, 23, a farm laborer renting his home. Olive is 18.

The 1930 census for Painesville, Ohio has William L Pierce, 33, married at 22, an electrician in a battery shop who owns his home on Kerr Ave. worth $5000 and a radio.

Olive is 28 and was married at 17. Their children are Donald L, 10 and Elaine J, 4.

A 1940 census has not been found. There is an Inglewood, California City Directory with William E Pierce, wife Olive, aircraft worker, home 113 W Hillcrest Blvd. Apparently the entire family moved to California about 1940.

## 5. Eva Parrish and Ira Conant Brainard

Eva Parish, 18 married Ira Brainard, 18 on 15 Sep 1904 in Lake County, Ohio.

The 1910 census for Painesville, Ohio has Conant Brainard, 25, married 5 years, a fisherman renting a home on Richmond Street. Eva P is 25 and had 3 children, 2 are living. The children are Clyde, 3 and Glenn, 11/12. An uncle is living with them.

The 1920 census for Painesville, Ohio has Ira Brainard, 33, a fisherman on the lake who owns his mortgaged home. Eva is 30. The children are Clyde, 13; Glen, 10; Lottie, 8 and Alfred, 6.

The 1930 census for Painesville, Ohio has Ira Brainard, 44, married at 19, a fisherman for a wholesale fish company who owns his home at 501 Lakeview. Eva is 42 and was married at 17. The children are Alfred, 15 and Olive, 6.

Eva May Parrish Brainard born 4 Oct 1886, died 3 Jan 1935 in Painesville, Ohio and is buried in Evergreen Cemetery. Ira C Brainard born 20 Oct 1885, died 6 Aug 1957 and is buried with Eva.

The 1940 census for Painesville, Ohio has Ira C Brainard, 54, graduated high school, a ditch grader for the WPA renting a home at 477 Elm Street for $14 per month. His 2nd wife, Minnie is 53 and completed 6th grade. Olive is 16 and completed 10th grade.

## 6. Clyde Brainard and Katherine Conklin

Clyde Ezra Brainard, 21, married Kathryn Marjorie Conklin, 18, on 7 Sep 1927 in Chautauqua, New York, just over the border from Ohio.

The 1930 census for Painesville, Ohio has Clyde Brainard, 23, married at 20, a laborer in construction renting a home at 136 Morse Ave. for $5 per month. Katherine is 19 and married at 16. Their son Clyde Jr is 1 3/12. Katherine's mother and 3 brothers are living with them.

The 1940 census for Painesville, Ohio has Clyde Brainard, 33, completed 8th grade, a truck driver for the city who owns the house at 136 Morse worth $1000. Katherine is 29 and completed 8th grade. Their children are Clyde, 11, completed 8th grade; Marjory, 9, completed 4th grade; Katherine, 7, completed 2nd grade; Carol, 4 and Larry, 1.

## 6. Glen Brainard and Marie Edna Starliper

Glen Brainard married Marie Starliper on 28 Nov 1927 in Chautauqua, New York.

The 1930 census for Painesville, Ohio has Glen Brainard, 20, married at 18, a painter living at 534 Chardon Street. Marie is 18 and was married at 16. Glen Jr. is 1 7/12.

The 1940 census for Painesville, Ohio has Glen Brainard, 30, completed 8th grade, a crane operator at a chemical plant renting his home at 115 Burton for $20 per month. Marie is 28 and completed 7th grade. Their children are Glen H, 11, completed 7th grade; Eva Marie, 8, completed 3rd grade and Shirley, 3. They have a lodger.

## 6. Lottie Pauline Brainard and Charles E Brown

The 1930 census for Painesville, Ohio has Charles Brown, 22, married at 20, a fire operator at a coffee plant renting a home at 560 Chardon for $22 per month. Lottie is 19 and married at 17. Their son, Charles Jr., is 1 2/12.

The 1940 census for Painesville, Ohio has Chas E Brown, 31, completed 11th grade, an expeller operator for a soybean plant renting his home at 425 Chardon for $10 per month. Lottie is 28 and competed 10th grade. The children are Charles, 11, completed 5th grade; Marilyn, 8, completed 2nd grade; Marvin, 4 and Stanley, 3.

## 6. Alfred Brainard and Anna Gergely

The 1940 census for Painesville, Ohio has Alfred Brainard, 26, completed 8th grade, a janitor for a savings bank renting a home at 578 Richmond Street for $15 per month. Anna is 27 and completed 8th grade. Their children are Joseph, 4 and Lois Jane, 2.

## 5. Lottie Isabelle Parrish and Arthur Allen / Fred Korth / Bert Peterson / George E Forgason / David Loveland

Lottie Parrish's daughter, Violet Parrish, was born in 1906 with an unknown father.

Lottie May Parrish married Arthur G Allen on 12 Aug 1909 in Ashtabula, Ohio. They were divorced soon after and both remarried in 1910.

Lottie Parrish Allen, 19, married Fred W Korth, 19, on 21 Apr 1910 in Lake County, Ohio. A 1910 census was not found.

The 1920 census for Ashtabula, Ohio has Bert Peterson, 42, a wet tacker at a tannery renting a home at 50 Adams Street. Lottie is 29. Violet Parrish is 12.

Lottie Parrish Peterson, 36, married George E Forgason, electrician, on 4 Oct 1927.

The 1930 census for Painesville, Ohio has George Forgason, 48, married at 45, a foreman in an alkali plant renting a home at 99 Grant Street for $35 per month. Lottie I is 38 and was first married at 16.

George E Forgason born 2 Apr 1882, died 7 Apr 1935 in Painesville, Ohio and is buried in Evergreen Cemetery.

Lottie married David Loveland between George's death in 1935 and the 1940 census.

The 1940 census for Painesville, Ohio has David Loveland, 63, completed 8th grade, a cemetery worker who owns his home at 156 Jefferson Street worth $2000. Lottie is 49 and completed 8th grade. Lottie's brother, William Parrish, is 68, completed 3rd grade and is living with them.

Lottie Isabelle Parrish born 7 Nov 1891 in Fairport Harbor, Ohio, died 13 Jun 1947 in Painesville, Ohio and is buried with George Forgason.

## 6. Violet I Parrish and Ludwig Santti / John M Hemming

Violet I Parrish, 18, married Ludwig A Santti, 22, a sailor, on 20 Nov 1923 in Monroe, Michigan. They were both from Fairport Harbor, Ohio. Ludwig's parents were from Finland. Violet would have been 15 or 16.

Ludwig Santti, 23, born 1901, died 5 Jun 1924 at Fairport Harbor, Ohio and is buried in Evergreen Cemetery near his parents.

The 1930 census for Painesville, Ohio has John M Hemming, 30, married at 26, an electrician in an alkali plant renting a home at 57 Kerr Ave. for $35 per month. Violet I is 23 and married at 19. Their daughter, Gloria is 1 6/12. A marriage record was not found.

The 1940 census for Painesville, Ohio has John Hemming, 40, completed 8th grade, an electrician at a chemical plant renting a home at 151 Morris Ave for $25 per month. Violet is 31 and graduated high school. Their daughters are Gloria, 11, completed 6th grade and Joanne, 8, completed 3rd grade. A lodger is living with them.

## 5. Alfred E Parrish and Mildred M Alfard

Alfred E Parrish, 18, married Mildred M Alfard, 18, on 3 Jul 1919 in Geauga, Ohio.

The 1920 census for Ashtabula, Ohio has Alfred Parrish, 24, a laborer who owns his mortgaged home. Mildred is 18. Alfred's father, Ezra is 69 and widowed.

The 1930 census for Painesville, Ohio has Alfred E Parish, 38, married at 25, a fisherman for a wholesale fish company who owns his home worth $3000 and a radio. Mildred is 29 and was married at 18. Their son, Albert, is 10. Alfred's father, Ezra is living with them.

The 1940 census for North Perry, Ohio has Alfred Parrish, 46, completed 5th grade, a farm laborer renting a home for $17 per month. Mildred is 38 and completed 8th grade. Their son George is 6.

Alfred Parrish born 11 Nov 1893 in Fairport Harbor, Ohio, died 24 May 1979 in Perry, Lake, Ohio and is buried in Perry Township Cemetery. Mildred Parrish born 1901, died 1981 and is buried with Alfred.

It has been difficult to determine what happened to Albert. He may have moved to Florida and served in the Air Force most of his life. There is no middle initial or parent's names to connect him.

### 4. Charles "Charley" Parish and Emma Jane Lamar Stafford

Charles Parish married Emma J Stafford on 1 Jul 1880 in Lake County, Ohio.

Emma born 1859, died 1896 in Fairport, Ohio and is buried in Evergreen Cemetery.

The 1900 census for Painesville, Ohio has Charles Parish, 43, born Apr 1857, widowed, a day laborer. Walter is 19, born Mar 1881, a day laborer. They have a housekeeper.

The 1910 census for Painesville, Ohio has Charles Parish, 57, widowed, not working, owns his home on 2nd Street. Walter is 28, single and working at odd jobs.

The 1920 census for Painesville, Ohio has Charley Parish, 64, widowed, a fish peddler who owns his home on Vine Street. His brothers Tom, 47, widowed, a road worker; Wayne, 44, single, a fish peddler and Chester, 61, widowed, a mill worker, are living with Charley.

Walter Parish married Gladys H Friend about 1922.

The 1930 census for Fairport Harbor, Ohio has Charles Parrish, 73, widowed, first married at 23, retired and owns his home at 110 Vine Street. Charles' son, Walter, 49, married at 21, an independent teamster. Walter's wife, Gladys is 23 and married at 15. Wayne, brother is 58 and divorced. Lucile, niece is 6.

Charley Parish born 30 Apr 1856 in Pulaski, New York, died 4 Nov 1931 in Fairport, Ohio of myocardial degeneration and circulatory failure. Walter Parrish was the informant. Charley Parrish is buried in Evergreen Cemetery.

The 1940 census for Fairport, Ohio has Walter parish, 59, completed 8th grade, a watchman on a WPA road project owns the house at 110 Vine Street worth $1500. Gladys is 33 and completed 8th grade. Two cousins, Lucile, 16, completed 9th grade, and Wanceda, 15, completed 8th grade are living with them. Wayne Parish, uncle, 69, divorced, did not attend school and is not working.

Gladys H Friend Parish born 13 Aug 1906 in Pennsylvania, died 4 Jun 1944 in Fairport Harbor, Ohio and is buried in Evergreen Cemetery. Walter Parish born 9 May 1881, died 19 May 1948 in Wickliffe, Ohio and is buried with his wife and parents.

## 4. Chester Parish and Almina Allen / Hallie Clute Bannon

Chester is 21 and living with his uncle, Deforest Parish in 1880.

Chester Parish married Almina Allen on 4 May 1894.

The 1900 census for Geneva, Ohio has Chester parish, 41, born Feb 1859, married 10 years, a fisherman. Almina is 30, born Jun 1869 and has 1 child still living. Allen Arthur, step-son, is 11 and born Jun 1888

The 1910 census for Geneva, Ohio has Chester Parish, 51, single, not employed but owns his home on South Ridge Road free and clear.

Chester and Almina were divorced before 1915. Chester Parish, 39 married Hallie Clute Brannon, 39, on 12 Apr 1915 in Ashtabula, Ohio. They parted before 1920.

In 1920 Chester is living with his brother Charlie.

Chester Parish born 2 Feb 1859 in Watertown, New York, died 22 Feb 1923 in Ashtabula, Ohio of influenza. He was divorced and the proprietor of a rooming house. The informant was Charlie Parish. Chester is buried in the potter's field section of Evergreen Cemetery, Painesville, Ohio.

## 4. Harriet "Hattie" Parish and Edward Whitely

The 1900 census for Painesville, Ohio has Ed Whitley, 38, born Feb 1862, married 17 years and renting a home on State Street. Hattie is 34, born Mar 1866 and has 7 children all living. The children are Jennie, 13, born Jul 1886; Mary, 11, born Sep 1888; Jackie, 10, born Jun 1889; Laura, 8, born May 1892; Eddy, 6, born Apr 1894; George, 3 born Mar 1897; and Mable, 8/12, born Sep 1899. Jackie, Laura and two babies died before 1910.

The 1910 census for Painesville, Ohio has Edward Whitley, 48, married 27 years, a laborer at odd jobs renting a home. Hattie is 43 and has had 11 children, 6 are living. Their children are Jennie, 24, a knitting mill worker; Edward, 16, a farm laborer; George, 13; Mabel, 11 and Chester, 8.

Edward "Ned" Whitely born 28 Apr 1862 in Ohio, died 10 Jul 1911 in Painesville, Ohio.

Harriet Parish Whitely born 5 Mar 1866, died 10 Nov 1915 and is buried with Edward. The place of burial is not known and there are no headstones.

## 5. Jennie Whitely and George L Moyer / James A Smith / Wilber L Clipp

Jennie Whitley, 25, married George L Moyer, 25, on 12 Sep 1911 in Lake County, Ohio.

George L Moyer died 20 Jan 1916 in Cuyahoga County, Ohio.

Jennie Whitely Moyer, 31, married James A Smith, 31, on 20 Oct 1917 in Lake County, Ohio.

The 1920 census for Painesville, Ohio has James Smith, 37, a conductor on a steam railway who owns his home at 323 St Clair Street free and clear. Jennie is 33 and her sons are Paul Moyer, 6 and George Moyer, 3 ½.

Jennie divorced James Smith before 1930.

The 1930 census for Painesville, Ohio has Jennie Moyer, 43, a sales lady at a department store renting a home on Prospect Street for $25 per month. Her sons are Paul, 16 and George L 13.

Jennie K Whitley Moyer married Wilbert L Clipp on 24 Oct 1931 in Buffalo, New York. Wilbert Leighton Clipp born 30 Sep 1878, died 23 Feb 1937 and is buried in Evergreen Cemetery, Painesville, Ohio. Jennie got the house.

The 1940 census for Painesville, Ohio has Jennie M Clipp, 54, widow, completed 6th grade, owns her home at 151 East High Street worth $6000. Paul Moyer, son is 26, graduated high school and an elect melter at Diamond Alkali. There are also 2 lodgers.

The 1940 census for Painesville, Ohio has George Moyer, 23, graduated high school, circulation agent for Plain Dealer Newspaper. Louise is 22 and graduated high school. Their son, Robert is 1.

## 5. Mary Mamie Whitely and Grover C Leigh

Mamie Whitley, 20, married Grover Leigh, 20 on 25 Jul 1907 in Lake County, Ohio.

The 1910 census for Willoughby, Ohio has Grover C Leigh, 26, a fireman on a locomotive. Mary M is 22. They are living with Grover's parents and sisters.

The 1920 census for Willoughby, Ohio has Grover C Leigh, 36, a butcher who owns his farm on Ridge Road. Mary M is 32. Their daughter Evelin M is 9.

The 1930 census for Willoughby, Ohio has Grover C Leigh, 45, married at 23, a cattle buyer who owns his farm on Ridge Road worth $10000. Mary is 41 and married at 19. Their daughter, Francis, is 9. Evelyn is away at college with no census record.

Mary M Whitely Leigh born 1 Sep 1887, died 30 Aug 1937 in East Cleveland, Ohio and is buried in Willoughby Village Cemetery, Willoughby, Ohio.

The 1940 census for Willoughby, Ohio has Grover C Leigh, 55, widowed, completed 7th grade, a painter who owns his home on Ridge Road now worth $2000. Frances is 19, graduated high school and a stenographer for a credit bureau.

The 1940 census for Cleveland, Ohio has Evelyn M Leigh, 29, completed 2 years college, a secretary for an automotive engineering firm and a lodger at the Knickerbocker Hotel on Euclid Ave.

Grover C Leigh died Nov 1958 in Willoughby and is buried with Mary.

## 5. Edward B Whitely and Margaret Carroll

The 1920 census for Painesville, Ohio has Edward Whitely, 25, working in railroad repair. Margaret is 24 and their son, John is 2. They are living with Margaret's parents and sisters.

The 1930 census for Painesville, Ohio has Edward Whitley, 36, married at 22, driving truck for a dairy and owns his home at 128 Carmody Drive worth $4500. Margaret is 34 and married at 20. The children are Mary E, 9; Margie A, 7 and Richard, 5. John, 12 is living with his mother's parents.

The 1940 census for Painesville, Ohio has Edward Whitely, 46, graduated high school, a nursery worker. Margaret is 44 and completed 10th grade. The children are John, 22, graduated high school, a nursery worker; Mary Ellen, 19, graduated high school; Margie Ann, 17, completed 11th grade; Richard, 15, completed 9th grade and Ronald, 8, completed 2nd grade. They are all living with Margaret's mother.

## 5. George A Whitely and Leona M Turner

George A Whitely, 21, a truck driver, married Leona M Turner, 22, a bookkeeper, on 13 Jul 1918 in Geneva, Ohio.

The 1930 census for Painesville, Ohio has George Whitely, 33, married at 21, a fireman for the fire department, renting a home at 315 Walnut Street for $35 per month and has a radio. Leona is 34 and married at 22. Their daughters are Evelyn, 10 and Jean 4.

The 1940 census for Painesville, Ohio has George Whitely, 43, completed 8th grade, a fireman for the city who owns his home at 315 Walnut Street worth $3000. Leona is 44, completed 8th grade and an elevator operator. Evelyn is 21, graduated high school and an elevator operator. Jean is 14 and completed 8th grade. Leona's sister is living with them.

## 5. Mable Whitely and Thomas M Lynch

Mabel Whitley married Thomas Morrison Lynch on 1 Aug 1918 in Lake County, Ohio.

The 1920 census for Painesville, Ohio has Thomas Lynch, 23, a switchman on the railroad renting a home at 114 Oswego Street. Mable is 20. Their son, James is 8/12. Mable's brother, Chester Whitely, 17 is a laborer on the railroad.

The 1930 census for Painesville, Ohio has Thomas M Lynch, 34, married at 18, a conductor on the steam railroad who owns his home at 28 Axtel Ave. worth $5000. Mabel is 30 and married at 16. Their children are James, 11; Thomas Jr, 7; Jack, 4 and Jane, 3.

The 1940 census for Painesville, Ohio has Thomas Lynch, 43, completed 8th grade, a brakeman on the Railroad who owns his home at 28 Axtel Ave. worth $3000. Mabel is 40 and completed 8th grade. Their children are James, 20, graduated high school, delivering for a grocery; Thomas, 17, graduated high school; Jane, 13, completed 8th grade; Donald, 8, completed 3rd grade; Sally, 5 and Dickey, 2. Jack may have died or may be staying with someone else.

## 6. Chester J Whitley and Laura Conley / Helen Cricket

Chester J Whitely, 19, married Laura B Conley, 20, on 31 Jan 1921 in Painesville, Ohio. Laura and Chester may have divorced

The 1930 census for Concord, Ohio has Chester Whitely, 25, married at 23, a laborer on the railroad and renting his home for $20 per month. Helen is 27 and was married at 25. Billy is 1 ½. Helen's brother and sister are living with them.

The 1940 census for Painesville, Ohio has Chester J Whitely, 38, completed 8th grade, a laborer on the railroad who owns his home on Madison Ave. worth $2000. Helen is 37 and completed 10th grade. Their children are William E, 11, completed 3rd grade; Ann M, 8 completed 2nd grade; Carol J, 7, completed 1st grade and Raymond E, 1. Helen's father is living with them.

## 4. Thomas Parish and Ruth E Green

Thomas Parish is with his parents in 1880. Lemuel, Thomas' father, died before 1900. Mary, Thomas' mother married Deforest parish in 1891. Thomas has not been found in the 1900 or 1910 census data.

Thomas Parish, 41, widowed, was living with his brother Charles in 1920 and working on the roads. There is not record of who he married or if there were any children.

Thomas Parish, 42, married Ruth E Green, 20, on 17 Nov 1921 in Ashtabula, Ohio.

The 1930 census for Ashtabula, Ohio has Thomas Parish, 57, married at 49, born in Canada, a basket maker who owns his home on Hamlin Drive worth $400. Ruth E is 39 and was married at 20. The children are Marian A, 12; Stanley P, 7; Richard R, 5; Grace F, 2 and Eilene I, new born. Ruth's brother, Donald Green, 17, is living with them. The age of Marian may not be right as she is not listed with her mother in 1920. Ruth is 18, single and living with her parents. It is also possible she was not listed because she was born out of wedlock and therefore hidden.

The 1940 census for Fairport, Ohio has Thomas Parish, 67, completed 8th grade, not working and renting a home at 192 Water Street for $15 per month. Ruth is 38 and graduated high school. The children are Stanley, 17, completed 10th grade; Richard, 15, completed 6th grade; Grace, 12, completed 5th grade; Eileen, 10, completed 3rd grade; Lloyd, 7, completed 1st grade; Marlene, 5 and William, 3.

The 1940 census for Columbus, Ohio has Marian Parish, 22, single, completed 7th grade, lived in Painesville in 1935 and currently a patient in the Institution for Feeble-Minded Youth at 1601 West Broad Street. This is a very large institution as there are 59 pages in the census records. Given Marian completed 7th grade she may have been institutionalized for other reasons including, epileptic, mental issues and making poor decisions. Sometimes girls were put in an institution and sterilized for being pregnant out of wedlock.

## 4. Wayne Parish and Myrtle Green

The 1880 census for Painesville, Ohio has Thomas, 10; Wayne, 6; Nathan, 4 and Lemuel, 1 living with their parents.

The 1910 census for Painesville, Ohio has Wayne Parish, 37, single, a hunter, living with Conant and Eva Brainard on Richmond Street. Eva is Wayne's sister Olive's daughter.

Wayne Parish, 48, was living with his brother Charles in 1920.

Wayne Parish, 52, married Myrtle Green, 18, about 1924. They had 2 daughters and were divorced before 1930.

Wayne, 58, married at 52, divorced, is living with his brother Charles in 1930. His daughter, Lucille, 6 is living with him. Wayne's other daughter Juanita, 5, is living with her mother who has remarried.

The 1940 census for Fairport, Ohio has Wayne Parish, 69, divorced, never attended school and living with George's son Walter and his wife Gladys. Wayne's daughters Lucille, 16, completed 6th grade and Juanita, 15, completed 8th grade are living with him.

Wayne Parish born 28 Aug 1871, died 25 Nov 1951 and is buried in Evergreen Cemetery, Painesville, Ohio.

## 4. Nathan Parish

Nathan Parish was born 23 Nov 1875 and died soon after the 1880 census. He is buried in Evergreen Cemetery, Painesville, Ohio.

## 4. Lemuel Parish and Mary Ellen Mack / Bessie Brainard

Lemuel Parish, 16, married Mary Ellen Mack, 16 on 11 Feb 1897 in Ashtabula, Ohio.

The 1900 census for Geneva, Ashtabula, Ohio has Lemuel Parish, 21, born Jun 1878, married 3 years, a fisherman who owns his mortgaged home. Mary E is 19, born Jul 1880 and had 2 children, one is living. Frankie R is 1 and was born Apr 1899.

Lemuel Parish, 28 divorced Mary Parish, 25, on 2 Jul 1905.

Lemuel Parish, 28 married Bessie Brainard on 26 Aug 1905 in Ashtabula Ohio.

Lemuel Parish born 29 Jun 1878, died 5 Mar 1910 in Geneva, Ohio.

## 5. Frank Ray Parish and Lydia M Cone

The 1910 census for Geneva, Ohio has Kate Mullen, 54, a grocery store proprietor who owns her home at 77 South Broadway Street free and clear. Frank R Parish, 11 is her grandson. Kate would be Frank's grandmother on his mother's side.

Frank Parish, 21, married Lydia Cone, 18, on 11 Oct 1915 in Westfield, New York. Frank would have actually been 16.

Frank Ray Parish register for WW1 on 12 Sep 1918. Frank was born 4 Apr 1899 and is working as a drayman (truck driver). His next of kin is Lydia Parish. They separated soon after.

Lydia M Cone Parish, 20, married William Kissman on 7 Mar 1919 in Ashtabula, Ohio.

The 1920 census for Pittsburg, Pennsylvania has Daniel Easton, 43, owner of a fish and poultry business renting a home at 807 Ohio Street. Mary (Mack Parish) is 40. Frank Parish, step-son, is 20, divorced and a store clerk at the fish and poultry business. Katherine Mullen is 65, mother-in-law, widowed and working as a housekeeper in a private home.

The 1920 census for Geneva, Ohio has William Kissman, 27, an auto mechanic, renting his home at 26 ½ West M Ave. Lydia (Cone) is 22. Raymond Parish, step-son is 2 9/12. Judith A Cone, mother-in-law is 61. Frank has a son Raymond. Lydia may have died soon after this census as William Kissman has another wife in 1930. It has not been possible to trace Raymond or his mother any farther.

Frank R Parish, 21, married Dorothy L Deering on 29 Jan 1921 in Ashtabula, Ohio. 1930 and 1940 census records were not found.

Frank Ray Parish, 63, died 18 Sep 1963 of a heart attack at B & W Tubular Products Plant in Koppel, Pennsylvania. His wife is Evelyn Logston Parish. Frank is buried in Union Cemetery, Steubenville, Ohio.

### 3. Deforest Parish and Adelia / Esther / Mary Jane Phillips Parish

Deforest Parish was with his parents in 1855. He married Adelia sometime before 1860.

The 1860 census for Brownville, New York has Deforest Parish, 26, a farmer. Adelia is 20 and Fred is 8/12.

The 1865 New York State Census has Deforest Parish, 31, first marriage, a farmer. Adelia is 25 and has had 3 children. Everett is 2. Fred and the other child must have died

Adelia and Everett may have died and Deforest married Esther.

The 1870 census for Watertown, New York has Deforest Parish, 38 and a laborer. Esther is 37 and keeping house.

The 1880 census for Painesville, Lake, Ohio has Deforest Parish, 41, a peddler of fish. Esther is 39. A nephew, Chester is 21, a peddler of fish and a niece, Ester is 23. All are born in New York.

Deforest Parish married Mary Jane Phillips Parish 17 Aug 1891 in Lake County, Ohio. Mary was the wife of Lemuel Parish. Lemuel and Mary were divorced about 1885.

The 1900 census for Painesville, Lake, Ohio has Deforest Parish, 63, born Aug 1836, married 8 years and working as a day laborer who owns his home free and clear. Mary J is 64, born Feb 1836 and has had 10 children, 8 are still living. The children are under Lemuel Parish.

The 1910 census for Painesville, Lake, Ohio has Deforest Parish, 72, married 25 years and a laborer on the streets. Mary is 72 and has had 10 children, 6 are still living.

There is no 1920 census or death information on Deforest. Mary is buried in Evergreen Cemetery, Painesville, Ohio. Lemuel is in the same cemetery.

## 4. Nathan Parish 3rd and Amelia / Dianthia Jewett

The 1860 census for Limerick, New York has Nathan Parish, 23, a farmer. Amelia is 18. Their son, Edwin is 1. They are the listing after Levi Carpenter and his family.

Nathan Parish, 24, registered for the Civil War on 1 Sep 1862 in Brownville, New York for 3 years. He was mustered in 11 Sep 1862 as a private in Company I Heavy Artillery. He deserted 11 Sep 1862. The explanation is "from Sackett's Harbor". He was a farmer, 5'10", with blue eyes and brown hair. His cousin Oliver died less than a year earlier in the Civil War.

Amelia died in 1865 and Edwin died in 1870. Nathan married Diantha in 1865.

The 1870 census for Albion, Oswego, New York has Nathan Parish, 29, a farm laborer. Diantha is 28 and the children are Frank, 5; Isabel, 4; George, 2 and Orin, 1.

The 1880 census for Elyria, Ohio has Nathan Parish, 41, a laborer. Diantha is 37. The children are Frank 18; Belle, 15; George, 12; Orrin, 10; Louise, 7; Sarah, 5; Martin, 4; Fred, 1.

The 1900 census for Painesville, Ohio has Nathan Parish, 57, born Feb 1842, married 35 Years, a ladder maker who owns his mortgaged home on 2nd Street. Diantha is 55, born Sept 1844 and has had 12 children 11 are living. The children are James, 17, born Sep 1882, a ladder maker; Nathan, 16, born Nov 1883, at school; Chester, 12, born Feb 1888, at school; Fred, 22, born Dec 1877, a ladder maker; and Orrin, 26, born Jun 1873, a ladder maker.

The 1910 census for Fairport, Ohio has Nathan Parish, 69, widowed, living on East Street in a home he owns. Chester is 21 and living with him.

Diantha Jewett Parish born 12 Jul 1844, died 26 Dec 1908. Nathan Parish born 12 Feb 1838 in Sackett's Harbor, New York, died 28 Dec 1917 of heart failure, in Fair Harbor, Ohio. He is buried in Evergreen Cemetery, Painesville, Ohio. Fred born 1877, died 1907.

Their son, Frank Parish born 1865, died 1 Oct 1881 in Vermillion, Ohio according to some ancestry trees. Nothing more could be found.

## 5. Isabel "Belle" Parish and Freeman Fifield

Belle Parish married Freeman Fifield on 16 Oct 1886 in Lake County, Ohio.

The 1900 census for Painesville, Ohio has Freeman Fifield, 33, born Aug 1866, married 13 years, a tug engineer who owns his home on 2nd Street free and clear. Belle is 33, born Nov 1866 and has had 2 children both living. The children are Estella (step-daughter), 15, born Jul 1885 and Bessie, 9, born Jul 1890.

The 1910 census for Painesville, Ohio has Freeman Fifield, 42, married 24 years, an engineer on a tug boat who owns his home on Plum Street. Belle is 43 and has had 2 children both living. Bessie is 19.

Belle Parish Fifield, 48, died 27 Mar 1914 in Fairport Harbor, Ohio. Freeman Fifield, 67, died 28 Mar 1934 in Fairport Harbor, Ohio.

## 6. Estella Florence Fifield and Edward R Stern

Estella F Fifield, 21, married Edward R Stern, 25, on 28 Sep 1909 in Chautauqua, New York. A 1910 census record was not found.

The 1920 census for Cleveland, Ohio has Edward Stern, 36, a coffee sales manager, renting a home on Kenmore Ave. Florence (Estella) is 30.

The 1930 census for Cleveland, Ohio has Edward Stern, 46, married at 22, a commercial traveler for plumbing renting a home on Crawford Road for $60 per month. Estella is 43.

The 1940 census for Cleveland, Ohio has Edward R Stern, 56, graduated high school, a salesman for a plumbing supply manufacturer and renting a home on East 107th Street for $110 per month. Estella is 51 and graduated high school.

## 6. Bessie Eugene Fifield and Andrew Manning / John "Jack" E Mog

Bessie Eugene Fifield, 20 married Andrew William Manning, 22, on 7 Sep 1910 in Chautauqua, New York. The marriage did not last long.

Bessie Fifield, 21, married John E Mog, 21, on 7 Dec 1911 in Lake County, Ohio.

When John E Mog registered for WW1 he had a wife and 3-year-old child. A 1920 census was not found. Ancestry trees have Faith Natalie (1912-1922)

The 1930 census for Painesville, Ohio has John E Mog, 38, a mechanical engineer for an alkali plant who owns his home at 400 Liberty Street worth $6500. Bessie is 35 and was married at 19. Their daughter, June P, is 5.

The 1940 census for Concord, Lake, Ohio has Jack E Mog, 45, graduated college, a mechanical engineer for heavy machinery who owns a home worth $6500. Bessie is 43 and graduated high school. June is 16 and completed 10th grade.

## 5. George Riley Parish and Claudous C Joiner

The 1900 census for Ashtabula, Ohio has George R Parish, 33, born Mar 1867, married 7 years, a fisherman renting his home. Claudie is 24, born Jul 1875 and has 3 children, all are living. The children are George W, 6, born Nov 1893; Loretta J, 4, born Sep 1895 and Gilbert, 2, born Sep 1897.

The 1910 census for Painesville, Ohio has George Parish, 43, married at 28, a horse trader who owns his home on 2nd Street. Claudous, 33, married at 18, has 3 children all are living. The children are George, 16; Loretta, 14 and Gilbert, 12.

The 1920 census for Painesville, Ohio has George Parish, 53, a wagon driver in a lumber mill. Claudous is 43.

The 1930 census for Fairport Harbor, Ohio has George Parish Sr., 63, married at 24, a laborer at a lumber company who owns his home at 614 2nd Street worth $3000. Claudous is 54 and married at 16. The grand children living with them are Raymond, 12 and Eileen, 10.

George Riley Parish born 12 Mar 1867 in New York died 16 Apr 1937 in Fairport Harbor, Ohio and is buried in Evergreen Cemetery. Claudous C Joiner Parish born 4 Jul 1875, died 30 Oct 1946 and is buried with George.

## 6. George W Parish and Elma H Hallen

George W Parish, 21 married Elma H Hallen, 21, on 29 Jun 1915 in Lake County, Ohio.

George William Parish, 23, born 10 Nov 1893 registered for WW1. He was married, living in Fairport Harbor and working at Diamond Alkali.

The 1920 census for Painesville, Ohio has George Parish Jr., 26, a boss in a mill who owns his home on 2nd Street. Elma is 25.

The 1930 census for Fairport Harbor, Ohio has George Parish Jr., 36, married at 21, a foreman at an alkali plant who owns his home at 314 East Street worth $3500 and a radio. Elma H is 35 and married at 20. They have 2 roomers living with them.

The 1940 census for Painesville, Ohio has George Parish, 46, completed 8th grade, a process operator at Diamond Chemical who owns his home on Main Street worth $4000. Elma is 45 and completed 8th grade. Their son, George, is 6.

Elma H Parish born 1894, died 1963 in Painesville, Ohio and is buried in Evergreen Cemetery. George W Parish, born 12 Nov 1893, died 15 Apr 1971 and is buried with Elma.

## 6 Loretta Parish and Alton J Dewey / Frank B Reid

The 1920 census for Cleveland Heights, Ohio has A J Dewey, 24, a superintendent in a rubber works renting a home. Loretta is 24. Their daughter, Lucile, is 2.

Loretta Parish Dewey, 27 married Frank B Reid, 27, on 27 Feb 1923 in Crawford, Ohio.

The 1930 census for Detroit, Michigan has Frank Reid, 39, married at 24, a manager in a steel plant renting a home at 5673 16$^{th}$ Street for $40 per month. Loretta is 34 and married at 19. Lucille Dewey is 11. Gilbert Parish, 32, widowed, a pattern maker for a casting company is living with them.

The 1940 census for Cleveland, Ohio has Loretta Reid, 44, graduated high school, a lodger who lived in Painesville in 1935 and a saleslady in a department store.

## 7. Lucille Dewey and Bauer / Ray A Hendershot

Lucile Dewey Bauer, 22, married Ray A Hendershot, 22, on 1 Jan 1940 in Cuyahoga County, Ohio.

The 1940 census for Cleveland, Ohio has Ray A Hendershot, 23, completed 3 years of college, a lab assistant in the enameling industry renting a home on East 78$^{th}$ Street. Lucille M is 22 and graduated high school.

## 6. Gilbert Parish and Cora E Barnes

Gilbert R Parish, 21, married Cora E Barnes, 21 on 4 Sep 1917 in Lake County, Ohio.

The 1920 census for Painesville, Ohio has Gilbert parish, 22, a laborer in the alkali mill renting a home on 2$^{nd}$ Street. Cora is 23. Their son, Raymond R is 1/12.

In the 1930 census Gilbert Parish, widowed, is living with his sister's family in Detroit. His children, Raymond and Eileen, are living with their grandparents. Cora did not die but divorced Gilbert. She died in 1941 with the same parents listed.

The 1940 census for Fairport, Ohio has Claudos Parish, 64, completed 4$^{th}$ grade and owns her home at 614 2$^{nd}$ Street. Gilbert Parish, son is 42, divorced, completed 8$^{th}$ grade, and a locomotive operator. Raymond, grandson is 21, completed 10$^{th}$ grade and a fireman at a lumber company. Eileen, granddaughter, 20, completed 10$^{th}$ grade and a clerk in a dime store.

## 4. Orrin Parish

Orrin Parish was living with his parents in 1900. He was farming with his brother Martin in North East, Pennsylvania in 1927 when he died.

Orrin Parish, 55, divorced, born Jun 1873, died 21 Oct 1927 of apoplexy and heart trouble. Orrin Parish is buried in Evergreen Cemetery, Painesville, Ohio. Nothing is known about his wife.

## 4. Louise Parish and Henry Leitze / Alfred Lewis Jr

The 1900 census for Glasgow College, Illinois has Henry Leitze, 38, born Apr 1862, married 9 years, a day laborer who owns his home free and clear. Lizzie is 28, born Nov 1871, has 2 children, both living. The children are George, 8, born Apr 1892 and Launa E, 4, born Apr 1896. Henry's mother, born in Germany, is living with them.

Louise Parish Leitze, 30 married Alfred Lewis Jr, 27, on 2 Nov 1903 in Lake County, Ohio.

The 1910 census for Chardon, Geauga, Ohio has Alfred Lewis, 33, married 7 years farming a rented farm. Louise is 36, married $2^{nd}$ time and had 3 children, 2 are living. The children are George Leitze, 17, labor on the farm and David Lewis, 3. Launa died before 1910.

The 1920 census for Fairport, Ohio has Alfred Lewis, 43, restaurant and pool (hall) keeper who owns his home on High Street free and clear. Louise is 46. Their children are David, 13 and Albert, 9. George Leitze, 27, son, labor in the restaurant and Mary, 19, daughter-in-law are living with Alfred. Two roomers are living with them as well.

The 1930 census for Fairport harbor, Ohio has Alfred Lewis, 55, married at 25, independent trucker who owns his home at 219 $2^{nd}$ Street worth $6500. Louise is 57 and married at 32. Albert Lewis, son is 19, married at 17, a sailor on the Lake. Albert's wife, Glady is 19 and married at 17. Their son, Donald N is 1 3/12. They are all living with Alfred and Louise.

The 1940 census for Painesville, Ohio has Alfred Lewis, 65, completed $5^{th}$ grade, a trucker renting a home at 256 Richmond Street for $25 per month. Louise is 67 and completed $6^{th}$ grade. Their grand daughter, Diane Lee Lewis, is 3 and living with them.

## 5. George Leitze and Mary / Katherine

George Leitze is living with his parents in 1910 and 1920. The 1930 census could not be found and there is no further record of Mary.

The 1940 census for Glasgow, Scott, Illinois has George Leitze, 48, completed $9^{th}$ grade, a farm laborer renting his home for $5 per month. Katherine is 45 and completed $8^{th}$ grade.

George Leitze, 50, born 27 Apr 1892, of Glasgow, Illinois registered for WW11 on 8 Apr 1946. His next of kin is Kate Leitze and he is working in Illinois for Eastern Panhandle Pipe Line Co. of Kansas City, Missouri.

## 5. David Lewis and Thelma Helen Herpy / Emma

David H Lewis, 21, married Thelma H Herpy on 2 Jul 1928 in Ashtabula, Ohio.

The 1930 census for Fairport Harbor, Ohio has David Lewis, 23, married at 21, an independent painter who is renting his home at 213 High Street for $20 per month. Helen is 20 and married at 18. Their daughter, Jeanette, is 1.

The 1940 census for Fairport, Ohio has David Lewis 32, completed 4$^{th}$ grade, a laborer for a coal dock company renting his home at 224 Seventh Street for $8 per month. Emma is 28 and completed 4$^{th}$ grade.

The 1940 census for Fairport, Ohio has Helen Lewis, 29, divorced, completed 11$^{th}$ grade, a waitress in a restaurant and renting part of a home for $15 per month. Her children are Jeanette, 10, completed 4$^{th}$ grade and David, 7, completed 2$^{nd}$ grade.

## 5. Albert N Lewis and Gladys Evans / Alma C Kerr / Dorothy

Albert Lewis married Gladys Evans on 30 Sep 1928 in Chautauqua, New York. Both were from Ashtabula, Ohio.

In 1930 Albert was living with his parents, a sailor on the lake and had a wife Glady and a son Donald N Lewis. There is no further information on Gladys or Donald.

Albert N Lewis married Alma C Kerr on 7 Aug 1932 in Chautauqua, New York.

The 1940 census for Painesville, Ohio has Albert Lewis, 28, completed 10$^{th}$ grade, a dredgeman (probably dredging the lake/river) and owns a home worth $2500. Dorothy is 25 and completed 3 years high school. Their daughter, Penelope, is 2.

## 4. Sarah Parish

Sarah Parish, 5, is with her parents in 1880. Nothing more could be found.

## 4. Martin Van Buren Parish and Sadie Wier

The 1900 census for Fairport, Ohio has Martin Parish, 23, born Aug 1876, married 4 years, a ladder maker who owns his mortgaged home on Second Street. Sadie is 23, born Sep 1876 and has 2 children, both are living. Their sons are Clarence, 3, born Aug 1896 and Lloyd, 2, born Sep 1897. Martin's parents are the next listing.

The 1910 census for Fairport, Ohio has Martin Parish, 34, married 15 years, a horse trader who owns his home on Second Street. Sadie is 34 and has 7 children, all living. The children are Clarence, 14; Lloyd, 12; James, 10; Sadie, 7; Martin, 5; Lillie, 2 and Jenetta, 2/12.

Jenetta Parish born 1910, died 1913 and is buried in Evergreen Cemetery, Fairport Harbor, New York.

The 1920 census for Fairport, Ohio has Martin Parish, 43, a hare dealer (rabbits) who owns his mortgaged home at 539 Second Street. Sadie is 42. Clarence is 23 and a brakeman on the railroad. Lloyd is 21 and a laborer on a vessel (boat). The other children are James, 19; Sadie, 16; Martin, 14; Lillian, 11 and Diantha, 7.

The 1930 census for Fairport Harbor, Ohio has Martin Parish, 53, married at 19, a real estate agent who owns his home at 541 Second Street worth $20,000 and a radio. Sadie is 53 and was married at 19. Sadie Barkinen is 27, divorced and a clerk in a drug store. Sadie's daughter Eva Joy is 5. Lloyd Parish is 32, single and an independent druggist. Lillian Maltbie is 22 and married at 22. Clarence Maltbie is 25, married at 25 and a draftsman at an alkali plant. Diantha is 18.

The 1940 census for Kinsman, Trumbull, Ohio has Martin Parish Sr. 63, completed 8th grade, a farmer on a farm he owns worth $4000. Sadie is 63 and completed 8th grade. Martin Parish Jr. is 34, completed 11th grade, a farmer, farming with his father. Norma is 32, completed 2 years college and Martin Jr's wife.

Martin V Parish born 18 Aug 1876, died 28 Jul 1942 and is buried in Evergreen Cemetery, Fairport Harbor, New York. Sadie Wier Parish born 1876, died 1952 and is buried with Martin.

## 5. Clarence Ray Parish and Lillian Marie Randasaw

Clarence Ray Parish, 21, born 17 Aug 1896 registered for WW1 on 5 Jun 1918. He is farming on his own and his father is next of kin. He did not serve.

Clarence Ray Parish, 25, married Lilian Marie Johnson Randasaw, 22 on 8 Dec 1921 in Lake County, Ohio.

The 1930 census for Greenfield, Erie, Pennsylvania has Clarence Parish, 34, married at 25, a horse dealer on a stock farm who owns his home on Station Road and a radio. Lily is 30 and married at 22. Donna, daughter is 14. I believe Donna is Lily's daughter by a previous marriage.

A 1940 census was not found. There is a Donna J Parish, 21, in an Iowa Institute for the Feeble Minded

Clarence R Parish born 17 Aug 1896, died 29 Oct 1988 and is buried with Lillie M Parish born 18 May 1899, died 2 Oct 1967, in Sherman Cemetery, Sherman, New York.

## 5. Lloyd W Parish and Bessie P Petrie

Lloyd William Parish, 20, a switchman on the B & O Railroad, registered for WW1 on 2 Sep 1918. He served from 11 to 19 Nov 1918.

Lloyd W Parish, 34, married Bessie P Petrie, 24, on 16 Jul 1932 in Ashtabula, Ohio.

The 1940 census for Findley, Ohio has Lloyd Parish, 41, graduated college, a pharmacist in a drug store renting his home at 633 Cherry Street for $30 per month. Bessie is 31 and graduated high school. Their daughter, Saundra is 2. Their maid, Naomi Check, is 18 and completed 10th grade.

Lloyd Parish born Sep 1897, died 8 Jul 1986 in Lima Memorial Hospital, Lima, Ohio.

## 5. James Nathan Parish and Sadie Gibson

James Nathan Parish, 18, born 12 Aug 1900, registered for WW1 on 12 Sep 1918. His next of kin was Martin Parish. According to the 1930 census he did serve.

James Parish, 19, is listed with his parents in 1920.

James N Parish, 22, of Painesville, Ohio, an electrician married Sadie Gibson, 22, of Painesville, Ohio on 25 Aug 1920 in Detroit, Michigan. Either they divorced or she died.

The 1930 census for Eagle, Hancock, Ohio has James Parish, 29, single, a farm laborer boarding with a farmer.

James Parish, 33, born 12 Aug 1900, died 28 Jun 1934.

## 5. Sadie Parish and Seth Donald Barkinen / Thomas G Dunn

Sadie Parish, 20 married Seth Donald Barkinan, 20, on 2 Jul 1923 in Lake County, Ohio.

In 1930 Sadie Barkinen, 27, is living with her parents, divorced, working as a clerk in a drug store and has a daughter, Eva Joy, 5. Evalyn J Barkinen was born 30 Apr 1924 in Lake County, Ohio.

Sadie Parish Barkinen, 28, married Thomas G Dunn, 27, on 26 Sep 1931 in The First Presbyterian Church, Monroe, Michigan.

A 1940 census was not found.

### 5. Martin "Buster" Parish and Norma Smith

Martin Parish and Norma Smith were married in 1939.

Martin and Norma are living with his parents in 1940.

Martin "Buster" Parish born 24 Aug 1905, died 11 Nov 1972 and is buried in Sherman Cemetery, Sherman, New York. Norma S Parish born 24 Dec 1908, died 9 Oct 1997 and is buried with Martin.

### 5. Lillie Parish and Clarence B Maltbie

Lillie and Clarence were married in 1929 or 1930. They are living with Lillian's parents in 1930.

The 1940 census for Andover, Ashtabula, Ohio has Clarence Maltbie, 33, graduated high school, a draftsman for a brass factory renting a home on East Main Street for $13 per month. Lillian is 31 and graduated high school. Their sons are Martin, 8, completed 2nd grade and William, 7, completed 1st grade.

### 5. Diantha Parish and Sam Sterling

Diantha Parish, 21, married Sam Sterling, 28, on 5 Jan 1933 in Detroit, Michigan.

The 1940 census for Cleveland, Ohio has Samuel Sterling, 35, completed 8th grade, a restaurant manager renting an apartment at 2015 East 90th Street for $55 per month. Diantha is 25, graduated high school and a cashier in the restaurant. Their daughter, Darlyne, is 6. They have a live-in maid.

### 4. Fred Parish

Fred Parish is with his parents in 1880 and 1900.

Fred Parish born Dec 1877, died 1907 and is buried in Evergreen Cemetery, Painesville, Ohio.

### 4. James Arthur Parish and Esther Elsie Miller

James A Parish, 25, married Esther E Miller, 17, on 28 Apr 1909 in Lake County, Ohio.

The 1910 census for Ashtabula, Ohio has James A Parish, 26, married less than a year, a laborer in a greenhouse renting his home on Benefit Street. Esther E is 18.

James Arthur Parish, 35, born 1 Sep 1883 registered for WW1 on 12 Sep 1918. He was a fish dealer, living at 24 Humphry, Ashtabula, Ohio and next of kin is Esther Elsie Parish.

The 1920 census for Ashtabula, Ohio has James Parish, 36, a huckster (salesman) for trucks who owns his mortgaged home at 24 Humphry Street. Esther is 28.

The 1930 census for Ashtabula, Ohio has James A Parish, 46, married at 25, a street huckster (door to door salesman?) who owns his home at 50 Jefferson Street worth $3000 and a radio. Esther E is 38 and married at 17.

The 1940 census for Geneva, Ashtabula, Ohio has James Parish, 56, completed 4th grade, a basket maker for the retail basket trade who owns his home on U S Route 20 worth $1500. Esther is 48 and completed 8th grade.

## 4. Nathan Parish 4th and Frances L Ganter

Nathan Parish, 20 married Frances L Ganter, 20, on 2 May 1908 in Lake County, Ohio.

The 1910 census for Fairport, Ohio has Nathan Parish, 23, married 2 years, a farm laborer who owns his home on 2nd Street. Frances is 21 and does not have children.

The 1920 census for Fairport, Ohio has Nathan Parish, 37, a laborer in a mill who owns his mortgaged home at 504 2nd Street. Frances is 35. Their daughter, Iris is 8.

The 1930 census for Fairport, Ohio has Nate Parish, 44, married at 24, an independent teamster who owns his home at 509 2nd Street worth $3500 and a radio. Frances is 42 and was married at 20. Iris is 18.

The 1940 census for Fairport has Nathan Parish, 55, completed 6th grade, an excavating contractor who owns his home at 509 2nd Street worth $2000. Francis is 52 and completed 6th grade. Their daughter, Iris Myers, is 28, graduated high school and a typist for the WPA. Robert Myers is 26 and graduated high school. Their children are Frances Jane, 4 and Robert N, 1.

Nathan Parish born 28 Nov 1884, died Jun 1968 and is buried in Riverside Cemetery, Painesville, Ohio. Frances L Parish born 1888, died 1969 and is buried with Nathan.

## 4. Chester Parish and Mary N Willberg

Chester Parish, 21, married Mary N Willberg, 18, on 5 Nov 1913 in Lake County, Ohio.

The 1930 census for Painesville, Ohio has Chester Parish, 42, married at 26, labor at a wrecking yard renting a home at 128 North State and has a radio. Mary is 34 and was married at 18. Their son, Ronald V is 14. Mary's brother and sister are living with them.

Mary and Ronald died 31 Dec 1938 and are probably buried in Evergreen Cemetery.

Chester Parish born Feb 1888, died 14 Jun 1961 and is buried in Evergreen Cemetery, Painesville, Ohio.

### 3. Margarette Parish

Nothing was found on Margarette Parish. She may have married and there is no record or she may have died before the 1850 census.

### 3. George R Parish and Eliza J Dorsey

The 1880 census for Adrian, Michigan has George R Parish, 37, a teamster. Eliza is 33. The children are Eliza G, 11 and George R, 5. His widowed father Nathan, 84, is living with them at 56 Henry Street.

The 1900 census for Adrian, Michigan has George R Parish, 54, born Jan 1846, married 32 years, a teamster who owns his mortgaged home at 45 Ormsby Street. Eliza is 52, born Aug 1848 and has 2 children, both are living. Their son, George R Jr is 25, born Mar 1875, married 1 year and living with his parents. George's wife is Minnie S, 26, born Jun 1874 and has 1 child who is living. Dorothy M is 1 and was born Dec 1898.

George R Parish born 28 Feb 1844, died 1 Dec 1904 and is buried in Oakwood Cemetery, Adrian, Michigan.

The 1910 census for Adrian, Michigan has Eliza Parish, 61, widow, has 2 children, both are living, a laundress in the home she owns free and clear at 45 Ormsby Street.

The 1920 census for Adrian, Michigan has Eliza Parish, 71 living in the home she owns free and clear at 617 Ormsby Street. George R Parish is 44, single and a laborer at the screen door factory.

Eliza J Dorsey Parish born 1 Aug 1848, died 20 Feb 1927 of a cerebral hemorrhage causing paralysis. The informant is her daughter, Eliza Hieber. Eliza is buried with George Parish in Oakwood Cemetery.

### 4. Eliza G Parish and John F Heiber Jr

Eliza Parish, 31, dressmaker, married John F Heiber, 32, laborer, on 7 Feb 1900 in Adrian, Michigan.

The 1900 census for Adrian, Michigan has John Heiber, 32, born Apr 1868, a day laborer renting his home at 53 Conrad Street. Eliza is 31 and born Jun 1869.

The 1910 census for Adrian, Michigan has John F Heiber, 43, married 10 years, a foreman in a screen door factory who owns his mortgaged home at 59 Chestnut Street. Eliza is 41 and has had 1 child who is living. Their son is Donald G, 9.

The 1920 census for Adrian, Michigan has John F Heiber, 52, a superintendent at the screen door factory who owns his mortgaged home at 613 Chestnut Street. Eliza G is 50. Donald G is 19 and a machinist at the screen door factory.

John F Heiber born 28 Mar 1867 in Germany, died 31 Dec 1926 in Adrian, Michigan of stomach cancer and is buried in Oakwood Cemetery.

The 1930 census for Adrian, Michigan has Eliza Hieber, 60, a widow who owns her home at 614 East Maumee Street worth $4000 and a radio. Donald is 29, married at 26 and an auto repair mechanic. Donald's wife, Virginia is 21, married at 18 and a bookkeeper at an electric, light and power company. They have a lodger.

The 1940 census for Adrian, Michigan has Donald G Heiber, 39, completed 8$^{th}$ grade, a maintenance man at an aluminum manufacturer who owns his home at 424 Comstock worth $3000. Virginia A is 31, graduated high school and a stenographer at a leather factory. Eliza G is 71, a widow and completed 8$^{th}$ grade.

## 4. George R Parish Jr and Minnie Stelzer

George R Parish Jr, 24, married Minnie Stelzer, 24, on 9 Feb 1899 in Adrian, Michigan.

George and Minnie had a daughter, Dorothy, Dec 1899. They were living with his parents in 1900. George and Minnie had another child in 1903 who died at 1 month.

The 1910 census for George R Parish Jr could not be found. It is uncertain what happened to Minnie and Dorothy. They are not buried in Oakwood Cemetery with George and the baby. A divorce or census records could not be found. George is listed as widowed by 1931.

George Riley Parish, 43, born 21 Mar 1875, a teamster, registered for WW1 on 8 Sep 1918. He was living with his mother at 617 Ormsby Street, Adrian, Michigan.

The 1920 census for Adrian, Michigan has Elisa J Parish, 71, a widow who owns her home at 617 Ormsby Street free and clear. George R Parish is 44, single and a laborer at the screen door factory.

George R Parish Jr, 56, widowed, born 21 Mar 1875, died 12 Aug 1931 of stomach cancer. The informant was Eliza Heiber. George is buried in Oakwood Cemetery, Adrian, Michigan.

## 3. Mary Etta Parish and Brown

Mary Etta Parish is living with her parents in New York in 1865.

Mary Etta Parish Brown, born 1844 died 22 May 1915 in Pittsford, Hillsdale, Michigan of dropsy of the heart and old age. Her parents are Nathan Parish and Polly Carpenter. Mrs. Elmer Letherer was the informant. She is buried in Leonardson Cemetery, Pittsford, Michigan.

This is the only verifiable information about Mary Etta Parish. It was thought she may have married Clement Brown but that turns out to be Mary Etta Mason Brown.

Mrs. Elmer Letherer is Mary Etta Brown Letherer. She may be Mary Etta Parish's daughter but the connection could not be made. The Marriage record for Elmer Letherer and Mary Etta Brown lists her parents as unknown.

The life of Mary Etta Parish is a mystery.

## 2.7. Rebecca Carpenter

Rebecca Carpenter was born in 1805 to Phillip Carpenter and Mary Rhodes. She died before 1844.

## 2.8. Daniel Carpenter and Elmina P Shepard / Mary

The 1850 census for Alexandria, Jefferson, New York has Daniel Carpenter, 45, a carpenter. Elmina is 35. Their children are William Wallace, 14, Olive, 10 and Delina 6.

The 1855 State of New York census for Alexandria, Jefferson, New York has Daniel Carpenter, 44, born in Washington County, a farmer who owns his farm with a frame house (many are log). Elmina is 36 and was born in Jefferson county as were all the children. The children are Wallace, 18; Olive, 15 and Delina, 12. They have lived in the same place 8 years.

The 1860 census for Brownville, Jefferson, New York has Daniel Carpenter, 52, a farmer. Elmina is 42. Their children are Wallace, 23, Olive 20 and Delina, 18.

In 1865 Wallace is married and living with his parents. The girls have left home and nothing more is known about them. Elmina P Shepard Carpenter born 1819, died 1867.

The 1880 census for Brownville, Jefferson, New York has Daniel Carpenter, 72, a farmer. His wife, Mary, is 37.

Daniel Carpenter born 20 Sep 1807, died 6 Sep 1893 and is buried in Stone Cemetery, Jefferson, New York.

## 3. William Wallace Carpenter and Florence M Bowman

Wallace Carpenter was eligible for the Civil War in 4 Jul 1863. Wallace was 26, born in New York, married, a sailor and now sailing. There is no evidence he served.

The 1865 New York State census for Brownville, Jefferson has Daniel Carpenter, 55, a farmer who owns his farm with a frame house. Elmina is 45 and had 3 children. William W is 28, a farmer and his wife, Florence is 19.

The 1870 census for Brownville, Jefferson, New York has Wm W Carpenter, 33, a farmer. Florence is 24. Living with them is Minnie Seacf, 4. Minnie may be the daughter of one of Wallace's sisters.

The 1880 census for Champion, Jefferson, New York has Wm W Carpenter, 43, a farmer. Florence M is 34. Minnie is 13 and their adopted daughter.

William Wallace Carpenter born 11 Apr 1837, died 13 Oct 1885 and is buried in Union Cemetery, Adams Center, Jefferson County, New York. Florence M Bowman Carpenter born 22 Jan 1846, died 30 Mar 1928 and is buried with William.

## 4. Minnie Seacf Carpenter and William H Hall

Minnie Carpenter and William Hall were married in 1892.

The 1900 census for Watertown, New York has William Hall, 32, born Dec 1867, married 8 years, a machinist who owns his mortgaged home at 12 Grant Street. Minnie is 31, born Oct 1868 and has one child, still living. Their son is Carl, 4, born Jun 1895.

The 1910 census for Adams, Jefferson, New York has William H Hall, 40, married 20 years, a truck farmer who owns his mortgaged farm. Minnie C is 42 and has had 1 child. Carl H is 14. Florence Carpenter is 64 and a widow with her own income.

The 1920 census for Adams, Jefferson, New York has William Hall, 52, a dairy farmer who owns his mortgaged farm. Minnie is 53. Their son Carl is 25 and labor on the farm. Florence Carpenter is 73, a widow, and mother-in-law. Florence died in 1928.

The 1930 census for Adams, Jefferson, New York has William Hall, 61, married at 22, a dairy farmer who owns his farm on Church Street and a radio. Minnie is 61 and was married at 22. Carl is 33, married at 25 and working on the dairy farm. Carl's wife is Pauline, 33 and married at 25. Their daughter is Shirley, 5.

The 1940 census for Adams, Jefferson, New York has William H Hall, 72, completed 8th grade, a farmer who owns his farm worth $6000. Minnie is 72, and completed 8th grade. Carl is 44, completed 8th grade and a farmer. Pauline is 41 and graduated high school. Shirley E is 15 and completed 8th grade.

William H Hall born 13 Dec 1867, died 24 Dec 1949 and is buried in Union Cemetery, Adams Center, New York. Minnie Seacf Carpenter Hall born 23 Oct 1866, died 20 Apr 1950 and is buried with William.

### 2.9. Orson Carpenter and Nancy Jane Duffin / Maria Phillips / Mary M Smith

Orson Carpenter and his descendants are in Chapter 11.

### 2.10. Cynthia Carpenter and Jonathan Elmer

Cynthia Carpenter and Jonathan Elmer were married about 1826 or 1827. Jonathan was a carpenter and worked in ship building at Sacketts Harbor later they moved to Pillar Point and Jonathan started farming.

The 1850 census for Brownville, Jefferson, New York has Jonathan Carpenter, 46, a laborer. Cynthia is 38. Their children are Silas, 23; Minerva, 22; William M, 18, a laborer; Melissa, 16, Washington, 13; Wellington, 13; Roxana, 10; Adelaide, 6; Arvilla, 4 and Elvira, 2. Nothing more could be found on Minerva.

Ruth Elmer was born in 1853 and died in 1856.

Wellington H Elmer born 1837, died 28 Apr 1859 and is buried in Dexter Cemetery, Dexter, New York. The stone is inscribed "Children of Jonathan and Cynthia".

The 1860 census for Brownville, Jefferson, New York has Jonathan Elmer, 58, a farmer with $1000 in real estate. Cynthia is 51. Their children are Silas, 32, a farmer with $900 in real estate; Washington, 23, a farmer; Roxana, 20, a seamstress; Adelaide, 17; Arvilla, 14; Elvira, 12 and Edward, 10.

Jonathan Elmer, 62, born 20 Jun 1803 in Vermont, enlisted 29 Dec 1863 in the New York 10th artillery, company K as a private. He was mustered out 5 Jan 1864 having been discharged for disability on 13 May 1864. Jonathan was in heavy artillery and spent his time guarding Washington DC. Jonathon's son Washington Rufus Elmer also served in the Civil War.

The 1870 census for Brownville, Jefferson, New York has Jonathan Elmer, 67, a farmer with $2340 in real estate. Cynthia is 61 and keeping house. The children are Elvira, 22, assisting keeping house; Edward. 19, a farmer and Alice, 15.

Edward D Elmer born 1850, died 25 Dec 1875 and is buried in Dexter Cemetery, Dexter, New York. The stone is inscribed "Children of Jonathan & Cynthia.

The 1880 census for Brownville, Jefferson, New York has John Elmer, 76, a farmer. Cynthia is 66 and keeping house.

Jonathan Elmer born 20 Jun 1803, died 2 Jan 1885 and is buried in Dexter Cemetery, Dexter, Jefferson, New York. Cynthia Carpenter Elmer born 1811, died 2 Mar 1887 and is buried with Jonathan.

### 3. Silas Elmer and Hannah

The 1870 census for Oswego, New York has Silas Elmer, 42, a carpenter with $600 in real estate. Hannah is 39 and keeping house. Their children are Harriet, 9, at home and William, 6 attended school.

The 1880 census for Oswego, New York has Silas Elmer, 53, a carpenter with a home at 164 West 5th Street. Hannah is 51 and keeping house. Their children are William, 14, at home and Freddie, 8. George Petri, 21, a clerk in a store and Harriet, 20 are living with her parents. Harriet has a daughter, Lulu, 2/12.

"Fredrick Elmer died at Oswego Hospital as a result of a fall from a second story window at his home. He was injured about the head, it was thought, but the physicians now believe that his spine was hurt as he lay as if paralyzed all day yesterday. He was taken to the hospital shortly before 6 o'clock and was then rapidly sinking. Elmer was born in this city on 7 Mar 1871 and was consequently 28 years of age. He was educated in the public schools. He is survived by his parents, a sister, Mrs. George Petrie and a brother William." 26 Jul 1899, Oswego Daily Times

Fred Elmer born 7 Mar 1871, died 25 Jul 1899 and is buried in Rural Cemetery, Oswego, New York.

The 1900 census for Oswego, New York has Silas Elmer, 71, born Oct 1828, married 52 years, a day laborer who is renting his home at 933 West 4th Street. Hannah is 70, born May 1830, and had 3 children, 2 are living. William is 34, born Jun 1865, single and a painter.

Silas Elmer born Oct 1828, died 6 Jul 1905 and is buried in Rural Cemetery, Oswego, New York. Hannah Elmer born May 1830, died 18 Aug 1919 and is buried with Silas.

### 4. Harriet "Hattie" Elmer and George Petrie

Harriet and George Petrie are living with Harriet's parents and have a daughter Lula, 2/12 in 1880. They are still living with her parents in 1892 and have two daughters, Lulu, 12 and Maude, 6.

The 1910 census for Oswego, New York has George Petrie, 51, married 30 years, a stone mason renting his home at 22 Mohawk Street. Hattie is 48 and Maud is 23.

The 1920 census for Oswego, New York has George Petrie, 58, a stone mason renting his home at 66 West Bridge Street. Hattie is 56. Maude is 27 and single.

The 1930 census for Oswego, New York has George E Petrie, 67, married at 18, an independent mason who owns his home at 39 East 5th Street worth $3000 and a radio. Hattie is 66 and was married at 18. Maude is 39 and single.

Harriet "Hattie" Elmer Petrie born 1860, died 8 Apr 1934 and is buried in Rural Cemetery, Oswego, New York.

The 1940 census for Oswego, New York has George Petrie, 81, completed 8th grade and renting a home at 132 ½ West 8th Street. Maude is 52, single and completed 8th grade.

George Petrie born 1859, died 1956 and is buried in Rural Cemetery, Oswego, New York. Maud Petrie born 1885, died 17 Sep 1970

## 5. Lulu May Petrie and Kirke Henry White

The 1905 New York State census has Kirke H White, 23, a foreman in a woolen mill living at 198 West 5th Street. Lulu M is 24. Their son Kirke is 3/12.

The 1910 census for Oswego, New York has Kirke H White, 29, married 8 years, working in underwear manufacturing, renting a home at 30 East Utica Street. Lulu M is 30 and has had 1 child who is living. Their son, Kirke, is 5.

The 1920 census for Oswego, New York has Kirke H White, 38, working in manufacturing and owns a home at 49 East Mohawk free and clear. Lulu M is 39. Their children are Kirke M, 14; Virginia L, 8 and Neil S, 2.

The 1930 census for Oswego, New York has Kirke H White, 49, married at 21, treasurer at Lastlong Underwear Company who owns his home at 129 East 7th Street worth $9000 and a radio. Lulu M is 50 and was married at 22. Their children are Kirke M, 25; Virginia L, 18 and Neil S 12. They also have a servant and her daughter.

The 1940 census for Oswego, New York has Kirke H White, 59, completed 8th grade, a partner at Lastlong Underwear company who owns his home at 133 East 7th Street worth $10,000. Lulu is 60 and completed 9th grade. Kirke M is 35, single, completed 5+ years of college and a private lawyer. Neil is 22 and completed 3 years college at Harvard. They also have a maid.

Kirke H White born 5 Mar 1881, died Mar 1969 and is buried at Riverside Cemetery, Oswego, New York. Lulu M born 1880, died 1976 and is buried with Kirke. Kirke M White born 1905, died 1985 and is buried with his parents.

Virginia White born 8 Sep 1911, attended Radcliffe college and Felix Fox School of Pianoforte. She performed with the Boston Symphony Orchestra. She married Stedman

D Tuthill, an attorney on 27 Aug 1935. They lived in Camden, New York where he was an attorney and she gave private piano lessons and performed classical piano. Virginia died 31 Jul 2014 and is buried in Forest Lawn Cemetery, Camden, New York. She was 102.

## 4. William Elmer

The 1910 census for Oswego, New York has Hannah Elmer, 64, widow, married 50 years and had 3 children, 2 are living. Her son, William, is 46, single and a painter. They are renting a home at 227 3rd Street. Hannah died in 1919.

The 1930 census for Oswego, New York has William Elmer, 65, single, a building painter, rooming in a home on 1st Street.

The 1940 census for Oswego, New York has William Elmer, 76, completed 7th grade, on pension and lodging at 34 West 2nd Street.

William Elmer born Jun 1865, died 25 Jan 1951 and is buried in Rural Cemetery, Oswego, New York.

## 3. William M Elmer and Mariette A Scott

William M Elmer married Mariette A Scott about 1860.

William Elmer, 31, a farmer, married, registered for the Civil War in June 1863.

The 1870 census for Brownville, Jefferson, New York has William Elmer, 38, a farmer with $2120 in real estate. Mary A, 27 is keeping house. The children are William, 7 and Freddie, 3.

Frank N Elmer born 1871, died 1876 and is buried in Dexter Cemetery with his parents.

The 1880 census for Watertown, New York has Wm M Elmer, 48, a huxter (salesman). Mary A is 37. Their sons are Wm H H, 17 and Fred M, 13.

The 1900 census for Watertown, New York has William Elmer, 68, born Feb 1832, married 40 years, a fruit merchant who is renting his home at 9 Jackman Street. Mariette is 57, born Mar 1843 and has 2 children both living. Their grandson, Frankie M, 12, born Feb 1888 and niece, Maud Soridan, 24, born May 1876, a milliner are living with William and Mariette.

The 1910 census for Watertown, New York has William Elmer, 78, married 50 years, a confectionary maker renting a home at 147 Jackman Street. Mary is 67, and had 3 children, 2 are living. William H, son, is 47, divorced, a retail merchant of pictures and furniture. Frank M, grandson, is 22, married 2 years and working with his father. Lillian,

Frank M's wife, is 22, has not had children and a clerk in a store.

William M Elmer born Feb 1832, died 1911 and is buried in Dexter Cemetery, Dexter, New York. Mariette A Scott Elmer born 1843, died 20 Dec 1919.

### 4. William Henry Harrison Elmer and Hattie M Lonsdale / Martha "Mattie" Poole Hurd

William Henry Harrison Elmer married Hattie M Lonsdale in 1887. Their son Frank M was born Feb 1888. Hattie M Lonsdale Elmer born 1869, died 1888 and is buried in Dexter Cemetery. It is not known if she died in child birth.

William H H Elmer married Martha "Mattie" Poole Hurd in 1889.

The 1900 census for Watertown, New York has William H H Elmer, 36, born Jan 1864, married 9 years, a fruit merchant renting his home at 11 Jackman Street. Mattie is 30 and has had 3 children, all living. Their children are Mildred, 9, born Aug 1890; Lincoln, 8, born Jun 1891 and Marietta, 1, born Aug 1898. They have a roomer living with them. Frank M is living with his grandparents.

Marietta Elmer, born Aug 1898, died before 1910.

William H H and Mattie were divorced between 1900 and 1910. Mattie may have had custody of her 2 remaining children.

In 1910 William H H, his son Frank M and Frank's wife are living with William's parents.

The 1920 census for Watertown, New York has William H Elmer, 56, proprietor of a grocery store and renting a home at 171 Jackman Street.

William Henry Harrison Elmer born Jan 1864, died 5 Sep 1927 and is buried in Dexter Cemetery, Dexter, New York with his first wife, Hattie.

### 4. Frank Monroe Elmer and Lillian Edith Hobbs / Ruth E Dorothy

Frank Monroe Elmer, 21, married Lillian Edith Hobbs, 22, on 30 Jun 1909. They are living with Frank's father and grandparents in 1910.

Frank Monroe Elmer, 29, born 13 Feb 1888 in Pillar Point, New York, registered for WW1 on 5 Jun 1917. He is married, a merchant and living at 315 Flower Ave. His store is at 150 Arsenal Street. Frank, a private, was inducted 20 Jul 1918 into 153 Depot Brigade until 30 Oct 1918 and then 48 Service Company Signal Corps until discharge. Frank was discharged 6 Dec 1918. He did not serve overseas

The 1920 census for Watertown, New York has Frank M Elmer, 31, an independent music teacher who owns his mortgaged home at 315 Flower Ave. Lillian E is 32, immigrated from Canada in 1892 and a merchant of music and books.

The 1930 census for Watertown, New York has Frank M Elmer, 42, married at 22, a merchant with a store who owns his home at 314 Flower Ave. East worth $8000 and a radio. Lillian is 43 and was married at 23.

The 1940 census for Watertown, New York has Lillian Elmer, 54, divorced, graduated high school, born in Canada, working in a laundry and living with her sister.

Frank M Elmer married Ruth E Dorothy on 12 Oct 1936 in Nassau, New York

A 1940 census was not found for Frank and Ruth.

Frank M Elmer born 13 Feb 1888, died 9 Oct 1960 and is buried in Milton Cemetery, Milton, Massachusetts. Application for a head stone was by Ruth D Elmer of Ithaca, New York on 19 Oct 1960. A flat bronze marker was approved and ordered on 25 Nov 1960.

Lillian Hobbs Elmer, born 1887, died 11 Jun 1973 and is buried in North Watertown Cemetery, Watertown, New York.

## 4. Mildred I Elmer and Fredrick A Isley

The 1910 census for Syracuse, New York has Mattie Elmer (William H H Elmer's 2$^{nd}$ wife), 39, widowed, married 17 years, had 3 children, 2 are living, a nurse renting her home at 113 ½ Palmer Ave. Mildred is 20, single and a bookkeeper.

Mildred I Elmer married Fredrick A Isley on 26 Jun 1916 in Syracuse, New York.

The 1920 census for Syracuse, New York has Fredrick A Isley, 34, a construction contractor who owns his mortgaged home at 334 Palmer Ave. Mildred I is 29. Their son, Fredrick E is 2.

The 1930 census for Syracuse, New York has Fredrick A Isley, 44, married at 31, a carpenter who owns his home on Delray Ave. worth $11,000 and a radio. Mildred I is 39 and married at 26. Their children are Fredrick E, 12 and Dorothy A, 8. Mildred's mother, Martha N Hurd, 59 is living with them.

Fredrick E Isley, 20, born 11 Aug 1918, enlisted 15 Jan 1938 in Headquarters Troop of the 121$^{st}$ Calvary, New York National Guard. He was separated 26 Mar 1940.

The 1940 census for Syracuse, New York has Fred A Isley, 54, completed 8$^{th}$ grade, a carpenter and painter with his own business who rents his home at 226 Rich Street. Mildred I is 49, completed 3 years high school and is a receptionist at a doctor's office.

Dorothy A is 19, graduated high school and a clerk in a drug store. They also have a lodger.

The 1940 census for Washington, DC has Fred E Isley, 22, single, graduated high school, a clerk-typist for the civil service commission and a lodger at 805 G Street SW.

Fredrick Arthur Isley born 2 Jun 1885, died 4 Nov 1955 and is buried in Woodlawn Cemetery, Syracuse, New York. Mildred Elmer Laming (she remarried) born Aug 1890, died 23 Jun 1960 and is buried with Fredrick.

## 4. Lincoln Grant Elmer and Anna G Witt.

Lincoln G Elmer married Anna Martha Witt on 23 Feb 1918 in Kings County, New York.

The 1920 census for Brooklyn, New York has Lincoln Elmer, 27, a machinery inspector renting part of a house at 481 49th Street. Anna is 26 and their son, Ralph is 2/12.

The 1930 census for Gouverneur, New York has Lincoln G Elmer, 37, married at 25, a photographer with his own business renting a home at 47 Babcock Street for $12 per month and has a radio. Anna is 36 and was married at 23. Their sons are Ralph F, 10; Richard M, 8 and Robert L, 1/12.

The 1940 census for Hailesboro, New York (near Gouverneur) has Lincoln Elmer, 47, completed 8th grade, a photographer who owns his home worth $700. Ann is 45 and completed 8th grade. Their sons are Ralph, 20, graduated high school; Richard, 18, graduated high school and Robert, 10, completed 4th grade.

Lincoln Grant Elmer born 1 Jun 1891, died 1 Apr 1979 in Lynchburg City, Virginia.

## 4. Fred M Elmer and Minnie Shaffert

Fred M Elmer married Minnie M Schaffert on 17 Jun 1891 in Watertown, New York.

The 1900 census for Watertown, New York has Fred Elmer, 33, born Dec 1866, married 9 years, a merchant renting a home at 1 Court Street, New Fair Banks Block. Minnie M is 28, born Jul 1870 and has not had children. They have a lodger.

The 1910 census for Watertown, New York has Fred M Elmer, 43, married 18 years, a retail merchant at a confectionary. Minnie M is 39 and has not had children. They are living with Minnie's mother at 231 Coffeen Street.

Fred M Elmer born Dec 1866, died 26 Jan 1919 and is buried in Dexter Cemetery, Dexter, New York. Minnie S Elmer born Jul 1870, died 13 Oct 1921 and is buried in Sanford Corners Cemetery, Calcium, New York as Minnie Shaffert wife of Fred M Elmer.

## 3. Melissa Elmer and Charles N Osborn

The State of New York census for 1855 has C N Osborn, 44, born in Thompkins County, a merchant. Melissa is 21 and was born in Jefferson County. Elnora A is 2 and was born in Oswego County. A clerk is living with them.

The 1860 census for Oswego, New York has Charles N Osborn, 49, a grocer with $3000 in real estate. Melissa is 25. Their son Charles A is 2/12. They have a domestic to help with housework. Elnora must have died between 1855 and 1860.

The 1870 census for Oswego, New York has Charles N Osborn, 60, a retired grocer with $8000 in real estate. Melissa is 34. Their son, Charles A, is 10.

An 1880 census was not found. An Oswego City directory for 1882 has Charles N Osborn, grocer at 69-71 E Cayuga, home 49 East 5th Street. Charles A Osborn is a clerk and boards at 49 E 5th Street.

It appears both Charles and Melissa died before 1900. They are not recorded in the Riverside Cemetery.

## 4. Charles A Osborn and Ada Hill

Charles A Osborn and Ada Hill were married about 1886.

The 1900 census for Oswego, New York has Charles A Osborn, 40, born Apr 1860, married 14 years, a grocer who owns his home at 69 Cayuga. Ada is 38, born Sep 1861 and has not had children. Chares owns his father's store.

The 1910 census for Oswego, New York has Charles A Osborn, 50, married 23 years, a retail grocer living at 69 Cayuga Street. Ada M is 48, has not had children and is a clerk in the grocery store.

Charles A Osborn born Apr 1860, died 1914 and is buried in Riverside Cemetery, Oswego, New York. Ada Hill Osborn Sweetland born 28 Sep 1861, died 22 Aug 1946 and is buried with Charles. Her second husband, Fred E Sweetland is in the same plot.

## 3. Washington Rufus Elmer and Helen V Burlingame 1837-1925

Washington Rufus Elmer, 29, born 27 Jan 1837 in Pillar Point, enlisted 29 Aug 1862 in the New York 10th artillery, company I. He was mustered in 12 Sep 1862. He had duty in Washington DC until May 1864 then joined the Army of the Potomac. He would have been at Cold Harbor, before Petersburg and at the siege of Petersburg. After a mine explosion on 30 Jul 1864 the unit was sent back to Washington DC. They were then moved to the Shenandoah Valley 27 Sep and the Battle of Cedar Creek on 19 Oct.

They remained in Shenandoah Valley until Dec when they went back to Washington DC. They were involved in the Appomattox Campaign 28 Mar to 9 Apr including the assault and fall of Petersburg 2 Apr. The unit was mustered out at Petersburg, Virginia 23 Jun 1865. Washington was discharged 7 Jul 1865.

Washington Elmer married Helen Burlingame on 12 Aug 1869 in Cuyahoga, Ohio.

The 1880 census for Rockport, Ohio has Washington Elmer, 40, a laborer. Hellen is 34 and their son, Lewis is 15.

Washington Elmer filed for a disability pension 28 Apr 1887. He served in 10th New York Heavy Artillery. Helen V Elmer filed for a widow's pension 30 Oct 1925

The 1900 census for Rocky River, Ohio has Washington R Elmer, 63 born Jan 1837, married 31 years, retired and owns his home free and clear. Helen is 54, born Feb 1846 and has 1 child still living. Lewis H is 31, born Sep 1869 and single.

The 1910 census for Rocky River, Ohio has Washington Elmer, 73, married 41 years, retired with own income. Helen V is 64. Lewis is 41 and single.

Lewis H Elmer born 5 Sep 1869, died 28 Mar 1918 of bronchial pneumonia with a contributory factor of Epilepsy and is buried in Lakeside Cemetery, Bay Village, Ohio.

The 1920 census for Rocky River, Ohio has Washington Elmer, 82, retired and owns his home at 19217 Lake Road. Helen V is 79.

Washington Rufus Elmer, born 27 Jan 1837, died 16 Oct 1925 of bronchial pneumonia and is buried in Lakeside Cemetery, Bay Village, Ohio.

Helen V Burlingame Elmer born 26 Feb 1846, died 18 Aug 1930 and is buried in Lakeside Cemetery, Bay Village, Ohio with Washington and Lewis.

### 3. Roxanna Elmer and Benjamin T Glassford

Benjamin T Glassford enlisted in the Civil War 17 Dec 1863 in Oswego, New York as a private. He served in the New York 9th heavy artillery, company L and was mustered out 14 Jun 1865 at Yorktown, Virginia. He was born in Canada.

Roxanna Elmer married Benjamin T Glassford in 1865. They went to Canada and returned 1879. An 1880 census was not found.

The 1892 New York State census for Oswego, New York has Benjamin T Glassford, 52, a carpenter. Roxanna Glassford is 50. Ada L Glassford is 30 and may be Benjamin's sister. She was born before Roxanna and Benjamin married.

Another part of the same 1892 census has Frank Glassford, 18, a carpenter and Fred Glassford, 13. It is unknown why the boys are listed separately.

The 1900 census for Oswego, New York has Benjamin Glassford, 61, born Aug 1838 in Canada, immigrated 1858, married 35 years, a carpenter who owns his home at 104 8th Street. Roxanna is 59, born May 1841 and had 5 children, 3 are living. Their son Fred F is 21, born Apr 1879 and a carpenter. They have a lodger.

Roxanna Elmer Glassford born May 1841, died 26 Feb 1903 and is buried in Riverside Cemetery, Oswego, New York.

Benjamin T Glassford is living with Fred in 1910.

Benjamin T Glassford born Aug 1837, died 1917 and is buried with Roxanna.

## 4. Frank Jule Glassford and Emma A Foley

Frank Glassford married Emma Foley 14 Feb 1894 in Oswego, New York.

The 1900 census for Rotterdam, Schenectady, New York has Frank Glassford, 26, born Jun 1873, married 6 years, a carpenter boarding with another family. Emma is 25, born Jul 1875, and has 2 children both are living. The children are Lola, 4, born Feb 1896 and Harold, 3 born Mar 1897.

The 1910 census for Schenectady, New York has Frank J Glassford, 39, married 16 years, a house carpenter. Emma is 36 and had 3 children, 2 are living. Their children are Lola, 14 and Harold, 13.

The 1920 census for Schenectady, New York has Frank J Glassford, 46, a contracting carpenter who is renting his home at 28 Odell Street. Emma is 45, and Venita is 5.

The 1925 census for Schenectady, New York has Frank Glassford, 52, a contractor. Emma is 51. Their daughter, Venita is 11. Frank's brother, Fred, is 47 and a carpenter.

Something must have happened to Emma between 1925 and 1930 as Frank and Venita are living with Lola.

Frank Glassford born Jun 1873, died 2 Dec 1959 and is buried in Vale Cemetery, Schenectady, New York.

## 5. Lola V Glassford and Raymond Miehl

Lola Glassford married Raymond Miehl on 3 Nov 1913 in Schenectady, New York.

The 1920 census for Schenectady, New York has Raymond Miehl, 23, a machinist in the electrical works renting part of a house at 20 Howard Street. Lola is 23. Their daughter, Lillian is 3. Raymond's father, Jacob, is 76 and not working. Raymond's brother, Earnest is 38 and a machinist at the electrical works.

The 1930 census for Schenectady, New York has Raymond Miehl, 34, married at 17, a building carpenter who owns his home worth $6000 at 1442 Hawthorne Street. Lola is 34 and married at 17. Their daughter Lilian is 14. Raymond's father, Jacob Miehl, is 89, was married at 17 and a laborer on the barge canal. Lola's father, Frank Glassford is 62, married at 20 and a building architect. Frank's daughter Venita is 15.

The 1940 census for Schenectady, New York has Raymond Miehl, 43, completed 8$^{th}$ grade, a builder who is renting his home at 408 McClellan Street. Lola is 43 and completed 8$^{th}$ grade.

## 6. Lillian Ruth Miehl and Oscar Held

Lillian R Miehl married Oscar Held on 7 Feb 1937 in Schenectady, New York.

The 1940 census for Schenectady, New York has Oscar Held, 25, graduated high school, an oil truck driver renting a home for $25 per month at 2406 Campbell Ave. Lillian is 23 and graduated high school. Their son Raymond is 1.

## 5. Harold Frank Glassford and Albina Fronek / Rose Keenan

Harold Frank Glassford, 21, born 24 Mar 1897 registered for WW1 on 5 Jun 1918. He was living at 128 Egbert Road, Bedford, Ohio and working for McMyler Interstate Company, Bedford, Ohio. His nearest relative is Frank J Glassford.

Harold F Glassford married Albina Fronek on 1 Jul 1918 in Cleveland, Ohio.

The 1920 census for Cleveland, Ohio has Harold Glassford, 23, a machinist in a shop. Albina is 23. Their daughter Leona is 6/12. They are living with Albina's parents.

The 1930 census for Cleveland, Ohio has Harold Glassford, 33, married at 21, a machinist in manufacturing who owns his home at 12818 Dove Ave. worth $5800 and a radio. Albina is 34 and was married at 22. Their daughters are Leona, 10 and Marie, 5.

Albina Fronek Glassford, born 1896, died 20 Mar 1931 and is buried in Calvary Cemetery, Cleveland, Ohio with her parents. Harold Jr was born and died in 1931. Albina probably died in childbirth.

The 1940 census for Cleveland, Ohio has Harold Glassford, 43, completed 8$^{th}$ grade, a machinist in a tool factory who owns his home at 3590 Sykora Ave. worth $3000. Rose is 39 and completed 8$^{th}$ grade. Marie is 15 and completed 9$^{th}$ grade. 3 of Rose's children are living with them.

## 6. Leona Glassford and Vernon C Wheeler

Leona Glassford, 20, married Vernon C Wheeler, 27, on 24 Jul 1939 in Cleveland, Ohio.

The 1940 census for Cleveland, Ohio has Vernon Wheeler, 27, graduated high school, a driver and salesman for a bakery. Leona is 20, completed 10th grade and a waitress in a restaurant.

## 5. Venita Glassford

Venita, 15, is living with her father, Frank Glassford and sister, Lola Miehl, in 1930.

A 1931 Schenectady directory has Glassford & Miehl Contractors working out of their home at 1442 Hawthorne. Venita is a student. A 1940 census has not been found. A 1947 Albany, New York city directory with Venita Glassford, waitress at New Steak House. Her residence is 11 Hall Place.

## 4. Fredrick Foster "Fred" Glassford and Mary Ann Moore

Fred Glassford married Mary Ann Moore on 15 Jun 1904 in St. Joseph Catholic Church.

The 1910 census for Oswego, New York has Fred F Glassford, 31, born in Canada, immigrated 1879 married 5 years, a carpenter in the railroad shops who owns his mortgaged home. Mary A is 30, has 3 children, all living and was born in New York. Their children are Roxie, 5; Lawrence, 3 and Richard, 1 6/12. Benjamin T Glassford, 72, widowed is living with them.

The 1920 census for Oswego, Oswego, New York has Fred F Glassford, 39, immigrated from Canada in 1883, a carpenter in the rail road shop with a farm on Plank Road. Mary A is 38. Their children are Marion R, 14; Lawrence F, 13; Richard J, 12; Edwin F, 10; Harriet M, 7; Mary A, 5 and Hazel R, 2.

This picture of Fred and Mary was probably taken in the 1920's.

The 1930 census for Oswego, Oswego, New York has Fred Glassford, 50, married at 24, a house carpenter who owns his home worth $2500 on Fruit Valley Road and a radio. Mary is 50. Their children are Lawrence, 23, owner dry cleaners; Richard, 21; Edwin, 19, a pattern maker at an iron works; Harriett, 17; Mary, 16 and Hazel, 12.

The 1940 census for Oswego, Oswego, New York has Fred Glassford, 60, completed 8th grade, a carpenter who owns his home worth $5000 on Highway 104. Mary is 60 and completed 8th grade. Hazel is 21, graduated high school and a saleslady. Harriet is 28, graduated high school and a school teacher.

Fredrick Foster Glassford born 14 May 1879 in Durham, Ontario, Canada, died 30 Mar 1941 of a heart attack and is buried in Riverside Cemetery, Oswego, New York. Mary Ann Moore Glassford born 24 Aug 1880, died 1 Jan 1963 of a stroke and is buried with Fred.

## 5. Marion Roxanne "Roxie" Glassford and George Corke

Marion R Glassford, 29, born 22 Mar 1905, left New York on 20 Jul 1934 for British and French West Indies, Virgin Islands, and British Guiana. She arrived back in New York 13 Aug 1934. She was living on Franklin Ave, Oswego, New York.

Marion R Glassford met George Corke in Bermuda and they were married on 28 Jun 1935 in Oceanside, New York. George was an officer on a British ship and eventually a captain. Marion graduated from Oswego Normal School with a certificate in special education. She taught in several school in New York State.

The 1940 census for Hempstead, Nassau, New York has George Corke, 38, completed 2 years college, a section manager at a department store renting a home at 12 Rockwell Place for $55 per month. Marion is 35 and completed 3 years college. Their daughter, Anita is 3.

This is a picture of Marion and George Corke.

## 5. Lawrence F Glassford and Leona Frances Wall

Lawrence F Glassford married Leona F Wall on 17 Sep 1938 in Oswego, New York.

The 1940 census for Oswego, Oswego, New York has Lawrence Glassford, 32, completed 11th grade and a painter who owns his home worth $6000 on Highway 104. Frances is 32 and completed 10th grade. Frances' mother, Leona Wellbourne, 56, lives with them.

## 5. Joseph Richard Glassford and Ann Humphreys

Joseph Richard Glassford graduated from high school in 1926. He graduated from Union College, Schenectady, New York when the depression hit. He went to Albany,

New York to get a master's in education but there were were no jobs. A 1940 census was not found but he must have been a student at the time. He went to South Carolina where he worked in a store and married Ann Humphreys.

## 5. Edwin F Glassford and Elizabeth M Robarge

Edwin F Glassford married Elizabeth M Robarge Donaldson on 13 Feb 1937.

The 1940 census for Oswego, Oswego, New York has Edwin Glassford, 29, completed 11th grade, a pattern maker in a machine shop renting a home on State Road for $10 per month. Elizabeth is 26 and completed 10th grade. Their children are Allan, 7, completed 1st grade (Elizabeth's son by a previous marriage) and Marilyn, 8/12.

## 5. Mary Agatha Glassford and Herbert Finch

The 1940 census for Oswego, Oswego, New York has Herbert Finch, 25, completed 8th grade, a laborer in construction renting his home on Highway 104 for $10 per month. Mary is 26 and graduated high school. Their son, Robert is 3.

## 3. Adeline / Adalaide "Addie" Elmer and Henry A Read

The 1870 census for Brownville, New York has Henry A Read, 32, farmer and sailor. Adeline is 26 and keeping house.

The 1880 census for Croghan, Lewis, New York has Henry Read, 41, a sailor. Adeline is 35. Their daughter, Minnie, is 7.

The 1900 census for Brownville, Jefferson, New York has Henry A Read, 61, born Sep 1838, married 34 years, a farmer who owns his farm free and clear. Adaline is 54, born Dec 1845 and has 1 child, still living.

Henry A Read born 1838, died 1906 and is buried in Dexter Cemetery, Dexter, New York.

Adeline Read is living with her daughter in 1910

The 1920 census has Adalaide Read, 73, widow, renting a home on Kirby Street. Hazael Ackerman, grandson, 20, is living with her.

Adaline Read born 1845, died 5 Dec 1925 in Dexter, New York.

## 4. Minnie C Reed and James W Ackerman

The 1900 census for Brownville, Jefferson, New York has James Ackerman, 31, born Jul 1868, married 7 years, a farmer renting his farm. Minnie is 26, born Jul 1873 and has 1 child, still living. Hazael R is 7/12, born Oct 1899.

The 1910 census for Brownville, Jefferson, New York has James W Ackerman, 42, married 16 years, a farmer renting his farm. Minnie C is 37 and has 1 child, still living. Their son, Hazael R, is 10. Addie Read, Minnie's mother, is 64, a widow and has 1 child, still living.

Hazael Read Ackerman, 18, born 28 Oct 1899, a student, registered for WW1 on 12 Sep 1918. His next of kin is Minnie Ackerman and they are living in Dexter, Jefferson, New York.

Minnie C Read Ackerman born Jul 1873, died 1918 and is buried in Dexter Cemetery, Dexter, New York.

Hazael R Ackerman married Maude A Burdick on 24 Dec 1921 in Syracuse, New York.

Hazael Ackerman born 1899, died 1924 and is buried in Dexter Cemetery, Dexter, New York. Cause of death is unknown.

### 3. Arvilla Elmer and Azariah Ackerman / William Philips

Arvilla Elmer married Azariah Ackerman about 1867. Azariah had been previously married to Louisa and had two sons, Charles and Franklin and was living with them in 1865. Arvilla and Azariah moved to Minnesota between 1868 and 1872.

The Minnesota State Census of 1 May 1875 for Waseca County, Minnesota has A P Ackerman, 49. Arvilla is 27. Their children are James, 7 and Minnie, 3. All are born in New York except for Minnie.

Azariah Ackerman died 12 Jul 1875 and is buried in Janesville Cemetery, Janesville, Minnesota. Arvilla returned to New York with her children and married William Philips.

The 1880 census for Dexter, New York has William Philips, 49, a grocer and dry goods merchant at 190 Factory Street. Arvilla is 29. The children are James, 12; Minnie, 9; Willis, 4 and Fanny, 1. Nothing more could be found on William, Arvilla, Willis or Fanny Philips.

### 4. James W Ackerman and Minnie C Read / Luella P Stone

The 1900 census for Dexter, New York has James Ackerman married to Minnie C Read. They were first cousins. Minnie died in 1918. See above.

The 1920 census for Brownville, Jefferson, New York has James Ackerman, 51, widowed, a farmer. Living with him are John Philips, 72, brother-in-law and Minnie Philips, 48, sister.

In 1930 James W Ackerman is living with his sister Minnie.

James W Ackerman, 63 married Luella P Stone, 65 on 2 Sep 1931 in Dexter New York.

The 1940 census for Brownville, Jefferson, New York has James Ackerman, 72, completed 8th grade, a farmer who owns his home at Route 1 Dexter, New York worth $600. Luella is 78, and completed 8th grade.

James W Ackerman born Jul 1868, died 7 Mar 1941 in Watertown, New York.

## 4. Minnie Ackerman and John Philips / William H Dopking

Minnie Ackerman married John Philips in 1889.

The 1900 census for Brownville, Jefferson, New York has John Philips, 55, born Feb 1845, married 11 years, a farm laborer renting his home. Minnie R is 28, born Feb 1872 and has 1 child, still living. Their daughter, Flora A, is 10, born Jan 1890.

The 1910 census for Brownville, Jefferson, New York has John Philips, 64, married 21 years, a fisherman on the lake who owns his home on Shore Road free and clear. Minnie R is 38 and has one child, still living. Flora A is 20 and single.

Flora A Philips born Jan 1890, died 8 Jul 1916

In 1920 John and Minnie are living with her brother James Ackerman.

John Philips born 1845, died 1921.

Minnie Ackerman, 50, married William H Dopking, 62, on 5 Dec 1923 in Jefferson County, New York.

The 1930 census for Brownville, Jefferson, New York has William H Dopking, 68, first married at 20, a laborer in a papermill. Minnie is 58 and first married at 18. James W Ackerman, 62, brother-in-law, widowed, first married at 25 and farming is living with them.

The 1940 census for Brownville, Jefferson, New York has Minnie Hopking, 68, widow, completed 4th grade, a farmer who owns her home worth $300 at Route 1, Dexter, New York.

Minnie Ackerman Philips Dopking born 16 Feb 1872, died 9 Oct 1951 and is buried in Dexter Cemetery, Dexter, New York.

## 3. Elvira Elmer and Alexander Johnston

Elvira Elmer married Alexander L Johnston about 1872.

The 1880 census for Martinsburg, New York has Alexander Johnston, 45, born in Ireland, a farmer. Elvira is 31. Their children are Minnie, 7; Mannoah, 5 and Goldie, 1.

The 1900 census for Buffalo, New York has Alexander Johnston, 65, born Feb 1835, married 28 years, immigrated 1849, a watchman who is renting his home at 314 Niagara Street. Elvira is 50, born Jul 1848 and had 4 children, 2 are living. Their children are; Goldie E, 19, born Aug 1880 and Everett E, 18 born May 1882, wood carver apprentice. Edward Johnston (Alexander's son by a previous marriage), 32, born Jan 1868, a laborer on the dock. Minnie and Mannoah died before 1900.

The 1910 census for Buffalo, New York has Alexander Johnston, 74, married 38 years, 2$^{nd}$ marriage, retired, renting a home at 359 Prospect Ave. Elvira is 62, has had 4 children, 3 are living (counting Edward, Alexander's son). Edward is 48, single, a real estate and insurance salesman. Goldie E is 29, single and a school teacher. They have 6 boarders.

Alexander L Johnston born 13 Feb 1835 in Ireland, died 22 Mar 1913 and is buried in Martinsburg Cemetery, Martinsburg, New York.

The 1920 census for Buffalo, New York has Elvira Johnston, 70, widow, owns her mortgaged home at 119 West Ave. Goldie is 38 and single. Edward is 60, single, step-son and a real estate agent. Everett W E is 37, single and running a laundry business. They have a boarder. Nothing more was found on Edward Johnston.

Elvira Elmer Johnston born 1848, died 3 Oct 1924 in Buffalo, New York.

### 4. Goldie Johnston

The 1930 census for Buffalo, New York has Goldie Johnston, 49, single, working at a business exchange and renting a home at 1261 Michigan Ave. for $35 per month.

The 1940 census for Buffalo, New York has Goldie Johnston, 59, graduated high school, not working and renting apartment 89 at 140 Verplanck. She has a male lodger.

### 4. Everett E Johnston and Ella

The 1930 census for Buffalo, New York has Everett E Johnson, 47, married at 43, a contractor for homes renting part of a home at 1262 Jefferson Ave. for $30 per month. Ella is 32 and was married at 29.

The 1940 census for Buffalo, New York has Everett Johnston, 57, completed 11$^{th}$ grade, a butler renting a home at 445 Franklin for $22 per month. Ella is 41, completed 8$^{th}$

grade and a cook.

## 3. Alice Elmer and George Loyd

The 1875 New York State census for Brownville, Jefferson, New York has George Loyd, 22, born in Canada, a farmer with a frame house worth $400. Alice is 20. Their son Charles is 6/12. The last name is sometimes spelled Lloyd, a more common spelling, but is more often Loyd.

The 1880 census for Cape Vincent, New York has George Loyd, 32, a track hand. Emily is 28. Their children are Lewis, 8; Damas, 6 and Charles, 5. Alice must have died and George remarried. George's second wife, Emily, had 2 children by a previous marriage. Nothing more could be found on George Loyd. He may have moved back to Canada.

## 4. Charles Wellington Loyd and Lillie M Starker / Louise

The 1900 census for Cleveland, Ohio has Charles Loyd, 24, born Dec 1874, widowed, a stationary engineer. He is living with his wife's parents John & May Hill.

Charles W Loyd, 25 married Lillie M Starker, 21, on 13 Nov 1901 in Coshocton, Ohio.

The 1910 census for Oxford, Coshocton, Ohio has Charles Loyd, 34, born 4 Dec 1874, married twice, married 9 years, a consulting engineer renting his home. Lilly M is 30, married once, has 1 child, still living. Their son, Rollin, is 6. They have a trained nurse living with them.

Lillie M Starker Loyd born 5 Aug 1880, died 27 Jul 1910 and is buried in East State Street Cemetery, Newcomerstown, Ohio. Rollin went to live with Lillie's sister.

Charles Wellington Loyd, 43, born 4 Dec 1874, registered for WW1 on 12 Sep 1918. He is a foreman at the Elyria Machine Company, his wife is Louise and he did not serve.

The 1920 census for Elyria, Ohio has Charles Loyd, 47, a tool maker in a machine shop renting a home at 341 12th Street. Louise is 29. Their daughter Ann is 2/12.

The 1930 census for Elyria, Ohio has Charles Loyd, 53, married at 23, a power foreman in a steel plant who owns his home at 1219 Lake Ave. worth $6500 and a radio. Louise is 37 and married at 22. Their daughters are Ann, 10 and Nancy, 2.

The 1940 census for Elyria, Ohio has Charles Loyd, 63, completed 10th grade, a foreman at US Steel Mill who owns his home at 1219 Lake Ave. worth $5000. Louise is 49 and graduated high school. Their daughters are Ann, 20, graduated high school, an inspector at Northern Ball Manufacturing and Nancy, 12, completed 6th grade.

Charles W Loyd born 4 Dec 1874, died 24 Jun 1942 and is buried in Ridgelawn

Cemetery, Elyria, Ohio.

### 5. Rollin Morrison Loyd

The 1920 census for Layfayette, Coshocton, Ohio has Rolland M Loyd, 16, living with his aunt Miranda Starker Aronhalt, uncle and cousins on a farm. He was attending Coshocton High School.

The 1930 census for Columbus, Ohio has Rollin M Loyd, 24, single, a salesman in a drug store lodging at 169 East Gay Street with many other people.

The 1931 Columbus City Directory has Rollin M Loyd apprentice at Walgreen Company, living at Crittenden Hotel.

A 1940 census was not found.

Ronald Morrison Loyd born 25 Nov 1903, died Jul 1970 in Chicago, Illinois.

### 2.11. Permelia Carpenter

Several Ancestry trees have Permelia Carpenter married to Amos Yeomans Shepard. I checked 6 census records. In all cases Amos and Permelia are born in Massachusetts. Permelia Carpenter was born in New York. I do not believe the Permelia that married Amos Shepard is the correct Permelia. Nothing could be found on Permelia Carpenter born 1814.

# Chapter 11

## Orson Carpenter

1. Orson (Orison, Orris) Carpenter (1811-1899) * (another source b. 1809)
+ Nancy Jane Duffin (1815-1848) (m.1830)
    2. Elizabeth E Carpenter (1834-1917)
   + Samuel Resseguie (1830-1905)
       3. Frank Samuel Resseguie (1858-1934)
      + Ella McMullen (1864-1920)
          4. Jessie E Resseguie (1883-1914)
         + Herbert A Hatfield (1879-)
             5. Beulah Hatfield (1907-1927)
             5. Lillian Ruth Hatfield (1911-)
              + Virgil L Nicklin (1909-)
             5. Esther M Hatfield (1914-1974)
              + Albert Lentz (1914-)
          4. Samuel J Resseguie (1885-1931)
         + Lucinda B Husen (1891-)
             5. Valda Resseguie (1918-1975)
              + Howard Gallant (1913-)
          4. Orson Resseguie (1887-1954) WW1
         + Nila Drucilla Kipp (1893-)
             5. Jay N Resseguie (1912-1994)
              + Mary Miner (1920-)
             5. Baby Boy Resseguie (1913-1913)
             5. Paul Kenneth Resseguie (1914-)
              + Marjorie Louise Wilson (1914-)
                 6. Roseanne Resseguie (1938-)
             5. Ella Resseguie (1918-1918)
          4. Daniel Robert Resseguie (1888-1946)
         + Nellie Henry (1888-)
         + Tressie Hunt (1894-)
             5. William Clyde Resseguie (1922-2005) WW11

             5. Dorothy Resseguie (1925-)
             5. Olive Resseguie (1926-)
             5. Ruth Resseguie (1928-)
             5. Donna Resseguie (1929-)
             5. Tessie Resseguie (1931-)
             5. Barbra Resseguie (1933-)
             5. Francis Resseguie (1934-)
   + Mary McMillon Salisbury (1857-1930)
    2. Hiram A Carpenter (1836-1841)
    2. William H Carpenter (1836-1900) Civil War

+Alice Eveline Wilcox (1839-1901)
    3. George H Carpenter (1857-1919)
   + Clara E. Bailey (1857-1902)
        4. Bertha E Carpenter (1882-)
       + Dennis Jackson (1887-)
        4. Linnie Eveline Carpenter (1890-1981)
       + Thomas Barnes (1884-)
       + Arthur James Jackson (1888-1955)
        4. Carl Bailey Carpenter (1898-1974)
       + Aileen Kelley (1903-1973)
           5. Thomas L Carpenter (1937-)
           5. Clark Lanny Carpenter (1939-)
   + Ida Slocum (1860-)
    3. Edgar Leone Carpenter (1860-1924)
   + Jessie E Tabor (1860-1935)
        4. Grace M Carpenter (1883-1960)
        4. Pearl M Carpenter (1885-1969)
        4. Ross O Carpenter (1890-1947)
       + Letha Leoma Kane (1897-1985)
           5. Ardis V Carpenter (1918-2000)
          + Emmett Moyer (1912-1981)
           5. Bernice I Carpenter (1919-1999)
          + Leroy G Harden (1916-1999)
              6. James A Harden (1938-)
           5. Edwill Carpenter (1922-2011)
          + Velma Harden (1923-)
           5. Geraldine Carpenter (1926-2002)
          + Donald Rowlson (1922-2006)
           5. Pauline Carpenter (1930-)
        4. Alma B Carpenter (1892-)
       + Frank Albert Gemmell (1891-1953) WW1
           5. E Jean Gemmell (1923-)
           5. L Richard Gemmell (1926-)
           5. Frank A Gemmell (1928-)
        4. Shirley Leone Carpenter (1896-1945)
       + Mary S Rowley (1902-)
           5. Bernita Carpenter (1922-)
           5. Marjorie Carpenter (1924-)
           5. Melburn K Carpenter (1927-)
           5. Willis Carpenter (1934-1945)
           5. Daniel Carpenter (1937-)
        4. Ralph T Carpenter (1897-1918) WW1
    3. Fred O Carpenter (1870-1940)
   + Ella Silvernail (1870-1943)
        4. Lucile C Carpenter (1905-)

+ Harold McDonald (1904-)
                5. Barbara Jean McDonald (1925-)
        4. William S Carpenter (1907-1936)
        + Laurene Cyphers (1915-)
                5. Dane Lu Carpenter (1935-1935)
        4. Facelia E Carpenter (1909-1981)
        + Russell L Bailey (1909-)
                5. Ronald Bailey (1934-)
                5. Janet Bailey (1938-)
        4. Virginia Carpenter (1911-)
        + Lacerne Mecorney (1906-)
        4. Evelyn L Carpenter (1914-)
        + Carlton Franklin Ohlerich (1914-)
        4. Robert D Carpenter (1918-)
        + Katherine Kelley (1919-)
                5. Janice Carpenter (1938-)
                5. Jacqueline Carpenter (1939-)
2. Sarah Jane Carpenter (1841-1905) *
+ George W. Bailey (1830-1890)
    3. Elba George Bailey (1860-1925)
    + Clara Greenfield (1867-) *
        4. George Washington Bailey (1895-1959) *
        + Mary Rose Berridge (1893-)
                5. Marjorie L Bailey (1923-)
        4. Marion Bailey (1906-1909)
    3. Ethie May Bailey (1866-1918)
    + Orestus Cheney (1863-1929)
        4. Caroline Mae Cheney (1888-1971)
        + Charles E Badgley (1880-1964)
                5. Russell A Badgley (1908-)
                5. Marcella W Badgley (1909-2000)
                + Fred Hagaman (1905-1985)
                        6. Dois Hagaman (1929-)
                5. Rachel Badgley (1911-)
    + Henry Henning (1858-1909)
    + Earnest H Root (1870-)
2. Mary Ett (Mariette) Carpenter (1846-1928) *
+ Michael E. Dillon (1846-1932)
    3. Fred J. Dillon (1874-1936)
    + Phoebe Parker (1889-1971)
        4. Parker Dillon (1914-1985) WW11
        + Beulah Kuhn (1912-2004)
        4. Clare Fremont Dillon (1920-) WW11
    3. Nina R. Dillon (1884-1916) *
    + Harry Sweezey (1880-)

                4. Michael E "Dillon" Sweezey (1913-2002)
                + Carla Belle Jewell (1914-)
                    5. Beverly Ann Sweezey (1936-)
                    5. Stephen J Sweezey (1937-)
                    5. Jewel K Sweezey (1938-)
+ Maria Phillips (1831-1857) (m. 1848)
    **2. Ellen Louise Carpenter (1856-1924) ***
    **+ Fred C. Stanley (1864-1939)**
        3. Mabel Stanley (1884-1945) *
        3. Orson Stanley (1885-1919) *
        3. Blanche Stanley (1887-1956) *
        3. Charlie Stanley (1889-1889)
        3. Mae Louise Stanley (1892-1945) *
+ Mary M Smith (1822-1889)

The * indicates they are pictured in the Orson Carpenter Family Photo taken between 1896 and 1899.


**1. Orson Carpenter and Nancy Jane Diffin / Maria Phillips / Mary Smith**

Orson Carpenter was born in Granville, Washington County, New York 25 Aug 1811. The same person is also called Orris and Orison. Orson is listed in the dictionary as a Germanic name meaning bear like. Orris refers to a root and Orison to a prayer. It is not known which version is his original name, although, he seems to have used Orson most of the time.

Orson Carpenter married Nancy Jane Duffin in 1830. They were probably married in Brownville, the town, or Pillar Point.

Their first daughter, Elizabeth, was born about 1835.

Hiram Carpenter died young. His stone reads: Hiram A son of Orison and Jane Carpenter died March 26, 1841 aged 5 years 1 month and 19 days.[16] He is buried in Stone Cemetery, Pillar Point, New York. Hiram would have been born 7 Feb 1836.

William H Carpenter was also born in 1836 according to most records. Some family trees have him born 25 Aug 1836 while others have 4 Sep 1836. It is not known how either date was obtained. William may have been Hiram's twin or he was born late in the year. There are no official records with a birth date.

Orson and Jane Carpenter owned 10 acres of land some time before 1837. On 7 Jan 1837, they sold half of the ten acres, 5 acres, to Julius C. McKee for $44. They sold the other half of the 10 acres to Medad Cook for $44. This land was bordered by land owned by Symon VanPatten and Nathaniel B Osborn. The description of the land says it is bounded by land owned by various parties and stakes in the ground. This makes it difficult to locate later with limited early maps of the area.

Orson and Jane then bought 25 acres of land 13 Jan 1837 from Simon VanPatten for $100. This land was located in 44W 23 and 24N range of Brownville Township. It appears the land was located along the east side of an old road, no longer there, between Middle Road and South Shore Road just west of Sherwin Creek. It also appears the land was adjacent to the original 10 acres sold just before this land was purchased. Deeds were written for the land and did not mention any buildings on the land. It would appear the 10 acres was more valuable because it included buildings. This area appears to have had several houses fairly close together on the oldest map available.[18]

Sarah Jane Carpenter was born 10 Apr 1840. Mary Ett (Mariette) Carpenter was born 6 May 1844. Her name was spelled several different ways during her life so it is not known what the original name was.

Nancy Jane Duffin Carpenter died about 1845-1848, leaving Orson with five children. Nancy Maria Phillips may have been enlisted to take care of the children soon after. It was the custom to marry soon after the death of a young mother so that the husband would have someone to take care of the children. The two older girls may have been old enough to help as well.

The 1850 census for Brownville, Jefferson, New York, taken 18 Jul 1850 has Orson Carpenter, 38, a farmer with $600 in real estate. The others listed without relationships are Nancy M 19; Elizabeth 15; William 14; Sarah J 10; and Maryette 5. There is another family living in the same house or at least on the same farm (Medad Cook, 53, a farmer, Roxy, 48, and Medad, 18). The Cooks appear to have been hired help although it is possible Orson Carpenter was living with them. This is the same Cook that Orson sold land to in 1837.

Nancy M Carpenter was thought to be Orson's daughter at first but is probably Orson's second wife, Nancy Maria Phillips. The age would be right for Maria and she may have gone by Maria most of the time rather than Nancy as her mother's name was Nancy. I have not found proof that Maria is Nancy Maria but the children listed in Orson's Obituary do not include a Nancy Carpenter. Orson is supposed to have married Maria Phillips 20 Aug 1848 according to one family tree.

The 1850 census also lists Joseph Phillips, 57, and his wife Nancy, 53. They are listed just before Orson and are obviously neighbors. The listing goes over the page and seems to have some errors as the children are not listed chronologically. The bottom of the 1st page has a male 21 and a female 20 (this could be Maria) over the page are Lydia, 14; William, 24, sailor; Abner or Allen, 17; Chester, 11 and Chittenden, 11. This would make the children: William 24, unknown male 21, Maria 20, Abner 17, Lydia 14, Chester and Chittenden 11.

A listing on Ancestry.com has Joseph Phillips born 1789 in Vermont, died 1863 in Adams, Michigan. Joseph's wife, Nancy Stebbins, was born 1798 in Fort Edward, Argyle, Washington, New York and died 20 May 1865 in Adams, Michigan. Their children are listed as: Lydia A. Philips, Jane Ann Phillips born 9 Sep 1817, Hannah Phillips 16 May 1819, Joseph Richardson Phillips born 12 Mar 1821 in Sackett's Harbor, New York, Daniel S. Phillips born 27 Sep 1823, William R. Phillips born 27 Apr 1825, John Albert Phillips born 16 Aug 1827, Almond Phillips born 9 Oct 1829, Maria S. Phillips born 7 Jan 1831, Chester R Phillips born 26 Jan 1839, and Roderick C. Phillips born 26 Jan 1839. Jane, Hannah, Joseph, Daniel and Albert would have left home by 1850. The rest seems to correlate.

This information seems to confirm that Maria Phillips parents are Joseph and Nancy Stebbins Phillips. It also seems that Maria was much younger than Orson. She would have been 19 in1850 the same age as Orson's oldest daughter (if he had a daughter Nancy). Maria may have started keeping house for Orson when his oldest daughters left home then married him later, something that was not unusual at that time.

**The Stebbins Family**

1. Daniel Stebbins (about 1755-) Revolutionary War
+ Ruth Goodwill (-)

2. Daniel Stebbins
2. John Alden Stebbins (1784-1830) War 1812
 + Phillips
    3. Nancy Stebbins (1798-1865)
     + Joseph Phillips (1789-1863)
        4. Joseph R Phillips (1819-1910) Civil War
         + Catherine Day (1838-)
        4. William R Phillips (1825-)
        4. John Albert Phillips (1827-)
        4. Almond Phillips (1829-)
        **4. Maria Phillips (1831-1857)**
         **+ Orson Carpenter (1811-1899)**
        4. Roderick Chittenden Phillips (1839-1915) Civil War
        4. Chester R Phillips (1839-) Civil War
    3. Daniel R Stebbins (1808-1850) built G P Griffith
     + Mary Palmer ()
    3. Solomon Alden Stebbins (1810-)
     + Rachel Maria Lincoln ()
    3. John Stebbins
    3. Mary Stebbins

Daniel Stebbins, born (1750-1760), and Ruth Goodwill were married 30 Mar 1787 in Wilbraham, Massachusetts. Daniel and a brother John Alden were born at Wilbraham a township near Springfield, Massachusetts. Daniel Stebbins served in the Revolutionary War and was with Marion in the Carolinas according to a source written in old English. *A Muster Roll of A Company of Militia from the County of Hampden to guard the stores at Springfield under the command of Capt. Gideon Burt are as follows.* (Several townships are listed along with Wilbraham). *18 men are from Wilbraham including Dan Stebbins, Zadok Stebbins, and James Stebbins.* This is from a hand-written document from the time but with no date. It can be assumed the other Stebbins are brothers or at least cousins. The Stebbins connection has been verified by DNA. The history goes further back in Massachusetts and Connecticut.

John Alden Stebbins, born 1784, the son of Daniel Stebbins and Ruth Goodwill, was in the War of 1812 from Fort Edwards, Vermont. Ft Edwards was at times considered part of Vermont until after the Revolutionary War when the state boundaries were settled. It seems the Carpenter and Stebbins families may have known each other from the Revolutionary War and Fort Edwards, New York.

John Alden Stebbins married a Miss Phillips and had 5 children all born at Fort Edward. They were: Nancy, born in 1798, married Joseph Philips; Daniel R, born in 1808, married Mary Palmer; Solomon Alden, born 31 Jul 1810, married Rachel Maria Lincoln; John unmarried; and Mary unmarried. John Alden Stebbins moved to Sackett's Harbor, New York about 1813 and was a blacksmith.

Soldiers from the Revolutionary War and War of 1812 were given land in New York State as payment for their service. Those from Fort Edward seemed to end up in Sackett's Harbor or Pillar Point, both are near Watertown, New York.

John Stebbins' son Daniel R Stebbins, born 1808, moved to Toledo, Ohio. In 1848 he built and partially owned the steamer G P Griffith. On 16 Jun 1850 the steamer departed Buffalo, New York heading for Toledo, Ohio with stops along the way. There were 326 passengers, mostly immigrants from England, Ireland, Germany and Scandinavia. The steamship had left Fairport, Ohio for Cleveland. At around 4 am on 17 June, sparks were reported shooting up from the smokestacks. As the ship headed toward shore the aft of the ship burned. The crew abandoned their posts causing the ship to stop about ½ mile from shore. Many passengers jumped into the water and drowned or were burned on the ship which was destroyed by fire. Daniel swam ashore and found a small boat which he used to rescue others. The Griffith is the 3rd worst disaster on the Great Lakes with 300 lives lost. Daniel was able to save a number of people before dying himself from burns. (Most of the above is from North America, Family Histories, 1500-2000; The Stebbins Genealogy. Nancy Stebbins father John Alden Stebbins was only about 14 when she was born. Something isn't right. I suspect the older dates not the order of names or the Nancy Stebbins information.)

Nancy Stebbins, born 1798 at Fort Edward, New York, married Joseph Phillips. Their daughter Maria was the 2nd wife of Orson Carpenter. Maria's parents moved to Michigan along with Orson and Maria Carpenter.

Joseph Phillips, born 1794 in Vermont, died 4 Jul 1863 in Hillsdale County, Michigan and was buried in Taylor Cemetery but later moved to Churches Corners Cemetery. His parents were Charles Phillips and Anna Stebbins Phillips. Nancy Stebbins Phillips, born 1798 in Vermont, died 1865 in Rollin, Lenawee, Michigan. She was the daughter of John Alden Stebbins. She is buried with her husband Joseph Phillips.

On 27 Feb 1851 Edward Stoman sold to Orison Carpenter for $107 a parcel of land that was part of the 43 and 44 west and 23 and 24 north ranges of Beaverland and bounded as follows: commencing in the middle of the road leading from Phillips Four Corners to Sherwin's Bay at a point at the NW corner of Joseph Phillip's land thence along the said Phillips land and land owned by Giles Douglas South 33 ¼ west 24 chains and 6 links to a stake and stones Thence south 38 ¾ west 12 chains and 55 links to a stake and stones at the north west of 5 acres contracted to A Becker thence north 31 west 24 chains 6 links to the center of said road, thence along the same north 57/4 east 12 chains and 50 links to the place of beginning. The rest of the deed is missing. [18]

This may be a house owned by Orson Carpenter near Pillar Point, New York. It is in the area of the above land deed. The house appears to be the right age and is as close to the right spot as could be determined by old maps. It is on the road from Phillip's Four Corners to Sherwin's Bay.

On 5 Mar 1853 Orison Carpenter and Maria his wife sold to James C Douglas for $800 a parcel of land in the 43 and 44 west and 23 and 24 north ranges with the same description as the land sold to Orson Carpenter by Edward Stoman on 27 Feb 1851, recorded in Book 100 of deeds page 105. The deed was signed by Orson Carpenter and Maria Carpenter on 25 Mar 1853. Maria was privately examined away from her husband and acknowledged that she executed this instrument freely and without compulsion of her husband. M Cook Justice of the Peace.[18]

The 1855, Brownville, New York census has Orson Carpenter, 46, born in Washington County, New York. Maria is 28 and was born in Jefferson County, New York. The children are William, 18; Sarah J, 15; and Maryette, 10. Maria was probably 24 but claimed 28.

Elizabeth Carpenter left home to marry Samuel Resseguie in 1854.

Orson Carpenter moved to Michigan from New York State in 1855[7]. His children William, Sarah Jane, and Mary Ette moved to Michigan with their father and stepmother. Elizabeth and Samuel moved to Michigan before 1863. Joseph and Nancy Phillips also moved to Michigan with them. They brought the family spinning wheel.

The spinning wheel remained in the family and is currently in the possession of Pam Bishop Smutek.

Orson bought the "family place" on the southeast corner of Gardener and Stewart Roads. Section 35 of Wheatland Township, Hillsdale, Michigan. Ellen Louise Carpenter was born there in 1857. Her mother died soon after and Orson married for the third time when she was three years old.

The 1860 agricultural census for Adams, Hillsdale, Michigan has Joseph Phillips owning 30 acres of improved and 40 acres of unimproved land with a value of $1200. The value of farming implements is $75. He has 2 horses, 3 milch (milk) cows, 1 other cattle, 3 sheep, and 3 swine (pigs) all worth $194. He has 40 bushels of wheat, 25 of rye, 100 of Indian corn, 23 of oats and 56 lbs. of wool. The standard 1860 census was not found.

The 1860 census for Wheatland, Hillsdale, Michigan has Orson Carpenter, 47, born in New York, a farmer with land worth $2500 and personal estate worth $400. His children are Mary E, 14, born in New York and Ellen, 3, born in Michigan. The following listing is Orson's son, William Carpenter, 26, born in New York, farm labor with a personal estate worth $100. Evelin is 21 and born in Michigan. Their son, George, is 1 and born in Michigan.

Orson Carpenter, 47, was married to Mrs. Mary Smith, 36, on 10 Dec 1860 according to Hillsdale County Probate Court records.

The 1870 census for Wheatland, Hillsdale, Michigan has Orson Carpenter, 56, born in New York, a farmer with $8600 in real estate and $1500 in personal property. Mary is 47, born in New York and keeping house. Their children are Marietta, 27, at home, born in New York and Ellen, 14, at school, born in Michigan. The listing above Orson's is his son, William Carpenter, 33, born in New York, a farmer with $2000 in real estate and $500 in personal property. Evaline is 28 and keeping house. Their sons are George, 12, at school; Edgar, 10, at school and Freddie less than a year at home. All the children were born in Michigan. William must have been living on a farm very close to Orson.

The 1880 census for Pittsford, Hillsdale, Michigan has Orson Carpenter, 67, born in New York, a farmer. Mary is 52, born in New York and with both parents born in New York. Their daughter, Ellen, is 21, born in Michigan with both parents born in New York.

Orson Carpenter's third wife had the following obituary:
Carpenter, Mary M 27 Sep 1889   Hudson Post
Mary M, wife of Orson Carpenter, died at her home in Wheatland, 20 Sep. Born at Portage, New York, Oct 1822, with her parents, she moved to Ohio, & then to Hudson, where she lived with her sister, Mrs. J H Carleton. In 1860 she married Orson Carpenter, who survives. Leaves 4 daus, & 1 son. Of her father's family, but 1 sis was able to attend the funeral.[7]

The 1894 State of Michigan Census, Wheatland Township lists Orson Carpenter 83 with Ella Stanley 36.

Orison Carpenter had the following obituary:
Hudson Post 1 Sep 1899

Orison Carpenter was born at Granville, Washington, New York, 25 Aug 1811 & died in Wheatland, Hillsdale, Michigan 27 Aug, aged 88. Lived near Pillar Point, New York until he moved to Wheatland. Married in 1830 to Mary Jane Duffin, who died in 1848, in New York. In 1849 he married Maria Philips, who died in 1857 in Michigan. In 1860 he married Mary Smith, who died in Wheatland in 1889. Five children from 1st union: Elizabeth Resseguie, of Dakota; Wm Carpenter, of Wheatland; Hiram Carpenter, died age 3; Sarah Jane Bailey, of Wheatland; Mary Ett Dillon, of Hudson Center, Michigan. One daughter from 2nd marriage, Ellen Stanley, of Wheatland.[7]

Orson Carpenter was buried in Maple Grove Cemetery, Hudson, Michigan with his third wife Mary. The stone is near that of his daughter Mariette Dillon.

The following picture was taken just before his death.

This is the home of Orson Carpenter, Orson is seated holding Mae Stanley.
From the left: Mabel Stanley Snyder, Blanch Stanley Gibbs, Sarah Carpenter Bailey
Orson Stanley, Met Dillon, Clara Greenfield Bailey, George Bailey, Ella Carpenter Stanley, Mae
Stanley Bishop, Orson Carpenter, Nina Dillon Sweezey

## 2. Elizabeth E Carpenter and Samuel Resseguie

Elizabeth Carpenter married Samuel Resseguie on 29 Oct 1854 in Jefferson County, New York.

The 1855 New York State Census for Hounsfield, Jefferson, New York has Samuel Resseguie, 25, a farmer who land with a frame house worth $100. Elizabeth is 21.

Samuel Resseguie, 33, a farmer from Bloomer Township, Michigan, married, born in Ohio, registered for the Civil War in June or July 1863. There is no evidence he served.

The 1870 census for Bloomer, Montcalm, Michigan has Samuel Resseguie, 40, a farmer with $8000 in real estate. Elizabeth is 36 and keeping house.

The 1880 census for Bloomer, Montcalm, Michigan has Samuel Resseguie, 49, a farmer. Elizabeth is 45 and keeping house. Their son, Frank, is 23 and works on the farm. Frank hasn't shown up before. He may have been adopted, possibly from a relative.

The 1870 census for Bloomer, Montcalm, Michigan has Frank Resseguie, 13, born in Michigan, and attending school. Frank was living with Perry Felch, a farmer, his wife, Almena, and their 2 children.

There is no real evidence as to whether Frank was the son of Elizabeth and Samuel or not. An 1860 census was not found. Frank may have been living with neighbors in 1870 because one of his parents was ill or otherwise not capable of taking care of him. He is most likely a relative and will be followed.

Samuel Resseguie born 27 Jul 1830, died 18 Jul 1905 in Bloomer, Montcalm, Michigan. Elizabeth E Carpenter Resseguie, daughter of Orson Carpenter, born 17 Jul 1834, died 20 Mar 1917 in Bloomer, Montcalm, Michigan of a broken hip caused by a fall on the ice in Carson City, Michigan. She is buried with Samuel in Carson City Cemetery.

## 3. Frank S Resseguie and Sarah Ellen "Ella" McMullen / Mary McMullen Salisbury

Frank S Resseguie and Sarah Ella McMullen were married 10 Aug 1880.

The 1900 census for Bloomer, Montcalm, Michigan has Frank Resseguie, 42, born Mar 1858 in Michigan, married 19 years, a farmer who owns his farm. Ella is 35, born Aug 1864 in Ohio and has 5 children, 5 are living. Their children are Jessie E, 16, born Oct 1883 in South Dakota; Samuel J, 14, born Jun 1885 in South Dakota; Orson, 13, born May 1887 in Michigan and Daniel, 11, born Dec 1888 in Michigan. All the children were attending school.

The 1910 census for Bloomer, Montcalm, Michigan has Frank S Resseguie, 51, married

29 years, a farmer who owns his farm free and clear. Ellen S is 47 and has 5 children, all living. Their sons are Samuel J, 25, a teacher in a public school and Orson, 23, a farm laborer on the home farm. Ellen's father, John McMillen, 78, a widower is living with them.

The 1920 census for Bloomer, Montcalm, Michigan has Frank S Resseguie, 59, a farmer who owns his farm on Quarter Line Road. Sarah E is 55. Their grandchildren, living with them are Beulah M Hatfield, 13; Lillian R Hatfield, 9 and Esther M Hatfield, 6. They are all attending school.

Ella died 18 Jul 1920 and is buried in Carson City Cemetery, Carson City, Michigan.

Frank married Mary McMullen Salisbury on 5 Jul 1924 in Stanton, Michigan. Mary was born 2 Jun 1857 and died 21 Feb 1930. She is Ella's sister.

The 1930 census for Bloomer, Montcalm, Michigan has Frank S Resseguie, 73, a widower and a farmer. Living with him are Ruth L, 19, granddaughter and Esther M, 16, granddaughter.

Frank S Resseguie, 76, widowed, born 31 May 1858, died 7 Sep 1934 of a concussion after a fall at home on 5 Sep 1934. His wife was Mary M Resseguie. The informant is John Resseguie of Carson City. He was buried 9 Sep 1934 in Carson City Cemetery, Carson City, Michigan.

## 4. Jessie E Resseguie and Herbert A Hatfield

Jessie E Resseguie, 20 married Herbert A Hatfield, 24, a farmer, on 8 Jun 1904 in Bloomer, Montcalm, Michigan.

The 1910 census for Crystal, Montcalm, Michigan has Herbert Hatfield, 30, married 6 years, a farmer. Jessie is 26 and has 1 child. Their daughter Beulah is 3.

Jessie Elizabeth Resseguie born 27 Oct 1884, died 9 May 1914 of puerperal septicemia in Crystal, Montcalm, Michigan. An infection after childbirth.

Herbert Albert Hatfield, 39, born 16 Aug 1879, registered for WW1 on 12 Sep 1918. He was working as a steamfitter for Toledo Shipbuilding Co. on Front Street in Toledo, Ohio. Three fingers were partly off left hand. Next of kin was Beulah Hatfield in Carson City, Michigan. His daughters were living with their grandparents in the 1920 census.

Beulah Hatfield born 1908, died 21 Feb 1927 of lobar pneumonia. She was single and an employee of University of Michigan Hospital. Beulah was buried in Carson City Cemetery on 24 Feb 1927.

## 5. Lillian Ruth Resseguie and Virgil L Nicklin

Ruth L Resseguie, 23, secretary, married Virgil L Nicklin, 25, salesman, on 18 Nov 1934.

The 1940 census for Carson City, Michigan has Virgil L Nicklin, 31, graduated high school, a salesman for a wholesale grocery who owns his house on Abbott Street worth $3000. Ruth L is 29, graduated high school and a secretary.

### 5. Esther May Resseguie and Albert Lentz

Esther May Resseguie, 26, a cook, married Albert Lentz, 26, a carpenter, on 21 Sep 1940. A 1940 census has not been found.

### 4. Samuel J Resseguie and Lucinda B Husen

S J Resseguie, 27, of Carson City, a school teacher, married Lucinda B Husen, 22, of Spaulding on 26 Jun 1912 in Saginaw, Michigan.

Samuel Jay Resseguie, 33, born 17 Jun 1885 registered for WW1 on 12 Sep 1918. He was a teacher in the Cadillac Public Schools and lived at 413 Prospect in Cadillac, Michigan. His next of kin was Mrs. Lucinda B Resseguie.

The 1920 census for Saginaw, Michigan has Samuel Resseguie, 34, employment manager at an employment agency. Lucinda is 29. Their daughter Valda is 1 10/12. A 1921 city directory has Samuel working at Employers Association of Saginaw Valley.

The 1930 census for Crystal, Montcalm, Michigan has Samuel J Resseguie, 44, married at 26, a farmer renting his farm. Lucinda B is 39 and married at 21. Velda E is 12 and attending school.

Samuel J Resseguie born 17 Jun 1885 in Day County, South Dakota, died 25 Apr 1931 of acute anemia and chronic vascular hypertension. The informant was Lucinda.

Valda Resseguie, 21, born 19 Feb 1918, married Howard Gallant, 26, born 9 Oct 1913 on 17 Aug 1939 in Steuben, Indiana. A 1940 census was not found.

### 4. Orson Resseguie and Nila Drucilla Kipp

Orson Resseguie enlisted in the Army 26 Jan 1907 for a period of 3 years. He was 22, a farmer and from Carson City, Michigan. He was in regiment HC. He was discharged 6 Jul 1908 from a fort in Nebraska. Nothing more is readable. Another military record has Orson Resseguie, private, regiment HC, company B, 4 Feb 1908 admitted Hot Springs US Army & Navy General Hospital, Arkansas. He must have been discharged after recovering.

Orson is living with his parents in 1910.

Orson Resseguie was married 30 Aug 1911 to Nila Drucilla Kipp. Nila D Resseguie filed for divorce 6 Jul 1915 for desertion. She had 2 children. Final action was 11 Sep 1916, dismissed, judicative action.

Jay B Resseguie was born 12 Jan 1912. Paul Resseguie was born 11 May 1914.

A Baby Boy was born and died 6 Jun 1913. A premature daughter, Ella, was born and died 12 May 1918. They are both buried in Carson City Cemetery, Carson City, Michigan.

Orson Resseguie born 2 May 1887, enlisted 20 Sep 1917 and was discharged 21 Apr 1919. He was a bugler in Battery F, 328th Field Artillery, 85th Division, AEF (American Expeditionary Force). According to an application for military headstone. The stone was delivered to Butternut, Michigan and placed in the Crystal Township Cemetery, Crystal, Michigan.

The 1920 census for Carson City, Michigan has Orson Resseguie, 33, a laborer renting a home. Nila D is 27. Their sons are Jay B, 7 and Paul, 5.

The 1930 census for Stockbridge, Michigan has Orson Resseguie, 39, single, married at 20, a carpenter rooming with Nellie Cantrell.

The 1930 census for Carson City, Michigan has Nila D Resseguie, 37, married at 18, doing housework in a private home and renting a home on Lincoln Street for $10 per month. Jay B is 18 and attending school.

The 1930 census for Home, Montcalm, Michigan has Kenneth P Resseguie, 15, attending school and living with Andrew Anderson, his wife and 2 lodgers as an adopted son. There is no evidence he was ever adopted but was boarding on the farm.

Nila Resseguie finally got her divorce from Orson on 28 Dec 1936. By then, there were no minor children and no alimony. The reason given was desertion and non-support although I suspect Orson was paying for Paul until he married.

Orson Resseguie born 2 May 1887, died 19 Aug 1954 and is buried in Crystal Township Cemetery.

### 5. Jay N Resseguie and Mary Minor

Jay B Resseguie, 26, a lineman, married Mary Miner, 18, on 1 Oct 1938 in Carson City, Michigan.

The 1940 census for Carson City, Michigan has Jay Resseguie, 28, married, graduated high school, a yardman in a refinery. Mary is 19 and graduated high school. Jay's father, Orson is 53, divorced, graduated high school and a scavenger.

## 5. Paul Kenneth Resseguie and Marjorie Louise Wilson

Paul Kenneth Resseguie, 22, married Marjorie Louise Davidson Wilson, 22, on 21 Nov 1936 in LaGrange, Indiana.

The 1940 census for Delhi, Ingham, Michigan has Kenneth Resseguie, 26, completed 10th grade, a tree trimmer for Consumers Power. Marjorie is 25 and graduated high school. Their daughter, Roseanne, is 2.

## 4. Daniel Robert Resseguie and Nellie Henry / Tressie Hunt

Daniel Resseguie, 21, a farmer, married Nellie Henry, 22, on 10 Feb 1910 in Carson City, Michigan.

Nellie filed for divorce from Daniel on 18 Aug 1911. Divorce was granted 17 Feb 1912 for willful failure to support, not contested.

Daniel R Resseguie, 31, a boiler maker's helper in Saginaw, married Tressie Hunt, 27 a stenographer in Saginaw on 18 Nov 1920 in Midland, Michigan.

The 1930 census for Saginaw, Michigan has Daniel Resseguie, 41, married at 31, an oil station attendant who owns his home at 1900 Collingwood worth $2000. Tressie is 36 and was married at 26. Their children are William, 7; Dorothy, 5; Olive, 4; Ruth, 2 and Donna, 8/12.

The 1940 census for Crystal, Montcalm, Michigan has Daniel Resseguie, 51, completed 8th grade, no occupation listed but owns his home worth $600. Tressie is 46 and completed 9th grade. Their daughters are Dorothy, 15, completed 9th grade; Olive, 14, completed 8th grade; Ruth, 12, completed 6th grade; Dona, 10, completed 4th grade; Tessie, 9, completed 2nd grade; Barbara, 7, completed 1st grade and Francis, 6.

A 1940 census for William could not be found. William Clyde Resseguie is in the Marine Corps Base, rifle range detachment in San Diego, California in 1942. Later records confirm the middle name. He probably enlisted in 1940 when he was 17.

Daniel Robert Resseguie, 57, born 3 Dec 1888 in Butternut, Michigan, died 9 Oct 1946 in Crystal, Montcalm, Michigan.

## 2. William H Carpenter and Alice Evaline Wilcox

William Carpenter married Alice Evaline Wilcox 27 Dec 1857 in Wheatland, Hillsdale, Michigan. Her parents were John Wilcox and Lucy Ann Piper.

The 1860 census for Wheatland, Hillsdale, Michigan has William Carpenter, 24, born in New York, a farm laborer. Eveline is 21 and born in Michigan. Their son, George is 1.

Civil War Draft Registration Records for Wheatland, Hillsdale, Michigan is a list of all persons of Class 1 subject to duty June 1863. William H. Carpenter, 27, married, a farmer, born in New York, former military service 4, is listed.

An 1890 Veterans Schedule for surviving soldiers in Wheatland, Hillsdale, Michigan has William H Carpenter, Private, Company B, Michigan 4th Infantry, served 31 Aug 1864 to 26 May 1866. A total of 1 year, 9 months 4 days

The 4th Regiment, Michigan Infantry organized at Adrian and Hudson, Michigan and mustered in 14 Oct 1864. They left for Nashville, Tennessee 22 Oct then went to Decatur, Alabama 26 Oct where they were attached to District of Northern Alabama, Department of the Cumberland. They defended Decatur against Hood's attack 28-30 Oct 1864. Duty at Decatur till 25 Nov 1864. Actions near Maysville and near New Market, Alabama, on 17 Nov at Duckett's Place and 19 Nov near Paint Rock River. They were moved to Murfreesboro 25-27 Nov and the defense of the Nashville & Chattanooga Railroad, Department of the Cumberland. Defended against Hood's attack on Murfreesboro 5-12 Dec then picket duty and guarding supply trains. Transferred to 3rd Brigade, 3rd Division, 4th Army Corps, Army of the Cumberland. Moved to Huntsville, Alabama, 15 Jan 1865 and duty there till 23 Mar. Duty at Knoxville, Strawberry Plains, Bull's Gap, Jonesboro and Nashville, Tennessee. Moved to New Orleans, Louisiana, 16 Jun - 5 Jul; thence to Indianola, Texas, 6-10 Jul and Dept. of Texas. March to Green Lake and duty there till 12 Sep. March to San Antonio 12-24 Sep. Camp at Salado Creek till Nov. Provost duty at San Antonio and other points in Texas till May 1866. Mustered out at Houston, Texas, 26 May, and discharged at Detroit, Michigan, 10 Jun 1866. The Regiment lost during service 7 Enlisted men killed and mortally wounded and 141 Enlisted men by disease a total of 148.

The 1870 census for Wheatland, Hillsdale, Michigan has William Carpenter, 33, a farmer with $2000 in real estate and can vote. Evaline is 28 and keeping house. The children are George, 12, at school; Edgar, 10, at school; and Freddie, 9/12. They are listed next to Orson Carpenter.

An 1880 census has not been found for Wheatland, Hillsdale, Michigan.

William H Carpenter filed for a Civil War pension 28 Jun 1897 as an Invalid and Alice filed 18 Jul 1900 as a widow.

The 1900 census for Wheatland, Hillsdale, Michigan has Alice E Carpenter, 60, born Jun 1839, a widow who owns the farm. Her son, Fred, is 30, born Jan 1870, married 9 years, a farmer. His wife, Ella E is 29 and born Aug 1870.

William Carpenter, born in 1836, died 4 Apr, 1900 of dropsy and heart failure in Wheatland, Hillsdale, Michigan. Alice Evaline Wilcox Carpenter, born 3 Jun 1839, died 30 Mar 1901, of cancer and is buried beside William in Maple Grove Cemetery, Hudson, Michigan.

### 3. George H Carpenter and Clara E Bailey / Ida Whicker Slocum

George H Carpenter married Clara E Bailey in 1877.

The 1900 census for Wheatland, Hillsdale, Michigan has George Carpenter, 42, born Oct 1857, married 19 years, a farmer who owns his farm free and clear. Clara is 42, born Aug 1857 and has 3 children, all living. The children are Bertha, 18, born May 1882; Linnie, 11, born June 1890 and Carl, 2, born May 1898.

Clara E Bailey Carpenter, born 11 Aug 1857, died 4 May 1902 of pulmonary tuberculosis. She is buried in Section Y, Maple Grove Cemetery, Hudson, Michigan.

George H Carpenter, 44, of Addison, a farmer, married Ida Slocum, 43, of Wheatland on 4 June 1903 in Hillsdale, Michigan.

The 1910 census for Woodstock, Lenawee, Michigan has George Carpenter, 50, married 7 years, second marriage, a farmer who owns his farm. Ida is 49 and has had 2 children both living. Their children are Bertha, 27, single, post office assistant; Linnie, 19, single; Carl D, 11, attended school; Clifford Slocum, 21, step-son, single, automobile worker.

George Carpenter born 2 Oct 1857, died 26 Apr 1919 of apoplexy very suddenly. He is buried in Maple Grove Cemetery with Clara.

### 4. Bertha E Carpenter and Dennis Jackson

Bertha E. Carpenter, 28 of Addison, married Dennis Jackson, 23 of Addison, a farmer, on 24 Nov 1910 in Addison, Michigan.

The 1920 census for Woodstock, Lenawee, Michigan has Dennis Jackson, 34, married, a farmer who owns his mortgaged farm. Bertha is 36. Dennis' parents Thomas, 59, and Carrie, 56, are living on the same farm. It is unclear who owns the farm.

The 1930 census for Woodstock, Lenawee, Michigan has Dennis Jackson, 41, married at 23, a farmer who owns his farm and a radio. Bertha is 47 and was married at 28. Roy Perkins, 12, a foster son is living with them.

Bertha Jackson filed for divorce 3 Mar 1936. She was divorced from Dennis Jackson 17 Feb 1937 in Lenawee County. Cause is listed as Extreme and repeated cruelty.

The 1940 census for Jackson, Michigan has Bertha E Jackson, 57, divorced, completed 8th grade, lived in rural Lenawee County in 1935, working as a housekeeper in a private home. She is living with her brother Carl Carpenter and his family.

Bertha Jackson filed for Social Security 23 Sep 1950.

## 4. Linnie Eveline Carpenter and Thomas Barnes / Arthur James Jackson

Linnie Carpenter, 20, of Addison married Thomas Barnes, 26, of Addison, a clerk, 3 May 1910 in Adrian.

Linnie Barnes filed for divorce from Thomas E. Barnes 6 Jul 1911 for non-support. The uncontested divorce was granted 11 Oct 1911.

Linnie Eveline Carpenter, 23, of Woodstock, married Arthur James Jackson, 25 of Somerset, a farmer, on 28 Feb 1914 in Addison, Michigan.

The 1920 census for Woodstock, Lenawee, Michigan has Arthur Jackson, 31, a farmer who owns his mortgaged farm. Linnie is 30.

The 1930 census for Woodstock, Lenawee, Michigan has Arthur J Jackson, 41, married at 25, a farmer who owns his farm and a radio. Linnie is 39 and was married at 23.

The 1940 census for Addison, Michigan has Arthur Jackson, 51, completed 9th grade, a farmer who owns his farm on US 127 worth $2000. Linnie is 49 and graduated high school. Leroy Perkins is 21, servant, graduated high school and a laborer on the farm. Roy was living with Bertha in 1930.

Arthur J Jackson born 1888, died 1955 and is buried in Dibble Cemetery, Wheatland, Hillsdale, Michigan. Linnie Carpenter Jackson born 9 Jun 1890, died 14 Jun 1981 in Jackson, Michigan and is buried with Arthur.

## 4. Carl Bailey Carpenter and Aileen Kelley

Carl Baily Carpenter, 20, of Addison, Michigan, born 19 May 1898, registered for WW1 12 Sep 1918. He was an operator in a munitions plant. Employer was Jackson Munition Corporation. His father is George H Carpenter of Addison. He is medium height and slender build with brown eyes and hair. He has had Infantile Paralysis (Polio) which has probably left him unfit for service.

Carl B. Carpenter, 23 of Addison, Michigan, a truck driver, married Aileen Kelley, 20 of Cement City, Michigan on 5 Sep 1923 in Cement City.

Newspaper clipping: Miss Arleen Kelley and C B Carpenter wed at Cement City.
    Cement City, 6 Sep – Carl B Carpenter of Addison and Miss Aileen Kelley were

united in marriage Wednesday at the home of the bride's mother, Mrs. Milo Kelley, of Cement City. Only the family of Mrs. Kelley were present, on account of the death of the bride's father, Milo Kelley on 23 Aug.

The ceremony was conducted by Rev. D M Halsey. The bride's gown was white silk Canton crepe.

The couple left for a trip to Detroit after which they will remain with the bride's mother for a short time but will make their home in Hudson later.

The 1930 census for Jackson, Michigan has Carl B Carpenter, 31, married at 24, a machine operator in a motor shaft factory who owns his home at 119 Hillside Ave. worth $5000 and a radio. Aileen is 26 and was married at 19.

The 1940 census for Jackson, Michigan has Carl B Carpenter, 42, completed 10th grade, a press operator in an auto parts factory who owns his home worth $3000 at 220 Hillside Ave. Aileen is 38 and completed 10th grade. Their sons are Tommy L, 3 and Clark L, 2/12. Beryl Highland is 27, sister-in-law, widowed, graduated high school, a sales lady for retail clothing. Bertha E Jackson, 57, sister is divorced, completed 8th grade and a housekeeper in a private home.

Aileen Kelley Carpenter born 8 Feb 1902, died 8 May 1973 in Lake County, Florida. Carl B Carpenter born 19 May 1898, died 22 Dec 1974 in Jackson, Michigan and is buried in Woodland Cemetery, Jackson, Michigan.

Obituary: Carpenter, Carl B Of 220 Hillside passed away in Foote Hospital Sunday evening, age 76. Surviving are two sons Tom of Clark Lake and Lanny of Jackson; six grandchildren; one sister Mrs. Linnie Jackson and one step brother Clifford Slocum both of Addison.

### 3. Edgar Leone Carpenter and Jessie E. Tabor

Edgar L Carpenter, 21, of Wheatland, a farmer and Jessie E Tabor, 22, of Pittsford, were married in Pittsford, Michigan on 15 Feb 1882.

The 1900 census for Pittsford, Hillsdale, Michigan has Edgar Carpenter, 39, born Aug 1860, married 18 years, a cream gatherer who owns his farm free and clear. Jessie E is 40, born Jan 1860, and has 6 children, all are living. The children are Grace M, 16, born Oct 1883; Pearl M, 14, born Nov 1885; Ross O, 9, born July 1890; Alma B, 7, born Jul 1892; Shirley, son, 4, born Mar 1896 and Ralph, 2, born Dec 1897. The four older children attended school 9 months in the last year.

The 1910 census for Wheatland, Hillsdale, Michigan has Edgar Carpenter, 49, married 28 years, a general farmer who owns his farm. Jessie E is 50 and has -six children, all are living. The children are Grace M, 26; Pearl M, 24; Ross O, 19, a farm laborer; Alma B, 17; Shirley, 14 and Ralph T, 12. The youngest 3 attended school.

Michigan Soldiers of the Great War has Ralph T Carpenter of Hudson, a corporal in the US Army, died of disease. Many soldiers died of the Spanish Flu. Ralph born Dec 1897, died 4 Oct 1918 in France and is buried in Suresnes American Cemetery and Memorial in Suresnes, Paris, Ile-de-France, France.

The 1920 census for Wheatland, Hillsdale, Michigan has Ed Carpenter, 59, a farmer on a general farm. Jessie is 59. The children are Grace, 36; Pearl, 34, a nurse in a hospital; Alma, 28, a school teacher in a district school; and Shirley, 23, a laborer on the home farm.

Edgar L Carpenter born 20 Aug 1860, died 2 Oct 1924 in Camden, Hillsdale, Michigan of a cerebral hemorrhage. He is buried in Maple Grove Cemetery, Hudson, Michigan.

The 1930 census for Wheatland, Hillsdale, Michigan has Jessie E Carpenter, 70, a widow who owns her farm worth $2000 and a radio. Her daughters Grace M, 46, a helper in the household and Pearl M, 44, a trained nurse in a private home are living with her.

Jessie E Taber Carpenter born 17 Jan 1860, died 7 Jul 1935 of an ovarian cyst and is buried with Edgar in Maple Grove Cemetery, Hudson, Michigan.

The 1940 census for Hillsdale, Michigan has Grace Carpenter, 56, completed 9th grade and Pearl, 54, completed 2 years college. They are living in a home they own worth $3200 at 20 Glendale Street.

Grace M Carpenter born Oct 1883, died 1 Jan 1960 and is buried in Maple Grove Cemetery next to her mother, Jessie Carpenter.

Pearl M Carpenter born 12 Nov 1885, died 10 Nov 1969 in Hillsdale and is buried with her parents and sister in Maple Grove Cemetery. Grace and Pearl never married.

## 4. Ross O Carpenter and Letha Leoma Kane

Ross O Carpenter, 26, of Wheatland, a farmer, married Letha Leoma Kane, 18, of Pittsford on 3 Dec 1916 in Pittsford, Michigan. His parents were Edgar L Carpenter and Jessie E Tabor. Her parents were Wm H Kane and Florence J Fellows.

Ross O Carpenter, 26, born 20 Jul 1890 in Hudson, Michigan, a farmer with a dependent wife, registered for WW1 on 5 Jun 1917 in Wheatland, Hillsdale, Michigan. He had a medium build and height with light blue eyes and dark brown hair.

The 1920 census for Rollin, Lenawee, Michigan has Ross O Carpenter, 28, a farmer who owns his mortgaged farm. Letha L is 22. Their daughters are Ardis V, 2 and Bernice I, 8/12.

The 1930 census for Rollin, Lenawee, Michigan has Ross O Carpenter, 40, married at 27, a farmer who owns his farm and a radio. Letha L is 33 and was married at 20. The children are Ardis, 12; Bernice, 11; Edwill, 8 and Geraldine, 4 7/12. The three older children attended school.

This picture of Ross and Letha Carpenter was taken in the 30s or 40s.

The 1940 census for Rollin, Lenawee, Michigan has Ross Carpenter, 48, completed 8th grade, a farmer who owns his home worth $3600. Letha is 42 and completed 8th grade. The children are Edwill, 20, single, graduated high school and working on the farm; Geraldine, 14, completed 10th grade and Pauline, 10, completed 3rd grade

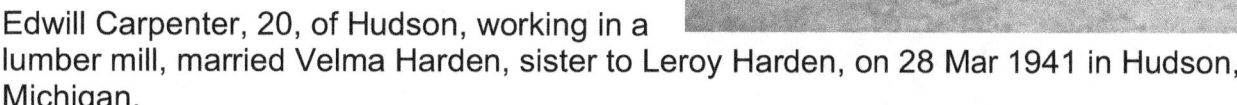

Edwill Carpenter, 20, of Hudson, working in a lumber mill, married Velma Harden, sister to Leroy Harden, on 28 Mar 1941 in Hudson, Michigan.

Geraldine Carpenter, 16, married Donald Rowlson, 19, in Addison, Michigan on 28 Dec 1941. War was approaching and many couples were getting married in hopes of avoiding the draft.

Ross O Carpenter, born 20 Jul 1890 in Hudson, Michigan, died 8 Jun 1947 in Hudson, Michigan and is buried in Maple Grove Cemetery. Letha Leoma Kane Carpenter born 22 Dec 1897, died 1 Apr 1985, and is buried with Ross in Maple Grove Cemetery.

### 5. Ardis V Carpenter and Emmett Moyer

Ardis Carpenter of Hudson, 22, born 17 Oct 1916, a stenographer, married Emmett Moyer of Hudson, born 8 Jul 1912, a farmer, on 10 Aug 1938 in Auburn, Indiana. Her parents are Ross Carpenter and Letha Kane. His parents are Jenva Moyer and Mary Adams

The 1940 census for Rollin, Lenawee, Michigan has Emmett Moyer, 27, graduated high school, a laborer on a farm. Ardis is 23, graduated high school and working at home.

### 5. Bernice I Carpenter and Leroy G Harden

Bernice I Carpenter, 18, of Hudson, married Leroy G Harden, 21, of Hudson, on 6 Aug

1937 in Hudson, Michigan.

The 1940 census for Hudson, Michigan has Leroy G Harden, 23, graduated high school, a laborer in a condensed milk factory who owns his home worth $1000. Bernice I is 21 and completed 10th grade. Their son, James A, is 2.

### 4. Alma Beatrice Carpenter and Frank Albert Gemmell

Frank Albert Gemmell, 25, born 17 Sep 1891, a mechanic for Hazen Manufacturing Company registered for WW1 on 5 Jun 1917. He did serve in WW1.

Alma Carpenter, 28, of Wheatland, a teacher, married Frank Albert Gemmell, 29, of Hudson, a moulder (factory tooling job), on 2 Oct 1920 in Hillsdale, Michigan.

The 1930 census for Wheatland, Hillsdale, Michigan has Frank A Gemmell, 39, married at 28, a veteran and a farmer. Alma B is 37 and married at 27. Their children are E Jean, 7; L Richard, 4 and Frank A 2.

The 1940 census for Wheatland, Hillsdale, Michigan has Frank A Gemmell, 48, graduated high school, a farmer who owns his home on Somerset Road worth $1500. Alma is 47 and graduated high school. The children are Jean, 17, graduated high school; Richard, 14 completed 9th grade and Frank, 12, completed 7th grade.

### 4. Shirley Leone Carpenter and Mary Sophia Rowley

Shirley L Carpenter, 24, a farmer, married Mary S Rowley, 18 on 1 Dec 1920 at Adrian, Michigan.

The 1930 census for Wheatland, Hillsdale, Michigan has Shirley L Carpenter, 34, married at 25, a farmer renting his farm. Mary S is 28 and married at 18. The children are Bernita A, 8; Marjorie J, 6 and Melburn K, 3.

The 1940 census for Wheatland, Hillsdale, Michigan has Shirley L Carpenter, 44, completed 11th grade, a farmer who owns his home worth $1000. Mary is 38 and completed 8th grade. Their children are Bernita, 18, graduated high school; Margery, 16 completed 9th grade; Melburn, 13, completed 7th grade; Willis, 6 and Daniel, 3.

Willis Burdell Carpenter, 11, born 30 Jan 1934, died 2 Dec 1945 in Adrian, Michigan and is buried in Maple Grove Cemetery, Hudson, Michigan.

Shirley Leone Carpenter born 1896 in Wheatland, Hillsdale, Michigan, died 3 Dec 1945 in Adrian, Michigan and is buried in Maple Grove Cemetery, Hudson, Michigan.

### 3. Fred Orson Carpenter and Ella Gertrude Silvernail

The 1900 census for Wheatland, Hillsdale, Michigan has Fred Carpenter, 30, born Jan 1870, married 9 years, a farmer. Ella G is 29 and born Aug 1870. They are living with Fred's mother Alice Carpenter who owns the farm.

The 1910 census for Hudson, Lenawee, Michigan has Fred O Carpenter, 40, married 20 years, a farmer who owns his mortgaged farm. Ella G is 39 and has 3 children, all are living. The children are Lucile C, 5; William S, 2 and Facelia E, 11/12.

The 1920 census for Moscow, Hillsdale, Michigan has Fred O Carpenter, 49, a farmer who owns his mortgaged farm. Ella is 49. The children are Lucile C, 15; William S, 12; Facelia, 10; Virginia E, 9; Evelyn, 7 and Robert D, 3.

The 1930 census for Pittsford, Hillsdale, Michigan has Fred Carpenter, 61, married at 21, a farmer who is renting his poultry farm. Ella is 60 and was married at 20. The children are Virginia, 19, a sales lady at a dry goods store; Evelyn, 15 and Robert, 12.

In 1940 Fred and Ella Carpenter were living with their daughter Virginia and her husband Lacerne Mecorney.

Fredric Orson Carpenter born 23 Jan 1870 in Wheatland, died 27 Apr 1940 in Jackson, Michigan of cardiac decompensation, carcinoma of lung and 50 years of asthma. Fred is buried in Maple Grove Cemetery, Hudson, Michigan. Ella Gertrude Silvernail Carpenter, born 19 Nov 1870 in Pittsford, Michigan, died 19 May 1943 in Jackson, Michigan and is buried with Fred. They were living with their daughter Virginia.

## 4. Lucile Carpenter and Harold McDonald

Lucille Carpenter, 19, clerk, married Harold McDonald, 20, inspector, on 18 Mar 1924 in Detroit, Michigan.

The 1930 census for Leoni, Jackson, Michigan has Harold McDonald, 26, married at 20, an inspector in a gear factory and renting a home at 108 Park Place for $25 per month. Lucile C is 25 and was married at 19. Their daughter Barbara Jean is 5.

The 1940 census for Michigan Center, Michigan has Harold H McDonald, 36, completed 10th grade, a dairy man for a Milk Company and renting a home at 641 9th Street for $20 per month. Lucile C is 35, graduated high school and a sales lady in a retail variety store. Barbara J is 15 and completed 8th grade.

## 4. William S Carpenter and Laurene Cyphers

The 1930 census for Pittsford, Hillsdale, Michigan has William Carpenter, 22 a lodger and working on the farm.

William Carpenter, 27, of Michigan Center, a machine operator married Laurene

Cyphers, 19, of Michigan Center on 9 Jun 1934 in Jackson, Michigan.

Dane Lee Carpenter born 4 Apr 1935, died 9 Oct 1935 in Foote Hospital, Jackson, Michigan. She was the daughter of William and Laurene Carpenter. She died of bronchopneumonia after 4 days in the hospital. She was buried in Woodland Cemetery.

William S Carpenter, a truck driver, born 16 Aug 1907, died 14 Nov 1936 in Foote Hospital, Jackson, Michigan of chronic myocarditis and cardiac failure. The secondary cause was valvular disease. His wife is Laurene Carpenter. The informant is Fred Carpenter, his father.

### 4. Facelia E Carpenter and Russell L Bailey

The 1930 census for Jackson, Michigan has Facelia E Carpenter, 20, a student nurse, living in the nurse's home at 1513 E Ganson Street. The nurse's home is part of Foote Memorial Hospital. Many people are living in the home and hospital.

Facelia Carpenter, 21, married Russell L Bailey, 21, on 23 Aug 1930 in Williams, Ohio.

The 1940 census for Blackman, Jackson, Michigan has Russell Bailey, 35, completed 10th grade, a life insurance salesman who owns a home at 3920 Clinton Road worth $2500. Facelia is 30 and completed 2 years high school. Their children are Ronald, 6 and Janet, 2.

### 4. Virginia Carpenter and Lacerne Mecorney

Virginia Carpenter, 26, married Lacerne Mecorney, 31, on 6 Aug 1937 in Jackson, Michigan.

The 1940 census for Jackson, Michigan has Lacerne Mecorney, 34, completed 9th grade, a machinist in aircraft and automotive industries renting a home at 801 Stewart Street for $25 per month. Virginia is 29 and completed 11th grade. Virginia's father, Fred Carpenter is 70 and completed 8th grade. Ella is 69 and graduated high school.

### 4. Evelyn L Carpenter and Carlton F Ohlerich

Evelyn Leanore Carpenter married Carlton Franklin Ohlerich on 31 Oct 1938 in Jackson, Michigan. They were divorced 7 Apr 1945 in Jackson, Michigan.

The 1940 census for Jackson, Michigan has Carl F Ohlerich, 26, completed 10th grade, an inspector for a muffler factory renting a home at 215 ½ Elm Street for $28 per month. Evelyn is 26 and completed 11th grade. Carl's sister, Belle, is 19 and graduated high school.

### 4. Robert D Carpenter and Katherine Kelley

The 1940 census for Blackman, Jackson, Michigan has Robert Carpenter, 23, completed 10th grade and a mechanic in a garage. Katherine is 21 and graduated high school. Their daughters are Janice, 2 and Jacqueline, 11/12. They are living with Katherine's widowed father and his 4 children.

## 2. Sarah Jane Carpenter and George W Bailey

The 1860 census for Wheatland, Hillsdale, Michigan has George W Bailey, 30, a farmer, with $1000 in real estate. Sarah J is 21. Both were born in New York.

George W Bailey, 33, a farmer, married, born in New York was listed 1 Jul 1863 as a possible soldier for the Civil War. He claimed general disability.

The 1870 census for Wheatland, Hillsdale, Michigan has George Bailey, 40 a farmer with $2000 in real estate. Sarah is 29. Their children are Elba, 10 and May, 4.

George W Bailey born 17 Sep 1830 died 18 Oct 1890 in Wheatland, Hillsdale, Michigan of blood poisoning and is buried in Maple Grove Cemetery, Hudson, Michigan.

Sarah J Carpenter Bailey, 64, born 10 Apr 1841, died 27 Jun 1905 of a liver disease. She was buried 29 Jun 1905 in Maple Grove Cemetery with George.

## 3. Elba Bailey and Clara Greenfield

Elba Bailey, 30, a farmer, married Clara Greenfield, 23, on 18 Feb 1891 in Hillsdale, Michigan. They were both from Wheatland, Michigan.

The 1900 census for Wheatfield, Hillsdale, Michigan has Elba Bailey, 39, born Jun 1860, married 10 years, a farmer who owns his mortgaged farm. Clara is 32, born Sept 1867 and has 1 child who is still living. Their son is George W, 5, born Apr 1895. George's mother, Sarah, 59, born Apr 1841, is living with them.

Marion Bailey born 13 Apr 1906, died 28 Apr 1909 from an accident. She was knocked down by a horse and then stepped on about noon. Marion died of hemorrhage of the lungs at 6pm the same day. She was buried in Hudson on 1 May 1909.

The 1910 census for Wheatfield, Hillsdale, Michigan has Elba Bailey, 49, married 19 years, a farmer who owns his farm free and clear. Clara is 42 and had 2 children, one is living. George is 15 and attending school.

The 1920 census for Wheatland, Hillsdale, Michigan has Elba Bailey, 59, a farmer on the home farm. Clara is 52,

Elba George Bailey born 17 Jun 1860, died 26 Aug 1925 of arteriosclerosis and cerebral hemorrhage. He was a farmer and the son of George Bailey and Sarah Carpenter. The informant is Clara Bailey. He was buried 29 Aug 1925 in Hudson, Michigan. Clara continued to live on the farm and is in the 1930 and 1940 census data. She died Jan 1955 and is buried with Elba George.

## 4. George Washington Bailey and Mary Rose Berridge

George Washington Bailey, 22, a farmer, married Mary Rose Berridge, 24, a school teacher on 29 Nov 1917 in Hudson, Michigan.

The 1920 census for Wheatland, Hillsdale, Michigan has George Bailey, 24, a farmer who is renting his general farm. Mary is 26.

The 1930 census for Wheatland, Hillsdale, Michigan has George W Bailey, 35, married at 22, a manager on a general farm. Mary R is 36 and was married at 23. Their daughter Marjorie L is 7. Paul Knight, 21 is a lodger and labor on the general farm.

The 1940 census for Wheatland, Hillsdale, Michigan has George W Bailey, 45, graduated high school, a farmer who owns his farm on Somerset Road worth $1500. Mary is 46 and graduated high school. Marjorie is 17 and completed 10th grade. They have hired hands living with them and working on the farm. Earl Cunningham is 27 and Gerald Bradley is 18. According to his daughter, George Bailey was a very progressive farmer and used tractors early. He would not have horses on the farm.

## 3. Ethie May Bailey and Orestus Cheney / Henry Henning / Earnest H Root

Ethie May Bailey, 17, married Orestus Cheney, 20, a farmer on 31 Oct 1883 in Wheatland, Michigan. They had a daughter Caroline Mae born 1887.

Ethie and Orestus divorced sometime before 1895. Orestus married Eva Spore 26 Feb 1895.

May Bailey Cheney, 29 married Henry Henning, 36, a farmer on 18 Feb 1897 in Clayton, Michigan.

The 1900 census for Hudson, Lenawee, Michigan has Henry Henning, 42, born Feb 1858, married 3 years, a farmer renting his farm. May is 34, born 1866, and has 1 child still living. Henry's son is Claude, 5, born Feb 1895. Ethie's daughter is Carrie Chenry, 12, born Oct 1888.

Claude Henning, 15, born 14 Jan 1895, died 24 Jun 1910 of anemia following measles and pneumonia. He is buried in Maple grove Cemetery.

Henry Henning, 50, born 18 Feb 1859, died 6 Oct 1909 in Hudson, Michigan. He is buried in Maple Grove Cemetery.

May Henning, 40, a widow, married Earnest H Root, 37, a farmer, on 28 Feb 1910 in Lucas County, Ohio.

The 1910 census for Wheatland, Hillsdale, Michigan has Earnest H Root, 37, married twice, a farmer renting his farm. May is 40 and married twice. Earnest's father, Erskine, 67, a widower is a farm laborer who works out.

May Bailey Root born 1866, died 31 Aug 1918 in Toledo. She is buried in Maple Grove Cemetery, Hudson, Michigan.

## 4. Caroline Mae Cheney and Charles E Badgley

Caroline Cheney, 18, married Charles E Badgley, 26, a railroad man on 3 Oct 1906 in Williams County, Ohio.

The 1920 census for Toledo, Ohio has Charles E Badgley, 39, a salesman in a furniture store, renting a home at 2428 Broadway Street. Carrie M is 31. Their children are Russell A, 12; Marella W, 11 and Rachel M 9.

The 1930 census for Toledo, Ohio has Charles E Badgley, 49, married at 26, a book salesman, renting a home at 1130 Harding for $40 per month. Caroline is 41 and married at 18. Their children are Russell A, 22, a laborer in trucking and Rachel M, 19 a file clerk in the telephone office. Also living with them is Fredrick D Hagaman, 22, son-in-law, married at 19 and a yacht fitter at a yacht Club. Marcella W, daughter, 21 and married at 18. Their granddaughter is Doris M, 10/12.

The 1940 census for Toledo, Ohio has Caroline Badgley, 50, married, completed 10$^{th}$ grade and renting a home at 2729 ½ 116$^{th}$ Street. Russell is 32, graduated high school and a spark plug salesman. Rachel is 27, graduated high school and manager of a retail department store.

Charles Badgley born 28 May 1880 in Clayton, Michigan, died 4 Oct 1964 in New Mexico.

Caroline Cheney Badgley, born 8$^{th}$ Oct 1888, died 1971 and is buried in Lauderdale Memorial Park, Fort Lauderdale, Florida.

## 5. Marcella W Badgley and Fredrick Hagaman

Marcella W Badgley, 19, married Fred Hagaman, 22, a boat builder, on 19 Jun 1927 in Monroe, Michigan. They were living with her parents in 1930.

The 1940 census for Toledo, Ohio has Fredrick Hagaman, 32, graduated high school, captain of a private yacht and renting a home at 2935 118$^{th}$ Street. Marcella is 31 and graduated high school. Doris is 10 and completed 5th grade.

## 2. Mariette Carpenter and Michael E Dillon

Mattie Carpenter, 26, married Michael E Dillion, 27, a farmer, on 4 Dec 1873 in Wheatland, Michigan. Rev B D Congling officiated.

The 1880 census for Hudson, Lenawee, Michigan has Michael Dillon, 33, a farmer, born in Michigan. Mary Ette is 33 and born in New York. Their son, Fredie, is 5.

The 1900 census for Hudson, Lenawee, Michigan has Michael Dillon, 54, born Feb 1846, married 27 years, a farmer who owns his farm free and clear. Mariette is 54, was born May 1846 and has 2 children, both are living. The children are Fred J 24, born Dec 1874 and Nina R, 15, born Dec 1884.

The 1910 census has Michael E Dillon, 64, married 37 years and owns his farm. Mariette is 65 and has had 2 children. Fred J is 36, single, and a manufacturer of cheese.

The 1920 census for Hudson, Michigan has Michael E Dillon, 73, owns his home at 316 East Main Street. Mariette is 74. Their grandson, Dillon Sweezey, 6, is living with them.

Marietta Dillon, born 6 May 1846 in Watertown, New York, died 12 Oct 1928 of an intestinal disorder. M E Dillon was the informant. She was buried in Maple Grove cemetery, Hudson, Michigan on 14 Oct 1928.

Her obituary appeared in the Hudson Post-Gazette on 16 Oct 1928.
Mrs Mariette Dillon died at her home on Main Street, 12 Oct. Burial in Maple Grove. Born in Watertown, NY 6 May 1846, she was the daughter of M/M Orson Carpenter who came to Wheatland when she was 10. She married M E Dillon. They had a son, Fred J Dillon, of SE of the city; a grandson, M E Sweezey, of Addison and grandsons, Parker and Clare Dillon, of SE of the city. A daughter, Mrs Nina Sweezey, died about 13 years ago. (1915)[7]

First names were often misspelled or several names were used. Before Social Security numbers, a legal name was not as important and could be changed easily.

Michael E Dillion born 28 Feb 1846, died 27 Apr 1932 in Hudson, Michigan and is buried with Marietta.

## 3. Fred J Dillon and Phoebe Parker

Fred J Dillon, 37, a coal dealer, married Pheo Parker, 24, on 4 Oct 1913 in Addison, Michigan.

Fred J Dillon, 44, born 29 Dec 1874, registered for WW1 on 12 Sep 1918. His nearest relative is Pheo Dillon.

The 1920 census for Addison, Michigan has Fred J Dillion, 46, a worker at a battery manufacturing company who owns his mortgaged home on Lake Street. Phoebe is 30 and their son, Parker M, is 5.

The 1930 census for Hudson, Lenawee, Michigan has Fred J Dillon, 54, married at 39, a farmer who is renting his farm and has a radio. Pheo is 41 and married at 25. Their sons are Parker M, 15 and Clare F, 9.

Fred J Dillon, born 29 Dec 1874, died 11 Nov 1936 in Addison, Michigan of apoplexy. Pheo Dillon is the informant. Fred is buried at Hillside Cemetery, Addison, Michigan.

The 1940 census for Addison, Michigan has Pheo Dillon, 51, completed 10th grade and owns her home on Jackson Street worth $500. Clare is 19, graduated high school and a farm laborer. Charles Parker, Pheo's father is 82, widowed and completed 8th grade.

Clare served in the Army during WW11.

## 4. Parker Dillon and Beulah Kuhn

Parker Dillon, 24, married Beulah Kuhn, 25, on 3 Apr 1937 in Indiana.

The 1940 census for Hillsdale, Michigan has Parker Dillon, 26, graduated high school, a baker in a bakery renting his home on Carlton Road for $15 per month. Beulah is 34, graduated high school and working as an inspector in a pants factory.

Parker Dillon born 21 Oct 1914, died 27 Oct 1985 and served in the Navy from 22 Jun 1944 to 23 Dec 1945.

## 3. Nina R Dillon and Harry Sweezey

Nina Dillon, 24, married Harry Sweezey, 28, a farmer, on 15 Jan 1908 in Hudson, Michigan.

The 1910 census for Rollin, Lenawee, Michigan has Harry Sweezey, 31, married 2 years, a farmer who owns his mortgaged farm. Nina is 26. Nina's uncle, Francis Dillon is living with them.

Nina R Sweezey Dillon, 32, born 29 Dec 1884, died 18 Feb 1916 in Rollin, Lenawee, Michigan of Tuberculosis. She is buried in Maple Grove Cemetery, Hudson, Michigan.

The 1920 census for Rollin, Lenawee, Michigan has Harry Sweezey, 41, widowed, a farmer who owns his farm on Manitou Beach Road. His son Dillon, 6, is living with his grandparents.

By 1930 Harry has remarried, owns a grocery store and is living in Lansing.

### 4. M E "Dillon" Sweezey and Carla Belle Jewell

The 1930 census for Rollin, Lenawee, Michigan has M E Sweezey, 16, a second cousin, attending school and living with Jay and Grace Crofoot.

M E Sweezey, 23, born 24 Apr 1913, a bookkeeper, married Carla Belle Jewell, 19, born 15 Jun 1914, on 12 Jan 1934 in LaGrange, Indiana. Carla's parents are Mace and Mildred Jewell.

The 1940 census for Hudson, Lenawee, Michigan has M E Sweezey, 27, completed 1-year college, a farmer who owns his farm. Carla B is 24 and completed 1-year college. The children are Beverly Ann, 4; Stephen J, 3; and Jewel K, 2.

### 2. Ellen Louise Carpenter and Fred Stanley

Ellen and Fred are in Chapter 12.

# Chapter 12

## Fred Stanley and Ella Louise Carpenter

1. Ellen Louise Carpenter (1856-1924) *
+ Fred C Stanley (1864-1939)
    2. Mabel Adell Stanley (1884-1945) *
   + Arthur Snyder (1879-1963)
       3. Harry Allen Snyder (1905-1980)
      + Geraldine June Black (1911-)
          4. Harry Allen Snyder Jr (1929-)
          4. Clare N Snyder (1934-)
      + Alice Lucille Fuller (1913-)
       3. Ruth E Snyder (1911-2001)
      + Gerald E. Allen (1912-1970)
          4. Virgil Allen (1934-)
          4. Howard B Allen (1936-)
          4. Dorothy M Allen (1940-)
       3. Walter C. Snyder (1915-1932)
       3. Helen Evelyn Snyder (1924-2006)
    2. Orson Stanley (1885-1919) *
   + Clydia Altensee (1888-1943)
    2. Blanche M Stanley (1887-1956) *
   + Elvin Sherman Gibbs (1878-1961)
       3. Fred S Gibbs (1906-1975)
      + Elsie M Cain (1911-)
          4. Roberta M Gibbs (1929-)
          4. Donna Jean Gibbs (1931-1990)
          4. Juanita Gibbs (1935-)
       3. Leon Gibbs (1908-1927)
       3. Edna Lucile Gibbs (1918-1984)
      + Harold Russell (1914-1959) WW11
          4. Elvin Russell (1937-)
          4. Ronald Russell (1938-)
          4. James Russell (1940-)
       3. Stanley Gibbs (1921-1992) WW11
    2. Charlie Stanley (1889-1889)
    **2. Mae Louise Stanley (1892-1945) ***
   **+ Charles T Bishop (1888-1954)**

*Pictured in Orson Carpenter Family Photograph taken between 1896 and 1899. (Page 356)

**1. Fred Stanley and Ella Louise Carpenter**

Fred C Stanley, 19, a farmer, of Wheatland and Ella Louise Carpenter, 20, of Wheatland were married 20 Mar 1884 in Rollin, Michigan. Rev. Bailey a clergyman officiated, Mrs. Mary Bailey of Rollin and Alma E Cerandall of Rollin were witness. Ella was actually 27 at the time but apparently didn't want to admit it.

Mabel Ardell Stanley was born 31 Oct 1884. Fred and Ella probably lived with the Carpenters at first until they could afford a home of their own.

Fred Stanley worked for a logging company in the mid1880s.
He is pictured standing on the ground on the far left. Others are unknown.

This was obviously an unusually large log to have a picture. The greatest production of lumber was in 1889. Most of the lower peninsula of Michigan had been logged out by the end of the 19th century and logs as large as this were a rarity. Most of the production was from smaller, younger trees. Fred worked away from home somewhere in northern Michigan. Lumberjacks worked long hours for $20 to $30 per month plus room and board. This doesn't seem like much but may have been the extra needed to help support his growing family.

Orson was born in 1885 and Blanche in 1888.
A son Charlie was born in 1889 and died soon after. The obituary appeared in the

Hudson Post.
Stanley, 18 Oct 1889, Hudson Post
The infant child of M/M Fred Stanley was buried last Sunday at Church's Corners. [7]

Ella Carpenter's father Orson Carpenter died in 1899. She inherited her father's farm. It was not in Fred Stanley's name but always in Ella's name.[6]

About this time Ella or her father bought a cylinder phonograph. It was later in the attic of the Carpenter place. The Bishop children, Ella's grandchildren played with it.

The 1900 census for Wheatland, Hillsdale, Michigan has Fred C Stanley, 35, born Dec 1864, married 16 years, a farmer who owns his farm free and clear. Ella L is 43, born Oct 1856 and had 5 children with 4 still living. The children are Mable, 15, born Oct 1884; Orson, 14, born Nov 1885; Blanche, 11, born Jun 1888 and Mae, 7, born July 1892. Orson, Blanche and May were all at school.

A School picture was taken about 1903 of the children attending the old brick Taylor School. Mae Stanley is standing 2nd from left next to the teacher.[6] The school only had classes through the 8th grade so Mae's older siblings, Mable, Orson and Blanche are not pictured.

A picture was taken probably in front of the George Klingensmith home in Pittsford about the time Mae Stanley started high school in 1906.

Mae Stanley is standing 4th from the right in the top rows. This appears to be a school class or choir. Pictures of this type were very popular in the early 1900's.

The 1910 census for Wheatland, Hillsdale, Michigan has Fred C Stanley, 45, married 26 years, a farmer on a general farm. Ellen is 52 and had 5 children 4 are living. Their daughter, Mae, is 17. Orson, Mable and Blanche have left home.

Mae Stanley graduated from Pittsford High School in 1910. This is her graduation picture.

The 1920 census for Wheatland, Hillsdale, Michigan has Fred Stanley, 55, a farmer who owns his farm. Ella is 61.

Ellen L Carpenter Stanley, born 23 Oct 1856, died 28 Sep 1924 of chronic valvular heart disease. She was buried on 1 Oct 1924 in Locust Corners Cemetery.

The 1930 census for Wheatland, Hillsdale, Michigan has Fred C Stanley, 65, a farmer who owned his farm worth $3000. Living with him are Fred S Gibbs, 24, grandson, a farm laborer; Elsie M, 19, grandson's wife and Roberta M, 1 3/12, great granddaughter. After this census Fred moved in with his daughter Blanche Stanley Gibbs.

Fred C Stanley, born 14 Dec 1864, died 14 Dec 1939, on his 75th birthday, at Thorn Hospital in Hudson, Michigan. Fred had been living at Manitou Beach, Michigan with his daughter Blanche. Fred was born in Wheatfield, Hillsdale, Michigan. His parents were John Stanley and Elizabeth Klingensmith both from Germany. The informant on the death certificate is Mable Snyder of North Adams, Michigan. Burial was in Locust Corners Cemetery on 16 Dec 1939 next to Ella. The cause of death was Later Pneumonia. He was admitted to the hospital just one day before he died.

## 2. Mable Stanley and Arthur Snyder

Mable Stanley was married to Arthur Snyder about 1901. This picture was taken around the time of their marriage.

The 1910 census for Wheatland, Hillsdale, Michigan has Arthur Snyder, 31, married 9 years, a farmer on a general farm, renting his farm. Mabel is 25 and has one child, still living. Their son, Harry is 4.

Arthur Snyder registered for WW1 on 12 Sep 1918. Arthur was 39, born 25 May 1879, a farmer and living at RFD # 2, Pittsford, Hillsdale, Michigan. His nearest relative was Mable Snyder.

The 1920 census for Wheatland, Hillsdale, Michigan, has Arthur Snider, 40, a farmer who owns his mortgaged farm. Mabel is 35. The children are Harry, 14, attended school; Ruth, 8, attended school; and Walter, 4 8/12.

The 1930 census for Wheatland, Hillsdale, Michigan has Arthur Snyder, 50, married at 22, a farmer who owns a farm worth $4000 and a radio. Mabel A is 45, married at 17 and an independent paperhanger. The children are Ruth E, 18, a helper in a private home; Walter C, 14, attended school and Helen E, 6.

Walter C Snyder, born 20 Apr 1915, died 23 Dec 1932 of Pleurisy and Streptococcus. The doctors had performed an operation on 20 Dec 1932 for emphysema of the left Pleura. He is buried in Locust Corners Cemetery. He was 17 years old.

The 1940 census for Wheatland, Hillsdale, Michigan has Arthur Snyder, 60, completed 8th grade, a farmer who owns his farm on North Adams Road. Mabel is 55 and completed 9th grade. Helen is 16 and has completed 9th grade.

Mabel Adell Stanley Snyder born 31 Oct 1884, died 20 Apr 1945 in Addison, Michigan. Arthur Snyder born 25 May 1879, died 11 Apr 1963 in Hudson, Michigan and is buried with Mabel in Locust Corners Cemetery.

### 3. Harry Allen Snyder and Geraldine June Black / Alice Lucille Fuller

Harry Allen Snyder, 21, of Wheatland, a clerk married Geraldine June Black, 16 of Wheatland on 12 Feb 1927 at the Wheatland Congregational Church.

The 1930 census for Wheatland, Hillsdale, Michigan has Harry A Snyder, 24, married at 21, a salesman in a general store renting his home for $3 per month. Geraldine J is 19 and married at 16. Their son Harry A Jr is 1 4/12.

Harry A Snyder filed for divorce from Geraldine J Snyder on 6 Jan 1938 which was granted for extreme cruelty on 2 May 1938. There were 2 children, Harry A Snyder, 9 and Clare N Snyder, 4.

Harry Allen Snyder, 33, born 4 Jun 1905 married Alice Lucille Fuller, 25, born 11 Nov 1913, on 7 May 1938 in Angola, Indiana.

The 1940 census for Wheatland, Hillsdale, Michigan has Harry Snyder, 34, completed 10th grade, a milk truck driver renting a home on Saunders Road for $5 per month. Alice is 26 and completed 10th grade. Harry's son, Clare is 6.

The 1940 census for Morton, Mecosta, Michigan has Norman Black, 62, a farmer. Emma is 48. Their grandson, Harry Snyder is 11 and completed 6th grade.

### 3. Ruth Emma Snyder and Gerald Elmer Allen

Ruth Emma Snyder, 20, married Gerald Elmer Allen, 20, on 24 Dec 1931 at the Auslon Church parsonage in Pioneer, Ohio.

The 1940 census for North Adams, Michigan has Gerald Allen, 27, completed 10th grade, a salesman for Rawleigh Products who owns his home at 207 Wilbur Street. Ruth E is 28 and completed 8th grade. Their children are Howard B, 4; Virgil, 6 and Dorothy M less than a year.

## 2. Orson C Stanley and Clydia Altensee

The 1910 census for Fairview, Frontier, Nebraska has Orson C Stanley, 25, newly married, a house painter renting his home. Clydia I is 22. Freddie Altensee, nephew, 3 is living with them.

Orson Stanley registered for WW1 on 12 Sep 1918. He was living at RFD 1, Allen, Hillsdale, Michigan where he was working as a self-employed thrasher. His nearest relative is Clydia Stanley.

Orson Stanley, 33, born 3 Nov 1885, died 5 Apr 1919, in Quincey, Branch, Michigan of influenza. The informant is Fred C Stanley. It may have been the Spanish Flu in the great epidemic of 1918-1919. Orson is buried in Locust Corner's Cemetery.

The following obituaries appeared in the Hudson Post-Gazette.

Stanley, Orson, 8 Apr 1919 Hudson Post-Gazette
Orson Stanley died at Allen, Michigan, Friday, from flu. His father, Fred Stanley, lives near Pittsford. Survived by his wife.[7]

11 Apr Post-Gazette - Orson C Stanley was born in Pittsford Township 3 Nov 1885, & died 5 Apr at his home in Quincey, aged 33. Spent early part of his life in Wheatland Township. Went to Neb in 1907, where on 7 Dec 1909, he married Clydia I Altensee. In 1911 they moved to Wheatland Township. Leaves his wife, parents and 3 sisters.[7]

## 2. Blanche Stanley and Elvin S Gibbs

Blanche M Stanley, 18, of Hudson, Michigan, married Elvin S Gibbs, 25, of Rollin, Michigan, a farmer on 23 Nov 1903. His parents were S N Gibbs and Mary Sherman. Her parents were Fred Stanley and Ella Carpenter. J I Nickerson of Adrian, M E minister officiated. Elbert Gibbs and Ada M Nickerson were witnesses.

The 1910 census for Wheatland, Hillsdale, Michigan has Elvin Gibbs, 32, married 7 years, a farmer on a rented farm. Blanch is 24 and has two children both are living. The children are Fred, 4 and Leon, 1 8/12. Fred and Ella Stanley are two families away.

Elvin Sherman Gibbs, 40, 6 Jan 1878, registered for WW1 on 12 Sep 1918. He is farming on his own with an address of Hudson, Michigan. Blanche Gibbs is next of kin.

The 1920 census for Wheatland, Hillsdale, Michigan has Elvin Gibbs, 43, a farmer who owns his mortgaged farm. Blanche is 33. Their children are Fred, 14; Leon, 11; and Edna C, 1 8/12.

Leon E Gibbs, 19, born 22 Jun 1908, died 1 Aug 1927. He was in a motor cycle accident 31 Jul 1927. He was thrown off the cycle. He was taken to Thorn Hospital in Hudson with a fracture of facial plate and skull. Leon was buried 3 Aug 1927 in Maple Grove Cemetery, Hudson, Michigan. The motorcycle slid in loose gravel on a dirt road while he was going too fast according to his cousin, George Bishop. George would not go near a motorcycle.

The 1930 census for Rollin, Lenawee, Michigan has Elvin S Gibbs, 52, married at 25, a farmer renting his farm. Blanche M is 42 and married at 16. The children are Edna L, 11, attended school and Stanley P, 9, attended school.

The 1940 census for Rollin, Lenawee, Michigan has Elvin Gibbs, 62, completed 8th grade, a farmer on a rented farm. Blanche is 52 and completed 8th grade. Stanley is 20, graduated high school and working on the farm.

Blanch Stanley Gibbs born 25 Jun 1888, died 28 Jun 1956.
Gibbs, Blanche   June 28, 1956   Addison Courier
Mrs. Blanche Gibbs, 68, Redford Rd, Manitou Beach, Rome Township, died at Addison Hospital. Born June 25 1888, daughter of M/M Fred Stanley. Leaves husband Elvin Gibbs of Manitou Beach; 2 sons Fred of MB & Stanley of Jerome; a daughter, Mrs. Harold Russell of MB; 19 grandkids & 10 great grands. Predeceased by her parents, 2 sis & a bro. Burial in Maple Grove, Hudson. Blanche's funeral was held at Rome Baptist Church.

Elvin Sherman Gibbs born 1878, died 2 Jul 1961 and is buried beside Blanche.

### 3. Fred S Gibbs and Elsa M Cain

Fred S Gibbs, 22, a farmer married Elsa M Cain, 17, on 27 Jul 1928 in Wauseon, Ohio.

The 1930 census for Wheatland, Hillsdale, Michigan has Fred C Stanley, 65, widowed, a farmer who owns his farm worth $3000. Fred S Gibbs is 24, grandson, married at 22, and a laborer on a general farm. Elsie M is 19, grandson's wife and married at 17. Roberta M is 1 3/12 and a great granddaughter.

The 1940 census for Rollin, Lenawee, Michigan has Fred Gibbs, 34, completed 7th grade, a farm laborer on a rented farm. Elsa is 29 and completed 7th grade. The children are Roberta, 11, attended school; Donna, 9, attended school and Juanita, 5.

Fred S Gibbs, born 27 Mar 1906, died 21 Jul 1975 at Manitou Beach, Michigan and is buried in Maple Grove Cemetery, Hudson, Michigan.

### 3. Edna Lucile Gibbs and Harold O Russell

The 1940 census for Rollin, Lenawee, Michigan has Harold Russell, 26, completed 8th grade, a farm laborer renting his home for $5 per month. Edna L is 21 and graduated high school. The children are Elvin A, 3; Ronald, 2 and James F, 5 months. Harold's mother and 4 children are living with them.

Harold O Russell enlisted in the Army 22 Jan 1944. He was given a less than honorable discharge 9 Jul 1949. The rank is private and branch is 877 Heavy Ordinance. He served in an automotive maintenance company.

Harold Russell born 15 Feb 1914, died 25 Jul 1959 and was buried in Woodstock Cemetery, Devils Lake, Michigan with a bronze marker furnished by the US Army. Application for marker was signed by Donald F Murphy.

Edna had 9 sons and 3 daughters with Harold Russell in 22 years. After Harold died, Edna married Leonard B LaCoe. Edna Lucille Gibbs LaCoe born 18 May 1918, died 16 Nov 1984 and is buried in Woodstock Cemetery, Addison, Michigan.

### 3. Stanley P Gibbs

Stanley was living with his parents in 1940. He served in WW11, enlisting on 21 May 1942 and discharged 2 Jan 1945.

### 2. Mae Louise Stanley and Charles T Bishop

Charles and Mae Bishop are in Chapter 16. Charles' mother was Katherine Müller. Her family is in Chapter 13. The Bishops are in Chapter 14 and Charles' parents are in Chapter 15.

# Chapter 13

## Christian Müller and Margaretha Essen

1. Christian G Müller (1833-1884)
+ Margaretha E Essen (1834-1905)
　　2. Louisa W Müller (1864-1931)
　　　+ Theodore H Damm (1861-1915)
　　　　　3. Theodore H Damm Jr. (1886-1954)
　　　　　　+ Charlotte B Hartmann (1892-1969)
　　　　　　　　4. Theodore L Damm (1920-2008) WW11
　　　　　　　　4. Robert W Damm (1922-1943) WW11
　　　　　　　　4. Charlotte Damm (1927-)
　　　　　3. Louis Damm (1890-1941) WW1
　　　　　　+ Mary Halpin (1894-1968)
　　　　　　　　4. May Damm (1925-)
　　　　　3. Luscada "Lucy" G Damm (1896-1979)
　　2. Christina H Müller (1866-1957)
　　　+ Adolf Wagner (1862 -1931)
　　　　　3. Louise Caroline Wagner (1888-1966)
　　　　　　+ Joseph Dewitt Baldwin (1887-1975)
　　　　　　　　4. Herbert D Baldwin (1908-1909)
　　　　　　　　4. DeWitt Baldwin (1913-1980)
　　　　　　　　　+ Helen (1908-1995)
　　　　　　　　4. Everett J Baldwin (1919-2001) WW11
　　　　　　　　4. Walter F Baldwin (1921-1992) WW11
　　　　　3. Anna C Wagner (1890-1969)
　　　　　　+ Frank Drinkwater (1892-1964)
　　　　　　　　4. Frank Drinkwater (1917-1996)
　　　　　　　　4. William Henry Drinkwater (1918-1997)
　　　　　　　　4. Anna Drinkwater (1920-2008)
　　　　　　　　　+ Clifford E Lee (1913-)
　　　　　3. Henry Adolph Wagner (1893-1965) WW1
　　　　　　+ Eleanor A (1900-1973)
　　　　　　　　4. Edward Wagner (1921-)
　　**2. Katherine Johanne (Katie) Müller (1869-1909)**
　　**+ Theodore Bishop (1868-1951)**
　　　　　**3. Charles T Bishop (1888-1954) Spanish American War**
　　　　　**+ Mae Louise Stanley (1892-1945)**
　　　　　3. Clara Bishop (1890-1962)
　　　　　3. Gertrude Bishop (1893-1964)
　　　　　　+ William O Saxton (1889-1950)
　　　　　　+ Fredrick K Cavalier (1920-1976
　　　　　3. Esther M Bishop (1894-1973)
　　　　　　+ Stephen Grandner (1889-1981)

                3. Theodore Bishop (1894-1976)
                  + Elizabeth Gulisippi (1894-1983)
          2. Margaret E Miller (1872-1946)
            + George O Baldwin (1871-1947)
                3. George Nelson Baldwin (1896-1978)
                  + Clairesse May Hawkins (1898-1984)
                      4. George Nelson Baldwin (1921-2011) WW11
                      4. Howard J Baldwin (1924-1988) WW11
                3. Harvey "Harry" Percy Baldwin (1899-1963)
          2. Ibe Henry Miller (1877-1941)
            + Ada L Capron (1879-1964)


**1. Christian Gustav Müller and Margaretha Essen**

A list of German Immigrant Passengers has a Christian Müller 19 from Gotha, landing 22 Jun 1853. Gotha is South east of Hanover and may have been part of Prussia, then or later. This could be our Christian Müller, the age is close and there is conflicting information about where he came from in different census reports. At that time, without birth certificates, an individual's age and place of birth were open to interpretation by whoever was giving the information.

The 1855 New York State census for New York City Ward 12 for Ward's Island Emigrants Refuge and Hospital has a long list of inmates. Christian Müller, 33, from Germany is an inmate of ward number 43, medical. The age should be 23 but could be wrong the next person is 23, so they may have been switched. There were 64 inmates in the ward.

Christian Müller became a naturalized citizen 30 Sep 1856. He is from Grand Duke Baden. No address is given for Christian but the witness is Henry Seger of 53 Suffolk Street, New York City. In 1855 Henry Seger, 36, a shoemaker, was living in a frame house with three other families. There was a total of 24 people in the dwelling, 5 were boarders. There were, 2 porters, a seamstress, a cooper, a seaman and 2 tailors. Baden, Wurttemberg and Bavaria are very close and were used interchangeably. Christian Müller may have gone north through Hanover and Gotha to sail out of Bremerhaven or Hamburg.

The 1860 census for New York City, Ward 8 District 3, has Christian Müller, 23, a baker from Bavaria. He is living with a master baker from Würtemberg, the baker's wife and 7 children and 3 other bakers for a total of 13 in the dwelling, all from some part of Germany. It appears to be a poor neighborhood with a mix of immigrants of all races. Christian's age would correspond to the 1870 census.

It is not known which of the above entries are our Christian Müller. Being detained for illness was not unusual even before Ellis Island. There are several Christian Müllers as it is a common name.

The 1860 census for New York City, 1st division 19th Ward lists Margaret Hesson 23, a servant from Bavaria. The head of household is 40, a brewer and from Bavaria. He has a wife and 5 children. Living with them are 6 men also brewers, a teamster, a man with no listed occupation, and 3 servant girls, a total of 18 people. Most are in their 20s or 30s and all are from Germany. They are in dwelling 1012, family 2162. This is the only family listed in the dwelling.

Others nearby in the census have several families in a dwelling. The census taker wrote down all the names so he could have easily heard Essen as Hesson. The same is true for passenger lists. They are all written by one person who may not have heard the name right and it seems often had poor handwriting. The above census information may not be our Margaretha but the conditions are typical for New York immigrants of the time. Dwellings may be an apartment building with several different apartments or a building with retail on the lower floor and living spaces above. The brewer and his renters probably lived above the bier (beer) saloon.

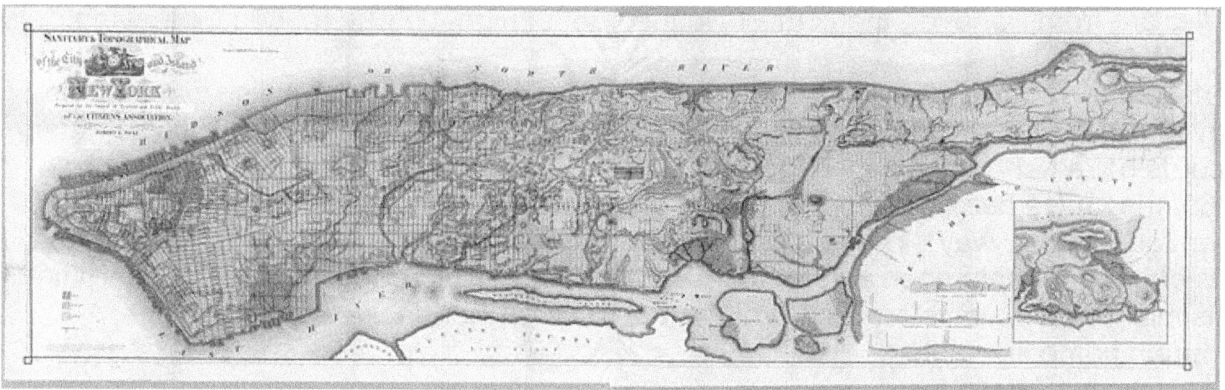

Immigrants from all over Europe landed in lower Manhattan and moved into crowded neighborhoods. Tenements usually consisted of a small back bedroom, a kitchen/living area and a front room with window. Many families rented out beds in the front room which may have included meals. At other times some type of home industry was carried out in the front room. Families did not have a whole apartment to themselves. Other buildings had retail space on the bottom floor and living space on the upper floors. All had shared outdoor toilets, 3 or 4 outhouses between buildings. The above map of 1865 New York shows the crowded conditions in lower Manhattan, left side of map. The small darker blue/green rectangle is the beginning of Central Park. North of there, to the right, is more open Harlem. At this time New York was only Manhattan Island and ended at the Harlem River, right side of map.

Margaretha arrived in 1855 but a passenger list was not found. Margaretha Müller became a naturalized citizen 8 Apr 1864. Her address was 50th street between 6th and 7th avenue. Her former nationality was Bavaria. Manhattan has a 50th street between 6th and 7th avenues just South of Central Park. This would place the Müllers in Manhattan in 1864. They may have wanted to be US Citizens before the children were born.

The 1870 census for Oyster Bay, Queens, New York has Chris Müller, 33, born in Württemberg, a laborer with $500 in real estate and $200 in personal estate. Margaretha is 32, keeping house and born in Württemberg. They have three daughters all born in New York, Louisa, 6; Augusta, 3 and Katie, 1. The parents of both were of foreign birth and Chris was a citizen eligible to vote.

The 1880 census for Oyster Bay, Queens, New York has Christian Miller, 48, a farmer from Prussia. Margaret E is 45, housekeeping and from Prussia. The children are Louisa W, 16; Christina H, 14; Catherina J 11, Margaret E, 8 and Ibe H, 4. All the children were born in New York. This listing is in conflict with the ages of the parents in the 1870 but may be more accurate. The place of birth, Würtemberg, is also different.

A daughters 1930 census listing has both her parents born in Hanover Germany. Hanover can refer to a region or a city. The city is directly South of Hamburg and West of Berlin. The region of Hanover was annexed by Prussia in 1866. The city of Hanover became the capital of the Prussian Province of Hanover. If Christian and Margaretha Müller are from Hanover, the conflicts in the 1850s might be one reason for leaving.

Christian and Margaretha must have been married about 1863 as Louisa was born in May of 1864. One source, a death index, has Louisa born in Manhattan while cemetery records have her born in Bethpage. Augusta (Christina), born 1866, and Katie, born 1869, may have been born in Manhattan or Oyster Bay, Long Island. No evidence has been found either way. The conflict over Württemberg or Prussia may mean that there was one parent from each and the census taker only wrote down the one he heard first. This may remain a mystery as it is difficult to trace further back especially with a common name like Müller.

Christian died in 1884 so he is not in the 1900 census which lists year of arrival in the United States. With no firm date of arrival, it is difficult to find a passenger ship which might have more information.

Christian wrote a will on 6 Jan 1884.
I Christian Gustav Müller of the town of Oyster Bay, Queens County, New York being of sound and disposing mind and memory, and considering the uncertainty of this life, do make, publish and declare this to be my last Will and Testament, as follows:
First after my lawful debts and funeral expenses are paid, I give device and bequeath to my wife Margaretha Müller all my Real Estate and personal property of what nature or kind or wheresoever situated of which I may die, for her use and benefit for and during her natural life.
Second – At the death of my said wife Margaretha – I direct and empower my executor here in after named to divide all of Real and Personal property there remaining among my five children, Louisa, Christina, Catherine, Margaretha and Henry Müller in manner following. To each of my four daughters one sixth part and to my said son Henry two

sixths parts of said estate then remaining. I hereby appoint my friend Edward G Raul MD to be executor of this last will and testament. The will was recorded in the Surrogate Court of Queens County, New York on April 9, 1884.

The gravestone in St John of Jerusalem Cemetery has:
IN MEMORY OF
CHRISTIAN G MILLER
BORN JAN 25, 1833
DIED FEB 22, 1884
HIS WIFE
MARGARETHA E MILLER
BORN SEPT 20, 1834
DIED AUG 9, 1905
GONE BUT NOT FORGOTTEN

According to the gravestone, they should have been 37 and 36 in 1870. Either the gravestone or the census is off. It is the same couple, as the names are unique. The name was changed from Müller to Miller later in life, or was the preferred name of the person buying the stone.[22]

Christian and Margaretha Miller are in Lot # 44 of St. John of Jerusalem Cemetery. The other burials on this lot have the last name of Baldwin. The last contact for this plot was a Baldwin in 1988.[23] There are other stones in St. John of Jerusalem Cemetery for Baldwin and Damm. Baldwin, George O (22 June 1871 to 16 Nov 1947) and Margaret (20 Sep 1871 to 2 Nov 1946). Louise or Louisa Damm died 8 Mar 1931 and is buried in grave 217 west of lot 119. South of the path by Harry Tutor of Hicksville, New York. Louis Damm born 10 Jul 1890, died 20 Apr 1941, was buried 23 Apr 1941 in grave # 246, North of his mother by Arthur White of Farmingdale, Long Island. George Baldwin and Louis Damm were both members of the Bethpage Fire Department.[22,23]
Charles T Bishop recited a ditty: "A Bishop took a Damm Wagon load of Baldwin Apples to the Miller". All the names were of relatives.

Margaretha was living with her son Henry in 1900. She was born Sep 1834 and immigrated in 1855.

The map of Oyster Bay Township, Nassau County, New York on Long Island, on the following page, although from 2000 may help locate the various members of the Müller family. Broadway and Stewart Avenues come nearly together just north of Baldwin Place. Central went through the village of Central Park at one time and connects with Hicksville Road just to the West of the map going NW. Although part of Bethpage now, all of these areas were part of Oyster Bay. The airport and plant were farther South but are now at the end of Grumman Road. Central Park Village became Bethpage.

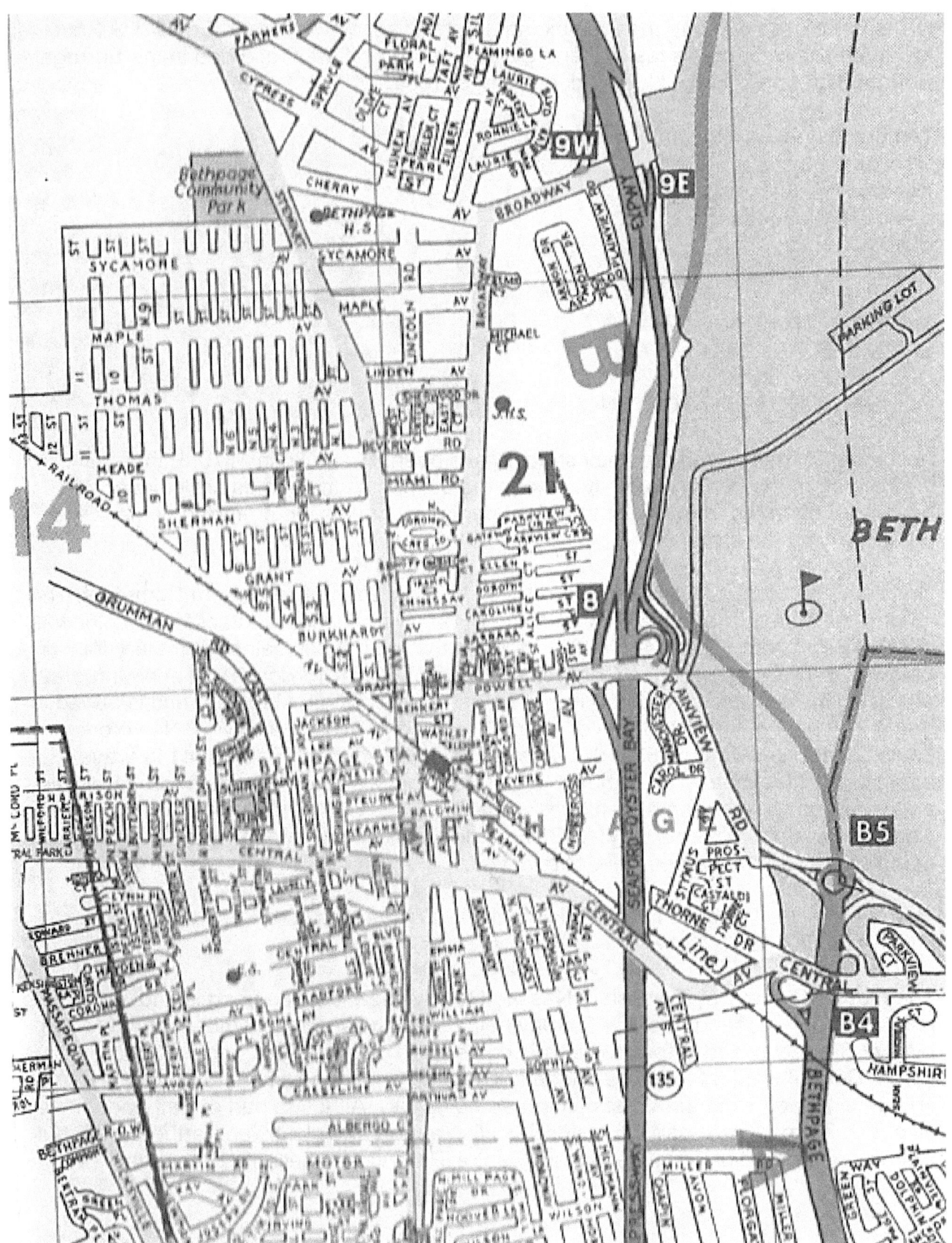

## 2. Louise W Müller and Theodore H Damm

Louise Müller married Theodore H Damm on 31 May 1885 in Kings County, New York.

The 1900 census for Brooklyn, Ward 18, Kings, New York has, Theodore Damm, 38, born Nov 1861 in New York with both parents born in Germany, married 15 years, a produce dealer renting a home at 303 Stagg Street. Louisa is 36, born May 1864 in New York with both parents born in Germany and has 3 children, all living. Their children are Theodore, 14, born Mar 1886, at school; Louis, 9, born July 1890, at school and Lucinda, 4, born Jan 1896.

The 1910 census for Brooklyn, Kings, New York has Theodore Damm, 47, married 25 years, a helper for a ship builder renting a home at 126 Ainslie Street. Louisa is 44 and has 3 children all living. The children are Theodore Jr. 24, a printing worker; Louis, 19, a chauffeur for a private family and Lucy G, 14.

Theodore Damm born Nov 1861, died 19 Oct 1915 in Manhattan, New York and is buried in St John of Jerusalem Cemetery, Wantagh, Nassau, New York.

The 1915 New York State Census for Central Park Village has Theodore Damm Jr, 27, a printer living on Central Avenue. Louisa is 51. Louis is 25 and a mechanic. Lucy is 19.

The 1920 census for Central Park, New York has Louis Damm, 29, a machinist in a garage who owns a mortgaged home on Harrison Ave. Louisa is 55 and a widow. Lucy is 24 and single.

The 1930 census for Central Park, New York has Louisa Damm, 65, widow, married at 21, hand sewing in a necktie factory renting a home at 12 Seaman Street for $30 per month and has a radio. Lucinda is 34, single and hand sewing in a necktie factory.

Louisa W Müller Damm died 8 Mar 1931 and is buried in lot 217 west of lot 119 south of the path, by Harry Tutor of Hicksville, New York. Louis Damm died 20 Apr 1941 and is buried in grave 246 North of his mother by Arthur White of Farmingdale, Long Island.[23]

## 3. Theodore Henry Damm Jr. and Charlotte B Hartmann

The 1925 New York State Census for Central Park, New York has Theo H Damm, 39, a printer living on Stewart Ave. Charlotte is 33. Their children are Theodore L, 5 and Robert W, 3.

The 1930 census for Central Park, New York has Theodore H Damm, 44, married at 33, a pressman in the printing press industry who owns his home on Stewart Ave. worth $7,500 and a radio. Charlotte is 38 and married at 27, The children are Theodore L, 9, attended school; Robert W, 8, attended school and Charlotte W, 3.

The 1940 census for Bethpage (Central Park), New York has Theodore H Damm, 54, completed 6th grade, a pressman in a printing plant who owns his home on Stewart Ave worth $7000. Charlotte B is 48 and completed 8th grade. The children are Theodore L, 19, completed 10th grade, a proof man in a printing plant; Robert, 18, graduated high school, a proof man in a printing plant and Charlotte, 13, completed 7th grade. Lucy, Theodore's sister, is 44, completed 8th grade and not working.

Theodore L Damm, born 1920, enlisted 13 Oct 1942 in the US Army as a private. His civil occupation was printing and he completed 10th grade. Theodore L Van Damm, born 16 Jun 1920, died 26 Mar 2008, was a Sargent in the US Army and is buried in St John of Jerusalem Cemetery. This is probably the same Theodore L Damm as it is a small cemetery. The addition of Van is puzzling.

Sgt. Robert W Damm, born 1922, enlisted in the Army Air Force 11 Nov 1942, died 17 Oct 1943, Rapides Parish, Louisiana. Sargent Damm served with the 469th Bomb Group, 796th Bomb Squadron. Killed when a B-17F Flying Fortress #42-3423 crashed on landing at the Alexandria Army Air Base, Louisiana. Seven other airmen also perished. Robert is buried in St. John of Jerusalem Cemetery.

Theodore H Damm Jr. born 2 Mar 1886, died 4 Aug 1954, and is buried in St. John of Jerusalem Cemetery. Charlotte Hartmann Damm, born 5 Feb 1892, died 25 May 1969 and is buried with Theodore.

### 3. Louis E Damm and Mary Halpin

Louis E Damm, 26, born 10 Jul 1890 in Brooklyn, New York, of Central Park, New York, registered for WW1 on 5 June 1917. He was a self-employed mechanic and supporting his mother. Louis was tall, slender with blue eyes and brown hair. His uncle, Henry Miller was the registrar. He served during WW1.

Louis Damm, 29, was living with his mother and sister in 1920.

The 1930 census for Central Park, Oyster Bay, Nassau, New York has Lewis Damm, 39, married at 33, a proprietor of a Printing Shop who owns his home on Kearney Ave. worth $10,000 and a radio. Mary is 36 and was married at 19. Their daughter, May, is 5.

The 1940 census for Oyster Bay, Nassau, New York has Louis Damm, 49, renting his home on Central Park Ave. for $25 per month. No education or occupation is listed. Mary is 43 and completed 8th grade. Their daughter, Mary is 15 and completed 9th grade. Mary's son, James P Gilson is 23, graduated high school and a laborer in the aircraft factory (Grumman). Lewis may have been sick as he died a year later.

Louis Damm, a WW1 veteran, born 10 Jul 1890, died 20 Apr 1941 and is buried in St John of Jerusalem Cemetery. The stone has only Louis Damm.

### 3. Luscada "Lucy" G Damm

Lucy Damm, born 12 Dec. 1896 in New York, died 3 Aug 1979 in Corinth, Orange, Vermont. She lived at Pike Hill working as a tie maker. She died of cardiac arrest and is buried in New Cemetery, East Corinth, Vermont. The informant was Charlotte Hanson. This could be Theodore H Damm Jr's daughter Charlotte. Charlotte may have married a Hanson, moved to Vermont and took her Aunt Lucy with her as Lucy would have had no other living relatives with the exception of Theodore L Damm.

### 2. Christina H Müller and Adolf G Wagner

The 1900 census for Central Park, New York has Adolf Wagner, 38, born Apr 1862, married 15 years, a foreman at a pickle works who owns his home free and clear. Christine is 33, born Oct 1866 and had 4 children, 3 are living. The children are Louise, 11, born Jun 1888; Anna, 9, born Nov 1890 and Henry, 6, born Sept 1893. Adolf Wagner is on the same census page as Theodore Bishop. Louise Wagner and Charles T Bishop were the same age. They lived close to each other and were probably friends.

The 1910 census for Central Park, New York has Adolf Wagner, 48, married 25 years, a foreman in a pickle works who owns his home on Broadway Street. Christine is 43. The children are Henry, 16, a laborer in a factory and Anna, 19. Louise has left to marry Joseph Baldwin. George O Baldwin is listed on the same page with his wife Margaretha.

The 1920 census for Central Park, New York has Adolf G Wagner, 57, a foreman in a canning factory who owns his home on Broadway. Christina H is 54.

By 1930, Adolf and Christine are living with their daughter Louise Baldwin.

Adolph Wagner, born 15 Apr 1862, died 15 Sep 1931 and is buried in Bethpage United Methodist Church Cemetery.

In 1940 Christine was still living with her daughter Louise Baldwin.

Christine H Wagner, born 26 Oct 1866, died Aug 1957 and is buried with Adolph.

### 3. Louise Caroline Wagner and Joseph Dewitt Baldwin

Louise Caroline Wagner, 20, married Joseph Dewitt Baldwin, 21, on 11 Jul 1908 in Nassau County, New York.

Herbert Baldwin, son of Louise and Joseph Baldwin born 11 Nov 1908, died 23 Apr 1909 and is buried in Bethpage United Methodist Church Cemetery. He died on a Thursday and the funeral was held at his parent's house in Central Park on Sunday. A newspaper clipping from the time says he was buried in Jerusalem Cemetery. He was moved later to be with his parents.

The 1910 census for Farmingdale, New York has Joseph D Baldwin, 23, married 1 year, a blacksmith who is renting his home on Railroad Ave. Louisa is 21 and had 1 child who is not living.

The 1920 census for Central Park, New York has Joseph D Baldwin, 32, a blacksmith with his own shop and owns his mortgaged home on Element Ave. Louisa C is 31. Their sons are Dewitt, 6 and Everett, 10/12.

The 1930 census for Central Park, New York has Joseph Baldwin, 43, married at 21, a carpenter in the building industry who owns his home at 161 Stewart Ave. worth $10,000 and a radio. Louise is 41 and was married at 20. The children are DeWitt, 16, a laborer in a restaurant; Everett, 10 and Walter, 8. Adolph Wagner, 67, father-in-law, married at 22 and Christine, 63, mother-in-law, married at 18 are living with him.

The 1940 Census for Bethpage (Central Park), New York has Joseph Baldwin, 53, completed 7th grade, a mechanic for the town highways who owns his home on Stewart Ave. worth $5060. Louise is 51 and completed 7th grade. The children are DeWitt, 27, completed 9th grade, a laborer; Everett, 20, graduated high school, a counterman at the army airport and Walter 18, graduated high school, a mechanic at an aircraft plant. Christine Wagner is 73, a widow, and completed 4th grade. They are seeing the advantage of education as each generation goes to school longer.

Joseph D Baldwin, born 14 Feb 1887, died 9 Jun 1975 and is buried in Bethpage United Methodist Church Cemetery. Louise C Wagner Baldwin, born 25 Jun 1888, died 2 Jun 1966 and is buried with Joseph.

De Witt Baldwin, born 1913, died 1980. He married Helen born 1908, died 1995.

Everett J Baldwin, born 7 Dec 1919, died 8 Nov 2001. He was an Army private in WW11, serving from 15 Jun 1943 to 26 Feb 1946 and is buried in Long Island National Cemetery.

Walter F Baldwin born 18 May 1921, died 27 Sep 1992. He served in WW11 from 1 Nov 1943 to 1 Apr 1946.

### 3. Anna C Wagner and Frank Drinkwater

Anna Wagner married Frank Drinkwater 15 Jun 1916 at the Wagner home on Broadway in Central Park, New York.

The 1920 census for Central Park, Nassau, New York has Frank Drinkwater, 27, a house mason, renting a home on Central Ave. Anna C is 29. Their sons are Frank, 3 and William H, 2.

The 1930 census for Central Park, New York has Frank Drinkwater, 37, married at 23, a brick layer who owns his home on Central Ave. worth $3500. Anna C is 39 and was married at 25. Their children are Frank, 12; William, 11 and Anna, 9.

The 1940 census for Bethpage (Central Park), New York has Frank Drinkwater, 48, completed 7th grade, a brick layer for a building contractor who owns his home on Central Ave. worth $4500. Anna is 49 and completed 7th grade. Frank is 22, single, completed 10th grade and a laundry worker. William is 21, single, completed 8th grade and a brick layers helper.

Frank Drinkwater born 1 Apr 1892, died 24 Jun 1964 and is buried in Bethpage United Methodist Church Cemetery, Bethpage, New York. Anna C Wagner Drinkwater born 6 Nov 1890, died 12 Mar 1969 and is buried with Frank.

### 4. Anna Drinkwater and Clifford E Lee

Anna Drinkwater married Clifford E Lee on 4 Aug 1939 in Bethpage, New York.

A 1942 Rockville Center, New York, City Directory has Clifford Lee (Ann) painter. They are living with his parents at 26 Lincoln Court.

### 3. Henry Adolph Wagner and Eleanor A

Henry A Wagner born 25 Sep 1893 in Central Park, New York was inducted 29 May 1918 for WW1 at Glen Cove, New York. He was assigned to the 152th Brigade as a private. He was honorably discharged 23 Oct 1918 with a 33 1/3% disability. There is no further explanation.

The 1920 census for Farmingdale, New York has Henry A Wagner, 26, a block operator on the railroad who owns his mortgaged home on Columbia Street. Elanor A is 19.

The 1930 census for Farmingdale, New York has Henry A Wagner, 36, married at 25, a veteran of WW1, working as a towerman on a railroad who owns his home at 16 Columbia Street worth $7800 and a radio. Eleanor is 30 and married at 19. Their son, Edward is 9 and attended school.

A 1940 census could not be found.

Henry Adolph Wagner, 48, born in Bethpage 25 Sep 1893 registered for WW11 on 26 Apr 1942. He is living at 16 Columbia Street in Farmingdale, New York and working for the Pennsylvania Rail Road in Jamaica, Queens, New York. Next of kin is Mrs. Eleanor Wagner. Henry is 5' 11", weighs 190 lb. and has blue eyes.

Henry A. Wagner, born 25 Sep 1893, died 18 Jan 1965. He served in The US Army during WW1 as a private. Henry is buried in Long Island National Cemetery 2040 Wellwood Ave. East Farmingdale, New York, Section 2d Site 780. Eleanor A Wagner, born 26 Mar 1900, died 6 Jan 1973 and is buried with Henry.

## 2. Katherine Müller and Theodore Bishop

Theodore Bishop married Katherine Müller and they had 5 children: Charles Theodore born 2 Feb 1888, Clara born in 1890, Gertrude born in 1893, and twins Esther M and Theodore born in 1894. Their story will be continued in Chapter 15.

## 2. Margaretha H Miller and George O Baldwin

The 1900 Census for Hempstead, Nassau, New York has George O Baldwin, 28, born June 1871, married 5 years, a blacksmith who owns his mortgaged home. Margaret H is 27, born Sept 1872 and has 2 children, both living. Their sons are George N, 3, born Oct 1896 and Harvey P, 6/12, born Nov 1899. A boarder, blacksmith, is living with them.

The 1910 Census for Central Park, New York has George O Baldwin, 39, married 15 years, an overseer of poor for the town who owns his home on Broadway. Margaretha is 39 and has 2 children, both living. Their sons are Nelson, 13 and Percy, 10.

The 1920 census for Central Park, New York has George O Baldwin, 48, a foreman for the State Roads who owns his home free and clear on Baldwin Place (just off Broadway, possibly the same house). Margaret H is 48. Harry P is 20 and a machinist in a machine shop.

The 1930 census for Central Park, New York has George O Baldwin, 59, married at 24, a superintendent at the water works who owns his home on Baldwin Place worth $20,000 and a radio. Margaret is 58 and married at 24. Her parents were both born in Hanover Germany. Harry P is 30, single and an electrician for an electrical contractor.

This same census, next page, has Lewis Damm on Kearney Ave (left of Stewart, 1st street N of Central on above map); Theodore Damm on Stewart Ave; Joseph Baldwin next door on Stewart Ave and his in-laws Adolph and Christina Wagner are living with him. A few pages farther we find Louise Damm living at 12 Seaman Ave. (right on Baldwin Place then south on Broadway to next street) with her daughter Luscada both doing hand sewing for a necktie factory. The descendants of Christian and Margaretha Müller did not stray far!

The 1940 census for Bethpage (Central Park) New York has George O Baldwin, 68, completed 4th grade, manager of the water district who owns his home on Baldwin Place in the same house as 1935. Margaret is 68 and completed 5th grade. Harry P is 40, completed 8th grade and an electrician doing private work. Theodore H Damm and Joseph Baldwin are still on Stewart Ave.

Margaret Miller Baldwin, of Bethpage, born 20 Sep 1872, died 2 Nov 1946, buried 5 Nov 1946 in lot #44 St John's of Jerusalem Cemetery. George O Baldwin, of Bethpage, born 22 Jun 1871, died 16 Nov 1947, buried 19 Nov 1947 in Lot # 44[25]

## 3. George Nelson Baldwin and Clairesse May Hawkins

George Nelson Baldwin married Clairesse May before 1918. She is his nearest relative on his WW1 registration dated 5 Jun 1918. George is working for Doubleday Page & Co. in Garden City, New York. They are living on Carl Street in Hicksville, New York. He is of medium height and build with brown hair and brown eyes. He did not serve.

The 1920 census for Oyster Bay, Nassau, New York has Nelson G Baldwin, 23, a bookbinder for Doubleday renting a home on Carl Street. Clairesse is 21. Russell Hawkins, 18, brother-in law, a bookbinder is living with them.

The 1930 census for Hicksville, New York has Nelson Baldwin, 33, married at 21, a bookbinder in a factory who owns his home on 5th Street worth $8000 and a radio. Clairesse is 31 and married at 19. Their sons are George, 9, and Howard, 6.

The 1940 census for Hicksville, New York has G Nelson Baldwin, 43, completed 8th grade, a bookbinder for a publisher who owns his home on W Cherry Street worth $6500. Clairesse is 41, completed 8th grade and an operator for a dress manufacturer. George N is 19, graduated high school and a mechanic's helper for an airplane manufacturer. Howard J is 16 and completed 10th grade.

George Nelson Baldwin, 46, born 2 Oct 1896, of 139 5th Street, Hicksville, New York, registered for WW11 on 25 Apr 1942. He was working for Country Life Press Corporation on Franklin Ave., Garden City, New York. He is 5'10" and weighs 145 lb. with brown eyes and hair.

George N Baldwin, 22, enlisted 9 Feb 1943 as a private for the duration of WW11. He graduated high school, was semiskilled in building aircraft, single, height 5'5" and weight 118 lbs.

Howard J Baldwin born 18 Mar 1924, died 2 May 1988 and is buried in Calverton National Cemetery, 210 Princeton Boulevard, Calverton, New York. He served as a corporal in the U S Army in WW11 from 16 Feb 1943 to 16 Sep 1945.

George Nelson Baldwin born 2 Oct 1896, died 18 Nov 1978 and his ashes are in grave 5 of lot 44. Harvey "Harry" Percy Baldwin born 11 Nov 1899, died 31 Dec 1963 and is buried in grave 8 of lot 44. Clarisse born 1898, died 30 Nov 1984 and her ashes are in lot 44. Clarisse was the information contact for St John's of Jerusalem Cemetery and lived in Venice, Florida. After that Howard Baldwin was the contact, last known address 127 S. Hillside Ave., Nesconset, New York 11767 but we lost contact in 1988.[23]

## 2. Henry E Miller and Ada Capron

Ibe H Miller in the 1880 census was known as Henry Miller the rest of his life. He even has the name Henry in his father's 1884 will.

The 1900 census for Central Park, New York has Henry Miller, 22, born July 1877, single, a servant, working as a store clerk. His mother, Margaret is 65, born Sept 1834, widowed and has 5 children, all still living. She immigrated to the US in 1855 and has been living in the US for 45 years. They are living with Henry and Dora Sengstacken, both German immigrants. He is working as a store keeper and they are renting their home which may be over the store.

Also, in the 1900 census is Ada L Capron, 20, born Aug 1879, a student, living next door to Theodore Bishop and Henry's sister Kate.

Henry Miller married Ada L Capron on 8 Jan 1901 in Kings County, New York.

Margaretha Müller died in 1905.

The 1910 census for Central Park, New York has Henry E Miller, 33, married 9 years, born in New York of German parents, a foreman for a paving company who owns his home on Suburban Land Road free and clear. Ada L is 29, has not had children and was born in New York with parents born in Rhode Island and New York. Alvin Nowse, grandfather is 96, widowed and born in New York. Fredrick Ronnuld, 75, widowed, born in Sweden. They (Ada) are taking in elderly men for income.

A 1915 census for Central Park, New York has Henry E Miller, 39, a butcher, living on Broadway. Ada L, 35 is doing housework. The next listing is the Joseph Baldwin family.

Henry E Miller, 42, born 5 Jul 1876, of Central Park, New York, registered for WW1 on 12 Sep 1918. He was employed by the State Highway Department and nearest relative is Ada Miller. He was tall, medium build with blue eyes and blond hair

The 1920 census for Central Park, New York has Henry E Miller, 44, a butcher in a butcher shop who owns his home on Broadway free and clear. Ada L is 40 and has 2 boarders.

The 1925 New York State Census for Central Park has Henry E Miller, 48, a butcher's helper, living on Broadway. Ada L is 44 and does not have boarders.

Henry and Ada moved to Wisconsin between 1925 and 1930. The 1930 census for Eau Claire, Wisconsin has Henry Miller, 53, married at 23, a packer for a book company who owns a home at 452 Lincoln worth $6500. Ada is 49 and married at 20. This may be why Ada was willing to travel to Michigan when all the other relatives thought it was far far away. The time in Wisconsin didn't last long as they were back in New York by 1935.

George and Jean Bishop had a double wedding with Agnes Bishop and Charlie Letherer in Jun 1936. They went to New York for their honeymoon. They visited Henry and Ada Miller who were living north of New York City. This picture may have been taken at that time or some time not much later.[6]

The 1940 Census for New Platz, New York has Henry Miller, 63, completed 8th grade, unable to work and owns his home at 431 Plattekill Road worth $4500. Ada L is 59 and a completed grade is not given. They were living right across the street from State University of New York at New Platz. The town is west of the Hudson River about half way between New York City and Albany. Agnes Letherer said they lived north of New York City when they visited in 1936.[6]

Henry E. Miller born 5 July 1877, died 9 Jan 1941 and is buried in Bethpage Cemetery, Farmingdale, Nassau, New York.

Ada L. Miller born 24 Aug 1879, died 15 Apr 1964 and is buried with Henry.

After Henry died "Aunt Ada" visited in Michigan and appears in several remembrances as well as at the 1950 Klingensmith reunion.

# Chapter 14

## Frank Bishof/Bischoff/Bishop and Mary Geiser/Kaiser

1. Frank (Franz) J Bishop (Bishof, Bischoff) (1832-1906)
+ Mary (Marie) Geiser (Kaiser) (1845-1912)
    **2. Theodore Bischoff / Bishop (1868-1951)**
    **+ Katherine Johanna Müller (1869-1906)**
        3. Charles Theodore Bishop (1888-1954)
        + Mae Louise Stanley (1892-1945)
        3. Clara Bishop (1890-1962)
        3. Gertrude L Bishop (1893-1964)
        + William O Saxton (1889-1950)
        + Fredrick K Cavalier (1890-)
        3. Esther Bishop (1894-1973)
        + Stephen Grandner (1889-1981)
        3. Theodore George Bishop (1894- 1976)
        + Elizabeth Gulisippi (1894-1983)
  + Grace Wild (1888-1965)
        3. Constance (1908-1908
        3. Leonard Bishop (1908-1917)
        3. Everet W Bishop (1911-1992)
        + Margaret Colwell (1915-1997)
  2. Katherine "Katy" Bischoff (1870-before 1951)
  + Frank Schwartz (1868-1946)
        3. Paul Adam Schwartz (1892-1967) WW1
        + Madeline C Engel (1893-1991)
            4, Gertrude (1923-)
        3. Florence Schwartz (1894-1925)
        + William Herman Loos (1889-1948)
            4. Leonard Loos (1915-1992) WW1
            4. Harry Loos (1918-)
            4. Madeline Kathleen Loos (1921-)
        3. Arthur L Schwartz (1904-1968)
        + Francis DeOdener (1905-)
            4. Arthur L Schwartz (1925-)
            4. Robert Schwartz (1926-1938)
            4. Marilyn Schwartz (1939-)
  2. Charles Erasmos Bishof (1872-between 1936 and 1940)
  + Minnie (1872-after 1949)
        3. Magdalena Mabel Bishof (1897-1982)
        + George Hemhauser (1896-)
            4. Vivian Hemhauser (1924-1997) WW11
        3. Walter C Bishof (1898-1965) WW1
        + Catherine Gallegher (1894-1972)

                4. Walter C. Bishof Jr. (1928-2001) WW11 & Korea
        3. Herbert Bishof (1899-1903)
        3. Raymond J Bishof (1903-1994)
         + Estella (1904-1991)
                4. Raymond J Bishof Jr. (1929-)
        3. Wilber C Bishof (1904-1982)
         + Mildred L Cooper (1904-1982)
                4. Col Wilber C Bishof (1930-2016) Korea thru Viet Nam
                4. Paul Bishof (1934-)
                4. Charlie Bishof (1939-)
        3. Albert H Bishof (1906-2005) Navy 1930s
         + Viola L (1905-1991)
        3. Harold E Bishof (1908-1991)
         + Ruth (1910-)
        3. Viola Bishof (1910-2003)
         + Melvin F Hass (1910-1986)
                4. Russell M Hass (1939-)
        3. Gladys Bishof (1914-2000)
    2. Frank Joseph Bishof (1878-1939)
     + Rose Kohl (1878-1964)
    2. George Bishof (1880-after 1951)
     + Lillian "Lillie" (1884-)
    2. Joseph Bishof (1880-)
     + Rose Hemhauser (1873-)
     + Anna A Diebold (1884-)
    2. Anthony "Anton" Edward Bishof (1883-1972)
     + Catherine Burger (1875-1941)
    2. Fredrick Theodore Bishof (1883-before 1941)
     + Lillian A (1886-after 1941)
        3. Fredric J Bishof (1909-1980) WW11
        3. Norman P Bishof (1912-)
    2. William Bishof (1890-1946) WW1
     + Bertha Hauser (1890-)
     + Mabel E (1890-)


## 1. Frank Bishof and Marie Kaiser

According to family legend, as told to me by Agnes Bishop Letherer and others, Theodore Bischoff was born in Haarlem, Kings County New York in 1868. He went to Bethpage, Long Island, New York when he was about 12 years old to work in truck farming. He remained on Long Island the rest of his life.[6]

It was discovered that New York marriage records go back to 1885 which should include Theodore Bishop's marriage to Katherine Müller. The records could not be found in a visit to the Nassau County records in Hempstead, New York on Long Island. The record could be obtained by sending money to the State of New York with the request but there were no guarantees as the money would cover the search whether or not the record was found. After a wait of one year, the following was received:

The State of New York marriage record from the Village of Hicksville, County of Queens is as follows:

| | |
|---|---|
| Groom: Theodor Bishof | Bride: Katharine Johanne Miller |
| Residence: Amityville, Long Island | South Oyster Bay |
| Age next birthday: 20 years | 19 |
| Occupation: farmer | |
| Place of birth: Amityville, Long Island | South Oyster Bay |
| Father's name: Frank Bishof | Christian G Müller |
| Mother's name: Marie Geiser | Margaritha Essen |
| Groom's first marriage | first |

Dated Hicksville, 10 Aug 1887
Signed by Theodore, Katie and two witnesses: A Wagner and Paul Sauer

There is also a certificate of marriage. It is from the town(ship) of Oyster Bay and the residence is listed as Hicksville, Long Island, New York. The marriage appears to have taken place in the township or county offices. Hicksville is just North West of Bethpage and appears to currently be in Nassau County but county lines and names changed over the years. The records are on the next 2 pages.

According to 1900 census data, Frank arrived in 1865 and Mary arrived in 1866. A passenger list was found that seems to be the right Frank Bishof. A Frz Bischoff, 32, arrived in New York 6 Sep 1865 on the Alamo from Bremen Germany. He had 1 bag and is listed as a shoemaker from Bavaria. He is number 56 on the list. The ship had 568 burthen (berths). There were 5 first class passengers and 5 second class passengers, the rest would have been in steerage. The age would be correct as Frank's birthday is 26 Nov 1832 according to death records.

Mary Geiser or Kaiser arrived in 1866 according to census records. The most likely passenger information I found was Marie Kaiser, 17, born about 1844 and traveling alone, from Kenzingen, Germany (part of Baden-Württemberg). She departed Bremen Germany on a sailing ship with one steam engine and an iron hull that held 60 first class, 110 second class and 400 third class passengers. The crossing took at least 12 days and they landed in New York on 28 May 1861. The age is right but conflicts with the date of arrival given in the 1900 census. Mary's memory may not have been accurate as she was trying to get all 12 children in the right order and birth dates. Marie would have been in the German tenements near Haarlem after she arrived.

# To the Bureau of Vital Statistics,
### STATE OF NEW YORK

Registered Number: 455

## RETURN OF A MARRIAGE

In the Town (Village) City of Hicksville County of Queens

1. Full Name of Groom, Theodor Bishof
2. Place of Residence, Amityville, L.I.
3. Age next Birthday, 20 years
4. 
5. Occupation, Farmer
6. Place of Birth, Amityville, L.I.
7. Father's Name, Frank Bishof
8. Mother's Maiden Name, Marie Walter
9. No. of Groom's Marriage, First
10. Full Name of Bride, Katharina Johanna Miller
    Maiden Name, if a Widow,
11. Place of Residence, South Oysterbay
12. Age next Birthday, 19 years
13. 
14. Place of Birth, South Oysterbay
15. Father's Name, Christian J. Miller
16. Mother's Maiden Name, Margaretha Esser
17. No. of Bride's Marriage, First

N. B.—At Nos. 4 and 13: If of other than the White Race, specify it. At Nos. 9 and 17 state whether 1st, 2d, 3d, 4th, Marriage of each. The signatures below of Bride and Groom, should be written out in full for the "given" and family names.

Dated at Hicksville, August 10th 1887

We, the Groom and Bride named in the above Certificate hereby Certify that the information given is correct, to the best of our knowledge and belief.

Theodor Bishof (Groom)
Katie J. Miller (Bride)

Signed in presence of H. Wagner
and Paul Schuett

# CERTIFICATE OF MARRIAGE

No. 4132

In the Town (Village) City of _Oyster Bay_ County of _Nassau_ Town of _Oyster Bay_

## STATE OF NEW YORK

**Hereby Certify,** that _Kristen Stephenson Willis_ and _Katherine Suzanne Miller_ were joined in marriage in our presence, in accordance with the Laws of the State of New York, on this _1st_ day of _August_ 1887, at _Hicksville_ Nassau Co. NY

Attest: Edward G. _____

P.L.S. Matthews

Witnesses to the Marriage:
A. Hagens, Hicksville, N.Y.
Paul Glassel, Hicksville, N.Y.

Residence,

. Frank and Mary were married in 1867 or 68. According to the 1900 census they had been married 32 years Jun 1900. Their first child, Theodore, was born Mar 1868.

They should be recorded in an 1870 census but I have not been able to find anything. The 1880 census for Amityville, New York has Frank Bishop, 47, a laborer renting his home. He was born in Bavaria and his parents were born in Bavaria. Mary is 34 and was born in Prussia as were her parents. Their children are Theodore, 12; Katy, 10; Charles, 8 and Frank, 2, all born in New York. This would agree with Agnes Bishop's story that Theodore moved to Long Island when he was twelve. Fritz Bischoff may have changed his name to Frank Bishof soon after he came to the United States.

The 1895 New Jersey State census for Ward 10, Newark, New Jersey has Frank and Mary Bishop both born in Germany (German male and German female are categories on the census). The next entry is a male between 20 and 60 the name may be Gask or Carl. The children are Frank, George, Joseph, Anton and Fritz (Fred) all are 5-20 male. The youngest is William a male under 5 years. Frank would have been 53 so the unknown male must be a brother or other relative not his father or maybe Marie's father but the last name is missing. Not much information but definitely our Bishops. The categories were German, Irish and other. They were in a German-Irish neighborhood with tenements as there were 2 families in the house.

The 1900 census for Ward 12, Newark, New Jersey has Frank Bishop, 67, born Nov 1832 in Germany, married 32 years, immigrated 1865, not a citizen, a day laborer, not employed for 3 months of the year and renting his home at 91 Hamburg Place. Mary is 54, born Oct 1845 in Germany, immigrated 1866, not a citizen and has had 9 children all living. The children are Frank, 20, born Mar 1880, a day laborer; George, 17, born Aug 1882, a plumber; Joseph, 17, born Aug 1882, a hat maker; Anton, 16, born Sept 1883, a hat maker; Fred,16, born Sept 1883, a hat maker and William, 10, born Jan 1890, at school.  None of the sons have been unemployed in the last year and all were born in New York. Two sets of twins a year apart must have been a handful! I doubt Frank or the older boys would have been much help. George is the only one with a trade, maybe an apprentice. They were living with two other families, a total of 19 people mostly from Germany. One was a Candy Store Keeper, the others were a box maker, a pattern maker, and 2 hat trimmers.  Others on the page also worked with hats. This was a tenement industry carried on in the largest room with everyone crowed in whatever space was left.

Frank and Marie's oldest son, Theodore, married in 1887 and stayed in Amityville on Long Island. Theodore had a job working in truck farming fields so there wasn't much incentive to move with the large family, besides there was Katie and her family. More about Theodore and Katherine in the next chapter.

Katy their only daughter married in 1899. Charles was alive in 1900 as Marie said she had 9 live children. Frank is the only child from the 1880 census who is still with his parents. Their youngest son, William was born in New York in 1890. They moved between 1890 and 1895. All of the children worked at a young age.

The name Bishop and Bishof seems to be used interchangeably. The older children may have been born Bischoff and the younger Bishof. Without much documentation, (Social Security numbers, driver's license) a person could change his name as desired. Theodore's marriage license has Bishof but he went by Bishop most of his life.

There is no known reason for Frank Bishof to move his family to New Jersey. There does seem to be a change of name with each move. Bischoff in Harlem or Manhattan, Bishof on Long Island, and Bishop in New Jersey although the children stayed with Bishof. I leave what prompted the moves up to your imagination. There are gaps in child birth before each move.

25 Hamburg Place - Hamburg Place School

The following pictures and map show where they lived in Newark, New Jersey.

This is a picture of the Hamburg Place School where the Bishof children may have attended when not working.

I did not find a picture of 91 Hamburg Place but it seems to have been surrounded by industry and retail stores with tenements above as in this early photo of 73-89 Hamburg Place. A current photo on Google Maps shows a building similar to the closest one in this photo.

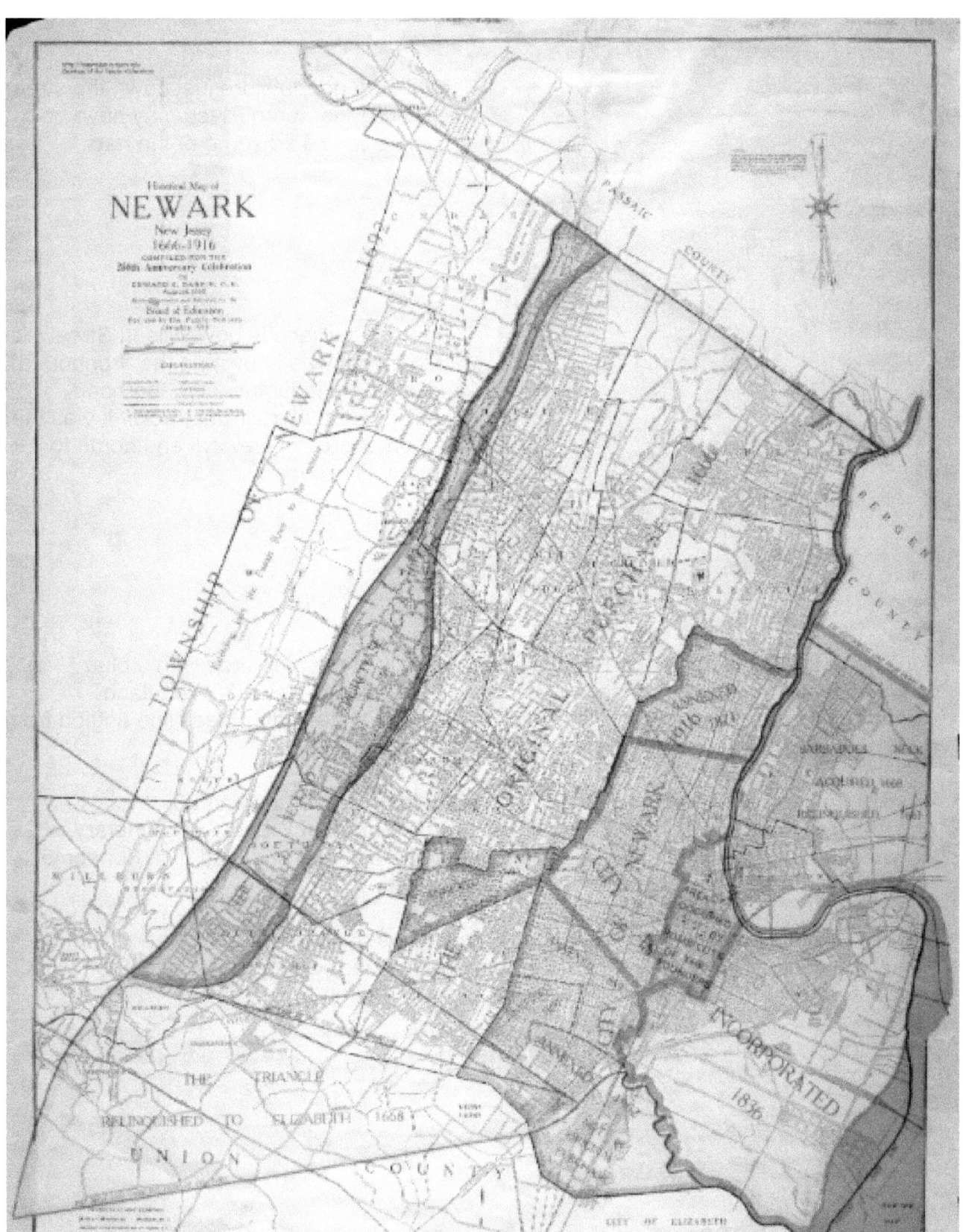

This dry goods store just down the street from 91 Hamburg Place may have been where they sold some of the hats.

Hamburg Place is now Wilson Street. It is in what was known as the "Ironbound" district, an industrial neighborhood surrounded by railroad tracks. It was the poorest area in Newark and home to many Germans.

Oppenheimer's Dry Goods - 108/110 Hamburg Place

Looking at the above map, the Bishofs lived primarily in the pink area with a blue border. Several streets go on an angle toward the center of Newark. Woodland Cemetery is just south of Springfield Ave. Springfield is the lighter black line angled from the South West through the yellow and pink and into the green.

Frank J Kaiser Bishof died 16 Feb 1906, age 73 years, 2 months and 20 days. According to this, he was born 26 Nov 1832. He is buried at Woodland Cemetery, Newark, Essex, New Jersey. He is the husband of Mary who survived him. For some reason, Mary's last name, Kaiser, is part of his name.

Using the wife's last name in the husband's name was a German tradition and indicates Kaiser was actually Mary's last name before she married. Geiser may have been what the person recording the marriage heard.

The following is a map of Woodland cemetery.

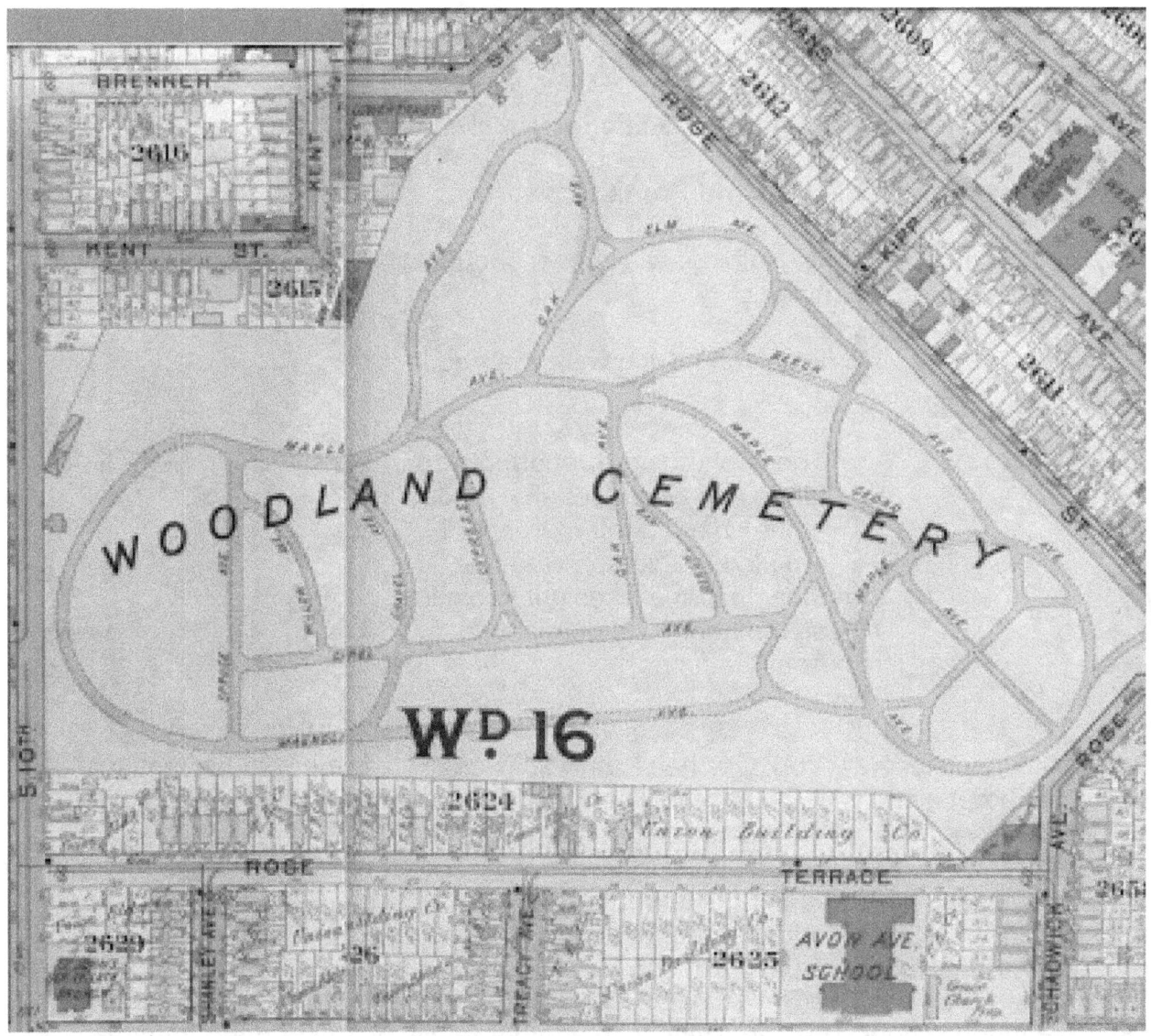

Wood lawn Cemetery was established in 1855 and was considered a rural cemetery meaning it's layout was not like the common church cemeteries. Rural cemeteries in the area, were built on the outskirts of town, surrounded by a stone wall, and featured natural rolling hills, curved pathways, landscaping and trees. Between 1870 and 1880 a two-story Gothic Revival brownstone gatehouse was built at the entrance. A majority of the earliest burials were of German people. At one point, it was called the "German Cemetery".

The 1910 census for Ward 10, Newark, New Jersey has Mary Bishoff, 65, widow, has had 12 children and 9 are living. We do not know the names of the other 3 children that died or when they were born. Mary is working as a housekeeper in a private home and living at 92 Garrison Street with 2 other families. She may be working for one of them. William is 20 and working as a tin smith for skylights.

There is a record of a Marie Bischoff, 66, dying 12 Dec 1912 in Queens, New York. She may have been staying with her daughter Katie when she died.

**2. Theodore Bishop and Katherine Miller are in chapter 15.**

**2. Katherine "Katy" Bischoff and Frank Schwartz**

Katy was born about 1870. Nothing was known about her until several family trees led to her husband Frank Schwartz.

Frank and Katie were married in 1889.

These photos are reportedly on fabric and were probably made at the time of their marriage. I am glad the person who has these had the foresight to digitize as the photo is delaminating from the fabric.

An 1880 census for New York City has Frank Schwartz, 11, living with his family at 621 East 16th Street along with 7 other families. The father is a cabinet maker and all the children are in school. The parents are from Bavaria.

The 1900 census for Borough of Queens, City of New York has Frank Schwartz, 31, born Sept 1868 in New York, married 10 years, a plumber renting his home at 542 Broadway. Katie is 30, born Mar 1870 in New York and has had 3 children, 2 are living. The children are Paul, 8, born Oct 1892, attended school and Florence, 6, born Feb 1894, attended school. They are living with another family of 7 where the father is a grocer and owns the dwelling. They are probably all living above the grocery store.

The 1910 census for Ward 3, Queens, New York has Frank Schwartz, 41, married 20 years, a plumber who owns his own business and renting a home at 152 Forest Ave. Katherine is 41 and has had 5 children, 3 are living. The children are Paul A, 18, an automobile apprentice; Florence M, 16, did not attend school and Arthur L, 6, attended school.

The 1920 census for Flushing, Queens, New York has Frank Schwartz, 51, a plumber who owns a mortgaged home at 152 Smart Ave. Katherine is 51. The children are Paul, 28, single, a mechanic working on automobiles and Arthur, 16, working in a repair shop for automobiles.

The 1930 census for Flushing, Queens, New York has F Schwartz Jr., 61, married at

26, a plumber who owns his home at 152 Smart Ave. worth $7000 and has a radio. Katherine is 60 and was married at 21.

The 1940 census for Flushing, Queens, New York has Frank Schwartz, 71, completed 8th grade and owns his home worth $4000 at 45-46 Smart Street. Katherine is 71 and completed 6th grade. Arthur L is 37, completed 7th grade and working for Dept of Sanitation in City of New York. Francis, daughter-in-law, is 35 and completed 9th grade. The grandchildren are Arthur L Jr, 15, completed 9th grade and Marilyn, 9/12. This is an area of 2 story homes so there may have been apartments on each floor.

Frank Schwartz born 18 Sep 1868, died 20 Sep 1946 in Queens, New York. It is not known when Katherine died or where they are buried.

### 3. Paul Adam Schwartz and Madeline C. Engel

Paul Adam Schwartz registered for WW1 on 5 Jun 1917. He was born 26 Oct 1892 on Long Island and is a chauffeur (mechanical) for American Auto. He claimed an exemption for making machinery for the US. He was a medium height and build with brown hair and eyes. Apparently, he did not get the exception as he is listed as a veteran later.

Paul was living with his parents in 1920 and was married later in 1920.

The 1930 census for Flushing, Queens, New York has Paul Schwartz, 38, married at 28, a veteran of WW1, a chauffeur for a factory. Madeline is 36 and was married at 26. Their daughter, Gertrude is 7. William Bischoff, uncle, 56, widowed, married at 25, parents born in Germany, a painter who owns the home at 159-12 59th Ave. worth $6200. This is further proof that Paul's mother was Katherine Bischoff. If William Bischoff was 56, he would have been born in 1874. William was born in 1890 which would make him 40. Probably Madeline gave the information and he looked old to her.

The 1940 census for Flushing, Queens, New York has Paul Schwartz, 48, completed 8th grade, an assembler in a factory and renting a house at 164-02 16th street for $40 per month, Madeline is 46 and graduated high school. Gertrude is 17 and completed 9th grade.

Paul A Schwartz, born 26 Oct 1892, died 14 Jan 1967 and is buried at Long Island National Cemetery, Farmingdale, New York. He was a corporal in the US Army during World War 1, service start date 30 Sep 1917. Madeleine Engel Schwartz born 12 Apr 1893, died 11 May 1991 and is buried beside Paul.

### 3. Florence Matilda Schwartz and William Herman Loos

Florence M Schwartz married William H Loos on 20 Sep 1913 in Queens, New York.

The 1920 census for Astoria, Queens, New York has William Loos, 30, a chauffeur at a storage Company renting a home at 563 Grand Ave. (5 families live at the same address). Florence is 25. Their sons are Leonard, 4 and Harry, 2.

Florence and William had a daughter, Madeline Kathleen in 1921.

Florence Schwartz Loos, born Feb 1894, died 12 Apr 1925, in Manhattan, New York.

William H Loos married Florence Dean 10 Oct 1925.

The 1940 census for Plattsburg Barracks (Crab Island) 28th Infantry Co. G, Building No. 30 has Leonard H Loos, 23, single, completed 10th grade, born in Astoria, Long Island, New York, a soldier in the US Army, worked 52 weeks in 1939 for $360.

Harry and Madeline were still living with their father in 1940.

Leonard Loos, born 21 Dec 1915, died 13 Aug 1992. He enlisted/served in the Air Force 4 Aug 1944 – 16 Nov 1945; 16 Jul 1947-26 Jul 1950; 27 Jul 1950- 30 Nov 1960.

### 3. Arthur L Schwartz and Francis DeOdener

Arthur L Schwartz married married Francis DeOdener on 12 Jul 1922.

The 1930 census for 3rd assembly, Queens, New York has Arthur L Schwartz, 27, married at 20, a machinist for a bus company renting part of an apartment at 119 8th Ave. for $40 per month. Francis is 25 and married at 18. Their sons are Arthur L, 5, attended school and Robert, 4.

Robert Schwartz, 12, born 1926, died 12 Mar 1938 in Queens, New York. Marilyn Schwartz was born in 1939.

Arthur and his family were living with his parents in 1940.

### 2. Charles Erasmos Bishof and Minnie Rukstuhl / Ruchstuhl

Charles Bishof married Minnie Rukstuhl on 26 Apr 1896 in Manhattan, New York. Their first child, Magdalena Mabel Bishof was born 7 Mar 1897 and baptized 25 Apr 1897 at the 1st German Presbyterian Church.

The 1900 census for Ward 7, Newark, New Jersey has Charles Bishof, 27, born Aug 1872, married 4 years, a teamster renting his shared home on Wilsey Street. Minnie is 28, born Apr 1872 and has had 3 children all living. The children are Mabel, 3, born Mar 1897; Walter, 1, born Aug 1898 and Herbert, 6/12, born Dec 1899. Charles may have moved to Newark with or soon after his parents but was not living with them in 1900.

Herbert F W Bishof died in 1903 in New Jersey.

The 1905 New Jersey State census for Ward #12, Newark has Charles E Bishof, 32, born Aug 1872, a teamster for a brewery renting part of a house at 17 Lentz Ave. (near Ferry Street) Minnie is 32 and was born Apr 1872. The children are Madeline, 8, born Mar 1897; Walter, 6, born Aug 1898; Raymond, 2 born Jun 1903 and Wilbert, 8/12, born Sep 1904.

A 1911 Newark, New Jersey City Directory has Charles E Bishof, driver, home 65 Hawkins.

The 1915 New Jersey State census for Newark has Chas E Bishof, 43, born Aug 1872, a driver renting a home at 517 Ferry Street. Minnie is 42 and was born Apr 1872. The children are Mabel, 18, born Mar 1897, a brush maker; Walter, 16, born Aug 1898, a druggist; Raymond, 11, born Jun 1903; Wilber, 9, born Sep 1904; Albert, 8, born Oct 1906; Harold, 6, born Oct 1908; Viola, 5, born Apr 1910 and Gladys, 1, born Apr 1914.

A 1917 Newark, New Jersey City Directory has Charles E Bishof, driver, home 517 Ferry. 517 Ferry Street is in the ironbound district. The current Google picture of this address looks like a remodeled 1800s structure with a store on the lower floor and 2 upper floors of apartments.

Pvt Walter C. Bishof of 517 Ferry Street, Newark, New Jersey enlisted 5 Mar 1918 in Quarter Master Corps, Auxiliary Regiment, Dep #333 and was discharged 4 Mar 1919.

The 1920 census for Ward 12, Newark, New Jersey has Chas E Bishof, 48, born in New York, parents born in Germany, a truck driver, living at 517 Ferry Street with 2 other families. Minnie is 48, born in New Jersey and both parents born in Germany. The children are Walter, 21, a heater in a shipyard; Raymond, 17, an electrician's helper; Wilber, 15, a painter's helper; Albert, 13; Harold, 11; Viola, 9; and Gladys, 5. All the children are born in New Jersey.

A 1922 Newark City Directory has Charles E Bishof, driver, home 517 Ferry.

The 1930 census for Newark, New Jersey has Charles Bishof, 57, married at 27, a machine operator at a celluloid company. Minnie is 57 and was married at 27. The children are Harold, 21, a carpenter in building construction; Viola, 19, a clerk in an insurance office and Gladys, 16. They are all living in the same house as Walter Bishof, 26 Stuyvesant Ave. Walter is renting part of the house to his father.

Charles Erasmos Bishof filed for an original Social Security Number, in Dec 1936, born 30 Aug 1872, Amityville, New York, father Frank J Bishof and mother Mary Kaiser.

In 1940 Minnie was living with her daughter Viola as a widow. Charles E Bishof died sometime between 1936 and 1940.

The 1949 Cedar Grove New Jersey city directory has Minnie Bishof, widow of Charles E, residence 16 Overlook Rd. It is not known when Minnie died.

### 3. Magdalena Mabel Bishof and George Hemhauser

Mabel Bishof and George Hemhouser were married in 1918 in New Jersey.

The 1920 census for Ward 13, Newark, New Jersey has George Hemhauser, 26, a toolmaker in a shop renting part of a home at 74 Richelieu Terrace. Mabel is 22. Joseph Bishof and his wife Rose are also renting in the same dwelling as well as a third couple. It appears to be a rental unit with an absentee landlord.

The 1930 census for Newark, New Jersey has George M Hemhauser, 34, married at 23, a toolmaker in a factory renting his home at 74 Richelieu Terrace for $45 per month and has a radio. Mabel M is 33 and married at 21. Their daughter, Vivian R, is 6. Joseph Bishof owns the home and is living there with his wife, step-children and mother-in-law. This home is a couple of blocks from Stuyvesant Ave.

The 1940 census for Irvington, New Jersey has George A Hemhauser, 49, completed 8$^{th}$ grade, a foreman at a paint manufacture renting his home at 27 Harrison Place for $30 per month. There are 2 other families in the same dwelling.

### 4. Vivyan Rose Hemhauser

The 1941 Newark, New Jersey city directory has Vivyan R Hemhauser an employee of Prudential Insurance Company, home at Irvington. A 1940 census was not found.

Vivian Hemhauser Arnold born 18 Feb 1924, died 5 May 1997, served in the military from 28 Feb 1944 to 14 Mar 1946. She is in several Marine Corps Muster Rolls serving in Company G of the Second Headquarters Battalion, Henderson Hall, Arlington, Virginia. She rose from Private to Sargent.

### 3. Walter C Bishof and Catherine C Gallegher

The 1930 census for Newark, New Jersey has Walter Bishof, 31, married at 25, a veteran, a machinist in a Railroad Shop who owns his home at 26 Stuyvesant Ave. worth $5000 and has a radio. Catherine is 34, married at 28, born in New Jersey with parents born in Ireland. Their son is Walter Jr., 2. Walter's father, Charles Bishof, 57, married at 27, not a veteran, working as a machine operator at a Celluloid Manufacturer is renting part of the home for $50 per month and has a radio. Minnie is 57, married at 27 and born in New Jersey. The children are Harold, 21, working as a carpenter in building construction; Viola, 19, a clerk in an Insurance office and Gladys, 16.

The 1940 census for Newark, New Jersey has Walter Bishof, 42, completed 8$^{th}$ grade, a helper machinist for Railroads renting a home at 50 Columbia Ave for $35 per month. Catherine is 45 and completed 8th grade. Walter Jr. is 12 and completed 8th grade.

The 1941 Newark NJ City Directory has Walter C Bishof (Catherine C) machinist Pennsylvania Rail Road, home 50 Columbia Ave.

Walter C Bishof, born 30 Aug 1898 in Newark, New Jersey, died 11 Jul 1965 East Orange, New Jersey. PFC Quarter Master Corps US Army WW1, burial Beverly National Cemetery, Beverly New Jersey. Catherine born 1 Jun 1894, died 17 Oct 1972 is buried with Walter.

Walter C Bishof Jr. born 31 Dec 1928, died 10 Mar 2001. He was a private serving in the US Army and Navy during WW11 and Korea. Walter is buried in Beverly National Cemetery.

### 3. Raymond Bishof and Estella

The 1929 Newark City Directory has Bishof, Raymond J fireman Newark Fire Department, home 145 Stuyvesant Ave.

The 1930 census for Newark, New Jersey has Raymond Bishof, 26, married at 23, a foreman for the city renting a home at 160 Alexander Street for $50 per month and has a radio. Stella is 26 and married at 23. Their son, Raymond, is 1.

The 1940 census for Newark, New Jersey has Raymond Bishof, 36, completed 8th grade, a city fireman, renting his home at 76 Sanford Place for $44 per month. Estelle is 36 and completed 8th grade. Their son Raymond is 11 and completed 6th grade.

The 1941 Newark City Directory has Raymond J Bishof (Estelle I) fireman Newark Fire Department, home 76 Sanford Place.

Raymond J Bishof Sr. born 1 Jun 1903, died 23 May 1994 and is buried in Ocean County Memorial Park, Toms River, New Jersey. Estelle I Bishof born 1904, died 1991 and is buried with Raymond.

### 3. Wilber C Bishof and Mildred L Cooper

Wilber Bishof, married Mildred L Cooper 3 Sep 1927 in Bronx, New York.

The 1929 Newark City Directory has Wilber C Bishof, plumber, home 66 Halsted.

The 1930 census for Newark, New Jersey has Wilber Bishof, 25, married at 23, a plumber at a plumbing company, renting his home at 66 Halstead Street for $45 per month and he has a radio. Mildred is 25 and was married at 23. Another family lives at the same address.

The 1940 census for Middletown, Monmouth, New Jersey has Wilber Bishof, 35, completed 6th grade, a pipe fitter in the plumbing industry who owns his home on Cedar Ave. worth $1400. Mildred is 35 and graduated high school. Their sons are Wilber, 9, completed 3rd grade; Paul, 6, completed 1st grade and Charlie, 1.

Wilber and Mildred's son Wilber C Bishof, born 3 Jul 1930 enlisted in the US Army 16 Oct 1947. Wilber served during the Korean War, took advantage of a college degree and was commissioned an officer in 1956. He rose through the ranks and served during the Viet Nam War where he received a purple heart and other honors. Wilber eventually became a Colonel and served at the Pentagon as well as in New Jersey.

A Social Security death certificate has Mildred Bishof, born 1 Aug 1904, died Aug 1982. Wilber C Bishof born Sept 1904 also died Aug 1982 according to one source.

### 3. Albert H Bishof and Viola

The 1929 Newark, New Jersey City Directory has Albert H Bishof, a sheet metal worker, residence 26 Stuyvesant Ave.

Albert H Bishop enlisted in the US Navy 7 Apr 1933 and started serving on the USS San Francisco 17 Jun 1935. He served at least through 30 Jun 1939 when he appears in a muster roll for the USS San Francisco. It is not known if he served during WW11. 1930 and 1940 census records were not found.

Albert H Bishof born 5 Dec, 1906, died 12 Aug, 2005 and is buried in Manasota Memorial Park, Brandon, Manatee, Florida. His wife Viola born 1905, died 1991 and is buried with him.

Albert H Bishof of 85383 Glendale, Marcopa, Arizona, born 5 Dec 1906, died 12 Aug 2005. His SS# was issued in New Jersey. This appears to be the same person possibly he was vacationing in Arizona.

### 3. Harold E Bishof and Ruth

The 1929 Newark City Directory has Harold E Bishof, a carpenter, residence 26 Stuyvesant Ave. Harold is living in the same place with his father in 1930.

Harold Bishof has not been found in a 1940 census.

Harold and Ruth Bishof returned to the USA from Bermuda on 9 Mar 1958. They were living at 6 Remer Ave. Springfield, New Jersey. Harold was born 3 Oct 1908 and Ruth was born 8 Oct 1910 in Newark, New Jersey.

A Social Security Index has Harold E Bishof born 3 Oct 1908, died 20 May 1991.

## 3. Viola K Bishof and Melvin F Haas

The 1929 Newark City Directory has Viola K Bishof an employee of PruIns Company, residence 26 Stuyvesant Ave.

The 1940 census for Lawrence, Mercer, New Jersey has Melvin F Haas, 30, completed 8th grade, an inspector for the State of New Jersey renting a home at 817 Brunswick Ave. for $35 per month. Viola K is 29 and completed 11th grade. Their son Russell M is 1 ½. Minnie Bishof, 67, mother in law, a widow, completed 7th grade, same house in 1935. Minnie moved in with Viola after Charles died.

A Montclair, New Jersey City Directory for 1959 has Haas, Melvin F (Viola K) analysis engineer, Summit and councilman 525 Pompton Ave Cedar Grove, home 94 Overlook road Cedar Grove. He was a Chemist in an earlier census.

Melvin Haas, born 1 Nov 1909, died May 1986 according to the SS death index. Viola K. Hass, born 24 Apr 1910, died 24 Jan 2003, Cedar Grove, Essex, New Jersey.

## 3. Gladys Bishof

Gladys is found with her parents in the 1930 census. She was not found in 1940 and nothing is known about her after that.

## 2. Frank Joseph Bishof and Rose Kohl

Frank Bishof and Rose Kohl were married in 1906.

The 1910 census for Newark New Jersey has Frank J Bishop, 31, married 3 years, a laborer in a celluloid shop renting a home at 35 Barbara Street. Rose is 31 and has not had children. Bertha Kohl is 27, sister-in-law and an operator in an electrical shop. Minnie Kohl is 25 and sister-in-law. Rose Körkel is 35, aunt, single, born in New Jersey, parents born in Germany and a forelady in a celluloid shop. Did Rose Körkel find work for Frank? The census isn't clear but Rose may have owned the mortgaged home which Frank seems to have been renting as head of household. A 1900 census has Rose Körkel, 66, as head of house; a daughter Rosie Körkel, 28; and Sophia, 18. The Kohl's are Rosie, 21; Bertha, 18; Minnie, 16 and Charles, 14. All are living with an uncle Frank Warner, 50, single. They are all related but those relationships are not clear.

A WW1 draft registration card has Frank Joseph Bishof born 26 Mar 1878, living at 102 Houston Street in Newark, New Jersey with his wife Rose. He is working as a headman for a celluloid company on Ferry Street in Newark. He is of medium height and build with gray eyes and light hair.

The 1920 census for Newark New Jersey has Frank J Bishof, 41, a foreman in a celluloid company who owns a mortgaged home at 26 Darcy Street, parts of which he is renting out to 3 other families. Rose is 41 and is not working outside the home.

The 1930 census for Tom's River, New Jersey has Frank Bishof, 52, married at 28, husband of sister-in-law, a salesman in an oil & gas station. Rose is 51, sister-in-law and married at 27. They are renting part of a house at 119 Horner Street. Jacob J. Lautenschlager, 50, widower, a salesman at a lumber company owns the house worth $10,000 and a radio. Mildred R Lautenschlager is 17, daughter and attended school. Rose is a sister-in-law to Jacob and aunt to Mildred. They may have been living together so that Rose could take care of her niece.

Frank Bischof, born 1878, died 1939, and is buried in Riverside Cemetery, Toms River, New Jersey. Rose Bischof, born 1878, died 1964 and is buried with Frank.

## 2. George Bishof and Lillian

George Bishof married Lillian about 1906.

The 1910 census for Ward 13, Newark, New Jersey has George Bishof, 29, married 4 years, born in New York, both parents born in Germany, working as a plumber at Sley Plumbing, out of work 8 weeks in the past year and renting a home at 719 South 18$^{th}$ Street which is shared with the owner and his family of 8. Lillie is 26 and born in New Jersey with both parents born in Germany. There is also a boarder listed with George. 719 South 18$^{th}$ Street intersects with Springfield Ave. near Woodland Cemetery. The area has old large multi-family houses.

George Bishof, 38, born 24 Aug 1880, registered for WW1 12 Sep 1918. George was a plumber working for Butterworth-Judson on Ave. R, Newark, New Jersey and living at 683 South 20$^{th}$ Street. His nearest relative is Lillian Bishof with the same address. He is of medium height and build with blue eyes and brown hair.

The 1920 census for Newark, New Jersey has George Bishof, 39, a plumber contractor who is renting part of a home at 683 South 20$^{th}$ Street which held 3 families. Lillie is 36.

The 1930 census for Newark, New Jersey has George Bishof, 49, married at 26, not a veteran, a plumber journeyman who owns a home at 102 Vermont Ave. worth $400. Lily is 46 and was married at 23.

George applied for a Social Security life claim 8 Jan 1952. His birth date is 24 Aug 1880 and birth place Amityville, New York. (the 1900 census has 1882) Life claim is probably when he took retirement. A 1940 census and death date have not been found. It appears they did not have children.

## 2. Joseph Bishof and Rose Hemhauser / Anna Deobald

The 1910 census for Ward 6, Newark, New Jersey has Joseph Bishof, 28, widowed, born in New York with both parents born in Germany. George was a finisher in a hat shop and had been out of work 15 weeks in the last year. He was living at 18 Hunterdon Street as a boarder. Rose Hemhauser, 36, widow, had 1 child still living, a jewelry polisher and is renting the home. Rose's son George is 15 and a jewelry polisher. It is not known who Joseph's first wife was.

Joseph Bishof married Rose Hemhauser in 1913.

The 1920 census for Newark, New Jersey has Joseph Bishof, 38, a hatter in a factory renting a home at 74 Richelieu Terrace. Rose is 47. Rose's son, George Hemhouser, 26, a toolmaker in a shop and his wife Mabel, 22, are living with them.

The 1929 Newark City directory has Joseph Bishof hatter home 74 Richelieu Ter.

The 1930 census for Newark, New Jersey has Joseph Bishof, 50, married at 48, not working but owns his house at 74 Richelieu Terrace worth $4000 and has a radio. His wife, Anna is 46 and was married at 44. Fannie Wagner is 18, step-child and working as a tracer for Insurance. Edward Wagner is 17, step-child, not working and did not attend school. Sadie Deobald is 76 and Joseph's widowed mother-in-law. Also living with them is George M. Hemhauser, 50, married at 23, working as a toolmaker in a factory and renting part of the house for $45 per month. George's wife, Mabel is 33 and was married at 21. Their daughter, Vivian is 6.

The 1941 Newark City Directory has Joseph Bishof (Anna A) hatter home 74 Richelieu Terrace. A 1940 census was not found.

Joseph Bishof claimed his Social Security 27 Jan 1947, born 28 Aug 1880 in Amityville, New York. A note has the same name on 8 Oct 1976. (the 1900 census has Aug 1882) It may have been hard to keep track of so many children. The SS date was given by the individual and should be more accurate.

## 2. Anthony "Anton" Bishof and Catherine Dries Burger

Anthony Bishof and Catherine Burger were married in 1906 in New Jersey.

Anton Bishop was actually Anthony according to Theodore's obituary. His WW1 draft registration card reads: Anthony Edward Bishof, 35, born 18 Sep 1882, of 133 Washington Street, Newark, New Jersey. His occupation is Bartender, employer Seidler in Cliffwood, New Jersey and nearest relative is Katherine, his wife. Anton is tall and of medium build with blue eyes and light hair.

The 1920 census for Ward 2, Newark, New Jersey has Anthony E Bishof, 37, born in New York with both parents born in Germany, a bartender renting a home at 133 Washington Street. Catherine is 43, born in New Jersey with both parents born in

Germany, her occupation is rooming house. She is working at a rooming house not having roomers or boarders in her own house.

The 1930 census for Irvington, New Jersey has Anthony E Bishof, 47, married at 25, born on Long Island, a painter of buildings and homes who owns his home at 220 40th Street worth $8000 and a radio. Catherine is 55 and first married at 17. Lillian Wheeton, 30, step-daughter, married at 19 and granddaughters Dorothy, 10, and Jean, 4 are living with them.

The 1940 census for East Orange, New Jersey has Anthony Bishof, 57, completed 7th grade, painting for Mutual and renting a home at 130 Chestnut Street. Catherine is 65 and completed 8th grade.

Anthony Edward Bishof, 59, born 18 Sep 1882 in Amityville, Long Island, New York registered for WW2 on 26 Apr 1942. He was living at 130 Chestnut Street, East Orange, New Jersey and the person who would know his address is Mary Collins 120 South Clinton Street, East Orange, New Jersey. His employer is P Widmark 305 Carroll Street, East Orange, New Jersey. He is 5' 11", weighs 195 lbs., has blue eyes, brown hair and a light complexion.

Several family trees have Catherine's death as 2 Jan 1941 and Anton's as Aug 1972.

## 2. Fredrick Theodore "Fred" Bishof and Lillian A

The 1915 New Jersey State census for Newark, New Jersey has Fredrick T Bishof, 32, born Sep 1882, a metal worker living at 64 Seymour Street. Lillian is 29 and was born Jun 1886. Their sons are Fredrick, 5, born Jun 1908 and Norman, 2, born Jun 1912.

Fredrick Theodore Bishof, 35, born 18 Sep 1882 and living at 64 Seymour Ave. Newark, New Jersey registered for WW1 on 11 Sep 1918. His occupation is sheet metal worker at Baker & Smith Company, Morgan Station, New Jersey. His nearest relative is Lillian Bishof (wife) of the same address. He is of medium height and build with gray eyes and brown, bald hair.

The 1920 census for Ward 16, Newark, New Jersey has Fred T Bishof, 37, born in New York, both parents born in Germany and a sheet metal worker who owns his home at 64 Seymour Ave. Lillian is 33, born in New Jersey, both parents born in Germany. Their sons are Fredric, 10 and Norman, 7. Two couples are renting parts of their house.

The 1924 city directory for Newark, New Jersey has Fredrick T Bishof cornice maker, living at 64 Seymour.

The 1930 census for Newark, New Jersey has Fredrick T Bishof, 47, married at 26, not a veteran, a metal worker in a building who owns his house at 64 Seymour worth $20,000 and a radio. Lillian A is 44 and was married at 23. Their sons are Fredric J, 20, single and working as a plumber in buildings and Norman P, 17, single, attending school and not working. There is another family living in the house.

The 1941 city directory for Newark, New Jersey has Lillian A Bishof, widow of Fredrick T Bishof living at 64 Seymour. Fredrick J Bishof, plumber and Norman P Bishof, working for Prudential Insurance Company are also living at 64 Seymour Ave. A 1940 census was not found.

The following is Fredrick's WW 11 Navy record.
The U.S. Marine Corps Muster Rolls, U.S. Naval Reserve has Fredric J Bishof, metalsmith 1st class, enlisted 31 Aug 42, (he was part of a replacement battalion for men in the hospital in Australia).
The Combat Casualty Detachment, 17th Marines (Engineer) was organized 11Jul 43, for the purpose of providing a distinct and separate administrative status for such personnel as the Third Battalion, Seventeenth Marines (Engineer) remaining at Melbourne, Victoria, Australia, authority Division Administrative Circular #2-43 dated 16 Jul 1943.
11-31, unless otherwise stated in remarks all men appearing hereon performed duty at Mt Marha, Camp Balconbe, Victoria, Australia.
Muster Roll of Officers and Enlisted Men of the U. S. Marine Corps, 20th REP BN % Fleet Post Office, San Francisco, California. From 1 July to 23 July 1943 inclusive.
U.S. Navy Metalsmith 1st Class Bishof, Frederick J.

A department of Veterans Affairs Death File Has Fredric Bishof born 6 Jun 1909, died 1 Dec 1980, served in the Navy from 24 Nov 1942 to 15 Oct 1945.

Norman P Bishof, born 23 Jun 1912. was living in Manasquan, New Jersey in 1997.

## 2. William Bishof and Bertha Hauser / Mabel E.

The 1910 census for ward 10, Newark, New Jersey has Mary Bischoff, 65, a widow who had 12 children, 9 now living, born in Germany, immigrated in 1866 and working as a housekeeper in a private home. Her son, William Bischoff, 20 is single, was born in New York with both parents born in Germany, working as a tin smith for Sky Lights. They are living at 92 Garrison Street with two other families.

William Bishof, 28, of 72 Christie St. and Bertha Hauser, 28, of 29 Bremen Street both in Newark were married 21 Jun 1918 according to New Jersey United Methodist Church Records. He was born in Amityville and is a police officer. Oscar L Joseph officiated. The witnesses are Harriet Zimmerman and John Zimmerman of 424 South 17th Street, Newark, New Jersey.

William enlisted 24 Jul 1918 and left for WW1 shortly after he was married. William Bishof, private first class, departed Bordeaux, France on 13 Jun 1919 and arrived in New York 24 Jun 1919 on the ship Alphonso. He had been working in Base Hospital Number 208. His wife is Bertha Bishof of 29 Marne Ave. Newark, New Jersey.

The 1920 census for ward 13, Newark, New Jersey has William Bishof, 30, born in New York, a policeman renting a home at 426 South 17th Street. Bertha is 30 and born in New Jersey with father born in Germany, mother born in New York. A step-son, Edward Kelly is 12 and born in New Jersey. They are living with 2 other families of three people each.

The 1930 census for Newark, New Jersey has William Bishof, 40, married at 28, a police officer who owns his home at 12 Norwood Street worth $5000 and a radio. Bertha is 40 and was married at 28. Edward Kelly is 21 and working as a chemist in a laboratory. Bertha Hauser, mother-in-law is 69 and a widow.

The 1941 Newark City Directory has Bishof, William, policeman, residence 344 Belmont Ave.

William Bishof, 52, born 14 Jan 1890 at Amityville, Long Island, New York, registered for WW11 on 26 Apr 1942. He is living at 344 Belmont Ave., Newark, New Jersey and his nearest relative is Mable E Bishof, same address. William is a police officer for the City of Newark, at Market and Reed Street, Newark, New Jersey. He is 5' 9 1/2", weighs 175 lbs. and has gray eyes and blonde hair.

Bertha may have died or they were divorced between 1930 and 1942. William then married Mabel E. Bishof sometime before 1942. A 1940 census was not found.

William Bishof died 3 Sep 1946 and is buried in Fairmount Cemetery, Newark, New Jersey. No other Bishofs are buried in Fairmount Cemetery.

Mrs. Mabel E Bishof of 344 Belmont Ave, Newark, New Jersey applied for a headstone for William Bishof, born Jan 14, 1890, died 3 Sep 1946. Enlistment 24 Jul 1918, discharge 28 Jun 1919, a Pfc. company B, Field Hospital 347, 87th division, New Jersey.

# Chapter 15

## Theodore Bishop and Katherine Müller

1. Theodore Bishop (1868-1951)
+ Katherine Johanna Müller (1869-1909)
    2. Charles Theodore Bishop (1888-1954)
    + Mae Louise Stanley (1892-1945)
        3. George Henry Bishop (1914-1983)
        3. Agnes Louise Bishop (1916- 2010)
        3. Dorothy Irene Bishop (1918-2002)
        3. Earl Charles Bishop (1921-2010)
        3. Edward Wayne Bishop (1923-1989)
        3. Robert Ellis Bishop (1925-2001)
        3. Leleah Marie Bishop (1930-1930)
    2. Clara Bishop Cornell (1890-1962)
    2. Gertrude L Bishop (1893-1964)
    + William O Saxton (1879-1950)
        3. Katherine Saxton (1910-1982)
        +Donald Newland (1907-1966)
            4. Lillian Newland (1934-)
            4. Barbra Newland (1936-)
            4. Katherine Newland (1938-)
            4. Louise Newland (1939-)
        3.Harold Saxton (1912-1996) WW11
        + Christine Manna (1914 or 13-2000)
            4.Gertrude Saxton (1937-)
            4. Robert Saxton (1939-)
        3. William "Bill" Saxton (1914-1997) WW11
        + Ida M Pangi (1914-1999)
            4. Ronald Saxton (1938-)
    + Fredrick K Cavalear (1890-) WW1
        3. Fredrick K Cavalear (1920-1976) WW11
        + Kathryn Suckee (1925-)
    2. Esther Bishop (1894-1973)
    + Stephen Grandner (1887-1981)
        3. Bertha V Grandner (1913-1997)
        + Sidney J Lockley (1905-1995)
        3. Stephen Theodore Grandner (1916-1978) WW11
        + Alma Mae Dewitt (1921-2008)
            4. Theodore W Grandner (1946-)
    2. Theodore Bishop (1894-1976) WW1
    + Elizabeth Gulissippi (1894-1993)
        3. Mary B Bishop (1924-)
        3. Elizabeth Bishop (1931-)

   + Grace Wild (1888-1965)
      2. two babies who died at birth
      2. Leonard Constantina Bishop (1909-1917)
      2. Everet W. Bishop (1910-1992)
     + Margaret Caldwell (1915-1997)
         3. Virginia Bishop (1933-)
         3. Grace Bishop (1934-)
         3. Charles Theodore Bishop (1936-1960) Korea

## 1. Theodore George Bishop and Katherine Müller / Grace Wild

The long-held story that Theodore was born in Harlem, New York was finally solved with the discovery of Theodore's Social Security registration.

Theodore Bishop applied for Social Security in late 1939. He was born 15 Mar 1868 in Harlem, New York. His parents are Frank Bishop and Mary Kyseir. Kyseir is a phonetic spelling of Kaiser.

This information is in conflict with his marriage license where his birthplace, Amityville, and mother's name are different. I believe this information is closer to the truth. His mother's name was Kaiser rather than Geiser and he was born in Harlem. Theodore and Katherine stayed in the Oyster Bay area when his family moved to Newark, New Jersey. Frank Bishop and the rest of the family moved to New Jersey between 1880 and 1895 probably because of hard times on Long Island. It does not appear they went for better living conditions. Frank and Marie were hard working immigrants all of their lives.

Harlem has an interesting history. Refer to the map on page 383. The original inhabitants were Manhattan and Lenape Indians. They came to the area to farm the flatlands in the summer. Several Dutch homesteads were established in the area but when hostilities heated up, they fled to New Amsterdam in lower Manhattan. Eventually the Indians left and the English replaced the Dutch changing the name from New Haarlem to Harlem. During the Revolutionary War the small agricultural town of Harlem was burned to the ground. Harlem was rebuilt with farmland estates. Many of the wealthy houses on the heights overlooked the Hudson River. The railroad came through which led a speculator to lay out streets, gas lines, sewer lines, and other facilities required for urban life. Piers were also built enabling it to become an industrial hub. Between 1850 and 1870 many large estates were auctioned off as the fertile soil was depleted and crop yields fell. Some of the land became occupied by Irish squatters. After the Civil War, starting in 1868, those coming north to Harlem were poor immigrants. Factories, homes, churches, and retail buildings were built at great speed. After a panic in 1873, property values fell and the City of New York began to annex the land as far north as 155$^{th}$ street. With the recovery in 1876, row houses as distinct from the previous free-standing houses were being constructed in large numbers. By 1880 an elevated railroad was to be constructed into Harlem. Urbanization and the disappearance of farmland may have sent the Bischoffs and Müllers to Long Island. Long Island offered truck farming so called because the produce could be trucked to railroads to feed a growing New York City.

Frank Bischoff may have worked in the fields in Germany. After getting off the boat, they would have lived and worked in lower Manhattan. They may have moved to Harlem to work in the fields before Theodore was born in 1868. They moved to Long Island by 1880 to farm there.

The 1892 New York State Census for Oyster Bay, Queens has Theodore Bishop, 24, a farmer; Katie, 22; Charlie, 4, and Clara 2.

The 1900 census for Oyster Bay, Nassau, New York has Theodore Bishop, 32, born Mar 1868, a farm laborer who owned a mortgaged house. Kate is 31 and born Apr 1869. The children are Charles, 12, born Feb 1888; Clara, 10, born Feb 1890; Gertrude, 7, born Jan 1893; Ester, 5 and Theodore, 5, both born June 1894. All are born in New York. Theodore and Kate's parents are also listed as being born in New York, possibly to seem more American.

Katherine died when Charles was 18 years old. Theodore Bishop purchased lot no. 56 in St John of Jerusalem Cemetery for $15 in 1906.[23] According to tradition; Theodore changed his and his children's last name to Bishop after Katherine died. The records would indicate the name change was much sooner. Soon after Katie's death, he married Grace Wild. They had a son Constantia.

The 1910 census for Bridgewater, Somerset, New Jersey has Theodore Bishop, 42, born in New York with both parents born in Germany, second marriage, married 3 years, a general farmer who owns a mortgaged farm. Grace is 23, born in New York with both parents born in New York, first marriage and has 1 child who is living. Their children are Theodore,16; Esther, 16; and Constantia, 1 3/12. Julia Holst is 72, a widow, an aunt, has not had children, born in Ireland with both parents born in Ireland, immigrated in 1870, cannot read or write and has her own income. Julia must have been Grace's aunt. Was it Julia's farm or her money that purchased the farm in New Jersey? Charles, Clara, and Gertrude are not living with their father. Charles joined the army in June 1908.

The 1915 New York State Census for Babylon, Suffolk, has Theodore Bishop, 47, a farmer at Pine Lawn, Long Island living on Conklin Street. Grace is 27. The children are Theodore, 20, farmer at Pine Lawn; Leonard, 6; and Everett, 4. Apparently, things did not work out in New Jersey because they are back on Long Island. Pine Lawn is an institution which was eventually made into a cemetery.

The New York Death Index has Leonard Bishop, 8, born 1909, died 10 Oct 1917 in Manhattan, New York. He may have been taken to Manhattan for medical treatment.

The 1920 census for Huntington, Suffolk, New York has Theodore Bishop, 51, widowed, a house carpenter who owns his farm on Half Hallow Road. His son Everett is 9 and is listed as his grandson.

By 1920, Grace had left. Everett was told she died although this is not true as he found her in Maine when he was an adult. She just couldn't live with Theodore or maybe it was the loss of her 3 children. The Wild family tree has her birth as 3 Feb 1888 and death 1965 in Elsworth, Maine. Her 1st husband was Theodore Bishop and 2nd was Curtis Wesley Johnson (1891-1962) married 1918.

Theodore Bishop born 15 Mar 1868, died in 1951 in Amityville. He is buried in St. John of Jerusalem Cemetery, 500 Wantagh Ave., Levittown, New York with his 1st wife Katherine.

There is a small church in St John of Jerusalem Cemetery, 500 Wantagh Ave., Levittown, New York. The cemetery and chapel have been granted landmark status. The chapel is being restored with grant money.[22] The sign out front identifies the chapel as a German Methodist-Episcopal Mission. The church was founded as a mission in 1856 and the building completed in 1865. The name dates back to when the area was known as Jerusalem. Old church records do exist but early ones are in German. A professor has done some translation.[23] The cemetery is in the Town of Hempstead.

Find A Grave has additional information added in 2014.

Theodore Bishop born 15 Mar 1868, died 14 Mar 1951 in Copiague, Suffolk County, New York. He married Katherine Miller on Wednesday 10 Aug 1887. He worked as a farmer and for a time worked in the Central Park (Old Bethpage) Pickle Works. Burial is in Saint John of Jerusalem Cemetery, Wantage, Nassau, New York. GPS (lat/lon) 40.71205-73.50314 Created by anonymous on April 9, 2014. An Obituary is included:

Theodore Bishop
Theodore Bishop who lived on Straight Path Road, next to the Lucas Farm for over 35 years, died at the Nassau-Suffolk Hospital in Copiague March 14. He was born in Amityville March 15, 1868. Funeral services were held March 15 at the Heling Funeral Home in Lindherst, with the Rev. A. E. Abben, pastor of the Community Presbyterian Church officiating. Interment was at the St. John of Jerusalem Cemetery in Wantagh.
Mr Bishop is survived by three sons, Theodore of Wantagh, Everett of Huntington, and Charles of Michigan; three daughters, Mrs Gertrude Cavalier of New Jersey, Mrs. Esther Gardner of Huntington, and Mrs. Clara Cornell of Brooklyn; and two brothers George and Anthony of Newark, New Jersey.

## 2. Charles T Bishop and Mae Louise Stanley

Charles, Mae and their family are in chapter 16.

## 2. Clara Bishop

Clara Bishop was born Feb 1890 according to the 1900 census. She left home after her mother died. Her father Theodore's obituary has her last name as Cornell.

The 1910 census for Queens, Queens, New York has Charles Cornell, 56, married 35 years, a lumber piler, renting his house. Louisa is 53 and had 3 children, 2 are living. Clara Bischoff is 20, servant, single and working for a private family. All of them are born in New York as are their parents. This is the correct age for Clara but it is interesting she is using the Bischoff last name. Possibly she was born a Bischoff and chose to maintain the name and not change to Bishof.

The 1920 census for Brooklyn, Kings., New York has Charles Cornell, 65, working as a laborer; Louisa, 61; and Clara, 29, daughter, single, not working. They are renting a home at 193 Hull Street; another family is also renting in the same building. It is not known if Clara was formally adopted or she just started using the name.

The 1930 census for Brooklyn, Kings, New York has Charles Cornell, 78, a laborer but is not currently employed renting a house at 850 Jefferson Ave. for $38 per month. Louisa is 72. Clara is 41, single, daughter and a saleslady in a department store.

This is a picture of Clara on a postcard she sent to Charles T Bishop. The date is unknown. The woman is Clara and looks like I remember her when she visited Michigan in the early 50s except, she was older. The postcard is in the possession of Anna Mae Letherer Bertalon.

Clara indicates the man "driving" the car is Mr. Cornell. This could be Charles Cornell, born in 1852 with James Henry Cornell, born in 1876 and 14 years older than Clara in the back seat. The two men do appear to be related with similar features.

A distant cousin found on Ancestry through DNA testing, said the man in the back seat was James Henry Cornell but didn't recognize the driver.

The 1940 census for Brooklyn, Kings, New York has Charles Cornell, 91, widowed, completed 5th grade, living in the same house in 1935, renting a home at 1258 Broadway. Clara Cornell, daughter is 50, single, completed 8th grade and not working.

Charles and Louisa Cornell's son, James Henry Cornell, 42, of 2168 Fulton Street, Brooklyn, New York, born 6 Feb 1876, an automobile mechanic, wife Dora Cornell, registered for WW1 on 12 Sep 1918.

The 1910 census for Brooklyn, Kings, New York has James Cornell, 33, married 15 years, a carpenter in buildings. Dora is 31 and has 3 living children. The children are James A 12; Harold R, 8 and Benjamin F, 5.

A 1920 census for Brooklyn, Kings, New York has James Cornell, 42, a mechanic in a garage renting part of a building at 211 Reid Ave. Dora is 40 The children are; Harold R, 19, a bookkeeper in a real estate office and Benjamin, 15, a clerk in a real estate office.

James Cornell born about 1876, died 3 Aug 1925, age 49, in Kings, New York.
Dora Cornell born about 1879 died 2 Mar 1930 in Kings, New York.

Charles Simeon Cornell, 92, died 22 Jun 1940. He was living at 1258 Broadway, Brooklyn, New York. Clara Cornell, daughter is the informant. He must have died soon after the 1940 census was taken. With James Cornell and his wife dead, Clara would be the only surviving "child". There were two grandsons. It is not known how the estate was divided.

This left Clara Bischoff Cornell free to visit her brother in Michigan.

## 2. Gertrude Bishop and William O Saxton / Fredrick Cavalear

The story of Gertrude Bishop and William Saxton is very complicated! Recent discoveries keep changing the story. There may be more yet to be discovered.

The 1880 census for Brooklyn, Kings, New York has William O Saxton, 26, born on Long Island, a bookkeeper living at 691 Lafayette Ave. Augusta is 26, born in New York and keeping house. The children are William O, 2 and Helen A, 8/12.

The 1900 census for Montclair, Essex, New Jersey has William Saxton, 44, born Oct 1855, married 24 years, a commission merchant who owns his home at 58 Highland Ave. free and clear. Augusta is 44, born Oct 1855, and has 4 children, all living. The children are William, 21, born Feb 1879, a clerk for his father; Chester, 19, born Jan 1881 and Robert, born Jan 1891. There are servants, a coachman and 2 domestics. The Saxton's owned property both in New York City and New Jersey. They raised and bought produce in New Jersey for sale in New York City.

The 1910 census for Manhattan, New York, New York, taken Apr 1910, has William Saxton, Jr. 32, married 7 months, a salesman in a produce store renting his home at 54 West 77th Street. Helen P is 25.

Gertrude C Bishop married William O Saxton, both from Ridgefield, Connecticut, on 9 Sep 1911 according to Connecticut Church Record Abstracts. He must have had a quick divorce from Helen (or not). Gertrude's daughter Katherine was born 15 Jun 1910. Gertrude would have become pregnant in September and William married Helen in September. Apparently, William married Gertrude because of Katherine. William's parents may have only known about Helen. It is probable, even likely, that Gertrude did not know about Helen until about 1915. With Helen in New York and Gertrude in New Jersey, it was possible to keep the secret until there were 2 babies at once. William was born 18 Sep 1914. Virginia was born 1 Mar 1915.

The 1915 New York State Census for New York, New York has William O Saxton, 36, merchant living at 410 West End Ave. Helen P is 26. Their daughter Virginia is 3/12. They have a maid living with them. William appears to be married to two wives.

Fred Cavalear, 29, single, born 4 July 1888 in Jersey City, New Jersey, registered for WW1 on 5 Jun 1917. He was living on East Main Street, Bound Brook, New Jersey and a house painter for Petti of Bound Brook, New Jersey. He is tall, medium build with blue eyes and light hair. He is listed on a troop transport, leaving Hoboken, New Jersey 19 May 1918. He was in an ambulance company.

Gertrude Bishop married Frederik Cavalear in 1919 in New Jersey.

The 1920 census for Bound Brook, Somerset, New Jersey taken 15 Jan 1920, has Fredrick Cavalier, 30, born in New Jersey, a wagon driver for a lumber company renting a home at 115 West Main Street, 4 other families live in the same building. Gertrude is 27 and born in New York. The children are Katherine, 9, born in New York; Harold, 7, born in New Jersey and William, 5, born in New Jersey. The two older children attended school.

The 1920 census for Manhattan, New York, New York has William O Saxton, 40, separated, a commercial marketer of eggs and butter renting an apartment at 146 Central Park West. His daughter, Virginia is 4 2/12. Louise Trant, a servant is living with them.

William Saxton's daughter, Virginia Saxton Macwillie, born 1 Mar 1915, died 23 Nov 1974 in Santa Fe, New Mexico. Her mother is Helena Paulina Beyerlieb Becker. Her father is not mentioned. Both Helen and Gertrude left William. Gertrude kept her children while Helen's daughter, Virginia, lived with her father and grandmother.

A 1925 New York State Census for New York City has William Saxton, 45, a produce merchant living in an apartment at 471 Park Ave. His daughter, Virginia is 10. His mother, Augusta is 73. His sister, Helen Benjamin is 40. An English governess is living with them.

The 1930 census for Bridgewater, Somerset, New Jersey has Fredrick Cavalear, 41, first married at 31, born in New Jersey, a veteran, a laborer in a nursery who owns a home on Field Ave. worth $2000. Gertrude is 37 and first married at 19. The children are Harold Saxton, 17, stepson, a laborer at odd jobs; William Saxton, 15, stepson and Fredrick Cavalier, 10, attended school. The 2 Saxton boys did not attend school.

The 1930 census for City of New York, Manhattan, New York has Agustine Saxton, 77, widow, first married at 25 renting an apartment at 471 Park Ave. for $500 per month. William O is 51, son, divorced, married at 30 and working as a wholesaler of butter & eggs. Helen Benjamin is 49, daughter and widowed. Virginia Saxton is 15, granddaughter and attended school. Living with them are Ellen T Crowley, maid and Katie F Shea, cook. According to this William O Saxton would have been first married in 1909 which corelates.

There is a social Security application for William O Saxton, spouse Gertrude Bishop, child William Ottis Saxton. Applications started to be processed in 1936. It appears William was claiming Gertrude and his son. Gertrude married Fredrick Cavalear in 1919.

The 1940 census for Bridgewater, Somerset, New Jersey has Fredrick Cavalear, 50, completed 3rd grade, a painter, worked 26 weeks in 1939, income $250. Gertrude is 47 and completed 8th grade. Fred Jr., 20, completed 8th grade, seeking work, a truck driver for a cement contractor, worked 16 weeks in 1939, income $150. The family is still living on Field Ave. in a home they own, valued at $2500. The family probably had a hard time during the depression but hung on to the house and somehow got by.

Fred Kinch Cavalear, 54, born 1 Jul 1887 in New Jersey registered for WW11 on 25 Apr 1942 in Somerset, New Jersey. He was living on Field Ave. in Finderline, Somerset, New Jersey, mailing address of R. D. #2, Box 95, Somerset, New Jersey. He did not have a telephone. His wife was Gertrude Cavalear of the same address. His employer's name was George Devine, Supervisor, WPA, Raritan, Somerset, New Jersey. He was 5' 3", weighed 145 lb. had blue eyes, brown hair and a scar on his right arm.

This picture has Clara Cornell or possibly Esther Grandner and Gertrude Cavalear, 3rd and 2nd from the right respectively. Clara and Esther looked a lot alike and both visited at different times.

From left to right, children in front row: Judy Bishop, Donald Letherer, Mickey Bishop, Margie Bishop, Anna Mae Letherer, Marian Bishop, Nancy Bishop, Carol Bishop
Back row: Agnes Letherer, Charlie Letherer, Bob Bishop, Corabell Bishop, Earl Bishop, Betty Bishop, Helen Bishop holding Wayne, Charles T Bishop, Clara or possibly Esther, Gertrude Cavalier, and Jean Bishop. George and Ed Bishop were taking the picture.

Gertrude Bishop Cavalier died 5 Apr 1964. It is not known when Fred Cavalear died but probably before 1946 as Gertrude traveled alone.

### 3. Katherine Saxton and Donald Newland

The 1930 census for Bridgewater, Somerset, New Jersey has Donald Newland, 23, married at 21, a truck driver for a construction company renting a home on Eastern Turnpike for $10 a month. Catherine is 20 and married at 18. This would indicate Katherine / Catherine was born in 1910 and married in 1928.

The 1940 census for Bridgewater, Somerset New Jersey has Donald Newland, 32, completed 6$^{th}$ grade, born in New Jersey, a laborer in a resin factory who owns his home on Somerset Ave. worth $1000. Katherine is 32, completed 8$^{th}$ grade and born in New York. Their children are Lillian, 6; Barbra, 4; Katherine, 2; and Louise, 8/12. All the children were born in New Jersey.

Donald William Newland, born 14 Sep 1907, died Apr 1966 and is buried in New Somerville Cemetery, Somerville, New Jersey. Katherine (Catherine) Saxton Newland, born 15 Jun 1910, New York, died 27 Mar 1982 Bridgewater, Somerset, New Jersey and is buried with Donald.

### 3. Harold Saxton and Christina Manna

The 1940 census for South Bound Brook, Somerset, New Jersey has Harold Saxton, 27, completed 6$^{th}$ grade, born in New Jersey, an automobile mechanic in a garage renting a house on Washington Street. Christine is 26, completed 6$^{th}$ grade, born in New Jersey. The children are Gertrude, 3, and Robert 9/12.

According to the official list of names of residents of Newark, New Jersey who served in WW11, Harold Nelson Saxton served in Co D 13$^{th}$ Regiment.

Harold Saxton, born 24 Jun 1912, died 11 Apr 1996.

### 3. William O Saxton and Ida M Pangi

In 1936 William Ottis Saxton Jr. (3$^{rd}$) applied for a Social Security number, born 18 Sep 1914 in South Bound Brook, New Jersey, died 29 Dec 1997, parents William O Saxton and Gertrude Bishop.

The 1940 census for Hillsborough, Somerset, New Jersey has William Saxton, 26, highest grade completed is blank, a private truck driver renting a home for $10 per month. Ida is 25, completed 8th grade and an operator in a dress shop. Their son, Ronald, is 2.

A 1942 city directory for Somerville, New Jersey has Saxton, Wm O (Ida M) foreman home 14 W Main.

World War 11 Navy Muster Roll has William O Saxton, enlisted 6/8/42 in New York, New York. Rating at date of last report is GM3c. V-6. Report is from U.S.S. Conway (DD507) on 9 Oct 1942.

At some point they moved to Phoenix, Arizona as William O Saxton is listed in the 1956 Phoenix, Arizona city directory as Saxton, Wm O (Ida M) Manager Butane All Fuel Service home 325 ½ N 18th Dr.

William Saxton, born 18 Sep 1914. died 29 Dec 1997 in Phoenix, Arizona and is buried in Resthaven Park West Cemetery. Ida M Pangi Saxton, born 19 Dec 1914 in Manhattan, New York, died 24 Jul 1999 in Phoenix, Arizona. There isn't a separate stone for William Saxton.

**3. Fredrick Cavalear and Kathryn Suckee**

Fredrick K. Cavalear, born 1920 in New Jersey from Somerset, New Jersey, enlisted 25 Mar 1942 at Fort Dix, New Jersey. Branch Immaterial–Warrant Officers, grade private, enlisted for the duration of the war. He had a grammar school education and had worked as semiskilled chauffeurs and drivers of bus, taxi, truck, and tractor. He was married, height 71", weight 151. Frederick Cavalear, served from 25 Mar 1942, until 22 Sep 1945.

Fred K Cavalear, 26, a maintenance man married Kathryn Suckee, 21, on 9 Mar 1946 in Alexandria, Virginia. His parents were Fred Cavalear and Gertrude Bishop of route 2, Summerville, New Jersey. Her parents were Wayne Suckee and Gizella Vrba of route 2, Plainfield, New Jersey. Michael Frasca, appointed by the Corporation Court of Alexandria, Virginia, married them on 9 March 1946 in Alexandria.

Fredrick Cavalear, born 5 Mar 1920, died 29 Nov 1976. His last residence was 08807 Bridgewater, Somerset, New Jersey.

## 2. Esther Bishop and Stephen Grandner

Esther Bishop married Stephen Grandner in 1912.

The 1920 census for Bridgewater, Somerset, New Jersey has Stephen Grandner, 37, a general laborer who owns his mortgaged home. Esther M is 25. Their children are Bertha, 7 and Stephen, 3. His parents are living next door.

The 1925 New York State Census for Huntington has Stephen Grandner, 36, dairying on Lower Half Hollow Road. Esther M is 30. The children are Bertha V, 11, at school; Stephen Theodore, 8, at school and Everett W Bishop, 14, at school. Everett Bishop is not living with his father but is living with his sister and going to school.

The 1930 census for Huntington, Suffolk, New York has Stephen Grandner, 42, married at 25, a laborer on a private estate and renting a home on Half Hallow Road. Esther is 35 and married at 17. The children are Bertha, 16, attended school; Teddy, 13, attended school and Everett Bishop, 19, a laborer on a truck farm. Sidney Lockley is, 24, a lodger and a laborer on a truck farm.

The 1940 census for Freeport, Nassau, New York has Esther Grandner, 46, married, completed 8th grade, born in New York, a nurse for a private family living on Atlantic Ave. She is living with Rosco and Katheryn Conklin and is probably taking care of Elizabeth Conklin, 87. The nursing being done by Esther did not require a degree or much training at that time. Families tended to get a woman to live in and take care of someone for little more than board and room. Stephen was not found in the 1940 census they may have been separated.

Dad, Helen, Wayne, Ed, Aunt Esther + Sid

Ed, Helen and Wayne Bishop took a trip to Long Island in 1948. Charles T Bishop went with them. They visited Ester Grandner, her daughter, Bertha and Sidney Lockly. Bertha must have taken the picture while they were at the beach.

Esther M Grandner, born 6 Jun 1894, died Oct 1973 in Florida and is buried in Saint John of Jerusalem Cemetery in Wantagh, Nassau, New York.

Stephen Grandner born 8 Nov 1887, died Nov 1981 with a last residence of East Orange, Essex, New Jersey.

### 3. Bertha V Grandner and Sidney Lockley

The 1940 census for Queens, New York City, New York has Sidney Lockley, 34, completed 10th grade, a ground service man for air lines lodging with other families at 3412 31st Ave. Bertha is 26, completed 8th grade.

Bertha and Sid may not have had children. They did not have children in the 1948 photograph. I remember Bertha and Sid Lockley coming to our house on Meridian Road, Hudson, Michigan in the summer of 1952. Sid was fascinated with the corner cupboard that was about to be installed in the new kitchen. He said it would make a roulette table. They were about my parents age.

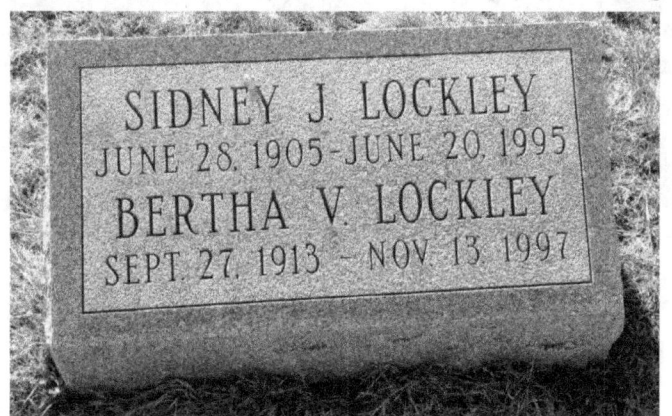

Sidney J Lockley born 28 Jun 1905, died 20 Jun 1995 and is buried in Saint John of Jerusalem Cemetery, Wantagh, Nassau, New York.

Bertha V Lockley, 84, born 27 Sep 1913, died 13 Nov 1997 in Deland, Volusia, Florida and is buried with Sidney.

### 3. Stephen Theodore Grandner and Alma Mae Dewitt

Stephen Grandner enlisted 19 Jan 1943 for WW11 and was discharged 7 Nov 1945. He must have gone to Tennessee for training married Alma then served in Europe.

Stephen Theodore Grandner, 27, married Alma Mae Dewitt, 21, on 24 Aug 1943 in Lauderdale County, Tennessee. The license states the Stephen is bound to the State of Tennessee in the sum of twelve hundred and fifty dollars. This is a very high price for a marriage license. Is it a bride payment? The bride did not sign, only Stephen.

Stephen applied for a social security number Dec 1945 in Florida. His parents are listed as Stephen Grandner and Esther Bishop.

Stephen and Alma had a son Teddy. Theodore W Grandner was born 28 Nov 1946. The address is 685 Half Hallow Road, Dix Hills, New York.

This picture is labeled Ted, Teddy, Alma, Aunt Esther and baby. It was taken in 1948.

Stephen Theodore "Teddy" Grandner born 8 Aug 1916 in Martinsville, New Jersey, died 2 Jun 1978 and is buried in Saint John of Jerusalem Cemetery, Wantagh, Nassau, New York. Alma Dewitt Grandner born 6 Oct 1921, died 7 Nov 2008 and is buried with Stephan. Stephen's last address was 11746 Huntington Station, Suffolk, New York.

## 2. Theodore George Bishop and Elizabeth Gillespie

Theodore went to work on the farm with his brother Charles after 1915.

Theodore George Bishop Jr., 22, born 6 Jun 1894 in Central Park, New York, registered for WW1 on 5 Jun 1917 in Wheatland, Hillsdale, Michigan. He was a farm laborer employed by Charles T Bishop, R#1 Hudson, Michigan. He was a medium height and build with blue eyes and light brown hair. He served in the Navy from 1 Apr 1917 to 18 Feb 1919.

The 1920 census for Bridgewater, Somerset, New Jersey has Theodore Bishop, 26, a laborer at the asbestos works boarding with other workers on Galeville Road.

Theodore G Bishop married Elizabeth Gillespie on 26 Jun 1920 in Manhattan, New

York, New York.

The 1930 census for Brooklyn, Kings, New York has Teddy Bishop, 35, married at 25 a painter for better stores who owns a home at 581 East 35th Street worth $10,000. Elizabeth is 37 and married at 27. Their daughter Mary B is 6.

The 1940 census for New York, Kings, New York has Theodore G Bishop, 45, completed 8th grade, seeking work but owns the home at 581 East 35th Street worth $6200. Elizabeth is 45 and completed 8th grade. The children are Mary, 16, completed 10th grade and Elizabeth, 9, completed 4th grade.

Theodore G Bishop born 6 Jun 1894, died 13 Nov 1976. Elizabeth Gillespie Bishop, born 12 May 1894, died 1 Aug 1983 and is buried in Mt Ararat Cemetery, East Farmingdale, Suffolk, New York.

### 3. Lenard Constantina Bishop

Lenard was born in 1909 to Grace and Theodore Bishop. He is listed in the 1910 and 1915 census records with his parents. He died 10 Oct 1917 in Manhattan where he was taken for treatment.

### 3. Everett Bishop and Margaret Caldwell

In 1925 and 1930 Everett was living with his sister Esther.

Everett Bishop married Margaret Caldwell on 23 Nov 1931 in West Islip, New York. His father moved in with them right away.

The 1940 census for Huntington, Suffolk, New York has Everett Bishop, 29, head of household, completed 8th grade, born in New Jersey, a dairy worker who owns a home on Straight Path worth $4000. Margaret is 25, completed 8th grade and born in New York. Their children are Virginia, 7, completed 2nd grade; Grace, 6 and Charles, 4. Theodore Bishop, father, is 72, completed 5th grade and is retired. They were all living in the same house in 1935.

Everett and Margaret's son, Charles Theodore Bishop born 16 Apr 1936, died 25 Aug 1960. He was a private in the US Army in Korea from 26 Aug 1953 to 11 Aug 1956. He died in a car accident and is buried at Long Island National Cemetery, 2040 Wellwood Ave., Farmington, New York, Section S Site 794.

Everett Bishop, 81, born 6 Sep 1910, died 19 Jun 1992 in Volusia, Florida and is buried in Fred Hunter's Hollywood Memorial Gardens East, Hollywood, Florida. Margaret Ann Caldwell, 82, born 24 Jan 1915 at Oyster Bay, Nassau, New York, died 19 Aug 1997 in Broward, Florida and is buried with Everett. Her parents were Joseph Caldwell and Annie Welsh.

In 1979 my son, Mark was interested in genealogy. My aunt wrote a two-page history of the Sawyer family. Our family took a trip east to find out more about The Sawyer and Bishop families. Essentially the beginning of the journey into genealogy. We visited Margaret Bishop at 61 W. Pulaski Road in Huntington Station, New York on Long Island. While there, Mark interviewed Margaret.

Margaret: Now old man Bishop, I lived with him for 20 years, I didn't appreciate him so much. His wife died when these first bunch of kids were in their teens; then a few years later he married my husband's mother, her name was Wild, Grace Wild and she was I think around 20, in her 20's, and he was like 45 with grown children at the time. But anyway, Charlie, claimed Theodore pushed the older ones out, so he went in the Army. Then he came back to Michigan and he met his wife and he stayed there and he didn't come back around here; so, we didn't see much of him. But I know a lot of his children had come down to Ester's and that was Charlie's sister. There was Esther, Gerdy, Clara, and Teddy and that's the five children of the first marriage which you would probably be most interested in.

Mark: No, I want to know the whole thing.

Margaret: The whole thing. I'll tell you as much as I can.

Mark: Was your husband the only child by the second marriage?

Margaret: No, she had four children but three died. One died about 8 years old, and the other two died right in birth. They are buried, they're I think in Bethpage Cemetery, the two young ones. The other one he lived to be eight, he's buried in Pinewalled, and of course my husband, he's the survivor of that family. You see it's like two families.

Nancy: Do you have the names of those first and second wives?

Mark: Yeah. I do. When did he marry the second wife?

Margaret: Let me see. Let me see if I can get back to that. Well my husband is going to be 69 in September and his brother would be older than him, he'd be two years older then him so that would be 71, probably 72 years ago, I don't know what year that would be.

Mark: Alright, when was your husband born?

Margaret: September the sixth 1910.

Mark: And yourself?

Margaret: I was born in Oyster Bay, Long Island here on January 24, 1915.

Nancy: I was thinking you would be more the age of my parents than my grandfather.

Margaret: Well, yeah. That's because that the original family, in other words those kids were, I don't know how old Charlie was when Theodore married his second wife. He must have been; Esther and them were around seventeen and then Charlie, he was older, I would say he married her when Charlie was in his 20's or so, he married again.

Mark: Now what is your name?

Margaret: What, first name, last name, or both?

Mark: both

Margaret: My name is Caldwell, Margaret Caldwell.

Mark: And you said you were born....

Margaret: Oyster Bay, I was born in Oyster Bay. You want to know where he was born?

Mark: Yep.

Margaret: Martinsville, New Jersey; there father had a big farm out there.

Nancy: I didn't know that. It was over in New Jersey.

Margaret: Yeah, my husband was born in Jersey, but I think the older ones were born here, around Bethpage. That's where they originally came from. Grandpa Bishop I think was born up in Harlem. I always called him Grandpa Bishop because he was around and the kids always called him Grandpa, so I always called him Grandpa Bishop.

Mark: His name was Theodore, right?

Margaret: Theodore.

Nancy: Do you know when he was born in Harlem?

Margaret: It was way back. Let me think he would be, he was 83 when he died, he has been…

Nancy: When did he die?

Margaret: …dead 29 years.

That was the end of Mark's transcription but Margaret did give us St. John of Jerusalem Cemetery as Theodore's burial place. We went to a funeral home to find the location and were able to visit his and several other graves while there. Margaret served us Long Island tea which the girls found a treat. It had sugar, something we didn't do at home. Margaret told us she was Irish and clashed with the stubborn German frequently. The most memorable quote by Margaret was: "It was no bargain when I married a Bishop". She was not happy that Theodore moved in right after they were married.

Everett Bishop, 81, born 6 Sep 1910 Martinsville, Somerset, New Jersey, died 19 Jun 1992 Volusia, Florida and is buried in Fred Hunter's Hollywood Memorial Gardens East, Hollywood Florida. Margaret A Colwell Bishop, 82, born 24 Jan 1915, died 19 Aug 1997 and is buried with Everett.

# Chapter 16

## Charles Bishop and Mae Stanley

1. Charles Theodore Bishop (1888-1954) Spanish American War
+ Mae Louise Stanley (1892-1945)
    2. George Henry Bishop (1914-1983)
    + Leona Jean Sawyer (1914-2013)
        3. Richard Charles Bishop (1937-1937)
        3. Marian Louise Bishop (1939-2020)
        3. Nancy Marie Bishop (1941- )
        3. Carol Ann Bishop (1944- )
    2. Agnes Louise Bishop (1916-2010)
    + Charles Letherer (1909-1992)
        3. Anna Mae Letherer (1942-)
        3. Donald Letherer (1944-)
        3. Mary Letherer (1945-)
        3. Shaila Marie Letherer (1947-)
        3. Lucille June Letherer (1949-)
    2. Dorothy Irene Bishop (1918-2002)
    + Leo D. Jennings (1917-1997) WW11
        3. Joe Jennings (1949-)
        3. Kay Jennings (1952-)
    2. Earl Charles Bishop (1920-2010)
    + Jennifer Elizabeth "Betty" Foreman (1922-2003)
        3. Earl Charles "Mickey" Bishop (1940-)
        3. Marjorie Diane Bishop (1941-)
        3. Judy Ann Bishop (1943-1968)
        3. Jacklynn Sue "Jackie" Bishop (1950-)
    2. Edward Wayne Bishop (1923-1989)
    + Helen Kincaid (1926-2014)
        3. Wayne Edward Bishop (1945-)
        3. Dianne Jeannine Bishop (1950-)
        3. Charles Leo Bishop (1955-)
        3. Lynette Marie Bishop (1961-)
        3. Scott Lynn Bishop (1962-)
    2. Robert Ellis Bishop (1925-2001) WW11
    + Corabelle Phetteplace (1927-1987)
        3. Barry Bishop (1947-2011)
        3. Pamela Bishop (1951-)
        3. Cynthia Ann Bishop (1954-1954)
    2. Leleah Marie Bishop (1931-1931)

## 1. Charles Theodore Bishop and Mae Louise Stanley

After his mother died, Charles left home and joined the army. He is reported to have served with Teddy Roosevelt's Rough Riders.[6] Roosevelt sent troops into Cuba to preserve order in 1906. The first president of Cuba, Tomas Estrada Palma, was a good president and honest man who was devoted to a program of "more teachers than soldiers". However, the question of his reelection in 1906 provoked a revolution and the intervention of the United States which lasted until 1909 when Gomez was elected president. It is not known if Charles went to Cuba but it seems doubtful.

Charles T Bishop, 21, born 2 Feb 1888 Long Island, New York, enlisted in the United States Army 19 Jun 1908 for 3 years. Occupation is teamster. He had blue eyes, brown hair and was 5 ft 10 inches tall. He joined the 7th Calvary, Troop L. He was discharged 16 Jun 1911 at Ft. McDowell, California. Comments were: short term, Pvt., very good and honorable discharge.

This is part of a picture of the 7th Calvary. The arrow points to Charles Bishop.

Charles told his son Robert that he left home because his father misused him. He was home during the summers to work on the farm. He was put out to work and fend for himself in the winter. By joining in June Charles avoided another summer on the farm. Charles went to the Philippines, China, and Japan. His son Robert went to the same places with the Navy in WW 11. Robert was very proud of that fact and said it brought his father and him closer together. [25]

The pictures of Charles Bishop in the military were provided by Robert Bishop.

This is a picture of Charles and some of his friends from the 7th Calvary. He is in the first row on the left.

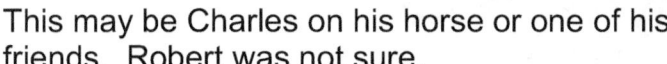

This may be Charles on his horse or one of his friends. Robert was not sure.

This picture is very definitely Charles T Bishop before he was married. He has a cigar in his hand. Later he smoked a pipe.

Charles bought this embroidered silk cloth while in the Philippines. It was made for the 7th Calvary and has a picture of their ship under the place for a picture of the individual. He framed the picture after he got home.

His military hat.

His insignia pin. 7th Calvary, Troop L.

These items are in the possession of Pam Bishop Smutek. There is also a commemorative book that has his name Charles Bischoff.

The 1910 census for Fort Riley Military Reservation, Kansas, taken 15 Apr, has Charles T Bishop, 23, soldier, born in New York with both parents born in New York.

Charles met Lee Horton from Michigan while in the service. Lee Horton enlisted 9 Nov 1908 in Ohio. Lee was an engineer and although the writing is unclear, he may have been assigned to the 7th Artillery. Lee was discharged 16 Nov 1911 from Ft McDowell, California. The comments were exceptional service, potential, rest is illegible. It has been thought Ray Dougherty was also in the army with Charles but Ray was born in 1901. They must have become friends later.

Charles Bishop may have written to Lee Horton's cousin, Mae Stanley, and decided Michigan might be a good place to settle. He came to Michigan and hired on to work for a family on Kelso road in Hillsdale County (1-mile south of Locust Corners).[6] Mae Louise Stanley was working for the same family, helping in the house. They met and eventually married.

On the left is Mae Stanley, Center back is Charles Bishop. The other couple may be Fannie Kester and Lee Horton or some other friends.

Charles T Bishop married Mae Louise Stanley on 6 Jun 1912 in Hillsdale, Michigan. Charles M Weaver, justice of the peace, officiated.

This picture of Charles and Mae was taken about the time of their marriage. The picture was taken in front of Mae's parent's house.

Mae and Charles had 6 children: George Henry Bishop was their first. George was born 23 Jun 1914. This picture is of the proud mother and her boy at about 1 year. Later children were doing good to get a picture as Mae became more and more busy.

Agnes was born 2 Jan 1916. Dorothy was born 13 Sep 1918.

In the fall of 1919, when George was 5 years old his mother took him to Taylor School, the same small country school both her and her mother had attended. George would be the third generation in that school. He went to school for 3 or 4 days but was very unhappy. The only other students were 8 big boys. There was no one his age. He asked his mother if Agnes could go with him. She had been his playmate as long as he could remember and the only person, he could think of to accompany him to school. The school teacher and Mae decided it would be better to send both George and Agnes the next year. The superintendent agreed. George would be 6 and Agnes would be 4. They were together the rest of their school years. Graduating from Addison High School in 1933.[6]

The 1920 census for Wheatland Township, taken 12 Jan lists Charlie Bishop 32, a farmer; his wife Mae 27, George 5, Agnes 3 11/12, Dorothy 2 4/12. They were living on a mortgaged farm in Wheatland Township but the location is not listed.

Earl was born 17 Jan 1920.

Edward was born 16 Oct 1923. This is his picture.

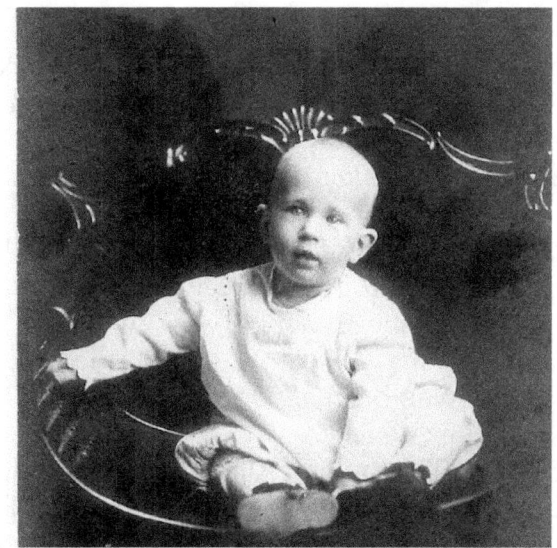

As soon as George was able, he was expected to help with chores. Charles would go out early to do the chores then come back in for a cup of coffee and tell George what needed to be done. Most days George and Agnes would go out to work in the fields or barn while Dorothy helped in the house.[6]

Charles always wore coveralls, summer and winter. He drank coffee hot in the morning then put the rest in a pail which he hung on the back of the wagon, and drank cold the rest of the day. He never drank water.[6] George didn't like being told what to do and never drank coffee because of what it symbolized for him.

This picture is of the coffee can used by Charles T Bishop. It is in the possession of Don and Jean Letherer.

Mae took the children to church. Charles only went when there was a special program. If Charles was busy, they would walk from the Somerset Road home to the Wheatland Church, a distance of about 3 miles. Sometimes a neighbor would bring them home or Charles would come get them.[6]

Ellen Louise Carpenter Stanley died 28 Sep 1924. The following obituary appeared in the Hudson Post Gazette:

*Stanley, Ellen L   Sep 30, 1924    Hudson PG*
*Mrs Ellen L Stanley, wife of Fred Stanley, died at her home NW of the city Sep 28. Burial at Locust Corners. Was 66, & leaves her husband, 3 daus, Mrs Mabel Snyder, Mrs Blanche Gibbs & Mrs May Bishop of Wheatland & 13 grandchildren.*

*Oct 3 Ellen Louise Carpenter was born in Wheatland twp. Oct 23, 1857. Married Fred C Stanley Mar 20, 1884 & they had 5 children, Mable, Orson, Blanche, Charlie\* & Mae. Charlie died in infancy & Orson Apr 5, 1919.*[7]

Robert was born 12 Dec 1925.

5 Sep 1926 the first Klingensmith reunion was held at Fred Stanley's place. Possibly because of Ella Stanley's death and folks were getting older. A poem was written for the occasion[12]. It is at the beginning of this book.

Leleah Marie Bishop born in 1 Apr 1931, died 17 May 1931 when she was 6 weeks old. Charles put her in a small casket and buried her at the feet of her Grandmother Ella Carpenter Stanley in Locust Corners Cemetery on 18 May 1931. The family was living on Somerset Road between Ames and Saunders Roads at the time. Directly east of where Agnes lived at the end of her life.[6]

This is a picture of the Bishop brothers and sisters which includes all six of them. From the left: Ed with Earl kneeling in front; George is in the center by the dog; Dorothy is next then Agnes with baby Bob. The picture was taken in the summer of 1927.

This picture is of the "Bishop boys" taken about 1928. They are from the left Earl, George, unknown, Ed, Unknown. The unknowns are probably Gibbs or Snyder cousins.

About this time, Charles got homesick. He wanted to see the relatives in New York. He hadn't seen any of them in 10 or 15 years. After thinking about it for some time, he decided to go. He took the train. After he came back, several relatives visited from time to time.[6]

It was discovered quite some time after this interview that Charles did have contact with his family. His youngest brother, Theodore George Bishop was living with and working for Chas. T Bishop in 1917 when he registered for WW1. Teddy, as he was known by family, fought in WW1 and went back to New York after he was discharged. It was about 14 years later when this picture was taken in Oct 1931 at the Hudson, Michigan Depot.

From the left Charles, probably Robert and Mae.

The family moved to Gardner Road when George started High School in 1929. George drove a 1924 Dodge Coupe to school according to an interview with Robert Bishop many years later.[25] I would think the move was somewhat later because there is a picture of Agnes in front of the Somerset road house in 1931 and the 1933 graduation picture of George and Agnes seems to be taken in front of the same house.

The 1930 census for Wheatland, Hillsdale, Michigan has Charles T Bishop, 42, married at 24, born in New York, a farmer who owns his general farm worth $3000. Mae L is 37, married at 19 and born in Michigan. Their children are George H, 15; Agnes L, 14; Dorothy I 12; Earl C, 10; Edward W, 7 and Robert E 4 4/12. All the children were born in Michigan and the older ones attended school. Everyone but Charles was listed as not working although that is not what I have heard. The family did not have a radio.

Radios were becoming popular. The family planned to get one as soon as the hogs were sold. The hogs got Cholera and the family had to wait another year for the radio.[27]

This is another picture of the "Bishop boys". A copy from Ed and Helen Bishop is not as close and labeled "Bishop Boys". Another copy of the same photo held by Jackie Bishop Salazar is more of a close up as shown here. Their father, Charles, is on the left. Edward is on the right. The boy in front on the cow is not a Bishop but probably a cousin. The boy in back seems to be Robert Bishop. In the background is the barn and silo on Gardner Road. It looked the same in the 1950s.

As young boys, Earl, Edward, and Robert had a 2-3-year-old Guernsey bull they rode like a pony. It pulled hay and carried the boys. Edward had a horse that he tried to put on a sleigh but the horse kicked it to pieces.[30]

The Taylor School was destroyed in a tornado in 1931. Robert started school that fall in the Hall house on the corner of US 127. (Helen Hall and her father Charlie lived 1 mile south on the West side of the road. Harry Snyder lived at the gas station across the corner from the Hall house.[25]

Agnes Bishop, 15, Sept 1931 in front of the Somerset Road house.

George and Agnes Bishop graduated from Addison High School in 1933. George is in the back row 5th from the left in a patterned sweater. Agnes is 3rd from the left in the center row, the first girl in the row.

This is a picture of George and Agnes on graduation day in 1933. It was taken in front of the Somerset Road house. George wore that suit for many years.

Helen Hall taught at the Addison High School while George and Agnes were there. She started teaching in Blissfield about the time Agnes graduated. There wasn't a normal school in Hillsdale so Agnes rode with Helen Hall to the normal school in Blissfield, Michigan. She boarded there, going to school during the week and helping out in the home. Charlie came to get her some weekends. It was a long way to go and gasoline was expensive. An elementary teaching certificate was granted after two years of normal school.[6]

This certificate was sufficient to teach in a county school. Agnes had to take three more classes to keep up her certificate. She could take them in Hillsdale. One class would renew the certificate for two years.[6]

According to another interview with Robert Bishop, the family moved to the Carpenter Place on Gardner Road about 1933. (This seems correct) Grandpa Stanley had been living there after Ella died but it never belonged to him, it was left to Mae, Blanch and Mable.[25]

Fred Stanley died in 1939. He lived the last 6 years with Blanche Gibbs. Mae bought the Carpenter Place by giving $500 each to her sisters Mable and Blanche.[6]

It would have taken some time to settle Ella Carpenter Stanley's estate.

Charles T worked on US 127 when it was put through. Both Charles and his horses were hired to run a slip scoop to grade the road.[6]

The following picture may be of men and horses that worked on the road. It could also be a gathering of local farmers to help another farmer harvest but that sort of group is less likely to have a picture taken. The State of Michigan would have the money to take the picture. Charles is in front 3rd from the left with a long dark jacket. Horses were used to work on US 127 according to other stories. The road went around a swamp/sink hole south of Hudson. Several horses were lost there.

George began dating Jean Sawyer, the daughter of Hattie and Jacob Camp "Camp" Sawyer, in 1934. This picture was taken in 1934 or 1935 outside the Wheatland Congregational Church.

Jean graduated from Hudson High School in 1932. She attended Ypsilanti Normal school for 1 year of a 4-year course to teach French. She dropped out because there were too many stairs. They aggravated the hip she broke in high school.

Agnes was dating Charlie Letherer, a farmer and neighbor. He was the son of Robin G and Lena B Letherer.

During the depression, the family barely got by most years. Mae would get a refrigerator as soon as times were better. George felt really bad that his mother didn't have a refrigerator to help with her never ending work. His mother finally got a refrigerator a few short years before she died. George kept the refrigerator after his father died.[27]

Dorothy graduated from Addison High School in 1936. She applied for a Social Security number June 1937.

By early 1936, the two couples, George and Jean; Charlie and Agnes, decided to get married. Agnes and Mae started planning. When they shopped for new dresses, Agnes got a pink dress and Jean a matching yellow dress. They were very nice but simple dresses that could be worn after the wedding. I remember a yellow crepe dress. It had flounced cap sleeves, a skirt that went below the knees and gathers at the bust line. The wedding date was set for June 1st. There was to be a wedding in the morning and a reception for friends and family in the afternoon. For some reason the wedding was moved up to 6 am according to Jean Bishop. No one ever said why the time was changed but I know George always liked to get an early start when traveling. According to Agnes the neighbors gathered in the afternoon and had a nice reception even without the newly married couples.[6]

George Bishop married Jean Sawyer in a double wedding with his sister Agnes and Charles Letherer on 1 Jun 1936 at his parent's home on Gardener Road. George

Burdick got out of high school to be a witness to the 6:00 am wedding, returning to school later that day according to Jean Bishop.[26] The two couples left on their honeymoon to New York State immediately after breakfast. George drove a new Chrysler car that had been bought with money George earned while living at home. The following notice appeared possibly as told by Mae Bishop:

### Letherer-Bishop
### Bishop-Sawyer

Charles W. Letherer and Miss Agnes Bishop, both of Wheatland township, and George H. Bishop, also of Wheatland township, and Miss Jean Sawyer of Hudson were united in marriage yesterday morning at 7 o'clock at the home of Mr. and Mrs. Charles T. Bishop of Wheatland township. Mr. and Mrs Charles T. Bishop are the parents of Miss Agnes Bishop, one of the brides, and George H. Bishop, one of the grooms. The Rev. A. W. Kauffman, pastor of the Hudson and Wheatland Congregational churches, officiated, using the single ring service.

Charles Letherer and Miss Agnes Bishop were attended by Earl Bishop and Miss Margaret Letherer. George Bishop and Miss Jean Sawyer were attended by George Burdick and Miss Dorothy Bishop. Following the service, a wedding breakfast was served for members of the immediate families of the two couples. Miss Dorothy Bishop and Miss Margaret Letherer served.

The two couples left immediately for a trip to New York City, Long Island and other places in the east. Both couples plan to make their homes in Wheatland township.

This is where they stopped the first night. A cabin in Erie Pennsylvania. Pictured are George, Jean and Charlie. Agnes must have taken the picture. Agnes had purchased a camera to take with them.[6]

Apparently, they didn't check the luggage, before they left home, as the men's pajama pant legs were sewn together according to George Bishop. Dorothy had played a trick on them.[27]

Picture taken by Agnes Bishop Letherer 2 Jun 1936.

Another picture taken by Agnes.

Jean Sawyer Bishop has her hand on the pump and Charlie is standing near her. The car is barely visible in front of them.

This is a picture of all four in front of a relative's house. George, Jean, Charlie, and Agnes. Someone else took the picture and wasn't very steady with the camera.

They visited Aunt Clara in Manhattan. George could not understand how anyone could live with the EL (elevated) Train going by the window every few hours. Long Island was nicer, quieter, but still busy. The whole trip was a real eye opener. There were stop lights, one-way streets and even clover leaves that were unheard of in Hillsdale County Michigan. They got lost looking for Central Park (Long Island not in Manhattan) and asked several policemen before finding the small town with most of the relatives. The police wanted to send them to the Park in Manhattan. They also stopped north of New York City to see Henry and Ada Miller. They may also have seen some relatives in New Jersey.

To the left is a picture of George and Jean looking at the Atlantic Ocean. Quite a sight for Michiganders.

When they returned from the Honeymoon, George's father insisted the Chrysler was his car because George was living at home when he bought it. George relented although Jean was very unhappy about the situation. George and Jean got the old Ford Model T instead of the Chrysler.[26] I learned about this when Jean was in her 80s. It made a big impression. George always bought Dodge or Chrysler products and never liked Fords.

George and Jean lived first at the Smith farm north of Bishop's near Addison. George earned $40 per week. They had one easy chair, a table with two chairs and a bed. Mr. Smith was the agriculture teacher in Addison.

Richard Charles Bishop was stillborn 8 Mar 1937.

In the spring of 1938, they moved to Camp Sawyer's farm on Packard Road south of Hudson. This is the farmhouse in 1938. A bedroom is on the left, living room in the center, and parlor on the right.

George, Jean and an unidentified man in front of the house on a Sunday afternoon in the summer of 1938.

Robert rode his bicycle 17 miles from his school in Addison to Packard Road south of Hudson on Friday evenings so that he could help on the farm on Saturday. He preferred working for George.[25]

Marian was the first grandchild and quite the event. She was born 9 Apr 1939 and adopted by George and Jean in June. They went to Ann Arbor to get Marian where she had been in an incubator and was now ready for a home. Much later Marian discovered she was born in Hudson's Thorn Hospital on an Easter Sunday to a mother who was recently married to a man who was not her father. They did not want the baby. Even though Marian was premature, she was kept on the small hospital for 5 days, then when she didn't die, she was taken to Ann Arbor and put in an incubator for pre-mature babies. Marian was very fortunate that she went to a home where she was truly wanted and loved.

Earl C Bishop married Jennifer Elizabeth Foreman on 17 Jun 1939.

This is Marian in the summer of 1939 with her Grandpa and Grandma Bishop. Charles Bishop is sitting in a wheelbarrow. I suspect he was handed the baby after he sat down!

A four-generation picture was taken in the fall of 1939. The four generations are Fred Stanley, great grandfather, seated; Mae Stanley Bishop, grandmother on right; George Bishop, father on left and Marian Bishop, the baby.

A picture was taken in late 1939. Earl is on the far left with Betty in front of him, Bob, Charles, Mae with Marian, Dorothy, Jean, possibly Leo to the back, Agnes and Charlie. George must have taken the picture.

In 1939 George started selling Kasco Feed from a barn on his farm. He was always more interested in business than farming according to Jean Bishop.

Fred Stanley died 14 Dec 1939.
The following obituary appeared in the Hudson Post Gazette:
Stanley, F C 15 Dec 1939 Hudson PG

Fred C Stanley, who has made his home with his dau, Mrs Alvin Gibbs of Rollin twp, for the past 6 yrs, died yesterday at Thorn hosp. Was 75 the day he died. Leaves 2 other daus, Mrs Arthur Snyder & Mrs Chas Bishop of Wheatland twp, 12 grandkids, 11 great grands, & 1 bro Jacob Stanley of Saskatchewan, Can.[7]

Fred C Stanley born 14 Dec 1864, died 14 Dec 1939 in Thorn Hospital, Hudson, Michigan. He died of later Pneumonia after only a day in the hospital. Mabel Snyder was the informant. He is buried in Locust Corners Cemetery with Ella.

After they were married, Earl and Betty lived with his parents until after Earl Charles Bishop Jr. "Mickey" was born 14 Mar 1940.

This picture is of Betty Bishop holding Mickey and Jean Bishop holding Marian. It was taken at George Bishop's farm in the summer of 1940.

Ed Bishop is on the left with Charles Bishop holding Marian in the center. The picture was taken on a warm summer day when many of the Bishop children were home as seen by the many cars.

The picture may have been taken because of the colt and 2 horses. Horses were still important in 1940. Charles Bishop used horses for some farming even after he had a tractor. Most of the many cars are from the 1920's or early 30s.

The 1940 census for Wheatland Township, Hillsdale, Michigan taken 13 Apr, has Charles T Bishop, 52, completed 8th grade, lived in the same place in 1935, a farmer who owns the farm on Gardener Road worth $12,000. Mae L is 48 and graduated high school. The children are Edward, 17, completed 11th grade and Robert, 14, completed 8th grade.

The 1940 census for Wheatland Township, Hillsdale, Michigan taken 15 Apr has Charles Letherer, 30, completed 8th grade, living in the same place in 1935, a farmer renting a home on Gardner Road for $5 per month. Agnes is 24, completed 2 years college and working as a grade school teacher. Charlie and Agnes lived on a farm about 2 miles north of Charles and Mae Bishop.

The 1940 census for Wheatland, Hillsdale, Michigan taken 29 Apr has Earl Bishop, 20, graduated high school, living same place as 1935 (Wheatland) a farmer renting his home on Wheatland Road for $7 per month. Jennie E is 17, completed 10th grade and lived in Lenawee County in 1935. Their son, Earl Jr. is less than a year. Later, Earl and Betty lived on a farm on Gardner Road just north of Charles Bishop's farm and south of Charlie and Agnes.

The 1940 census for Medina, Lenawee, Michigan taken 10 Apr has George Bishop, 25, graduated high school, same place in 1935 (they weren't but were on a farm), a farmer who owns his farm with another income source. Jean is 26 and completed 1-year college. Their daughter, Marian, is less than 1 and born in Michigan. A E Widdiefield is 60, a lodger, graduated college, born in Canada, a naturalized citizen, lived in rural Lenawee in 1935 and a spice salesman. I remember talk about the eccentric Widdiefield who threw his teeth out with the water he used for washing. He left a clock and rocking chair with my parents. They are still in the family.

The 1940 census for Hudson, Michigan taken 20 Apr has Dorothy Bishop 22, graduated high school, was living in Jackson Michigan in 1935 and a stenographer in an electrical power office. Ruth Marvin is 28. They are renting an apartment at 315 ½ Main Street for $7 per month. The apartment was in the building next to the D&C dime store across the street from the Consumers Power office where bills could still be paid in the 50s.

This picture has Charles in the coveralls he frequently wore, smoking a pipe, George looking at the old truck they have just loaded on a wagon, his dog Ted and Edward sitting on the wagon. I am sure they put tires back on the truck and got it running.

This appears to be the same truck with Jean, Ted the dog and Marian.

This picture is from a summer outing in 1941. George is taking the picture. The couple on the left are Sacketts, Agnes is in the middle holding Marian, Charlie to the back and Jean Bishop on the right.

Ed Bishop is holding his niece Marian. Someone is in the background. I believe the car is the Ford George was driving after their honeymoon.

13 Oct 1941 Margie Diane Bishop was born in Hillsdale, Michigan to Earl and Betty Bishop.

21 Oct 1941 Nancy Marie Bishop was born in Hudson, Michigan to George and Jean Bishop.

Dorothy Bishop met Leo Jennings in the late 1930s. He joined the Army and was home on leave in late November of 1941.

On Sunday, 7 Dec 1941, Robert went to Wirt's store on Church Road in Wheatland or Churches Corners. They had a radio and heard President Roosevelt's address. Pearl Harbor had been bombed. A day no one forgot. Leo Jennings had been in the Army Medics, right after Pearl Harbor he switched to the air core.[25]

Leo Jennings of Californis (stationed there) enlisted in the Air Corps on 25 Mar 1942.

Agnes Bishop and Charlie Letherer were married almost six years before Anna Mae Letherer was born 16 Jan 1942. The miracle baby they had wanted for so long.

George Bishop is holding Marian and Jean is holding baby Nancy on a Sunday in the spring of 1942.

It must have been a Sunday or some special occasion as George never wore a suit during the week. It is the same suit he had for graduation and wore for many years. I like Jean's hat and diaper bag!

Aunt Ada (Charles Bishop's Aunt) must have made a visit in the summer of 1942 as she is shown here with all the grandchildren. Mickey is on the left then Marjorie, Nancy and Anna Mae on her lap and Marian on the right. I'm not sure why she is sitting in front of the car. She is in a chair, not on the bumper.

This picture of Nancy and Marian was taken about the same time as the one with Aunt Ada. Marian has on the same dress. Marian's crossed eyes were corrected with surgery when she was 3, after this picture. March 1943 according to Helen's diary.

This picture is of Ed Bishop and Helen Kincaid, on the left, when they were dating. The other couple is Dick (?) and Helen Rawlson, Helen Kincaid's best friend in high school.[30]

Helen said there was always room for more at the Bishop table. Helen didn't know how Ed's mother, Mae Bishop, did it but there was always enough food for everyone. It may have been because everyone looked around to see how many there were and how much food before serving themselves. They all knew how to make it stretch after the depression.

Mae joined the Royal Neighbors of America an organization to enrich the quality of life for women and those they care about through life insurance and fraternalism. She bought life insurance for all of her grandchildren (at least while she was alive). The Royal Neighbors would have meetings the whole family attended although the children had to go play elsewhere when the adults had a business meeting. I remember Stanleys, Snyders, Gibbs, Bishops and possibly other neighbors in attendance.

A picture was taken of the Charles and Mae Bishop family in late fall 1942. Bob is on the left, Ed behind, Mae, Earl, Dorothy, Charles barely peeking through, Agnes and George behind.

Robert Bishop with Marian and Mickey in Nov or Dec 1942. The van in the background is George Bishop's first feed delivery truck. It was previously a Quality Cleaners truck. He painted over the Cleaners and put on Feed.

Pictures were taken outside at this time, even in the snow.

A picture of the grandchildren taken in the winter of 1942-1943 with Marian and Mickey in back. Margie, Anna Mae and Nancy are in front.

Another picture, with the whole family. It is hard to tell but back row appears to be Betty, Earl, Jean, Charles, Mae, Leo, Helen, Agnes, George, Charlie. In the front row Bob, Nancy, Marian, Mickey, Dorothy holding Margie, Anna Mae. As usual Ed took the picture.

Leo Jennings was home from the Air Force for Thanksgiving or Christmas 1942, He was stationed in Texas. He may have been in training with the change from Army to Air Force. He also trained other soldiers.

Possibly the first picture of Grandbabies on George's truck. Nancy is on the left with Marian in the middle and Anna Mae on the right.

Helen Kincaid started keeping a diary in January of 1943. She was 16 and a junior in high school. The following excerpts give an idea of what it was like in 1943 with no TV, cheap movies, visiting, and people still wrote letters. Not everyone had a telephone and long distance was expensive. Popcorn and Ice cream were treats. The war was on everyone's mind with young men leaving and victory uncertain.

Helen was the daughter of Leo Arthur Kincaid (1881-1961) and Jeanette "Nettie" Covell (1887-1973). Harold is her oldest brother and married to Jessie. Cullen is the second son in the family, he married Ruth after the war. Martha, known as Metha, married Lloyd Myers and they had a son Robert. Claude married Ellen in 1946 and is often mentioned as writing letters home. Mildred married Harold in January of 1942 and they had a daughter Karen. Helen is the youngest. She was dating Ed Bishop. Diary entries are in italic.

January 1, 1943: *We were home all alone today but Ed, Metha, Lloyd came over, we had a good time. Mother isn't feeling so good yet today, I did the ironing.*

January 3 *Ed came over for dinner. Mildred & Harold, Karen came in the afternoon. We took Dorothy to Adrian tonight. Went to see Ellen tonight too.*

It was not uncommon for folks to drop in on family and friends. Dinner was at noon. Not everyone had a car so those who had a car offered rides to those who didn't.

January 4 *I got the best news I have heard in a long time. Ed got a 6-month deferment. Ma went to the doctor today. I didn't go to school.*

January 5 *I went to school today. Metha, Lloyd & Bobby were over. Harold is supposed to come home tonight, nothing happened besides that.*

January 6 *Ed came over and we went to the show. Nelda & Dick went with us. We had a swell time. I went to school.*

January 7 *I went to school – We sure had a lot of fun at noon. Dick Smith left today for the Army. Mildred and Harold came down today.*

January 8 *We went to a party over to Eileen Moskers. Had a good time. I stayed home today. Harold & Mildred & K was here for dinner.*

January 9 *Ed came over we went to the show and after to Ed's folks. Went to town in the afternoon. I got a new pocketbook tonight.*

January 10 *Ed came over and we went to church. We went to Hillsdale today.*

January 11 *Ed started working nights today. We went to school today. Didn't do much in school today. Got a letter from Claude.*

January 13 *We were reviewing today for semester exams. Mom & Dad got the rest of Mildred's stuff and brought them home. I didn't see Ed today.*

January 15 *I had my exams today. I got B- in History. Ed came over for dinner, mother said. I sure would like to see him.*

January 17 *I went to Hillsdale with Ed. Mildred and Karen came home to stay, I sure feel sorry for her. We didn't do much of anything.*

Harold had left for the Army.

January 18 *Went to school, got sick 3 times had a lot of fun. I was sick all day. Karen is sure sweet.*

January 19 *It sure was an awful day. I didn't go to school as the bus didn't go. I wrote a letter to Ed. Mildred got Harold's address.*

January 20 *I didn't get to go to school as we can't get out yet. I didn't hear from Ed either. Is Karen sure getting fat.*

January 21 *We did the washing. Still can't go to school. Karen is the best little thing at night. I got a card from Ed.*

January 22 *Metha and Lloyd were over tonight. Karen is 24 inches long. Got a letter from A J. Mildred got her letter from Harold.*

January 23 *We went to town today. I wrote 3 letters tonight. I got a new notebook. We received a letter from Claude.*

January 24 *Ed came over for dinner. I sure was glad to see him. We went to church and had more fun.*

January 26 *Dick Peterson went for his second exam. I went to school had Student Council. Dick was rejected.*

January 27 *I received a letter from Ed. Went to school. I sure was glad to get my letter.*

January 31 *We went up to George and Jean's, Dick P & Helen went with us we sure had fun. We got stuck.*

February 1 *Mother's Birthday is today, she is 56, Collen's is tomorrow. We went to school. It sure is icy.*

February 3 *I got a letter from Ed. I wrote to Harold & A J tonight. We won the game last night with Cement City.*

February 4 *I didn't get a letter today from Ed. We went over to Metha, Lloyd and Bobby's tonight. Went to school today.*

February 5 *I'm going to basketball game tonight with Hudson and Addison. We won 24-38. We sure had a good time.*

February 7 *We went to the show this afternoon. Took Dorothy back to Adrian tonight.*

Feburary 8 *Ed had his teeth pulled tonight, nothing else happened.*

February 9 *Ed's teeth are hurting him. Robert told me today.*

Feburary 10 *Ed came over but we didn't go anyplace. We got Claude's picture today.*

Feburary 11 *Ed was over for supper. I went to school today but I didn't want to.*

February 14 *Ed came over this afternoon and we went to his sister's. Had a good time.*

February 15 *We started school on slow time today, nothing else happened.*

February 17 *I went to Adrian today got 2 new dresses and material for a skirt. I like them very much.*

February 18 *I went to school. Mary Bills is sick with the flu.*

February 19 *We went to the basketball game and dance in Addison, tonight we took Nelda M with us.*

February 20 *Ed came over we went to town. I had my eyes tested and my glasses need to be changed.*

February 21 *I mopped today. Ed is supposed to come over for dinner. He came.*

February 22 *Mildred & K didn't come home today either. I went to school.*

February 23 *We got a letter from Claude, I got one from Betty. Went to school.*

February 24 *We had our Junior-Senior Banquet tonight It was very nice. Ed came after me. Bobbie is over the measles & Chicken pox.*

February 26 *Ed came over tonight. Went to school. Had a test in History, Was it hard.*

*Maybe Mildred will go to Texas. I hope she can. Mildred came home today.*

February 27 *We cleaned the house. I worked on English. Ed came over tonight. We went to the show.*

February 28 *Nobody was here for dinner. Ed came over and we went over to Metha and Lloyd.*

March 1 *Went to school. Ed was supposed to quit today. Nothing else happened.*

March 2 *Ed quit today. He went down to George's today, Robert said.*

March 3 *Ed didn't come over he had to go to work to grind feed. Went to school. Metha L & B came over tonight.*

March 4 *Went to school. Nothing else happened. Got a letter from Claude & Harold.*

March 5 *Helen Rawlson came home with me we went up to Addison tonight.*

March 6 *Went to the show. Ed came over and was I glad to see him.*

March 7 *Ed came over this afternoon. He gave me a two-dollar bill. (Do I ever like [added above] Love him)*

March 8 *Mildred got a letter from Harold and she is going to Texas Wed. I got a letter from A J. He thinks he will get to come home.*

March 10 *Mildred & Iona & Karen left for Texas this morning. Went to a party on Herb Peterson tonight. Ed came after me.*

March 11 *Went to school. I forgot my dinner today. Was I mad. We got a letter from Claude and some snapshots of him. Donna Patrick's Birthday.*

March 12 *Went to school. Herb Peterson was up there. Ma and I went to the show. It was pretty good. I got a card from Mildred.*

March 13 *I got my engagement ring tonight it is very pretty and am I happy.*

March 14 *Went to Jackson after Marian. Went to Bishop's for dinner. Went to the show tonight "Young & Willing" was the name of it.*

Marian Bishop had eye surgery for crossed eyes when she was about 3. Her mother, Jean didn't drive so frequently someone else took her when George was working.

March 15 *Well today is my birthday I'm 17 years old. Got a letter from A J and Mildred.*

March 16 *Robert treated Barbra & I to a black out. It was swell. Went over to Metha's and Lloyds tonight. Had popcorn.*

March 17 *Ed came over tonight with some ice cream. Nothing else happened.*

March 18 *We got a letter from Claude & Mildred and I got a card from Mildred. I wrote to her tonight.*

March 19 *We got a letter from Claude and Aunt Elizy and card from Mildred. Mildred has a new hat and permanent. Went to school.*

March 20 *Went downtown this afternoon. Ed came over tonight. We went to the dance. Had a lot of fun.*

March 21 *Ed came over for dinner. Dick & Helen went with us to church at Sand Creek. Stemens were over to. Today was Betty Howland's Birthday*

March 22 *We got a letter from Mildred and Claude. Metha & Lloyd came over tonight, had popcorn.*

Mach 23 *We got a letter from Claude & Mildred again. Went to school. Nothing else happened. Dick P went to the doctor.*

March 24 *Ed came over tonight we went to Adrian, he bought a tractor. We got a letter from Claude today.*

March 25 *Today was Mr. Gray's birthday. Got a letter from Claude. We didn't do anything else.*

March 26 *Mr. Randel's wife had a baby boy – name Richard James. Dick was up to school after Helen.*

March 27 *We went to the dance. I had a nice time. I've been sick all day. We went over to see A J Bradstreet. He looks nice in his uniform.*

March 28 *We went to church this morning. Was over to Bishop's for dinner. Helen & Dick came over this afternoon. We went for a ride. Did chores tonight.*

March 29 *We got a letter from Claude & Mildred. I finished my blouse. Ellen called tonight.*

Mach 30 *Went to school. We got a letter from Claude & Mildred.*

March 31 *Went to a surprise party on Jean Bishop, today was her birthday. Mildred &*

*Karen went to see Claude.*

April 1 *Today was April Fool's day. We went to see Spring Fever it sure was good.*

April 2 *We go a letter from Claude. I wrote him and Harold a letter tonight.*

April 3 *Went to town this afternoon I got a new pair of shoes. We went to the dance. Had a nice time.*

April 4 *We went to Jackson with Dick after Helen R. We went to Star Spangle Rhythm. Then we came to Hudson and seen Commandoes Strike at dawn. We had a nice time.*

April 5 *We got a letter from Mildred. I got my book for English "Wild Geese Calling".*

April 6 *We got a letter from Claude & Mildred. I got one from Geraldine. Helen wasn't to school.*

April 7 *Ed came over and we went down to George's Jean was papering.*

Wall paper was cheaper than paint and covered the cracks in the plaster. Most homes were wall papered, mostly by women.

April 8 *We got a card from Mildred. I don't know when they are coming here. We had a lot of fun at noon.*

April 9 *Nothing happened. We got a letter from Aunt (?) today. A J Bradstreet was moved to Mississippi.*

April 10 *We went to Bettie Lynn's Shower tonight. They sure got a lot of nice things.*

April 11 *Ed came over about 4 o'clock and we went for a ride. Nelda & Charley came over and sat in the car with us.*

April 12 *Helen didn't come to school. She was sick. Claude thinks he will be moved soon.*

April 15 *Helen came back to school. She had a cold in her eyes. We had Chapel today. We went to the show tonight. Ma & I did.*

April 16 *Helen wasn't to school today again they went to Jackson. Nothing happened.*

April 17 *We went to the dance Earl and Betty went with us. We had more fun. Lot of the kids were there.*

April 18 *We were over to Bishops for dinner. Helen & Dick came over in the afternoon.*

*We went to the show at night.*

April 19 *Mildred and Ione are supposed to start for home tonight. We didn't have any school Wed. I started my dress. We haven't heard from Claude yet. G R is going to have a baby.*

April 20 *Well Mildred got home but they stayed down to (?) Metha and Lloyd came over. Mother & Dad got a new stove at Hammonds.*

April 21 *Mildred came home today. We went over to Metha & Lloyd's. Ed came over and we went to the show.*

This picture is Mildred, Helen's sister, and her daughter, Karen.

April 22 *We had a farewell party for the Taylors at school. I got ready to go to Jackson.*

April 23 *Dick came after me and we went to Jackson. We went to the show at night. I was in Jackson*

April 24 *We were downtown today Helen got a white dress. We stayed home and all took a bath.*

April 25 *Ed & Dick came up. Ed and I didn't get along very good. We went to the lake at night.*

Apparently, they also brought her home from Jackson. Helen stayed in Jackson for the weekend with her friend Helen R. Jackson is about 30 miles from Hudson.

April 26 *Went to school. I sure was tired. We got a letter from Claude he is in Pittsburg, California. I got a letter from Herb.*

April 27 *We got a letter from Claude. We got our linoleum and stove down.*

April 28 *Ed came over we went to the show. We had more fun.*

April 29 *Mildred got a letter from Harold. We got two new chairs. Metha, Lloyd, Bobby are over. Did Metha ever make me mad.*

May 1 *We went to the dance didn't we have fun. Nothing else happened.*

May 2 *Ellen came out for dinner. Ed & I took care of Karen. Mildred & Ellen, Ma & Dad went to the show.*

May 3 *I stayed home tonight getting ready to run the rest of the week.*

May 4 *Thelma came over and wanted me to go to church super. Then Ed came over and I wasn't to home. Ed's Aunt Ada came today.*

May 5 *Ed came over we had a lot of fun. We went to the show.*

May 6 *We hung a May basket on Arlene & Dick Joughin's. We had a lot of fun.*

May 7 *Tonight was our J-hop we made swell. I went with Norma Smith.*

May 8 *Tonight Ed and I went together two years. We went up to the dance we had a fight but got along ok, I guess.*

May 9 *I went over to Ed's folks for dinner. Dick & Arlene J went to the show with us the name was Bambi. It was cute.*

May 10 *We got a letter from Claude his mail is censored so we don't know where he is.*

May 11 *Nothing happened today. Mildred got a letter from Harold. We have a test in History.*

May 12 *Bill Klinger got home tonight. Ed came over we went down town. Had lot of fun.*

May 13 *Mildred & I went down to Thelma Harden's tonight we had fun, Mildred got a letter from Harold.*

May 14 *We hung a May basket on Harry and Thelma. Arlene and Dick came with Ed. We only have another week of school. I got my working permit today.*

May 15 *We had more fun tonight. Then we have had in a long time. We went to the dance. There were four couples of us.*

May 16 *We went to Baccalaureate tonight then we went to Seneca. We had quite a nice time. There were four couples of us tonight too.*

May 17 *Gee am I tired. I think I'll go to bed early tonight. I got a letter from Alverda. Jesses pigs have the Hog Cholera and he has lost 50 pigs.*

May 18 *Nothing happened I had an English exam today. We painted in Home Ec.* (Home Economics a general how to run a home class with sewing, cooking, etc.)

May 19 *We went to graduation night.*

May 20 *I stayed home tonight and Ma & Mildred went to the show.*

May 21 *We had a history test today and I got 80. We had a Home Ec. test too. Ed came tonight we went to Addison graduation.*

Robert Bishop graduated from Addison High School in 1943. He was too young to enter the Navy that summer but enlisted on his 18th birthday, 12 Dec 1943. Government records say Robert served from 24 Mar 1944 until he was discharged 8 Jun 1946. There are several Robert E Bishop's, there may be some confusion. I believe his military # was 951 94 51. He served on the USS Roi.[25]

This is a picture of Robert's ship.

May 22 *I was sick all day. We went to the dance tonight. Ed heard about his deferment.*

May 23 *Ed came over for dinner. About 4 we went over to his place. We went up to Agnes' at night.*

May 24 *It sure seemed funny not to go to school. I got a card from Ed's Mom. It's raining today.*

May 25 *We have been house cleaning. We got Karen's new bed up today. I popped corn tonight.*

May 26 *Ed came over tonight. His Mother got home from Texas. Dorothy was married Saturday. She bought me a sofiner (?) All he talks about is getting married.*

Dorothy Irene Bishop married Leo Jennings May 22, 1943 while he was on leave in Texas. Dorothy returned home to work until Leo was out of the service.[28]

This is Dorothy and Leo's wedding picture

May 27 *We went to town this morning and over to Metha's this afternoon. Mildred heard from Harold.*

May 28 *We ironed. Millie, Ma & Ellen went to the show tonight. I wrote a letter to Betty Howland.*

May 29 *We went to the dance. We saw A J & Phyllis. Ed's been sick. The same thing I had last week.* There are several references to being sick. This may have been a cold which didn't stop her from visiting or going to a dance.

May 30 *We went up to Agnes' for dinner. We had lots of fun with the kids at Hudson, A J has to go back tomorrow.*

May 31 *We hung a May basket on Ed and he was sick. Helen R stayed all night with me we are going to Adrian to see about a job.*

June 1 *I went home with Helen R Dick came after us. I drove all the way from Addison. (a little over 10 miles)*

June 2 *Dick came after us. He took me over to Ed's. I stayed all night so I can go to Toledo tomorrow. (about 60 miles)*

June 3 *Ed and I went to Toledo we had lots of fun. I helped him pick & shell corn and I got a lot of dishes today.*

June 4 *I took care of Karen tonight. I mowed the grass. Mildred got a letter from Harold.*

June 5 *We went downtown tonight. We went to the dance. I didn't have much fun.*

June 6 *We went over to Metha's today for a farewell party on Happy. We went over to Bishop's tonight.*

June 7 *We, Virginia, Helen & I, went to look for a job. We got one working in a restaurant making 65¢ hour. We start Friday.*

June 8 *Were we surprised Cal came home tonight were we glad. Mildred got a letter from Harold he thinks he will be sent to Ohio.*

June 9 *I got my permanent today. Ed came over tonight. Metha Lloyd & Bob came over too. We had ice cream.*

June 10 *Well here we are in the big city of Adrian. Have a nice room on 415 Allis Street with Mr & Mrs. Sherman. We start work tomorrow am I tried tonight.*

June 11 *Here is our first day of work and am I tired. I like it OK Jess & Lou are swell.*

June 12 *Another day of work. Richard came up after us. Ed had to plow so I went to the dance with Helen.*

June 13 *Ed came over this afternoon. We were over at Metha's for supper Ed brought us both back and did we have fun.*

June 14 *I liked my work today. I made 30¢ in tips. I wrote to Ed. Helen had some trouble tonight.*

June 15 *I made 50¢ in tips. I got my first check I made $9.10. I wrote to Ed.*

June 16 *Another day of work. I got a letter from Ed. It sure was silly but I liked it.*

June 17 *Do I ache and feel awful.* (partial and crossed out words)

June 18 *I made 60¢ in tips. I worked 11 hours today.*

June 19 *Ed and Dick were up tonight. We had to take Virginia back to Hudson.*

June 20 *I had to work today. Ed didn't like it too well. I got 85¢ in tips today.*

June 21 *I was home today and Ed took us back. It seemed good not to have to work.*

June 22 *Well we worked again today. I wrote a letter to Ed. I had to iron tonight. I made $42.41*

June 23 *We went to Hudson and Ed and I had a long talk. I cried after I went to bed. Ed wants to get married.*

June 24 *I worked today got a letter from Ed. Was I ever glad.*

June 25 *I got 2 new dresses. I like both of them. Dick came down and took us girls for a ride.*

June 26 *Ed and Dick came down and some (?) chased up all over were they ever dirty talking things.*

June 27 *We went over to Bishop's and waited for George and Jean to get out of church. I worked too.*

June 28 *Dick brought us back. I had my hair set. Nothing else happened.*

June 29 *I got $30.82 today. Boy am I tired. I am going to bed tonight early.*

Helen received a post card post marked July 9.

Dear Helen,
Just a line this morning in answer to your letter yesterday. You can make some sandwiches for Sunday if you want to or get some cookies, if it would be easier. I guess Agnes and Charlie are going with us. If they decide they can't go, perhaps your Father and Mother would like to.

Be seeing you.
Mother Bishop.

It seems Ed was not the only one pushing.

July 13 *I made $28.59*

July 20 *I made $27.05.*

The diary ends here. Helen was torn about getting married before finishing school. Many years later, she rather wished she had finished school. There was a lot of uncertainty at the time with a war on.

Judith Ann Bishop was born to Earl and Betty August 12, 1943.

Edward Bishop of Hudson, Michigan married Helen Kincaid of Pittsford, Michigan in Hudson on 16 Oct 1943. Serg F. Hammon, minister Hudson-Wheatland Congregational Church officiated. Witnesses were Robert Bishop and Mrs Harold Hammond (Helen's sister).

This is their wedding picture.

The following certificate, not received until 1945, may have been part of the reason for marriage. Men who were married were generally not drafted. With the war in Europe winding down in 1945, the Army may not have needed so many men. Ed did have a heart murmur.

Donald Letherer was born to Agnes and Charlie Letherer on 19 Jan 1944.

```
                                SELECTIVE SERVICE SYSTEM              App. not req.
                                                                      ORIGINAL
    Local Board No. 1
    Lenawee County          091
                            001           CERTIFICATE OF FITNESS
    220 W. Maumee St.
    Adrian, Michigan
    (Local Board date stamp with code)

         Edward           Wayne            Bishop              13455
      (First name)     (Middle name)     (Last name)        (Order number)

    I hereby certify that the above-named registrant has been given a preinduction physical examination
    and found:

    1. ☐ Physically fit, acceptable for general military service.
    2. ☐ Physically fit, acceptable for limited military service.
    3. ☑ Rejected, physically unfit.
    4. ☐ Rejected, physically fit but unacceptable for other reasons.

       JAN 23 1945
    (Date of examination)           Name    S. A. MOORE, Maj. Inf., Comdg.
                                                     Induction Station Commander.
                                    Rank
    DSS Form 218 (Rev. 6-8-44)  GPO 16-39685-1  Station    Detroit 7, Michigan
```

Helen & Beauty  43

Helen had a horse called Beauty. They are in front of Ed and Helen's first house.

Not long after, they moved to a farm on North Adams Road. Helen saved money for a bedroom set but they had to buy a cow instead. I remember going to their farm about 1947 and Helen had her bedroom set. I was impressed! It was a very 40's set with a round mirror on the dressing table and rounded corners everywhere.

A picture was taken of Mae and Charles Bishop near the back door of their home in May 1944. The pictures taken at the 1944 Klingensmith Family reunion are some of last with Mae and her sisters.

Carol Ann Bishop was born to George and Jean Bishop 20 May 1944.

It was a caesarian birth at Thorn Hospital in Hudson. Jean stayed in the hospital for 2 weeks then came home by ambulance. Nancy was in the dining room when the ambulance pulled up to the side porch. It was scary to have her mother and baby Carol arrive in an ambulance. She remembered that moment the rest of her life. A neighbor girl, Mabel Robey stayed with them for a month to help take care of the family.

May, 1944

A picture was taken of George and Jean Bishop's three girls later that year or early 1945. Carol is on the left with Nancy in the center and Marian on the right.

Wayne Bishop was born to Ed and Helen Bishop 28 Jan 1945.

Mae Bishop was diagnosed with cancer in 1945.

A picture was taken of Mae and some of the family in the spring of 1945. Back row left to right, George, Mae, Agnes, Jean holding Carol with Earl behind her. Front row, Margie, Marian, Anna Mae, Mickey, Donnie, Judy, Nancy, Charley. Betty may have taken the picture.

Robert was in Hawaii when the news of his Mother's illness reached him. His commander could not let him have leave because there was a war on but he could have him transferred. Bob was transferred 22 May 1945 to San Diego. Soon after he arrived in San Diego, he managed leave and headed for home.[25]

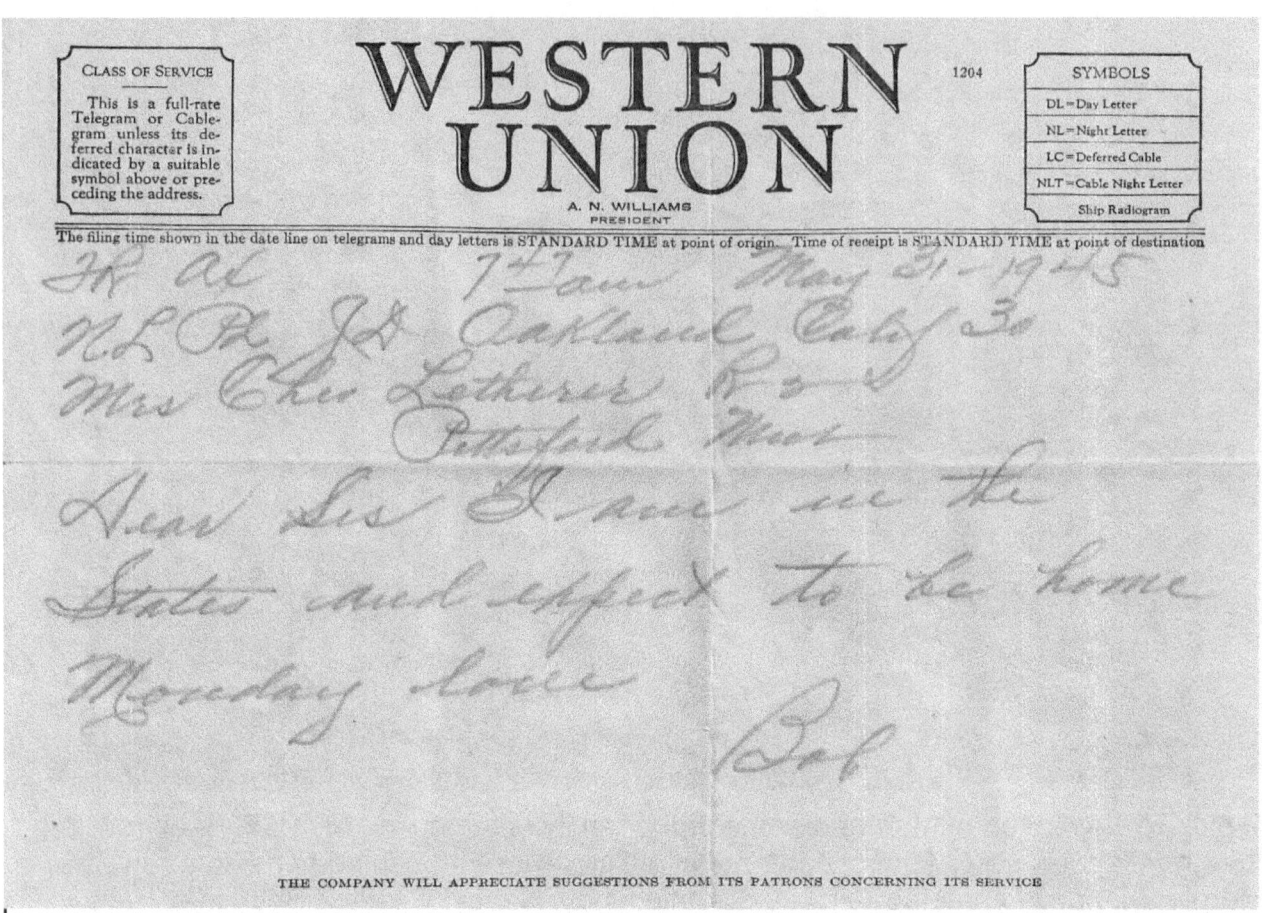

One day in the summer of 1945, Nancy and Anna Mae were at Grandpa Bishop's house, standing in the living room. There were two small bedrooms off of the living room. Agnes had a syringe with a long needle. She went into the first bedroom where it was dark and gave an old lady the shot. Nancy and Anna Mae found that very scary!

MAY BISHOP, 53, DIES TODAY AT WHEATLAND HOME            Hillsdale Daily News
      Hudson, Aug. 20 - Mrs. May L. Bishop, 53, a lifelong resident of Wheatland township, died at 7 o'clock this morning at her farm home. She was born July 19, 1892.
      Surviving besides the husband, Charles, are two daughters, Mrs. Agnes Letherer of Wheatland, and Mrs. Dorothy Jennings of Hudson; four sons, George Bishop of Medina, Earl of Wheatland, Edward of Addison, and Robert in the U. S. Navy; a sister, Mrs. Alvin Gibbs of Manitou Beach; nine grandchildren, and several nieces and nephews.
      The body was entrusted to the Charles E. Brown and Son Funeral home where arrangements are pending word from the son who is in military service.[31]

On the back side of the newspaper clipping:

ROAD TRAFFIC LEAPS 50 PCT.
State Police Announce Traffic Rules Will Be Tightened

Lansing, Aug. 20 - Automobile traffic on Michigan highways leaped 50 to 100 per cent over the weekend as drivers were lured onto the roads by full gas tanks and hot weather, Capt. C. G. Scavarda, head of the state police traffic division, estimated today.[31]

The war in Europe was over and gasoline was more available. The rest of the state was seeing a brighter future just when Mae died.

Mrs. Bishop's Funeral Services on Thursday
Hillsdale Daily News
Hudson, Aug. 21 - Funeral Services for Mrs. May Bishop who passed away Monday, will be held Thursday afternoon at 3 o'clock (E. W. T.) At the home, 5 miles northwest of Hudson. The Rev. H. R. Yongberg will officiate and burial will be in the Locust Corners cemetery.[31]

Bishop, Mae L   Aug 23, 1945   Hudson Post Gazette
Mrs Mae L Bishop, 53 wife of Chas Bishop, died at their home NW of Hudson Mon. Born July 19, 1892. Burial in Locust Corners cem. Leaves husband, 4 sons, Robert, in Navy; Geo of Medina, Earl of Wheatland, & Edward of Addison; 2 daus, Mrs Agnes Letherer of Wheatland & Mrs Dorothy Jennings at home; 1 sis, Mrs Alvin Gibbs of Manitou Beach & 9 grandkids.[31]

The 9 grand children would have been: Marian, Nancy, Carol, Mickey, Marjorie, Judy, and Wayne Bishop, Anna Mae and Donald Letherer.

A summer day about 1946. Earl put some of the cousins on Grandpa's mules, Jack and Jill. From the left, Anna Mae, Mickey, Earl holding the mule's heads, Marian and Nancy. George's truck is in the background.

George's new (to him) truck must have been a big event because both Helen and Bob had pictures taken with it, both are holding Wayne.

Stones lined the edge of Grandpa Bishop's lawn at intervals. Here the cousins are sitting on the stones. From the left: Judy, Mickey, Margie, Marian, Anna Mae, and Nancy with George's truck in the background.

The whole family rode in the truck. George drove, Jean was on the other side of the bench seat, Marian sat between them straddling the gear shift, Carol was on Jean's lap, and Nancy stood between her mother's knees and the gear shift, bumping her head on the ceiling.

Mary Louise Letherer was born October 31, 1945.

One time when Bob was home from the Navy, he brought a Navy outfit for Mickey. This is a picture of the proud Navy men!

Earl's family had a picture taken later in 1945 or early 1946. From the left, Margie, Earl, Mickey wearing his Navy uniform, Betty, and Judy.

In

March of 1946, the following appeared in the Hillsdale Daily News:

## BISHOPS MADE SCHOOL RECORD
### Fourth Generation Attends Taylor District School

Pittsford, March 23, - When young Mickey Bishop entered the Taylor district school in Wheatland Township last fall, he added a star to the family school history by becoming the fourth generation to attend the same school.

Preceding him in the Taylor school have been his great-grandmother, his grandmother, and his father. His grandmother, Mae Stanley Bishop, later graduated from Pittsford high school, and was well known in and around the village. The father Earl Bishop completed his education in the Addison high school.

From previous generations on down, the family has been affiliated with the Wheatland Congregational church. All four generation representatives have been born and grown up in the district; two generations were born in the same house; and two died there. Charles T. Bishop, the grandfather, a two-farm landowner in the district, plans to remain here, so the family honor roll in the Taylor school may increase with the years.

The family home was the scene of a gala occasion recently when Mickey celebrated his sixth birthday anniversary. He entertained 33 schoolmates and friends for a birthday dinner, with the teacher, Mrs. D. Kelly, of Hudson as a special guest.

Table decorations and place markers in St Patrick's green, added to the attractive setting. Pleasing to his guests were the decorated birthday cake, and the two kinds of ice cream served for dessert. And Mickey was thrilled with his numerous gifts.

Co-hostesses with Mrs. Bishop in entertaining the group of youngsters were Mrs. Kenyon Wirick, Mrs. M. Lendronies, and Mrs. Russell Leffingwell.

Mickey's dad returns this week from East Lansing, where he has been taking a short course in heating and air-conditioning. His mother is a popular singer in this locality.[31]

The four generations going to Taylor school were Ella Carpenter, Mae Stanley, the Charles Bishop children and some grandchildren including Earl and Mickey Bishop and Robert and Barry Bishop.[25]

50 years after Mae Stanley graduated from Pittsford High School, Anna Mae Letherer graduated from the same school followed by many grandchildren and great grandchildren.

Ed Bishop and Wayne at the North Adams Road Farm. In the spring 1946 mud!

One time when Bob was home from the Navy, he stopped by to visit Earl then he left to go to Hudson Hospital where Corabelle worked. Marjorie came in the house crying because Bob didn't take her but took Judy. They realized Marjorie fell off the car running board when Bob left but her younger sister Judy managed to hang on. Earl left in a hurry but was not able to catch them until Bob stopped at the hospital. Judy had held on all the way and was not hurt.[25] She was only 3 years old.

Robert Bishop was discharged from the Navy 8 Jun 1946.
When he got out of the Navy, Bob and Corabelle came to visit at George's farm. Everyone was in the dining room. Bob was very handsome in his uniform and Corabelle was young and pretty. Marian was enthralled! She was sure she wanted to marry a sailor when she grew up. Nancy was there too and noticed the small white fuzzy dog. It was a happy day for all.

Leo Jennings also returned when the war was over. He had a job in Cincinnati, Ohio. George loaded his big truck with all of Dorothy and Leo's belongings and they drove to Cincinnati. George and his truck moved many family members. He got an early start and they made it in one day. A real accomplishment on the roads at that time.

George Bishop built a swing set for his girls under the maple trees in front of the Packard Road home. A slide was added after this picture was taken.

A family gathering was held at George and Jean's Packard Road home. A table was made on the side lawn using crates. From the left Corabelle Bishop, Agnes Letherer, Jean Bishop, and Aunt Ada Miller. In front are Anna Mae Letherer, Nancy Bishop, and Marian Bishop. Carol Bishop never liked having her picture taken and was probably hiding behind her mother.

This picture was taken on a Sunday in the fall of 1946. In the back from the left: Agnes, Charlie, Bob, Corabelle, Earl, Betty looking back at him, Helen holding Wayne, Charles, Charles' sisters Esther and Gertrude, Jean. In front: Judy, Donald, Mickey, Margie, Anna Mae, Marian, Nancy and Carol.

A separate picture of Bob and Corabelle was taken the same day.

Robert E Bishop, 22, and Corabelle Phetteplace, 22, were married on 26 Apr 1947 in Indiana.

Shaila Marie Letherer was born to Agnes and Charlie Letherer 25 Jul 1947.

Barry Bishop was born to Bob and Corabelle Bishop 26 Sep 1947.

The George Bishop family had their picture taken. George, Marian, Nancy and Jean holding Carol. Navy dresses were popular.

The Letherer and Bishop cousins had their picture taken on the front of George's truck. From the left are Donny Letherer, Marian Bishop, Carol Bishop, Nancy Bishop and Anna Mae Letherer.

Marian was taking piano lessons. At the 1947 Bishop family Christmas celebration, she received "Bell Bottom Trousers," her first piece of sheet music. She wore out the paper from playing it so many times. It was her all-time favorite! Christmas was held at Grandpa (Charles) Bishop's home.

When the gathering was at Grandpa's the house had to be cleaned. Several families gathered a week or so before and cleaned, especially the parlor which was seldom used. About 1950 they decided it was easier to hold Christmas at other homes.

Wayne was about 3 when Ed decided he needed a hunting gun. They were living on the farm near North Adams and the war was just over. The only way to get a gun was to order it through Montgomery Ward. Ed went to Hillsdale to pick it up. He laid the box on the kitchen table and carefully removed the tape and wrappings. It was a shotgun. Ed took it from the box with Wayne and Helen watching. He pointed it toward the ceiling, put in a shell, and cocked. The gun went off blowing a hole in the ceiling! That gun went back in the box and right back to Hillsdale! Ed was always safety conscious and was not having a gun that went off prematurely. Wayne Bishop's memories 4/14/2014.

Ed and Helen moved to Maple Grove St. in Hudson in 1947.

Wayne with his dog at the Maple Grove Street home.

Edward, Helen, Wayne and Charles Bishop went to New York in 1948 to visit relatives.

This is a picture taken at Jones' Beach. From the left Charles Bishop, Helen with Wayne in front, Ed and Bertha Lockley. Look back to the previous chapter to see relationships.

They met Grandpa Bishop (Theodore) once. He was up on a roof and Ed's dad said "Dad this is your grandson". He grunted and that was it. The only time Ed met him.[30]

Henry and Eleanor Wagner called on Bertha one day the week we were on Long Island so we met them. Bertha and Sid moved to Florida, so no more Long Island trips for us. Dad's sister Gertie, we met in New Jersey but can't remember her married name and she was married twice. Clara came here also but can't remember her last name as she married late in life and lived in New York City.[30]

Esther's son Theodore "Ted" his wife Alma, and son Teddy as well as another baby (I don't have a name) came to visit.[30]

Grandpa Bishop must have taken this picture. His car is in the background.

Jean Bishop is pointing at the camera, Carol, Marian and Nancy are looking at the camera.

Joe Jennings was born 9 Apr 1949 and adopted by Dorothy and Leo Jennings soon after.

George and Jean Bishop left the farm on Packard Road and moved to Hudson on Memorial Day 1949. Nancy had been sick since Christmas time and being alone on the farm was just too much for Jean. George always moved on Memorial or Labor Day because it was the only non-Sunday day in the summer he did not work.

Lucile June Letherer was born to Agnes and Charlie Letherer the 4th of July 1949. Nancy remembered watching her for a while one day. That was the first baby she remembered babysitting.

Carol started Kindergarten in Hudson in the fall of 1949. Nancy had a teacher, Mrs Clark, who visited her at home for 3rd grade. By the fall of 1950 Nancy could finally go to school again. She really liked her teacher, Mrs. Austin.

Esther Grandner's daughter was Bertha Lockley, according to Robert Bishop she acted like Edith Bunker.[25]

Jackie Bishop was born 26 Apr 1950 to Earl and Betty Bishop

Diane Bishop was born 18 May 1950 to Ed and Helen Bishop

Early in the summer of 1950, men started digging out the large stone in the woods south of Grandpa Bishop's house. It was larger than they thought because so much was underground. The Bishop children played on it for many years. The stone was finally loaded on the large, low, trailer of a truck. It moved slowly north on Gardner Road until they were just north of Charlie and Agnes Letherer's farm. Then it went through a small bridge in the dirt road. They were stuck for days. We all went to see the sight! Finally, it arrived at its destination, Hidden Lake Gardens near Tipton, Michigan. The stone was buried to the same depth as they found it in the woods. The gardens have been enlarged and changed over time but the stone is still there. About the same as this photo taken that summer before a plaque was put on the stone.

large Stone at Hidden garden

Pamala Bishop was born 29 Apr 1951 to Bob and Corabelle Bishop

Kay Jennings was born 23 Sep 1952 and was adopted by Dorothy and Leo Jennings soon after.

The Earl Bishop family had their picture taken about 1952. In the back from the left are Judy, Mickey and Margie. In front are Betty holding Jackie and Earl.

These cousins played together often in the summer. The picture was taken in late summer, Aug or Sep. In back with blanket over them are Anna Mae Letherer, Marian Bishop, Nancy Bishop and Don "Donny" Letherer. In front are Shalia Letherer, Carol Bishop, Mary Letherer and Lucille "Lucy" holding the corn.

As 1953 was coming to a close, the annual Christmas gathering of the Bishop's was held at George and Jean's place on US 127, south of Hudson. All of George's brothers and sisters decided to buy their father a new suit for Christmas. It seems that he did not have a decent suit to wear for some occasion. At the Christmas gathering a picture was taken of the grandchildren with Grandpa in the big gray rocker.

The Bishop cousins in 1953: standing in back row: Marian Bishop, Marjorie Bishop, Mickey Bishop, Anna Mae Letherer, Nancy Bishop, Donny Letherer, Wayne Bishop Next row: Shaila Letherer standing by chair, Mary Letherer in chair beside Grandpa Bishop, Jackie Bishop on his lap, Judy Bishop on arm of chair holding Pam Bishop, Barry Bishop with toy. Sitting on the floor in front: Lucille Letherer, Carol Bishop holding Joe Jennings, Diane Bishop. Kay Jennings, 3 months old, was sleeping in the bedroom.

The same day with the Aunts & Uncles included.
Back: George Bishop, Agnes Letherer, probably Charlie Letherer behind, Mickey Bishop in front of Earl Bishop Marjorie Bishop, Anna Mae Letherer, Nancy Bishop, Betty Bishop, Corabelle Bishop holding Pam Bishop, Marian Bishop with a platter of food, Jean Bishop. Middle: Carol Bishop, Donny Letherer, Leo Jennings holding Joe Jennings, Mary Letherer Grandpa Charles T Bishop, Jackie Bishop, Judy Bishop, Diane Bishop, Barry Bishop, Helen Bishop. On floor: Wayne Bishop, Shaila Letherer, Lucile Letherer, Dorothy Jennings.
Ed Bishop took the picture and Bob Bishop must have also been taking pictures.

Charles T. Bishop died on 8 Jun 1954 from head injuries sustained in a car accident in January of that year. The funeral was his first occasion to wear the new suit.

## CHARLES T. BISHOP

Charles T. Bishop, 66 years old, ill since an automobile accident in January, died Monday night in the Hillsdale Community Health Center. He was in University hospital for five days before being removed to the Hillsdale hospital.

Mr. Bishop was born Feb. 2, 1888, in New York state and came to Michigan with his parents when a child. He is survived by four sons, George, Earl and Edward of Hudson, and Robert of Hillsdale; two daughters, Mrs. Charles Leather of Wheatland township and Mrs. Leo Jennings of Cincinnati. Eighteen grandchildren also survive along with three sisters, Mrs. Ester

Grander of Long Island, N. Y., Mrs. Clara Ehling of Brooklyn and Mrs. Gertrude Kay of Summerville, N. J., and two brothers, Theodore and Everett, both of Long Island.

Mr. Bishop was a veteran of the Spanish-American War and a member of the Wheatland Congregational church,

Funeral services are today, Thursday, at 2p.m. in the Charles E. Brown & Son Funeral Home in Hudson. The Rev. W. E. Dudley, pastor of the Wheatland Congregational church will officiate. Burial will be in the Locust Corners Cemetery. Pallbearers are: Earl Bates, Ed Swander, Archie Bradstreet, Harold Holmes, Russell Leffingwell and Byron Ames.[28]

The obvious mistake is that he didn't come to Michigan as a child with his parents.

The following notice appeared in the paper:
STATE of MICHIGAN The Probate Court for the County of Hillsdale
In the Matter of the Estate of CHARLES T. BISHOP, Deceased
At a session of said court, held on December 27th 1954
Present, Honorable Thelma V. Uran, Judge of Probate.
Notice is Hereby Given That the petition of George H. Bishop, Administrator of said estate, praying that his account be allowed and the residue of said estate assigned to the persons entitled thereto, will be heard at the Probate Court on January 20th, 1955, at 10 a.m.
It is Ordered, that notice thereof be given by publication of a copy hereof for three weeks consecutively previous to day of said hearing, in the Hillsdale News, and that the petitioner cause a copy of this notice to be served upon each known party in interest at his last known address by registered mail, return receipt demanded, at least fourteen (14) days prior to such hearing, or by personal service at least five (5) days prior to such hearing.
(Signed) Thelma V. Uran, Judge of Probate.
A true copy
Bernadine Wade, Clerk of Probate, Dec. 29, Jan. 5, 12.[31]

When everything was settled, Robert Bishop bought the farm with the help of George. Robert designated a Saturday when the family could come and get what they wanted. According to Robert he only allowed the one day. Pam has the phonograph and spinning wheel that no one else took, they weren't in a real obvious place.[25]

Cynthia Bishop was born to Corabelle and Robert Bishop November 1954 and died Jan 1955. Marian, Nancy, Anna Mae and Marjorie were pall bearers. Cynthia is buried in Locust Corners Cemetery.

Chuck Bishop was born 23 Feb 1955 to Ed and Hellen Bishop.

Lynette Bishop was born 29 Mar 1961 to Ed and Helen Bishop.

Scott Bishop was born 21 Nov 1962 to Ed and Helen Bishop

Judith Ann Bishop / Miles / DeFrance, 24, died 15 Jan 1968 at the Portsmouth Naval Hospital in Portsmouth, Virginia. She was married to Donald DeFrance and working at

Birtchard Dairy as a secretary. The cause of death was Darvon Poisoning from an over dose of Darvon. Darvon was a narcotic pain medicine that was finally withdrawn from the market in 2007. A major side effect was heart arrhythmias. At the time, she was said to have had a heart attack.

A picture of the six Bishop brothers and sisters was taken not long before George died. Back row: Earl Bishop, Ed Bishop, Robert Bishop. Front row: Agnes Bishop Letherer, George Bishop, Dorothy Bishop Jennings. They must have gotten together for some event as the men have boutonnieres. The ladies may have taken off their flowers.

George Henry Bishop died 17 Apr 1983 in Adrian, Michigan.

Edward Wayne Bishop died 17 Aug 1989 at St Joseph's Hospital, Ypsilanti, Michigan.

Robert Ellis Bishop died 26 Oct 2001 in Adrian, Michigan.

Dorothy Bishop Jennings died 19 Nov 2002 in Lexington, Kentucky.

Agnes Louise Bishop Letherer died 21 May 2010 in Hillsdale, Michigan.

Earl Charles Bishop died 4 Dec 2010 in Hillsdale, Michigan.

Barry R Bishop born 26 Sep 1947, died 4 Oct 2011 in Hudson, Michigan

# References

1. A Concise History of Germany; Mary Fulbrook, Cambridge University Press 2002

2. Fragen an die deutsche Geschichte; an exhibition organized by the German Bundestag, German Bundestag Publications Section, 1989

3. Cambridge Illustrated History of Germany; Martin Kitchen, Cambridge University Press 1996

4. New York passenger lists, 1820-1957 (Pauline out of La Havre, France)

5. Information and photos from Jim Richardson

6. Interviews with Agnes Letherer July 15, 2000-2003

7. A Peep Into The Past, Marjorie Blanks, 2000.

8. History of Hillsdale County, Michigan with illustrations and biographical sketches of some of its prominent men and pioneers; Everts and Abbott, Philadelphia, 1889

9. Miscellaneous Births in Hillsdale County, Michigan: Vivian Lyon Moore, 1962
    some are from Trinity Church Records (Lutheran)
    some are Hillsdale County Records

10. Marriages of Hillsdale County Prior to 1867 by Vivian Lyon Moore, Hillsdale, MI 1947

11. Hillsdale Records Vol. 3 Re to Z

12. Klingensmith Family Reunion poem by Elizabeth Klingensmith Southern

13. Eighteenth Century Documents *of the Nine Partners Patent* Dutchess County, New York; compiled by Clifford Buck and William McDermott, edited by William McDermott, collections of the Dutchess County Historical Society, Volume X, Gateway Press, Inc.

14. Information from Dutchess County Historical Society

15. History of Jefferson County, New York; Hough 1854

16. Gazetteer of Jefferson Co., NY – by Hamilton Child, Published July 1890, P. 295 and other information from the Watertown Historical Society

17. Revolutionary War Pension File, Claim # 14275 Philip Carpenter

18. Deeds and maps located in Watertown, NY

19. Fort Plain Nelliston History 1580-1947, Nelson Greene, Fort Plain-Nelliston Historical Society, 1947, Reprinted by Fort Plain Printing Inc. 1987

20. General George Washington in the Mohawk Valley Summer 1783; Deborah J. Skivington, October 2002, printed by Kinko's, Albany, NY

21. Brothers in Arms, A Time of Terror, Part Three; J. Abner, 2005

22. Observations during visits to St. John of Jerusalem Cemetery, Wantagh, Nassau Co., New York

23. Communications, letters and phone calls, with Lynn Deere caretaker of cemetery records for St. John of Jerusalem Cemetery, 2001-2003

24. Certificates from Office of the Town Clerk, Hempstead, NY; and certificates from State of New York Department of Health, September 14, 2004

25. Interview with Robert Bishop March 2000, August 8, 2000 and March10, 2001

26. Memories of Jean Bishop

27. Information shared by George Bishop.

28. Information and newspaper clippings from Kay Jennings Miller, 2002

29. Interview with Earl Bishop,

30. Information from Helen Bishop, October 2001.

31. Contained in scrapbooks made by Gladys Fedigan Sawyer and held by the Hudson Museum.

www.ingramcontent.com/pod-product-compliance
Lightning Source LLC
Chambersburg PA
CBHW082019300426
44117CB00015B/2276